LEO TOLSTOY

Resident and Stranger

**Sources and Translations Series
of the Harriman Institute
Columbia University**

The W. Averell Harriman Institute for Advanced Study of the Soviet Union, Columbia University, sponsors the *Sources and Translations Series* in the belief that important works of Russian and Soviet history, literature and criticism, as well as memoirs and other source materials not readily available before (or available only in incomplete or inadequate form) should be made accessible to specialists and a general reading audience—either in skillful English translations or, when the occasions warrant, in the original languages. It is hoped that such publications will contribute to a knowledge and understanding of Russian and Soviet history and culture, as well as to an enhanced respect for the craft of translations.

Richard F. Gustafson

LEO TOLSTOY
Resident and
Stranger

A STUDY IN FICTION
AND THEOLOGY

Princeton University Press
Princeton, New Jersey

Library of Congress Cataloging in Publication
Data will be found on the last printed page of this
book
ISBN 0-691-06674-4
ISBN 0-691-01473-6, pbk.

First Princeton Paperback printing, 1989

This book has been composed in Linotron Trump
Clothbound editions of Princeton University Press
books are printed on acid-free paper, and binding
materials are chosen for strength and durability
Printed in the United States of America by Princeton University Press, Princeton,
New Jersey

10   9   8   7   6   5   4   3   2

To Robert A. Maguire

Contents

Contents · viii

Acknowledgments

THERE are many institutions that have supported me over the years in my work on this book. The American Council of Learned Societies sponsored a year of freedom to read Tolstoy (1969-1970), The National Endowment for the Humanities another year to write the first draft of this study (1976-1977). Through its summer seminar program for college teachers, the Endowment also funded my participation in a seminar on Eastern Christian Thought, conducted by Professor Yaroslav Pelikan of Yale University (1979). The W. Averell Harriman Institute for Advanced Study of the Soviet Union at Columbia University (formerly the Russian Institute) gave me financial assistance during three leaves of absence devoted to this study, and Barnard College of Columbia University paid for the expenses involved with the preparation of the manuscript. To all I am most grateful for their enduring support.

Several people have helped me in the publication of this book. Bob Howard shared with me my early enthusiasm and involvement with Tolstoy; Spencer Means my anxiety and joy over completion. Professors Deborah Milenkovich of Barnard College and Robert L. Jackson and Yaroslav Pelikan of Yale University read the manuscript and offered encouragement and sound advice. Candice Agree painstakingly typed the long and not so neat manuscript. To all of them I am most grateful. Most of all, however, I am indebted to my colleague and good friend, Professor Robert A. Maguire of Columbia University. He has not only read my work with his sharp critical eye, but has been there all the years with his generous ear, creative erudition, and unfaltering assurance. To him in thanks I dedicate this book.

Preface

IN Russia art is a serious affair, for art is at the heart of its religion. Russian Orthodoxy involves above all the holding up of right images for the believers to contemplate. Since these icons are pictures of the divine reality present to us, they contain all the theology one needs. Medieval Russian culture bequeathed to the modern world no systematic statement of its faith; the beliefs and longings of the people are expressed, rather, in the sensuous imagery of its "theology in colors." Art, which the radical critic Vissarion Belinsky thought was "thinking in images," is that beauty which Dostoevsky thought would save the world. In the nineteenth century, by the time Russia had already begun to move into modernity and into more Western ways, the art of the icon had fallen into decline, no longer capable of expressing the salvific beauty. Systematic theology, however, was still not quite available to the culture. What passed as theology were but slightly dressed-up versions of Western systems of thought, Catholic and Protestant. Only with Alexey Khomyakov and really only toward the end of the nineteenth and the beginning of the twentieth centuries did the Russian people start to give systematic expression to their religious beliefs in the works of Vladimir Solovyov, Nicholas Fyodorov, Pavel Florensky, Nicholas Berdyaev, Sergey Bulgakov, Nicholas Lossky, and Simon Frank. What came between the icons and the theology was literature, narratives of the human situation.

Narratives may be one of the best forms of theology. They certainly are the oldest. Most people's first verbal expressions of their religious beliefs come in the form of stories. If they are very old, we call them myths. In nineteenth-century Russia this sense of the theological role of human narratives was still operative; indeed it may still be so. The images created by artists were taken seriously as words which reveal the Truth. But this sense of the revelatory quality of verbal art coexisted with an increasing secularization of the society, especially of many of its intellectuals, and most particularly of that peculiar Russian class, the intelligentsia, who sought to enlighten and reform the culture of Russian Orthodoxy solely within the secular sphere, even while they were nurtured by that culture, many of them having been former seminarians, like their later grotesque parody, Joseph Stalin. The intelligentsia were the major readers and critics of this literature. They saw in fiction images revealing the Truth, but they saw through a glass darkly. They read the narratives as stories of sin and redemption, but limited the implications of these stories to the social, political, and economic realms. Like their Soviet successors, they closed their eyes to the theology of their literature.

It is in this context that we must see the emblematic realism of Tolstoy. Tolstoy's literary works cannot be separated from his religious world view; they are the verbal icons of it. Art for Tolstoy too was a very serious affair. Indeed his fiction represents a world in which not only are moral values made explicit but a world in which the divine is seen to dwell. His narratives tell of the divine call to love and man's response to that call. But Tolstoy's works have not often been seen in this way. In this sense Tolstoy has fared even worse than Dostoevsky. Although simplified by Soviet criticism and the nineteenth-century critical tradition on which it draws and trivialized in the West by the association with Freud, to modern Russian Orthodox theologians and others not threatened by the religious nature of his art, Dostoevsky has emerged as the primary Russian Orthodox theologian of the nineteenth century. That Dostoevsky was an artist and expressed his theological vision in images only makes him seem more a theologian to the Orthodox. But Tolstoy fought the formal Orthodox Church, rejected many of its doctrines—at least as he understood them—and in his outraged contempt, not unmixed with a very strong affection, managed to get himself officially excommunicated. Russian Orthodox theologians, to the extent that they discuss Tolstoy, turn to him, not as one who holds up right images, but as one who must be criticized for the errors in his images, not to mention his ideas or ways. So Tolstoy has been left to the intelligentsia and its critical tradition culminating in the Soviet notion of "critical realism." Tolstoy is understood mainly as a writer interested in psychological analysis of characters seen embedded in the social, historical, and economic realities of their times and hence typical of their times. His religious views, to the extent that they are perceived in his work, are considered an abberation. In the West Tolstoy has fared no better, for he is read within the context of the Western literary movement we call realism. Much of what is central to Tolstoy seems embarrassing to Western critics. Often it is passed over in silence or dismissed as unconvincing. What is there is commonly not seen because Tolstoy is judged by the canons of a kind of realism he did not intend to write.

Tolstoy himself believed that Russian literature was fundamentally different from Western literature. He considered that all Russian literature from Pushkin to Dostoevsky stands outside the "forms of the novel, narrative poem or novella" and insisted that *War and Peace* was "not a novel, not an epic, still less an historical chronicle" as these terms are understood in the European tradition (16,7;1868). While such statements may be exaggerations, they do point to a fundamental reality. In Russian literature the forms of Western literature are taken over, reworked, and transcended. The example of Dostoevsky is to the point. He began his literary career with a translation from Balzac. He was especially devoted to thriller fiction and detective stories. The enigmatic, the suggestive, and the melodramatic became vehicles for him to convey the psychological drama of faith in the modern world. He transformed murder stories into narratives of the loss of faith and the search for God. Likewise with Tolstoy, he experimented with a variety of literary structures. Each major work before the conversion takes its origin in an established Western literary genre, the Bildungsroman, the romance, the fictional memoir, the epic, the novel. But these genres are reworked, more or less successfully, to accommodate the religious stories that are being told. After the conversion Tolstoy abandoned the Western genres and moved to the creation of his own, a tendency in him from the beginning, seen in the fragment *A History of Yesterday* and such works as *Two Hussars* and *Three Deaths*. In the emblematic *Master and Man* he created the type of his art, a form that is uniquely his and the form that he had all along used to transform the Western genres. The history of Tolstoy's style is the story of his fiction becoming more and more emblematic. That this late work resembles an allegory or seems to be an extended parable or appears to represent a world in which characters, nature, man-made objects, and the plot event are all emblematic, embodying and revealing spiritual values and events in this world simply tells us that this work is a most clear realization of Tolstoy's quest to find a way to tell the story of God's love that is coming to be in this world.

Based on a close reading of the fiction and diaries, as well as on an original reconstruction of Tolstoy's theology seen in the light of Eastern Christian thought rather than under the influence of those Western thinkers many believe are formative, this book explores the relationship between Tolstoy's psychological life, his verbal icons, and his religious world-view. It doggedly disagrees with two generally held assumptions. While received opinion says that there are two Tolstoys, the pre-conversion artist and the post-conversion religious thinker and prophet, this study is anchored on the conviction that Tolstoy is not two, but one. I have found no evidence in the ninety published volumes of his work to suggest the radical shift in attitudes or theoretical understanding many have deduced from reading *A Confession*. Likewise, contrary to the common belief that Tolstoy was simply a moralist, my reconstruction of the theology shows a range of thought from ontology and epistemology to aesthetics, ethics, and political theory, all grounded in personal religious experience. It is with this all-encompassing theological view that the fiction is shown to be connected in various ways. Part One of this book studies the relationship of characters and plot events to Tolstoy's metaphysics and ethics; Part Two explores the fictional representations of inner experience and various states of consciousness in relation to Tolstoy's epistemology, aesthetics, political theory, and theology of prayer. Furthermore, the poetics of Tolstoy's fiction, worked out in some detail throughout the book, are shown to flow from the theological content. Narrative technique and verbal devices are studied in connection with the reader's experience of the text and hence with the prophetic intent of the fiction. The whole book attempts to demonstrate the coherence in all of Tolstoy. I believe it thereby reveals a new Tolstoy.

Translation and Transliteration

ALL translations from Tolstoy have been made especially for this book. In translating the fiction I have paid especial attention to reproducing the syntactical peculiarities of Tolstoy's style. With both the fiction and the non-fiction I have striven for terminological consistency; where this has been impossible to reproduce, I often quote the original in parentheses. All translations are based on the best editions available. Parenthetical references in arabic numerals refer to the authoritative Jubilee Edition, *Polnoe sobranie sochinenij* (Moscow, 1928-1958): the first numeral to the volume, the second to the page, and the third to the year of composition, or, if relevant, publication. The reader should know that volumes 1-45 contain Tolstoy's fiction and non-fiction, including variant texts, early drafts, and unfinished works. Volumes 46-58 contain the diaries, and volumes 59-89 the letters. Volume 90 is a supplement. One later edition in twenty volumes, *Sobranie sochinenij* (Moscow, 1960-1965), has more textually sound versions of the fiction. I have used this edition for all the fiction, *A Confession*, and *What Is Art?* but so that the reader might locate quotations in any edition or translation I do not cite by page number. Parenthetical citations in roman numerals refer to the sections of the given work: the first numeral in capital letters refers to the largest division of the work ("volume" or "part"), the second to the second largest division ("part" or "chapter"), and, in the case of *War and Peace*, the third numeral refers to the smallest division. The commonly used Maude translation of *War and Peace* is sectioned differently from the Russian version: Books One to Three equal I, i-iii; Books Four to Eight equal II, i-v; Books Nine to Eleven equal III, i-iii; Books Twelve to Fifteen equal IV, i-iv; the first and second epilogue equal E, i-ii. Generally I put parenthetical references at the end of the sentence which first contains a quotation. All quotations that follow are found in the same place and no further citation is marked, until, of course, there is a change of place.

I have used a twofold system of transliteration from the Russian Cyrillic alphabet. With direct quotation of Russian words and in all footnotes and bibliographical references I opted for a version of the system commonly used in linguistics. The following table indicates how the fifteen letters which give rise to variations in transliterations are rendered in this system:

е	e	щ	shch
ё	ё	ъ	ʺ
ж	zh	ы	y
й	j	ь	ʹ
х	kh	э	e
ц	ts	ю	ju
ч	ch	я	ja
ш	sh		

For proper names I have chosen the more popular variant of this system, which writes "y" for "j," "yo" for "ë," "sky" for the ending "skij," and omits symbols for the hard and soft signs. Some proper names have been given in their English form, i.e., Nicholas instead of Nikolay.

I often feel that a plain truth wants to pass through me and demands to be expressed by me, but that I still have not been able to cast it in the most intelligible form. This truth is stupidly simple: it is better for people to live not each for himself but for all, as God wants it. Maybe I'll be able to say it. Of course, not so that I'll be praised or that I might rejoice in what I have done, but so that I will have done what I ought to. (55,173;1905)

Part One

STORIES OF HUMAN RELATEDNESS

Love is life itself because it is its purpose and its law.
(49,116;1884)

Chapter One

RESIDENT AND STRANGER

Life is like the steps a baby takes from the moment his mother
lets him out of her arms until she picks him up again.
(52,60;1891)

Art is the microscope under which the artist puts the secrets of
his soul in order to show people those secrets that are common
to all.
(53,94;1896)

TOLSTOY was a man of many crises. Throughout his long and
full life, from his youthful Caucasian adventures and military service, his enthusiastic pedagogical endeavors, his inspired period of literary creativity, his histrionic mid-life conversion, his intense im-
mersion in matters theological, and his tortured attempts to reshape
himself and the world, culminating in the tragic drama of his married
life, he was moved by one continually reiterated experience. "I feel
that I am perishing—that I am living and dying, that I love life and
fear death—how can I be saved?" (48,187;1878). And with these repeated crises came the Tolstoyan questions: "Why am I alive? What
is the cause of my existence or of anything at all? What is the purpose
of my existence or of anything at all? What does the division of good
and evil that I feel in myself mean and why is it there? How am I to
live? What is death?" Few men, and especially men of such noble position and privilege as Count Leo Tolstoy, have lived life thus on the
brink. "I am tumbling, tumbling downhill to death and scarcely feel
the strength to stop," he wrote but a year after his marriage and just
before beginning *War and Peace*. "But I do not want death, I want and
love immortality" (48,57;1863). Tolstoy's crises of death call to life
now and forever. For Tolstoy, however, life is life only when it is
spent in meaningful labor. "The consciousness of the continuous
process of dying is useful because one cannot have this consciousness without the consciousness of life which evokes the necessity of

using one's dying life for some task" (51,15;1890). This task of life Tolstoy eventually came to understand as the "mission" on which he, like Christ or anyone else, has been sent: he must "serve and instill the truth not only in people but in the whole world" (*mir*) (63,207;1885). In his pedagogy, fiction, and journalism his duty is to "bring his reason into the world." The content of this "truth" and "reason," however, can always be reduced to the Christian idea of love. Tolstoy's crises at the brink of death, then, are moments of purposelessness and meaninglessness which flow from a sense of duty to others neglected and a mission of love which has failed.[1]

These crises continually called Tolstoy to a clarification of his duty and his mission. He found his answer in faith. Tolstoy's faith, however, rests not quite in "the substance of things hoped for, the evidence of things unseen" (Heb.11:1). Rather, his faith arises from the "consciousness of one's position in the universe" (*mir*) and the actions that follow therefrom (35, 170;1902). His search for faith in the face of death becomes a quest for an identity which will reveal his true vocation. His faith is thus a matter of conscience, of that call from an authentic future to an authentic self. His life is thus a matter of finding his place (*mesto*), task (*delo*), and destined purpose (*naznachenie*) within the unfolding universe, a drama of the self in search of a vocation that will be meaningful not just to itself but to the whole of existence. In the end the "inevitable, necessary and sufficient faith" Tolstoy found was the "faith in the fact that God or the One that sent me into the world (*mir*) exists, that I am His product, His worker, a particle of Him, and that what will happen with me is what ought to, the faith of a child in its mother who is holding him in her arms" (54,52;1900). At the start, when he was beginning his now famous diary, he turned inward to seek that "reason" which was to be "drawn into accord" and "merge with the whole (*tseloe*), the source of everything" (46,4;1847). With this turn inward he found and then recorded his first clarification of that faith which would save him:

---

[1] The formalist critic Boris Eikhenbaum was the first to stress the role of continuing crises in Tolstoy. He considered the "real foundation of these crises" to be the "quest for new artistic forms and a new justification of them." Boris Eikhenbaum, *Skvoz' literaturu*, "O krizisakh Tolstogo" (Petersburg, 1923), p. 69. I believe this interpretation is at best backward. The crises were moral and religious, and they led to reevaluations of literary forms.

What is the goal of a person's life? . . . The goal of a person's life is the most possible enabling in all directions of the development of all that exists (*vsë sushchestvujushchee*). . . . If I look at nature, I see that everything in it is constantly developing and that every component part in it unconsciously enables the development of the other parts. Man, since he is just such a part of nature but endowed with consciousness, ought just as the other parts to strive for the development of everything that exists but consciously using his mental abilities. . . . When I look at these mental abilities of man, that is at the soul of every person, I find the unconscious striving which comprises the necessary need of his soul. . . . From the point of view of theology, I find that almost all peoples recognize a perfect being the striving to attain which is the goal of all men. And so it seems I can accept without error as the goal of my life the conscious striving for the development in all directions of all that exists. I would be the most unhappy of men if I did not find a goal for my life, a common (*obshchaja*) and useful one, useful because the immortal soul, once it has developed, naturally turns into a being which is higher and corresponds to it. (46,30-31;1847)

In this first articulation of his identity as a striving soul that corresponds to and turns into a higher being and his vocation as the development of all that exists, Tolstoy lays down the foundation for his doctrine of person, his doctrine of work, and his doctrine of God. His own life and works gloss this first confession of faith.

What is striking about Tolstoy, then, is not the contradictions in his life and thought that many have found with great ease, but the consistency of his crises and the questions they brought to his mind. Tolstoy's life is shaped by his quest for faith, his need to clarify who he is and what he must do. In the Caucasus and again on his return home, in his school and in his study, during his solitary walks in the woods and in his encounters with the peasants, in his literary creations and his diary entries, he returned again and again to this theme of faith first articulated in 1847: the nature of the soul, the purpose of its "unconscious striving," its role in the development of "all that exists," what he later will call the All (*vsë*), and the soul's goal of development into "a being which is higher and corresponds to it," the "merging" of a part with the "whole." Furthermore, for Tolstoy, who believed that the "task of life is perfection" (*sovershenstvo*) (52,140;1894), this vision of the universe in the process of development provides the model for his own life of self-perfection. The underlying image is centrifugal. Life is the process of striving outward in all directions from some imagined center toward the fullness of the circle of "everything that exists." The striving soul "develops" by unfolding itself (*razvitie* means "development," "unfolding," "unwinding") to its completion. For Tolstoy this "process of perfection" (*sovershenstvovanie*), for which Christ's exhortation "Be ye perfect as your heavenly Father is perfect" (Mt.5:48) later became the proof text, requires the nurturing of the seed of the self, the "eternally growing soul" (52,155;1894), by weeding away whatever hinders its growth, a process of continual clearing of consciousness and conscience through ever more precise articulations of the self. Tolstoy's whole life takes its shape from this paradigmatic action: his early rules for behavior, his lifelong habit of weight lifting, his obsession with reworking his manuscripts, his tendency in his diaries to return to the same sets of ideas just to write them out more precisely, his repeated moments of repentance followed by firm resolve for right action, his self-instructing message of "death, humility, silence" written on his fingernail, his attempt to acquire the practice of perpetual prayer in order to reform himself, his theological belief in salvation through "effort"—all stem from the great need to find and form the self, to discover, nurture, and reveal the perfection already within. "He who has understood that all life depends on a more or less dull or sharp knife, for him every sharpening is important and he knows that there is no end to this sharpening, that the knife is a knife only when it is sharp, when it cuts what it must cut" (25,226;1886). Tolstoy's real mission is the continuous articulation of identity and vocation. Only in death will he find his true and complete self. "However old or ill, however much or little you have done, your whole life's task has not only not ended, but not yet received its final decisive meaning until the last breath" (51,20;1890).

This process of articulation unto death provides the key to reading Tolstoy. "I am all that I have written" (83,547;1885), he wrote, and to understand his life's text as well as his life's task we must see it whole. Just as in any human utterance a sound takes its meaning only from within the total statement, so any Tolstoyan text takes its meaning only from within the complete oeuvre. To understand any part of his life's text, a story or novel, an essay or tract, a diary entry or a letter, we must see the particular set of words in their relationship to all his words. The pattern of this relationship is shaped by the process of articulation. The primary rule in reading Tolstoy, therefore, is that the later clarifies the earlier. This does not mean that an earlier work of art is better than a later one or vice versa. It does mean, however, that an earlier work may be an experimental version of a later one and that later works may reveal the hidden patterns and meanings of earlier ones. This primary rule of reading also does not mean that the later philosophical and religious essays, not to mention the letters and diaries, are to replace the great novels and stories in our estimation of Tolstoy's accomplishment. It does mean, however, that we must grasp the clearest articulations of Tolstoy's view of the world if we are to understand the vision embodied in his great fictions. Tolstoy himself believed this was the correct way to approach his literary works (66,188-89;1892).

Tolstoy attempts to understand and express his experience of life by trying out images and working out ideas. The diaries record experience and analyze it; they move from experience to idea. The fictions create images grounded in his inner life; they move from experience to image. A diary entry elaborating some metaphysical concept may begin or end with a humble simile, an image which is meant to embody the abstract idea. A work of fiction, for example *War and Peace*, may include an abstract dissertation on the idea imaged in the story. Even the essays often begin with an image which contains the seed for the idea to be argued. The pattern of articulation which governs Tolstoy's life in general, however, moves from experience to image to idea. It is significant, in this respect, that while creating his most complex fictions, *War and Peace* and *Anna Karenina*, Tolstoy virtually abandoned his diaries and wrote no essays. In this period of his life he recorded and analyzed life only in the novels. Tolstoy's best fiction is an image of his experience that contains his view on life. Therefore, just as beyond Tolstoy's art there is the clarified idea of faith embodied in it, so behind his art there is the experience of the search for that faith, the quest for identity and vocation. Before we can study Tolstoy's fictional images articulated in the idea beyond them, we must attempt to define the pattern of experience behind them.

TOLSTOY'S EXPERIENCE OF LIFE

Tolstoy's most ideal image of himself, his most cherished sense of life, his most firm conviction of faith, flow from his urge and desire to belong. His many years of family life rooted in Yasnaya Polyana surrounded by his wife and many children testify to this deep-seated need to feel himself a part of a community. If in his later years he so vehemently asserted his universal citizenship and so loudly preached the ideal of human relatedness, this assertion and this preachment grew from an expanded sense of residency in the whole world. Just the thought of the millions of people in Africa and Japan unknown to him, "alien" (*chuzhie*) to him, so terrified him that he had to believe that "they and I are one, as are one with me those now living, who have lived and who will live and I live through them and they through me" (52,62;1892). Tolstoy the Resident belongs in and to a world which belongs to him. His best sense of self is realized in this reciprocal belonging. He is called to be at one with all.

In the mythology of his life, the first image of this sense of human relatedness appears in the game of "ant brothers" the five-year-old Tolstoy used to play with his brothers. One day his older brother Nicholas announced that he knew of a wonderful secret that would make all men happy by eliminating disease, misery, and anger: all would love one another and become "ant brothers." But the secret was written on a green stick buried by the road at the edge of a ravine in the Zakaz forest. The boys were so taken with the story that even without the stick in hand they used to play "ant brothers," huddling together in shared love and tenderness under a shawl draped over two chairs. Tolstoy never forgot this game; it symbolized to him his highest ideal and best self. "The ideal of the 'ant brothers' clinging lovingly to one another only not under two armchairs draped with shawls but of all the peoples of the whole world under the wide dome of heaven, has remained unaltered for me," he wrote in his *Memoirs* (34,387;1905). "As I then believed that there was a little green stick whereon was written something that would destroy all evil in men and give them great blessings, so I now believe that such truth exists among people and will be revealed to them and will give them what it promises." In a grand and highly significant symbolic gesture Tolstoy requested that he be buried at the spot of the green stick and to this day there he lies.

The image of all people huddled together loving one another haunted Tolstoy all his life. It represented the ideal to which he was drawn and the perfection toward which he would strive. He later discovered the ideal in the Enlightenment principles of equality and fraternity and himself believed that his conversion grew from a heightened awareness of these eighteenth-century ideals (52,158;1894). The controlling idea of his thought is unity. But the unity with others that Tolstoy experiences transcends the Enlightenment idea. Tolstoy's "unity" is a cosmological and metaphysical reality. "The tenderness and ecstasy we experience in contemplating nature is the recollection of that time when we were animals, trees, flowers, the earth. More precisely, it is the awareness of the unity (*edinstvo*) with everything, which is hidden from us by time" (55,217;1906). For this Tolstoy life's moments of unity with everything strike the only truthful chord. "I am walking along the hard road, while at my side brightly dressed peasant women are walking home from work singing most lively. A moment between tunes and the measured thump of my feet against the road becomes audible and then again the song rises and again fades off and the thump of my steps. That's good. In my youth without the women something used to sing inside me always and often. And everything, the sound of my steps, the light of the sun, the fluttering of the hanging birch branches, and everything, everything was accomplished (*sovershilos'* also means "made perfect") as it were to the tune of the song" (52,30;1891). The Resident belongs to a world harmonized into accord, made perfect because all participate together in the one song of life. For him music is the art and metaphor of this unity.

The theme of this unifying song of life is love. The Resident belongs when he loves. Ethically, of course, this belonging is expressed in service to others. If the young Tolstoy could exclaim, "If three days pass during which I do nothing for the good of the people, I will kill myself" (47,4;1854), the older man reflects that "the only happy moments of my life were those in which I gave my whole life over to serving the people" (54,94;1901). The Resident participates in the life of others and often finds his mission in labor done for the common good. But the peak experiences of life, the moments that reveal Tolstoy's ideal way of being in the world, are marked not by ethical action or duty, but by a sense of ecstatic love for all. "I am vividly feeling . . . the joy, calm, and bliss of the state of love for all. Only in such a state is everything in life and death good" (56,24;1907). In this ecstatic state Tolstoy discovers his true belonging. "What incomparable amazing joy—and I am experiencing it—*to love* everyone, everything, to feel this love in oneself or better to feel oneself by means of this love. How everything we with our spoiled taste consider evil is destroyed, how everything, everyone becomes close, one's own" (*svoi*) (56,153;1908).

No experience is more telling for Tolstoy. He spent his life attempting to sharpen the self which was shaped by its love for others. Because he sensed in this something of his true mission, because he saw in this something of his ultimate identity and final vocation and therefore heard in it the call of the divine, Tolstoy kept on urging himself toward this experience, attempting to articulate it more perfectly. "You rush about and struggle just because you want to float in your own direction. Yet right beside you, near everything, there flows unceasingly always in the same direction the divine endless stream of love," he instructed himself in his diary (53,167;1895). "When you are really exhausted in your attempts to do something for yourself, to save and safeguard yourself, abandon all your own directions, throw yourself into that stream and it will bear you off and you will sense that there are no barriers, that you are eternally calm and free and blessed." "Free will," Tolstoy the Resident therefore concludes, "is nothing other than the true, eternal divine life which we receive, with which we can commune in this life. . . . It is God within us, working through us. I am free when I merge (*slivajus'*) with God, and I merge with God when I suppress in myself everything that hinders love and when I yield to love" (53,49;1895). Tolstoy finds his ultimate self only when he loses himself and becomes "merged with God," in communion with divine life, a part of the "divine endless stream of love" where he freely and truly belongs.

Tolstoy's most cherished moments of that "joyful, gladsome feeling of love for everyone and everything" (57,119;1909) resemble the ecstasies of mystical prayer when the self loses and finds itself in union with the divine all. The experience is profoundly religious and in various forms finds expression throughout Tolstoy's life. Characteristically, his first recorded moment of prayer contains the seeds of these later experiences of the divine:

The sweet feeling I experienced while praying cannot be communicated. I read my usual prayers . . . and then remained in prayer. If prayer is defined as petition or thanksgiving, then I was not praying. I desired something lofty and good but what I cannot communicate, although I was clearly conscious of what I desired. I wanted to merge (*slit'sja*) with the all-embracing Being. I begged Him to forgive my trespasses, but no, I did not beg for I felt that if He gave me that blessed moment, then He had forgiven me. I begged and at the same time felt there was nothing to beg for. . . . I gave thanks, yes, but not in words or thoughts. In one feeling I united everything, supplication and thanksgiving. The feeling of terror (*strakh*) disappeared completely. I could not have distinguished any simple feeling of faith, hope, or charity from the general feeling. No, that one feeling I experienced yesterday was love for God, that exalted love which unites everything good in itself and negates everything evil. (46,61-2;1851)

In prayer, in the moment of merging and the feeling of love for God, the "terror" of existence, the sense of tumbling downhill to death, disappears. Love is the affirmation of life. Even more striking in this first prayer is the simplicity and purity of the love. No guilt or doubt mars the feeling. Tolstoy's trespasses do not block the flow of his own love because his love is the flow of God's love in him and for him. And Tolstoy assumes a God who loves him. To believe that God is not merciful and forgiving, that He does not love him, would be tantamount to not believing in God. In his first recorded prayer Tolstoy reveals that for him the sense of merging and belonging, the ability to love, rests on a foundation of firm acceptance, on the conviction that he is loved. His later theology is built on this experience of merging and on this idea of love for him.

A true Resident, however, is involved in a world which is involved with him. The relationship is reciprocal. For Tolstoy this seemed logical: "The human being's highest happiness is to be loved and therefore that desire is placed within the human being (in perverted form this is expressed as ambition and vanity). In order to be loved, obviously, it is necessary for one to love" (54,188;1903). But for Tolstoy this logical relationship grew into a vision of community. "God wanted us to be happy, and for that reason He placed within us the need for happiness, but He wanted us all to be happy together and not individually. That is why people are unhappy if they strive for happiness individually rather than in common." This community of love rests on mutuality. Christian love is for one another. That is the meaning of one of his favorite proof texts: "Let us love one another. Love is from God and everyone who loves is the son of God and knows God" (I Jn. 4:7). This sense of love as mutual, reciprocal, and communal culminates in Tolstoy's firm belief that "we cannot be saved separately, we must be saved all together" (71,307;1898). Tolstoy the Resident, who experiences the unity of all in moments of ecstatic prayer and preaches the ideal of human relatedness, hopes for the universal salvation of all together.

TOLSTOY'S CRISES when he senses that he is perishing and seeks to be saved turn, however, on a loss of love for him. "I feel alone and want love" (55,160;1905) is the varying refrain of his diaries, where he recorded the many moments when he suffered the loss of God. "I cannot become conscious of God, and everything has become lonely, meaningless, and terrifying" (57,125;1909). Without God Tolstoy loses his sense of reciprocal relationship and destined purpose. "The other night in bed I somehow started thinking about life and God and the meaning of life and God stopped being clear and I was overcome by the horror of doubt. It was terrifying. My heart sank, but it didn't last long. The main horror of the doubt was that it was impossible to pray, that no one would hear, that nothing was necessary. Not the horror of death, but the horror of meaninglessness. It didn't last long. The first ray of hope shone in what is always the foundation of everything: from Whom and What I have come, there do I go and will I arrive" (54,198;1903). In the God who loves him he finds his origin, goal, and home; in doubt he is lost and alone. "Not to live with God is to be orphaned, to feel alone" (56,42;1907) he observes in a moment of what he calls the "feeling of being orphaned" (55,102;1904). For Tolstoy the loss of God is commonly experienced as this "feeling of being alone, orphaned and unfree" (56,42;1907). His crisis of conversion recorded in A Confession resulted from "the sense of terror, of being orphaned, of loneliness midst everything alien (chuzhoe) and the hope for someone's help" (xii). The Resident's world makes sense because he belongs to it and it belongs to him. He is secure because he is supported, protected, and accepted by a world of which he feels himself a part. The Resident belongs to the family of man and is a son of the Father who loves him.

Lev Nikolaevich Tolstoy was an orphan. His mother died before he was two, his father before he was nine. Along with his brothers and sister, he was brought up by the women of the family, his grandmother and two aunts, and they gave him the attention and affection they could, but the sense of a family residence was lost. Tolstoy was so affected by his orphanhood and the consequent deprivation of parental love and sense of lost homestead and family that even at age 23 he fantasied his future marriage as a return to the idyllic childhood he never knew. His favorite aunt becomes "grandma" to his children, living upstairs in grandmother's room, and "everything in the house is as it used to be in the same order in which it was in father's lifetime and we continue the same life only with roles changed. . . . I take the role of papa, although I do not expect ever to deserve it, my wife, the role of mama, our children, our role" (59,160;1852). For Tolstoy family life promises a secure world without any acquaintances to "pester" them with "visits and gossip," a world where nothing can disturb the intimacy and affection of the closed family circle.

Nothing, that is, except its loss. Once upon returning home to an empty Yasnaya Polyana six years later, Tolstoy was overcome by just such a feeling of the loss of this "family of his imagination and dreams" (60,260;1858). "I am a widower. I have lost the whole family that was living here." To him, however, this lost family is no "invention" of his fantasy, but the "ideal," the "most precious thing in life" without which he "does not want to live." In this black moment of abandonment, alone without his resurrected family circle, Tolstoy would hold a "requiem service for everything" so that there would be "no prayers left" in his heart. The early loss of his parents thus impressed on Tolstoy's young mind the desirability of a loving family and the readiness of death to snatch it away. Later, the death of his favorite brother was traumatic. Life, Tolstoy learned early, is a process of being abandoned. Love is a risk and easily lost. However, the abandonment and loss of those who love me make no sense, he seemed to reason, unless it could be that I am at fault, that they abandoned me because I did not love them enough or in the right way. How can I love so that I will be loved and not be abandoned? This is the question that pursued Tolstoy the orphan all his life. His marriage was the first answer to this question, the fulfillment of his fantasy of the resurrected family circle. In his later years, as the fantasy faded into reality and lost its power to fulfill, these questions returned with increased intensity and urged him toward his God.

All Tolstoy's major heroes, except Natasha and Nicholas Rostov, are orphans; many experience the loss of a parent.[2] Tolstoy's Christ is a bastard with no known earthly father; the virgin birth is a later legend designed to mask the stigma and the Sonship with the Father a "bright, abandoned" child's explanation to his friends, all of whom have fathers in the flesh (24,49-52;1884). For Tolstoy the feeling of belonging and the security of residency are associated with parental presence and providence. His relationship with his God is founded on the Abba experience; he trusts in His love and relies on His help. "You know God not so much by reason or even by the heart, but by the sense of total dependency on Him, like the feeling a nursing child has in his mother's arms. He knows not who holds him, warms him, feeds him, but he does know that there is this someone and moreover that this someone loves him" (52,157;1894). The loving, caring mother whom one does not know is the constant model for Tolstoy's God. "Over and over again from various directions I came to recognize that I just could not have appeared on this earth for no reason, cause, or meaning," Tolstoy argued in A Confession, "that I could not be the fledgling fallen from its nest that I indeed felt I was. Even as I, a fallen fledgling, lie on my back and peep in the tall grass, I peep because I know that I was borne, hatched, warmed, fed, and loved by my mother. Where is she, that mother? If I have been abandoned, who has abandoned me? I cannot deny that I was born of someone who loved me. But who is that someone? Again God" (xii). Tolstoy's firm feeling of care, comfort, and concern, his sense of belonging and hence his own capacity to love and ability to accept love without fear of its loss, have been lost in his past. To be saved he must resurrect this idyllic world. His quest for perfection, the Kingdom of the Father, returns him to his mother's embrace. "A dull melancholy state all day. Toward evening this state changed into a tender feeling, a desire for affection, for love. As in childhood I longed to cling to a being who loved me, who took pity on me, and to weep tenderly and be consoled," Tolstoy wrote but four years before his death. "But who is

---

[2] In Russian one is considered an "orphan" (sirota) with the loss of one parent.

that being to whom I would cling so? I go over all the people whom I love, and none will do. To whom can I cling? I'd like to make myself small and cling to mother as I imagine her to myself. Yes, yes, mommy, whom I had not even yet called by that name since I couldn't speak. Yes, she, my most exalted concept of pure love, not that cold, divine type, but a warm, earthy, motherly love. That's what my better but tired soul yearns for. Yes, mommy, come cuddle me. All this is insane, but it is all true"(55,374,1906). The Resident of the whole world with his ecstatic love for all would belong in his mother's arms. If that is insane and impossible, then in sonship with the Father, however "cold" it may be, Tolstoy will find his true identity and vocation, in his Father's Kingdom his only residence.

TOLSTOY the orphan wants to love and belong but cannot. He is a Stranger. Throughout his life in one way or another he destroyed most of the social or personal relationships he had managed to establish. He served in the military, only to make it the object of his satirical wit and then later to seek to abolish it and the whole governmental order it supports. He broke out into the literary world at a young age, became an accepted member of the literary establishment of the day, only to withdraw abruptly from it and then later to portray the literary profession as a form of parasitism and prostitution. He rejected his own literary masterpieces. He fantasied about family life throughout his young adult years, but married late and enjoyed some years of mixed family happiness, only to find that life a hindrance to his own. Later the modicum of connubial bliss turned into a continual blitz from which in the end he had to escape. He formed relationships with two fellow writers, Turgenev and Fet, only to spoil them. He had no real friends with whom he shared his inner life and was suspicious of the motives of those close to him. He did not trust or love others easily. He could not bear opposition to his opinions. He shared his inner self only with his diary, which then became the medium of communication between him and those close to him, especially his wife, until he felt so threatened by this that he had to establish various forms of secret diaries, some of which he hid in his shoe. In the end the only person in the world he felt he could trust was his fanatic follower and disciple, Vladimir Chertkov, a man who proved his devotion by his total support and agreement.

The man who had a need to belong and an urge to love all led a life estranged from the world, focused not on others but on himself. Although he lived in a large household community, loved to romp and play with children, and had a special capacity for a penetrating understanding of others, even of animals, Tolstoy the Stranger spent most of his time alone. Furthermore, throughout his life, he not only destroyed the relationships he established, he also self-righteously and even self-pityingly blamed his resultant isolation on others. Long before his years as an isolated prophet and twenty years before the public conversion, he sensed the pattern and supplied the formula. "I have no friends. None. I am alone. I used to have friends when I served Mammon, but now when I serve the truth none" (48,40;1862). The tone of this statement is petulant. Tolstoy is annoyed that others do not respond to his righteousness, just as later outrage finds its way into his moral tracts and diary entries because he is frustrated by the failure of love in the world and the refusal of people to try his theory of love. But the underlying failure is really Tolstoy's, and again characteristically he formulated the psychological law which governs him. "When a person judges another for lack of love, then it almost always means just that that person himself has become cold to people from a lack of love and is pained by this" (52,148;1894). Tolstoy's judgments on the world, tinged with the outrage of his pain, are the cries for universal love from a man who does not love universally.

This psychological drama of Tolstoy's failed residency was played out within the social and economic boundaries of the world into which he was born. Count Leo Tolstoy was fated by his noble origins to a life separated from the vast majority of the people, the peasants among whom he lived. Despite his sense of mission to the world, there was no way he could participate in the life of the very people, who, he saw, made his or any life possible. Every effort he made— teaching their children, joining in their work, dressing like them, writing for them—turned out to be but a symbolic gesture void of effective content. All his life he suffered from a sense of idleness amidst luxury, believing that "everyone works except me" (58,44;1910). This "inequality of wealth and excess midst poverty" he believed was "the secret tragedy of my life" (56,39;1907). For him the world in which he lived was based on a principle of human disrelatedness, a fundamental failure of love. "How can we love, when our whole life is grounded in evil? . . . We live by oppressing our brothers. Before we can love, we must stop living off their sufferings" (52,270;1906). Thus in the public arena, as in the private, Tolstoy the aristocrat suffered from the outrage of his pained failure to love others. The Resident of Russia lived in fated isolation from her people.

Tolstoy does not just fail to love others. From his earliest days he also felt himself unloved and unwanted. "Why does no one love me?" the young man of twenty-two asked himself. "I am not a fool, nor a freak, nor an ignoramus, nor a bad person. I cannot understand it" (46,169;1853). In his moments of youthful insecurity, as later in his crises of confidence and faith, therefore, Tolstoy felt both unlovable and unloving. "I feel that I cannot be pleasing to anyone and that everyone is hard for me to bear" (46,149;1852). This failure to be loved and to love feeds on itself. Early on, Tolstoy claimed that "for me the main sign of love is the fear of giving offense to or of not being liked by the beloved, really a fear" (64,237-38;1852). Tolstoy knows that he loves only because he wants to be loved. But then when he does not sense that the beloved loves him, he feels "hostility" toward her. The failure of love ends up as anger. He is hostile because he is not loved, but since he does not feel lovable, he cannot but be angry. Tolstoy the Stranger, who was subject to outbursts of rage, a feature he bequeathed to such disparate heroes as Nicholas Rostov and Father Sergius, is hostile to the world.

Tolstoy's hostility stems from his deep-seated self-loathing. The first extended self-portrait of the Stranger focuses on his unattractiveness.

What am I? One of the four sons of a retired lieutenant-colonel, from age 8 left without parents to the care of women and outsiders . . . from age 18 on my own without much capital, any social position, and especially any rules, a person who has messed up his affairs to the extreme, spent the best years of his life without purpose or pleasure, and finally exiled himself to the Caucasus . . . and then to the army without means except salary, without sponsors, without the know-how to live in society, without understanding the service, without any practical abilities, but with a lot of self-esteem. Well, that's my social position. But what about my personality? I am ugly, awkward, slovenly, and socially inept. I am petulant, boring to others, immodest, in-

tolerant, and bashful like a child. I am almost an ignoramus. . . .
I am intemperate, indecisive, inconstant, stupidly vain, and fervent, like all people without character. I am not brave. I am careless and so lazy that idleness has become an invincible habit. . . .
I am honest, i.e. I love the good, . . . but I love glory more. I am
very ambitious. . . . I am not modest and therefore I am proud in
myself but bashful and shy in society. (47, 8-9; 1854)

In this picture drawn nearly one-third of his way through life, Tolstoy stresses his sense of alienation and isolation. He lists what he
does not have and describes himself negatively. Tolstoy portrays a
man who cannot get along in the world. He believes himself unlikable and worthless, yet is proud and vain. He judges himself profligate
and lazy, yet is immodest and ambitious. He sees himself estranged
from society, yet craves recognition from it. The negative image
screens the self-centeredness. Tolstoy is filled with self-love. The
negative image is calculated to struggle with Tolstoy's central flaw,
that "vanity" which he understands as "self-love transfered to the
opinion of others," a person's "love for himself not as he is but as he
shows himself to others" (46,95;1852). At the same time, however,
this negative self-portrait cultivates an obsession with self. Thus
filled with such vain self-love, Tolstoy himself not only does not love
others, but he neither truly loves himself nor does he feel himself
loved by others. This dialectic of a negative love of self coupled with
a sense of failure of love from others both grounded in a vanity which
"poisons all existence"pursued Tolstoy all his life.

Tolstoy the Stranger contradicts Tolstoy the Resident. The Stranger stands in opposition to the world around him and finds his sense
of self not in acceptance but rejection. The man who resided at Yasnaya Polyana with a strong sense of roots and home also harbored
fantasies all his life of abandoning that home for the road to pursue
the quest of a religious wanderer. The Christ he fashioned from the
Gospels is a "vagabond" and "person without a home" (*bezdomovnik*) (24,198-201;1881). Although he rarely commented on the Old
Testament, Tolstoy gave this telling reading of the Book of Jonah:
"Jonah is a prophet who wants to be righteous all alone and distances
himself from depraved people. But God shows him that since he is a
prophet, he is needed to communicate his knowledge of truth to sinful people and therefore must not run from these sinful people but

live in common with them" (23,413;1884). The Jonah who "wants to be righteous all alone" until God shows him that in this he is "escaping from his destined purpose" is Tolstoy the Stranger, who indeed declared "I am Jonah" (23,461).

The Stranger lives outside the bond of human relatedness. He does not want to participate in the world or be dependent on anything outside himself. "Shall I ever become independent of outside circumstances?" the nineteen-year-old Tolstoy asked himself. "In my opinion that is real perfection, for in a person who is not dependent on any outside influence, the spirit by its own need will necessarily surpass matter and then the person will reach his destined purpose" (46,32;1847). A month before he died Tolstoy still held to this belief, now essential for his piety. "One must be like a lantern shut off from external influences—the wind, insects—and thus pure, transparent, and glowing warmly" (58,117;1910). In this conscious attempt to remove himself from the sphere of others' experience, Tolstoy even sought to abstract himself from his own. "I often look upon life completely detached, as if I were not participating in it. Only with such a view do you see it correctly" (54,144;1905). Tolstoy becomes a pure spirit who glows warmly and sees clearly because he is disengaged from all that surrounds him and happens to him. The Stranger is not related to others.

Tolstoy turned this isolation into a positive force for good. He experienced his ecstasies of love for all during his walks in the woods by himself. Solitude became so valuable that he believed that "in a heap, a crowd, a gathering there is accomplished only evil. Good is done only by each single person separately" (53,7;1895). He felt that "a person is strong only when he is alone" (52,53;1891). For Tolstoy the Stranger, then, freedom comes not as for the Resident in loving others but in separating himself from others. "One psyche submits to the influence of another psyche, so a person is free only when alone" (41,551;1904). Thus Tolstoy suffered from "the feeling of being captured, of unfreedom, of coercion" (34,393;1905). He believed in his autonomy and suffered from that "feeling of captivity" one senses in dreams when "you want to run or strike out and your legs collapse and you struggle powerlessly and weakly," a feeling that never "leaves the best of us even when awake" (48,106;1865). For Tolstoy the Stranger strength and freedom come only with release from external pressure or outside limitations, the "captivity of the body" (43,301;1907).

In the mythology of Tolstoy's life, alongside the image of the boy huddled lovingly together with his "ant brothers" should be placed the image of the babe recalled by the fifty-year-old man. "I am bound, I want to stick my hands out but I cannot. I cry and weep. . . . Some people are standing bent over me, above me. . . . They are alarmed by my cries but do not untie me. To them this seems necessary (that is, that I be bound), while I know it is not and I want to prove this to them so I let forth a cry repellent to myself but irrepressible. . . . What is memorable to me is not my cries, my suffering, but the complexity, the contradiction of the impression. I want freedom; it hinders no one, and they torment me. They pity me and tie me up, and I who need everything, I am weak and they are strong" (23,469-70;1878). Not united with others under a shawl spread over a chair, this Tolstoy is separated from others, bound up in himself by the swaddling they have placed on him. He realizes himself not in communion with those around him but in release from the constriction of those who surround him. Their pity and concern torment and restrict him. In his torment the Stranger is alienated from those who love him.

The Stranger is the direct opposite of the Resident. This opposition, expressed in Russian as the opposition of "one's own, native" (*svoj, rodnoj*) and "someone else's, alien" (*chuzhoj*), is fundamental to Tolstoy's psychological experience. The two exist, however, in a dialectical relationship: the extreme of one evokes the other. Solitude calls out solidarity. "I avoid people; they bother me," Tolstoy the Stranger observes of himself in the first person, and then the Resident goes on in the next sentence to instruct the Stranger in the second person. "But you live only through people and for people. If people disturb you, then there is nothing for you to live for. To remove yourself from people is suicide" (51,47;1890). But likewise not to remove himself from people was also a form of suicide, so that Tolstoy found himself in a characteristic psychological double bind. He needed to love and be loved, to have the sense of validation and security that residency in a community gives, and at the same time he found it so difficult to love and let himself be loved that he retreated into himself and in his self-centeredness alienated others. He transformed residency in a community into a form of internal emigration.

This syndrome played itself out in many areas of his life and defines Tolstoy's way of being in the world.

Tolstoy the Stranger lives his life separated from the life around him. At one extreme this is the man who forever analyzes his experiences, looking at his life rather than living it. This spectator keeps diaries. Such self-scrutiny includes the consciousness of what others think of him, but this concern for others is directed only at himself. The Stranger is the aristocrat who takes pride in his heritage, feels himself superior to the majority of his peers and contemporaries, and lashes out angrily at all forms of "coercion" (*nasilie*) which threaten to limit or mold his being—church, state, press, educational institutions, and bureaucratic organizations. He is caustic in his iconoclasm. He lashes out at what seems to him "not right" (*ne to*). Tolstoy the Stranger lived through four major intellectual movements which captured the minds of nineteenth-century men—Hegel, Darwin, Marx, and Nietzsche—but remained aloof from them, attacking them while being fundamentally ignorant of them. Even in art what was new and popular he dismissed as a fad: Wagner, Baudelaire, Mallarmé. The Stranger lives by saying nay. At the negative extreme, the Stranger loses his sense of living, feels that he has no purpose in his present world, discovers in his estrangement from others a form of emptiness and worthlessness, and fears that annihilation and death are devouring his every minute.

Tolstoy the Resident lives to the fullest, assured that his life has meaning and purpose because he is participating in the activity of the world around him. In his school, in his creativity, in his family, in his sonship with the Father, the Resident finds his security and worth. He is involved, enthusiastic, trusting. In mowing hay with the peasants and sewing bast shoes alone, in emptying his chamberpot and dusting his room, the Resident of Russia, dressed in peasant clothes and eating simple food, feels himself a part of the people, creating life along with the rest. Analysis yields to experience, and he lives spontaneously in the moment. In this moment the Resident belongs and has faith. He has no fear of death and feels his life but one form of the eternal life where he resides forever. The Resident says yea. At the positive extreme, he feels the "force of life" coursing through his veins and enthuses with the "joy of life" to which he calls himself and all others. "Rejoice! Rejoice! Life's task, its destined purpose is joy. Rejoice in the sky, the sun, the stars, in grass, trees, animals, and people. Take care lest this joy be dispelled. When joy is dispelled it means somewhere you have erred. Find the error and correct it. . . . Be like children—rejoice forever" (50,144;1889).

NEKHLYUDOV'S IMAGE OF LOVE

Tolstoy believed that "the work of art flows from the state of the artist's soul" (30, 215; 1889). From his earliest days his "main interest" in reading lay in the "character of the author as expressed in the work" (46,182;1853). In literature and even in philosophy he sought "only the soul, the mind, the character of the person writing" and was convinced that the deeper the author drew from himself, the more his work would seem "like yourself, familiar to you and common to all" (66,254; 1892). Now the "character of the author" Leo Tolstoy needs to love. This love is the "truth" in art which shows the "way," "the one narrow path of the divine will leading to life" (26,308;1886). To get on the path to this truth, Tolstoy taught in his *Christian Doctrine*, is the "task of life" which all men are "called to participate in," a task which consists of replacing the division and discord (*nesoglasie*) in the world (*mir*) with union and harmony (*soglasie*), a task accomplished by the increase of love for all in oneself and in the world (39,127;1896). With this increase of love in himself, a person "collaborates" (*sodejstvujet*) in the Divine task which is being accomplished in the world, the "establishment of the Kingdom of God." The truth in art, therefore, is not the "truth of what is" but the "truth of the Kingdom of God, which is close at hand but not yet here" (26,308; 1886). The work of art reflects the "character of the author" in his search for the "Kingdom of God." The stress is on the process of the search. "The artist must be a person who quests so that the work itself will be a quest. . . . Only if he quests, does the viewer, listener, or reader merge with him in his search" (54,74;1900). The fundamental action and value in Tolstoy's fiction is the quest for love. The Stranger becomes a Resident.

This fundamental action is well illustrated in simple form by the early short piece *Lucerne* (1857). A Russian nobleman named Nekhlyudov arrives at the latest and best tourist hotel in Lucerne. In this alien place he is annoyed by the modern, "four-cornered, five-storied" buildings that destroy the old charm of the street and clash with the natural environment. He is upset by the English tourists who overrun the resort, all decked out in local costume. He is at odds with the "strangely grandiose and yet inexpressively harmonious and soft nature." Nekhlyudov arrives on the scene, angry with the world he finds himself in. He is a Stranger. Feeling superior to the other strangers in the place, however, Prince Nekhlyudov retires to the solitude of his chambers. Alone, he is roused by the beauty of the nature he sees from his window to express an "excess of something" which wells up in his soul, the desire to "do something unusual, to embrace someone," even "tickle and pinch" him. He is moved by nature to feelings of love for others. Then, as he stares out into the world of nature, the scene expands outward until "everything is inundated" with the flow of air and light: ". . . not one completed line, not one distinct color, not one moment the same, everywhere movement, symmetry . . . an endless mixture and variety . . . and in all calm, softness, unity (*edinstvo*), and the necessity of beauty." The expanse of nature becomes an image of the whole universe, the harmonious world in which he would dwell. He experiences the call to be a Resident.

With his moral mission to love and his metaphysical vision of unity, Nekhlyudov then descends to the dining room to share his first meal with the other guests. But he sees in their faces only "an awareness of their own well-being and a total absence of attention to everything around that does not directly relate to their own person," and he reacts with annoyance at their "propriety" and "privacy" based on the "absence of a need for intimacy." In the world he finds himself in, Nekhlyudov sees others as strangers, self-absorbed and self-interested, isolated in their sense of self, and incapable of love. They make him feel "stifled," and he recalls a childhood experience when, guilty of a prank, he was punished by being set down on a chair all alone while he could hear his brothers playing merrily in the other room. To Nekhlyudov estrangement is the punishment for a crime and salvation the happy accord of all brothers. Why, he wonders, do the strangers deprive themselves of life's best pleasure, "the enjoyment of each other, the enjoyment of a human being?" He recalls his past in Paris, where dinners at his former residence were different. There "everything was in common" (*obshchee*), and "we related to each other in a human fashion." However, the unity and human harmony recalled but lost only make him feel "sad, cold, lonely, and depressed." Thus deep down in his soul and back in his past Nekhlyudov feels a closeness to others; here, right now, his mission of human relatedness is frustrated by the self-enclosure of others.

He goes for a walk. While strolling along, Nekhlyudov hears the sound of some "strange but very pleasant" music which immediately restores his interest in life. In his merriment he "suddenly" sees the beauty of nature anew and for the first time hears her sounds: the frogs croak and the quails whistle. The music too grows clearer and louder, and soon Nekhlyudov sees before him its source, a "dark little man" singing a Tyrolian song. Nekhlyudov is totally transformed. His "indifference to everything in the world" is replaced "suddenly" by a "need for love, a fullness of hope, and a joy of life (*radost' zhizni*) without cause." Music restores the call of the Resident.

What follows is a comedy of errors. Taken by the "dark little man" and his song, Nekhlyudov is incensed at the other tourists' indifference to him, mockery of him, and, worst of all their failure to toss him a tip. He feels as though he himself has been rejected. The "dark little man," in need and unwanted, gives Nekhlyudov a chance to put his stifled feelings of love for others into action. This he does with a vengeance. He invites the wandering singer, who looks like a "working man," for a drink at the hotel dining room. Nekhlyudov must display his charity as an example to the Englishmen. Even the waiters are outraged and try to stop it, which only arouses Nekhlyudov's "vanity" and "self-love" to the point of "spite" (*zloba*). He'll show them. A duel of wills ensues. In the fight for equal rights, however, Nekhlyudov, who always refers to the singer as a "little man" (*chelovechik*), condescends where he would communicate, insults where he would respect, and takes where he would give. In his act of love Nekhlyudov is centered on himself.

The "dark little man" goes off into the night, and Nekhlyudov is left alone, still hoping to make his point. But the opportunity does not arise, and Nekhlyudov "all, all alone" turns inward and to himself delivers himself of a long, angry harangue against the "cruelty" and "injustice" of all these people. He argues that in these times of "progress and civilization," with the flowering of "freedom and equality" and the development of this "rational, self-loving association" called civilization, "vanity, ambition, and profit" have replaced the "simple, primordial feeling of person for person" and destroyed that need for true "loving association which is instinctual." The rule of law, he insists to himself, destroys love. "Life is incommensurate with law," the product of our "unfeeling mind," which knows only "imagined knowledge." He would have us turn then to that "infallible guide," the "blessed voice" within, which is the "universal spirit that penetrates us all together and each separately," "that same spirit which orders the tree to grow toward the sun, the flowers to fall off in autumn, and us unconsciously to hug one another." Lucerne with its resident aliens is for him an image of modern life, Western individualism, a rational utopian association, the social contract of laws and rights, a society built not on human nature's inherent urge toward love, but on the mind's "one-sided" attempt to make distinctions "in the eternally moving, infinite, infinitely jumbled chaos of good and evil." Lucerne is the emblem of the City of Man. It is not where he can belong.

But then, as his sermon is winding down, the voice of the "little man" singing in the distance breaks through the "dead silence of the night," and Nekhlyudov turns his attention to himself. He sees a contradiction in his spiteful tirade. The "little man" has "no reproach, nor spite, nor remorse in his soul," so who is Nekhlyudov to say that these people behind their "wealthy walls" do not have in their souls just as much "joy of life" (*radost' zhizni*) and "harmony with the world" (*soglasie s mirom*) as he does? It is Nekhlyudov's own anger that has separated him from the Englishmen and destroyed his vision of a harmonious world. Nekhlyudov now sees himself a "miserable worm," attempting to understand the laws of the Spirit, while only "He" can fathom the "infinite harmony" in which we all move in seeming contradictions. He concludes, however, that even with his spite he is somehow answering "the harmonious need of the eternal and infinite." With his view of the universal spirit guiding us all, resolving our contradictions in an infinite harmony, grasped only by the Divine, Nekhlyudov in the end finds a world large enough for him to belong in it.

The fundamental action of *Lucerne* is a mission of love, but it is a mission misunderstood because Nekhlyudov is barred from love by his alienating anger. He projects his estrangement onto others and takes on as his cause the demonstration to these others of his own great love. When this fails in deed, he turns to the word and creates a critique of human civilization which sees self-love as the glue of the

commonwealth and postulates an inherent urge to human relatedness in all, available to each in the depths of his consciousness. But
then toward the end Nekhlyudov discovers the error in his ways and
his views: his anger right now blinds him to the harmony of the
world. The story embodies the "character of the author" Leo Tolstoy
in a most remarkable way. It tells the tale of the Resident and the
Stranger even as it looks forward prophetically to the course of Tolstoy's life, the shape of his works, and the essence of his ideas.

The full title of this story is "From Prince D. Nekhlyudov's Notes.
Lucerne" and the piece is presented as a diary entry of July 8 recording an event of the preceding day. Now Tolstoy's own diary for July 7
in fact records in barest outline the event which is represented in the
story:

> Night. It's cloudy. The moon is breaking through. I can hear
> some fine voices, two bells on the avenue, a tiny person with a
> guitar is singing Tyrolian songs and very well. I gave him some
> money and invited him to sing opposite . . . [the hotel]. Nothing
> happened, he walked off mumbling something, and the crowd
> followed him, laughing at him. . . . I caught up with him and
> asked him to . . . [the hotel] for a drink. We drank, the doorman
> started to laugh, and the waiter sat down. This infuriated me. I
> cursed them and became very agitated. (47,140-41;1857)

The very next day Tolstoy recast this experience into an image, one
close to the final story, because the "impression" of the event had so
sparked his "imagination" that he could not "separate himself from
it" until "he had expressed it in words" and because he hoped that
the "impression," if "sincerely transmitted," "would affect the readers even a hundredth of what it did him" (60,199-212;1857). An actual event in Tolstoy's life is transformed into an image in order to
articulate, not the event, but the feelings and ideas the event evokes.
The transformation from experience to image releases Tolstoy from
the obsessive "impression," but this catharsis of expression has an affective purpose: Tolstoy wants others to share his version and vision
of life. *Lucerne*, with its diary form and first-person narration, accomplishes this in a most direct fashion, and it is clear that the purpose of the tale is not the telling of the event but the sharing of the
view on the event. But all Tolstoy's art serves this same prophetic intent. The image attempts to accomplish what later the idea will do.

The art is the image of experience and the "unconscious creation" of a world-view articulated in his later works and days (52,6;1891).

NIKOLENKA'S TALE OF LIFE

Lucerne reveals the "character of the author" Leo Tolstoy in his sincerity and in his quest, even in his self-contradiction and self-justification. But from early on Tolstoy preferred a less direct representation of the "character of the author." "The most pleasant works are those in which the author, as it were, hides his personal view and at the same time remains constantly true to it wherever it is revealed" (46,182;1853). In *Lucerne* the only disguise is the name of the character. But in his first extended fiction, the autopsychological trilogy *Childhood, Boyhood, Youth* (1852-57), which is a reworking of the form of a Bildungsroman, Tolstoy not only disguised his name, but ascribed his acquaintances' experience of life to his hero and endowed other characters with his own.[3] He hides his "personal view" by mixing it up with others'. It is not the story of Tolstoy's early years. But this distortion of personal experience conceals only to reveal, for throughout this work Tolstoy does remain true to the "character of the author." The trilogy portrays the quest of an "eternally growing soul" for his lost harmonious residence.

Childhood opens three days after the young hero's tenth birthday, but the happy moments when Nikolenka had enjoyed his "marvelous presents" are destroyed in the very first sentence of the work when Nikolenka's tutor, Karl Ivanych, swats a fly just above the boy's head, thereby knocking over the icon of his guardian angel and arousing the child from sleep. This first-person narrative thus begins with an awakening, a sudden shift in awareness. The sleepy boy, annoyed at being disturbed, sees himself the special victim of his tutor, who, he imagines, spends his life planning ways to torment him; even the tutor's dressing gown and tasseled skullcap seem offensive. Happiness is removed to the past, and angered, the child sees himself

---

[3] The term "autopsychological" was first applied to the trilogy by Lydia Ginzburg in her monumental study of psychological prose, *O psikhologicheskoj proze* (Leningrad, 1971), p. 314. I believe the term aptly suggests Tolstoy's basic manner of writing throughout his career. I include within the concept of psychological experience all moral and religious life of the author.

hindered and hurt by those who should care for him. But as the child shakes off the drowsiness, he recovers his former feeling of love and devotion to Karl Ivanych, and on the next page somewhat shame-facedly the boy sees the very tassel on his tutor's skullcap as a sign of his goodness. Nikolenka awakens to life. The morning sun shines through the windows, his brother Volodya laughs gaily, and the moment of alienation becomes a moment of at-onement. Nikolenka feels loved. This sense of security and belonging pervades the rest of the chapter, which culminates in a glimpse of another world beyond. The boy looks out the window of his classroom to see the road, the lime trees, the meadow, the woods, and the terrace where his mother sits and chats with the other grownups. He feels that his lessons keep him from this paradisical garden and his mother's comforting pres-ence, and he dreams of the day when he will be grown up and can be "with those whom he loves" (i). Alienation replaces at-onement. Ni-kolenka now sits in the room estranged from the world in which he would reside. The garden beyond the window of the family residence at Petrovskoe contains the happiness he must have. The whole tril-ogy moves toward a clarification and acquisition of this happiness imaged in this garden.

Childhood is made of a sequence of events which reiterate one ac-tion: the character is suddenly thrust from a familiar and caring world into a strange and alien state from which he escapes into a re-stored realm of love. Karl Ivanych is to be fired and then the beloved tutor, it is decided, will be kept on. Nikolenka spills a pitcher of *kvas* on a tablecloth and for punishment Maman's favorite and all-loving servant Natalya Savishna rubs his face in it until he cries from fury, but then she admits her guilt, begs forgiveness, and gives the boy some candy. He weeps from love and shame. Nikolenka leaves home and Maman to visit grandmother in Moscow, where he is introduced, among other things, to the social world of name-day parties and the conventions of dancing. The band strikes up the familiar strains of a mazurka, and the child's sense of estrangement in an unknown world without Maman and home is overcome by the lively melody and he begins to dance. But as he yields to the music and whirls around the floor, he sees one of the onlookers staring at his feet. "That glance killed me." Thus alienated he begins horsing around "neither in time to the music nor in accord with anything else," until all begin to stare at him. Nikolenka's father reprimands him and then dances off with the boy's partner, to the loud applause of all. Nikolenka feels totally defeated. "Everyone despises me and always will. Every road is closed to me, the road to friendship, love, honor, all is lost!" But this moment of utter rejection and betrayal is then immediately transformed.

> If Maman were here she would not have blushed for her Niko-lenka. And my imagination carried me far off in pursuit of her beloved image. I recalled the meadow in front of the house, the tall lime trees in the yard, the clear pond over which swallows swirled, the blue sky in which there were hanging white transparent clouds, the fragrant stacks of new-mown hay. And many other peaceful, happy memories drifted through my distraught imagination.

The memory of Maman overcomes the present moment of alienated despair. Her "beloved image" recalls the paradisical garden, only now the glimpse of the world beyond moves outward to the pond and haystack and toward the blue sky and white clouds. As the child's views of the world grows, his horizons expand until they will encompass all of nature. The harmony of the natural world here remembered in a moment of isolation and dejection restores well-being. The Stranger becomes the Resident.

The autopsychological nature of Tolstoy's fiction can be seen in this image of the garden. The image runs through the trilogy and contains its high meaning. But this garden is itself based on a real one that had a specific moral and religious meaning for Tolstoy.

> This morning I was strolling round the garden and as always I recalled Mother, "mommy," whom I do not remember at all but who has remained for me the holy ideal. I have never heard a bad thing about her. While walking through the birch groves, as I was approaching the grove of nut trees, I saw in the mud the imprint of a woman's foot and thought of her, her body. But I could not imagine it. Everything bodily would defile her. What a good feeling I have toward her. How I would like to have that feeling toward all, women and men. And it's possible. In dealing with people it would be good to think of them like that, to feel toward them like that. It's possible. I'll try. (56,133;1908).

The garden is the place where "mommy" is recalled. To Tolstoy "mommy" has one meaning: she is the one he can love. In the garden Tolstoy recalls that he can love others and feels called to love others.

In the garden he resolves himself to right action. "It's possible. I'll try." In the garden, therefore, Tolstoy comes to a clear awareness of identity and vocation. The garden is the place of faith, an image not of the physical world, but of the universe of love in which he would reside. In Tolstoy's works all great moments of faith, the epiphanies of clarification of identity and vocation, take place in the expanse of nature which this garden represents.

The theme of childhood is expressed in a series of paràdigmatic actions: love is lost and then restored. These actions are, of course, versions of the fundamental action, the Divine task which seeks to replace division and discord with union and harmony. What is characteristic of the paradigmatic action of *Childhood*, however, is the location of the harmonious experience at the terminal points of the action. This imagination of paradise at the beginning and end of experience is enhanced by the peculiar mode of narration in the work. *Childhood* opens with an immediate moment in the life of a young boy, seemingly told by him, but in fact the work is narrated from a distance in time by the young man Nicholas Irtenev recalling his lost past. The act of memory spans the period of loss and connects the distant moment of love with its final recollection. In the remembrance Irtenev returns home to mother. But he cannot remember her except in one ideal form: her eyes that express "kindness" (*dobrota*) and love and her hand that "so often used to caress him" and that he "so often used to kiss" (ii). In reverie Irtenev recalls and restores a world of reciprocal love. The central chapter of the work, entitled "Childhood," focuses on Irtenev's memories of this "happy, happy, irretrievable time" when his mother's "tender hand" would stroke his hair or tickle him, when he would nuzzle up to his mother's bosom and whisper that he loved her, when she would kiss him most tenderly and tell him never to forget her (xv). At night, praying before the icon, he recalls, his "love for her and his love for God somehow strangely merged into one feeling." At the center of the work, Irtenev recaptures his best moment.

While made of recollections which restore the past, *Childhood* focuses on loss: the loss of innocence, imagination, aesthetic sensitivity, and religious sensibility. The culminating event is the death of Maman, the ultimate loss, the privation of love. What Nikolenka feels most, however, in this first encounter with death in Tolstoy's fiction, are his own failings. He does not know if his grief is sincere and fears it may be but a show of vanity, that feeling "most strongly grafted onto human nature" (xxviii). Although in her death Maman abandons him, he doubts not her love, but his own. Not in himself but in Maman's servant, the all-loving Natalya Savishna does Nikolenka see genuine grief and hence true love. Untouched by self-interest, Natalya Savishna lives her life in care for others and dies as a result "without regret or fear," having thus "accomplished the best and greatest task in life." *Childhood* ends not with loss of love, then, but with Irtenev's remembrance of the one who loves him and the one who knows how to love. His "last sad memories" restore this love to him and show him his own life's task. The form of the work transforms the tale of loss into a resurrection of a lost paradise.

CHILDHOOD depicts a series of events from two typical days in Nikolenka's life. The first day is at home, the second day at grandmother's house. *Boyhood* moves the action out of the family residence for good. Nikolenka abandons Petrovskoe. Maman's death thrusts the fledgling out of the nest into an alien world where even the familiar becomes estranged. Papa seems to pay no attention to Nikolenka, grandmother does not love him for himself but only as a reminder of his mother, Karl Ivanych dons a wig and looks so "strange and silly" that Nikolenka is surprised he had not noticed this earlier, and an "invisible barrier" appears between the boys and girls (iv). Nikolenka fights with his older brother, and they see each others' torment but "hide" from this understanding and for a whole day refuse to admit their guilt or ask forgiveness: "Now all is over between us; we are at odds forever" (v). Nikolenka's poor relation and friend Katenka realizes that "not forever will they live together" (*vmeste*), and he finds it hard to imagine how they will live "apart" (*vroz'*) (iii). *Boyhood* tells of life lived without mother's comforting embrace. The world of human relatedness is lost, and Nikolenka becomes a Stranger.

But *Boyhood* opens with a journey away from death and loss to the "joyous feeling of consciousness of life (*soznanie zhizni*), satisfaction with the present and hope for the future" (i). The springtime nature bathed in a "calmly joyful light" reflects Nikolenka's mood. The journey into the future, however, brings Nikolenka into contact with unknown people, and he is disturbed that they "have nothing in common with me . . . and that they may never be seen again." As the journey proceeds, this moment of alienation issues forth as "God's wrath," a thunderstorm which momentarily stops the travel (ii). A fantastic "human-like being" with crooked legs approaches the carriage and thrusts into the window the red stump that remains of his arm. The utterly alien creature terrifies the young boy, but one of the servants gives alms to the "pitiful creature," who then moves on his way. This moral expression of charity and compassion for others is followed by a clearing of the storm and a total transformation of both self and nature. "My heart was smiling as was the refreshed and rejoicing world of nature." Bewitched by the "wondrous fragrance of the forest after the spring storm," Nikolenka bursts forth from the carriage to romp in nature. He moves outward from self and toward other. The journey of discovery leads to another level of awareness which is a heightened return to the sense of hope and belonging. The sadness of parting becomes joy, the gloom of the storm, ecstasy, the alienation, at-onement. Love turns life into joy—but not for long. In direct contrast to *Childhood*, *Boyhood* opens in a calm and joyous key which is lowered and then raised to an exalted height from which everything then falls and collapses. There is no memory to resurrect the lost "consciousness of life," only moments when you "stop the activity of your mind and try to convince yourself that there is no future and that there has been no past" (xiv).

Boyhood represents the experience of life as rejection and betrayal by others. Karl Ivanych is finally fired for good, and his tale of life now told at length is the paradigm of Nikolenka's experience of boyhood. The tutor sees himself as the eternal stranger, "unhappy even in his mother's womb," an "alien (*chuzhoj*) even in his own family" (vii). He considers himself an orphan, "loved and caressed" only by his "kind mother." But even she cannot save him from what he believes is his fate. His unloving stepfather scolds and punishes him for his brother's and sister's misdeeds, sends him off at age 14 to be an apprentice, and later lets him be drafted into the army in place of his stepbrother, the "only son." Karl Ivanych then spends a life of forced wandering away from home only to end up caring for Nikolenka until now once again he is pushed out of the nest where he hoped he belonged. The tutor tells this tale with sentimental and self-pitying tears in his eyes, but it is clear that Nikolenka hears it as his own story. He then proceeds to make it come true. The paradigmatic action of *Boyhood* tells of the increase of division and discord in the world.

At the center of *Boyhood* is sin, the failure to accomplish one's task and do one's father's will. Nikolenka wanders out from his lessons, is caught by the music teacher, and then nearly fails a history examination. Then, a little later, when his father gives him the keys to get something from a drawer in his study, Nikolenka lets curiosity get the better of him and opens his father's briefcase, only to break off the key in the lock. Even the thought of this "new crime" is terrifying and the fear of being caught begins to spoil his perceptions (xii): he begins to feel "superfluous, left out" (xiii). And then the music teacher does tell on him. Rejected, betrayed, and ashamed, Nikolenka is about to be punished, when out of spite he strikes his tutor with all his childish might (xiv). He is dragged upstairs to the closet, having earned his solitary confinement. Sin leads Nikolenka to the isolation of the closet, from which he can hear the merry sounds of the children playing in the other room. He resembles Nekhlyudov in *Lucerne*. He also resembles his creator, who forty years later recalled the experience from which this autopsychological image was created. "Everyone is feeling fine, but I am depressed and cannot get hold of myself. Just like the feeling when St. Thomas locked me up and I heard from the closet how merrily they were laughing" (53,105;1896). Confinement in the closet is the emblem of banishment from the Kingdom of God, the punishment for the sin against others.

For Nikolenka the isolation leads to a fantasy of rejection and revenge. Maybe he is not the son of his mother and father, but an "unfortunate orphan, an abandoned child taken in out of mercy" (xv). This misfortune, he assumes, comes not from his fault but, like Karl Ivanych, from fate. His imagination takes hold, and he conjures up a confrontation with his father, who is forced to admit: "I have adopted you and if you are worthy of my love, then I will never leave you." Nikolenka professes his eternal love but insists that he himself must "leave home" because "no one loves him." The fantasy continues, and Nikolenka joins the army, where he becomes a general whom the Tsar himself will grant any favor he would wish. The favor he wishes is revenge on his hated "enemy," St. Jerome. Nikolenka's solitary thoughts turn from revenge to the injustice of his punishment, and he begins to doubt God. Then he dies. Nikolenka's soul takes off on its flight outward and toward heaven, where he sees "something amazingly beautiful, white, transparent, long," his mother. "That something white (*beloe*) surrounds and caresses" him, but he cannot kiss her hand nor feel her tickling him. They both then fly off "higher and higher" until the fantasy collapses and Nikolenka awakens to the reality of his punishment and shame. With his admission of guilt, he begins a self-confrontation and starts on the path to his youth.

YOUTH opens with a moment of moral awakening. Already toward the end of *Boyhood*, Nikolenka had met his new friend Nekhlyudov, a correct, rather rigid young man who knows the rules of moral life and attempts to guide young Nikolenka to right action. The friend embodies Nikolenka's awakening conscience; he represents the "exalted adoration of the ideal of virtue and the conviction that man's destined purpose is continual self-perfection" (xxvii). Nekhlyudov is the voice of mission. *Youth* begins with the internalization of Nekhlyudov's view of life. As in *Boyhood*, the opening time is spring, but now sitting in the classroom of his Moscow residence, Nikolenka looks out onto the back garden, which speaks to him "about something new and beautiful . . . about beauty, happiness and virtue," which are "one and the same" (ii). This intuition of some unifying principle in nature and man leads immediately to a review and revision of life: "How bad I was in the past, how good and happy I might and can be in the future. . . . Right now, right this very minute I have to make myself into another person and begin life differently." This firm resolve to change Irtenev then compares to another moment of awakening. "Have you ever lain down and fallen asleep on a gloomy, rainy summer day and awakened at sunset, opened your eyes to see through the expanding rectangular window . . . the rain-soaked shadowy lilac-tinged vista of a lime tree lane and the damp garden path lit by bright slanting rays and heard suddenly the merry life of birds in the garden and seen insects weaving through the openings in the window while glittering in the sun and sensed the aroma of the air after the rain and thought 'How could I not be ashamed to sleep through such an evening' and quickly jumped up to go into the garden to rejoice in life?" This, he tells us, is the "image" of the new awakening. *Youth* returns Nikolenka to the paradisical garden beyond the window of his childhood classroom and thus opens up the path to the joy of life.

Nikolenka repents of his past, but the past of which he speaks is not the distant idyll that represents the ideal. He regrets the "sad times when the soul silently submitted to the power of life's lie and depravity." Nikolenka rejects this immediate past in order to find a better life in the future. "It seemed so easy and natural to me to sunder myself from my past, to alter or forget everything that had been and to begin my life and all its relationships completely anew, that the past did not burden or bind me. I even enjoyed loathing my past and tried to see it darker than it was. The blacker the circle of memories of the past, the purer and brighter did the pure, bright point of the present stand out and the rainbow colors of the future unfold" (iii). *Youth* reverses *Childhood*'s attitude to the past and repents of *Boyhood*. Now like the Nekhlyudov of *Lucerne*, Nikolenka begins to hear that "blessed, joyous voice" that speaks out against all "untruth" and "exposes his past." He even feels "repelled by himself," but his "remorse is so merged with hope for the future that there is nothing sad in it." The despair of boyhood led to a wasteland; only repentance shows the way to the garden where he will find his youthful "daydreams": love for "her," love of being loved, and hope for fame and success. The paradigmatic action of *Youth* is repentance: it recalls and rejects a discordant past in an effort to create a harmonious future.

This paradigmatic action of *Youth* takes the form of examination. Nikolenka examines himself in order to confess before his Easter communion. He even does it twice. He is then examined by others in order to enter the university. This test passed, he moves out into the world, revisiting the relatives who had visited him in *Childhood*; now he tests them and himself against them. He makes new friends at the university and judges himself by their standards. In this he finds himself lacking, and so in order to make his way toward fame and success he abandons Nekhlyudov's path toward right action for a life of *comme il faut*, living the way others say he should. In his need for acceptance and recognition, he loses sight of his mission. He seeks no higher vocation and finds his identity in being *comme il faut*. The "eternally growing soul" stops.

Nikolenka realizes that he is not participating in the life around him and that his new philosophy leads to a dead end only when he examines himself upon his return to his childhood past, the family residence at Petrovskoe. Placed at the center of *Youth*, the return to Petrovskoe is the central paradigmatic action of the work and the culminating event of the whole trilogy. After the long separation, Nikolenka finally confronts himself. The whole experience is an examination in which he recalls and rejects the past in order to create a harmonious future. As he awakens the morning after his arrival, he "suddenly" feels the "caress of the dear old house" and wonders how "we, the house and I, could have been so long without each other?" (xxviii.) The "house joyously receives him in its arms"; in his return he is again accepted and loved. He then strolls through his past, and the rooms remind him of the drama of his childhood, the fears and joys, the all-permeating love, and the loss of that love. The first response to his return home ends with the memory of suffering and death. This memory of lost love must be rejected.

In a chapter entitled "Youth," therefore, Nikolenka moves outward from the house toward the world of nature outside, where he recovers from the sense of loss and breathes in nature's "force of life" (*sila zhizni*, xxxii). The journey back to Petrovskoe reaches its climax and meaning, however, only when Nikolenka returns to the paradisical garden of *Childhood*, which now reappears, but filled with the sights and sounds of the "force of life": animals and people abound in the scene, the minute details marking the moment of attention to the "force of life." But then as Nikolenka awaits the appearance of "her," the one who loves him and whom he loves, the scene takes on a "strange significance, the significance of a beauty too great and a happiness somehow incomplete."

> But the moon would rise higher and higher, brighter and brighter in the sky, the rich lustre of the pond steadily swelling like a sound would become clearer and clearer, the shadows darker and darker, the light more and more limpid, and as I would gaze upon and listen to it all, something would tell me that even she with her bare arms and passionate embraces was far, far from the only bliss (*blago*), and the more I would look at the high full moon, did true beauty and bliss seem to me higher and higher, purer and purer, nearer and nearer to Him, the source of all beauty and bliss, and tears of some unsatisfied but tumultuous joy would well up in my eyes.

This vision of the moon filling the heavens and earth with light takes his attention away from "her" and Nikolenka discovers that "love for her" is not the highest "bliss." In the world transformed by light, he finds "Him," the "source of beauty and bliss," the true one who loves him and the one whom he loves. The happiness in the garden is the experience of the Divine. Waiting for the woman in white, Nikolenka is overcome with "joy" and finds God.

> And still I would be alone and still it would seem to me that nature in her mysterious grandeur, the luminous and enticing circle of the moon which had for some reason rested in one distant, indefinite place in the pale blue sky while being present everywhere and seemingly filling the immensities of space, and I, an insignificant worm already defiled by all the petty, wretched human passions, but with my might power (*sila*) of imagination and love—still it would seem to me at those moments as though nature and the moon and I, we were one and the same.

The image of the garden expands to the "immensities of space." Returning to the place of love, Nikolenka finds himself in the All. He discovers his true position in the universe. He finds his identity in an identification with everything that exists. But he is not God, nor is God everything. God is the "source of beauty and bliss," the one from whom all good things flow. Like the moon, which is a circle and center of attention and yet dispersed by light throughout, Nikolenka belongs to all of nature but is separated from it in his mighty love for what is also beyond nature, the "source of the beauty and bliss," God. In relation to God, Nikolenka is an "insignificant worm defiled by human passions." But while Nikolenka is miserable in his passions, he is mighty in his "imagination and love." He has the "power" (*sila*) within. In his identification with everything that exists Nikolenka raises to a new level the consciousness of the "force (*sila*) of life" he experienced earlier in the garden.

Five pages later this exalted moment of at-onement in the paradisical garden is obliterated for good by the devastating news that papa is about to remarry. "I was disturbed by the idea that an outsider, an alien (*chuzhaja*) and especially a young woman without any right would suddenly take the place . . . of my dear deceased mother!" (xxxv) Even nature conspires in this desecration. The trees and bushes seem desperate to depart, tearing themselves up by their roots, and the leaves fall from the trees as if in a race with each other to get away. The "force of life" is gone, and the garden is ravaged by destruction and death. Nikolenka leaves home for the university. But while the feeling of "being a member of a large society was very pleasant" to him, he has difficulties in belonging. (xxxvi) "Everywhere I felt the link which united that whole youthful society, but with sadness I felt that somehow that link had passed me by." He tries to be friendly with the students outside his own special circle and economic class, but he does not find the link nor become a member of that "large society." The examinations are given at the end of the first year, and he fails. Remorse returns. Nekhlyudov again appears on the scene, and with renewed fervor Nikolenka once more looks to his "rules of life" in his quest for right action. With this failure and this firm resolve this first tale of life comes to an end.

THE PARADIGMS OF LIFE

"For a work to be absorbing," Tolstoy believed, "it not only should have one idea guiding it, but it must also be imbued with one feeling" (46,214-15;1853). Behind the complex psychology and rich texture of Tolstoy's fictions there is a unity of experience shared by the author and his characters. This thematic unity is embodied in the paradigmatic actions which comprise the bulk of each piece. The meaning of the work, the "one idea guiding it" and the "one feeling" with which it is embued, is most clearly revealed at the physical center of the narrative: in *Childhood*, the resurrection of a love through the memory of Maman; in *Boyhood*, the loss of love through the sin against father; in *Youth*, the effort to rediscover the self and shape its future by a return to the parental residence. Seen in this way the trilogy is shaped by a pattern of reversal and return, a dialectic which, as we shall see, plays a major role in Tolstoy's thinking. Both *Childhood* and *Youth* reverse a loss of love by a return to it in a new form. *Boyhood* reverses the love of *Childhood*; *Youth* seeks to reverse the loss of love in *Boyhood*. Just as each of the three parts of the narrative alternate variously moments of at-onement and moments of alienation, so the whole trilogy moves by a dialectic of reversal and return to love, culminating in the moment back home, in the garden, in an experience of mystical union with God followed by a denouement of reversal into isolation, failure, and banishment. The pattern of this tale of life outlines the story of the Resident and the Stranger and provides the shape for Tolstoy's three major novels. These novels comprise a second triology of life.

As *Childhood* tells of an idyllic world tragically lost and magically retrieved through memory, so *War and Peace* recounts the story of the homeland invaded and desecrated by a foreign enemy who is then defeated and expelled triumphantly by the residents of the land. The paradigmatic action of the novel revolves around a reversal and a return: harmonious life is brought to ruin and then wondrously restored. This paradigmatic action shapes the public and personal plots. Indeed Tolstoy represents Napoleon's entry into Moscow as a metaphoric violation of female purity. Napoleon sees Moscow's "big, beautiful body quivering with life" and believes that "une ville occupée par l'ennemi ressemble à une fille qui a perdu son honneur." (III,iii,xix). But in losing her honor Moscow finds it: the residents abandon their home to save it. The historical narrative parallels the main story of human relatedness, Pierre's and Prince Andrew's quest for Natasha's love. Like Moscow, Natasha Rostova "quivers with life" and young love and then nearly loses her honor in captivity to her enemy, Anatole Kuragin. Placed at the end of the first half of the work—that is, at the center—the seduction of Natasha is, even in Tolstoy's own assessment, the "crux of the whole novel" (61,180;1867). But Natasha too is saved by and with the residents of the land. Her enemy is expelled from Moscow, her honor is retrieved, her love is returned. Natasha's victory over her own violation restores Prince Andrew's alienated love and rewards Pierre's abiding affection. *War and Peace* tells of the expulsion of enmity and thus imitates the task of life.

War and Peace is not organized around the vicissitudes of one character, but one character is central to the whole book and embodies its meaning. Natasha Rostova is given and earns, exudes and personifies the "force of life" (*sila zhizni*) (IV,iv,xx) which other major characters pursue or pervert. Her experience of life represents an ideal mode of being in the world, the blessed state in the universe of the novel. Natasha is the child we are all called to be like. "I note the merriment (*veselost'*), boldness, freedom, and majesty (*tsarstvennost'*) of young people and even more so of children," Tolstoy noted when near seventy. "In us oldsters our sins have humbled us, have covered over that divine force (*bozhestvennaja sila*) enclosed in us. Children cannot help being self-assured and free. They must be that way because they bear in themselves the divine principle (*bozhestvennoe nachalo*) not yet sullied by life—all possibilities" (*vse voz-*

mozhnosti) (53,51;1895). Natasha Rostova is the incarnation of this "divine principle" and the emblem of the "divine force" of life. She is the one "whom everyone always loves" (II,v,vii).

The "crux of the whole novel" entails a reversal of and a return to Natasha's blessed state of love. Her betrayal of love leads to an illness whose symptom is the loss of "joy in life" and a withdrawal into isolation (III,i,xvii). Living "life without life," Natasha becomes a Stranger. But then, just as the Rostovs hear that Napoleon is approaching Moscow, Natasha goes to church. She hears the deacon begin the service, "In harmony (*mirom*) let us pray unto the Lord." "In harmony—all together, without distinction of class, without enmity, united in brotherly love, let us pray," she responds in her heart. In this response Natasha penetrates to the central meaning of life and the ideal mode of experience the novel represents: she prays for human relatedness. *War and Peace (Vojna i mir)* depicts the victory over war and enmity, division and discord, the triumph of peace. But "peace" (*mir*) in Russian and in this novel means many things: the absence of war and enmity, calm, harmony, union, all people together, the commune, the world, the universe. "Peace" implies the accord of all people, each with each, the harmony of all together at one. This "peace of all people among themselves" is the "Kingdom of God on earth" (23,370;1883). This "peace," which in Christian terms is the peace of Christ, is, furthermore, the grand accord of everything that exists, the total unity of All destroyed only by our acts against it. This "peace," then, is the beginning and end of all reality; the Divine task of replacing discord with harmony is an act of restoration to "peace." The task of life for Tolstoy, therefore, is the "return of the world to peace" (*vozrozhdenie mira k miru*) (5,256;1856).[4] All this Natasha seems to intuit at her prayer in

---

[4] In the Eastern Christian tradition, this "peace" has ontological and epistemological significance: "peace" is the foundation of reality and the inner core of consciousness. This is made most clear in the excellent study of Eastern Christian literature by S. S. Averintsev, *Poetika rannevizantijskoj literatury* (Moscow, 1977), pp. 84-128. The Russian language reflects this dual significance of "peace" in the one word *mir*, which has two basic directions of meaning, inner calm ("peace") and total unity ("world" or "universe"). Pre-revolutionary orthography distinguished these two directions. Etymologically and phonetically the words are the same, and modern orthography makes no distinction. In this study I try to translate the first direction of meaning as "peace" and the second as "world" or "universe" (Tolstoy preferred this translation in philosophical passages: 67,114; 1894). The significance of this complex concept for *War and*

church. The remainder of her career in the novel is devoted to the restoration of this "peace."

This paradigmatic action of the restoration of harmony governs the novel not only as a whole but also in its parts. This is well illustrated in the delineated segment of Natasha at the ball (II,iii,xiv-xvi). The sequence begins with Natasha's involvement with everyone else: she would "get them all dressed as well as possible" and almost forgets about herself. She arrives at the ball in expectation of others' involvement with her. But then all of a sudden she is overcome with a fear that "no one will approach her." She falls into a despair in which she feels "all alone in this forest, in this alien (*chuzhdyj*) crowd, interesting to no one, needed by no one." Her whole life, past, present, future, then passes her by: Prince Andrew strolls past without noticing her, Anatole Kuragin glances at her "as if he were looking at the wall," Boris goes by twice and turns away each time. Then Pierre, seeing her despair, brings Prince Andrew up to her and the two dance off. Natasha is "happier than ever before in her life," in "that most exalted state of happiness when a person becomes completely kind and beautiful and does not believe in the possibility of evil, unhappiness, or grief." Now "in her eyes all at the ball are kind, nice, good people who love each other, who could not hurt each other and therefore everyone must be happy." The rhythm of the scene, like many others in the work, as we shall see throughout this book, reenacts the paradigmatic action of the novel: the world of human relatedness is lost and then restored to a new maturity.

The delineated segment of the hunt is the most complex example of such a paradigmatic action (II,iv,iii-vi). Not without the usual domestic tensions, the Rostovs start out all together, the Count, Nicholas, Natasha, Petya, Uncle, Danilo, and the jestor Nastasya Iva-

---

Peace, but not for all of Tolstoy, has been pointed out by Soviet scholars, who have noted that although early editions of the novel spell the title as "War and Peace," the single instance of the title written in Tolstoy's own hand spelled "world" not "peace." For the full complexity of the word in the novel see Ja. S. Bilinkis, *O tvorchestve L.N. Tolstogo* (Leningrad, 1959), pp. 195-279; S. Bocharov, *Roman L. Tolstogo "Vojna i mir"* (Moscow, 1963), pp. 49-53; E. Zajdenshur, *Vojna i mir L. N. Tolstogo, Sozdanie velikoj knigi* (Moscow, 1966), pp. 66-70; S. Bocharov, "Mir v *Vojne i mire,*" *Voprosy literatury* VIII (1970), 76-90; and G. Ja. Galagan, *L.N. Tolstoj: khudozhestvenno-eticheskie iskanija* (Leningrad, 1981), pp. 20-22, 93-99. The etymology was established by V. N. Toporov, "Iz nabljudenij nad etimologiej slov mifologicheskogo kharaktera," *Etimologija* (Moscow, 1969), pp. 18-21.

novna. No social, gender, or species distinctions divide the group. "The dogs know their master and name. Each hunter knows his task (*delo*), place (*mesto*), and destined purpose" (*naznachenie*). All of a sudden a wolf appears. But the Count, already a bit tipsy, is so busy trying to get another snort from his snuff box that he misses his chance. Then the wolf dashes off in Nicholas' direction. "Hope turns into despair" as Nicholas immediately begins to pray to God that his dog will get the wolf "right in front of Uncle's eyes." Nicholas fails and Danilo moves in for the catch. Then a fox appears on the scene and everything gets confused; even the dogs get scattered. Nicholas looks up and sees a stranger (*chuzhoj*), their neighbor Ilagin, whom the Rostovs have been battling in court for some time. Nicholas considers his neighbor his worst enemy. But Ilagin apologizes for being on the Rostov land, praises Nicholas' dog, and invites them all to come hunt at his place. The neighbors become friends. Then they go off to Ilagin's to hunt hares, Ilagin preaching a philosophy of the hunt that excludes envy and rivalry. But in the heat of the hunt this philosophy fades. Each hunter cries out at the same time to his own dog in a "voice not his own," urging the dog on to the catch. The hare is caught and Natasha "joyously and ecstatically squeals so loud that it rings in her ears. With this squeal she expresses what the other hunters are expressing in their own simultaneous conversations. Natasha perceives the harmony of all together. Her squeal marks this final moment of belonging which is triumphant because each belongs in his own way.

The delineated segment of the hunt moves from high hope to moral failings to repentance to triumphant harmony, and thus imitates the action and embodies the meaning of *War and Peace*. The theme of the hunting scene is the triumph over alienation. Each of its three parts represents a moment of division or discord overcome. In the first section the moral failings which isolate the aristocratic masters from their tasks nearly ruin the catch until Danilo the servant reconciler steps in to save the day. This first part of the hunt reflects the image of war in the first half of the novel, where the battles of 1805 are presented through the isolated aristocratic characters' experience of them, and victory, such as it is, is accomplished through the efforts of Danilo's counterpart, Captain Tushin. In the second section of the hunting sequence there is no hunting, but, rather, Danilo's triumph is spoiled by an alien neighbor whose repentance by apology expels a long-standing enmity. This interlude is central, placed between the moments of hunting, just as Natasha's scene of sin and repentance is central to the war, placed as it is between the battles of 1805 and 1812. In the third part of the hunting sequence the individual strivings for victory are reconciled in a moment of accord. As in the war of 1812, where final victory is won through guerrilla warfare, this scene represents the special mode of relatedness which underlies the whole novel: the vision of a providential harmony in which everyone and everything does its own task and thereby participates in the victorious outcome of the whole. Like the guerrilla warfare, the second hunt is the image of the idea expressed in the epilogue: "As the sun and each atom of ether is a sphere in its size incomprehensible to man, so each person (*lichnost'*) has within himself his own aims and yet has them in order to serve the common aims incomprehensible to man" (E,i,iv). The sequence of the hunt moves toward the paradigmatic restoration of that peace which is the harmony of all together and at one.[5]

THE EPILOGUE TO *War and Peace* pictures this peace. Prince Andrew has died, returned to the "source of love" from which he learned he came, and lives on as a hero in his young orphaned son's imagination. The Stranger is gone. Pierre, who ever seeks the meaning of life, is married to Natasha, the embodiment of the "force of life," and Nicholas, who ever seeks the serenity of hearth and home, is wedded to Princess Mary who dreams of the road that leads to the "eternal haven" where there is "eternal joy and bliss" (II,iii,xxvi). These four main characters brought together in one final scene close the novel even as they reconcile the various tendencies of their creator: the urge to understand is united to the exuberance of experience, the need for family and home combined with the urge to reli-

---

[5] This reading of the hunt follows in part the analysis given by S. Bocharov in his excellent book *Roman L. Tolstogo "Vojna i mir"* (Moscow, 1963), pp. 19-33. He treats the hunt as an example of what I call a "delineated segment" and shows how this segment is related to the whole. My conception of "paradigmatic actions," while different from Bocharov's in definition and terminology, is at bottom in accord with his understanding of the relationship of parts to whole in the novel. I have extended this idea to the other two major fictions and given it a foundation in Tolstoy's psychology and theology. For another treatment of this issue, see E. K. Brown, *Rhythm in the Novel* (Toronto, 1950), pp. 78-84.

gious quest. Snatched from the time flow of the life of the novel, the epilogue glimpses a picture of two happy families seemingly residing all together and at one. *Anna Karenina* reverses the picture. Eventually all the characters in this novel come to share Alexey Karenin's predicament when "he experiences the feeling you would experience upon returning home and finding your home locked shut" (II,ix). *Anna Karenina* focuses its attention not on harmony restored but on the pervading discord of this world. "All happy families resemble each other, every unhappy family is unhappy in its own way" (I,i).

The opening paragraph of *Anna Karenina* alludes to the word "home" eight times but speaks of the failure of residency. Dolly is locked in her rooms, Stiva has not been home for three days, the children are running all about the house, and the servants are quarreling with each other. They all feel that "people who have chanced upon each other in some inn are more linked together than they."All their communication is about separation, and the paragraph ends with departure from the home. "There is no meaning in their living together." Stiva awakens to the realization of this confusion and his assessment of the "drama": "I am at fault, but not guilty." Yet despite his fundamental honesty and hatred of "falsity and lies" (iii), in order to attempt to reestablish harmony, he tells Dolly that he is guilty and asks for forgiveness. Dolly sees the lie. She feels hurt and rejected and wants punishment and revenge. She wonders whether it is possible for them "to live together" since inside she feels hatred and estrangement (iv). "Even if we remain in the same house, we are strangers (*chuzhie*), strangers forever." Neither knows "what to do" but Stiva believes that all will somehow "shape up." His sister Anna arrives, there is a reconciliation, and then the drama of Stiva and Dolly fades into the background of the novel as it slowly disintegrates again into a confusion from which they cannot be saved.

Like *Boyhood*, *Anna Karenina* begins with the discovery that life is not the harmony it seemed and with the expectation that life can be made into the harmony that I want. Both works in this sense begin with the hope of love. They culminate in despair over a sin which leads the central characters in each into a world of solitary confinement filled with thoughts of revenge. The rhythm moves from the hopeful possibilities of a new residency to the actuality of isolation, from the dream of at-onement to the reality of alienation, from anticipation to frustration. The delineated segment of Kitty at the ball, so different from the ball in *War and Peace*, illustrates this paradigmatic action (I,xxiii-iv). Kitty arrives at the ball, all expectation: everyone wants to dance with her, and the first quadrille is already promised to Vronsky, who surely will propose. A waltz begins to play, Vronsky approaches hesitantly, but finally asks, they dance off, and the music stops. "She looks at his face, so close to her, and long after, many years later, that look full of love which she gave him and which he did not respond to tore her heart with tormenting shame." This one sentence, which steps out of the narrative sequence, captures the feel of the whole work, from the moment of hope to endless shame. But for Kitty there is still the quadrille. Again they dance, but nothing significant is said. Later she sees Anna and Vronsky talking together and her unconscious suspicion and fear begin to surface. "The whole ball, the whole world, everything in Kitty's soul becomes covered in mist." The mazurka begins and Kitty is overcome with "despair and horror." There is "no hope" that Vronsky will ask her. Anna and Vronsky dance by and in order to say something to Kitty, Vronsky murmers, "It's a nice ball." On his face Kitty sees "embarrassment and submission, like the look of an intelligent dog who is guilty of something." And Anna seems "horrible and cruel in her alluring charm," somehow "alien and demonic." With this, Kitty, who is the controlling consciousness of the ball scene, just drops out of the text of the scene. The delineated segment moves from Kitty's hope of love to her despairing aloneness. The same rhythm controls the mushroom-picking romance of Varenka and Sergey Ivanovich (VI, iii-v).

Despair hovers over the major characters in the novel, but it does not readily conquer because they share Stiva's belief that everything will "shape up." What keeps Kitty going from dance to dance is her hope after hope. *Anna Karenina* moves forward through just such false hopes. Harmony is never truly achieved and therefore it cannot be lost or restored. Rather, each failure of harmony is forgotten in the light of a new false hope. Vronsky is in the depths of despair. Rejected by Anna in her sick-bed reconciliation with her husband, shamed before the man he shamed, embarrassed at his own failing career, Vronsky takes a gun to himself. The suicide fails, but it does at least, he believes, "redeem his guilt" (IV, xxiii). Still, the despair does not pass because what Vronsky wants he cannot have. Anna is lost to him forever and he must go to Tashkent to pursue his career. Then the next day Betsy stops by to tell him that Karenin will give the divorce. "Not bothering to accompany Betsy to the door, forgetting all his decisions, not asking when it will be possible or where the husband is, Vronsky takes off immediately for the Karenins. Seeing nothing and no one, he rushes up the stairs and quickly, almost restraining himself from running, he goes into her room. Not thinking, nor noticing whether there is anyone else in the room, he embraces her and begins kissing her all over, face, hands, neck." The hope of reconciliation thrusts Vronsky from his despair in his room right into Anna's arms, all in one short paragraph. And Anna responds to the passion. "Yes, you have possessed me and I am yours." The terrifying memory of all that has happened only increases the passion and the hope. They will be "like husband and wife," a "family." With these great expectations the first half of the novel ends.

At the center of *Anna Karenina* false hope still springs eternal. This is true even of Kitty and Levin, whose marriage opens the second half of the novel. In the midst of the momentous bliss of the wedding ceremony, as the deacon reads the words, "by love joined in union them that were separated," Levin is struck by the "depth of meaning" in the phrase and glances over into Kitty's eyes to see if she shares his feeling (V,iv). He believes she does, but she does not. Kitty is not listening to the service and does not understand the words. For her the experience is emotional, the sense of joy in the fruition of all her hopes and desires, and she yields to the emotion. For Levin the experience is intellectual, the realization of the profound, even metaphysical, meaning of the event and he understands the relationship anew. Joined, they are still separate. At the center of *Anna Karenina* the two couples are reconciled after a separation and now it would seem for good. But each joining, whether licit or illicit, is marred by the isolation that distances the characters from each other. In the second half these high hopes fade: Anna and Vronsky drift into antagonism, and Kitty and Levin, shown mostly in moments of disagreement, end up spiritually isolated from each other, as Levin moves to his vision of the "Master" all alone. In *War and Peace* moments of harmony are genuine; in *Anna Karenina* harmony is elusive and often illusive.

The delineated segment of the hunt is the most complex example of the paradigm of life in *Anna Karenina* (VI, vii-xii). The three hunters, Levin, Stiva, and Veslovsky—an unlikely combination of person-

alities—start off in a good mood. Levin feels "joy in life" as he tries
to forget Veslovsky's flirtation with Kitty. But the first day of the
hunting episode is marked by division and discord. The three men
never go out together and there is no common task. Rivalry and envy
spoil the mood. Levin is nice to Veslovsky, but this only increases his
antagonism toward him. Even the music of the hunt sounds chaotic.
There is no harmony. Rather, each of the hunters is interested only
in himself. Levin charitably lets his guests have their way, but resents them for it. Veslovsky is oblivious to the drama he is in and as
a result he has a good time. Stiva avoids the drama around him and
as a result he makes a good catch. All three are isolated from each
other.

These three styles of estrangement are then raised to another level
during the evening interlude in the peasant's hut, where the three
men begin to talk. The conversation turns to the economic and social
questions which in fact pervade the novel. This conversation raises
the questions of the whole work. How can I be myself and yet belong
to others? How can I reside in a world of others and still feel myself
fulfilled? The three men represent the three alternative answers that
the novel shows. Veslovsky does what he wants for himself, but does
not belong. He has fun but no moral imagination. Like Sappho Stoltz
or Yashvin, he is only a guest resident in this world. Stiva too does
what he wants, but he maintains a facade of involvement. He is at
fault but does not feel guilty. Like Betsy Tverskaya or Countess
Lydia Ivanovna, he is a false resident in this world. Levin is tormented about what he wants, but he must participate and feel that
he belongs. He does not want to feel guilty. Like Anna, Karenin, and
Vronsky, he is a failed resident. But this Levin cannot accept. In the
third part of the sequence, therefore, he joins in a common task.
Levin and Laska, master and servant, work together, the servant
doing the will of the master, the master succeeding through his servant's labor. The hunting episode ends with the new image of life's
task, one that requires abandoning the former hopes for life's joint
venture. It is only a moment in Levin's experience, but it prefigures
his career in the novel, where in the end he will find his own "master" and his final hope for resolving his gnawing sense of failure.

As in *War and Peace*, the hunting episode in *Anna Karenina* begins with high hopes for a common fulfilling experience and a time
of being all together. But in *Anna Karenina* these hopes have a false

foundation and quickly collapse into the separate realities of the estranged participants. No triumphant harmony emerges from the rivalry and envy. Rather, the distance separating individuals expands throughout the scene, and in the end the moment of triumph is achieved only in isolation from others. The delineated segment of the hunt reiterates the action of the whole novel.

PRINCE DMITRY NEKHLYUDOV is just waking up. The door opens and the chamber maid enters the room with a note reminding him that today is the day he starts his jury duty. He dawdles over his mail which recalls to him his innocent youth, but now he must face the day, the letter, and the law, and go off to court. He arrives and learns that it is a murder trial. Some prostitute, it seems, has poisoned one of her clients. She takes the stand and gives her name—"Love." (I,ix). "No, it can't be, but how could it be 'Love?' " The judge too knows that is not her name, asks her real one, and she answers "Katerina Maslova." "No, it can't be," Nekhlyudov says again to himself, but now he knows. The prostitute and alleged murderer is his own Katyusha, his aunt's innocent young ward with whom he fell in love one summer in his idyllic youth and whom three years later he seduced and forgot. "Love" is on trial. Nekhlyudov, a failed artist in crisis over his vocation, is to be found guilty. Thus begins *Resurrection*.

In a flashback, the only extended use of this device in Tolstoy's fiction, the narrator then tells the story of Nekhlyudov's first love, but not as a direct recollection by Nekhlyudov. The tale is told in the language and from the point of view of the narrator's absolute truth. During that innocent summer Nekhlyudov had been in the "ecstatic state" when a young man for the first time becomes aware of the "beauty and significance of life," when he sees the "possibility of the infinite perfection of himself and the whole world," and when on moonlit nights walking in the garden he is overwhelmed with the "joy of life" (I,xii). He met Katyusha and believed that his feeling for her was "but one manifestation of that joy of life which at that time filled his whole being." Then he went off, joined the army, and three years later returned one spring just before Easter a new, but not better, man. Gone was the "joy and ecstasy of fathoming the mystery of God's world" (I,xiii). Gone was his love and need for "communion with nature." Gone was his "real self," his "spiritual being." Now he was just his "animal self," with "pleasure" and "insanity of egoism" ruling his life. He goes to his room to freshen up. There's a knock on the door and in she walks "the same, but nicer than before," all smiles and dressed in white, holding two towels and a new bar of fragrant soap, "large, fuzzy, and Russian." Easter comes and they go to church. The "joyful" refrain of "The passover of the Lord, rejoice, o ye people" rings out, and as Nekhlyudov looks at Katyusha with her "joyful" expression and "white dress," he sees that "what sings in his heart sings in hers also." They leave, sharing with others the Easter greeting and kiss, "Christ is risen," "Verily, He is risen." Katyusha kisses a beggar and the chambermaid kisses Nekhlyudov. "All are equal today." Then Nekhlyudov and Katyusha exchange the Easter kiss. This moment is fixed forever in Nekhlyudov's memory. He sees her "love not only for him but her love for everyone and everything, not just everything good, but everything in the whole universe" and in this love "he merges with her." That night, as the fog rolls in off the river and the thawing ice crackles in the distance, the "animal self" wins out and Nekhlyudov seduces the woman in white. "The waning moon dimly lights up something black and terrible" (I,xvii). The next day Nekhlyudov slips Katyusha one hundred rubles in redemption of his sin and leaves, abandoning his idyllic innocent love forever.

The opening sequence of Nekhlyudov's career in *Resurrection* embodies the theme of the work: resurrection is the awakening of a forgotten self from the sleep of life. The hero discovers he has a double past and a double nature, his recent profligate life, his "animal self," and his distant, idyllic moment of love, his "spiritual self." Now he is lost, his mother is dead, his artistic career a failure, his prospective marriage not resolved in his own mind. He does not know what to do. But then he knew: he was involved in the issues of the world around him, giving and sharing; he was certain of his path of perfection; he loved and was loved; he knew the "joy of life." Then he was a Resident, now he is a Stranger. Life has tarnished the image of his distant idyllic past. The paradigmatic action of the novel, therefore, is awakening and recollection. The hero repeatedly awakens to the hard realities of the letter of the law only to recall his own participation in the letter of the law. He examines his relationship to government institutions, the land, the peasants, sexuality, and family life. By the process of discovering his failings in these realms, he clears his path to return to his former innocence. Like *Youth*, therefore, *Resurrection* rejects a discordant past in an effort to create a harmonious future. But in *Resurrection* this future is a return to a more distant, idyllic past forgotten by all but the narrator. The action of *Resurrection*, therefore, moves from the narrator's truth given, to the truth perceived and accepted by the hero, and then to the hero's attempt to realize that truth in right action. Katyusha's "love for everyone and everything" is the narrator's truth forgotten by all, which Nekhlyudov and Maslova too will perceive and accept in themselves through a series of moments of awakening and recollection. These repeated resurrections urge them toward right action. What is central in the novel is the perception and acceptance of the given truth within oneself. These moments of awareness slowly uncover identity and vocation. The heroes clarify their faith through the resurrection of their lost past love. They reverse themselves and return to a mature version of their idyllic love.

The central action of the novel is the return to the family residence. At the middle of the novel Nekhlyudov goes back to the scenes of his primal innocence and sin. He looks out onto the darkening garden, hears the nightingales in the distance, sees the rising moon and flashes of heat lightning which illumine the house and flowering garden. A thunderstorm is threatening, but he feels "happy," "joyful," and "glad" (II,viii). He recalls the summer he spent here as an innocent youth and recovers his past. "The best moments of his life" return: the "child weeping in his mother's lap, as she is about to depart, promising her always to be good and never to cause her pain; the "fourteen-year-old praying to God to reveal the truth to him"; he and his old friend Nikolenka Irtenev resolving together "to try to make all men happy." He now knows "what he must do." The rain begins. What he does not understand is why. "Why were there my aunts? Why did Nikolenka Irtenev die and I live? Why was there Katyusha? and my insanity? Why was there the war and my whole profligate life afterward? To understand all of it, the task of the Master, is not in my power. I can only do His will written in my conscience. That is in my power and that I know for certain." He feels himself "not a master but a servant." Nekhlyudov returns to the primal scenes of innocence and sin and finds faith. In the garden refreshed by the rain he perceives and accepts his identity and vocation. He admits his guilt and sees his path to salvation. He will seek right action.

Resurrection recalls *Youth*, from which Nekhlyudov, the voice of mission, is resurrected. In *Youth* Nikolenka Irtenev too has a double past to which at the beginning he awakens. *Youth* too is built on a series of encounters with reality, examinations, tests, and trials, which lead Nikolenka on his path to himself. Both works return at the center to the childhood residence where in the garden the hero is illumined by faith. Both works end with the hero moving from the garden out into the world and discovering the discrepancies between his best self and his attempts at right action. Both works begin in spring. In *Resurrection*, however, the opening spring vista, like the flashback, is presented not as a direct experience of the hero but as the narrator's absolute truth. This is the given. The "tenderness and joy of spring" represent the forces in nature which make the grass grow through the cracks in human civilization (I,i). No matter how people have "huddled together" in cities and "disfigured the earth," paving the land with stone, tearing up the trees, scaring away the animals and birds, befouling the air with coal and gas fumes, "spring is spring even in the city." Spring continually returns joy and gladness to the earth.[6] "Gladsome are the plants and the birds and the insects and the children." But people remain unaware. "They deceive and torment each other." Searching for "power over each other," they do not see what is "sacred and significant in the spring morning, the beauty of God's universe (*mir*) given for the good (*blago*) of all beings, the beauty which disposes all to peace (*mir*), harmony, and love." Resurrection begins with the act of perceiving and accepting the good of God's universe given to all. With resurrection one becomes a Resident.

The trilogy *Childhood, Boyhood, and Youth* rehearses the paradigmatic action of the three major fictions because it imitates, as do they, the psychological drama of the Tolstoyan crisis. This drama un-

---

[6] The expression "joy and gladness" is rendered in both Russian and the liturgical language Church Slavonic by the same phrase *radost' i vesel'e*. These words and the adjectival, adverbial, and verbal forms based on the same roots abound in Tolstoy's language. He believed that the experience of "joy and gladness is one of the manifestations of the will of God" and spoke of the "sanctity of gladness" (55,120;1905). It is not usually possible, however, to translate these words and keep the Biblical overtone. This is especially true of the words related to "gladness." I translate this group variously: "gladness," "merriment," "gaiety." I shall often give the Russian in parentheses.

folds in three scenes: the idyllic past, the barren present, and the future of hope. In the center of this drama stands the Stranger, but it commences and concludes with the Resident. The fictional characters, male and female, obsessively act out this drama in three scenes, but not necessarily in the same order. In the beginning there is love—parental, romantic, or marital. This love is then lost through abandonment, rejection, betrayal, or death. This loss of love leads to a crisis of alienation which stems from a self-centeredness that grows into a sense of meaninglessness. Despair and death loom before the eyes. But then at the depths of despondency something happens which casts the past into a new light. The characters see their guilt, repent of their black past, and, thus reversed, start out in a new direction which will, it is hoped, return them to the lost paradise. This drama, repeated in the lives of almost all of Tolstoy's major characters and reiterated paradigmatically in many, many scenes in his fiction, is the tale of life of the "character of the author."

Chapter Two

THE CAREER OF LIFE

There is an "I," there is an "it." The relationship of "I" to "it" is "thou." "Thou" is life.
(56,356;1908).

IN his first attempt at a philosophical essay Tolstoy argued that his experience of life resulted from the interaction of the "I" and the "non-I" (1,226;1847). His basic assumption was that the relationship between self and other involves what he called love. Not surprisingly, then, in his simplistic and moralistic "Rules" for life from this same period, Tolstoy asserted that the "source of all feelings in general is love, which can be divided into two classes: love for self . . . and love for everything that surrounds us. All feelings which have as their source love for the whole world" (*ves' mir* also means "all people"), he continued, "are good; all feelings which have their source in self-love are bad" (46,267;1847). At this point he excluded from his examination of the kinds of love any religious notion of love for God because "one cannot call by the same name a feeling which we have toward beings like ourselves or lower than ourselves and the feeling we have toward the Supreme Being, who is unlimited in space, time and power (*sila*) and is incomprehensible to us." God, it would seem, is wholly other.

Five years later Tolstoy recast his first conception of the relationship of self to other into the language of traditional Christian moral philosophy, with its dichotomous body and soul. "The attraction of the soul is the good of one's neighbors. The attraction of the flesh is the personal good (*lichnoe dobro*). The riddle of contradicting aspirations rests in the mysterious union of soul and body" (46,140;1852). "When the attraction of the soul collides with the attraction of the flesh, then the first ought to prevail because the soul is immortal, as is the happiness (*schast'e*) it acquires" (46,167;1853). The Christianized version of the ethical relationship between self and other varies only slightly from the earlier articulation in the

"Rules," but the difference is telling. In the "Rules" self-love is bad, love of others is good; in the Christianized restatement there are two kinds of good, the "personal good" and the "good of others." Tolstoy seems confused in his attitude toward the self and other. The Stranger believes in the primacy of the "personal good"; the Resident is moved by the soul's attraction to the good of others for the acquisition of happiness. Tolstoy spent his life clarifying his conception of the self in its relation to the other.

Tolstoy's heroes are thrust into the midst of this conflict. Life, for them as for their creator, consists in the pursuit of happiness. "The attaining of happiness is the course of the soul's development." But in what this happiness consists the heroes do not know. The fictions thus all open with the hero at a juncture in his life when he starts out on a mission to ascertain and acquire the happiness which will develop his soul. During this mission the hero will explore the possibilities of happiness: pleasure, material well-being, fame, altruism, love. He will stumble upon the inevitable opposition between self and other and in the end bump up against the Divine.

OLENIN'S QUEST FOR LOVE

Olenin, the hero of *The Cossacks*, Tolstoy's last (1863) major work before *War and Peace*, is a typical Tolstoyan Stranger. He has no ties with the world, "no family, no homeland, no faith, no needs" (ii). At twenty-four he has not chosen his life's career and does not feel he has accomplished anything. He "believes in nothing and accepts nothing." This alienated nihilism does not turn him into a "morose, bored, and argumentative" malcontent, however, because he is attracted to fame and pleasure, which he pursues up to the point of involvement. Since his highest value is freedom, however, he shrinks from the involvement the moment it starts to require any "labor, struggle," or "feeling" from him. Olenin participates in the world in which he resides by taking from it and then taking off from it. His story begins and ends with a departure.

The Cossacks opens with Olenin celebrating his departure from Moscow for the Caucasus, where, like many a Romantic literary hero, not to mention his creator, he expects to make a new life for himself as a cadet in the army. In contrast to the burgeoning daily life of the working people of Moscow with which the novel begins, Olenin's habitual style of life is captured in the image of his farewell party, the late hours, the abundance of food and drink, the idleness, and the endless conversations about life. He is a man of the flesh. But the conversation depicted at the beginning of the story embodies its central concern. Olenin and his friends are discussing love. Olenin, it seems, has won the heart of a young woman, but has not been able to bestow his in return. His friends believe he is "guilty" before the young lady because he will not accept her love (i). According to them, "to be loved . . . gives just as much happiness (schast'e) as to love and is sufficient for a whole lifetime once it is achieved." But Olenin sees it differently.

> Why shouldn't I myself love? Why do I not love? No, to be loved is a misfortune (neschast'e), a misfortune when you feel guilty because you do not give what you cannot even give. . . . I feel as though I had stolen that feeling . . . but I cannot repent. . . . Can I be guilty if I am not able to love? . . . It's true, I have not loved. Yet I have the desire to love, a desire stronger than any other. I again wonder whether there even exists such a love.

From the beginning, then, Olenin stands out from the crowd. In the past, it seems, like his friends, he was able to enjoy the physical pleasures of life and find fulfillment in the attention of others. He assumed, it seems, that their attention was a response to his worth and therefore defined his meaning and purpose in life. But now Olenin needs to "establish his freedom" (ii). He is at the time in his life when the "force (sila) of youth" is calling; he is now aware of his "capacity to desire and do." In crisis over his vocation, Olenin starts off on a mission of love.

At his parting, Olenin is moved, not by his friends' love for him, but by his own "love for himself." When he arrives in the Caucasus he is overwhelmed by the beauty of the mountains, which reaffirm and represent for him this fundamental faith in his own "power" (sila) and "youth" (iii). To him they recall all his literary, romantic images of Cossack life. As he takes up his new residence in the Caucasus, these same mountains surround his being, and he is filled with the "youthful feeling of the joy of life without cause" (xi). Olenin encountering the mountains resembles Nekhlyudov in Lucerne, who, upon hearing the Tyrolian song, was thrust "suddenly" from his "indifference" into the experience of the "fullness of hope and a joy of life without cause." In Tolstoy's fiction this sudden joy of life without cause is always a sign of the presence of the Divine within, a presence usually not recognized by the characters. But here Olenin does believe that the old self, with its failure to love, is gone. "Here, as a new man among new people, he has been able to earn a new, good opinion of himself." His faith in himself is now justified. "The mountains, the mountains, the mountains pervade everything he thinks and feels." Olenin hears the call of his true vocation; he is ready to love. He is to enter a world of human relatedness.

As Olenin enters the Cossack world he encounters an enigmatic old man, a "merry" man of the flesh who "loves everyone." While Uncle Eroshka in reality is a liar and a drunkard whose life is based on economic self-interest and personal pleasure, to Olenin he seems a kind and generous man who represents the wisdom of the Cossack people. He knows how to live. While blind to Eroshka's more reprehensible ways, Olenin listens to his words. Eroshka has an enlightened vision of the providential harmony of all which he has transformed into an amoral world of personal satisfaction. In Eroshka's view "God has made all for the joy of man" (xiv). In his theology of the natural goodness of all creation, "there is no sin in anything," a principle which no doubt helps him justify his own lying and cheating. It also helps excuse his penchant for the delights of the fair sex, since to him women exist for man's pleasure. "To eye" or "play around with" or "love" a woman is "no sin, it's salvation" (xii). Woman "is made to be loved and rejoiced in." This follows from the natural goodness of all creation, as does the brotherhood of all men. It is from his sense of the unity of all that Eroshka loves all, a principle which has yielded him many oath brothers (*kunaki*) and much economic gain. In his universal brotherhood, he is the free-loader. But Eroshka sees that men's concepts of property and nation divide them from each other and incidentally spoil his life of living off others. With civilization "falsity" enters the world (xiv). Even the animals, who can settle down anywhere, know better. Man's "law" has violated God's creation. But still there is no punishment, for you live and die and "grass will grow on your grave, that's all." Even in their "falsity" men return to the natural harmony of God's world. Eroshka's vision of the goodness of creation leads to a world in which everything exists for the self, whose purpose is pleasure and end is death.

In the central chapter of *The Cossacks* Olenin confronts Eroshka's vision of providential harmony and personal good. The day before, while hunting pheasants, he and Eroshka had stumbled on a stag's lair and frightened the beast away. Now Olenin returns to the lair, shooting some pheasants along the way. In the cool of the stag's lair, where the mountains are no longer visible, "thinking about nothing, desiring nothing," Olenin is "suddenly overcome with such a strange feeling of happiness without cause and of love for everything that by old childish habit he begins to bless himself and give thanks to someone" (xx). This experience of sudden "happiness without cause" and "love for all," neither sought nor earned, reveals to him a new truth, not quite Eroshka's. "Suddenly it occurs to him with particular clarity that I, Dmitry Olenin, a being distinct from all other beings, am lying here alone, God knows where, in that place where the stag lived." Olenin in the stag's lair ("stag" is *olen'* in Russian) confronts his essential aloneness. He then thinks of the trees, young and old, of the pheasants who may recall their "murdered brothers," and of the mosquitoes buzzing around, "each one a Dmitry Olenin distinct from all as I am." "And it becomes clear to him that he is in no way a Russian nobleman, a member of Moscow society, a friend and relative of so-in-so and so-in-so, but simply just such a mosquito or pheasant or stag as those living now around him." In his distinctness and aloneness Olenin discovers his similarity to all. Furthermore, as he strips away the covers of his social self, he finds his own mortality. "Like them, like Uncle Eroshka, I will live and die. He speaks the truth: 'only the grass will grow.' "

But Eroshka's vision of life and death leads Olenin to an awareness not only of his mortality and aloneness; in his mortality he finds kinship with all living beings. No longer are other people those who love him and whom he cannot truly love, now others are those who are like him. For Olenin this raises anew the question of the purpose of life. Whether the new sense of identity as a distinct being like all other distinct beings means that he is, as Eroshka seems to believe, "just an animal . . . and nothing more" or even that he is a "frame in which is placed a part of the one divine being," still the purpose of life is happiness. "One must live, one must be happy." With his new but not yet clarified sense of identity Olenin discovers a new definition of "happiness."

Happiness is living for others. That's clear. The need for happiness is innate in man, therefore it is legitimate. If you attempt to satisfy it egotistically, that is, by seeking out for yourself riches, fame, the comforts of life, love, it can happen that circumstances will arise in which it will be impossible to satisfy those desires. Therefore, these desires are illegitimate, not the need for happiness. What desires can be satisfied regardless of external conditions? Love, self-sacrifice.

Olenin reshapes Eroshka's vision of natural brotherhood and mortality into an ethic of self-sacrificing love, an ethic diametrically opposed to Eroshka's. He resolves the dilemma of his life by reversing his former ways. He will become involved. But this resolution of his vocation to love rings false. The highly intellectualized argument sounds like a rationalization. Olenin has not yet clarified his vocation to love because he has not yet resolved his identity, his "position in the universe" as a bit of matter or a particle of the Divine. In the lair he loses sight of the mountains. Olenin's quandary, which was revealed to Tolstoy in precisely this form in a dream, will be resolved, Tolstoy thinks, only when "happiness" is understood as the "greatest possible seizure of the Divine" (48,83;1862). But Olenin's reversal is only the first step to his self-discovery and his own apprehension of the Divine. In the Tolstoyan universe identification with the other precedes identity of self.

OLENIN resolves the dilemma of his identity in his confrontation with Eroshka's theory of sexual permissiveness. Upon his arrival in the Caucasus Olenin meets a beautiful Cossack girl, Maryanka, whom from the start he casts in his idealized image of a female noble savage. Puzzled yet attracted by her shy flirtations, he soon learns that she is engaged to the handsome young brave, Lukashka. In Olenin's fantasy Lukashka is everything he would be, just as Maryanka is everything he would have. As a result of his idealization, Olenin cannot understand Lukashka's sexual adventures nor Maryanka's ambivalences. To Olenin they are the natural people: they "live like nature, they die, are born, copulate, are born once more, they fight, drink, eat, rejoice and again they die. . . . They have no other laws" (xxxvi). He has accepted Eroshka's view as an adequate description of Cossack life and fails to see the main point, that Cossack mores and Moscow mores are not really very different. Even so he honors the engagement of Lukashka and Maryanka, thereby preserving his ideal image of both. Lukashka, sensitive to Olenin's estrangement, offers him friendship and Olenin, anxious to put into practice his "recipe for happiness," makes him a present of his horse. This extravagant expression of self-sacrifice is not understood as a gesture of love; Lukashka becomes suspicious of Olenin's motives, as do the other Cossacks. At best they stand in awe of Olenin's wealth. The practice of self-sacrifice leads to isolation.

Still Olenin has the Maryanka of his dreams. He loves her, he believes, as he "loves the beauty of the mountains and the sky" (xxiii). This fantasy love is soon brought to the test when Prince Beletsky, a Russian nobleman from Moscow who has not yet discovered his identity with the mosquitoes, pheasants, and stags, arrives on the Cossack scene, as Russian noblemen usually do, for wine, women, and song. The Cossacks understand him and like him. Soon Beletsky arranges a party and Olenin is cajoled into attending. Awkward at first, he is soon thinking dangerous thoughts. 'What I formerly thought is all nonsense—love, self-sacrifice, Lukashka. There is only one thing, happiness. He who is happy is right" (xxv). Thus Beletsky awakens in Olenin a new sense of self-interest, not to mention a touch of erotic desire. Olenin needs a new "recipe for happiness." He is ready to move to a new awareness of identity and vocation.

Olenin's happiness does not come, however, in embracing Eroshka's theory of sexual permissiveness. That is not the love he desires "stronger than any other." His happiness comes in his new faith found in the Cossack wilds. The moment of faith is not shown: there is no epiphanic clarification of identity and vocation. Rather, in the rationalistic and rationalizing manner so characteristic of him, Olenin writes of his new faith in a letter addressed to his friends back home but not sent because "no one would understand what he wants to say and besides there wouldn't be any reason for anyone else to understand" (xxxiii). Like Tolstoy with his incessant articulations of his experience, Olenin tries to explain to himself what has happened to him, what this life and this happiness are. Formerly he saw himself marred by his "complex, inharmonious deformed past," a "weak, corrupted creature," while Maryanka to him was "happy, like nature consistent, calm, true to herself." He did not believe he could love her. "I admired her like the beauty of the mountains and the heavens. . . . Then I sensed that the contemplation (*sozertsanie*) of that beauty became a necessity in my life, and I began to ask myself whether indeed I did love her. But I found in myself nothing like the feeling I expected." But then, he writes, one day after returning home "I caught sight of her, my hut, Uncle Eroshka, and the snowy mountains . . . and I was seized by such a strong new feeling of joy that I understand everything. I love that woman with real love for the first and only time in my life. . . . I am not guilty because I have loved. It has happened against my will." In his quest for love, Olenin moves from self-sacrifice to contemplation to a sudden seizure of joy against his will.

Olenin proceeds to characterize this seizure of joy in a passage that is one of Tolstoy's most significant fictional articulations of the experience of the Divine.

It's not the ideal, so-called exalted love which I had experienced formerly, nor that feeling of attraction in which you admire your own love, feel the source of your feeling in yourself, and do everything yourself. I have experienced that too. Still less is it the desire for pleasure. It's something else. Perhaps in her I love nature, the personification of all the beauty of nature, but I am not in control of my will. Some elemental force (*stikhijnaja sila*) loves her through me (*chrez menja*). The whole of God's world (*ves' bozhij mir*), all of nature, presses that love into my soul and says: love. I love her not with my mind, not with my imagination, but with my whole being. Loving her, I sense myself an integral part of the whole of God's joyful world. . . . Self-sacrifice— that's all absurd nonsense. It's all pride, a refuge from unhappiness deserved, salvation from envy for another's happiness. To live for others, to do good. Why? When in my soul there is only love for myself and the sole desire to love her and live for her, to live her life. Not for others, not for Lukashka do I now desire happiness. I do not love these others now. Formerly I would have said that's bad. . . . Now I do not care. I do not live independently, but rather there is something stronger than me which is guiding me. I suffer, but formerly I was dead, now I am alive.

Discoursing with himself in order to discover himself, Olenin defines a new attitude to self and other experienced in his seizure of joy. Self-sacrifice is rejected as a subtle form of pride and a device for coping with one's own failure and others' success. From his psychological analysis of his former moral stances, Olenin moves toward a new way of being in the world which can best be described as mystical. For Olenin the beautiful mountains expand to include "all of nature," "all of God's world"; the emblematic expanse of nature represents everything that exists, the All. Maryanka, on the other hand, grows into the "personification of all the beauty of nature"; the feminine figure represents the incarnation of the idea and value of "all of God's world." Maryanka and the mountains, however, do not remain external objects which Olenin contemplates. Rather, Olenin both loves the embodied idea of "all of God's world" and feels that "all of God's world" loves the incarnated idea "through him." Knowing becomes loving, and the subject and object merge. This experience of harmony endows Olenin with a sense of belonging. In this moment of mystical union Olenin discovers a renewed sense of self that admits its weakness but combines in paradoxical fashion self-esteem with a self-renunciation which sees "something stronger" guiding him. Olenin resembles Nikolenka in the garden, the "insignificant worm" with the "immense mighty power (*sila*) of love," except that Olenin feels the "elemental force (*sila*) love through him." As Nikolenka sensed his oneness with nature and the moon, his residence in the universe, so now Olenin feels himself an "integral part of the whole of God's joyful world." He knows who he is and what he must do. Olenin has attained the "greatest possible seizure of the Divine" and now truly "lives." This mystical moment of contemplative residence in God's universe—his moment of "life"—only heightens the sad fact of the denouement of his drama. He returns to his daily existence "alone" and "unloved" and still in quest of love (xlii).

The Cossacks is a romance in which the hero goes in search of love. But the quest and its fulfillment are undercut by the narrator's irony and the hero's self-consciousness. We see Olenin in the stag's lair, but this experience is then alienated by the self-conscious articulation of its meaning. The final love is found in a moment of seizure of the Divine, but this is not shown. In its stead we have the hero's letter about the seizure. The narrative manner of *The Cossacks* reflects the Tolstoyan dilemma. The story is about the quest for spontaneous, unself-conscious love, but this story is told by an ironic narrator who doubts this quest and who focuses on the self-consciousness of the hero. *The Cossacks* is the story of a would-be Resident told by a doubting Stranger.

PRINCE ANDREW'S DISCOVERY OF LOVE

Like Olenin, Prince Andrew enters the world of *War and Peace* disenchanted with his past and bored with his life. His wife Lise loves him, but Prince Andrew does not love in return. Nor can we imagine that he ever did, since Tolstoy does not tell us how or why Prince Andrew married Lise. Indeed, all our information about Prince Andrew's past comes solely from the narrator's telling portrait of Prince Andrew's father. Of his mother, long dead, we learn nothing. Prince Bolkonsky embodies the eighteenth-century world. He lives an enlightened life, with faith in reason and autonomy, with skepticism tempered by firm belief in abstract principles symbolized by Princess Mary's daily geometry lessons, and with deistic assumptions of a clockwork universe and machine-man marked by his own ludicrously precise daily schedule and the routine presence of the house architect. Prince Andrew—the narrator always refers to him with this formal title—is a child of his father in every way. He has the mind of a master: he believes in himself, distrusts emotion, and has a firm faith in the power of his reason to shape reality. He is a skeptic and at best a deist. When Prince Andrew finds himself in a state of crisis over his inability to love, like Olenin he abandons the love and seeks another life. He will find a new way of being in the world and a new meaning for life by trying out a new vocation. But Prince Andrew enters the novel on a negative mission: he is to abandon his family and home and thus rid himself of that past which is the source of his estrangement. He must dispel the mind of the master. His main task in the novel will be to overcome the lessons learned from his father. Since he seeks a substitute for his impoverished enlightenment heritage, his quest is philosophical and religious. Prince Andrew undertakes a journey of spiritual discovery.

The father's moral lesson emerges in the son's meditation on the purpose of life just before the battle of Austerlitz. In the face of death, Prince Andrew is in quest of glory.

> I don't know what will happen then, I do not want to know, nor can I. But if I want that, if I want glory, if I want to be known to men, if I want to be loved by them, then it is not my fault if I want that, if I want that alone. I'll never tell anyone, but, my God, what am I to do if I love nothing but glory, love from people. Death, wounds, the loss of family, nothing frightens me. However dear and close people are to me—my father, sister, wife, the people most dear—still, however terrible and unnatural it seems, I would give them up immediately for a minute of glory, of triumph over people, for those people's love for me, people whom I do not know and will not know, for the love of just those people. . . . I love and value only the triumph over them all. I value that mysterious power (*sila*) and glory which is floating right here above me in the mist. (I,iii,xii)

The hidden meaning of Prince Bolkonsky's embittered exile, his sense of failure, his need for self-justification, and his hope for rehabilitation, has not been lost on his son. All action springs from self-interest: what seems to be self-sacrifice for one's country is but a covert form of a need for recognition and power. The purpose of life is to be loved by others; exile and isolation are signs of failure. To be happy, one must participate in the arena of action. Along with this perverted sense of duty, Prince Andrew also inherited his father's stubborn belief in himself, his insistence on his own interpretation of events, and his disdain and scorn for the opinion of others. The self lives for others but at the same time has no love for those others, only for itself. Prince Andrew's quest for glory is doomed to failure because his destined purpose in life is to overcome this inheritance of egocentrism.

Prince Andrew's true mission is revealed to him in battle after his valiant effort to lead the troops to victory. Bleeding on the battlefield near death, his "Toulon" now past, Prince Andrew glances outward and toward the sky.

> Above him there was no longer anything but the sky, the lofty sky, not clear but nevertheless immeasurably lofty with grey clouds gliding calmly across it. 'How calm, peaceful and solemn,

not as it was when I was running, shouting, and fighting . . . , not at all like that do the clouds glide across that lofty, infinite sky. How is it I didn't see that lofty sky before? How happy I am that I've seen it at last. Yes! Everything is emptiness, everything is deception except that infinite sky. There is nothing, nothing except it. But even it is not, there is nothing except the calm, the peace. Thank God." (I, iii,xvi)

Prince Andrew's career in the novel is the articulation of the meaning of this moment of revelation, when he discovers the expanse of nature in which he resides. At first he passes out and then comes to, looking again for the sky, only to see standing above him his hero and model, the man loved by all, Napoleon. "His head ached, he felt that he was bleeding and above himself he saw the distant, lofty, and eternal sky. He knew that it was Napoleon, his hero, but at that moment Napoleon seemed to him such a little insignificant person in comparison with what was happening between his soul and that lofty, infinite sky" (I,iii,xix). The first result of Prince Andrew's encounter with the emblematic sky is the rejection of his model of successful glory. The "vanity and joy of victory" now seem insignificant in comparison with the "lofty, just, and kind (*dobroe*) sky."[1] Prince Andrew intuits in the heavens new values. He has begun the process of abandoning the psychological ideals of life imparted to him by his father and embodied in his hero.

But the experience is not at all clear to him. He hardly understands the meaning of that eternal, just, and kind sky. He knows somewhat vaguely what he does not want any longer. But what is the meaning of the calm and peace he has experienced in that lofty, unending expanse dotted with clouds but without any sight of the sun? He takes out the golden chain with the little icon his sister had given him to wear. Contemplating the icon, Prince Andrew confronts his skepticism for the first time. His unbelief is accompanied by an intuition of and desire for something which transcends the emptiness and de-

---

[1] The word "sky" (*nebo*) also means "heaven." The religious significance of this expanse of nature is further marked by the axiological adjectives "just" and "kind." The adjective "kind" (*dobryj*) includes the idea of "tenderness of character" and "doing good for others." The abstract noun based on the root of this word (*dobro*) is one of Tolstoy's names for God. The moral value of "kindness" or "goodness" (*dobrota*) is one of the high ideals of Russian Christianity. It is what Nikolenka in *Childhood* sees in Maman (ii).

ception of life as he has known it. To be sure, he can find no name for this God he now intuits in the sky; neither "force" (*sila*) nor "All" nor "nothing" captures the "majesty" of the "incomprehensible but most significant" something he has experienced. But now Prince Andrew knows that he cannot grasp everything with his mind. The experience of the sky has revealed to him a new way of seeing the world and of being in the world. The remainder of his career in the work, therefore, is devoted to the quest for the meaning of that "force" or "All" or "nothing" that he discovers in the eternal, just, and kind sky.

Prince Andrew's experience of the sky changes his perspective on his past. He not only rejects his former hero, but now he is aware of his former failings and open to the possibility of love. Thus when Lise dies in childbirth he is thrust into a state of relentless remorse for his past and deep despair for his future. What finally shocks him out of his depression is his encounter with Natasha. On his way to the Rostov's Ryazan estate Prince Andrew sees an old, gnarled oak tree that speaks to him of the deception of "spring, love, and happiness" (II,iii,vi). The emblematic oak is the voice of death calling him to isolation and indifference. But as he approaches the house he hears a "cheerful feminine shout" and sees a young girl running toward his carriage. "When she spied the stranger (*chuzhoj*), without looking at him she ran back with a laugh" (II,iii,ii). Pained, Prince Andrew takes note of the girl, who takes no notice of "his existence," so "happy" is she "with her own no doubt stupid, but cheerful and happy life." That evening, unable to sleep, Prince Andrew goes to the window and looks out into the night. "His eyes become fixed on the sky." He hears the voices of two young girls speaking, one of them glorying in the night and the moon and wishing to fly off up into the sky. The next day he leaves and on his way home he passes again the old oak, now beginning to bud. At the sight of the tree "all transformed" Prince Andrew is "suddenly" overcome with a "vernal feeling of joy and renewal without cause" (II,iii,iii). Now, however, Prince Andrew does not want to live his life for himself alone. He does not want the girl "who wanted to fly into the sky" to be "separate from his life." He wants "my life to reflect on everyone and everyone to live together with me."

Natasha, who stumbles into the novel making "everyone laugh against their will" (I, i, viii) is on a mission to create the harmony of all together, and Prince Andrew heeds her call. When he visits her in Moscow he again senses the "presence of a special world (*mir*) completely alien (*chuzhdyj*) to him but filled with some sort of joy unknown to him," only now that "world is not alien" for he "has entered it and found new pleasure" (II,iii,xix). Then Natasha sings.

> Prince Andrew grew silent and unexpectedly felt that tears were about to choke him, a thing he had thought impossible for himself. He looked at Natasha singing and in his soul something new and happy took place. He was happy and at the same time sad. There certainly was no reason for him to weep but he was ready to weep. About what? His former love? The little Princess? His disenchantments? His hopes for the future? Yes and no. The main thing he felt like weeping about was the sudden vivid consciousness of a terrifying contrast between something infinitely great and unlimited in himself and something narrow and physical (*telesnoe*) which he himself was and she too. This contrast caused him torment and joy as she sang. (II,iii,xix)

In Natasha's song Prince Andrew discovers a new identity. He senses the spirit within. He returns home for the night but cannot fall asleep because he feels "so joyful and new in his heart, as if he had gone from a stuffy room out into God's wide-open world." "Why should I bustle about in this narrow, closed frame," he wonders, "when life, all of life with all its joys, is open to me?" With this new hope in the spirit, he decides that "it is time to live and be happy." Almost immediately after this night he declares his love and he and Natasha become engaged.

What has happened to Prince Andrew is a total but unconscious transference of the experience of at-onement with the eternal, just, and kind sky onto the "girl who wanted to fly up into the sky." For Prince Andrew Natasha embodies the "force," the "All" or the "nothing" he could not understand. In her presence he discovers the spirit. In his relationship with her he will enter that "alien world," "God's wide-open world," and find a new life of joy and happiness, but not yet. Listening to Natasha sing, however, he does have the paradoxical experience of insignificance and greatness, limitedness and unlimitedness, non-freedom and freedom, characteristic of the peak moments of other Tolstoyan heroes. He resembles Nikolenka, who experienced an idealized feminine figure associated with the sky and the moon and God while feeling himself both an "insignificant worm" and a "mighty power of love" in the "immensities of space." And he resembles Olenin, who loves and lives for the first time when through Maryanka he feels himself an "integral part of the whole of God's joyous world." All three heroes envision their idealized feminine figure in an emblematic expanse of nature, Nikolenka in the garden, Olenin in the mountains, Prince Andrew in the sky. For all three the woman embodies some "force" or "meaning" they intuit in nature. But Nikolenka and Olenin end their career with this intuition. Prince Andrew continues on his odyssey through life. He has more to learn.

What Prince Andrew must learn is the meaning of that "something narrow and physical" that he has now sensed he is. After a return home just before the battle of Borodino, he walks along a hot dusty road and passes a pond where some soldiers are bathing.

> He glanced at the pond from which shouts and laughter were emerging. The small pond, darkish from the green undergrowth, had obviously risen about a foot, flooding the dam, because it was filled with wallowing, white, naked, human bodies of soldiers and their brick-red hands, faces, and necks. All that naked, white, human flesh, whooping and laughing, was wallowing in that dirty pond like carp stuffed into a boiling pot. That wallowing suggested a certain merriment and was therefore especially saddening. . . . On the banks, on the dam, in the pond everywhere there was white, healthy, muscular flesh. . . . "Flesh, the body (*telo*), *chair a canon*," he thought as he looked also at his own naked body and shuddered not so much from the cold as from the incomprehensible repulsion and fright he felt at the sight of that huge number of bodies flopping about in the dirty pond. (III,ii,v)

The emblematic "dirty pond" reveals the meaning of Prince Andrew's experience of "something narrow and physical" in himself and even in Natasha. The physical (*telesnoe*) is the body (*telo*) itself. Even a healthy, muscular body is but cannon fodder: all physical life leads to death. What is worse, Prince Andrew sees that no one is aware of this. The soldiers whoop and laugh, and in their merriment do not care that the pond is muddying their white flesh. On his return to his family residence, therefore, the hero on a mission to abandon his home discovers the reality of flesh and decay and death. His remaining task in the novel will be to find some transcendence of this material realm.

This heightened awareness of death, coupled with the news of his own father's death, thrusts Prince Andrew into a new depression. In the "cold, white light of day, the clear thought of death" everything "suddenly" loses meaning for him (III,ii,xxiv). "Love! That girl who had seemed to be filled with mysterious forces (*sily*). How I loved her. . . . O what a child I was." He recalls his father's life, secure in Bald Hills: he thought that was "his place, his land, his air," and then Napoleon came and "Bald Hills collapsed along with his whole life." His face expresses his mood of "hostility." Pierre appears and Prince Andrew tells of his disenchantment with the military: the leaders give orders, but there is no relationship between their plans and the events of battle. The masters do not control history with their minds. Furthermore, the "game of chess" the leaders think they are playing is nothing but murder (III,ii,xxv). "Ah, my friend, of late it has become hard for me to live. I see I have begun to understand too much." What Prince Andrew has begun to understand in his depression is Tolstoy's view of war as a machine of death. This understanding marks the end of his military vocation. But then that night as he is falling asleep Prince Andrew recalls Natasha's "animated, agitated face" one day as she was trying to tell him what happened to her while out picking mushrooms, but couldn't find the right words to convey the feeling (III,ii,xxv). He smiles the smile he smiled then and thinks, "I did understand her, not just understand but I also loved in her that force of soul (*dushevnaja sila*), that sincerity, that openness of soul, yes, her soul itself which seemed bound by the body. I loved her soul itself so strongly, so happily." With his death-dealing vocation at an end, Prince Andrew stumbles on the key to transcendence, the "force of soul" he loved in Natasha. But Prince Andrew then "suddenly" remembers "him." This memory of his enemy destroys the memory of the soul he loved. Prince Andrew has yet to learn the significance of the key to transcendence.

This Prince Andrew learns only when he is wounded. At the first-aid station the sight of all the wounded men merges into one "impression of a naked bloody human body" (III,ii,xxxvii). In this mass of bodies he senses someone known to him. "Several of the doctors' assistants were leaning on the man's chest to hold him down. A white, large, plump leg was twitching rapidly all the time in feverish tremors. The man was sobbing and choking convulsively. Silently two doctors, one of them pale and trembling, were doing something to the man's other leg, the red one." The doctors then remove the shell from Prince Andrew's wound and he faints from the pain. He comes to and one of the doctors leans over and kisses him on the lips. With this kiss Prince Andrew feels a "bliss he had not experienced for a long time. In his imagination he saw not as if past but as if present all the best, happiest moments of his life, especially in his most distant childhood when he would be undressed and put to bed, when his nanny would sing to him and rock him to sleep, when he would bury his head in the pillows and feel happy just with the consciousness of life." The man with the one white leg disrupts these recollections of the lost idyllic past of love with an agonized moan that makes Prince Andrew feel like weeping with "childlike, kind (*dobrye*), almost joyful tears." The kindness he saw in the sky is experienced within. Not yet establishing the man's relationship to "his life" Prince Andrew "suddenly" recalls a "new, unexpected memory of the pure and loving world (*mir*) of childhood." He remembers Natasha at the ball. Once he has reexperienced the time when he was loved and when he loved, Prince Andrew immediately recognizes Anatole Kuragin, his enemy, and "an ecstatic compassion and love for that person fills his happy heart." He learns his identity and knows his vocation. He weeps "tender, loving tears for people, for himself, for their errors and his." He comes to a new understanding of life. "Compassion, love for our brothers, for those who love us and those who hate us, love for our enemies. Yes, that love which God preached on earth, which Princess Mary taught and which I did not understand. That is what I missed in life and that is what would remain for me were I to live." Prince Andrew's "child-like, kind, and joyful tears" show him the meaning of the kind sky above and Natasha's "alien world" here on earth. Prince Andrew discovers that the key to transcendence is the love that forgives.

But Prince Andrew has not articulated for himself the full meaning of this "life" he now discovers in his love for all, including his enemy, the man with the white leg. Later, when he is near death, now being nursed by his beloved Natasha, he has still another revelation of the truth he has been seeking. Natasha walks into the room where Prince Andrew is lying in a state of delirium and he sees her but dimly, as "something white at the door." This "something white" (*beloe*) sets off a train of thoughts about love, "not that love which loves for some quality, purpose, or reason, but that love which I expressed for the first time when near death I saw my enemy and nevertheless loved him. I experienced that love which is the very essence of the soul and for which there is no need of an object" (III,iii,xxxii). The white light of day, the white leg of his enemy, and the "something white" at the door reveal the truth of life. The kindness and justice Prince Andrew intuited in the eternal sky, discovered in Natasha's "force of soul" and experienced in his tears of forgiveness, are the moral and metaphysical values which transcend material existence even as they are immanent and essential in that existence. This learned, Prince Andrew extends his hand to the "white sphynx"; having forgiven his enemy, he now forgives his beloved, the woman in white. He becomes reconciled with love and life. And then he dies.

The depiction of Prince Andrew's dying is Tolstoy's first attempt to portray a death scene as a discovery of self and life, a final articulation of identity and vocation. The experience is a conversion only in the sense that accepted categories of experience become turned around: "this life" is seen as the oppressive "pressure of life"; death in the sense of a terminal point becomes an "awakening from this life" to a new mode of experience characterized by a "joyful and strange lightness of being"; this new mode of experience involves the "principle of eternal love," which is now called "life" (IV,i,xvi). The fear of death disappears because death is transformed into "life" and "this life" becomes a kind of death, a sleep from which one awakens. As with Olenin, the transformation of the categories of life and death becomes possible only through the experience of "free, eternal love."

Prince Andrew's "free, eternal love" is a love which has no external cause or object. This love, which is the "essence of the soul" and immanent to material existence, is a spontaneous and unmotivated giving forth of self to other. The self is moved by nothing outside it, and the other is not to be understood as the object of the love, if by object is meant a motivating recipient of the action. Prince Andrew's love is not love as understood in "this life," where we love what we are attracted to or need. That love he had for Natasha and it turned quickly into something ugly. His new sense of love is an active force reaching out to receive the other, a form of self-expression and identification with the other. Thus he reinterprets his relationship with

Natasha. "He vividly imagined Natasha to himself, not as he imagined her formerly with just her alluring charm (*prelest'*) which was joyful to him, but for the first time he imagined her soul. And he understood her feelings, her suffering, shame, repentance" (III,iii,xxxii). Prince Andrew loves Natasha not because he is drawn to her as an embodiment of what he needs but because she is her "force of soul," her love. In his love he gives forth of self and forgives. Prince Andrew's love, which both expresses self and identifies with the other, stands in sharp contrast to love in "this life": "To love everything, everyone, always to sacrifice oneself for love meant to love no one, meant not to live this earthly life" (IV,i,xvi). Prince Andrew's new conception of love precludes exclusivity because for him to love everything and everyone is "to love God in all manifestations" (III,iii,xxxii); he loves no one particular person or thing, only the manifestation of God in them, the "force of soul" he sees in Natasha, the woman in white who embodies the divine principle. Thus on his deathbed Prince Andrew discovers the limitations of love born of desire and the freedom of love expressed as gift.

Prince Andrew, who suffers from the mind of the master, is prone to abstract thought, and it is fitting that his deathbed experience of self and life should be accompanied by an attempt to articulate the experience in words. The words are "onesidedly personal" and too abstract, as words tend to be, but Prince Andrew's final "thoughts" do capture something of the discovery.

> Love? What is love? Love hinders death. Love is life. Everything, everything I understand, I understand only because I love. Everything is, everything exists only because I love. Everything is unified by it alone. Love is God, and to die means that I, a particle of love, return to the common and eternal source. (IV,i,xvi)

In his experience of "love," of both Anatole and Natasha, Prince Andrew has discovered the right relationship between self and other, between his soul and that eternal, just, and kind sky. The "essence of his soul" is love and the "general and eternal source" of all, God, is love. Everything and everyone is a manifestation of the God who is love and all is united by this love. Love is the transcendent universal that is immanent to all existence. Love understood as the expression of self, the essence of the soul, and the identification with the other, which is also a manifestation of God, such love is true life and such life precludes death. On his deathbed Prince Andrew discovers a metaphysical vision of what really is. The words seem inadequate to the vision, and Tolstoy, as we shall see, will attempt to clarify them, but these words are for Prince Andrew the clearest verbal articulation of the metaphysical truth he now knows because he has lived it. Prince Andrew loves.

PIERRE'S DISCOVERY OF LIFE

Monsieur Pierre enters the novel loving everyone. Awkward and ill-at-ease during Anna Sherer's gathering, he nevertheless plunges into conversation and, although he has just returned from study abroad, he immediately participates in Petersburg life. Pierre enters the novel to be at home. Prince Andrew, with his "defined dry features" (I,i,iii), stands apart, taking in the world through his lorgnette, alienated from all by his cynical self-centeredness. Pierre does not close himself off from others. "He glanced at everyone and smiled. His smile was not like other peoples' smiles which fade off into nonsmiles. On the contrary, whenever he smiled, then suddenly in one moment, the serious, even somewhat morose, look on his face disappeared and there appeared another look, child-like, kind (*dobroe*), even somewhat silly, as if asking forgiveness" (I,i,iv). Pierre intuitively understands from the beginning the meaning of the kind and just sky. His smile reflects his way of life: open, considerate and tender, eager for fun, indulgent of self, and drawn to others. Unlike Prince Andrew, who has turned inward, Pierre moves out into the world, carousing, drinking, gambling, whoring. While a self-indulgent man of the flesh, Pierre is never self-centered. Indeed he is easily lured on by others. Things happen to Pierre because he is open to people. He is ever involved with others.

Yet while Pierre spontaneously reacts to things that happen to him, his conscious moral concern for others and need for authenticity to himself always destroy the spontaneity of his moods and movements. Lured into marriage, Pierre questions his motivation. Angered by Dolokhov's insulting behavior, Pierre cannot find him guilty of any wrongdoing, knowing that he might have done the same thing himself. Pierre shoots Dolokhov and wounds him, but considers the duel stupid and false: "I shot at Dolokhov because I considered myself insulted. Louis XVI was executed because he was considered a criminal while a year later the ones who killed him were executed also for the same reason. What is bad? What is good? What should one love, what hate? What should one live for and what am I? What is life? What is death? What force (*sila*) governs all?" (II,ii,i.) When his love betrays him, Prince Andrew retreats into himself and nurtures hatred for his enemy and pity for himself. Pierre spontaneously strikes out at the enemy of his love, but then, uncertain of the rightness of his action, he falls into depression. In his crisis he asks the Tolstoyan questions and finds the Stranger's answer. "You die and it will all be over. You die and you find out everything or stop asking." The man who comes home to participate in life, Pierre enters the novel "in search of something" (I,i,ii). Because he needs to understand the meaning of everything, in his quest for belonging he is continually frustrated and constantly confronted with crises of faith. These crises raise the questions of identity and vocation. The illegitimate son of Count Bezukhov embarks on a mission to comprehend life. But, unlike Prince Andrew, who must learn what he must do, Pierre, who knows this intuitively, must discover who he is. Prince Andrew leaves home to find his vocation; Pierre comes home to find his identity. Pierre is the only major Tolstoyan hero who keeps on changing his name.

Pierre's first major crisis turns him away from others and toward himself. But then at precisely the moment of his philosophical estrangement, as he sits in a station house waiting for the next carriage on his journey, there appears before him an old man with wrinkled skin and a skull-and-bones ring on his finger. The emblematic fellow traveller is Bazdeev the Freemason. Confused by his spontaneous trust for the man and distrust of his freemasonry, Pierre expresses his fear that they "will not understand each other": "My image of the whole universe (*vsë mirozdanie*) is the opposite of yours" (II,ii,ii). The old man soon discovers that the source of Pierre's crisis is lack of faith in God: "You do not know Him, my lord, and therefore you are unhappy. You do not know Him, but He is here, He is in me, He is in my words, and He is in you." Pierre's disbelief, Bazdeev argues, shows only that he does not know himself. Pierre, who needs an "image of the whole universe" in order to know who he is, immediately accepts the arguments of this "alien person." "He believed and experienced a joyful feeling of calm, renewal, and return to life." Once his depression is dispelled, Pierre is ready to hear the words of Bazdeev's revelation.

> God is not apprehended by the mind but by life. . . . The highest wisdom and truth (*istina*) are as it were a most pure liquid which we desire to receive unto ourselves. . . . Can I receive this pure liquid into an impure vessel and judge of its purity? Only by the inner purification of myself can I retain to some degree of purity the liquid I receive. . . . The highest wisdom is based not on reason alone, not on those worldly sciences of physics, history, chemistry, and so forth into which intellectual knowledge is divided. The highest wisdom is one. The highest wisdom has one science, the science of the whole (*nauka vsego*), the science which explains the whole universe (*mirozdanie*) and the place man occupies in it. In order to contain that science in oneself, it is necessary to purify and renew one's internal man and therefore, before knowing, it is necessary to believe and perfect oneself. For the attainment of these goals there has been implanted in our soul the light of God called conscience.

Pierre, Bazdeev argues, has got things backwards. In order to have a true "image of the universe," you cannot begin with your own isolated powers of reasoning and abstraction. In order to understand the whole, you must first understand your own "place" within the whole. The "highest wisdom" begins with self-knowledge. However, the self you must know is the "internal man," the renewed self, and the knowing is not with the mind, but through the "light of God" within you. Pierre must find his true identity by first learning a new way of being and seeing. He must turn inward. To accomplish this, Bazdeev recommends "purification." This advice is repeated at Pierre's initiation into the brotherhood. "Turn all your attention to yourself, place chains on your feelings and seek bliss not in passions but in your heart. The source of bliss is not without, but within you" (II,ii,iii).

Like Olenin in his encounter with Uncle Eroshka, Pierre hears what he needs from Bazdeev. He transforms the call to turn inward into his image of the whole universe. Standing on a raft, on a journey toward Prince Andrew's home, Pierre counters Prince Andrew's doubting estrangement with this ecstatic vision of residency derived from his experience of freemasonry.

You say that you cannot see the the kingdom of good (*dobro*) and truth (*pravda*) on earth. I too have not seen it; nor is it possible to see if you look at your life as the end of everything. On the *earth*, right on this earth (Pierre pointed to the floor), there is no truth; everything is falsehood and evil. But in the universe, in the whole universe (*vo vsem mire*) there is a kingdom of truth, and we who are now children of earth are eternally children of the whole universe. Don't I feel in my soul that I comprise a part of that huge harmonious whole (*tseloe*)? Don't I feel that I comprise one link, one step from the lower to the higher beings in which the divinity, the highest force (*sila*), if you wish, manifests itself? If I see, clearly see that ladder leading from plant to man, then why should I suppose that this ladder, the bottom end of which I cannot see, stops with the plants? Why should I suppose that this ladder breaks off with me and does not lead farther and farther to higher beings? I feel that I not only cannot disappear, since nothing disappears in the universe, but that I always will be and I always have been. (II,ii,xii)

Pierre's "kingdom of good" is the "whole universe" which includes life on this earth but extends beyond, without limitation in space and time. Each particular thing that exists "on the earth" also participates in the "eternal" life of this "whole universe." The Divinity is this "harmonious whole" even as it manifests itself in each particular thing within the whole. All particular things are in movement toward "higher" levels of being which are more perfect, fuller manifestations of the Divine. To Pierre this means that there is no death as we know it, just eternal movement toward the Divine. In the course of the novel Pierre will internalize this "image of the universe" so that it gives meaning to his life and thus shows him who he is.

Pierre's ecstatic vision does not eradicate the source of Prince Andrew's alienation from others and from himself. He still feels the loss of his wife, who has suddenly disappeared "*there* in the *nowhere*." What convinces Prince Andrew is Pierre's gesture outward and toward the sky, which evokes Prince Andrew's own encounter with the eternal, just, and kind sky. He is moved toward residency by the recollection of his own best past. Because the ecstatic speech leads to this gesture and this recollection, the ride on the raft is a journey of spiritual discovery and a return home. In the scene that follows at the

Bolkonsky homestead, Bald Hills, the meeting with Princess Mary and her "God's people," the two opposed heroes reach their highest level of understanding and affection for each other. Pierre is loved by all, and at home Prince Andrew finds a sense of reconciliation with himself and others rare for him. It is a moment of belonging. The delineated segment moves paradigmatically from the initial moment of friendship to the estrangement in their dialogue to this heightened harmony.

Pierre's enthusiasm fades into depression when he hears of Prince Andrew's engagement to Natasha and at the same time learns of Bazdeev's death: "all the joy of his former life suddenly vanished" (II,v,i). But the event which robs Prince Andrew of his new faith in life and leads him to the despair of the "white light" of day and death—Natasha's flirtation with Anatole—is the very event which offers Pierre the opportunity to rediscover his own faith. To Natasha in her moment of need he gives of himself spontaneously and selflessly and from this love he receives a hundredfold.

> It was cold and clear. Above the dirty, darkish streets, above the black roofs hung the dark starry sky. Only when he looked up at the sky did Pierre cease feeling the humiliating baseness of everything worldly compared with the heights now reached by his soul. As he entered Arbat Square in the immense expanse of the starry dark sky, surrounded and sprinkled on all sides by stars, but distinct from all of them by its nearness to the earth, its white light, and its long up-raised tail, there hung the brilliant comet of 1812, the very comet which foretold, so they said, all sorts of horrors and the end of the world. But for Pierre that bright star with its long radiant tail aroused no feeling of terror. On the contrary, his eyes wet with tears, Pierre looked joyfully at that bright star, which seemed to have flown on a parabolic line with inexpressible speed across the immeasurable expanses and then suddenly, like an arrow which pierced the earth, to have fixed itself here in this one spot it chose in the black sky, and after energetically raising its tail, to have stood still shining and displaying its white light midst the other innumerable glimmering stars. It seemed to Pierre that this star fully responded to what was in his own softened and enheartened soul now blossoming into a new life. (II,v,xxi)

With this experience and precisely this passage the first half of the novel ends. In between Natasha's sin and her repentance Pierre encounters the sky. With his vision of the "white light" he crosses Prince Andrew's path: he too experiences the opposition of the worldly and the transcendent. But in his glance outward and toward the sky, Pierre resembles most Nikolenka, for, like him, he has a vision of a body of light which is the center of the sky and the focus of attention, yet dispersed throughout the "immensities of space" by its own shining rays. His metaphysical "image of the whole universe" has started to shape his vision of that universe. In the second half of the novel Pierre will find his identity within this whole universe, just as Prince Andrew will find the universe of love within himself.

The careers of the two heroes move in opposite directions, Prince Andrew toward his death and Pierre toward a new sense of life. Just as the energizing "white light" Pierre sees shed by the comet of 1812 contrasts with Prince Andrew's "white light" of day and death, so throughout the novel the two heroes' moments of alienation and at-onement alternate in opposite rhythms. In this sense they are at odds with each other. Furthermore, for each of the heroes the relationship between experience and his awareness of the meaning of experience is totally different: the self-centered Prince Andrew, ever estranged, undergoes an inner experience of the sky in isolation from others only to move toward a conscious, even philosophical, understanding of the meaning of that experience by means of an act of love; the self-indulgent Pierre, ever residing in the world of others, adopts a metaphysical view of reality from another, preaches this worldview to others, only to move toward the inner experience of that reality for himself. Prince Andrew begins his quest with an inner experience of something metaphysical and ends it with an outward moral gesture; Pierre begins his quest with an encounter with the moral teaching of another and ends it with an inner experience of metaphysical reality. Prince Andrew proceeds from within to without, thereby overcoming his self-centeredness; Pierre proceeds from without to within, thereby overcoming his other-centerdness.

Pierre's procession outward to others reaches its extreme when Napoleon invades Moscow. He adopts a new identity: he would be the savior of Russia by assassinating her enemy. But l'russe Besuhof ends up in captivity, turned in upon himself. Removed from life, forced to witness the execution of his fellow prisoners, himself led to the brink of death, totally in the control of others who themselves are but victims of a system not of their making, Pierre for the second time in the novel falls into despair.

> From the moment Pierre witnessed those terrible murders committed by people who did not want to commit ,them, it seemed as though the mainspring on which everything depended and which made everything seem vital (*zhivoe*) had suddenly been wrenched from his soul and that everything had collapsed into a pile of meaningless rubbish. Although he did not acknowledge it to himself, his faith had been destroyed, his faith in a well-ordered universe (*blagoustrojstvo mira*), in the human soul, in his own soul, and in God. Pierre had experienced this before but never so strongly as now. Before, when such doubts came over Pierre, those doubts had their source in his own guilt. And in the depth of his soul Pierre felt then that salvation from that despair and those doubts lay in himself. But now he felt that it was not his guilt that caused the universe to collapse before his eyes, leaving only meaningless ruins. He felt that to return to faith in life was not in his power. (IV,i,xii)

At this moment Platon Karataev appears. At Pierre's first crisis, when his own guilt led him to doubt life, Bazdeev revealed a teaching about a new attitude to self. Now when Pierre, who naturally trusts others, has come to doubt these others and as a result the order of the whole universe and even God Himself, Platon Karataev bodies forth a new relationship between self and other. Karataev does not see himself distinct from others. "His life as he saw it had no meaning as a separate life. It had meaning only as a particle of the whole (*chastitsa tselogo*) which he constantly felt" (IV,i,xiii). Karataev's life embodies the "image of the whole universe" Pierre ecstatically shared with Prince Andrew on the raft. This Pierre intuits in the movements of Karataev's hands in which Pierre felt "something pleasant, calming, and round" (IV,i,xii): to Pierre the "well-ordered (*blagoustroennoe*) movements" of Karataev's hands seem "intended to embrace something," even though in fact they are removing the covering from his legs (IV,i,xiii). In baring himself, Karataev embraces others. He is focused on himself, but he is not isolated or self-centered. In fact, in a spontaneous and unmotivated response to Pierre,

Karataev immediately offers him a gift of a potato. Unlike Pierre, however, the "round" Karataev, the "particle of the whole," is open to others but not led by them. He is detached from others and therefore free. "He loved and lovingly lived with everything life brought to him, in particular with people, not with any particular person, however, but with those people who were in his presence." In this passionless involvement, which includes a concerned response to others, Karataev is the emblem of love, of universal love that flows freely from the soul untouched by passion and suffering. The "particle of the whole" is the real self.

In his encounter with Karataev, Pierre learns the secret of "purification." He finds the "calm" and "harmony with himself" he had been seeking in his carousing and drinking, in his freemasonry and philanthropy, and in his erotic love for his wife, all that he now knows he was "not called to" (IV,ii,xii). Through Karataev's example Pierre learns to tear off the trappings of his "external man" in order to find "absolute internal freedom." In captivity Pierre is led to a new faith in the "force of life" (*sila zhizni*), which he now experiences profoundly within himself in a scene central to his whole career (IV,ii,xiv).

> The sun had set long ago. Brilliant stars had flared up here and there along the sky; as in a fire the red glow of the sky and the immense red sphere wavered (*shar kolebalsja*) wondrously in the greyish haze.... Pierre sat down on the cold earth ... and for a long time stayed there thinking. More than an hour passed. No one disturbed Pierre. Suddenly he burst into his broad, good-natured laugh so loudly that from various sides astonished people glanced over toward that strange, obviously solitary laughter. "Ha, ha, ha!" laughed Pierre. And he spoke out loud to himself; "The soldier didn't let me pass. They caught me, they locked me up. They held me in captivity. Who? Me? Me? Me—my immortal soul! Ha, ha, ha! Ha, ha, ha! "... The full moon was high in the bright sky. The woods and fields which formerly had been invisible beyond the camp now opened out in the distance (*vdali*). And still further (*dal'she*) beyond the woods and the fields there appeared the bright, swaying, infinite distance (*dal'*), beckoning to itself. Pierre looked up at the sky, into the depths of its retreat-

ing, sparkling stars. "All that is mine, all that is in me, all that is me!" he thought.

The imagery expands outward in a fashion we have already seen in the peak experiences of Nikolenka and Olenin. Here, of course, the imagery refers back to Pierre's own experience of the comet of 1812, the "bright star" and the "white light" that echoed and evoked the new sense of life in his soul. Only now Pierre moves further outward—this passage stresses the notion of distance (*vdali, dal'she, dal'*)—and further inward. The expanse of nature becomes the All, and Pierre realizes that the ultimate other, the All, is his, is in him, is him. Significantly this experience of at-onement with the All occurs at Pierre's most extreme moment of physical and emotional alienation from others, just as Prince Andrew's "love" is learned at the most extreme moment of detachment in dying. Pierre's sense of identification with the sky and moon again recalls Nikolenka, except that while Nikolenka feels the moon and the night and he are the "same," Pierre feels "the All is in him." In the relationship of self to other, Pierre does not experience an identification so much as a realignment: he is no longer subject to the other, because the other is not outside him but in him. Prince Andrew redefines the relationship of self to other by reassessing the other, Pierre by reassessing the self. In captivity Pierre moves paradigmatically from his usual sense of belonging to severe alienation to this high moment of residency in the All.

From this moment on, Pierre's ethical values and, more importantly, his behavior change. Pierre the man of the flesh is no more. The childish self-indulgence is outgrown once and for all. Nor is Pierre led by others, for "in captivity Pierre learned not with his mind but with his whole being, through life, that man is created for happiness and that happiness is within him," hidden only by the excessive trappings of his external life (IV,iii,xii). Pierre has begun to know Bazdeev's God. But Pierre cannot attain this highest wisdom and happiness until he learns the love of death. His last lesson will be that there is "nothing in the world that is terrifying." Karataev dies and Pierre is as detached from the event as Karataev himself. Even death cannot destroy that happiness within. Pierre's "image of the whole universe" is complete. It appears to him in a dream.

"Life is all. Life is God. Everything shifts and moves and that movement is God. While there is life, there is pleasure in the self-awareness of the Godhead (*samosoznanie bozhestva*). To love life is to love God. It is most difficult and most blessed to love this life in its sufferings, in innocent sufferings."

"Karataev," came to Pierre's mind. And suddenly there appeared, as though alive, the long-forgotten kindly old teacher who taught Pierre geography in Switzerland. "Wait a bit," the old man said, and he showed Pierre a globe. The globe was a large wavering sphere without any dimensions. The whole surface of the sphere consisted of drops pressed densely together. These drops were all moving, shifting, and now they merged from several into one, now they separated from one into many. Each drop was striving to expand (*razlit'sja*), to seize the most possible space but the others striving for something were trying to compress it, sometimes destroying it and sometimes merging with it. "That is life," said the old teacher. "How simple and clear," thought Pierre. "How could I have not known that before."

"God is the center and each drop strives to spread out in order to reflect Him to the greatest extent. It grows, merges, is compressed and destroyed at the surface, sinks to the depths and floats up (*vsplyvaet*) again. Like him, Karataev, he expanded (*razlilsja*) and disappeared. Vous avez compris, mon enfant?" asks the teacher. (IV,iii,xv)

This dream is the culmination of Pierre's metaphysical quest. It is also one of Tolstoy's most important fictional images of his metaphysics of life. Pierre's old geography teacher knows the secret of Bazdeev's "highest wisdom," that "most pure liquid we receive unto ourselves." In his dream Pierre attains an inner understanding of the abstract teaching. The dream moves from idea to image. The thoughts about life—"life is all," "life is God," "to love life is to love God"—are transformed into a dream image of life, the wavering liquid sphere which is Pierre's final internalization of the "pure liquid" of truth. But Pierre would not have been able to receive that "pure liquid" had he not been subjected to the sufferings of life epitomized in his captivity, when in that pivotal experience he discovered a new alignment of self and other as he internalized another "wavering sphere," the glowing moon whose red fire overflowed (*razlilos'*) the horizon and filled the expanse of nature. In the dream this sphere becomes the sphere of life, made of expanding and overflowing (*razlit'sja* means both) drops that somehow overflow a sphere that has a center and yet no fixed dimensions. The globe of life is a container without limiting form, all content. This dream image of life eliminates the very notion of death. The wavering liquid sphere without dimension is composed of tiny liquid drops that expand and contract, move inward toward the center that is God and outward toward the surface that is everyday life as we know it. Death is understood anew. Karataev's death is but the overflowing of an expanding drop of liquid, a spilling into the center which is God and the source from which the liquid drop may once again float up to the surface we call life. Karataev has simply disappeared. Prince Andrew discovers "love" and dies; Pierre discovers "life" and lives on.

TOLSTOY began his philosophical quest for life and happiness with the simple moral maxims that oppose the "personal good" to the "good of others," assuming that the boundary between the two "goods" was clear and distinct. But in his fictional renderings of the moral experience of Nikolenka, Olenin, Prince Andrew, and Pierre, Tolstoy reveals the complexity of his vision: for them the "good of others" turns out to be a covert form of the "personal good." And then once this is learned or at least sensed, each of the four characters has a third experience of "the good" which involves some new alignment of self and other. In this third stage the boundary of the other is extended to include eveything, the All, and then the self is seen in some way related to this other. The Enlightenment's commonsense distinction between or the Empiricists' confusion about self and other is subjected to what seems to be the Romantic correction of Identitätsphilosophie.

These three possible stances of the self toward the other, explored in the fictional careers of four major characters, are articulated in a full-blown theory of human and historical development that Tolstoy made explicit some twenty-five years after he completed *War and Peace*. Working from the unexpressed but very characteristic assumption that phylogeny recapitulates ontogeny, Tolstoy postulated in *The Kingdom of God is Within You* (1893) three historical ages which repeat the pattern of the three ages of man (28,69-85). This theory of historical development has a psychological foundation, since all activity, it is assumed, must have some clearly defined motivation that results from an intuition of total reality. This psychological base has moral implications that in their turn lead to metaphysical assumptions. Each age has its own "understanding of life" (*zhizne-ponimanie*), which includes its own psychology, ethics, and religion. Tolstoy's theory of the three ages of man articulates the meaning of the careers of his characters.

The first age of mankind is called the personal (*lichnoe*) stage, because at this point the motivation (*dvigatel'*) for action is the satisfaction of the "will of the personality" (*volja lichnosti*). All activity stems from self-interest. The personal age, a metaphor for the primitive savage, childhood, and the time from pre-history up to early antiquity, revolves around the satisfaction of the desires of the "animal self" (*zhivotnoe ja*): one is fed or feeds oneself, is warmed or warms oneself, is protected or protects oneself, is loved or loves oneself. The personal stage, whether in childhood or the primitive world, sees no boundary between self and other because the other belongs to the self. To recognize nature as nature, for example, one has to sense its separateness, but in this stage the self has not yet recognized the other as such and so it and nature are perceived as the same thing: "I am nature" (23,471). The understanding of life characteristic of this personal age is reflected in its religion, which centers around appeasement and reconciliation of the Godhead with oneself or the worship of oneself in the form of imaginary "personalities" of numerous gods who themselves live solely for the satisfaction of their own wills, gods, in other words, created in the image of man. In the personal age the other exists solely for the self. Everything else belongs to me. Uncle Eroshka embodies and reveals this personal stage of human experience.

The personal stage, thus, attains a kind of harmony because the self in its total self-centeredness knows no other from which it can be alienated. For the child or the primitive all that exists is its "personality." Tolstoy's category of the "personality," however, is not a simple one. First of all, it includes the basic, natural drives for food, sex, shelter, work, and rest that comprise the "animal self." To the extent that these animal needs are satisfied "unconsciously," Tolstoy argues in his *Christian Doctrine*, they give satisfaction and happiness (*blago*) (39,133). But such unconscious existence is for Tolstoy rather theoretical, because even the child or the primitive is aware of its body (*telo*), and such awareness of the "physical self" (*telesnoe ja*) transforms the unconscious drives into an "ineradicable attraction to the good of the personality" (39,131). The awareness turns in on itself, and satisfaction becomes an aim rather than a result. The concept of "personality" includes, therefore, the "animal self" and the "physical self"; it is associated with the body and its passions for self-satisfaction. In Tolstoy the concepts of "personal" (*lichny*) and "personality" (*lichnost'*) always carry the connotation of self-love. Tolstoy's doctrine of person, therefore, must exclude everything "personal."

The "personality," even of the child or the primitive, also includes the "habits" passed on by the culture to all its members and which are to them but "second nature" (28,280). What is "personal" has been shaped by the milieu. In many of his tracts, especially *What's To Be Done?* and *The Slavery of Our Times*, Tolstoy attacks the notion of "needs" (*potrebnosti*) because he is so acutely aware of the repressive character of these needs: culture increases the needs and redirects the drives of the human "personality" and thus enslaves human beings. Natasha's simple and touching love for ice cream (but not carrot flavored) is learned, as is Pierre's taste for drink, but both are examples of the dictates of the "will of the personality." This will, then, is not the same as the will of the self, although to one living at the personal stage of life it will seem so. Man is called to move beyond this state of false harmony between self and other.

The second age of man, called the pagan (*jazycheskoe*) or social (*obshchestvennoe*), reverses the stance of the first. If in the personal stage man recognizes life "only in himself," in his own personality, then in the second stage he recognizes life only in others, in "an aggregate of personalities" (*sovokupnost' lichnostej*), such as tribe, family, clan, church, state, or "humanity" (28,70). In the pagan or social stage, which is a metaphor for civilized man, youth through middle age, and the course of history from antiquity to the present, the self sacrifices its own good for the will of the "aggregate of personalities." The understanding of life characteristic of the pagan stage is reflected in its religion, which rests in the exaltation of the heads of aggregates—ancestors, founding fathers, sovereigns, bishops—and the worship of gods, who are the sole protectors of one's family, clan, church, or state. The meaning of life is found in the aggregate. The self exists solely for the other. I belong to everything else. The psychological motivation for such a life, however, is still self-interest. At best we are moved by "glory," which is the desire to be praised by others for doing useful and good things; at worst by "vanity," which is the desire to distinguish oneself before others by insignificant or even evil deeds. And even when glory and vanity play no role, we still live for others who are extensions of ourselves: "To love oneself is natural . . . ; to love my tribe, which supports and defends me, my wife, who is the joy and helpmate of my life, and my parents, who gave me life and brought me up—all this is natural. This love, although nowhere so strong as love for oneself, is very common. To love one's clan or fellow countrymen for oneself, for one's pride, although no longer so natural, is still quite common" (28,82). The pagan or social stage also presupposes a "natural" but false harmony of self and other which must be overcome.

In all this theorizing Tolstoy assumes that all life is motivated by self-love and that all "motives" (motivy) for love are found in the self's need or use of the object loved. The course of life and history have not changed the nature of love, but extended the boundaries of the object loved. Tolstoy draws a line, however, between love of some defined group of people and love of "humanity," for "humanity" like "fraternity" is a "fiction," an abstraction, not an object to be loved. The notion of one for all and all for one is fine, he thinks, but "there are no motives for it." At one and the same time Tolstoy is attacking the Enlightenment assumption of "humanity," the revolutionary assumption of "fraternity," and all the various socialist theories—utopian and otherwise—of the nineteenth century. We cannot love everyone because there is no motivation to do so. The extension of the boundaries of love leads to an impasse: "The natural course from love for self to love for family, clan, fellow countrymen, and then to the state characteristic of the social understanding of life has made people aware of the necessity of love for a 'humanity' which has no boundaries and merges with everything that exists, that is for something which evokes in man no feeling. The social understanding of life has led to a contradiction that it cannot resolve." The glory and vanity that move one to live for others in the pagan stage, while still egocentric, turns out to be, however, the "medicine" that will cure men of the totally self-centered view of the first stage; man's egocentric nature will lead him to a point where he cannot love what he sees he should love (45,247;1910).

Much of Tolstoy's fiction is devoted to an analysis of people who live with a mixture of these two different understandings of life. The character may be in a conscious state of conflict between them. More often, though, Tolstoy centers on the capacity for deception: we present our self-love to ourselves and others as some more or less disinterested love for others. The "personal" is masked as the "social." "No one can desire the good of another," Tolstoy wrote in his diary of 1880. "It's impossible. Just as you cannot desire to sneeze for another. It's a lie and the source of all evil. If someone says he desires something for the general good, find out what *he* wants and you'll understand" (48,323). In his fiction Tolstoy attempts to "find out what *he* wants" even as *he* weaves a web of rationalizations around his own desires. In his theorizing the two categories of personal and social tend to merge into one: the "personality" pursues its happiness for pleasure or profit in the fulfillment of its bodily desires, in its use of the things of this world, and in its love for people.

The major male characters in Tolstoy's fiction move through a career of life which imitates the Tolstoyan course of history. In different ways Nikolenka, Olenin, Prince Andrew, and Pierre all enter the life of their fictional worlds at the "personal" stage. Each soon suffers from a dissatisfaction with his life and seeks a solution in living for others. In the main their life is complicated by the conflicts that arise from these two "understandings of life." But then all four characters experience a moment of transcendence when they seem to overcome the impasse of their lives. These special times of peak awareness correspond to Tolstoy's third age of human experience, the "universal" (*vsemirnoe*) or "divine" (*bozheskoe*) stage, the metaphor for realized personhood, adulthood, and the historical period which should result from the proper understanding of the teachings of Christ (28,69-70). With this "understanding of life" life is found, not in the individual personality or in a group of personalities, but in the "source of eternal, undying life, God." The boundary of the other is extended to the extreme; the other becomes the "All, everything that exists, God" (*Vsë, vsë sushchestvujushchee, Bog*). This formula for the other which Tolstoy repeats over and over again throughout his later period implies a totally new conception of reality and morality, even while it seems to reiterate Tolstoy's earliest name for reality, "everything that exists." This God includes the self. This everything is not everything else. This everything is what I belong to and what belongs to me. Thus, while the second "social" stage reversed the stance of the "personal" one, the third "universal" stage returns to the first one, the "original consciousness of self," and the self is again at the center, only now in its transfigured form as the "divine personality." This uncovering of the "divine personality" is the purpose of life and history; it is the true discovery of self.

The motivation for all activity in this divine stage is "love," but this is no longer the love of the "personality" for its own pleasure or profit. In the universal stage egocentric love is transformed. Tolstoy's articulation of this new stage of love repeats Prince Andrew's formulation.

> The Christian teaching returns man to his original consciousness of himself, only not himself as animal but as God, as the divine spark, himself as the son of God, as a God just like the Father but contained in an animal covering. This consciousness of himself as the son of God whose main characteristic (*svojstvo*) is love, satisfies therefore all those demands for the expansion of the arena of love made upon him by the social understanding of life. Thus with the ever greater expansion of the arena of love for the salvation of the personality, love was a necessity and attached itself to certain objects, oneself, the family, society, humanity; in the Christian understanding of life love is not a necessity and is attached to nothing, for it is an essential characteristic (*sushchestvennoe svojstvo*) of the human soul. A person loves not because it is advantageous for him to love so-and-so or so-and-so, but because love is the essence (*sushchnost'*) of his soul. . . . Happiness (*blago*) is received not because he loves so-and-so, but because he loves the principle (*nachalo*) of everything—God, whom he is conscious of in himself as love and therefore he loves everyone and everything. (28,85)

The third stage of life resolves the question of identity and vocation. Happiness comes to him who knows his true self and what naturally flows therefrom. The divine stage of life is the state of faith. Entry into this third stage is attained by contact with the divine personality, the knowledge of yourself as a "particle of the whole" or as a "particle of love." Tolstoy's doctrine of person teaches that the person is spontaneous love for others unhindered by the personality. This "true self" (*istinnoe ja*) is what is hidden by the "physical self"; it is the "internal man" unencombered by the "external man." This "divine principle" (*bozhestvennoe nachalo*) resides in each and all; it is what is "common" (*obshchee* and not *obshchestvennoe*, "social") as opposed to what is "personal" (*lichnoe*). To live in this divine state is "to live according to God" (*po-bozh'i*) which means "to live for the good (*blago*) of your self not separated from other beings" (53,19;1895). This is the state of human relatedness. In the divine state there is no division or discord. In the universal state there is only union and harmony. In the third state of human life you reside in the All and the All resides in you. This state is the Kingdom of God within and abroad. All four major fictional heroes, Nikolenka, Olenin, Prince Andrew, and Pierre, glimpse this Kingdom of God.

THE GOD OF LIFE AND LOVE

When Prince Andrew in his dying learns that "life is love" and that he is a "particle of love" returning "to the common and eternal source" and when Pierre learns from Karataev that he is a "particle of the whole" and then intuits in his dream of the globe of life that "life is God," the literary heroes are articulating a metaphysical vision of reality fundamental to their creator. The autopsychological images express the author's experience of God. But, never satisfied with his articulations, Tolstoy spent the last thirty years of his life attempting to clarify the fictional images of this metaphysical vision which he came to believe was at least one way of understanding the "profound metaphysical meaning" of the teaching of Christ (23,423;1884). The later articulations of his metaphysics, however, Tolstoy usually left buried in his diaries because he believed that, after all, metaphysics are a private affair, since we all see metaphysical reality "through our own prism" (63,155;1884). No doubt he is right in this, and for this very reason Tolstoy's mature metaphysical views will clarify for us not only the doctrine of God expressed in *War and Peace* but also the "prism" through which Tolstoy views all of life.

Tolstoy was drawn to abstract thinking about moral and religious issues throughout his whole career as a writer. His first literary efforts (1847) were attempts at philosophical analysis of ethical ideas. The diaries kept during the first two critical periods of his life, 1852 and 1858, contain the seeds of all his later religious concerns. In his essays on education, written in 1862, he first confronted the concept of "coercion" (*nasilie*) which later became central to his moral and religious imagination. In working out the theory of history for the epilogue to *War and Peace* he approached his first non-fictional articulation of his doctrine of God. In his letters to Strakhov in the 1870's, in his *Confession* and in his theological interpretation of the Gospels in the early 1880's, he clarified for himself this same teaching. From 1890 until his death he became obsessed with his idea of God and man, and in his voluminous diaries of that period he recorded his finest articulations of his doctrine. Despite all these efforts, or perhaps because of them, Tolstoy's metaphysical vision is not easy to get to understand. He left no systematic treatment of his ideas, primarily because he did not believe in the possibility of a truthful system. "A philosophical system has within it not only the thinker's mistakes but the mistakes of the system" (48,344;1870). If for Tolstoy "truth is fragmentary and incomprehensible" (345), then the diaries were especially suited to his quest for truth. Whereas the essay published or the letter sent fixed his view, at least in the minds of others, the diaries allowed him to return again and again to the questions that perplexed him. Only in the diaries does one see Tolstoy's mind at work. His method of repeated articulations, however, creates the major difficulty in getting to understand his thought, because, instead of one clearly argued presentation, there are many, many statements of the same view, sometimes apparently contradictory, and usually told from different angles, within different contexts, and in different vocabularies. The doctrine must be distilled from the diverse articulations of the idea.

The fragmentary character of Tolstoy's metaphysical ideas, as indeed of most of his religious and theological ideas, is further exacerbated by the way he thought of philosophy. Tolstoy was violently opposed to academic philosophy and theology and their technical languages used to discuss what were for him vital questions of life and death. It always seemed to him that such thinking just came from books. He believed the mode of discourse used in academic philosophy was really designed to correct peoples' concepts about reality and then, by logical deductions made from these corrected concepts, to lead people to the view of reality that the particular author or age considered correct (62,220-225;1875). Genuine philosophical or theological discourse, of which the only practitioner recognized by Tolstoy was Plato, does not entail the implied realism and rationalism in this attitude toward concepts nor the assumed propaedeutical function of such writing. True philosophical or theological discourse must emerge directly from our subjective experience of our reality. Furthermore, Tolstoy believed that the "basic concepts" of philosophy, which include "my body, my soul, my life, my death, my desire, my thought, I feel pain, I feel sad, I feel good, I feel joyful," are the same for all human beings, and therefore he could not imagine that philosophy should seek to change them (62,222). The purpose of philosophy is not to change but to clarify the "basic concepts."

In order to deal with philosophy, then, Tolstoy begins with himself. He attempts to clarify for himself the "basic concepts" which he experiences "directly in his inner world." In this he is a characteristic Eastern Christian theologian.[2] The articulations in his diaries, as well as in the fictions, then, are the records of these attempts at clarification. Knowledge about the "external world" is based on this "internal" awareness of the basic concepts. All knowledge about the experience of others is projection. Only the assumption that the "basic concepts" are the same for all, it would seem, keeps this method from slipping into utter solipsism. This method is further complicated by another assumption. Tolstoy believes that since these "basic concepts" are known directly, they should not be dissected or distinguished nor related by logical or causal connection. They are known "only in their totality" (*tsel'nost'*) (62,223). True knowledge exists when these "basic concepts," which are "equal among themselves," are "harmoniously united in one whole" (*tseloe*) (62,224). Total knowledge is simply the best, the most harmonious, combination of the "basic concepts": "the cogency of philosophy is based on harmoniousness." How this "totality" and "harmony" are to be expressed, Tolstoy never quite makes clear. It is not surprising, then, that the majority of his articulations end in failure, dismissed with such phrases as "not clear," "very poor," "it didn't work out," "nonsense," often followed by the self-reassuring "mais je m'entends."

Tolstoy thus assumes that one can have a view of the world in all its totality and harmony in one's mind, even though one does not have the right words or the right order of words to express this view.

---

[2] Eastern Christian thought is often "mystical." Theology is understood as the verbal articulation not of concepts but of personal experience. This point is made most clearly and eloquently by Vladimir Lossky in his seminal work *The Mystical Theology of the Eastern Church* (London, 1957), pp. 7-22.

The view is the experience, the "basic concepts" in their "totality." The view is not a logically presented argument, nor are the "basic concepts" reducible to single words. Rather, the "basic concepts," a fundamental subjective experience of our own reality, are given various names, depending on the point of view the person wishes to convey and the context in which he is speaking. It is very often hard to know how metaphorical or how literal Tolstoy means his names to be. An artist first of all, he was very aware of the metaphorical character of all language, and, while compelled to attempt to express reality in words with precision, he knew the impossibility of the task.

Tolstoy's awareness of the metaphorical character of all language and his belief in the primacy of the fundamental "basic concepts" may be seen most simply perhaps in the application of this method to the exegesis of the New Testament. The evangelical "names"— God, Spirit, Son of God, Son of Man, light, and understanding (Tolstoy's first attempt to translate *logos*)—Tolstoy insists, all refer to the same "basic concept," but as seen from various points of view. "When it is spoken of as the principle (*nachalo*) of everything, it is called *God*; when it is spoken of in relation to the flesh, it is named *Spirit*; when it is spoken of in relation to its source, it is named the *Son of God*; when it is spoken of as its manifestation, it is named *Son of Man*; when it is spoken of as compliance to its reason, it is named light and understanding" (24,168;1884). Whatever we may think of such exegesis, the method is significant for Tolstoy's own use of language. For example, the "basic concept" of self has many names which fall into two general classes reflecting the primary duality of the human experience of the self as body and mind. If the one self is "physical," then the other is called "spiritual"; if the one is "external," then the other is "internal"; if one is "animal," the other is "divine"; if one is "personal," the other is "common"; if one is the "body," the other is the "soul." The words would suggest a reified dualism that Tolstoy does not mean to imply and a complexity of thought which is not truly appropriate. Since Tolstoy is so suspicious of the ability of words to express reality, he tends to be negligent in his terminology. The unsystematic use of the names for "basic concepts" is what makes his attempts at coherent presentations of his view difficult to grasp. Even his best philosophical work, *On Life*, suffers from these failings inherent in the method.

However unsystematic, subjective, and phenomenological, this method rests behind all Tolstoy's statements about metaphysical and religious reality. When we read that "love is God" or "life is God," we must realize that the statements of identity are a form of tautology and metaphor. "I say that 'to love,' 'to want' ('to desire,' the 'will') and 'to live' are the same thing and at the same time not the same thing. This is one of the applications of the philosophical method which does not use logical deductions, but tries to convince by the correctness of its combinations and concepts" (62,229). Because of this method, incidentally, Tolstoy felt few compunctions about also saying, as he often did, that "God is life" and "God is love." Now it is certainly possible to make distinctions between the different words for the "basic concept," but these distinctions do not necessarily clarify the expression of reality. Of course Tolstoy was himself able to make distinctions: "to desire is a temporal concept because one can only desire what will be: to live is a spatial concept for when we say 'life,' 'it is living,' we are only thinking about a space encompassed by life; to love is a causal concept because one can only desire what one loves and live only because one loves" (62,229-30). But Tolstoy was highly suspicious of this "philosophical jargon," even though he himself was not innocent of it in his own philosophizing. To get at Tolstoy's metaphysics, as well as his religious and theological thought, however, one must get beyond the jargon and the language and the metaphors to find the "basic concepts" where we should expect there will be lurking the "character of the author."

THE "BASIC CONCEPT" fundamental to Tolstoy's metaphysical view is the concept of God. It is certainly true that this concept of God always remained somewhat foggy for him. But a few years before he died he was still complaining about this lack of clarity in his conception (55,262;1906). In his brighter moments, however, he was aware that God could never be a clear concept because, as Bazdeev taught Pierre, "He is not apprehended by the mind but by life." "God is an x," wrote Tolstoy the old man, "yet although the meaning of this x is unknown to us, without it it is impossible not only to solve but even to formulate any equation. Life is the solving of the equation" (55,98;1904). Still Tolstoy felt compelled to articulate the "concept of God." For this "basic concept" Tolstoy had many names: from the point of view of the activity through which we know Him, God is "love," "life," the "force" (sila); from the point of view of the moral standard He is, God is the "truth" and the "law"; from the point of view of the totality which He comprises, God is the "All" (*Vsë*), the "whole" (*tseloe*), the "good" (*dobro*), "perfection"; from the point of view of the origin of everything which He is, God is the Father, the "principle" or "beginning" (*nachalo*), the "source" (*istochnik*); from the point of view of our subjective awareness, God is "consciousness," "reason," "freedom," "happiness" (*schast'e, blago*). While these names for the "basic concept" are important for understanding Tolstoy's thought, it is most important first of all to accept the apophatic correction Tolstoy always subjected himself to. He fills his diaries not only with statements of the type "God is . . ." but also the negatives of those statements: "God is not love" (58,143;1910); "the concept of life is not attributable to God" (54,135;1902); "the conception of the eternal, infinite being of God as a conscious being is just as incorrect as the conception of Him as a physical being" (54,159;1903). This apophaticism helps Tolstoy eliminate the anthropomorphic tendencies in his phenomenological method. At bottom Tolstoy the theologian knows that God is wholly other from the names he gives Him.

> That God whom I am not so much conscious of nor know but whose existence is inevitable for me, although I can know nothing about Him, except that He is, that God is for me ever *Deus absconditus*, unknowable. I am conscious of something non-temporal, non-spatial, non-causal, but I have no right to name that God, i.e., to see God and His essence in non-materiality, non-spatiality, and non-causality. That is just the highest essence in which I participate (*prichasten*). But the Principle (*Nachalo*), *principiium* of this essence can be and must be completely different from me and totally unavailable to me. . . . God is unknown to me, but my destined purpose (*naznachenie*) in Him is not only known to me, but my participation in Him constitutes the unshakable foundation of my life. (55,51;1904)

God's fundamental and full reality lies beyond human knowledge and is not available to analysis or comparison with anything in human experience. Yet this *Deus absconditus* is not alien to human life. Rather, for Tolstoy man participates in God. This notion of human participation in the divine, which is modeled on the Platonic *methexis* of particular things in the idea, reflects Tolstoy's Eastern

Christian understanding of man's relationship to God. In brief, this tradition portrays a human being who shares in the divine qualities, but who attains his true humanity and thus participates in the Divine only when he himself manifests those qualities. In this Eastern Christian view of man, therefore, there can be no opposition or conflict between nature and grace. By definition and creation man is in some sense divine. But in this view God's gift is man's task. In the above quotation, therefore, Tolstoy is saying that while man cannot know God with his mind, he can, like Bazdeev, know Him through his life. Man knows God to the extent that he realizes his "destined purpose in Him." But Tolstoy does not speak of such traditional divine attributes as justice, mercy, reason, freedom, purity, incorruptibility, or even love. Rather, Tolstoy speaks in metaphysical terms and finds the fundamental divine attributes in what is beyond the commonsense world of space, time, and causality, beyond matter and movement. These terms in which Tolstoy casts so much of his theological thinking are determined by the frame of reference of his imagined opponents, the enlightened or positivist materialists whose world of matter and movement seemed to toss the Christian God to the winds. In his theologizing Tolstoy attempts to demonstrate and describe a mode of being and a Being which transcend the eighteenth- and nineteenth-century materialist conceptions of man and the universe, and then, in the fashion of Eastern Christian thought, he goes on to explore the way in which creation participates in this transcendental world. His God remains unknowable, but still we know this God through our participation in Him.

This notion of participation in God underlies Tolstoy's "basic concept" of God. True, he believed that "a religious person's conceptions of God were continually being destroyed and replaced by newer and higher understandings" because this was the way he himself experienced God (53,222;1899). But the sense of participation in God is the constant and key to his conceptions. For Tolstoy the concept of God is always known inwardly, through the self's primary intuition of itself as a part of the whole. "I am a part, He is the All (*Vsë*); I cannot understand myself except as a part of Him" (52,49;1891). This synecdochic sense of self and God lies at the heart of Tolstoy's way of thinking about reality. God is always understood as the All, the self as part of the All. Nikolenka, Olenin, Karataev, Pierre, and Prince Andrew all share, although each in his own way, this fundamental experience with Tolstoy. This primary intuition of this "basic concept" is the essential religious experience, at least as Tolstoy defined it in *What Is Religion and Where Lies Its Essence?*: the clear awareness of one's "relationship to the whole universe (*ves' mir*) infinite in time and space yet understood as one whole" (*kak odno tseloe*) (35,161;1902). In his youth Tolstoy tended to speak of the All as "everything that exists" in this world we know with our senses and of God as a being out there, somewhere else, even though his experience, to judge from his prayers, did not make this distinction so clear; later at times he even seems to understand the All more in terms of all people, humanity (*ves' mir*, "the whole universe" also means "all people"); but most often, and his conversion marks the decisive clarifying point but not the *terminus a quo*, he understands the All as that which is infinite in space and time, yet not bounded by the categories of space and time. From this intuition of reality all Tolstoyan metaphysics follows.

> There is Something that does not pass on or change, in short something non-spatial, non-temporal, and not partial but whole. I know that it is, I am conscious of myself in it, but I see myself limited by a body in space and by movement in time. I imagine my human ancestors for a thousand centuries, and even before them their animal ancestors and the ancestors of the animals; I imagine that all that was and will be in infinite time. I also imagine that I occupy with my body one definite place in infinite space, and I know not only what was and what will be, but that all that, both in infinite space and infinite time, all that is me. (56,42;1907)

This late articulation of Tolstoy's understanding of God, man, and the universe combines the view imaged in Pierre's two peak moments: his rapturous discourse on the kingdom of truth and his ecstatic discovery of his immortal soul. In this late version the original category of self and other with which the young Tolstoy began his philosophical career has completely changed its complexion because of the primary intuition of God as the whole which is not the sum of its parts but their container. If God is the whole which contains the infinite universe and I am not just a part of that universe but a participant in the whole, Tolstoy reasons, then there is nothing else but this whole and nothing other than me. There is a sense in which I am

God and God is me and a sense in which God is everything and there is no everything else. The physical universe and all these ancestors and animals in their bodies limited in space and time which did, do, and will exist as parts of the universe are contained in the whole and yet are not that "something that does not pass on or change." Tolstoy's God is an Absolute and a Being which permeates and contains all the particular things which comprise Him. This God is the All which includes all that it is not within it. The All is both A and non-A. However, in the logic of Tolstoy's All, A and non-A do not exclude each other; they necessarily coexist and are, as we shall see, correlatives. This is the basic intuition and paradox on which Tolstoy builds all his metaphysics. "The universe is not God; the universe is the manifestation of God" (56,57;1907), but "either God is not at all or the only thing that is is God" (57,217;1909). Tolstoy's doctrine of God, as much of his theology, is shaped by this "antinomian" dialectic so characteristic of Eastern Christian thought.[3]

The most significant names for this God who is the All were first pronounced by Prince Andrew and Pierre. Tolstoy's God is the God of Life and Love. A characteristic Eastern Christian thinker, Tolstoy does not build his metaphysics on a philosophical conception of abstract being. His doctrine of God flows from the evangelical notions of Life and Love. These words, then, do not connote pious sentiments. For Tolstoy Life and Love are technical terms which serve as the foundation of his metaphysics. "I define life," Tolstoy wrote to Strakhov in 1876, "as the separation (ot"edinenie) from the rest of a part that loves itself" (62,243-44). Each such "separation" (ot"edinenie) is a "unification" (ob"edinenie). Life is understood in this most significant articulation as a process of what seems to be the self-creation of particular things, "parts" which are united and centered apparently by themselves. The process of centering and unify-

[3] For a useful discussion of the "antinomian" dialectic of irrationality in Eastern Christian theories of knowledge, see V. V. Bychkov, *Vizantijskaja estetika* (Moscow, 1977), pp. 14-64. This principle was introduced consciously into the tradition of modern Russian thought by Pavel Florenskij, *Stolp i utverzhdenie istiny* (Moscow, 1914), pp. 15-50 and 143-165. See also his article "Razum i dialektika," *Bogoslovskij Vestnik* IX (1914). This dialectical method is one of the major features shared by Russian religious thought and Marxist philosophy. See Gustav Wetter S. J., "Russkaja religioznaja filosofija i Marksizm," in N. P. Poltoratskij, ed., *Russkaja religiosno-filosofskaja mysl' XX veka* (Pittsburgh, 1975), pp. 99-116.

ing is what is called love, a reaching out to and an embracing of the other as thyself, an act which is simultaneously self-expression and identification with the other. The All, in this view, is the infinity of such unifications conceived as "one live whole" (*odno tseloe zhivoe*) which "embraces" everything. Life can be defined, then, as "unity (*edinstvo*) in multiplicity and multiplicity in unity" (55,137;1905). For Tolstoy, however, this "concept of something infinite and alive which unifies everything in itself is a clear contradiction," by which he means that, unlike the particular things contained within, the All could not unify itself by a process of separation from the rest because there would be no rest to separate from (62,243-44). Everything does not mean everything else. For Tolstoy this very "contradiction is the living and loving God" (*Bog zhivoj i Bog ljubov'*). Tolstoy is puzzled less by this contradiction, however, than by the fact. "What is this eternal, infinite, almighty God, who has become mortal, limited and weak? Why did God divide Himself up within Himself?" (53,131;1897). For this Tolstoy has no answer. Despite all his efforts to fathom the mysteries of this God of Life and Love, Tolstoy had to remain content with the knowledge that in this world "whatever we know is nothing other than just such divisions (*delenija*) of God." For him this means that what we call "matter in space and time" turns out to be the "contact of the limits of our Divinity with Its other divisions" and what we experience as "birth and death are transitions from one division to another." Whatever is, is a part of God and even in its coming and going it participates in the All.

The underlying assumption in this metaphysics of Life and Love is motion. "Not *cogito ergo sum*, not the inherence of space and time, but everything moves: a word which expresses something outside movement equals zero" (7,132;1868). Tolstoy dismisses what he understands to be the idealism of Descartes and Kant because he insists on the reality of motion. But this motion is not understood as random movement: it goes outward and toward. With motion thus assumed, Tolstoy conceives of a particular thing, what he calls a "being" (*sushchestvo*), not as an inert entity or atom but as an act and an action. A particular thing is a motion which goes out of itself toward something other, uniting this other to itself. Because Tolstoy imagines particular things as actions rather than entities, when he studied Newtonian physics he immediately questioned the concept of attraction. He rejected a world of passive bodies which "quasi attrahuntur" and replaced the concept of attraction with what he called a "striving toward union"(*soedinenie*) (48,131-33;1872). In Tolstoy's imagination everything moves outward and toward. This movement outward and toward is Life and Love. The fictional representations of characters at peak moments when they glance with their eyes and move with their hearts outward and toward the emblematic garden, mountain, or sky are images of this idea of a being who participates in the Divine by the fundamental action of Life and Love.

The assumption of motion in the metaphysics of Life and Love implies that there is no such thing as a separate, distinct being. By definition a being comes to be only in its movement outward and toward other. The "fundamental self" is defined in *On Life*, therefore, as "that which loves this and does not love that" (26,404;1886). The self exists only in conjunction with the other. In order for there to be A, there must be non-A. "What am I?" Tolstoy could thus ask himself and then answer, "I am nothing in and of myself. I am only a certain relationship, only my relationship really exists." (55,194;1906). Raised to the absolute beyond time and space, being would mean being for and belonging. "However strange it may be to say," Tolstoy observed, "if I were the All, then I would not live, I would just be for someone" (*dlja kogo-to*) (55,226;1906). But beings exist in time and space; they live in relationship "to everything and to the All," to all particular being-relationships and to the "totality" of such particular being-relationships (55,194;1906). The career of life is thus an endless process of belonging of an "eternally growing soul."

> I see myself in time and space as a unified (*ob"edinënnaja*) part of some infinite whole (*tseloe*) in which I see like parts unified by something and similar to me; I call them people or live beings or even plants. This [mode of] existence which is unified by love and which I am conscious of in myself and see in other beings I call life. Love gives this life; i.e., it unifies everything that constitutes one in time and space. I see the same sort of unifying principle of love in all particular (*otdel'nye*) beings. In this life, the more I live, I begin more and more to love something which is outside of me and does not constitute me: I love things and people and most of all something abstract—the good (*dobro*, *blago*) as I understand it—and less and less do I love what . . . had

constituted and does constitute me, my life in this world. From this . . . I conclude that my ever-decreasing love for this life and ever-increasing love for something outside this life is the movement of transition from this life to another not available to me until I have entered it. I assume that what really is appears to me as the *All*, God, and that in this All there are manifested (*projavljajutsja*) various units of unification (*edinitsy ob"edinenija*), various levels of love (*stepeni ljubvi*) which make beings what they are. I am one of those unified beings. In a former existence, while not being a human being, I loved what constitutes human spiritual being and moved from the lower level of existence to that which I loved. Now I love something higher and will move to that form of existence which corresponds to my love. The forms of existence may be infinite in number. In my father's house are many mansions. (53,62-3;1895)

This remarkable conception of the career of life rests on a vision of infinite motion outward and toward the "good" (*dobro*), "happiness" (*blago*); life is love for other. This articulation of Life, therefore, is really a clarification of Pierre's image of the globe of life. There are two modes of being, the All and the "units of unification" or "levels of love." These two modes of being correspond, on the one hand, to the living globe without dimensions, the formless container which is all content, and, on the other, to the liquid drops which keep on striving to reflect the Divine to the greatest extent possible. The conception of the universe in either articulation is at root neo-Platonic, as is so often the case in Eastern Christian thought. What truly is is the whole, the "totality of things" which is not just "all things" (53,41;1895). But all things for Tolstoy—the "parts," "particles," "unifications," "levels," and "manifestations"—are not Plotinian emanations from the One nor gnostic descents into matter. Each particular thing is a unification into a whole which participates in the life of the Whole. The analogy that serves Tolstoy throughout for describing the synecdochic relationship of part to whole is organic, the cell to the body. "I am the same as the Father, as Christ said, but I am His organ, the cell and the whole body. A similar relationship" (50,144;1889). In Tolstoy's imagination the All is "one live whole," a living being, and the "parts" are the organs or cells of the whole body. The inorganic is simply that which in no way seems to be similar to me and to my sense of participation in life (62,244;1876). In fact, however, "everything is alive. All things are organisms. We do not recognize some as such only because they are too large, like the earth, the sun, or because they are too small, like particles of minerals or of crystals" (54,170;1903). Whimsically Tolstoy wondered if "to a flea" his "toenail seemed inorganic" (53,179;1898). This organic imagination of the metaphysics of Life and Love places Tolstoy from the vantage point of modern Western thought closer to the Romantics and Spinoza than to the enlightened thinkers of the eighteenth century, with whom he is perhaps too often compared, or the positivists of his own time, with whom he is probably not compared enough. But this organic imagination of metaphysical reality, which after all has evangelical roots even for Tolstoy, might best be seen in the context of Eastern Christian thought. This organic metaphor serves to express the concept of participation which pervades this intellectual tradition and most appropriately suits a metaphysical vision based, not on the philosophical concept of being, but on the evangelical concept of life.

Tolstoy's vision of the All that contains all the particles may suggest at first glance a pantheistic universe in which the traditional personal God of the Judeo-Christian tradition disappears. But Tolstoy himself, like many another Eastern Christian thinker, does not accept the allegation of pantheism (all is God).

They say that God has to be understood as a person (*lichnost'*). In this there is a great misunderstanding: personality is a limitation. A man knows himself as a person only because he comes in contact with other persons. If a man were alone, he would not be a person. These two concepts are mutually dependent: the external world, other beings, and personality. If there were no world of other beings, a man would not recognize the existence of other beings. Therefore a man in this world is not thinkable other than as a person. But how can one say of God that He is a person, that God is personal? The root of anthropomorphism rests in this. Of God one can say only what both Moses and Mohammad said, that He is one, but not one in the sense that there are no other gods; in relation to God there can be no concept of number and therefore one cannot say of God that he is one (1) in the sense of number, but in the sense that He is one center (*odnotsentrenen*), that He is not a concept but a being, what the Orthodox call, in contrast to the pantheistic God, the living God, i.e., the highest spiritual being living in everything. He is one in the sense that He exists as a being to whom one can turn to . . . , in the sense that there is a relationship between me, a limited person, and God who is incomprehensible, but a being. For us the main incomprehensibility of God consists precisely in the fact that we know Him as an indivisible (*edinoe*) being, that we cannot know Him otherwise, and yet an indivisible being filling everything (*vsë*) with Himself we cannot understand. If God is not indivisible, then he is dispersed and He is no more. If He is indivisible, then we automatically imagine Him in the form of a person and then He is no longer the highest being, no longer the All (*vsë*). But still in order to know Him and lean on Him, it is necessary to understand Him as filling everything and at the same time as indivisible. (53,118-19;1896)

Tolstoy's doctrine of God is panentheistic (all-in-God). His God is in everything and everything is in God, but God is not everything and everything is not God. Rather, God is everything taken together as "one live whole." This God is beyond the world of space and time but includes within Him all the world of space and time. This God is not personal, although He contains within Himself everything personal. This God is both A and non-A. In scholastic terms, therefore, Tolstoy's God can have "accidents" in some sense distinct from His "nature" and His essence is not in every sense equivalent to His existence. This God is not Absolute Being but the Being that includes both being and becoming. This Being lives. The "Something that does not pass and change" contains within Him all passing and changing. The panentheistic God is both transcendent to and immanent in the world. Tolstoy's God exists only as a relationship to the world, just as the world exists only as a relationship to God. God and world, like self and other, are mutually dependent correlatives. The world "turns to" God, but the world is also the fulfillment of God's creative possibility. The "one live whole" comes to be in the world. God lives, He "lives with us and through us, all beings in the universe" (55,92;1904). Tolstoy's God, thus, holds all creation in His one living and loving embrace.

But Tolstoy's God is not the Creator. The idea of creation in the sense of a moment of beginning and the notion of creation *ex nihilo* were to Tolstoy "superstitions that have confused all our metaphysical concepts" (52,131;1894). For him the universe could not have begun in any meaningful sense of the word, because it is all that exists, God. Creation *ex nihilo*, a concept that does not exist for the Chinese or the Japanese, Tolstoy believes, is also incompatible with the Christian God, "a particle of Whom lives in me and comprises my life." In place of God the Creator Tolstoy puts God the Source. All things come from God and all things return to God. The universe is the process of reversal and return. Thus "the universe is not created. It is being created. And life is nothing other than the process of creation" (52,140;1894). God the Source, thus, offers the possibility of Life. "Nature or God always acts in the same way. Neither it nor He makes anything already finished; they make the possibility of accomplishment (*sovershenija*), not the tree but the seed" (49,128;1886). For Tolstoy every being is a "seed" of God, a potential being, and "we [all beings] create the universe according to God's will" (52,140;1894). By participating in "God's will," which is nothing other than His movement out of Himself to embrace all other as Himself, every being moves from potentiality to actuality outward and toward the creation of the universe.

The universe being created, however, is not the world of matter and movement in space and time, although that world is included in the universe. The world of matter and movement is the form of existence manifested within the All which human beings, like Prince Andrew, experience as "this life." The personality is the self that belongs to "this life" and hence is limited by its existence in the extended world. Seen from the point of view of intellect rather than will, personality is that which knows within the categories of space, time and causality. In "this life" the personality is "defined," "determined," and "limited" (*opredelën* means all three) by these categories. The world of matter and movement in space and time is what the personality knows. "The limits (*predely*) of my being appear to me as matter. The changes of my being appear to me as movement. The limits of my being in relation to other beings appear to me as space. The changes of my being in relation to the changes of other beings appear to me as time" (54,106;1901). But Tolstoy does not mean by these words—and they are but one example of many articulations of his conception of matter, movement, space, and time—

that the extended world is simply his idea or representation. For Tolstoy the extended world exists as the limit of a being's movement outward and toward. In "this life," therefore, "man is a manifestation ... in a limited state of the divine being" (55,25;1906), a "temporal and spatial manifestation of something non-temporal and non-spatial" (53,190;1898).

Tolstoy conceives of the universe which is being created as a dialectic of separation and belonging. Every particular being is both apart from the whole and a part of the whole. Particularity is opposed to participation. In this view "the material universe, moving matter, is just the form of my separation (*otdelenie*) and of the separation of all beings from each other" (55,79;1904). Thus the personality is opposed "to the All, i.e., to God and all humanity, to everything living, everything" (57,53;1909). It is "what hinders the merging of my soul with the All" (58,99;1910). In Tolstoy's metaphysical imagination, therefore, there are two modes of being: "one of separateness (*otdelënnost'*) from the All, the other of unity (*edinstvo*) with the All" (55,234;1906). A particular thing is a movement outward and toward which stops or is stopped by any or all other movements outward and toward. Separation, therefore, is characterized actively by a being's "inability to merge" (*neslivaemost'*) and passively by its "impenetrability" (*nepronitsaemost'*) (54,165;1903). A particular thing is a separate, limited, and isolated being. It is an individual. In "this life" the monad is made all of windows and doors kept shut. But for Tolstoy, whose metaphysics of the All is an argument against Western materialism and individualism, the individual, particular thing is not what truly is. In "true life" a being must be for and belong. Tolstoy believed, consequently, that what had been lost in the understanding of Christianity was the "very essence of Christ's teaching, sonship with God" (56,127;1908). Not adoption but sonship. A particular thing is by nature (and by grace, there is no difference) a part of the whole. To Tolstoy Christianity is a doctrine of the "participation in the Divine life given" to all beings. The unity of all things with the All precedes the separation from the All. This separation is experienced because the windows and doors are kept shut. When opened, when merged and penetrated, a particular being resides in the All. Such moments of merging and penetration, the moments of belonging, are moments of "true life" experienced within "this life." It is in such moments that the personality overcomes the "illusion of particularity, of its separateness from the universe" (*mir*) (53,190;1898). In "this life," "true life is made from those moments pooled together, without everything that divides them" (54,83;1901). "True life" is in this sense beyond the realm of space and time, matter and movement. It is also beyond all other possible forms of existence because "true life" is the life of God. To the extent that a particular being truly lives, it participates in the Divine life.

The purpose of "this life" is to attain more and more "true life," the "greatest possible seizure of the Divine," as Tolstoy phrased it while writing *The Cossacks*. The Stranger is called to be a Resident. "The aim of life is the penetration of all its phenomena by love, the slow, gradual conversion of evil life into good life. This is the creation of true life, for true life is just life which is loving" (53,22;1895). To accomplish this true and loving life a particular being must move farther outward and toward. The personality must "transfer" itself into "another person, animal, plant, even a stone" and thus "reestablish the unity among beings which has been as it were destroyed" (52,101;1893). It must transcend its limitations. The goal is to transfer oneself into "everything, to merge (*slit'sja*) with God, with the All." This transferal is the return to the original unity, a process that is without end. The career of life moves from the original at-onement to alienation back towards at-onement following the pattern of reversal and return.

This career of life doubly reflects the doctrine of salvation characteristic of Eastern Christian thought. This tradition assumes that, to use the famous statement of St. Athanasius, "God was made man that we might be made God" (*De incarnatione verbi*, 54,3). Salvation is deification. This deification is understood as the process of participation in the divine life which results in the transfiguration of mortal life. The transfiguration of Christ on Mt. Tabor is the perfect icon of this deification. This deification is not the same as imitation. Deification is not an imitation of something other than self. Deification implies not just the strict following of external, moral teachings, which in the end is rewarded with eternal life. Rather, deification entails a total transfiguration of self, a turning away from all personal passion, desire, perception, and reasoning which returns you to your life "in God." Deification is the total manifestation of the true self.[4]

---

[4] On the central significance of the doctrine of salvation as deification in Eastern

Tolstoy's conception of the career of life follows the pattern of this doctrine of deification. It assumes an "eternally growing soul" which exists in a process of increasing participation in true life and ends up becoming one with the All. However, when this doctrine of deification is generalized into a metaphysical vision, as with Tolstoy and other Eastern Christian thinkers, it leads to a cosmic conception of the purpose of life wherein all things on earth are seen in the process of return to their divine source. The deification of everything becomes the transfiguration of reality. The end of life is God "all in all" (I Cor. 15:28), a phrase which echoes as a proof text throughout Eastern Christian thought. Salvation thus seems universal and inevitable. Such was the vision of Origen, the first Father of Eastern Christianity, and his notion of *apokatastasis* ("restoration, re-establishment"), although duly condemned, pervades Eastern Christian thought in many disguises.[5] In Tolstoy, the Origenist *apokatastasis* recurs in a dialectical form. All beings are a part of God and apart from God, but all beings by nature strive toward union and thus in the end merge in the All. Tolstoy's metaphysical vision, thus, refracts the traditional doctrine of deification and the ancient hope of universal salvation, even as it reflects his own sense of estrangement and need to belong.

The doctrine of universal salvation seems to assume a world of necessity and a God whose mercy becomes inescapable. Human freedom is lost. Tolstoy attempts to overcome this apparent fall into slavery by expanding the notion of time. Just as he imagines a universe which is ever in motion, so he conceives of a universe unbounded by time. God is that universe which goes outward and toward forever. This is the eternal process of accomplishment (*sovershenie*) and perfection (*sovershenstvo*) in which everything participates. "The universe moves, perfecting itself. Man's task is to take part (*uchastvovat'*) in this movement, to submit to it and collab-

---

Christianity, see Jaroslav Pelikan's indispensable work, *The Spirit of Eastern Christendom* (volume two of his *The Christian Tradition*) (Chicago, 1974), pp. 10-16 and *passim*. Also John Meyendorff, *Byzantine Theology* (New York, 1974), pp. 163-164 and *passim*.

[5] The best discussion of the Eastern Christian conception of the "restoration of all things" (and the difference between this idea and the Western Christian conception of "reform") is by Gerhart B. Ladner, *The Idea of Reform* (New York, 1967), pp. 63-132 and *passim*.

orate with it" (sodejstvovat') (53,193;1898). Human freedom consists in the choice to participate and assist in this eternal process. Evil is the result of the refusal to participate and collaborate. But Tolstoy assumes that with enough time—forever—the choices for perfection will be made. Thus by expanding the limit of time, Tolstoy preserves the possibility of free choice and yet assures the inevitability of the accomplishment. By the logic of the All there is no way in which a part of the whole can ever or forever fall outside the whole.

> I, each living being (and everything is alive), am a particle of the All incomprehensible to me, a part which is expanding its limits, establishing a greater and greater connection (svjaz') with the All.

> I was
> I have become
> I am becoming

And thus it is for everyone always and without ceasing. My limits, i.e., what separates me from the All, I cannot understand other than as matter in space. My expansion of my limits I cannot understand other than as movement in time. Time is the possibility of more or less expansion of the limits. Freedom consists in my being able sooner or later to accomplish (sovershit') my expansion: to approach perfection (sovershenstvo). In this way I can collaborate (sodejstvovat') in the most certain realization of the Kingdom of God. For God it is accomplished (sovershilos'); for Him there is no time. But for me time exists in order that I might participate (uchastvovat'), that I might contain within myself more or less participation. (54,75-76;1900)

The dialectics of estrangement and belonging upon which Tolstoy builds his metaphysics rests on a temporal dialectic of process and completion. To the extent that a being is apart from the whole it is only in process, it has yet to complete itself, to attain deification, to merge with the All. For all particular beings life is process, the "movement toward happiness" (55,98;1904). For the whole, for God, however, there is no process, there is only completion and "life is happiness" (zhizn' blago). Therefore from God's point of view "everything that seems to us yet to be accomplished (sovershist'sja)

and everything that seems to us already accomplished, all that neither was nor will be but is. We just experience what is as we see the
light of a star which reaches us just now" (55,219-20;1906). The paradox of our life is that everything moves, but the movement is just
the "removal of the covers (*snimanie pokrovov*) from the one, immobile, truly existent (*sushchij*) Divine Spirit" (56,21;1907). But, despite all Tolstoy's statements apparently to the contrary, his God is
not just this "one, immobile, truly existent Divine Spirit." Tolstoy's
God is the All, the completion which has resulted from the process.
The God of Life and Love is the paradoxical being who separates
Himself from the rest and yet embraces everything within Himself.
This God is not an abstract principle removed from the world any
more than He is a Creator totally distinct from creation or a Ruler
totally superior to His subordinates. For Tolstoy there is a God and a
Kingdom of God (self and other), but there is no God without the
Kingdom of God. If God is Life, then God lives.

> The universe (*mir*) consists of separated parts of the Godhead.
> Matter and movement make for this separateness. . . . Matter
> and movement exist only for us separated beings. For God there
> is no matter or movement, but there is an innumerable quantity
> of separated beings which we can know only in space . . . and
> time . . . but which exist for God without space and time.
>
> All separated beings by their nature (*svojstvo*) strive to expand
> and transfer into other, higher separations. In that is our life. For
> God, though, they are already expanded and have transferred
> into a second, a third, an infinite number of forms of life. We are
> experiencing this. . . . Our life consists in the transferal from one
> life to another, eternal movement, eternal resurrection, eternal
> growth. In this is life and happiness (*blago*). In essence, for God
> everything stands still, everything is immobile and non-mate-
> rial, but there is life. What kind? We cannot understand or know.
> (55,12-13;1904).

The concept of life assumed in this vision of eternal life adds the
element of time to the static notion of life as the separation from the
rest of a part that loves itself. Now "life is continual creation, i.e., the
formation of new and higher forms" (54,49;1900). Each particular
thing is a process of expansion and merger in which the merger is the
completion and end of the former particular thing and the creation of

a new and greater particular thing. "A drop that merges with a larger drop, a puddle, stops being and starts to be" (53,231;1899). God is the completion and perfection of this process: the living liquid sphere in Pierre's dream of the globe of life. Tolstoy thus understands the evangelical concept of life as "eternal movement, eternal resurrection, eternal growth." Birth and death are transformed into a process of reversal and return, and yet this "process of life is not without purpose" because, "although life as it were returns to its beginning, it returns different from what it was when it began" (55,73;1904). The "process of birth and death" is therefore not to be understood as the "process of arising out of nothing and destruction into nothing," even though this is what may seem to be to us. After all, "the caterpillar sees its own withering but does not see the butterfly that will fly out of the caterpillar" (54,49;1900). To Tolstoy this means that "death is just such a metamorphosis, one which depends on another separation from the universe, on another personality" (53,211;1898). Furthermore, for Tolstoy, "everything we see and know belongs to this law of life, of birth and death" (55,73;1904). The process of birth and death is the process of expansion and merger which governs the universe. There is no annihilation or meaningless return because "every being while living is achieving the good (*dobreet*), that is, is becoming more and more conscious of his unity with other beings, with the universe, with God" (55,9;1904). Everything is becoming the All.

Tolstoy's God of Life and Love is an Eastern Christian God. The concept of God as an abstract idea of absolute being has been replaced by a God who dwells in the world of change even as He transcends it. In this view the "umbilical cord which unites" the universe "with God" has not been broken (50,90;1889). There is no God without His Kingdom and there is no Kingdom except the one that is coming to be. The shackles of the Aristotelian excluded middle have been abandoned, and the concept of God the All can contain the paradoxical fullness of life and death, movement and rest, change and immutability. The ancient Greek philosophical association of perfection and divinity with immutability which pervades many Western theologies in various guises has been replaced by a conception of perfection as perpetual progress. The "eternally growing soul" moves ever outward and toward, becoming more and more like God. And God is the container of all the "eternally growing souls," who lives His life through them. From the Western point of view, Tolstoy seems to bring the enlightened conception of the perfectibility of man and the modern idea of progress into his theological world-view. His concept of life resembles Hegel's "principle" of life. But Tolstoy's understanding of the evangelical notion of eternal life as "eternal movement, eternal resurrection, eternal growth," is really an ancient Eastern Christian conception. Gregory of Nyssa, the most profound of the Fathers of Eastern Christianity, was the first to understand the participation in the Divine leading toward deification as an eternal expansion of the soul. Borrowing from St. Paul, he called this process *epektasis*, a word which implies both a sense of contact with God (Gr. *epi-* "at, toward") and movement out of self toward what is ever beyond (Gr. *ek-* "out of"), movement outward and toward.[6] In Gregory of Nyssa's view— and this became paradigmatic for Eastern Christian thought—the locus of perfection is both the past and the future, the creation and paradise that is coming to be, when God will be "all in all." Origen's *apokatastasis*, the simple idea of the restoration of the past, is thus transformed into an eternal process of creation leading to the paradise which Gregory of Nyssa, much like Leo Tolstoy with his vision of the ant brothers and his ideal of the green stick, believed must come, "when all men shall be made one, when all will look to the same end, when God will become all in all, and all evil will be destroyed, and all men will be united together in harmony by their participation in the Good."[7] The deification of everyone and the transfiguration of the world is imagined as the communal harmony of all together, at one in their participation in the Divine Life. The highest ideal of Eastern Christian thought, then, is the incarnation of the God of Love in all of life. Tolstoy's metaphysics are grounded in this high ideal, and his ethics, as we shall see, are designed to bring this high ideal right down to earth.

[6] For a discussion of this doctrine of perpetual progress, see Jean Daniélou S.J. and Herbert Musurillo S.J., *From Glory to Glory* (New York, 1979), pp. 56-71.

[7] *Ibid.*, p. 288.

Chapter Three

THE STRUGGLE FOR LOVE

If you relate to people through your spiritual, divine self . . . ,
you will attract them to you and be attracted to them; if you
relate to them through your physical, personal self, inevitably
there will be estrangement, struggle, and suffering.
(55,68;1904)

IN *The Cossacks* and *War and Peace* the heroes seek to learn who
they are. They discover their identity in relationship to the All but
find their vocation only at the end and in abstract visions. They do
not live or work in the ordinary, everyday world of Russian upper-
class reality. Both fictions assume that, once faith is apprehended,
one's career in this life should be resolved, as it is in the epilogue to
War and Peace, in family happiness. One's true vocation is not questioned. The happiness of love simply comes to those who are married
and devoted to family living. *War and Peace* was written in the first
years of Tolstoy's own marriage.

Anna *Karenina* was written during the period when Tolstoy's major crisis was fomenting. For him the family was ceasing to be the
fantasy fulfillment of his need for love. He had to seek his goal else-
where. In this novel, which is the autopsychological image of his experience, he shifts his focus onto the earlier assumptions of family
happiness in order to explore the causes for the failure of the fantasy.
"Love," he still believes, "is the main purpose and happiness on
earth" (60,122;1856). But in *Anna Karenina*, as in the earlier work
Family Happiness (1859), Tolstoy turns his critical attention to the
modern assumption that romantic passion is the first step to marital
love and family life, and he explores the age-old confusion between
romantic love and the Christian idea of love. Tolstoy now raises the
question, not of identity, but of vocation. The characters do not ask
themselves "Who am I?" but "What must I do?" Like Olenin, they
want to love, but they do not quite know how to. They are represented, however, not in some extraordinary, distant time or place on

some metaphysical quest for identity and divinity, but here and now in ordinary times in the everyday circumstances of upper-class Russian life. The men work and play in the mundane world; the women care for the children and engage in charity or chatting. They all seek love. *Anna Karenina* explores the possibilities of careers in this life and represents people in crisis over their vocation to love.

But the characters do not confront their identity, and their quest for their vocation, as a result, is flawed. They do not find faith. They live in a world where they are divided within themselves. The men are torn between their work and their women; the women are torn between marriage and romance. Their choice of career in life revolves around a decision to live for others, regardless of self, or to live for themselves, regardless of others. This unresolved division is reflected in what Tolstoy called the "new psychology: not how a person thinks and desires, but how it seems to him that he thinks and desires" (48,89;1868). What they seek is not necessarily what they really want or need, and thus in their quest they err. From their mistakes they suffer, and, although they seek happiness, they find accommodation, frustration, and failure. The inevitable career through the three stages of life fades away, and people are caught between living for self or living for others. They strike out on careers, be it romance, family, or work, only to discover that this career does not lead them to the happiness of love. In this discovery they suffer, and from this suffering they learn, some tragically too late.

MASHA'S DESIRE TO LIVE

Masha, the heroine of Tolstoy's long first-person narrative of life recollected, *Family Happiness*, is a typical Tolstoyan character in crisis over life. The seventeen-year-old girl's mother has just died and, since her father passed away so long ago that she cannot remember him, she is now an orphan with no one to foster the assurance and self-esteem she needs to move into her young adulthood. The family home at Pokrovskoe is filled with "gloom," "death, and sadness" and Masha suffers from the "feeling of anguish, aloneness and boredom" (i). She wants nothing. "I am like a shadow without a task, without a thought, without desire." Then in late winter her father's former friend who has been appointed her "guardian" arrives and tries to instill in her a renewed interest in life. Sergey, a rather stodgy, settled man of middle years, has long loved her, and now Masha is thankful that he has come. He speaks to her "as a father or uncle," warns her "not to despair," and promises to return in spring "to examine" her. He departs, and Masha's despairing "why" disappears. Life is to be lived "in order to be happy," she now believes, and the "old, gloomy Pokrovskoe home suddenly seems filled with life and light."

Sergey begins to visit regularly in order to teach Masha how to love. To his instruction she responds in order to earn his love. She learns "to look at the servants and peasants completely differently than before" (ii). For seventeen years, she realizes, she had been a "stranger" (chuzhaja) among them. Now she sees the people who serve her are just like her. With this new sense of identification with others, the world in which she lives becomes "new and beautiful" for her; "the only certain happiness in life is living for others." She now believes Sergey has revealed to her "a whole life of joys in the present." In her prayers she "thanks God for all the happiness He has given her." Through her guardian's love Masha has begun to learn to love.

But Masha, who has a romantic imagination and fantasies a Byronic hero, wants Sergey to declare his love to her. Instead, he delivers himself of a speech against romantic declarations. "It will always be a lie. What kind of revelation is it that a person loves? As though once it is said something will click and wham! he loves. As though as soon as he pronounces the word something extraordinary must happen, portents of some kind, and all the cannons salute" (iii). But Masha, and because of the form of the work we really know only her version of reality, needs the drama of declaration, moonlight and all. When no declaration comes forth, therefore, convinced that "he is mine," she decides to fast and prepare herself for communion on her birthday, when she believes she will become his fiancée. What Masha wants, she will get.

In reshaping herself in the image of Sergey's love, however, Masha discovers a new world within herself and for a moment attains a love she did not seek. In church the familiar surroundings recall her past even as they now seem "sacred" and "full of profound meaning" (iv). She listens to the prayers and prays to God to "enlighten" her. When the prayers of repentance are read, even her innocent childhood seems dark in comparison with the present "bright state of her soul."

She repents of her dark past and begs forgiveness. She feels blessed, "as if some sort of light and warmth had suddenly entered her heart." Life and light fill her soul. This moment of enlightenment leads directly to action, a desire to help others, sacrifice herself for them, even give them the right of way on the road and be dirtied by the dust from their wheels. With her piety of humble and humiliated action for others, she sneaks off to leave "all her money" on the windowsill of some poor peasant. She is filled with "joy," thinks of death, and "at that moment loves warmly and passionately everyone on earth, including herself." She reads the Gospels, and "it seems to her that it is simple to love everyone and to be loved. All are so good and meek." She thinks of her one "enemy" and writes a letter begging her forgiveness. "Why are they all so good to me? How have I earned such love?" she wonders at her own reconciliation. When she takes communion, she feels "such full happiness" that she is afraid to lose it. This "full happiness" of "love for everyone" raised Masha to the "heights of spirituality," to a whole new "world" (*mir*) which Sergey would not understand because it is "higher than him." In her "love for everyone, including herself" Masha has soared past her "guardian"; she begins to resemble Natasha and Katyusha.

Still, Masha believes she wants romance. When Sergey continues in his indirection, expressing his fear of a love which seeks excitement, not life, Masha sees through his fears and declares her love for him. Masha attains her happiness, and they decide to marry. Still, Sergey cannot believe that her notion of happiness is the same as his. His settled ways and years separate him from her youthful needs for adventure. Blinded by her fantasies of romance, Masha imagines he is wrong and that they share the same view of life and love. Despite her conviction, just before the wedding Masha is overcome with doubt, fearing a life "without" all the trappings of her past (v). As she thinks of the "new life" that awaits her she feels herself "a stranger to herself." The wedding itself only heightens this confusion: she does not understand the words and his kiss seems "strange, alien." "Is that all?" she wonders. They take off in the carriage, but sitting next to him she feels "outrage and fear," even resentment, for his assurance in their love. But he takes her hand, and she reassesses her fears as but symptoms of her love: in fact she is, she thinks, "all his," "happy in his power over her." With these words the first half of the story ends.

Looking back at her life as she retells it, Masha recounts the story of her own fragile sense of self in terms of her confusion over how to love. Her moment of enlightenment does not lead her to a new way of being in the world but only encourages her in her pursuit of romance. To live for others, she thinks, means to live for her beloved; to sacrifice for others, she thinks, means to yield to his power over her. But the problem with Masha's romantic view of life rests in this notion of power which emerges at the center of the novel. She thinks she wants a hero to sweep her away and to teach her how to live, but she also wants him to be her possession. She pursues the one who will overpower her, but her hidden quest is that he be "mine" and that she be not just his equal but "higher" than him. This conflict in her purposes destines her to failure. Her inability to see this conflict destines her to resentment. The marriage as romance is doomed.

For Masha married life from the very beginning is a disappointment. While she thought that in marriage she was going to find a way to express herself, the "labor, fulfillment of duty in self-sacrifice and life for another" she had fantasied turns out to be self-seeking: marriage results in a "self-loving feeling of love for each other, a desire to be loved . . . and the forgetting of everything on earth." (vi). Marriage is no vocation. Their "happy little world" (mirok) seems narrow and self-interested in comparison to the "whole new world" (mir) of love that she felt in her moment of enlightenment. At the center of the story Masha loves and is loved, but in the wrong way. Thus when Sergey returns to his private world of work, discontent sets in because she is left alone. She is happy but now needs "labor and sacrifice." Her love, she feels, has stopped still and is no longer growing. She needs "movement." She has an "excess of energy" (izbytok sily) and needs "struggle" and "danger." "I want to live, to move and not stand in one place and feel time passing through me. I want to go forward with each day; each hour I want something new." Masha wants a love that is eternally growing, but all she has is her love for her husband. She must move and move on. "I want to live."

They move to St. Petersburg, and Masha moves into society. She takes up a career in "real life" (vii). She goes to a ball, and there she attains new heights. Now she is the "center around which everything moves." "Everyone . . . makes her feel they love her." This "love for me" now "for the first time" gives her confidence in herself. She again feels "higher" than Sergey and now believes she loves him even more. Her "pride and self-satisfaction" lead her to believe her social success is "for him, just in order to sacrifice it for him." Life in Petersburg leads to a "struggle for generosity," in which she believes that denying herself social pleasures is the expression of her love for him, while he believes the very move to the city is an act of sacrifice on his part. So when Sergey is not touched by Masha's self-denial, seeing no sacrifice in it, Masha believes that he just wants to insult and humiliate her, when she is "guilty" of nothing. "Ah, so there's the power of a husband." She refuses to "submit." She will go to the next party even without him.

> At that moment I feared and hated him. I had a lot I wanted to tell him to avenge all the insults, but if I had opened my mouth I would have started to weep and have fallen down before him. I left the room in silence. No sooner had I stopped hearing his steps, than I became horrified at what we had done. I was terrified that our relationship, which comprised all my happiness, would be broken forever. "But has he calmed down enough to understand me when I extend to him my hand in silence and look at him," I thought. "Will he understand my generosity? What if he says my grief is pretended? Or will he accept my repentance and forgive me with a consciousness of his righteousness and a proud calm? And why did he, whom I love so, so cruelly insult me?"

In her desire to live, Masha has stumbled into the abyss of self-love. Everything she does she does for herself but believes it is for others. The truth becomes insult and repentance an act of generosity. Her husband turns into a powerful and self-righteous enemy standing in the way of her life. She wants to live, but he will not let her. Love fades into resentment. Even when she gets her way and they go to the party together, she sees in him only his "pride" and her "judgment of him" lies "like a crime" on her "conscience," creating "an abyss that separates them from each other." In her self-centered universe her husband is guilty, but she suffers for the sin.

"Their life and their relationship changed from that day" (viii). Three years pass in their new urban world. Masha now accepts that they each live in a "separate world alien to the other." A child is born, but she experiences no joy of motherhood. They all live in profound estrangement. Masha slips back into depression. Then one summer they go abroad to take the waters. At this point *he* appears. The Italian Marquis D., who looks like Sergey, only "better," will rescue her from her boredom and call her back to life. Like her guardian, the Marquis too has a philosophy of love, but this love he understands differently. "I cannot help loving; without that there is no life. The only good is to make life into a romance." Masha is attracted and repelled. The Marquis does not have the look of "kindness" (*dobrota*) and "ideal calm" she sees in her husband; in him there is "something crude, something animal," but she senses his passionate "love" and thinks constantly of him "against her will." Then one day she goes with her friend Lady S. to a musicale, but the ball of life is over. Masha is no longer the "center around which everything moves." Lady S., younger and prettier, has stolen her place. All of a sudden Masha is alone. "Everything and everyone seemed stupid and boring" and she has "bad feelings" in her heart. At this point an erotic urge takes over. The Marquis finds the moment and declares his love, but Masha feels only hatred and alienation. "Shame" overcomes her, and she rushes off; that very evening she takes the train to rejoin her husband. She recalls their past and feels her "guilt" before him even as she resents him for not keeping her from this horrible experience. Passion cannot restore her love.

Masha and her husband return home. She has another child, but the alienation lingers. They return to Pokrovskoe, her family residence and the locus of her moment of enlightenment, but now against the background of her past Masha sees that she is the same person as before, except that she has "no love, no desire for love, no need for labor, no satisfaction with herself" (ix). The "religious ecstasies" are gone, as is her "love for him." She has lost the "fullness of life." The return to the garden of her childhood residence does not lead to a moment of at-onement with all of nature. Instead she again asks "why?" Again she sees her husband guilty, his allowance of freedom the cause of her sin and loss of love. She will not accept responsibility for her life and her love. Instead, she accepts the end of her "romance with her husband." He is no longer her "lover," just her "old friend." And she turns her attention for the first time to her child. He is "mine, mine, mine," she thinks as she covers the baby's face so that the father cannot look into it. "No one but I" can do that. With this assertion of her power and definition of her domain, a "new" and "happy life" begins, and with this the story ends.

Family Happiness is a paradigmatic work. It tells the story of a woman's career in the Tolstoyan universe. Within herself, when not depressed by the loss of life and love, Masha is filled with exuberant yet humble love for all. She knows the joy of life. Her greatest moment is in church. When her "guardian" appears, however, Masha adapts herself to him. She passes from an innocent girl filled with love for all, and a desire to realize this love in the world, to a devoted wife living by and off her husband and his idea of love. But Masha is a discontented wife because in the process she has lost her sense of self and duty. Stagnation sets in, and she feels the "desire to live." This desire loses in its translation into action, because for her to live now means to be loved by people in society. When this fails to fulfill her, Masha grasps at her original romantic fantasy, but shies away from the sexual expression it entails. Once the sexual urge is exorcized she settles into a new and final way of life; she becomes a mother. She will live for and through her children. In all four roles—wife, society lady, lover, and mother—Masha attempts to earn love by living for others. The fragile self is lost, but not in some identification with the All. She has no encounter with emblematic nature. Rather, Masha approaches her career in life with a "pagan understanding of life." Even her encounter with sexuality is related to her need to live for others. True, Masha bears a divine self within, but her "understanding of life" is limited, and, although she changes, she does not grow toward the discovery and seizure of the Divine.

This paradigmatic sequence of events is repeated by other major heroines, but never in the same order. Natasha is the innocent child who loves all; she becomes aware of this in church. She does pass through the ball of life and the seductive musicale and in the epilogue she becomes a wife and mother. Princess Mary is the embodiment of the innocent maiden in love with all, moved to a piety of humble self-sacrifice and devotion to others. But even she goes through a moment of romantic fantasy and erotic desire and in the end is rescued by a "knight" who whisks her away into marriage; like Natasha she is transformed in the epilogue into a wife and mother. Kitty also bears within the instinctive love for all which is hidden from her view by the ball of life, where her romance fails. She becomes a wife and mother. Katyusha is the very image of "love for everyone and everything," but at her high point in church she is seduced and sent off to an erotic existence which is no romance and later in prison in Siberia to a life in a society which is no ball. In the end she becomes a wife but not a mother.

Most women in the Tolstoyan universe, however, do not move through such a career in life. Rather, we see them fixed at one of its stages, caught in their limited roles in their "pagan understanding of life"; they live only for others. Vera Berg, Natasha's sister, is simply a wife, totally devoted to her husband, completely self-centered even as she lives for another. Anna Sherer and Betsy Tverskaya live continually in the ball of life, just as Helen and Sappho Stoltz embody the erotic solution to the "pagan understanding of life." Sonya lives only for others, but also for her own good; Varenka lives only for others, which is her only good. Countess Rostov and Princess Shcherbatskaya are mothers and old friends of their husband. Dolly Oblonsky stands out from these secondary female characters because she is both a discontented wife and a dissatisfied mother. The significance of these failures surface on her way to visit Anna which is Dolly's journey of discovery. What Dolly discovers in her fantasy is her desire for a romance that has as its source resentment and as its goal revenge. In this she resembles Anna.

ANNA'S BATTLE FOR LOVE

Anna Karenina enters the novel on a mission of reconciliation. She is the one who is to clarify guilt and foster forgiveness. Count Vronsky enters the novel on a mission of obedience to his mother, following her script of amorous pursuits. But as Vronsky is about to board the train to greet his mother, Anna walks past him and he notices "something affectionate and tender" in the expression on her face (I,xviii). Simultaneously they both look back at each other. Vronsky sees a "suppressed animation" in her glance and an "excess of something" which "fills her whole being." From this point on Vronsky begins to pursue a new affair. What Anna sees in Vronsky we are not yet told. But Anna's first action in the novel is a suppressed flirtation, a "sparkle in her eye" she "deliberately" tries to control but which "against her will shines forth in her scarcely noticeable smile." In the polite banter that ensues, Anna "tosses" Vronsky "the ball of coquetry," which he "picks up," and Vronsky's mother cannot help but express rather "banally" her love for Anna, who is so "very nice." Anna steps from the train into the world of romance.

The meeting of Anna and Vronsky is marked by a violent mishap. A watchman, either "drunk or too bundled up from the cold," is run over by a train he did not hear coming. His wife, who, despite her many children, is for some reason at the station, throws herself on his mangled body in a gesture of grief and despair. Through self-indulgence or self-protection one person has unintentionally but irrevocably destroyed himself and ruined the life of those for whom he cares and to whom he is responsible. Oblonsky "suffers" at the sight, "apparently near tears." What is awful to him is the tragedy of material poverty that he foresees. Anna too is moved enough to wonder whether "something might be done for" the widow. But neither does anything. Vronsky is "silent," "serious," and "completely calm," but in response to Anna's concern he "immediately leaves the train" to give two hundred roubles to the widow. Anna's "lips are trembling and she can scarcely hold back her tears." "An ill omen," she says, but her brother dismisses her unclear prognostication and draws her attention to their task. Anna asks her brother about Vronsky, only to learn of his relationship to Kitty. "Shaking her head, as if she were trying to drive away something superfluous that was bothering her," Anna finally turns to her mission. But the violent mishap that marks this meeting has marred the mood. Anna arrives on the scene full of "animation" and "decisiveness," but departs with a sense of doom. The meeting traces the course of Anna's romance and reiterates the paradigmatic action of the novel.

The violent mishap is an ill omen of Anna's failure and her fate. Through self-indulgence and self-protection Anna brings ruin to herself and to those for whom she cares and to whom she is responsible. The death of the watchman, who is "drunk or too bundled up from the cold," is the emblem of her sin. It returns to haunt her dreams. Anna's sin is that she lives for herself and enclosed in herself. On the one hand, the mishap of Anna's life will result from her self-indulgence, her desire to live regardless of others. In the very face of human tragedy, both the death of the watchman and the failed marriage she has come to reconcile, Anna embarks on a romance. Like Vronsky, she even uses the circumstances of these tragedies to foster the romance. On the other hand, the mishap of Anna's life will result from her self-enclosure, her failure to confront or reveal herself. Thus that very evening, when Kitty comes to visit her at Dolly's, Anna tells what she learned of Vronsky from his mother: Vronsky is a "knight," a "hero" (I,xx). But Anna does not tell of his gallant act of charity performed in response to her words because it bespeaks "something touching her and something which ought not to be." Thus in her first spoken words about Vronsky Anna tells of his heroic character, but she does not reveal his heroic act of charity nor confront her interest in his heroism. She hides from another the hero's relationship to her and from herself her relationship to the hero. She thinks she hates falsehood, but that is only how it seems to her that she thinks. Falsehood is her fatal flaw. Anna is not honest with others or herself, however, because she has suppressed her guilty conscience. Her self-indulgence entails her self-protection. She sees, disapproves of what she sees, and therefore cannot let herself see. Thus aware of her self-indulgence but unable to break through her self-protection, Anna seals her fate. The tragedy of the watchman who does not watch is the emblem of that suppression of conscience which results in death.

This suppression of conscience defeats Anna's mission of reconciliation. She listens to Dolly's outburst of frustration over her "position" (I,xix). Her face appears to express "genuine sympathy and love." But Anna places the burden of reconciliation on Dolly. She claims to know her brother's "character," his "capacity" for "total infatuation" and then "total repentance," and, although she does not understand, she believes that he holds the women of his affairs in "contempt," while he cherishes the "sanctity" of his home and wife. Anna thus attempts to clarify her brother's guilt, but not to him. She expects Dolly to forgive fully, but we do not see her confront her brother or make him confront himself. She does not learn what the reader already knows: Stiva does not repent of his adulterous act, has lost his erotic interest in his wife, and regrets only that his wife has found him out. By not confronting Stiva's guilt, Anna can tell Dolly what she wants to hear, and Stiva is protected from responsibility. Anna thus consoles the victim but condones the victimizer. She treats her brother's guilt, therefore, exactly as she will treat her own. Brother and sister are both "at fault but not guilty. In that rests the whole drama" (I,i).

Unlike her brother, however, Anna's drama results from the suppression of her guilty conscience. To attain forgiveness Stiva can readily admit to Dolly that he is "guilty," because he does not wholly believe in his guilt (I,iv). Dishonest with his wife, he is "honest in relation to himself" (I,ii). Anna lies, especially to herself. Thus, when boarding the train to return home, she can think, "Well, it's all over (vsë koncheno), and thank God," while the only thing that is over is her visit to Moscow (I,xxix). But her flirtation with Vronsky during her visit has made Kitty her "enemy," while she has failed to take this seriously, asking Dolly to fix things up. "I am not guilty, or guilty just a bit," she tells Dolly, who notices the resemblance with Stiva (I,xxviii). Furthermore, Anna's encouragement of Vronsky leads to his further pursuit of her, even while she feigns disinterest in the pursuit and innocence of the motive for pursuit. But Anna knows that she is responsible for Vronsky's continued interest and Kitty's sudden hatred. Seeing that she is responsible for her actions, however, Anna will not face the consequences of her action nor take action to be responsible. She waves her hand and wishes her involvement away. "It's all over" is the phrase she repeats at critical moments in her life in order to justify to herself the suppression of her watching conscience.

ANNA'S MISSION and romance in Moscow is a journey of discovery. When she returns home, Karenin's ears are all of a sudden too big and her son does not fit the ideal image she has of him. On her visit to St. Petersburg Dolly had noticed "something false in the whole arrangement of their family life" (I,xix). Now Anna feels "dissatisfied with herself" and becomes conscious of the "state of pretence" in which she has been living (I,xxx). Still, her first evening back home she spends reading an English novel, while waiting for her husband. At the stroke of midnight Karenin calls her to their chambers: "It's time, it's time" (I,xxxiii). All is as it was, except now Anna sees. "Still, he is a good man, just, kind, and remarkable in his sphere," she thinks to herself, "as if she were trying to defend him before someone who had blamed him and said that it was impossible to love him." But Anna does not confront this disenchantment nor her defensive accusations. She just retires to their chambers, the "animation" and the "fire" now suppressed. This first scene of the Karenin arrangement of family life once again traces paradigmatically the line of the story from high hopes to despair.

Karenin tries to confront the issue (II,ix). When he asks Anna about the flirtations, she pretends not to get his point and tells him to stop cracking his knuckles. When Karenin argues that her behavior is socially improper she takes this as an expression of his lack of love for her and then tells him he is not well. When Karenin warns her that their lives are united by God and that any violation of the union brings "retribution," Anna claims not to know what he is talking about and suddenly feels very tired. When Karenin begs her to listen to him, her husband who loves her, Anna doubts his ability to love. "If he had not heard that there was such a thing as love, he would not have used that word. He does not even know what love is." Throughout this scene, the second one shown between Anna and Karenin, Anna is lying to herself and to Karenin—only now she knows that she is. She is "amazed at her own capacity for lies" and feels herself "dressed in an impenetrable armor of lies," but she is possessed by some "invisible force" which keeps her at it. Her self-indulgence entails her self-protection. Since Anna cannot be guilty even when she is at fault, however, she finds a new mechanism for evading responsibility. She trivializes Karenin's emotions and then turns them against him. He is the one who is guilty. Their "new life" has begun, and Karenin feels like "an ox who has lowered his head obediently and is awaiting the axe he feels raised over him" (II,x). Anna's realization of her capacity to lie leads not to truth but to a new way of spreading falsehood. She creates others in her own worst image. Her prophecies, therefore, are all self-fulfilling.

The representation of this "new life" is followed in the text by the post-seduction scene, Anna's and Vronsky's "entry into a new life" (II,xi). Vronsky has attained "the single desire of his life," and Anna has fulfilled the "impossible, terrible, and therefore all the more fascinating dream of happiness." But Vronsky stands above Anna, his face pale and his lower jaw trembling, and Anna "lowers her once proud, merry but now shamed head," "stoops over," and almost "falls from the sofa where she was sitting onto the floor" at Vronsky's feet. "My God, forgive me," she exclaims, "pressing his hand to her bosom." Anna feels so "guilty" that all she can do is "humiliate herself and beg forgiveness." Anna thus enters her "new life" histrionically, acting out a scene of reconciliation. She begs forgiveness but not from the one she has wronged. She feigns contrition to herself in order to find a way out of her guilt. Then, raising herself up, she pushes Vronsky away and says, "It's all over. I have nothing left but you. Remember that." With this dramatic and decisive dismissal of her past, accompanied by a gesture of rejection and a veiled threat, Anna casts the responsibility for her future onto Vronsky. She waves away her world of human relatedness and takes possession of her hero's hand "forever." But not really. Anna acts out the role of a person who understands her desperate "position" and chooses her flawed future, but she hides from the "complexity of her feelings," refuses to talk of her "happiness," and dreams of her "two husbands who lavish their affection on her." Her "new life" with Vronsky thus begins a new state of pretence.

Anna's pregnancy puts this new state of pretence to the test (II,xxi-xxiii). In his attempt to confront Anna with the issue, Vronsky, like Karenin, stumbles upon her impenetrable self-protection. As with Karenin, Anna hides behind a mocking tone and treats lightly Vronsky's seriousness. She dismisses Vronsky's desire to "end it," however, by mimicking Karenin's imagined response to Vronsky's solution. The Karenin she creates in her dramatic rendering is the Karenin she needs. "He's not a man, but a machine, and an evil machine when he's angry," she says, as she "makes him at fault for everything bad she can find in him and does not forgive him anything because of that terrible fault which makes her guilty before him." The more Anna hides from her suppressed guilty conscience, the worse Karenin must be and therefore the less she can forgive him. The falsehood of projection precludes the possibility of forgiveness because it displaces guilt. This displacement of guilt is Anna's major mechanism of self-protection. With Karenin, however, the displacement takes place only in Anna's mind. She imagines it and resents him for it, but Karenin does not feel guilty. With Vronsky, Anna transfers the guilt. She makes him feel solely responsible for the dilemma. In this, histrionic silence is her best weapon. That is why Anna refuses to speak of what is the real issue: her inability to accept the loss of her son as a result of her choice to pursue her romance. All Vronsky sees is her misery in which he now feels so implicated. Thus when Anna consoles him by saying that "he has ruined his life for her," Vronsky can only feel the opposite. Her silent suffering makes him feel she has "sacrificed everything for him." "He cannot forgive himself for her unhappiness." The transferral of guilt is complete.

The steeplechase marks the successful displacement of guilt. Vronsky, the hero and conqueror, is represented in this emblematic race of life as the driver, the jockey who "guides the movements of the horse" (II,xxv). He is responsible for the outcome of the struggle. The steeplechase is depicted as a series of attempts to overcome the obstacles to a successful outcome. Toward the end, the rider notices that to "his horror," he has fallen behind the horse, not keeping up with her movement by making a "hasty, unforgivable movement" himself. "Suddenly his position has changed." The horse is falling, and all his "efforts" to save her are "in vain." Standing over the fallen Frou-Frou, his face "disfigured with passion," in exactly the same way he stood over the fallen Anna in the post-seduction scene, Vronsky kicks the horse in the belly and exclaims, "What have I done! The race is lost. And it is my fault, shameful and unforgivable." Like a bad dream, the steeplechase thus reveals to Vronsky his worst fears. He has made a wrong movement, and his position is changed. He has spoiled his career, made Anna unhappy and pregnant, probably destroyed her honor and her life, and therefore his. Vronsky assumes total responsibility and accepts the displaced guilt. But the kick in the belly betrays his resentment. The steeplechase paradigmatically reiterates the basic rhythm of the novel, from high hope to despair.

Vronsky's failure forces Anna toward a truthful position. She confesses to Karenin with a vengeance: "I love him. I am his mistress. I cannot stand you. I am afraid of you. I hate you. Do with me what you wish" (II,xxix). Anna thinks she can stop being the wife of her husband. "Well, thank God it's all over with him." But Anna's truth is twisted by her resentment. She thinks she hates Karenin, but she is in fact afraid of his failure to forgive. She also feels "hostility" toward Vronsky, but she is in fact afraid of his failure to love. The twisted truth reveals to Anna only her confusion. "Split in two" Anna "sometimes does not know what she fears and what she desires and whether she fears and desires what was or what will be" (III,xv). When the maid enters to tell her of her son Seryozha's stolen peach Anna immediately resolves her confusion by recalling her "at times sincere although much more exaggerated role of a mother living for her son." "Let her husband shame her and throw her out," she thinks. "Let Vronsky grow cold and continue to lead his independent life (she again thinks of him with annoyance and reproach); she will not abandon her son. She has a goal in life." In resentment for the feared loss of love and forgiveness, Anna turns her son into a weapon in her battle for love. She clarifies her son's guilt and forgives him the stolen peach. They are reconciled. But this reconciliation only reminds Anna that "they will not forgive her." This failure of forgiveness she then casts onto the expanse of nature. "She looked at the tops of the poplars wavering in the wind, their leaves washed and glistening in the cold sun; she understood that they would not forgive her, that everything and everyone would have no pity for her, just like the sky and these trees." In her only encounter with nature, Anna sees not Prince Andrew's "eternal, just and kind sky," but the merciless heavens of her own creation. She projects the feared failure of forgiveness onto the All.

But Anna is the prisoner of her projections. She cannot find forgiveness because she will not clarify her guilt, and she is compelled to displace her guilt because she fears the failure of forgiveness. Caught in this bind of failed reconciliation, Anna reviews her past. The story of her marriage, which has never been told, is now rehearsed, but for a purpose. Anna needs to prove that she is a victim. Assuming that she has always been right, she sees herself victimized by a Karenin who always thinks he is "right" (III,xvi). He has failed, she now thinks, to heed her need for love. Did I not strive "to find a justification for my life?" Did I not "try to love my husband and then my son when I could not love my husband?" But I am "alive," I am "not guilty." "God has so made me that I need to live and to love." With this twisted truth Anna casts her self-justifying assurance of righteousness onto Karenin and then sees herself the victim of this projected righteousness. The victim then feels justified in victimizing. "But no, I won't allow him that pleasure. I'll tear apart that web of lies he wants to entangle me in," she shouts with a vengeance and then bursts into tears, "weeping as punished children do." But Anna is the naughty child who will not admit to herself that she is naughty because she knows that she is naughty.

This absence of truth precludes the possibility of reconciliation. Without truth guilt cannot be clarified nor forgiveness fostered. Rather, in Anna's failed relatedness the guilt is suppressed by projection, and forgiveness is replaced by resentment. The logic of this flawed love rests on a consistent dialectic of behavior. In each relationship Anna suffers from the sense of her own failure. She has violated her family arrangement with Karenin and refuses to enter into a new arrangement with Vronsky. She fails both of them because of her self-indulgence: she wants to remain a respected member of so-

ciety and retain the role of wife and mother, yet she wants the freedom to pursue fully and openly her romance with Vronsky. Before
each she feels guilty because of the other. But Anna cannot continue
this self-indulgence if she confronts the contradiction. So seeing, she
cannot see. Her self-indulgence entails her self-protection. Anna
must therefore thrust the failure onto the other. At first, she experiences this transferral as disenchantment: Karenin has big ears and
Vronsky is not a hero. They fail her. Upon this failure Anna then
casts her own: she projects her falsehood onto Karenin and her hostility onto Vronsky. With the failure thus transferred, Anna feels resentment. But since this resentment is the result of Anna's own
sense of guilt not confronted, the more she indulges herself as the
contradictions of her conflicted desires unfold, the more she must
project her guilt and feel resentment. This dialectic of guilt and resentment shapes the pattern of Anna's story. In the end the dialectic
comes to its inevitable conclusion. Guilt not clarified leads to suicide, and guilt transformed into resentment turns into revenge. In his
assumption of full responsibility, Vronsky is brought to suicide; in
his righteous resentment Karenin is tempted by revenge. But Anna,
tormented by her guilt and burdened by her resentment, commits suicide in an act of revenge. Self-indulgence leads her to the destruction
of herself; self-protection leads her to the destruction of others. Her
flaw seals her fate.

Failed relatedness can be reconciled only through the clarification
of guilt and the fostering of forgiveness. This is Anna's mission
which was interrupted by her romance. But then, at the end of the
first half of the novel, her childbirth fever raises anew the task she is
to perform. In a delirium of delusion she revels in her guilt and begs
forgiveness, but all histrionically in the presence of Vronsky. But
"suddenly" Karenin is transformed into a "blissful state of soul
which suddenly gives him a new happiness he never experienced before" (IV,xvii). While "he had not thought that the Christian law he
wanted to observe all his life had required him to forgive and love his
enemies," now "the joyful feeling of love and forgiveness of his enemies fills his soul." Karenin learns what Prince Andrew learns. He
gets down on his knees, rests his head in Anna's arms, and "weeps
like a child." He confesses to Vronsky that he had desired Anna's
death and wanted "revenge," but that now he wants "to turn the
other cheek," "to give away his shirt when they take his coat." He

will not abandon her nor reproach her. Karenin thus purges himself of his guilt and resentment. "For the first time in his life," therefore, he feels "tender compassion," "pity for her," and "repentance of his desire for her death" (IV,xix). The "joy of forgiveness makes him suddenly" aware of the "alleviation of his sufferings." "What had seemed unresolvable when he judged, reproached, and hated, now becomes clear and simple when he forgives and loves." Karenin is "calm and in harmony with himself." It seems that the mission of reconciliation has been accomplished.

At the center of the novel, however, the mission of reconciliation fails. Karenin's forgiveness is flawed by his false position. He forgives but cannot act on his forgiveness. He is ruled, not by the "blessed, spiritual force" (sila) which guided him in his forgiveness, but by "another, crude, and more powerful force," the force of other people's opinions. He forgives only because he believes Anna has changed. His forgiveness is given forth conditionally. Anna's clarification of guilt is likewise flawed. She admits that "there is in me another self, one I fear" but believes that now "I am not that one" (IV,xvii). Yet Anna does not act on this clarification of guilt, because in it she has not been honest to herself. She acts out her role of repentant sinner only in order to rid herself of her guilt in the face of death. Her guilt is clarified conditionally. The conditions by which Anna limits her admission of guilt and Karenin his forgiveness defeat the mission of reconciliation. But the first half of the novel ends, as did the first failed mission of reconciliation, with new false hopes. Anna is reconciled with Vronsky.

KARENIN'S flawed forgiveness returns to torment him. Anna and Vronsky go off to Italy, and Karenin "sees his position clearly for the first time and is horrified" (V,xxi). "As if in reward for all that he now turned out to be alone, shamed, ridiculed, needed by no one and despised by all." Karenin's failed reconciliation results in his isolation. He becomes cynical. "Everything in the world is evil" (V,xxv). Furthermore, the "merciless" world fails to forgive him his failure. "He felt that people would destroy him as dogs kill a tormented dog squealing from pain" (V,xxi). Karenin's sin against his relatedness returns as his suffering. Karenin is thus subjected to the inexorable law of sin and suffering which is acted out in the second half of Anna's story. He suffers from his sin.

Anna retreats from her failed relatedness into a new form of self-indulgence. In the land of fantasy she is "happy and full of the joy of life" (V,viii). Anna fears only the "loss of his love." But Anna does not see that Vronsky's "realization of his desire" leads only to his boredom. He follows his mother's script. The heroine of this romance wants to possess the one who has swept her away, but the hero needs to move on to more adventure. In Italy, moreover, Anna's fantasy of romance totally excludes her role as mother, but she does not admit this clearly to herself and will not confront this with Vronsky. The escape to Italy fails because Anna and Vronsky do not understand their relationship in the same way and do not share their differences with each other. At the opening of the second half of the novel, therefore, Anna and Vronsky resemble Dolly and Stiva. Anna's failed mission of reconciliation returns as her fate.

Anna's violation of relatedness leads to a total loss of relatedness. Back in Petersburg she retreats into her "impenetrability" and seems "cold" and "annoyed." Vronsky believes that she is tormented by her social rejection, but she is not. Anna just wants to see her son. "Her grief was all the stronger because it was lonely. She could not and would not share it with Vronsky" (V,xxix). Anna's self-protection returns as self-isolation. She thinks "she knows" (the narrator repeats the phrase three times) what Vronsky thinks about what she will not tell him. In her falsehood she is turned in upon herself and can see the world only as it is twisted by her guilt and resentment. The relationship which excludes all other people now forces her to exclude all others. She sees her son, but leaves thinking, "Yes, it's all over and again I am alone" (V,xxxi). Anna's self-indulgence, which entailed her exclusion and abandonment of others, returns as her exclusion and abandonment.

Anna, like Masha, attends a musicale, where her isolation, she hopes, will come to an end (V,xxxii-xxxiii). The battle that follows marks the return of Anna's sin against her husband. In dreamlike fashion the scene reiterates the flawed relationship with Karenin. At first Anna acts out her old role of the unrepentant one who loves in defiance and resentment. Vronsky is cast into Karenin's position. He is the one who interferes with Anna's life. Anna feels she hears her husband speaking. The roles are then reversed. Vronsky, like Anna, is the one who reproaches and is annoyed. Anna, like Karenin, is forced to convince herself of the assurance of love in order to convince herself of her own unchanged security. Thus Anna is punished for her sin against the relationship with Karenin by being compelled to relive it with Vronsky.

Vronsky entered Anna's life a "conqueror," but she loves him when she sees "submissive, slavish devotion" written on his face. Her love gains power over the object of her love which she would possess. At the very moment when her fantasy of an English romance is fulfilled in the country idyll, therefore, Anna's need to enslave the beloved returns as her suffering, and she feels caught: "What woman, what slave could be to such an extent a slave as I am in my position?" (VI,xxiii.) She now becomes the victim of Vronsky's freedom. The battle ensues on new grounds. Vronsky goes off to the elections, but his "right to freedom" "offends" Anna and reminds her of her "humiliation" (VI,xxxii). To her his freedom means that she is abandoned. So Anna sends for Vronsky on the pretext that their daughter is seriously ill. While afraid of Vronsky's reaction, Anna needs the proof of his presence and her power over him. She sees he will not "forgive" her deception. Then, when Vronsky tells her he must go off on business, she insists she must go with him. Vronsky takes Anna's insistence as a "threat," and Anna takes the "cold, angry look" she sees on his face as Vronsky's unforgiving retreat. Anna's need to exercise power over Vronsky returns as Vronsky's power over her.

Anna's rage at this fantasied loss of power and love leads to the fulfillment of the fantasy. Vronsky is off gambling with his old friend Yashvin, and Anna believes he is doing this because "he wants to prove to me that his love for me must not interfere with his freedom." Vronsky returns. Anna's face is "cold and hostile"; Vronsky seems ready "for a fight." But Vronsky, seeing Anna's anguish, extends his hand to her. "She is pleased with this gesture of tenderness. But some strange power of evil does not let her yield to her attraction, as if the conditions of the battle would not allow her to submit." Anna accuses Vronsky of being "hostile" to her. Vronsky, seeing her "despair" and hearing the innuendo, takes her hand and kisses it, promising to do anything to make her happy. Anna feels the "triumph of her victory," but sees in Vronsky's cold expression that he "does not forgive her victory." The battle for love now comes to the surface, but Anna's victory is transformed into her defeat. The "spirit of evil and deception" that possessed Anna and Karenin in their "new life" recurs in its overt form as "the evil spirit of battle."

Anna's feigned indifference with Karenin surfaces as her histrionic weapons of despair and innuendoes of suicide. Vronsky's gestures of reconciliation resemble Karenin's. He responds to Anna's position while not yielding his own. Instead of the "loving harmony of family life," they live in "discord" (VII,xxiii). Anna's failure with Karenin returns as her failure with Vronsky.

Anna's voyage to death is her last journey of discovery. She knows, she thinks, the meaning and purpose of life. "All is untruth, all is lies, all is deception, all is evil" (VII,xxxi). There is only one real thing. "We all want something sweet and tasty. If not candy, then dirty ice cream" (VII,xxix). All seek only their own pleasure, and "nothing is merry or amusing, everything is vile." Religion is a hoax hiding the fact that "we all hate one another." She replaces Karenin's position of forgiveness with Yashvin's rule of life: "He who sits next to me wants to leave me without a shirt and I him. Well, we all fight and in this we find our pleasure" (VII,xxv). "The struggle for existence and hatred is the one thing that unites us" (VII,xxx). "Now that's the truth" (VII,xxix). The gambler's vision merges in her mind with the Darwinian struggle for existence to explain the "meaning of life and human relationships" (VII,xxx). In his love for her, Vronsky, she now thinks, was only seeking "satisfaction of vanity," the "pride of success." And in her own love for him she was only seeking power over the "submissive dog" she now again recalls in Vronsky's expression. In their romance, each sought their own needs and thus went their own ways. "I am the cause of his unhappiness, he of mine. "Are we not all tossed into the world just to hate each other and therefore to torment ourselves and others?" The sin against truth returns as sinful truth.

Anna's truth is the result of her own experience and the product of her own making. Tolstoy considers Anna's final vision of life the inevitable conclusion to be drawn from life understood as individual self-fulfillment. The pursuit of happiness for yourself alone, regardless of others, which in the end is what the fantasy of romance entails, inexorably leads to a world of struggle and strife. Individualism inevitably turns into a Hobbesian war of each against each and a Darwinian struggle for existence. Anna discovers what Tolstoy called in his essay *On Life* "the fundamental contradiction of human life":

Every person lives only in order to feel good, for his own happiness (*blago*). If he does not feel the desire for his own happiness, he does not feel himself living. . . . A person feels life only in himself, in his personality, and therefore in the beginning it seems to him that the happiness he desires is just the happiness of his personality. It also seems to him in the beginning that he is the only one who truly lives, just him alone. Other people's lives seem not the same as his, . . . but just one of the conditions of his own existence. If he does not wish them evil, that is just because the sight of suffering destroys his happiness. If he wishes them good, . . . that is just because the happiness of others increases his own. But then in the course of striving to attain his own happiness a person notices that his happiness depends on other beings. . . . He sees that they all, people and even animals, have the same conception of life as does he. He sees that each living being must be as ready as he is to deprive all other beings of their greater happiness, even of their life, for the sake of his own little happiness. This understood, he automatically concludes . . . that all the innumerable beings of the world in order to attain their own aim are ready any minute to destroy him . . . and therefore he sees that his personal happiness which he has understood as the sole aim of his life not only cannot be acquired easily but will certainly be taken from him. The more a person lives, the more this understanding is confirmed by experience, and he sees that the life of the world in which he participates and which consists of personalities bound together but desiring to destroy and devour each other, this life not only cannot be for his happiness, but will certainly be a great evil. (26,324-5; 1887)

The meaning of Anna's story rests in her final discovery of this Tolstoyan truth. Her life enacts the fundamental contradiction inherent in any life lived regardless of others: it leads to spiritual and physical death because it pits person against person. Anna's story is not a tale of social oppression or a drama of failed liberation. Tolstoy, it should be recalled, insisted that people have no rights, only responsibilities (55,216;1906). While embedded in a realistic fiction, Anna's story is a parable of self-indulgence. An ordinary person living in the failed reality we all share, Anna abandons her flawed human relatedness to which she is responsible in pursuit of happiness for herself. This quest for self-fulfillment regardless of others puts her in conflict, first with Karenin, later with Vronsky. In the end Anna becomes the victim of her own self-centered adventure. Her romance turns into a battle for love: imagery of violence, pain, and destruction marks her story. But Anna is not destroyed by others, and self-indulgence is not her fundamental flaw. Anna is not punished by Tolstoy for her sexual fulfillment. In a fuller sense, Anna's story is a moral tragedy of self-enclosure. She is cast from a world of unconscious well-being into a world of conscious misery because in her pursuit of love she hides from her own truth. For her the self-indulgence conflicts with the world of flawed human relatedness. Anna's truth is that in her way she does care for Karenin and her son. But, seeing this, she cannot see. Thus self-protective, Anna must hide her feelings and spread a web of lies in order to realize her desire to live. This falseness, which is her flaw, returns in the end as her weapon and her punishment. She comes to the truth, but it is a lie. Her story embodies and reveals the meaning of Tolstoy's words apparently spoken to Father Amvrosy, the elder at the famed monastery Optina Pustyn: "When we are in God, i.e., in truth, then we are all together; when we are in the Devil, i.e., in falsehood, then we are all separate" (51,23;1890).

LEVIN'S SEARCH FOR FAITH

Levin enters the novel on a mission to find his love. Like Anna an orphan, "deprived" of family life and the "memory of his mother," Levin has "in fact fallen in love with the "Shcherbatsky home and family" (I,vi); it is now a "question of life and death" that he marry the youngest daughter, Kitty (I,x). Upon his arrival in Moscow Levin learns that Kitty has gone ice-skating, and he goes off to the rink to find his love. He recognizes her in the crowd by the "joy and fear" he feels in her presence (I,ix). "The place where she was seemed to him an unapproachable holy spot, and he saw her, like the sun, without even looking." Her smile transforms him to a "magical world where he feels himself tender and soft, just as he remembers himself on rare occasions from his earliest childhood." In her presence he utters his first prayer of the novel, "Oh Lord, my God, help me, teach me," and he leaves her presence with "the smile of triumph and happiness shining in his eyes" (I,x). Levin's love for Kitty, however is "not love." "I have been in love," he claims, sounding like Olenin, "but this is not that. It's not what I feel. Some external force (sila) has taken possession of me, and I see that without this there is no life."

For him Kitty is a "pure innocent being" before whom he becomes aware of his "sins" and feels "unworthy." His "only consolation" is his favorite prayer: "Not according to my deserts forgive me, but according to Thy mercy." Kitty, he believes, is the "only one who can thus forgive him." In his love Levin raises Kitty to the divine: to her he will reveal his guilt, and by her he will be forgiven. In Kitty he will find reconciliation. But at the beginning of his story Levin understands his sins as sexual transgression and worthiness as sexual innocence. His mission to find his love is destined to fail because he has failed to comprehend his love.

Levin's failure is embodied and revealed at the restaurant repast with his best friend, Stiva Oblonsky. These two men "love each other," even though they do not like or respect each other (I,v). They condescendingly smile at each other's way of life and fail to understand or accept each other's mode of labor. This distance is firmly established at the banquet scene, where "alien to each other in everything," the two friends discuss love (I,x). To Stiva love and sexual passion are one and the same. He sees his failure of residency solely as a result of his wife's fading physical attraction. The "terrible drama" of life for him results from the conflict between his wife's "rights" to his erotic attention and the freely given pleasure from his latest fancy. "A roll sometimes smells so good you can't hold yourself back." To Levin there is no drama in this. For him there are, he argues, two kinds of love "which Plato defines in his *Symposium* (i.e., *Banquet*; Russian *Pir*), and both these loves serve as a touchstone for people." Stiva's "non-platonic" love, based on sexual passion, is an exchange of pleasures and hence no drama, while "platonic love is clear and pure because. . . ." Levin can go no further. The mind of the master fails. At the banquet which opens his mission to find his love, Levin stumbles over his own theory of love. His own "sins" against love contradict the exalted image of the love he needs. Stiva thinks that Levin needs to be a "whole (*tsel'nyj*) person," one whose life "occupation always has a goal (*tsel'*), for whom love and family life are one and the same," but that is Stiva's projected vision of his own ideal solution. It is only the goal Levin thinks he needs. In his confusion over his theory of love and hence his mission to find his love Levin ends up alone. The banquet concludes with "each one thinking only of his own business, one having nothing to do with the other." The scene moves from the high hope of two friends commun-

ing to the sense of division in their conceptions of love and thus reiterates the paradigmatic action of the novel.

The narration represents the encounter with Stiva as the first
event in Levin's story, but in fact upon his arrival in Moscow Levin
goes immediately to visit his half-brother, Sergey Ivanovich Koz-
nyshev, with the intention of consulting him about his mission. Sergey Ivanovich, the urban intellectual, has company and they are discussing the latest theories about the fashionable philosophical
problem of the mind-body relationship. At question is the theory of
knowledge, the epistemological foundations for any "conception of
reality" (I,vii). Is our "consciousness of reality the result of sensations" from the external world or from our "impressions" of those
sensations, or is there a "special organ for the transmission of our
conception of reality?" The intellectuals are latter-day empiricists.
To Levin, who has kept up with these philosophical problems, the
discussion misses the point because his brother and his friends do
not see the relationship between the questions they raise and the
"meaning of life and death." But Levin himself has no answers to
these questions. He is just annoyed. Levin's failure to clarify his own
"conception of reality" or the way to know it is the first flaw in his
mission to find his love.

The second flaw is his failure to visit his other brother, Nicholas.
From Sergey Ivanovich, Levin learns that Nicholas, who has squan-
dered what money he had, fallen into bad company, and quarreled
with his brothers, has returned to Moscow but does not want to see
his brothers. Levin is relieved because he would prefer to "forget
about his unfortunate brother" (I,viii). But Levin is also tormented by
this forgetting, and throughout the banquet discussion of love the
image of his prodigal brother surfaces in his mind to remind him of
his own "wickedness." On his mission to find his love Levin forgets
his own unforgiven brother. But the mission fails, and Levin is in the
"terrible position" of being rejected and unloved. He recalls his
brother, reassesses his relationship to him, and goes directly from
Kitty's refusal to his brother's place (I,xxiv). On the way Levin mentally reviews his brother's past, his rigid religiosity in his youth and
his fall into depravity. Misunderstood and unloved, Nicholas came
to believe that "everything in the world is bad and horrid." Himself
rejected, Levin now sees that he must not reject. From his suffering
he learns. He decides that he must tell his brother "everything and

get him to tell all and then show him that I love him and therefore understand him." With this first step toward reconciliation with his brother, Levin begins his "new life" in which he can "make of himself anything possible" (I,xxvi). When he returns home he once again begins lifting weights. He is "not guilty" and is ready "to struggle to live better, much better" (I,xxvii).

But Levin is wrong. He believes his "new life" can be found in his work, the caring for his estate and the book he is writing. He seems to have abandoned his mission to find his love. Levin fails to achieve any "blessed calm" from his career as master and author, however, because he has not understood his mission. Levin feels a conflict between his need for his work and his need for a wife. When one fails or flags, the other takes hold. But Levin's undertaking in the novel is to learn that his "conception of marriage" as the "main task of life on which all happiness depends" is as incorrect as his belief that his work as master and author can give him "blessed calm." Levin's failure to understand his mission comes from his faulty understanding of himself. His task, therefore, is to learn who he is in order to know what he must do. Unbeknown to him, his mission to find his love is a quest for faith.

The failed relationships with his brothers are the emblems of Levin's flaws. His quest for faith, therefore, entails a reassessment of these relationships. Sergey Ivanovich, who loves the country and needs a rest, decides to visit Levin and his "new life" so that he can "do nothing for a few days" (III,i). The visit bothers Levin. Sergey Ivanovich's vacation attitude to the country trivializes what Levin now looks upon as his "place of life" and "field for labor." What is worse, the urban intellectual is convinced from his occasional chats with peasants that he "knows the people" and what to do for the "common good" (*obshchee blago*). To Levin the "people" are the main participants in the "common labor" and share with him the "common task." So convinced is Levin that he understands the peasants and their role in agriculture that he is writing a book about it. He believes his book deals with the "common good" and that it will effect a "bloodless revolution": "Instead of poverty, common wealth and satisfaction; instead of enmity, harmony and unity of interests . . . , first in the little circle of our district, then in the province, then in all of Russia, then in the whole world" (III,xxx). With his mind the master will change the world. Thus Levin in fact shares with his brother a concern for the "common good" and is annoyed at his brother because he sees in him his own flaw. For all his talk about his special relationship with the peasants, at bottom Levin resembles his brother, for both turn the human and social problems into intellectual endeavor. They both have the mind of the master. Neither truly participates in the "common labor," and Sergey Ivanovich's physical idleness and isolation marked by the fishing line he holds is really Levin's lot too. Levin's confusion surfaces in this visit with his brother which culminates in an argument. Annoyed, Sergey Ivanovich pulls in his fishing line and, angered, Levin goes off to mow some hay with the peasants in order to feel he participates in the common task. This enmity between the brothers begins the process of disclosing Levin's misconceptions of himself and his task.

This process is furthered by Levin's encounter with peasants engaged in the common task. Later that summer he goes out to the fields to observe the gathering in of the hay. There is something wrong, however, and the master suspects that his peasants have taken more of the harvest than is their due. Angered that he is being cheated, Levin argues with the elder and settles himself on a haystack to watch the workers. His eyes fall on a newly married couple "merrily" working together, and their "expression of strong, youthful, recently awakened love" revives his good spirits (III,xi). As the work comes to an end, the peasant women form a circle and burst into song as they leave for home "with their rakes on their shoulders, glistening in their bright colors and crackling with their resonant merry voices" (III,xii). As they pass by Levin on his haystack, he feels a "cloud with the thunder of merriment" move over him and "seize him and the haystack on which he lay and all the other stacks and piles of hay and the whole meadow out to the distant field. All began to move and waver to the measure of that wild, gleeful song." With the common labor completed, the world is brought into harmonious accord. But not for Levin. From the seizure of gladness the master is estranged. He is "envious" of the "healthy merriment" and would like to "take part in the expression of this joy of life" but the sudden joy of life passes Levin by, and he is left with the "heavy feeling of anguish over his aloneness, his physical idleness, and his hostility to that world" (mir). Now, however, "especially under the influence" of the young couple joined in mutual loving labor it occurs to Levin "for the first time" that he must replace his "burdensome, idle, artificial, and personal life" with "that attractive life, toilful, pure, and common."

But Levin does not understand the meaning of the seizure of gladness that passed him by. He realizes he has been called to change his life, that he must abandon the "personal" for the "common."[1] He believes, he thinks, that his "former dreams of family life were nonsense." In the uncertainty of the moment he looks outward to the heavens and toward a cloud formation he sees as a "pearly shell." In the expanse of nature Levin discovers what seems to him his call. He gets up from the haystack and walks toward the road. At just this moment Levin hears the bells of an approaching carriage. Like Prince Andrew upon his first encounter with Natasha, he sees Kitty, "looking past him at the rising dawn, bright and pensive, wholly filled with a graceful and complex inner life alien to him" and believes that "there is only one being in the world capable of concentrating for him all the light and meaning of life." "Suddenly" all his other attempts to resolve the "riddle of his life" disappear. He again looks to the sky, but the emblem of his call is gone; he believes he has resolved the riddle. He loves Kitty. That, he believes, is his mission. This hope is false, however, and Levin's mission to find his love is again destined to fail because he mistakes his personal love as his mission.

At the center of the novel Levin marries Kitty. But just before the wedding, Levin must go to confession. The second half of *Anna Karenina* begins with the question of Levin's faith. "My chief sin is doubt," Levin tells the priest (V,i). "Sometimes I even doubt the existence of God." When the priest tries to argue the existence of God from the beauty of creation, Levin remains politely silent because he

[1] Most interpretations of this passage stumble over the word "common" (*obshchij*). In Tolstoy the "common" is often perceived and imaged in the "people" (*narod*). Therefore it is assumed, especially by Soviet critics, that the word "common" signals the peasantry. Rather, the word "common" refers to what is common to all; it is experienced in the moment of being all together at one which Tolstoy and his heroes often perceive in peasant life. But the "common" cannot be attained for Tolstoy or his heroes in peasant life. For them the experience of the "common" is acquired in love. The concept of the "common" is theological; the "common" is what is attained in the third stage of human existence. In the above passage Levin perceives this mode of being all together in peasant life, just as Pierre perceives it in "they," the soldiers in battle. Both are tempted for a moment to try to attain the experience of the "common" by joining the people. They confuse the particular manifestation for the general idea. Both learn better.

"does not feel it proper to enter into a philosophical discussion with a priest." The mind of the master is momentarily checked by the sense of propriety. But then, when the priest suggests that in the future he will have his own children who will ask him about the mysteries of creation and death, Levin is touched. The priest reminds him that he is "entering upon a time of life when he must choose his path." Levin leaves his confession feeling that the "nice, kind old man" is not so stupid. Levin "now more than ever feels a certain vagueness and impurity in his soul." He decides to resolve his "relationship to religion," but not now. To clarify his faith Levin will have to redefine his mission to find his love.

This redefinition begins with his marriage to Kitty. Confusion immediately surfaces. While he believes that Kitty "concentrates for him all the light and meaning of his life," Levin feels that the "pleasure of love" should not interfere with his work (V,xiv). "According to him, he was to do his work and rest from it in the happiness of love." Levin has failed to integrate his love and his task. The first result of this perceived failure is a reappraisal of his work. "Formerly his task had been his salvation from life" (V,xv). Now his work serves to stay his guilt for a life too full of pleasure. But not for long.

A letter arrives, and Levin learns that his brother Nicholas is dying. Nicholas had visited Levin in the country, during his period of retreat into "new life." Levin's "conception of reality" yielded to an inner recognition of death. He began to feel that "it is time to die," and he saw "in everything only death or the approach toward it" (III,xxxii). "Darkness covers everything," he came to see, and he grasped at his "task as the only thread to guide him in the darkness." Nicholas' visit brought Levin to despair. "This whole world of ours, you know, is but a bit of mildew which has grown on a tiny planet. And we think that we can do something great, ideas, deeds. It's all but grains of sand" (V,vii). But Kitty's light and life conquered this darkness, and Levin again forgot his brother, the emblem of his mortality.

Now death is at hand, and Levin must confront it. For Levin the "terrifying body" of his dying brother stymies all action (V,xvii). He wants to help but believes that "help is impossible" (V,xviii). This assumption of helplessness "angers" Nicholas because to him it expresses a failure of sympathy and understanding. But he is not quite right. In the face of death Levin feels helpless because to him help means, not facing death and confronting his brother, but stopping the process of death itself. He is the master who can control life. Levin's fear of death follows from this flawed understanding of life. Kitty knows better. She senses the dying man's needs and offers him comfort and solace. In the face of death Kitty gives forth of herself. And this Levin learns. As the hour of death approaches, Nicholas asks Levin to sit with him. Nicholas extends his hand, and Levin grasps it. The "question of death" recedes as Levin turns his attention to "what he must do now, right now" (V,xx). In giving forth of himself "now, right now," Levin has found his love. His brother's death "renews his terror over the enigma as well as the closeness and inevitability of death," but his "wife's presence" saves him from "despair" and thus "regardless of death he feels the necessity to live and love." In confronting his brother's death, Levin does not solve the intellectual "question of death," but he does affirm his own mortality and reappraise his mission to find his love. He clarifies his identity and vocation.

The stumbling block for Levin is suffering. The mind of the master cannot comprehend or control it. Levin just feels helpless. He does not know that for Nicholas the torment of suffering turns death into happiness defined as the fulfillment of a desire, because he does not understand the relationship between desire and suffering. Desire is the result of the awareness of "suffering or deprivation" (V,xx). "Pleasure," "fulfillment," "happiness" depend upon the experience of their absence. They are correlatives. Pain is not an evil but an essential element in the dynamic of living, the continual quest for happiness. If we did not suffer, we would not desire, and, therefore, we would not seek the fulfillment of the desire, and there would be no life, just meaningless existence. So argues the narrator, but none of this does Levin grasp as he clasps his brother's hand. But then several months later Levin once again finds himself confronted with an incomprehensible and mysterious event, now not death but birth. Levin's experience of Kitty's giving birth marks a new stage in his comprehension of suffering.

She suffered and seemed to be complaining to him about her sufferings. At first by habit he felt that he was guilty. But the tenderness in her look told him that she not only did not reproach him, but that she loved him for these sufferings. "If not me, then who is guilty for this?" Levin thought automatically trying to find the perpetrator of the sufferings in order to punish him, but there was no one guilty. She suffered, complained, and triumphed in these sufferings, took joy in them and loved them. He saw that something beautiful was taking place in her heart, but what it was he could not understand. It was beyond comprehension. (VII,xiii)

Levin learns that the sufferings at the extremes of "this life," at entrance and exit, at the moments of change between "the earthly and the non-earthly," have nothing to do with guilt and punishment (VII,xv). There is suffering but no guilt or projection, no resentment or revenge. Kitty "triumphs" in her suffering, as in the chapter preceding the birth scene, Anna "triumphs" in her "victory" in the battle with Vronsky. But, unlike Anna, who takes for herself, suffers from each fulfillment of the taking, and punishes others for the suffering, Kitty gives forth of herself, and accepts the pain as part of her love. For Levin this is all "beyond the usual conditions of life" (VII,xiv). The birth and the death are "openings through which there is shown something higher. In each case what was being accomplished happened with difficulty and torment, and in each case with the contemplation of something higher his soul was incomprehensibly raised to heights which he had formerly never even known, what his understanding (*rassudok*) could no longer keep up with." In his confrontation with the acceptance of suffering, the positive act of giving of self, Levin approaches the limits of his masterful mind. He, the man who does not believe, can only repeat his prayer, "Lord, forgive me and help me." The child is born, and Levin sees that Kitty has given forth "something strange, red, and wavering," a "helpless being" for whom Levin feels "pity" (*zhalost'*) and "fear" lest it be harmed (VII,xvi). Faced with this "strange, wavering, red being" Levin senses "a new area of vulnerability." The naked babe is for Levin the emblem of his own helpless being. Pierre sees the wavering red sphere in the sky and finds his "image of the whole universe"; Levin sees the "red, wavering" infant and finds his image of himself. The master is naked and helpless.

In his encounter with death and birth Levin becomes "terrified of life," now that he has no "knowledge of what it is, whence it comes, or what it is for" (VIII,viii). His former "convictions" and "way of thinking" no longer seem to give him the "knowledge he needs." The mind of the master is shaken. What strikes him, however, is that he, the man who does not believe, prayed at the moments of crisis and in those moments of prayer he believed. Levin's discovery of his help-lessness turns him toward faith, but this faith contradicts his whole conception of reality and he finds himself in "disharmony with him-self." For months his conception of reality torments him: "In infinite time, in infinite matter, in infinite space, a bubble organism sepa-rates itself and that bubble is maintained for a while and then bursts and that bubble is me" (ix). This "non-truth" now seems to be the "cruel mockery of some evil force" which is leading him to suicide. Levin's wrong conception of life returns to provoke the ending of his life.

Levin is not Anna, however. He does not twist truth into an armor behind which he hides from himself and others. In his nakedness he is open to the truth that will reveal to him who and why he is. In his most depressed moment he too takes a journey of discovery, going off to the fields to watch the workers, but there he talks with a peasant whose words contain the truth he needs: "People are different, one lives just for his own need, just for his belly, but another, like the righteous old man Fokanych, lives for his soul and remembers God" (VIII,xi). These words release in Levin a host of "unclear but signifi-cant ideas." To him they mean that "one must not live for what we understand, for what attracts us, for what we want, but for some-thing incomprehensible, for God, whom no one can understand or define" (VIII,xii). "Reason" explains and justifies "life for the belly," but "life for truth, for God" is not reasonable. "Reason reveals the struggle for existence and the law demanding the suffocation of all who hinder the satisfaction of my desires," but the "love for another is not reasonable." What Levin learns is that the correct conception of reality is not knowable by reason because the good falls out of the nexus of cause and effect. "If the good has a cause, then it is not good; if it has a result, a reward, then it is not good. Therefore the good lies outside the chain of cause and effect." It is this "good," this "truth," this "God," this love, which Levin now becomes aware of. When Levin examines this experience, however, he discovers a paradox: "I have discovered nothing, I have just recognized (*uznal*) what I know (*znau*)." This new knowledge, he now sees, knowledge "by the heart, by faith" (xiii) is not "acquired," but "given to him and to all, given because there is no place to get it from" (VIII,xii). It has always been there within him. "He has understood the force" (*sila*) which "gives him life." "He has been liberated from illusion and sees the Master." Levin looks up to the "cloudy sky" (VIII,xiii). The expanse of nature becomes for him the emblem of the dilemma of knowledge: "Do I not know that it is infinite space and not a round vault? . . . Yet, despite my knowledge of infinite space, I am undoubtedly right when I see the firm blue vault, more right than when I strain to see beyond it." What Levin knows with certainty from within, by "his heart," must be the right "conception of reality." He sheds the mind of the master.

This certainty is not shaken by the arrival of his brother, Sergey Ivanovich. Rather, Levin looks forward to the confrontation with his brother, now convinced that with his new conception of reality his "relation with all people will be different." Levin will find his love. And he does, but not in the way he expects. His brother has not changed, and Levin still feels his estrangement. Now, however, Levin sees that others are wearing an "impenetrable armor" and that he is "naked" (VIII,xvi), that despite the disturbances from reality around him, "the spiritual force (*sila*) he has again become aware of has remained whole within him" (VIII,xiv). His mission to find his love is reappraised for the last time. His brother leaves, a storm arises, and Levin is overcome with fear for his wife and child. Again he feels helpless, again he prays, but he now "knows that he loves" (VIII,xviii). He knows that even though he will still get angry with the peasants, argue with his wife, and disagree with his brother, that even though there "will be a wall between the holy of holies of his soul and others, even his wife," now, "despite anything that can happen," his "life is not meaningless" as it had been before but has the "unquestionable meaning of the good he has in his power to invest it with" (xix). He may still be estranged, but now he knows that his mission to find his love has always been a mission to learn to love.

Anna's story ends in hatred, Levin's in love. The novel consistently juxtaposes the stories of these two people, who meet each other only once and that briefly, because it tells the stories of the two possible ways of being in the world. *Anna Karenina* contrasts the career of the "personality" and the career of the "divine self." The artist Mikhaylov's painting of Pilate and Christ embodies and reveals these two modes of being and is the emblem of the book (V,xi).[2] Anna's story tells of her becoming solely a "personality"; Levin's story tells of his uncovering his "divine self." Both suffer from flawed knowledge, Anna from her self-justifying reason, Levin from the mind of a master. The flawed knowledge results in flawed conceptions of the purpose of life: Anna lives for her love regardless of others, Levin lives for his marriage and work. But throughout the novel Anna intensifies her flawed way of seeing, while Levin dispels his. From his suffering he learns. A change in the way of seeing the world results in a change in the way of being in the world. Anna does not change her way of seeing or being. She suffers, but she does not learn. She defines her identity solely by her need to be loved and understands her vocation solely as the battle for that love. Anna has no faith and never goes to church.

THE THEOLOGY OF SIN AND SUFFERING

The epigraph to *Anna Karenina* reads "Vengeance is mine, I shall repay." A puzzle to many, this epigraph seems to imply the existence of a God of retribution who would then stand in a direct contrast to the God of Life and Love.[3] But Tolstoy does not believe in a vengeful deity. The concept of a punishing God, he wrote as early as 1852, "results from the awareness of man's weakness" (46,135). The young Tolstoy understands "punishment" as "injustice," a kind of "threat in which man sacrifices a doubtful good to a certain evil." It is a form of "vengeance," which he believes "man cannot determine because he is too limited." His doctrine of God is not yet clear, but the

[2] The role of this painting in the novel has been discussed by E. N. Kuprejanova, who sees these moral categories for Tolstoy's conception of character. See *"Vojna i mir i Anna Karenina"* in volume two of *Istorija russkogo romana* (Moscow-Leningrad, 1964). In her important work *Estetika L. N. Tolstogo* (Moscow-Leningrad, 1966), Kuprejanova explores in detail the relationship of Tolstoy's moral imagination to his fiction. For this approach see also B. Bursov, *Lev Tolstoj, Idejnye iskanija i tvorcheskij metod* (Moscow, 1960) and G. Ja. Galagan, *op.cit.*

[3] For some of the major contemporary readings of the epigraph, which discuss as well earlier interpretations, see B. Ejkhenbaum, *Lev Tolstoj: semidesjyatye gody* (Leningrad, 1960), pp. 160-173; B. I. Bursov, *Lev Tolstoj i russkij roman* (Moscow-Leningrad, 1963), pp. 103-109; E. G. Babaev, *Roman L. Tolstogo "Anna Karenina"* (Tula, 1968), pp. 56-61; and G. Ja. Galagan, *op.cit.*, pp. 147-148.

twenty-three-year-old Tolstoy admits a "strong desire" to get his "concept of God as clear as his concept of virtue." Forty years later, sounding like Levin in his final discovery, Tolstoy could assert with assurance: "To do good (*dobro*) while not considering God as an avenger is the only true profession of God. Attributing concerns about rewards and punishment to God is a denial of Him and for oneself a total deprivation of the possibility of doing good. Doing good for the sake of the good, that is God" (51,44;1890). Tolstoy's God must not only be beyond the categories of space and time; He must also be beyond the all-too-human conception of psychological causality, reward and punishment. This human "conception of responsibility for one's actions, of reward and punishment," Tolstoy considers to be the "awareness of serving God as one's true good (*blago*) and of the deviation from that service as evil, transferred into the realm of time" (55,225;1906). In "true life" there can be no divine reward or punishment as ordinarily conceived because "there is no time for calculating when to reward or punish" (51,88;1890). God does not give His love forth when we are virtuous and mete out punishment to us when we are sinful, nor does He calculate our good deeds and our evil deeds by some equation to be solved in a heaven or a hell outside space and time. God is Love and Life; He gives forth and forgives. "If God does evil, then He is not good (*dobryj*), He is not love, and if He is not good, then He does not exist" (53,32;1895). The evil God, the one who avenges, punishes, and causes suffering, is our creation, necessary to us for our own self-justification. "People so convince themselves that the bad they do is good that when they experience evil (*zlo*) they blame God rather than themselves, and therefore in the depths of their souls they consider God evil, i.e., they deny Him and as a result receive no consolation from Him." That is Anna's story. To Tolstoy such self-justification is self-destructive as well as God-denying. Yet it has been encouraged, he believes, by the Christian Church, which has modeled its God on the Old Testament image of a wrathful God and failed to grasp fully Christ's teaching about "true life" and the Master's relationship with His workers (24,512;1884). Tolstoy's theology of sin and suffering is part of his lifelong attempt to ground his understanding of Christianity and the doctrine of God in his own reading of the four Gospels "divorced from the Old Testament and St. Paul" (55,262;1906).

Tolstoy understands sin as an act of separation from the God of Life and Love and a violation of the divine principle of love. There is, therefore, only one kind of sin and one kind of evil, the "disassociation (*razobshchenie*) of people" from God and each other (63,114;1883). In one sense, then, a human being in and of himself, if that were a real possibility, is not sinful. "It is not individual people who are evil, stupid, or guilty, but the world" (*mir*), all people together (57,87;1909). "When a person is alone, it's easy for him to be good. But let him come together with others and he becomes bad. And the more people come together, the harder it is to stay away from evil" (57,89;1909). The world as we know it then is sinful, and "the world (*mir*) without sin exists only in the ideal" (55,204;1906). Since metaphysically all particular beings in this world are separations from the All, and their destined purpose is to return to the All, all beings are sinful in their separation and virtuous and happy in their process of returning, their sense of overcoming the separation. "People have been given the possibility of the complete happiness (*blago*) of life. If it were not for sin, they would possess and use it. Now, however, while there is sin, people must strive to correct it. And at the present state of the world . . . the true happiness of human life lies in this correction of sin" (55,203-04;1906). People who have no "conception of sin" and do not guide their actions by their "fear of sin," and this includes "all so-called enlightened people," do not lead a human life (58,99;1910). Instead of understanding that "they are all and nothing," they "think they are something," and from this sense of self as something comes all sin (56,88;1907). To Tolstoy sin results from our mistaken identity, a misunderstanding of our position in the universe and hence of the actions that follow therefrom. Sin is a failure of faith.

Human identity can be located in one of two conceptions of the self, the "animal self" and the "spiritual self." "A person cannot live a life of the spirit, however, if he does not consider himself sinful, and he cannot lead a life of the flesh if he does not consider himself just" (*prav*) (53,104;1896). The establishing of one's true position in the universe depends upon the recognition of one's sinfulness and guilt; all false positions result from a sense of one's justness. "A Christian is always guilty in almost everything" (52,113;1894). But even though "a Christian cannot justify himself" (52,113), we all want to feel just, and therefore "we all justify ourselves even though it is better for us, for our soul, to feel ourselves guilty" (56,46;1907). In fact "nothing so softens the heart as an awareness of one's guilt, and nothing so hardens it as an awareness of one's justness" (53,206;1898). The proper assessment of guilt and justness is the first essential for an "eternally growing soul." "A person can judge himself in only two ways: he can consider himself completely just or completely guilty. He who considers himself completely just is the one who does not want to change his life and uses his reason to justify what has been, and he who considers himself completely guilty is the one who wants to perfect himself and uses his reason to understand what must be" (52,151;1894). The stories of Anna and Levin revolve around these two different forms of self-judgment.

True identity requires the admission of guilt to others and to yourself. Even "when you doubt you are guilty," you should "consider yourself guilty" (57,45;1909) because if you "look hard enough" you will discover your guilt behind your doubt (56,159;1908). The greatest threat to the clarification of identity, therefore, is falsehood, especially falsehood to yourself. "Lying to yourself is always a distortion of truth, a retreat from the demands of life" (53,104;1896). Even people who are "not guilty" because "they do not see the true meaning of life" and therefore cannot willingly violate it, people who are "blind, not like owls, but like puppies," are obliged to do "the one good thing they can, not to lie, not to dissemble" (54,88;1904). To dissemble to yourself or others is always to act for others, to live not for God but for human glory; and it always involves self-justification and results in alienation from those before whom you dissemble, from yourself, from other people, from God. The most harmful falsehood is the projection of our guilt onto others, when "it seems to us that things are bad for us not because we are bad but because others are guilty" (51,77;1890). Such "blame of others takes the responsibility away from us" and locks us up in our false selves. Furthermore, the failure to admit one's guilt not only precludes "salvation from your sins," but usually leads to a "new sin," because "when others point out your sins to you, you just get angry at them" (53,154;1896). The more falsehood, the more you must retreat and hide from others. "A person who cannot admit his own sins is a capped, hermetically sealed vessel which allows nothing into itself" (53,107;1896). Falsehood leads to total self-enclosure; the truth of guilt, which is to say "humility" and "repentance," "opens the cap and makes you capable of perfection, of happiness" (*blago*). Anna lives by falsehood; Levin discovers the truth of guilt.

To Tolstoy the only perfection is love; the only sin, the lack of love, which is the "disassociation of people." There is no need, then, to imagine a God who rewards perfection and punishes sin, nor a hereafter when this is done, because virtue is its own reward, and sin its own punishment. "A person is born, lives and dies alone, and alone not in some unknown world but in this one, he receives his reward for a good life and punishment for a bad one" (57,46;1909). The reward for love is love, the feeling that you belong and are not alone; the punishment for sin is the loss of love, the feeling that you are estranged and alone. People, therefore, are "punished not for their sins but by them" (77,123;1907). The sin returns as your suffering and your punishment. Tolstoy, therefore, takes the expression "Vengeance is mine, I shall repay" to mean that "only God punishes and that only through the person himself" (44,95;1910). But we should not interpret this as a statement about the nature of God. Tolstoy is speaking of human psychology. This understanding of the return of sin as punishment, therefore, provides Tolstoy with a way of understanding his own crises when he feels the loss of God:

> All night and early morning I was visited with what seemed an unprecedented state of coldness, doubt of everything, of God, of the truth of my understanding of the meaning of life. I did not believe in myself and could not evoke that awareness by which I used to live and do live. Only now this morning I have recollected myself and returned to life. It was all a punishment for unkind, unloving feelings which I allowed myself on the preceding days. And it serves me right. However strange it is to say, the knowledge of God is given only by love. Love is the only organ for knowing him. (57,131;1909)

The loss of faith, the false assessment of who you are and what you must do, the failure of your mission of love and reconciliation, is punished by a loss of faith. The return to faith, the proper assessment of your position in the universe as a particle of love and the acts of love that follow therefrom, is rewarded with the return to faith. As the title of his story says, *Where Love Is, There Is God*; where not, there is self and sin and suffering. Anna's story plays out the law of the return of sins as punishment; Levin's story plays out the law of the reward of love for love.

The law of the return of sin as punishment and suffering, however, does not seem to explain natural or moral evil. After all, there is natural evil; there are earthquakes, droughts, floods, disease, wild wolves on the loose, and the pangs of birth. These are, Tolstoy insists in *On Life*, the "necessary conditions of existence" (26,433;1887). And certainly there is suffering that is the result of the actions of others, not of myself. There is the moral evil of war, poverty, injustice, and the institutionalization of this injustice in education and business, church and state. Am I not a victim of this evil, rather than its cause? Is my life not one unceasing series of meaningless torments? Why should I live if the necessary conditions of existence are stacked against me? Such are the obvious questions the theology of suffering from one's sins brings to fore. But these are the questions of the Stranger. They assume that a person acts in total isolation from others, from past and future, from nature, history, and culture; they assume that a person is motivated by himself alone, that he is the center of everything, that he is an individual. But a person is a particle of the whole. Sin and suffering can be comprehended only within the context of the community of beings, the "world" (*mir*). Sin is the flaw of human relatedness.

Tolstoy's understanding of sin can be understood only within the context of the Eastern Christian conception of sin. In this tradition there is no original sin understood as some debilitating disfiguration of the moral self, inherited as it were by the genes. The person is not by nature evil and hence is in no need of any extra grace in order to be saved. What is inherited from Adam in the Eastern Christian conception is death, not sin. We are all mortals. It is understood that like Adam we all sin, but this sin is our individual act and our responsibility: like Adam *possimus non peccare*.[4] This understanding of original sin is related to the Eastern Christian doctrine of person and hence to Tolstoy's theological anthropology; to this I shall return in the next chapter. What is significant for Tolstoy in the Eastern Chris-

[4] For a clear discussion of the Eastern Christian understanding, see John Meyendorff, *op.cit.*, pp. 143-146. Some of the complexities hidden in this are discussed by Jaroslav Pelikan, *op.cit.*, pp. 294-295. The Russian theologian Sergey Bulgakov gives a modern and Russian reading of this doctrine in "On Original Sin," *The Journal of the Fellowship of St. Albans and St. Sergius* VII (1929), 15-26.

tian understanding of original sin is that we all sin. He is not interested in any metaphysical explanation of why we all sin. There is "sin of the world" (*grekh mira*), and we all "participate" in it (26,434;1887). Furthermore since "people live not separately but in society, . . . all suffer from the sin of each" (53,228;1899). But Tolstoy believes, however, that the relationship between the person who commits sin and the suffering caused by sin will never be clear to us. Whatever the apparent causal relationship seems to be, therefore, all we can know for certain is that we sin and we suffer. If I look at my life as my own individual existence solely, he argues, then suffering from natural or moral evil always seems meaningless and unjust and evokes "despair" for myself and "animosity" toward others (26,429;1887). If I look upon my life as a participant in the "life of the world" (*zhizn' mira*), I will see that my "sins, whatever they may be, are the cause of my sufferings, whatever they may be." We suffer from our sins and for each other.

This theology of sin and suffering, which places individual experiences within the context of the "sin of the world" and the "life of the world," allows Tolstoy to separate the pain in suffering from the suffering itself. "A person who recognizes the relationship between his own sin and suffering with the sin and suffering of the world is freed from the torment of the suffering" (26,430). There will always be suffering, but the acceptance of suffering as the result of sin gives it meaning, and this meaning releases us from the real torment, which is not the physical pain but the senselessness of the pain. "The torments of suffering are experienced," therefore, only when a person "separates himself from the life of the world by not seeing his sins through which he has borne suffering into the world; he does not consider himself guilty and therefore rebels against the sufferings which he bears for the sins of the world." When we do not admit our guilt, we feel the pain of our suffering. The pain of suffering is felt only when we "attempt to break the chain of love for our ancestors, our contemporaries, and our descendants, the chain which unites human life with the life of the world" (26,431).

This theology of sin and suffering is embodied in the life and story of Platon Karataev. Karataev was a peasant with a good master who "himself went out to mow" (IV,I,xii). But, once, Karataev went beyond the borders of his master's land to get some wood for himself and he was caught. He was "beaten, tried, and sent away to the army." Yet this turned out to be "not grief but joy," because it saved his younger brother, who had a wife and five children, from having to abandon his responsibility to them. "Had it not been for my sin, my brother would have had to go." Karataev sins, but he suffers for others. He finds meaning in his suffering. His favorite story, therefore, is a narrative of salvation through suffering for others. The story he repeatedly and "joyously" recounts "in ecstasy," which is the same story Tolstoy retold as *God Sees The Truth But Waits*, is the tale of a merchant falsely accused of a murder and sent to a prison camp, where after years of suffering for "his own sins" he meets the real murderer. This murderer confesses to the authorities in hopes of bringing release for the merchant who has "innocently suffered in vain," but fails because in the meantime God has shown his "forgiveness" by granting the merchant his true release in death (IV,iii,xiii). Karataev's tale contains the "mysterious meaning" of his own life. His sense of being a "particle of the whole" leads him to an intuition of the meaning of sin and suffering. He knows that we suffer from our sins, not for our own good but for the good of others, and that because we suffer for others, even as a result of our own sins, we will be granted God's forgiveness. Our sin and suffering are removed from the ordinary conception of the causal nexus of reward and punishment but in our suffering we are reconciled.

FOR TOLSTOY suffering is not an evil. Pain, he argues like Levin's brother Nicholas, exists only in correlation to pleasure. All pleasures in life are purchased at the cost of pain to oneself and others; the "two opposite conditions are aroused the one by the other and necessary the one for the other" (26,425;1887). If sufferings were evil, then so would be pleasure, and all life would be an evil that we should escape. Anna and Levin both come to this conclusion at some point in their experience. To Tolstoy suffering is the correlative of pleasure. It is a "painful sensation which arouses activity to dispel the painful sensation and to evoke a state of pleasure." In animals and human beings, therefore, "suffering is what moves life" (26,426), the "necessary condition of life" (26,433); "without it nothing good like birth (the comparison is evangelical) can happen" (55,282;1906). "What we consider evil for ourselves," therefore, "is most often a good we do not yet understand" (45,437;1910). When we understand, we see that "suffering, loss, death are all good. Suffering produces happiness and joy, just as work produces rest, pain produces the awareness of health, and the death of dear ones produces the awareness of duty, our own death, peace" (49,98;1884). Thus understood, "human life as we know it is a wave all bedecked with shining and joy." Pain produces the joy of life.

Pain also preserves life. On the physical level, the experience of pain is a danger signal, an "indication of a deviation from the law which governs life" (26,433). Without such suffering there would be no knowledge of the "law" of life. On the spiritual level this "law" of life, of course, is love, and suffering, therefore, is the signal of the absence of and need for love. In the face of the suffering of others, apparently, there can be only one appropriate response, "aid" for the sufferer and "alleviation" of the suffering. In this sense the "task of life" is "spontaneous loving service to those who suffer and the destruction of the general causes of suffering" (26,434). This is the meaning of Platon Karataev's potato. This "loving service" is what Kitty knows and Levin learns.

How are we to respond, however, to our own sufferings? What is the appropriate reaction to the danger signal? First of all, "suffering" (stradanie), we must realize, comes from some "passion" (strast'); suffering, therefore, signals experience in the physical, material, personal realm. "One can suffer only in the body; the spirit knows no suffering" (56,147;1908). The experience of suffering reveals a failure of identity, the assumption that our personal, physical material self is our true self. If "I suffer and desire" in a "moment of passion or attraction," however, I can "conquer" the passion and alleviate the suffering by separating "my true self" from the "troubled waters of passion" (53,108;1896). The first appropriate response to suffering is the clarification of the self. "We say that suffering is evil, but if there were no suffering, a person would not know where he ends and what is not he begins" (45,438;1910). Suffering gives knowledge of our boundary and limitation. Suffering reveals the barrier between self and other. Without suffering, therefore, there could be no faith or true life. "Suffering is the friction of life without which there would be no life nor what the essence of life consists in, the liberation of the soul from the body, the mistakes of the body, from the sufferings connected with the body" (56,108;1908). "Calamities and misfortunes" create the "possibility of true life" (58,95;1910). Suffering leads to the "struggle of the soul with the body," the "conquest of the body by the soul," and "life itself." Thus, when properly understood and appropriately confronted, all human passion and "all material sufferings (which are inevitable as is death itself) only destroy the boundaries which hamper our spirit. In destroying the illusion of our materiality, they return us to the inherent human awareness of our life in our spiritual rather than our material being" (54,142-43;1902). In suffering we discover our true self. That is why, when calamities and misfortunes occur, the peasants say that "God has visited" us.

Suffering leads to self-knowledge only if it is accepted. To accept suffering is to use it. When in moments of grief or illness, the peasants say "God has taken note even of me," they mean that "suffering itself can be used for the eternal task of life" (54,193;1904). Suffering may provide a "test" of progress, for we can see "to what extent we are living a life of the spirit, not of the flesh" (57,178;1909). Every moment of woe can serve as an "examination" or "verification" of "how firm we are in what we know and profess" (45,436;1910). Most importantly, suffering is useful because "from what we call evil, from woes, illness, and suffering we learn (uchimsja) to remake our animal self into our spiritual self" (45,438;1910). "God teaches (uchit) men through suffering" (52,66;1892). This pedagogical conception of suffering places Tolstoy directly within the ancient Eastern Christian tradition. Wisdom through suffering is, of course, a classical Greek idea, as old at least as Aeschylus. But this idea was fastened to the concept of *paideia* and reshaped into a theology of redemption by Origen, who passed it on to the Greek fathers. For Origen, God is a great teacher and the universe is his classroom. Origen believes the pain of life teaches men their radical insufficiency and helplessness before the God on whom all depend.[5] Origen's pedagogical conception of suffering surfaces in Tolstoy's theology of sin and suffering, even as it shapes the careers of Levin and, as we shall see, Ivan Ilych too.

To Tolstoy, God's greatest teaching device is illness. "Illness is given to man as a beneficent indication of the fact that his whole life is bad and that it must be changed" (53,82;1896). "The fact that we are burdened by illness just shows that we are not living the temporal life along with the eternal life as we ought, but that we are living the temporal life alone" (53,171;1897). Illness confronts us with the fact

[5] For a discussion of Origen's theology of suffering, see Jean Daniélou, S.J., *Origène* (Paris, 1948), pp. 271-283.

of eternal life, because it "prepares us for death." Since death is but a "transition to another life," however, "illness prepares for the transition." All our woes, but most especially illness, "help unglue us from this world and ease the transition to a new life." This is what Natasha and Kitty experience; it is what Levin learns from his brother Nicholas. Through suffering we are reborn to the spirit.

No suffering teaches, however, if we do not understand that "all life is a spiritual feat" (*podvig*) (53,122;1896). If we are tormented by "poverty, illness, infidelity of a spouse, slander, or humiliation" and we just "pity ourselves," then we will be "the most unhappy of the most unhappy." Life understood not as a spiritual feat but as the fulfillment of our personal desires for life leads to frustration and defeat. This is what Anna experiences. But if we see that "what gives us grief and seems to hinder our fulfilling our task of life is our task of life" and what we are "called to," then instead of "depression and pain there will be energy and joy." This is what Levin learns. It is the meaning of the Cross. "The cross sent to us is what we have to work on. Our whole life is that work. If the cross is illness, then bearing it with submission; if it is insults from people, then being able to repay evil with good; if it is humiliation, then humbling oneself; if death, then the thankful acceptance of it" (45,443;1910). For Tolstoy "everyone has his own cross, his own yoke, not in the sense of a burden, but in the sense of the destined purpose of his life, and if we look upon the cross not as a burden but as our destined purpose, then it is easy to bear." In our suffering, our cross, we must see, not our punishment, but our purpose.

The greatest suffering in life for Tolstoy is one's own death. But death, he argues, is also no evil. Rather, "death is the destruction of the self in the sense of a separated and hence material being" (54,121;1907). But this metaphor of destruction is misleading, since it suggests something negative. Tolstoy, therefore, prefers to speak of the "illusion of destruction," because in death what is destroyed are the "bounds" which limit the true self. With death this true self is "liberated like compressed gas" and "enters into new unifications." We should recall his aphorism: "A drop that merges with a larger drop, a puddle, stops being and starts to be" (53,231;1899). Death, then, is "good because it delivers from their own personal self those who have understood all the narrowness and unfreedom of the separation from the All, which is connected with that self" (56,47;1907).

If "this life" is the process of "liberation" from limitation, "disclosure of the unknown," "removing the covers," then "death is the last disclosure of this life" (55,239;1906). What is disclosed at death is the true self. "If you have understood not just with your mind but with your whole inner experience of life that life, its meaning and happiness, consists only in the liberation of the spiritual foundation which has been darkened, dirtied over, and buried under, . . . then death can be imagined only as the complete liberation of that spiritual principle from all that covers it, from the limitation of the flesh" (55,282;1906). Death is the destruction of the "personality" and the discovery of the divine self.

Since "this life" is understood as a process of liberation and disclosure, Tolstoy believes "all life from childhood on is the process of dying" (umiranie) (56,91;1907). To understand and live life aright, then, is ever to remember death. "The foundation of a reasonable, religious understanding of life is momento mori, the mindfulness of death, not even so much the mindfulness of death as the understanding of the brevity and fleetingness of life" (55,106;1904). Such mindfulness of death calls us to the "best use of the time that remains" (56,85;1907), and therefore is "the life for which there is no death" (57,111;1909). As for Levin, the awareness of death calls us to live and love right now. The remembrance of death, then, is the remembrance of God (55,83;1904). Furthermore, if we remember that "we are living means we are dying," then we know that "to live well means to die well" (49,60;1883). The "fear of death," then, is really the awareness of a life badly lived (55,75;1904). In fact, "you can measure the goodness of a person's life by his fear of death." To Tolstoy, the "teaching about reward in heaven and punishment in hell" really means that the "reward" for a good life is "fearlessness" in the face of death, the "punishment" for a bad life is "terror."

Still, if "I am aware of myself as dying" and "a person's life as well as the life of all of humanity and the whole universe is the process of approaching death," the basic question of existence is "what is this dying?" (55,182;1906). To Tolstoy, dying (umiranie) is "mortal (smertnaja) life." Therefore we should understand that "at the beginning dying is the ever greater understanding together with the development of lust which darkens the understanding, and toward the end dying is the quelling of lust, the illumination of understanding, and self-perfection. In general, therefore, dying is nothing other than ever more illumination." Dying is the very process of growth, the perpetual reversal and return on the journey toward the discovery of truth, the illumination of understanding we call love. Dying is life. The journey is not direct, and we fall by the wayside of our lusts, but the end of the journey is always certain, the illumination of everything in love. All deaths in Tolstoy, even Anna's, terminate in some form of illumination. In the journey of our mortal life, even when all else has been darkened by our lusts, the last moments of dying call forth the "greatest effort for the liberation of the soul by the manifestation of love," and consequently our dying is "the most opportune time to liberate the soul by means of love" (56,92;1907). If not before, then at our death, we come to faith, that illuminated understanding of who we are and what we must do. In death we finally define our "mission" (65,118;1890). In death as in suffering we are reborn to the spirit.

The Death of Ivan Ilych (1886), Tolstoy's first major fiction after *Anna Karenina*, is a story of sin and suffering and death, and therefore it is a tale of the loss and recovery of love and a narrative of "mortal life." It is an emblem of dying. The work opens with the announcement of Ivan Ilych's death, but the first chapter focuses on Peter Ivanovich, Ivan Ilych's "closest" friend, the one for whom "everything is too far away." Peter Ivanovich does not know "what meaning this death could have" nor "what he must do." In the face of death he reacts to others in his routine manner: he grasps at the opportunity to fill the "place" vacated by their departure. The task of life for him is the quest for a bigger and better place, regardless of others, and in this he resembles all others. On this resemblance all friendship indeed is founded, for these people are the ones who like each other because they are alike. They share the belief that life must be "pleasant" and "proper," that one does what others do and likes what others like, and life for them is the striving to be alike in order to be liked. They live for others in order to live for themselves. When Peter Ivanovich reads a message of contentment on his dead friend's face, he does not understand that Ivan Ilych has accomplished his mission, because he is solely concerned with his own behavior. When he hears from Ivan Ilych's wife the details of suffering and dying, he thinks not of his friend but of himself and goes off to play cards. Peter Ivanovich is the one who is distant even when close, whose task of life is the quest for another place, not the quest for his task in his place and who, instead of remembering death, plays cards. He does not know how to live or love and death for him is terrifying. He resembles most Ivan Ilych.

Ivan Ilych is not an orphan. He is the son of one whose life is a "career" which leads to a "position" where he can no longer "fulfill any essential duty" but continues "to get fictitious places and non-fictitious thousands" to "a venerable old age" (ii). The father's task of life is just to move from place to place, living by the "inertia of salary," and Ivan Ilych feels called to become like his father. Ivan Ilych's early life, then, is moved by every "change in job": "New institutions appeared, new people were needed, and Ivan Ilych became that new person." His job, he believes, has nothing to do with his "private life." He develops the "device of distancing himself from all circumstances that do not touch his job" and thus separates himself from his task. He is distant even when close. He changes his physical image to fit the new life and gets married because others think it is "correct" to do so and, besides, it is "pleasant" for him.

> The very process of marriage and the first period of married life with its conjugal kisses, new furniture, new dishes, and new linen went so well right up to his wife's pregnancy that Ivan Ilych began to think that marriage would not only not destroy but even improve the mode of easy, pleasant, merry, yet always proper and approved life which Ivan Ilych considered inherent to life itself. But then, from the first months of his wife's pregnancy, there appeared something new, unexpected, unpleasant, difficult, and improper which he had not expected and from which he could not separate himself.

Ivan Ilych's marriage reveals his flaw. He fails to understand what life is; when it appears, it seems the very negation of what he thinks it is. Life understood as a career will inevitably stumble on the facts of life and death. For one whose understanding of life is thus flawed, the facts do not fit the expectations and seem to be the negation and adversary of life. The syntax of this paragraph reflects the theme of the whole work: what seems positive becomes negative and what is expected is the opposite of what happens. The central word here, as in the whole work, is the adversative conjunction "but" (no). *The Death of Ivan Ilych* is the story of twisted values that in the end get turned right. The key words "position," "task," "life," and "death" change their meaning in the process, and in the end which is the beginning we see that Ivan Ilych's dying is his position, task, and life, while his conception of this position, task, and life is his death. In this story of conversion, the very words get converted in their meanings.

When the "complex and difficult task" of marriage fails, Ivan Ilych finds himself drowning in "a sea of silent enmity and alienation." To protect himself he becomes "impenetrable" to his wife's emotional outbursts. He returns to his work, which now becomes "his world" (*mir*) and "the whole interest of his life." But then, just when he has worked out the "relationship" to his marriage, his world of work falls apart. The "salary is not sufficient for life" (iii). That year of 1880—the year of Tolstoy's most serious crisis—is "the most difficult year in Ivan Ilych's life." "Everyone abandoned him." "For the first time" he experiences "boredom and unbearable anxiety." He must "seek a new place," a "new arrangement of his life," and "punish those" who have betrayed him. He journeys to St. Petersburg, where his quest is crowned with success. Now "his enemies are shamed," they "envy him his position," and "everyone loves him." Ivan Ilych marks the triumph of his punishment and revenge with a new apartment whose arrangement "grows and grows to the ideal" he has set, and his living room begins to "be like all other living rooms." But then, just when he is hanging the last drapery, he falls from the ladder of his successful arrangement of life. From this point on Ivan Ilych's own world tumbles down upon him, and he becomes ill.

In his illness Ivan Ilych suffers from the arrangement of life he had achieved. "Every spot on the tablecloth . . . annoyed him," and he "suffered from the apartment" he had arranged. As the pain increases, he goes to the doctor, who treats him as he had treated defendants in the courts and diagnoses his illness as a "wandering" kidney and a "blind" intestine. He experiences "doubt," "terror," and "despair," but no one like him understands what is so unlike them and they think that "he is guilty." His wife works out a definite relationship to his illness in which she too sees him "guilty," and at work he becomes the one who is soon "to vacate a place." The life he had arranged with its new furniture, its "device of distancing himself" from his task, its self-protective relationship to his marriage, and its unending quest to fill the vacant place, returns as his suffering, just as his diagnosed illness is the judgment on his blind and wandering life. None of this, of course, does he see. He just suffers from his sins, alone as he always was. But then, at the center of the work, Ivan Ilych looks in the mirror and sees the "changes" (v). He overhears the judgment that "he is a dead man," and he realizes the truth of his dying. From this point on his suffering begins its teaching task.

Suffering shows Ivan Ilych that others "do not know or take pity" on him and that in his dying as in his living he is alone. Suffering shows him that he is indeed like everyone else, like Caius in the syllogism, the mortal who must die. Suffering shows him that the facts of life and death are neither proper, nor pleasant, and that with urination and defecation we must live and die. Suffering shows him that "no one will take pity on him because no one even wants to understand his position," and so they all lie to themselves and others (vii). Suffering shows him that truth comes out twisted, as it does from his wife, because it is all self-centered: "She did everything for him only for herself and told him that she was doing for herself what she was really doing for herself in such an incredible way that he had to understand just the opposite" (viii). Suffering shows Ivan Ilych who he has been and what he has done: draped in the self-protective arrangement of his life, he has lived only for himself, even though he has not known himself. Suffering untwists the truth, but not completely.

What completes the lesson of suffering is the lesson of love. The servant Gerasim, the only figure in the story shown without family or friends, is the one who knows how to live and love because he accepts the facts of life and death. Gerasim knows that "we will all die" (vii) and that in the face of death one can offer solace and comfort but no remedy. Gerasim's presence stays Ivan Ilych's pain and terror, but his absence as a result heightens the dying man's sense of isolation and abandonment. In Gerasim's absence Ivan Ilych "pities himself" and "weeps like a child" (ix). Gerasim's departure, the loss of love, brings Ivan Ilych to the despair which will turn him around. "He wept over his own helplessness, his own terrifying aloneness, over the cruelty of people, the cruelty of God, over the absence of God." But then, he "stopped weeping and breathing and became all attention," listening to the "voice of his soul" which recalls his life of love as a child. "But the person who had experienced that pleasantness no longer exists; it was as it were a memory of someone else." The course of his life becomes clear: "The further, the deader" but "the further back, the more life, the more good in life, the more of life itself" (x). His life in quest of place after place has in fact been a "series of increasing struggles flying faster and faster toward the end, the most terrifying suffering," the "terrifying falling, shock, and destruction" of death. Gerasim's love teaches Ivan Ilych the ultimate truth that he himself is guilty of destroying his own life. There is no God who is tormenting him. He is tormented because he is not like Gerasim.

What Gerasim knows is that the task of life is not to seek place after place, but to see his task in his place. He lives not by the "inertia of salary" (zhalovanija), but by his ability to "take pity" (zhalet') on others. He knows in what way we all are alike and how we all need to be liked, but he does not seek to be alike or liked. Because he identifies with others without needing to be like them or liked by them, he is able to give spontaneously and freely of himself. From Gerasim Ivan Ilych learns that to live does not mean to be loved but to love. The "aloneness in the populous city amidst his numerous acquaintances and family, the aloneness fuller than it could be anywhere, at the bottom of the sea or in the bowels of the earth" (x), Ivan Ilych learns, comes from his deadly life: he isolated himself and then wanted to be pitied by others for his own self-isolation. What must be done is "to take pity" on others. This Ivan Ilych experiences when his hand touches his son's head, his son grasps it and kisses it, and Ivan Ilych feels "pity" for him. The pain and the death disappear in the act of pity which is Ivan Ilych's illumination and rebirth to life. To this concept of "pity" we shall turn in the next chapter.

The Death of Ivan Ilych is an emblematic story of crisis and conversion. Written just before the completion of the major philosophical work *On Life*, this autopsychological prose fiction tells of the discovery of life in the face of death. It is the fictional image of the "arrest of life" (ostanovka zhizni) which, as Tolstoy would have it in *A Confession*, was the immediate cause of his major crisis and conversion. All of a sudden the Tolstoyan questions started to rise relentlessly to the surface of his consciousness, and he fell into an arresting despair which led to his illumination (iii). In *A Confession* Tolstoy attempts to articulate this "arrest of life" by this clarifying simile:

There occurred what occurred with everyone sick with a deadly internal disease. At first there appear trivial signs of indisposition to which the sick man pays no attention, then these signs reappear more and more often and merge into one ceaseless suffering. This suffering grows and, before the sick man can glance back, he becomes aware that what he took for an indisposition is what is for him more important than anything else in the world—death.

The simile then supplies Tolstoy with the metaphor for the first fiction he completed after *A Confession*.[6] The story, therefore, is grounded in Tolstoy's experience, embodies his image of the experience, and reveals the later articulated idea drawn from the experience. *The Death of Ivan Ilych* in this sense represents Tolstoy's art in its most typical form.

[6] The parallel between this passage in *A Confession* and *The Death of Ivan Ilych* was first pointed out by Rimvydas Silbajoris in his excellent article "Human Contact and Tolstoy's Esthetics," *Papers in Comparative Studies*, The Ohio State University, Columbus, Ohio, Vol. I, No. 1, 1981, p. 39, n. 23.

Chapter Four

THE WAY TO LOVE

Remember, you are not standing still but passing through; you
are not in a home but on a train taking you to your death.
(45,449;1910)

A journey is an emblem of life.
(53,117;1896)

THE CRISIS recorded in *A Confession* was Tolstoy's turning
point in self-articulation. His sense of purpose and meaning which he
had found in his participation in cultural and family life faded into
the ever-present question "why." "My life stopped. I could breathe,
eat, drink, and sleep, and couldn't help breathing, eating, drinking,
and sleeping, but there was no life because there were no desires
whose satisfaction I could find reasonable" (iv). The source of his
depression, he came to see, was his own failure to participate in true
life and true love. In the black past, Tolstoy now believed, he had
spent his days for himself, deceiving himself in the process, believing
that what he was doing gave meaning to his existence. He was like
the animals. "The goat, hare, and wolf exist in such a way that they
must eat, multiply, and feed their families and when they do this, I
am firmly convinced, they are happy and their life is reasonable. But
what must a human being do? He too must procure life, just like the
animals, with one difference: that he will perish if he attempts to
procure it alone. He must procure it not for himself but for all" (xi).
In what sense he or anyone could "procure life for all" and how this
could be salvation from death became Tolstoy's central questions.
The answer, he believed, could be learned only from the people, the
majority who "create life" (x), not with him and those like him, the
"rich and the learned" (xi) who in fact do not even procure life for
themselves but live as "parasites" on life. What the crisis made clear
to Tolstoy was that his way to life and love in the face of death was
ill-chosen and ill-conceived. He learned what Levin learned. His ma-

ture years were spent attempting to articulate the right way, the "inclinations of which had always been in him" (x). He sought to be redeemed.

Tolstoy the artist also underwent a crisis of values. His former major works, which were after all articulations of the "character of the author" with his "eternally growing soul," likewise seemed to be unclear, poorly written, even wrong in their views. They, like him, had been far removed from the majority of people, too focused it seemed to him on the life of the rich and learned and too derivative of their modes of fiction, the Bildungsroman, the romance, the epic, and the novel. This he had to change. In *Death of Ivan Ilych* he chose a central character from the world of lower officialdom; in *Resurrection* Prince Nekhlyudov, now depicted as a failed artist, shares the burden of the tale with Katerina Maslova, a servant, prostitute, and prisoner; in *Master and Man* a petty merchant and his servant take the focus formerly given to figures drawn closer to Tolstoy and those of his class and milieu. As he strove to represent new types of people in his fiction, his method of representation seemed to change. He practiced writing parables and fables in imitation of the style of the literature of the folk. He created forms, as in *Death of Ivan Ilych*, *Master and Man*, or *Resurrection* which had no clear link with the literary genres of the educated classes. But in his art, as in his life, Tolstoy's later style reveals the "inclinations that had always been in him." The more the characters are removed from him, the more they stand for all, including him. The more the works move away from the traditions of realistic fiction, the more they reveal the peculiar features of his realistic fiction. In the manner and purpose of the late tales we find the key to the nature of Tolstoy's art.

NEKHLYUDOV'S PATH TO REDEMPTION

Resurrection is a story of sin and redemption. The sin, as always, is a failure of human relatedness, but in this work the violation of love is not seen in an epic war of peoples or in the romantic battles within the family. Now the master-and-servant relationship is violated by a romantic one, and the violation leads to an expanded arena of sin. The psychology of flawed love with its guilt and resentment, judgment and reproach, self-pity and hatred, still obtains, only now it is projected as well onto the whole society, whose institutions are seen as the embodiment of the violation of human relatedness. The path the resurrection must lead to is a redemption of the society, which in its institutions has broken the contract of human relatedness. The net of love must be all-embracing. The redemption of society can be attained, however, only through the redemption of each individual. Nekhlyudov's path is the way to love for all.

Resurrection opens, we should recall, with Nekhlyudov's awakening to the fact of his violation of love. The "astounding chance event" that brings him to the trial of "Love" and hence of his past at first evokes in Nekhlyudov a fear of shame and a retreat from his responsibility (I,xxii). "He would not admit to the feeling of repentance that was beginning to speak inside him. He imagined this was a chance event that would pass and not disturb his life. He felt like a puppy who had messed in the apartment and whose master had grabbed him by the collar and was rubbing his nose in the mess he had made." Nekhlyudov does not see the significance of what he has done and so pulls away from the awareness of his guilt, which "in the depths of his heart" he does feel. But then that evening, after dinner with his would-be fiancée Missi, "returning home along the familiar street," Nekhlyudov reexamines his relationship with Missi, which now seems but a part of his whole spoiled life: "shameful and vile, vile and shameful" (I,xxviii). He arrives home, goes into the living room, where his mother had died three months before, and seeing her portrait he "recalls" her life and death, his desire for her to die in order to relieve him of the sight of her suffering, his embarrassment for her life imaged in this portrait with her bared shoulders and arms, a portrait which itself recalls to his mind his would-be fiancée Missi. "It's shameful and vile, vile and shameful." Then "suddenly" he thinks of Maslova: he "recalls" the young Katyusha "in the white dress," their pure "love," his best self, his sin, and now himself "all in lies." He would free himself from his "shameful and vile" past. He needs, he knows, a "cleansing of his soul," by which he means a "psychological state in which after a long period of time he suddenly recognizes a slowing down or even a cessation of his inner life and undertakes to clean out the dirt that has accumulated in his soul and is the cause of the cessation." To liberate his eternally growing soul, Nekhlyudov believes he must "tear off the lie which is binding him"; he must tell Missi the truth of his intentions; he must tell Katyusha that he is "guilty before her" and "beg her forgiveness"; perhaps he even should "marry her if that is necessary." He looks outward toward the "moonlit garden" and from the expanse of nature breathes in the "life-giving fresh air" and pronounces it "good." Nekhlyudov leaves the trial of "Love" on a mission of reconciliation, which to him means a task of repentance and redemption. His sin against love has returned to teach him the way to love. This segment after the first day in court reiterates the paradigmatic action of the work: the journey to the past awakens a truth revealed in the expanse of nature.

Maslova leaves the trial of "Love" "amazed" that the very men who used to eye the prostitute so fondly now "so cruelly judge" the prisoner; they now "blame her" even though she is "innocent" (I,xxix). But then that evening while trying to go to sleep she thinks about the consequences of her incarceration: she may get too thin and the men will stop looking. "Love," the prostitute, knows who she is and what she must do. Maslova then thinks over her day and her life, but not of her terrible past, "all memories of which she had buried" (I,xxxvii). From the sin against love she hides. The buried past, however, is then told, but not as a recollection by Maslova. It is the narrator's truth to which she has not yet awakened. Maslova's "terrible dark night," we now learn, is not Nekhlyudov's. What lies buried in her is not the moment of sexual violation and the one-hundred ruble redemption of the sin. She had after all given herself to him. For Maslova the "terrible dark night" is the moment of total abandonment by the one whom she loved and who loved her. It seems that a few months after the fatal night of his sin, Nekhlyudov returned again to the country but not to Katyusha. Bearing his child and still believing in him, hearing that he is at the train station on his way back to Petersburg, Katyusha goes off "on the dark, rainy, windy night in fall" to see Nekhlyudov. Through the window of the compartment she sees him sitting in his "velvet seat," playing cards with his fellow officers and laughing over something. She taps at the window, but the train takes off. She runs after it, but the last car passes, and Katyusha is left "with no defense." She decides to throw herself under the train, but the child to be born moves in her womb and "suddenly everything that had tormented her and made her life seem impossible, all her anger at him and her desire to get revenge if only by her own death, suddenly all that passed." She returns home "wet and muddy," but for her the "spiritual crisis" of her life begins with that moment. "She stopped believing in the good. She became convinced that everything said about God and the good is said only to deceive people. He whom she loved and who loved her, this she knew, had abandoned her," and now she knows that "all live only for themselves, for their own pleasure and that all the words about God and the good are deception." In life she now knows "people do evil to each other and they suffer." Because she has been abandoned by her love, Katyusha loses her sense of human relatedness. Gone is her Easter ecstasy of "love for all." But none of this does Maslova recollect, and when the next day she attends the divine liturgy in the prison she understands all the "chants, prayers, and candles" as do all the other prisoners, as a "mysterious force by which one can acquire great comforts in this life and in the future life" and the failure to acquire these comforts through this "mysterious force" as an "accidental failure" (I,xl). The mystical moment of "love for all" has been transformed into magical ritual performed for your own good. Maslova leaves the trial of "Love," not yet knowing that she is on a mission of recollection, which will lead to her resurrection through forgiveness.

The first stage of the journey of awakening consists of three encounters between Nekhlyudov and Maslova. Nekhlyudov, impelled by his need for repentance and redemption, uses his privilege to obtain a meeting with the prisoner. Not even yet recognizing who he is, Maslova the prostitute sees by his clothing that he is "a rich man" and automatically "smiles" (I,xliii). He begins to speak stumblingly, but Maslova recognizes him "by the expression on his face." Her smile fades into a frown. "Without any intonation, as if it were a memorized lesson," Nekhlyudov "shouts out in loud voice" that he has come to beg her forgiveness. He wants, he says, to "do what he can," to "redeem his sin," but she keeps on saying "that's all over." Then "suddenly she looks at him and smiles unpleasantly, alluringly, sorrowfully." For a moment Katyusha recalls the young man she had loved, but then Maslova sees him again solely as "one of those who use beings like her when it is necessary and whom beings like her have to use as profitably as possible for themselves." She smiles again and asks him for some money. He reaches for it, and he, the one who first paid her, now judges her: "she is a dead woman." He again begs her forgiveness; she grabs the money from his hand;

and he feels that "there is in her something hostile to him which is protecting her as she is now and hindering him from penetrating to her heart." But, "amazingly," this only attracts him more to her; now he wants to "awaken her spiritually," not "for himself, but for her." The first attempt to redeem the sin results in awakening Maslova to her past and her hostility. But Nekhlyudov, while judging her a dead woman, still is moved to continue his attempt, seeing in it some altruistic deed. Maslova recollects Katyusha, and Nekhlyudov would resurrect Katyusha.

Nekhlyudov arrives at his second visit with the firm intention to proclaim the plan of redemption he failed to mention the first time. "I want to expiate my sin, not in words but in deeds. I have decided to marry you. I am obliged before God to do this" (I,xlviii). Maslova looks frightened and frowns angrily. "Get away from me. I am a prisoner and you are a prince and there's nothing here for you. You want to save yourself through me." Nekhlyudov smells liquor on her breath. His presence, he sees, has brought to her consciousness her ugly past, but the memory is so tormenting that she has to drown her sorrows in wine. He violated her in the past, and he torments her in the present. As he leaves the prison, he comes to a new sense of his "guilt" (I,xlix). "Had he not attempted to expiate and redeem his act, he would never have felt the full weight of his sin, nor would she have felt all the evil done to her." He can no longer take comfort in his own "repentance" nor have any assurance that what he is doing will do any good. Maslova's drunken outburst has revealed the depths of his self-centered quest for redemption, Nekhlyudov's presence, the depths of her anger and resentment. The whole thing is just "terrible." Nekhlyudov seems to have lost hope.

But then, at the center of the novel, Nekhlyudov returns again to see Maslova. Gone is the "feeling of solemnity and the joy of renewal" with which he began his journey of redemption. (I,lix). Now the impending meeting arouses "terror, even a sense of repulsion towards her." Now his intention not to abandon her torments him. However, Maslova comes up to him all "calm and meek" and "begs his forgiveness" for her behavior at the last meeting. She still insists that "he will leave her, that's for certain" and again refuses to marry him. Nekhlyudov still sees an "evil look" on her face, feels that her refusal is a sign of "hatred" and a failure to forgive his act, but now he senses something "good and important." Maslova's ability to ask his forgiveness for her drunken behavior restores Nekhlyudov's faith in her. She tells him she will drink no more and will take the job in the hospital he has arranged for her. "She is a completely different person," Nekhlyudov believes, now "convinced of the invincibility of love." The second half of *Resurrection*, as we saw in Chapter One, begins with Nekhlyudov's return to the family residence and his awakening to a new sense of faith. The first half ends with a triumph of mutual forgiveness. Nekhlyudov and Maslova both see some of their own guilt and ask to be forgiven. Their motivation may be suspect, their sense of their sin uncertain, their resolve for the future unsure, but each has made a gesture toward the other; each has, if only for a moment, stopped judging the other as a fixed entity, Nekhlyudov's "dead woman" and Maslova's "rich man." Once they stop judging the other and admit some of their own guilt, they approach reconciliation. The first half of the novel, then, culminates in the simile which asserts the "fluidity" of human behavior. "People are like rivers, the water in all is the same, everywhere one and the same, but each river is now narrow, now swift, now broad, now calm, now clear, now cold, now muddy, now warm." No person is a fixed entity; no one is good or bad, intelligent or stupid. These are just our judgments of people, our assessments of their character based on actions we may not even understand. In fact people change and therefore there is always hope and the water flows in all. Nekhlyudov's despair over his mission of reconciliation is dispelled, but he has yet to understand the real task of repentance and redemption.

Nekhlyudov's understanding of his task begins with a series of strange chance events in which his past returns to him to enlighten his path to redemption. While walking along the street, he passes a bar, and through the window amidst the dirty tables and the sweaty people with flushed, stupefied faces he sees one man, with raised eyebrows and pouting lips, staring into space, trying to remember something (II,x). Then "suddenly" he hears his name, looks up, and sees the smile and white teeth of his former army friend Shenbok, the very friend who had accompanied him on his fateful visit to his aunt's that Easter long ago. Nekhlyudov now sees his former friend anew, living off the labor and money of others, interested only in good food and horse racing, oblivious to the significance of Nekhlyudov's quest for justice. To Nekhlyudov, Shenbok is a man of the flesh. Shenbok asks Nekhlyudov for his address and then "suddenly his face becomes serious, his eyes stop still and his brows rise." He is trying to recall where Nekhlyudov used to live. But Nekhlyudov sees in the "vacant expression on his face" the image of the man in the bar. The man of the flesh who has forgotten where Nekhlyudov comes from merges with the picture of the man who is trying to remember something. Thus the return of Shenbok leads Nekhlyudov to a new image of himself and his sin. His fateful act was but the result of an empty, spoiled life. Drugged by the surfaces and surfeits of life, he had become vacant, staring into space, trying to remember, although he did not know this, where he came from. To expiate his sin by never abandoning Maslova, even by confronting Missi with the truth of his intentions, even by resolving the issue of his wealth and ownership of the land, will not redeem that inner emptiness, the sense of lostness, of not remembering where he comes from or who he is. The task of redemption must take a new course.

In Petersburg Nekhlyudov goes to the Senate, where he meets by chance another old friend from his student days, Chief Prosecutor Selenin (II,xxiii). Selenin was a man who had found his mission to service early in youth, a person who had believed this service could be best realized through institutions of governmnent. He tried, but, no matter what he did, he "felt that it was not at all what he expected nor what ought to be." But he could not extricate himself from his mission because he was afraid to disappoint those who had helped him and, besides, seeing himself in uniform gave him "pleasure" and bolstered his "self-esteem." Like all upright men of his time, Selenin took a critical approach to institutional religion and believed in "spiritual freedom." But life kept confronting him with the formalities of religion, and he had either to pretend or to remove himself from those situations. He firmly believed he was right in his belief in "spiritual freedom," but, just to be sure, he began to study the "unreasonable": he read theology, learned about the dogmas of the Church, slowly let himself believe them in order to be able to observe the formalities of religion and thus to be able to be like everyone else. But he believes in order to belong. He yields his "spiritual freedom" because he fears isolation from the human community. The dogmas he studied, therefore, are dogmas which deny individual knowledge of truth in favor of the communal experience of it. He reads Khomyakov. Furthermore, for Selenin the formalist, the letter and the dogma are important, if not valid, because they allow him to feel just without having to suffer through to justice. All is done by and through the letter and the dogma. When Nekhlyudov confronts him with Maslova's predicament, Selenin only sees the failing in formal procedures and changes the subject. He had heard that Nekhlyudov was supposed to attend the visiting preacher Kizavetter's talk the day before and he too had been invited but could not go. "Annoyed that Selenin had changed the subject," Nekhlyudov tells him angrily that, yes, he did attend and left in repulsion. What repelled Nekhlyudov was Kizavetter's doctrine of sin and redemption.

> Our sins are so great, the punishment for them so great and in-evitable, that it is impossible to live in anticipation of this pun-ishment. Let us just think, oh dear brothers and sisters, let us just think of ourselves, of our life, of what we are doing and how we are living, how we anger the loving God and how we force Christ to suffer, and we will understand that there is no forgive-ness, there is no way out, there is no salvation, that we are all condemned to perish. . . . But there is the blood which was shed for us by the only Son of God, Who gave Himself up to torment for us. His torment, His blood saves us" (II,xvii)

Selenin tells Nekhlyudov that this doctrine of redemption from sin by Christ's blood is one of the dogmas of the church in which he be-lieves. Nekhlyudov is amazed: "Selenin, who had once been a person close to him and loved by him, suddenly became, as a result of this short conversation, alien, distant, and, if not hostile, then incompre-hensible" (II,xxii). In this encounter with Selenin, the image of his best past, Nekhlyudov uncovers a new truth about the world in which he has lived but not known. What seems to hold this world together is a kind of faith which assumes the existing order is justi-fied in order to justify participation in it, a participation needed in or-der to feel the sense of belonging. The letter of the law and the dogma of the church give firm assurance that this participation, however unjust, is justified. This world does not need to be redeemed because, he believes, it has been redeemed. All is permitted, thanks to Christ's blood. In his encounter with Selenin, Nekhlyudov discovers that the letter of the law and the doctrine of redemption remove the need for responsibility for your actions and therefore eliminate the very no-tion of sin. What remains is to clarify his notion of sin.

This clarification begins when Nekhlyudov meets Mariette, a

seemingly sweet and agreeable young woman who, although married, is well practiced in the art of flirtation. Soon they are chatting, "not only like old but even exclusive friends who understand each other amidst the crowd that does not understand them" (II,xxiv). They make a date for the theater. But then that night, lying in bed recalling Maslova's cause and all the questions tormenting him, "suddenly Mariette's face" flashed before his mind. Everything became confused. The sin of sexual passion which he believed he had been expiating has returned and he again has yielded. He falls asleep with a sense of failure, as "after a big loss at cards." But then the next morning he awakens to the "vileness" of the day before. This vileness, he now sees, however, consisted of no evil act. It was the evil thought that was vile. "An evil act one can repent and not repeat, but evil thoughts beget evil deeds" (II,xxv). The return encounter with his erotic self reveals again a new sense of sin. Sin is not one's past acts but one's present thoughts. The implications of this for his task of redemption are not yet clear, but Nekhlyudov now feels that "however new and difficult what he intends to do may be, it is the only possible life for him now and that however easy and ordinary it would be for him to return to his former ways, that would be death." The erotic temptation, he believes, was a kind of oversleeping, "when you don't quite want to sleep but loll around awhile and snuggle in your bed, even though you know that it is time to get up for the important and joyful task awaiting you." Nekhlyudov's metaphor returns him to the opening scene of the story and marks the beginning of his awakening to a true grasp of his sin. His real task of redemption is at hand.

This task is then dramatically revealed. Nekhlyudov goes to see Maslova at the hospital where she is working, but she is not there. She got "in trouble," it seems, with a physician's assistant, and the doctor had her sent back to prison (II,xxix). Nekhlyudov is "pained" because he feels "shamed" and "ridiculous" for having assumed that Maslova had experienced any change in her soul. She is just "a depraved woman who knows how best to use" him. He leaves the hospital thinking that still his "conscience demands the sacrifice of his freedom for the redemption of his sin," and so he assures himself "with angry obstinancy" that he must marry her, "if only in a fictitious marriage." When he arrives at the prison Maslova appears "again as formerly dressed in white." Nekhlyudov "wanted to treat her as he did the last time, but he *could not* take her hand as he wanted to; she was now so offensive to him." He looks at her tears with "injured pride" and "hatred," while "in his soul two feelings were struggling, good and evil, pity for the one who was suffering and wounded pride." The first wins out. "Suddenly at one and the same time he feels himself guilty and takes pity on her." He leaves the prison feeling what he "had never experienced before: calm joy, peace and love for all people." Nothing Maslova does, he believes, can shake this love, because he "loves her not for himself but for her and for God." What Nekhlyudov does not know is that Maslova is innocent of the "trouble," that he has again judged her and found her guilty, that she knows this but remains silent because she does not believe he could believe her again, that her tear is shed for the love she in fact has for him but which, she believes, since he judges her, he does not have for her. In Nekhlyudov's "pity" for Maslova there is still the assumption of her fallenness, a judgment of her character born of his guilt for his sins against her. About to follow her to Siberia, Nekhlyudov is still the prince and Maslova the prisoner. His love for all others is flawed by his judgment of another. His present thoughts are still bad.

Then his sister, whom he had not seen since his mother's death, comes to see him. He remembers her from the days when she loved his dead friend Nikolenka Irtenev, and in their shared love for him they experienced "what was good in them, what united all people" (II,xxxi). His sister returns from his childhood of belonging, but now, like him, Nekhlyudov believes, she is spoiled. She has married a man motivated only by the desire "to show himself off before people," and Nekhlyudov does not like him or approve of his influence on his sister. When he gets together with his sister and brother-in-law, the inevitable disagreement ensues. Nekhlyudov's offensive manner makes his brother-in-law defensive. If Maslova is being punished, then she must be guilty, because the system of justice has as its aim justice. The brother-in-law calls a thief a thief, believes in punishment and the right to property, and cannot understand why Nekhlyudov tries to work within a system of justice he feels is unjust. But Nekhlyudov notices toward the end of this angered tirade that there is a tear in his brother-in-law's eye. Nekhlyudov leaves "confused," wondering if he has really changed since in being right he has wronged his brother-in-law and hurt his sister. He wakes up the next

morning "repenting what happened with his brother-in-law" and resolved to straighten it out. This encounter with his sister and
brother-in-law raises anew Nekhlyudov's task of repentence and redemption, for his brother-in-law, like Selenin, represents to him the
sin of sins, the participation in the world of unjust justice, and Nekhlyudov's contempt of this sin of sins has seemed to him but the
expression of his love for justice. Now he sees that in his attempt to
redeem his sin by taking up Maslova's cause, he too is guilty of this
complicity. His anger, as a result, has no justification. In his outraged
righteousness, in which he of course resembles the Nekhlyudov of
Lucerne, he has in fact judged his brother-in-law and caused him
pain. His present thoughts may be right, but they are still bad and in
his judgment of others he is still guilty.

The culminating point in Nekhlyudov's mission of reconciliation
comes the next day as he begins his journey to Siberia. He is on a
train. It is a hot summer day. The prisoners are being mercilessly
marched along the torrid pavement toward their punishment. Standing between two cars on the open train platform, watching the fields
and roadbeds pass by, Nekhlyudov "suddenly" recalls seeing one of
the prisoners just left to die because he had not the strength to go on.
"He was murdered, but worst of all no one knows who murdered
him" (II,xl). "No one is guilty and yet people are murdered and murdered by the very people who are not guilty of their death." Like
everyone else the guards see only their "obligations" to what they
judge to be just, and lose sight of the fundamental "relationship of
person to person," the feeling of "love for man" (*chelovekoljubie*).[1] A
storm rises and it begins to rain. "Everything seems to be covered
with lacquer, the green gets greener, the yellow yellower, the black
blacker." "More, more," shouts Nekhlyudov as he "rejoices in the
fields, orchards, and gardens coming to life under the beneficient
(*blagodatnyj*) rain."[2] With the rain comes the sudden joy of life. With

[1] "Love for man" (*chelovekoljubie*) is one of the major spiritual values in the Eastern
Christian tradition. The most common liturgical name for God is the "Lover of Man"
(*Chelovekoljubets*). "Love for man," therefore, is the way to participate in the Divine.
The word should not be confused, as it often is by Western scholars, with the idea of
philanthropy in the modern English sense, although of course it is a calque of the
Greek *filanthrōpia*. Tolstoy's theology is built around this idea of "love for man," but
to my knowledge this is the only instance of his use of the liturgical word.

[2] "Beneficient" (*blagodatnyj*) is an adjective derived from the noun *blagodat'*, which

the rain also comes a new awareness and a new acceptance. "They who serve are impenetrable to the feeling of love for man, like the parched earth to the rain. . . . They are immune to compassion like the stones to vegetation." Unless you receive the rain of "love for man," you will not grow the greenery of compassion. The impenetrability and immunity come from the letter of the law. "These people accept as law what is not law; they do not accept the eternal, immutable, pressing law that God has written in the hearts of men." Nekhlyudov penetrates to the absolute truth, the truth always there and always being given, the truth which in some sense he has always known, even way back in *Lucerne*. Only now Nekhlyudov realizes that the letter of the law or Kizavetter's doctrine of redemption are no different from his own ideas of justice and redemption. They all allow "people to treat people as things." But there is, he now believes, no "position" in which one can "relate to people without love." "Just allow yourself to relate to people without love, as you did yesterday with your brother-in-law," he tells himself, "and there are no limits to the cruelty and brutality toward other people, nor to your own suffering, as I have learned from my whole life." The narrator's opening image of absolute truth, the inevitable return of spring and greenery despite the paved hardness of human society, awakens in Nekhlyudov himself, and he sees that his or anyone's only sin is his lack of love right now, that his or anyone's only redemption is to love right now. Refreshened by the rain and the "awareness of the higher levels of clarity he has achieved in the question that has been bothering him for a long time," Nekhlyudov rides off to Siberia, to a "new world" and "new people" on a new journey of discovery. His experience recalls his old friend Nikolenka's journey away from home in *Boyhood* and his discovery in the rain of an act of charity, which releases a sudden joy of life and a new sense of the expanse of nature.

Maslova in Siberia is a changed woman. In her friend Marya Pa-

---

is the word for "grace." It is striking in this passage, especially since it is a rare word in Tolstoy's vocabulary. The Christian concept of grace as he knew it from his reading in theology displeased Tolstoy for two reasons: in its scholastic expression it absurdly divided up what could only be indivisible and in all its expressions it seemed to weaken the idea of responsibility. See the discussion of grace in his critique of Orthodox theology (23,225-239;1884). To my knowledge Tolstoy never uses the word "grace" (*blagodat'*) in his discussion of grace. For Tolstoy grace is called "God's love" and "God's life."

vlovna, in the one who has ascertained that love does not mean "sexual love," in the one who has discovered that the "sport of charity" is a "habit" to be acquired, the "effort" of which is the "task of life," in the one who has learned how to love, Maslova finds a model for herself (III,iii). From Simonson, from the one who loves Maslova just as she is, not as he judges she is, and for no purpose other than to love, from the one who sees that "everything in the universe is alive, nothing is dead" and that the "task of man is to support the life of the whole and all its parts," from the one who loves and knows what life is, Maslova finally learns she is "Love" and is loved. The love that was abandoned is resurrected not by a love given to resurrect but by a love given freely. Maslova once more feels that she belongs. She has finally recalled Katyusha. Upon meeting her again, Nekhlyudov approaches anew the heights of love for all, "pity and tenderness not only for her but for all people." But now this feeling opens up in him a "flood of love which formerly had no way out." He becomes "sympathetic (*uchastlivyj*) and attentive to all people" (III,v). But still an obstacle remains on his way to love. He has met and befriended a former revolutionary who is now a prisoner and dying from consumption; Nekhlyudov cannot fathom the punishment and the suffering. In the face of death Nekhlyudov goes to town for help. He rides off to the river and gets on a raft, where he meets a "short, raggedy old man." The old man has "no name, no place, no homeland, nothing" (III,xxi). He is, it seems, a "vagabond." He has "no father, no mother, except God the Father and Earth the Mother" and no age because "he always was and always will be." He answers to no one except himself, but goes where God leads him. But the God who leads him "has never been seen," although he has made manifest his only-begotten Son, who exists in the bosom of the Father and the self he answers to is the "one spirit in you, in me, and in him," so that by answering to this self "all are united." The old man is "free" and is to be called "Man." On the raft journeying to the aid of a dying man, perplexed over the questions of death and suffering, Nekhlyudov encounters an emblem of the divine self passing through life, but what the old man's theological utterings mean he does not yet comprehend.

Nekhlyudov fails to understand the emblem of Man because he still wants "to live" by which he means he wants "a family, children, a human life" (III,xxv). Once again he goes to Maslova, hoping against hope that here is his solution to his desire "to live," but Maslova does not understand his way of thinking. He still would serve her, he says, but she corrects him, not her but us. Her last words to him are "forgive me." Confused, Nekhlyudov leaves and goes home to bed, but, not being able to sleep, he takes up the Gospel and has his final awakening. He reads the words of Matthew 18, and the "inner voice of his whole being" tells him the meaning (III,xxviii). After his conversation with Man, the image of the divine self, he now sees that the "simple, certain truth" is that the "only certain salvation from the terrible evil from which people suffer" comes when people see that "they are always guilty before God and therefore are not capable of punishing or correcting others." His attempt to resurrect Katyusha was fundamentally no different from the punishment meted out to criminals. Both proceed from self-serving judgment of others. This he now knows. Because "there are no people who are not guilty," the only thing people can do is what Christ told Peter to do, "forgive always and everyone." With this new awareness of the forgiveness first learned at the center of the novel, Nekhlyudov sees the task of his repentance and redemption and is ready to start anew his mission of reconciliation of all for always.

Nekhlyudov's mission of reconciliation stands in opposition to Anna's. Her story, as we have seen, is a process of increasing hiding from her sin against human relatedness. She denies her guilt even to herself and, instead of forgiving, she resents and takes revenge. In the end she is not redeemed but condemns herself to death. Nekhlyudov, on the other hand, seeks to be redeemed. He is saved, not because he is more worthy, but because he makes the effort to be saved. He begins with a flawed conception of sin as a past act, a single, individual violation of love he can correct. Through a series of moments of partial awareness of truth from which he does not hide, the sinner learns that he lives in a world of violated human relatedness embodied in its very institution of justice and that he himself even now, right now, is violating love. Through life the sinner learns that in order for his soul to keep on growing, he must participate in the redemption of this unjust world, not by expiating some past act of his, nor by judging the unjust world around him, nor by justifying this unjust world through a belief in some mythological past redemption, but by clearing himself of his judgments so that he can right now help to create human relatedness. Reconciliation comes with the clarification of guilt, the realization that we are all sinful, and the fostering of forgiveness, the unconditional giving forth of the beneficent rain of love for all given to us. Reconciled, we are redeemed.

THE THEOLOGY OF REDEMPTIVE LOVE

The doctrine of person upon which Tolstoy rests his theology of redemption is that, by nature untouched by sin, every living being is a loving being, a particle of the whole, like Christ, a son of the God of Life and Love. "A person who is bitter or vicious is not in a normal state; only a person who loves is; and only in a normal state can one do good and see things clearly" (60,75;1856). Even though this normal state of love may seem hidden by our sins and our lusts, all beings are atoms of love for all. By nature, therefore, all beings strive outward and toward each other. "We are all attracted to the all and each other like the particles of one body" (53,106;1896). What hinders the perfection of love for all, the union of all in the all, is the imperfection of each: "Our lack of polish, our roughness, our corners, hinder our union. The attraction already exists, it has nothing to do, one has just to polish oneself, to rub out the corners." The corners of our human existence are our personal bodily passions, lust, all the love for self which covers over the divine love for all within us. "The foundation (osnova), life is the divine particle we are aware of as love. To the extent that our animal passions come loose, to the extent that the crust of animality dries up and falls off, to that extent there is set free the divine principle, the love which is and was in childhood and youth the essence of life, but then was covered over and transformed by the passions" (55,282;1906). All true life then is "resurrection . . . , the raising of love from the grave of the body" (56,74;1907), "from the grave of the personality" (56,77;1907). With this resurrection from the grave of the personality, we are redeemed.

Tolstoy's doctrine of person as a divine core covered by the crust of animality finds its source in Eastern Christian anthropological thought. This tradition bases its theology of man on the Biblical idea of creation in the image and likeness of God. The person is by nature an image of the Divine, whose task it is to be like God in his personality (likeness). Since He is God, Christ is understood to be the perfect image and likeness of God. Eastern Christian thought, as a result, tends to use the doctrine of Christ's person as the model for its doctrine of the human person. This is especially true among Russian religious thinkers in the tradition of Vladimir Solovyov and his idea of God-manhood. The notion of creation in the image and likeness of God gives Eastern Christian thinkers two important options: (1) they have a model of the person which is grounded in a God-given and stable center (image) but allows for free movement and change (likeness) and (2) they have a model of the person which is grounded in an inherent but God-given goodness (image) but allows for the deviation from that goodness called sin. Many seemingly contradictory statements can flow from this model of the person. For example, in Eastern Christian thought man is by nature and by grace good, but man is also sinful. He is Dmitry Karamazov's riddle of the ideal of the Madonna and the ideal of Sodom. Tolstoy himself held just such a view. In the Eastern Christian tradition sin, original and otherwise, is understood as a dark mark on the image—metaphors of rust, dust, dirt, and paint abound—and the cleansing of the image is the act necessary for its restoration. Nekhlyudov calls this process the "cleansing of the soul." The point is, however, that the image remains intact, covered by sin, but waiting to be uncovered. All uncovering restores the image of divinity, and the redemption of life comes with that salvation through restoration called deification. For Tolstoy this process often calls forth the telling metaphor of removing the covers from what is. All human creation is the negative act of restoration which reveals the given. This is what the artist Mikhaylov in *Anna Karenina* knows. Anna remains covered in her armor; Levin removes his covers and in the end stands naked. In the Eastern Christian tradition uncovered, we are redeemed.[3]

Tolstoy's journey through the three stages of human life leads to

[3] I have given a generalized statement of a very complex and rich tradition in which there are many different opinions. The literature on the Eastern Christian theology of the image is vast. For the best introduction to the early formation of this idea and to the basic bibliography, see Jean Daniélou, S.J., *Gospel Message and Hellenistic Culture* (London-Philadelphia, 1973), pp. 387-425. For a more popularized treatment, see George A. Mahoney, S.J., *Man the Divine Icon* (Pecos, New Mexico, 1973). A sound modern interpretation of the tradition by a Russian theologian can be found in Vladimir Lossky, *op.cit.*, pp. 114-134. See also his essay "Image and Likeness," published in his *Orthodox Theology: An Introduction* (Crestwood, New York, 1978), pp. 119-137. For some of the ramifications of this idea, see the collection of his essays *In the Image and Likeness of God*, ed. by J. H. Erickson and T. E. Bird (Crestwood, New York, 1974). See also the succinct discussion of this idea in John Meyendorff, *op.cit.*, pp. 138-150. On the relationship of this idea to icons (images), see Leonid Ouspensky, *The Theology of the Icon* (Crestwood, New York, 1978).

the uncovering of the divine self. The drama of human existence, however, comes from the struggle between the "crust of animality," all our involvement in our physical existence, the passions and concerns associated with our fated quest for success, security, and survival and the "divine particle of love" which is our only success, security, and survival. Human nature is divided, but not into a Cartesian body and mind. Human nature exists through two modes of being in the world, being for self and being for all. The body, the personality, the crust of animality, is the form or limitation of human existence in this life which results from being for self. This is a necessary condition of this life. Tolstoy's notion of the crust of animality reworks Gregory of Nyssa's conception of the garment of skin.[4] The crust of animality is being for self, which is not true life. Being for self hinders true and eternal life, which is being for all. The crust of animality ends in death. True life is attained, therefore, by tearing off the crust of animality, by getting loose from animal passion. Being for all is released by overcoming the passions of being for self. The goal, however, is not stoic *apatheia*, if this is understood as passionless detachment from everything else. The goal is to set loose love for all, our self and everything else. This resurrection of our love for all is called "enlightenment" (*prosvetlenie*); it is the "removal of the covers from what is" (55,82;1904). To the extent that we are enlightened, that we love "all in all," we "are God" (56,78;1907). Deification is our vocation.

> To be like God, one has to desire nothing and fear nothing, just love. As soon as one loves, one does not desire anything or fear anything. To be like the God Jupiter, God the creator, or the God of Sabaoth, is obviously an insane pride and sin, but to be like the God whom we know only through love and reason is not only no sin but a necessity in order to get rid of suffering and be calm and joyful. To be like God one need only love. To love one need only open up and take off what has shut off the source of living water, the divine life which is in us. (54,39;1900)

What shuts off the flow of the living water of divine life within us, being for all, is being for self, "pride, vainglory, self-esteem, self-ex-

---

[4] For a discussion of Gregory of Nyssa's doctrine of person, see Daniélou and Musurillo, *op.cit.*, pp. 10-23.

hibition, lack of humility. One touch of this personal feeling and the flower of love about to open closes" (52,84;1893). This "concern for yourself, for your personal life is the theft of the time and power (*sila*) which belong to the master, as when a bailiff buys himself a place near his master's and then takes the cattle and seed and everything else from the master's place to his own" (51,80;1890). The most dangerous and widespread form of this concern for yourself, paradoxically, however, is vanity, "doing everything for other people's opinion," the desire for approval (57,68;1909). This concern for people's opinion is particularly powerful because it "substitutes for religious feeling" and "borders on love, mainly on the desire to be loved, but represents itself in the form of love for others. 'I do not act contrary to people's opinion in order not to anger them and I do it according to their opinion in order to do something pleasant for them.' " *Love for* turns out to be a desire for *love from*. This is the central problem Tolstoy faces in his theology of love. The greatest happiness in life is to be loved, *love from*, but the only way we can acquire *love from* is to express *love for*. However, if we express *love for* in order to acquire *love from*, the intention of the *love for* spoils the *love from*. We then can experience approval, perhaps even fame, but no true sense of belonging or involvement. We want to participate in the world, belong to others, and experience human relatedness, but if we seek to participate and belong we will find only ourselves. How can we love our neighbor as ourself but not for ourself?

IN ORDER to grasp his God of Life and Love, Tolstoy constructed a metaphysical picture of God and the whole universe in some sense beyond or outside the categories of space and time. Likewise, in order to comprehend sin and suffering in this world, Tolstoy fashioned an explanation of the human experience of evil which placed God in some sense beyond or outside the category of causality. God does not mete out punishment. So also with love. The good, that is, love, must also be removed from the causal nexus. God does not offer a reward. This is what the peasants who reap the hay know and what Levin learns in the end. In a rare and therefore telling comment on an Old Testament story, Tolstoy makes precisely this point:

> Moses did not see the promised land which he led his people to.
> I love that allegory. We often regret that we do not see the fruits

of our labor, but not seeing, doing without the expectation of a reward, is the necessary, most essential condition of any good deed. (56,25;1907)

The Church's teaching about heaven and hell beyond this world, Tolstoy argues, express in "metaphoric (*obraznaja*) form" this same truth, that "the good can have no real, actual reward" (63,390;1886). *Love for* must not be understood as love for any purpose or profit. The simple golden rule—do unto others as you would have others do unto you—must be purged of all utilitarian motivation. Good works are not good if they are done to make you or others feel good. Philanthropy either assuages your guilt before others or quells their resentment of you. *Love for* cannot be motivated by a fear of loss of *love from* or for the purpose of acquiring *love from*.

For Tolstoy, then, all "moral activity is always independent of utility, i.e., it is outside space and time" (54,141;1902). A moral act does not arise from the will of the personality, the self that exists in space and time and measures by cause and result. "If a person considers the results of an act, then the motives of the act are not religious ones" (53,180;1898). Religious motivation comes, not from a concern for results, for purpose, profit, or even fear of punishment, all of which are after all always unknown and unpredictable, but from the inner assurance of doing what you ought to do, your own sense of mission in regard to all, even and especially when it may seem regardless of all. This mission, however, is your own mission only to the extent that you are not your personality, the self that seeks its own purpose and profit and avoids punishment and pain.

> I was taking my morning walk and praying and felt with particular clarity the possibility of life without the expectation of a reward (I have never had the fear of punishment), but just in order to fulfill my destined purpose. Like the cell of a body. Not to expect retribution for my acts, to desire nothing but the fulfillment of my destined purpose, to see in that everything, both the beginning and the end of everything which is necessary for a good life. (55,47;1904)

What we ought to do is only the expression of who we really are. Who we really are is not our personality, but our divine self, God's love for all in us, but hidden by the coverings of our passions and purposes.

To fulfill our destined purpose, therefore, is not a positive accomplishment for which we are to be rewarded. It is a negative act, a renunciation of our own passions and purposes which allows God's love to be accomplished through us. The good that we do, the love we give forth, therefore, has no merit in it.

Having fulfilled all that he ought, a human being has only not done evil, he is only not guilty. He can be not guilty, but there is no merit in this. . . . You are crossing a bridge which has been prepared for you and you can do nothing. You can not drown, but you cannot fly above the water. And if you cross and do not fall in, then there is nothing to be proud of. Be satisfied that there is a bridge and you are crossing it. Try to cross it better. That's all. . . . All moral teaching lies in this. (55,132;1905)

Still, even though acts of love have no merit, it is not quite accurate to say that love has no reward. While there is no reward for love, there is reward in love. Just as we are not punished for our sins but by them, so we are rewarded not for our good deeds but by them. "There is no more joyful state than goodness, love. It's reward is right now" (*sejchas*) (56,31;1907). If *love for* is experienced "in eternity, in the present, in the non-temporal moment" then it is its reward (56,96;1908). And since love is its own reward, it is also its own motivation.

They say that the good needs no reward. That is correct if you understand reward as external, in the future. But without reward, without the good giving what a person strives for, what motivates (*dvizhet*) him, without it giving happiness (*blago*), it would not be necessary to do good. It's a question of remembering what is true happiness. True happiness is not in something external or future, but in something internal and present, in the improvement of the soul. It is both the reward and the motivation. (54,108-09;1901)

Love, then, is not beyond causality, but a special form of it. To be sure, there is no external result which serves as the aim or purpose of *love for*. Rather, since *love for* must be understood outside time and space, by which Tolstoy means that time and space must be reduced to the mathematical minimum of the infinitely small point, *love for* is in this moment and in this place both cause and result, the labor and the reward.

If *love for* is outside the causal nexus as ordinarily understood, however, then it also follows that *love for* could not be a "predilection" (*pristrastie*) (58,110;1910) for a particular person or group of persons nor an attraction to or preference for the "object of love" (53,10;1895). This is what Prince Andrew learns. If *love for* is understood as an activity which singles out particular beings from the totality of particular beings, then this *love for* is in fact determined, limited, and evoked by the object loved. Such love is caused, and there can be no real spontaneous giving forth of self. But "there is nothing to evoke love for; you just have to remove what hinders the manifestation of it" (56,45;1907). *Love for* is not *love of*. The confusion of these two types of love, Tolstoy believes, is the particular confusion of the modern era, where "nothing is ranked higher than exclusive love, and true love is just called hypocrisy" (58,40;1910). The "moral person struggles with being-in-love (*vljublënnost'*) and exclusive love, while the immoral person indulges them" (53,191;1898). It is this exaltation of exclusive love which Tolstoy believed modern culture, particularly most modern literature, and especially novels, indulged in and which, as we have seen, he examined and condemned in *Anna Karenina*.

Still, *love of* particular beings is not necessarily an evil. To be sure "being-in-love," passionate or erotic love, is a most pernicious form of love because the love is evoked by the object and therefore one needs the object to have the love. The preference for the object becomes obsessive, and as a consequence the one in love feels a need to possess or control the object. Both Masha and Anna experience this. There is another kind of exclusive or preferential love, however, which at its best borders on *love for*. "Love for our children, spouses, and brothers is the model of that love which ought to be for all" (58,117;1910). This sort of "particular, exclusive love for neighbor is necessary only in order to show how one should love all. To see in prostitutes our daughters and to suffer for them just as we would for our beloved daughter" (57,75;1900). Such exclusive love can serve as an example only if it is not *love of* the object nor a covert form of *love from*, but a limited form of *love for*. Just as suffering accepted is the way to learn who you are, so exclusive love for family and friends is the way to learn to love as you should. Through suffering you discover your identity; through loving family and friends you discover your vocation.

The preferential love we have for those close to us, however, can never be the real type of *love for*. *Love for* by definition has no bounds or limits. But preferential love, even if it seems a spontaneous giving forth not evoked by the object, is still bound by the object. Preferential love can be rejected and possibly turned into suffering, resentment, and hatred. Preferential love can diminish; *love for* is "ever growing" (56,375;1908). Peferential love almost always has some hidden form of *love of* the object or expectation of *love from* the object. "Attachment to or affection for those who are useful, pleasant, or comforting to me can in no way be love. Pagans do the same thing. So do dogs" (50,127;1889).

For Tolstoy "the only real love is the one whose object is unattractive" (53,45;1895). Therefore the real type of *love for* is love for the enemy. "To love our enemies, to do good to those who do us evil . . . is only the natural attraction of a person who has understood the essence of love. To do good to those who love us, to love those who love us is not love and does not give that special, singular, and greatest bliss (*blago*) which is characteristic of love. That bliss is given only by loving people who do evil" (56,97;1908). The "sweetness of this love . . . is in reverse proportion to the attractiveness of the object of love" (53,100;1896). Only in love for the enemy is there the guarantee that there is no hidden love of the object or covert desire of love from the object. The only love that is certainly not at bottom a form of self-love is love for those who hate us. Therefore "divine love, love for God, is known only through love for our enemies" (56,104;1908). This is what Natasha knows instinctively as she prays for her enemies but not for their defeat.

Love for the enemy is the type of *love for* because it is certainly not love for human glory; it is not an appeal for approval. The more you cultivate love for the enemy, the more you grow in *love for*. In order to grow in love, therefore, one must not hide from one's enemies but make use of their enmity. To free oneself from the temptation of "human glory," you should "rejoice at every manifestation of enmity (*neljubov'*) toward you" and desire from people "humiliation and shame, enmity and hatred" (51,28;1890). This is how Tolstoy understands the piety of holy foolishness (*jurodstvo*). The fool for Christ's sake is the one who seeks humiliation from others to test and perfect his love for those others. But this quest for humiliation could itself be a subtle if perverted form of a need for human glory, so that humiliation and offense not so much sought for as accepted, especially when they are unjust, make the kind of "involuntary holy foolishness" Tolstoy believes is "the best school of the good" (53,218;1899). Karenin's love for the enemy is flawed precisely because it was a love in the "eyes of the world"; he could not bear the humiliation and shame his enemy unjustly caused him. Karenin was not practiced in the school of foolishness.

Love for the enemy is the type of our *love for* because at root it is a negative form of love. Love for the enemy is not a reaching out to the object, but a clearing within oneself of any resistance to the object. You cannot force yourself to experience *love for*; you cannot call it forth; all you can do is "concentrate all your energy on not not loving, on not allowing into your soul any hostile feelings" (52,66;1890). Love for the enemy is "negative love, not doing (*nedelanie*) what is against (*protiv*) love"; the "main characteristic of Christian love is love for those who abuse us, for the enemy, non-resistance" (*neprotivlenie*) (56,55;1907). Love for the enemy expresses itself in non-action, non-resistance to the evil of the enemy. What Tolstoy learned through self-scrutiny is that all action against and resistance to evil are rooted in anger, in hatred, in non-love, not in *love for*. Non-resistance to evil is the law of action that follows from the real type of *love for*.

> Yes, yes, to love our enemies, to love them that hate us is not an exaggeration, as it seems at first; it is the basic idea of love. Just as non-resistance, turning the other cheek, is not an exaggeration or a metaphor but the law, the law of non-resistance without which there is no Christianity, so there is no Christianity without love for those who hate us, precisely for those who hate us." (56,55;1907)

The way to love is to love when you do not love or are not loved. This is what Olenin learned. It is the fundamental idea in Tolstoy's theology of love. Tolstoy does not preach a love for sinners. For him the sinner is an abstract idea, and he had no inner need to judge distant others such as prostitutes or murderers as sinners. These he could love, at least abstractly and intellectually. Tolstoy preaches a love for those whom I judge have sinned against me. The enemy is the one I do not love because he does not love me, and non-resistance is the action of love when I am not loved. Love of enemy and non-resistance to evil, therefore, are expressions of *love for* not filtered through or blocked by the personality. Love must be "liberated from everything personal, from every slightest bit of predilection for yourself toward the object of love" (37,221;1908). "Every loving response to evil" comes from the "destruction of the personality." Such love, which is manifested only with the shedding of the crust of animality, gives the "highest bliss," the destruction of "all suffering" and the "main scarecrow that evokes all resistance, the fear of death." In the moment of true *love for* you live with others, not separated from them by your personal desires or fears, in the highest bliss of belonging which cannot be taken away even by your enemy or the scarecrow of death.

LOVE for the enemy is the type of *love for*, but it is not the way to complete expression of *love for*. *Love for* always means love for all. "Love is not exclusive attachments, but a good rather than evil relationship with every living being" (53,172;1897). *Love for* all includes "love for people, animals, nature, and yourself" (57,32;1909). This love for all is what is meant by love for neighbor.

> If you say that birds, horses, dogs, and monkeys are completely alien (*chuzhoj*) to us, then why not say that primitive people and black people are alien to us? And if you deem such people alien, then with the same right the black people can deem whites alien. Who is the neighbor? The answer is simple. Do not ask who is the neighbor, but do for everything living what you want to be done for you. (45,50-51;1910)

There is no way to make a distinction among living beings, or gradations of human beings: insects, plants, Zulus, Balus, Cossacks, Frenchmen, children, old senile people, idiots, "there are no boundaries. I am thankful to Darwinism for that" (51,14;1891). The real love for all, then, is "love for neighbor, equal and the same for all" (54,150;1902), "without the slightest distinction among the fiercest enemy, the somewhat unpleasant person and the most sympathetic person" (51,74;1890).

This love, equal and the same for all, cannot be imagined as some program for the future or some idealistic position one takes vis-à-vis the world. Love for all is "right-now love" (sejchasnaja ljubov') (56,168;1908). Love for neighbor is love for the one right near you (blizhnij, "neighbor," literally, "the one near you"). *Love for* occurs only in the present point in space and time, here and now. "The time is right now, this minute, the person is the one with whom you are dealing right now, and the task is to save your soul, i.e., to do the task of love" (53,199;1898). This is what Nekhlyudov learns in his experience of the beneficent rain of love for man: his violation of love for his brother-in-law is his real violation of the task of love, not his distant past, but his "right now." Natasha, who wants her love "right now, this minute," knows this intuitively.

What is most characteristic of this "right-now love" is that it is creative of love. Right-now love increases the amount of love through the manifestation of love. "As soon as love is manifested, it increases love right now, immediately in the one to whom it is manifested. This manifestation in the one loved then increases the love of the one loving, so that love grows of itself. This cannot help but be, because this love is God" (54,12;1900). The here and now is a reciprocal moment, and the event of love is a feed-back event. You love, but not in order to be loved; your love for the other returns to you as love for you which you then return again and which is then returned again, *ad infinitum*. In right-now love, to love and to be loved merge and nurture each other. This reciprocal, feed-back event of right-now love is the experience of God's love, right now within you. Since God's love is His love for all, eternally going out from Him and eternally returning to Him, in an ever-increasing embrace of everything which He is, the unceasing act of love which He does, your experience of God's love within you in your right-now reciprocal love for neighbor is the experience of an increase in love, a moment of growth for your eternally growing soul, your participation in the Kingdom of God coming to be.

Still, we can ask, what is the content of this *love for*? Is *love for* just the negative action of removing your resistances to the other, simply a letting go and letting be? Or can this negative action be related to a human emotion, even if its first cause is divine? What is the psychological experience or feeling a human being can identify with this *love for*? For Tolstoy, the answer to the proper content of *love for*, as so often, lay in the wisdom of the Russian people preserved in their language, the word that reveals. *Love for* is a kind of compassion.

In the language of the people "to take pity on" (*zhalet'*) means "to love" (*ljubit'*). This is a correct definition of that kind of love which more than anything else unites people and evokes their loving activity. There is love when upon seeing the beauty, the truth, the joyfulness of a person or any being, you feel your unity with that being and want to be him. This is the love of a lower being for a higher one. There is also a love, and it is most necessary, which is the transferal of self into another, suffering person, compassion, the desire to help him. This is the love that takes pity on. The first love can change into envy, the second into repulsion. The first love is love of God, saints, the best people, a love which is characteristic of human beings. It is especially important, however, to develop in oneself the second kind of love and not let it be perverted into repulsion. In the first kind of love we regret (*zhaleem*) that we are not like those better than us, in the second we regret that people are not like us: we are healthy, whole; they are ill, crippled. And in this regard it is especially important to try to develop in oneself such a relationship with the spiritually as well as the physically ill, the depraved, the errant, the proud. Do not get angry with them, do not argue with them, do not judge them, and if you cannot help them, then take pity on them for those spiritual qualities and illnesses which they bear not less but more burdensomely than physical ones. (55,278-79;1906)

For Tolstoy there are two fundamentally different kinds of love, *love of* a being perceived to be greater or better than yourself, who serves as a model for you or as an object you wish to attain. You desire to merge with or be identified with this higher being, and the experience of identification is an experience of expansion and improvement. Such love is part of the process of self-perfection. At its lowest level such *love of* desires the object for the pleasure or profit it offers: this *love of* may mask as *love for* and conceal the desire for *love from*. At its highest, however, this love is the *love of* God. This *love of*, Tolstoy believes, is inherent in human beings, what is characteristic of them at their best in their humanity and in their personality. This *love of* resembles Plato's eros. But *love of* is not *love for*; it is not God's love. God's love by definition could never be love of a higher being nor love based on desire. God's love can only be a free giving forth of self to all. God's love for man is compassion: "to take pity on people means to love in God's way" (po-bozh'i) (53,106;1896). Love for the enemy and love for neighbor means to identify with them, not because you want to be like them or liked by them, but because you want to give of yourself to them, to help them. The minimum of help, the negative action from which this compassion-love begins, is the clearing of your own anger, hatred, fear, or judgment, all your resistance to them. But this clearing of resistance is precisely what forgiveness is: "to forgive means to stop judging and hating" (53,70;1895). God's love is compassion, and compassion is forgiveness. Ivan Ilych sees the white light, feels the sudden joy, and learns that there is no death when he takes pity and thus forgives.

To love in God's way we have to take pity on others, which begins with our forgiveness of them. But since this forgiveness is the cessation of our judgment and hatred of others, it is really the cessation of our own violation of love, the end of our sin. "If I could forgive everyone everything, then this very state of forgiveness, of reconciliation with the whole world (mir), would wipe away all traces of my sins in the world" (51,104;1890). The past acts called sin are not black marks against me but against others, and they are erased by me in the present moment when I stop sinning against others, when I forgive. This means, however, that when I forgive, I am forgiven. "Our sins are forgiven only if we forgive all from our heart, i.e., if we love all. If you get to love, then all is conquered and former sins are unbound and do not hinder" (51,73;1890). Furthermore, since the violation of love is my sin and forgiveness the cessation of my sin, then the act of forgiveness is not in fact a forgiveness of others but of myself. Once you have cleared yourself of your judgments of the other, "you will see the divine essence of his love and you will not have to nor should you forgive him; you will just have to forgive yourself for not loving God in the one in whom He is and for not seeing God because you did not love" (53,12;1895). To "take pity on," then, is not to pity the other in a condescending fashion, still less to pity yourself, but so to end your judgment of the other as a personality that you will see their divine self which in no way need be forgiven, since it is forgiveness itself, the giving forth of self. Once you have "taken pity on" the other in this sense, then what follows is to forgive yourself your past acts, which separated you from others, your failure to see God in them, which resulted from your failure to love them. But this act of

self-forgiveness is nothing other than a tearing off of the crust of animality from your own divine self, a discovery of the particle of God's
love within. Our self-forgiveness is God's forgiveness of us in us. Furthermore, since with the recovery of our divine self we uncover
God's love for all in us, our experience of this love for all is our love
of God. The two types of love merge; the human *love of* is transformed by the divine *love for*. To tear away the crust of animality
does not mean to annihilate our self, but to transform it. God's love
for all in us transfigures our *love of* and we become "like God."

For Tolstoy, therefore, God's love is compassion, which is His forgiveness of all, which is our justification and redemption. This
means that our forgiveness of each and all in any moment of right-
now reciprocal love for neighbor is the experience of God's forgiving,
redeeming love in us. In our forgiveness we experience reconciliation, and in our reconciliation we are redeemed. There was no past
act of forgiveness or redemption. Christ is not our redeemer, but the
type of our redemption. With His forgiveness, which is His love for
all, especially the enemy, the one who killed Him, He conquered all,
all death, all sin, and thus showed us the way to our redemption, our
way to love. The model of this doctrine of redemption comes from
the Eastern Christian tradition. In the West redemption has long
been considered a kind of reparation. Christ redeemed man by taking
on all human sin and offering Himself as a sacrifice which established the atonement of God and man. But in the East redemption is
understood as the victory of Christ over death and the other satanic
forces which hold men captive. The cross is the symbol, not of
Christ's Passion and death, but of His resurrection and the eternal
life won for all.[5] Tolstoy's theology of redemptive love is cast in this
Eastern mold. But for Tolstoy faith in a past act which was effective
of our redemption and, to the extent that we hold that faith, a guarantee of our salvation, is a faith that robs us of our responsibility, our
duty, our vocation, and therefore ultimately of our identity. To him
Kizavetter's theology of redemption is the absurd extreme of such a
faith. For Tolstoy real faith understands that true redemption is ours,
given to us to be accomplished. The sin of the world is forgiven al-

[5] The issues involved in the definition of redemption are discussed clearly by Jaroslav Pelikan, *The Emergence of the Catholic Tradition (100-600)*, volume one of *The
Christian Tradition* (Chicago, 1971), pp. 141-152. See also volume two, pp. 137-139.

ready, but the forgiveness we have not yet experienced. The forgiveness of the sin of the world is ours to achieve; it will be given when all forgive each other. The doctrine of redemption, which is the doctrine of Christ's work, becomes the doctrine of work for all. Only in our acceptance of our relatedness will we uncover God's love for all. "We must be saved all together."

TOLSTOY's lifelong theological task was to describe the religion of Christ, "purged of faith and mysteriousness" (47,37;1855). To do this he sought not only to get beyond the dogmatic theology of the Orthodox Church as he knew it, but also, as we recall, to rid Christianity forever of what he believed was the Hebraic conception of a wrathful God taken over from the Old Testament and the Hebraic interpretation of Christianity he believed was the legacy of St. Paul. But, four years before his death, quite typically, he was becoming "more and more occupied with the idea of divorcing the Gospels from the Old Testament and St. Paul," which he admits is what "in part I have unconsciously done" (55,263;1906). What he in fact did, and not so unconsciously, was to exclude the Old Testament from scriptural revelation and to purge the Gospels of what he did not need or find intelligible. In place of the epistles of St. Paul he put the first epistle of John the Divine. The essence of Christianity, purged of mystery and the Hebraic tradition, lay for Tolstoy in an ethic and metaphysics of love. This love is God and the logos of the world. Our experience of this love given to us becomes our task of creation in the world.

Tolstoy's theology is his finest articulation of his ideal way of seeing and being in the world. This theology, however, was not derived directly from scripture; the ideas emerge primarily from Tolstoy's experience. That his ideas are shaped by the tradition of Eastern Christianity only proves the point, for Tolstoy experienced life within that tradition. His theological understanding of reality—his view of God and the universe, of sin, suffering and death, of forgiveness, redemption and reconciliation—was forged in the smoldering furnace of his own life. From his fundamental estrangement and need for belonging, Tolstoy shaped his notion of the God of Life and Love. From his firm belief in self-perfection, he moved to an image of an eternally growing soul. From his primal experience of relatedness lost, he derived an interpretation of sin as disassociation among people. From his confrontation with his own forms of disassociation, he saw his way to love. From his need for approval, what he called "human glory," he fashioned his understanding of genuine love as a right-now reciprocal act given forth to the one whom you are with. From the stubborn, self-centered mind of the master who knows better and petulantly judges others, he shaped a conception of love as the clearing within the self of one's own anger, resentment, and judgment, in short, love as forgiveness. Tolstoy found justification for his theological views in the Gospels, but his interpretation of the Gospels rests on attitudes and assumptions which he discovered within himself and then brought to the texts. The truth of the Good News is never doubted, but Tolstoy's theology is shaped by and from his experience. His religious ideas are not a new discovery of his later years, when he consciously studied religious and theological works; his later ideas, including his understanding of such works, are the clarified articulations of what he learned throughout his years is the meaning of life and therefore the way to love.

In his theology Tolstoy had to confront three central doctrines of Christianity, at least as he understood them: creation, original sin, and redemption. In each case, he came to see, our misunderstanding of the truth these doctrines may contain or be concealing arises from the assumption that they refer to some past act. But for Tolstoy any past act could at best be our understanding of some past act and in any case is our particular separation of an event from the totality of events and therefore an inevitable falsification of the reality of the whole. In the understanding of past acts, we assume a kind of cause-effect relationship which is contrary to the logic of the All. The All is that which is coming to be the All. The universe, and in some sense God too, is *im werden*. Tolstoy does not quite share the Greek assumption that pure being is superior to becoming. To the Greeks becoming implied deficiency. For Tolstoy becoming is the process of perfection and therefore the life of the Divine. To him there is no God outside the unfolding universe and therefore no God the Creator outside everything else. God, what is, is the All, the everything that is being created by everything else which is His instrument of creation. The sin of the world, the sum total of moral and physical evil, is neither of God's creation, as usually understood, nor the result from or consequence of a past act of original sin by any one person or even by Adam-Man. The "sin of the world" is the present residue of imperfection which impedes us on our path to perfection. Suffering from the "sin of the world" is our medicine and lesson. Since there is no past act of original sin, there is no need for a past act of redemption. Through our suffering from our sin we see our sin and learn to overcome it now. In our present moment we can stop sinning, which means we can start loving. In our love our sin is forgiven, we are all reconciled, and therefore we are redeemed.

In his theology of becoming, which is a theology of perfection, Tolstoy turns away from doctrine as teaching about past acts, divine or human. In the logic of the All, there is no past or future.

> One must desire only what is being accomplished (sovershaetsja) in the present (nastojashchee, also means "the real"). To desire in the past is regret, remorse; to desire in the future is fantasies, plans. And in the present one can desire only one thing: to fulfill in the best possible way one's duty (dolzhnoe), i.e., for a slave, the will of the master; for a person, the will of God. (55,178;1908)

This experience of the present moment, of the real, is the experience of doing the will of God, the experience of love. Tolstoy's religion looks not to past guilt or past redemption nor to future salvation, but to "happiness (blazhenstvo) on earth" (47,37;1855) in right-now love. What is hidden in the experience of the present moment —"Christ's teaching is the moment: live in the present" (48,327;1880)—we shall see in the last chapter of this book.

THE JOURNEY OF DISCOVERY

The first artistic articulation that Tolstoy attempted after his major crisis and the period of theological study that ensued was the short, unfinished work The Notes of a Madman (1884). Like Lucerne, this piece, at least in part, can be traced to a specific experience in Tolstoy's life, one that occurred just after he finished War and Peace. While on a trip to buy an estate, Tolstoy stopped over in the town of Arzamas, and that night, as he wrote to his wife, ". . . it was two in the morning, I was very tired, wanted to sleep, and wasn't in pain. But suddenly I was overcome with an anxiety, terror, and horror I had never experienced before" (83,167;1869). The Arzamas terror was a moment of extreme estrangement from life, the sense of horror at the scarecrow of death, a crisis of vocation experienced upon the completion of a major work. The moment corresponds in kind, therefore, to the crisis recorded in great detail in *A Confession*, the crisis of vocation after *Anna Karenina*. In Tolstoy's quest for perfection of his eternally growing soul, success calls forth a scrutiny of the path he has followed and a fear of failure in the face of death. Quite appropriately, then, *The Notes of a Madman* incorporates the Arzamas terror into a literary image of the Tolstoyan crisis. The madness consists of the transformation of a Stranger near death into a Resident of life. The work is autopsychological.

The unnamed hero of the first-person narrative is thirty-five years old, which is according to Tolstoy the "most difficult, critical age," (57,93;1909). At about this time in life the "development and growth of the body is coming to an end and the development and growth of the spirit should be beginning," although most people do not see this and continue to focus their concern on their physical development only. The madman is no exception. He had his moments of "sexual passion" and spent some time in pursuit of women. He had, in short, loved like everyone else, except in his innocent childhood. Then, as he now recalls, all loved each other and he despaired when people did not love. This despair over the loss of love was the first symptom, he says, of his present illness. When the housekeeper got angry with nanny, he was "so overcome with horror," so pained by what seemed terrifying and incomprehensible, that he hid his head under the blanket while recollecting the moment one of the servants had beaten a boy. This "despair" recalled to him his aunt's stories of Christ's passion: "they crucified him, beat him, tormented him, but he kept on praying and did not judge them." "The people were evil, but He was good" (*dobryj*). This image of love and goodness the madman never forgot.

The madman then tells the story of his madness. Once, not too long ago, he took a trip to a neighboring province to purchase an estate. He was enjoying the ride, night came, he dozed off, and then "suddenly he awoke." "Why am I going? Where am I going?" he "suddenly" wondered, realizing that there was "no need to go into that distance" where he could "die in an alien (*chuzhoe*) place." The Stranger wakens to the question of faith. Terrified, he drove on to the town of Arzamas to spend the night. The "square, white room" with the "red drapery" on the window depresses him, but he lies down to go to sleep. "Again he is awakened" by that overwhelming anxiety, the sense of being lost without purpose on a journey toward death in a foreign place. Only now he sees that he is on the journey because he is "running away" from something, from himself, who "will be neither increased or decreased" by that purchase he is to make. "I am always with myself" and "I can't stand myself." The "voice of death" speaks up, and he feels torn apart. "My whole being felt the need and right to life, while at the same time I felt that death was being accomplished within me." "There is nothing in life, only death." "The red, white, square terror" turns his attention away from his purchase, and he sees himself for what he has been, "without a drop of goodness" (*dobrota*). He feels "anger at himself and what made him this way." He thinks of the God whom he had long forgotten, and automatically begins to pray. The next day he returns home to his routine, but now "everything is boring." He begins to go to church.

Again the madman goes on a business journey, this time to Moscow. Again he finds himself in a "narrow room," and "suddenly" he is overwhelmed by the "Arzamas terror." Only now the thought of a life that ends in "death, the destruction of everything," raises the question of faith. "If You are, reveal to me why I exist and who I am." He begins to pray for an answer but gets none. "If You existed, You would have told me, but You do not exist, there is only despair and I do not want that, I do not want that." He again returns to his routine, but now knows that he has an "unresolved question." He increases his church attendance, even fasts and communes, but "just in case."

Again he goes on a trip away from home, this time to hunt. "It's winter and snowy out in the woods" and "suddenly" he "feels that he has gotten lost." He becomes frightened, and both the Arzamas and the Moscow terror return now a hundredfold. "Death here? Why death? What is death?" Again he wants to "reproach God, but now "suddenly" feels that he "dare not," that he "ought not to," that he "alone is guilty." He begins "to pray for His forgiveness" and feels "loathsome to himself." He then comes to, gets up, and quickly finds his way. The terror is gone, and he feels "joyful." In the expanse of nature he comes to the sudden joy of life. He goes home to his room to pray, "begging forgiveness and recalling his sins." On this third journey the madman learns that he has no "drop of kindness," not because of what has been done to him but of what he has done. He repents and sees who he is, but not yet what he must do. Then once again, and finally, he goes off on a journey to buy an estate as he had done at the beginning. On the way home, however, he encounters an old woman who tells him of her dire "need." He comes home and "suddenly becomes ashamed." His "profit," he realizes, is "based on her poverty and misery." "Suddenly" he is "enlightened with the truth." The peasants are "people like us." "Suddenly something that had long pained him seemed to be torn away, as though something were being born," and he feels "joyful." He again experiences the sudden joy of life. The covering of his passion for profit is rent asunder and he no longer sees himself separated from the people. Again he goes to church, and "suddenly" it becomes clear "that all this ought not to be, that it is not, and if it is not, then there is no death or fear." The "light completely enlightens him," and he walks out onto the porch, gives away all his money to the beggars, and strolls home, chatting "with the people."

The *Notes of a Madman*, because it is unfinished and somewhat schematic in its detail and psychology, lays bare a central feature of Tolstoy's fiction. In this autopsychological work Tolstoy did not choose to focus on his one experience of the "Arzamas terror." Rather, he represented the disguised character, an abstract figure who lives for his own profit, through selected scenes separated by time but in the narrative strung together to create an image of psychological development. In the major fiction such scenes are interrupted by other elements in the narrative; here in the simple tale they are not. This psychological development is represented through a series of cumulative questions that come to the character "suddenly." These sudden questions raise the issue of faith. They ask who he has been, what he has done and who he should be, what he should do. The questions of faith glance backward and forward. The answers to the questions entail a negation: he learns that what he has been doing is not what he must do. The process of change requires the destruction of what is "not right" (*ne to*), the dispelling of illusions of the self, the shedding of the covers that hide you from yourself. Each critical moment results in a rejection of some old assumption or habit or view which leads to a new way of being. This is the process of tearing off the crust of animality. The loss of the animal self becomes the discovery of the divine self. In the end he uncovers his original goodness. This journey of discovery can be defined, then, as a series of cumulative crises in which the character discovers a negative which he then sheds with the resultant release of the positive.

The experience of sudden questions of faith mark the turning points on the journey of discovery. What is significant is the suddenness of the questions. "Suddenly" is one of the most common adverbs in the story, as in Tolstoy's language in general. It is not at all clear psychologically why the character asks the question at this moment or in this place. The moments of sudden question occur, however, outside the routine of daily life. They are shocks of recognition, awakenings to the immediate surroundings, which to the character become emblematic of the world in which he resides, a barren room or an expanse of nature. The sudden questions of faith are asked in a moment of assessment of self and other by the voice of conscience, which appears as the "voice of death" but asks the questions of life. The critical questions of faith are sudden because they are this voice of conscience, the divine self which is not a personality and has no psychological motivation. To the person they just happen spontaneously. The sudden question, like the sudden joy of life, is an experience of grace.

These cumulative moments of revelation are the process of learning by life, not by the mind. This process of learning is the ordering principle of the journey of discovery. But this journey of discovery is the ordering principle of the characters' experience in all of Tolstoy's longer narratives. Thus *Notes of a Madman*, the work composed just after the conversion, articulates in a simple image the deep structure of Tolstoy's major fictions. The main heroes, Nikolenka, Olenin, Prince Andrew, Pierre, Levin, and Nekhlyudov, all, although variously, go through such a series of cumulative revelations which result from sudden questions of faith posed by their lives in moments freed from custom and routine, often in the face of death. These revelations lead to new ways of seeing and being for all. The hero of *A Confession* takes the same journey. But the pattern of this journey also reflects Tolstoy's idea of the path to redemption, the way to salvation through the uncovering restoration called deification. The structure of the journey of discovery is the structure of the process of salvation. And this is so because the autopsychological fiction is grounded in the same moral and religious life from which the theology grew. In Tolstoy the experience is tried out in a fictional image and worked out in a theological idea.

THE PERFECT type of Tolstoy's fiction is *Master and Man*. This late (1895) narrative is an emblematic journey of discovery and a parable of the way to love. Vasily Andreevich Brekhunov, a "local merchant of the second guild," is the one who thinks he is the master (i). He is in a most profound sense, therefore, a liar and a braggart. His name (*brekhun*) suggests both. He "boasts to himself and rejoices in himself and his position" (vi). He certainly thinks he is not like everyone else. "With me it's not like with them others where you gotta wait and then there's bills and fines. We go on honor. You serve me and I'll not abandon you" (i). He believes he is a "benefactor." This kind master lives for all and loves his neighbor as himself. "I desire for you as I do for myself." Brekhunov lives according to his conscience and will do no harm to a soul. "Let the loss be mine. I am not like others" (ii). Brekhunov the master has no doubt about himself or his virtue as a master. He knows who he is and what he must do. The church elder, he seems a man of faith.

Because he is the master, Brekhunov is the one to whom the world belongs. But to the merchant master the world that belongs to him is the sum total of his acquisitions. For him, then, to live (*zhit'*) means to acquire (*nazhit'*), and the task of life is to acquire for himself as much as possible. At the center of the story, therefore, he visits with an old man whose son wants a share of his father's land, and Brekhunov gives him his sound advice: "As for sharing, my friend, don't give in. You have acquired it, you are the master" (vi). The master is the one who is removed from human relatedness. The height of Brekhunov's spirituality, as a consequence, "the one thing that comprises the aim, meaning, joy, and pride of his life" is the contemplation of the process of acquisition, "how much money he had acquired and could still acquire, how much money other people he knew had acquired and did have, and how they did and do acquire it, and how he, like them, could still acquire a great deal of money." The emblems of himself, then, are his "house with the tin-roofed barn" and his two fur coats. The contemplation of these acquisitions gives him the confidence of his accomplished mission. "What have I done in fifteen years?" he asks himself, as he limns his possessions. "And how did it happen? Because I remember my task, I strive, not like others, and then the task gets done. . . . Labor and the Lord will give." Brekhunov is content, "satisfied with everything that belongs to him and everything that he has done" (i). The merchant master is the one to whom the world belongs because, he believes, he has accomplished his task. God gives His grace, but Brekhunov believes he is self-sufficient. The master does not need others.

Because he is the one whose task is to acquire, Brekhunov lives off the past and for the future. His mental life consists in summing up the past and calculating the future. He lives by his watch and for a goal. This goal he sees ever ahead of him; he constantly strives for it. Thus he spends his life for some future acquisition which in the future will become his past accomplishment, the sign that he has lived and lived well. His son is not the one he loves and who loves him but the one "who in his thoughts he always calls his heir" (i). Brekhunov is a successful merchant master, however, because, although he is content with his past, he must ever keep on the move. His characteristic phrase is "Forward march" (da i marsh). Furthermore, the successful merchant not only sees his task still ahead, he knows the way to it. He could even go it alone, he believes, and he certainly knows how to get there. He definitely has the mind of a master and does not know that Christ teaches us to live in the present.

Master and Man tells the story of a man on a mission of acquisition, removed from the world of human relatedness. Brekhunov and his servant Nikita go off into the snow and cold because the master feels he "has to go" (iii). While the master thinks he knows the way, Nikita is the one whose task is to try to stay on the road. Nikita is the man, the "worker," the "non-master" (i). He is the one who has "no home," but lives out in the world, with people (v ljudjakh). He has the sense of human relatedness. He is known for his hard work and, although he does not care for his job, "he has to live until he finds another place and he takes what is given." A drunkard, he does not now drink; a husband and father who provides for his family's care, he silently lets his wife continue her affair with the cooper. Nikita has no possessions or aspirations. He has no past he can live off of and no future he would want to live for. Nikita lives in the present, although he does not know this. He is where he is and lives where he lives and does what he does. At the center of the story, when the master tells the master how to be a master, Nikita drinks his tea and keeps warm. On the journey Nikita knows that he does not know and cannot know the direct path to the goal, but he does trust to his horse and listen to the wind; he tries to follow them. When he fails, however, he is neither surprised, annoyed, or dismayed. He knows he is helpless. Nikita did not want to go on this trip and has nothing to gain for himself, but he is there, and he is his master's servant and his master wants it, so he keeps on trying to stay on the road. Nikita, like his "kind and obedient" horse, is the one who does the will of the one who sends him (v). He is a man of the Lord.

Since he is the one who does the will of the one who sent him, Nikita knows how to live and love. He lives his life, not trying to get to the goal of his desires, but by responding to the needs of the moment, both for himself and others. His characteristic phrase is not "forward march" but the name with which he addresses others, "dear heart." He is known for his "kind" (*dobryj*) nature (i). This kindness is expressed in his treatment of his horse. He feeds and tends her with loving care. When Brekhunov and Nikita are overcome by the snow and the cold, Brekhunov cares for himself, Nikita for his horse. He is guided by one idea: "it will be warmer for you" (vi). When on their journey, they encounter the ones who are celebrating the holiday, racing gaily along to wherever, Brekhunov is buoyed up by their spirits and feels ever more strongly the urge to march forward; Nikita is astounded at those "Asians" who beat their horse so violently (iii). When he believes he is dying, he calls to Brekhunov, asks that his final wages be given to his "boy or his wife, it makes no difference," and then begs forgiveness from the master (ix). He has no fear of death and in the end lives on. Nikita, who knows he is the servant called to do his master's will, even when the master seems to have abandoned him, is the man of faith.

Master and Man is a journey of discovery, not for Nikita but for Brekhunov. The men get lost in the emblematic expanse of nature because Brekhunov keeps thinking he knows the way, seeing his goal just ahead of him. Over and over again—"again" is a key word in the story—Brekhunov espies "something black" which he hopes will be what he is after or a marker on the path to what he is after; what he sees keeps on turning out to be fragments of the lonely, desperate, abandoned world: some vines, an isolated tree, frozen wash on a clothesline, a tall wormwood "desperately reeling in the wind" (viii). Each time they chase after the image of Brekhunov's desired goal, they get lost; often they find themselves back where they started. Because Brekhunov cannot learn from his suffering, the quest for the goal of his desire ahead in the future becomes a crescendoing vicious circle until Nikita realizes they must stop right there and spend the night. At this point Brekhunov becomes overcome by "fear" for his life (vi). He now repents of his past, which for him means regretting he had not stayed with his master friend, where it was "quite warm and merry" (iii), and that he had brought along Nikita whom he sees as the cause of his problem (vi). To stay his fear, Brekhunov does what he always does: he gets busy and moves on; "Forward march." He rides off on the tired horse, abandoning Nikita in search of the goal of his desire. The vicious circle begins again. Brekhunov gets off the tired horse, determined to find the road all alone, but now the horse abandons him and he is "alone," buried alive in a snow drift, pinned down by the weight of his two fur coats (vii). His sin has returned as his punishment.

But Brekhunov is resurrected from his snowy grave. At the turning point in his journey he realizes he has "lost his way." No sooner does he see that he is lost than he again sees "something black," but now he sees, not the image of his desire but of his goal: his horse guided him back to Nikita. His "fear" somewhat past, he busies himself caring for the horse in order to keep his mind off his fear. At this point Nikita calls to him, makes his dying request and begs forgiveness. "Suddenly" Brekhunov starts digging Nikita out of the snow and then lies down on top of him to keep him warm. He even resorts to his usual boasting, "that's how we are," but then "to his great amazement" he can no longer speak, and tears flow from his eyes. Like Karenin in his moment of forgiveness he experiences a "majestic tenderness" but Brekhunov thinks the tears prove that he had "really gotten frightened." He does not view his act as a sacrifice but a "weakness" and therefore sees no great merit for him in it. Because of this he experiences "joy he had never felt before." His dream that follows clarifies this experience of the sudden joy of life: "the one he has been waiting for has arrived," but he is not the one he expected but "someone else," "the very one who called him and told him to lie on Nikita." Now he knows that "he is Nikita and Nikita is him, that his life is not in himself but in Nikita, that if Nikita is alive, he is alive." The merchant master is dead. But there is miraculously born another, who speaks of Brekhunov in the third person, who cannot fathom why "Brekhunov had been occupied with what he had been occupied," who himself "now knows what the task is." In his act of love here and now Brekhunov discovers who he is and what he must do. In a profound sense in his own action, but despite himself, he becomes a man of faith.

Master and Man may well be Tolstoy's most disguised piece of autopsychological fiction, but still, like his other works, it is an image of his experience of life. It is not based on a specific documented event as is *Lucerne*, nor does it work out a moment of encounter with death, as does *The Notes of a Madman*, but it is quite literally a trying out in images of Tolstoy's most profound experience of his faith. Like *The Death of Ivan Ilych*, it gives narrative form to a metaphoric statement of Tolstoy's dilemma. This statement was made in *What Is My Faith?* written some ten years before the story.

> I am lost in a snowstorm. One [person] assures me, and it seems to him so, that warm fires and a village are just right ahead, but it just seems to him and to me because we want it. When we go toward the fires they are not there. But another [person] takes off through the snow. He walks around a bit, comes out on the road and shouts to us, "Don't drive anywhere, the fires are in your eyes; you'll get lost everywhere and you'll perish. The firm road is right here, I'm standing on it and it will lead us out." Now that's not much. When we believed in the fires flashing in our blinded eyes, there was always just ahead a village, a warm hut, salvation, rest while here there's just a firm road. But if we listen to the first we'll surely freeze, while if we listen to the second we'll surely get out. (23,400-01)

In this metaphoric statement the one person ("I") lost in a storm which is an emblem of life suddenly becomes two different selves: one who represents his desires, the other the certitude of the way; one who represents the personality, the other the divine self; one who leads to death, the other to the way out of death. In the story these two selves are fleshed out as two separate characters, Brekhunov and Nikita. These characters are given a place in the social and economic milieu of Russian life of the mid-nineteenth century, and they are endowed with a simple psychology based on two opposed moral and religious attitudes to the world. The Tolstoyan drama of the call to true life, of the desire for relatedness and the need to be a Resident, is then cast into the form of a journey of discovery, and Brekhunov, the personality, goes through a series of cumulative awakenings, including hearing the voice of death, until in the end he truly encounters Nikita, the emblematic divine self who is the one who loves, and suddenly Brekhunov discovers the way. *Master and Man* is a parable made from Tolstoy's inner experience of the unceasing struggle to find his way to love, of his continuing discovery of his mission, which is not his teaching, his family, his art, or being the master, but the inner divine call to love his neighbor as himself.

This representation of the self as two different selves embodied in two different and opposed characters, one of whom is called to be like the other, is not new. It is just a fine articulation of a method which underlies all Tolstoy's major fictions. As we have seen, in them, but of course variously, Tolstoy represents his struggle for faith by opposing two sets of characters: on the one hand, Nikolenka, Olenin, Prince Andrew, Pierre, Levin, and Nekhlyudov; on the other hand, Maman and "she," Maryanka, Natasha, Kitty, and Katyusha. The female figures are all emblematic residents who embody and reveal the way to divine love. In the later, short fictions these female figures are replaced by male peasants who serve the same function as do the emblematic figures of the beloved in the genres of the rich and learned. Natalya Savishna is the first such figure, both female and peasant. All Tolstoy's major heroes are representations of the personality lost in life, but on a journey of discovery with or in search of an emblematic self. At the end of the journey, only in moments and just in the moment, they encounter their emblematic divine self and see the way to love. *Master and Man* is the perfect type of this autopsychological and theological prose that I call emblematic realism.

THE POETICS OF EMBLEMATIC REALISM

Realism, as understood in the nineteenth century, reflects a human reality that is shaped by the world in which people reside. Social, economic, and historical forces mold the individual, and God, at best, simply transcends the world. In this realism, furthermore, human psychology is understood as the complex interactions of a conscious being with this formative world and there is no God within. Tolstoy did not accept this deterministic and materialistic conception of human reality. He always defined himself in opposition to the non-spiritual and often outraged anti-religious world-views of those who dominated the intellectual life of his generation. For Tolstoy the human being is a conscious being, not separate from the material and historical world, but free from it to reside in the Divine. Furthermore, for him reality is the world not separate from God; reality is God's life coming to be in its acceptance and rejection. Tolstoy's concept of reality includes the concept of God. Reality reflects the Divine because God is in the world and the world is in God. Thus everything in the world speaks of the Divine. "God has a different language," said Tolstoy, "a different means for communicating His will. The means is the whole life of the external world (*mir*) and what is placed in our soul" (56,25;1907). Of what is placed in our soul I shall soon speak. Here it is important to note that for Tolstoy the world is the expression of the Divine. Reality is God's language, His word and His world. Life is revelation, and reality is emblematic.

Tolstoy's concept of reality grounded in his panentheism stands in direct opposition to the concept of reality assumed by nineteenth-century realism. Because he had his "unconscious, stupid desire to know and speak the truth," he considered the literature of his day, even before writing *War and Peace*, a "beautiful lie" (60,258;1860). Tolstoy's literary task, therefore, was to transform the nature of realism. His realism, like his reality, is emblematic. Because he sees that the world is the embodiment and revelation of spiritual truth, his representation of that world must embody and reveal that truth. He tends to read allegorically. He interprets scripture in the Alexandrian tradition: the narratives and parables are allegories of spiritual life. The story of Moses' failure to reach the promised land, we might recall, is to him an "allegory," and even the ideas of heaven and hell are a "metaphoric (*obraznaja*) form." Tolstoy also reads life emblematically. He receives a flashlight pencil as a gift and pronounces it an "emblem of life" because it works like life: "Unscrew it, set free what covers the light in your soul and you will live in a light that illuminates for you what you need to see and to know in order to act and only what you need in order to act" (57,175;1909). The humble object embodies and reveals the moral and spiritual truth of all being in God. The imagination that saw this flashlight pencil as an "emblem of life" created *War and Peace* and *Anna Karenina*.

Tolstoy's emblematic imagination is iconic. In the Eastern Christian tradition all art is an icon of divine reality. The icon is an image which embodies and reveals divine truth. (The Russian *obraz*, like the Greek *eikōn*, means both image and icon.) The perfect icon is Jesus Christ, the Image of God on earth. He is the Word made flesh, embodied to reveal. Man, created in the image and likeness of God, is called to deification which is his likeness to the Image of God. A saint is "very like" (*prepodobnyj*). An icon of a saint, therefore, is an image of an image of the Image of God. Art is not once removed from the reality it imitates, as in Western conceptions of mimesis. In the Eastern Christian tradition art is thrice-removed from reality. An emblem is precisely such an image thrice-removed. The art of emblematic realism is made of verbal images of natural and human images of the Image of God, which is His life coming to be in its acceptance and rejection. Tolstoy's emblematic fiction is a verbal icon of his God of Life and Love.

Emblematic realism resembles allegory.[6] In allegory the represented reality is an abstract moral or spiritual quality which is signified by verbal images which seem to refer to the world as we ordinarily understand it. The sign "dragon" signifies evil. In emblematic realism, however, the represented reality is not an abstract or spiritual quality. The represented reality includes the world as we ordinarily understand it, in all its psychological, social, economic, and historical complexity. It is realism. But the concept of reality is expanded beyond the material and historical world to uncover the Divine within and abroad. History, culture, nature, and human psychology transcend their material bounds, and the spirit is disclosed. In Tolstoy's emblematic realism, therefore, the signified is this expanded reality which itself embodies and reveals moral and spiritual truth to the characters and the readers.

The reality Tolstoy represents is the world of human relatedness. He shows all people together or in their failure to be together. This is the image of God's life and love in its acceptance and rejection. The three major fictions, however, depict the world of human relatedness in three different realms. *War and Peace* looks at this reality from the point of view of the structural opposition on which the whole work is built: the world of human relatedness is divided up into the enemy (war) and the residents (peace). The foreigners and all like them embody and reveal a way of being in the world diametrically opposed to that of the residents. The foreigners fail in their relatedness, the res-

---

[6] In the generalizations about allegory I have been guided by Angus Fletcher, *Allegory, The Theory of a Symbolic Mode* (Ithaca, 1968).

idents do not. The heroes move from failure to the relatedness of the residents. In *Anna Karenina* the realm of relatedness is not abstract patriotism, but the mediating structure of the family. The novel explores the causes and results of the failure of residency in family situations. In *Resurrection* the world of human relatedness expands: the institutions of judgment and punishment known as the system of criminal justice embody and reveal the truth of social life. All three works explore our failure to live together. They all speak of our sin against love. In *War and Peace* this failure is opposed to the success of the residents, who embody and reveal true life, the experience of being together at one right here, right now. The Russian people are the emblem of successful human relatedness here and in all Tolstoy's fiction and thought. This reality of human relatedness in its success and failure is represented in the complex manner of realism, but even in its complexity that reality is emblematic of moral and spiritual value.

In Tolstoy's fiction there is only one plot event: all works embody and reveal the way to love. The fundamental action of the works, as we have seen, replaces the "division and discord in the universe with unity and harmony." The fictions tell the same story of life. People come together only to be separated by a misunderstanding or a misdeed which results in a failure of relatedness experienced psychologically as annoyance, resentment, estrangement, anger, even hatred. One or more of the characters then undergoes an extraordinary experience which sets him free from the routine of life and off on a journey of discovery through a series of cumulative revelations in which he learns something new about himself and others. This new sense of self dispels the disharmony within and the people come together, if only for a moment, at a higher level of accord. Such is the story of Nikolenka, his loss of Maman and discovery of "she," and more clearly of Olenin and Maryanka, Masha and Sergey, Prince Andrew and Natasha, Pierre and Natasha, Levin and Kitty, Nekhlyudov and Katyusha, Ivan Ilych and his family, Brekhunov and Nikita. Anna, Karenin, and Vronsky experience the opposite. Tolstoy's fiction tells one story, the story of the growth or decline of human relatedness, the increase or decrease of love for all in oneself and the world. These narratives of human relatedness are emblematic stories of God's life coming to be.

Within the longer fictions, the trilogy and the three novels, there is another kind of repeated action that I have called paradigmatic. Each work is built around a variation of the fundamental action, which defines the theme of the story. *War and Peace* moves from relatedness to its loss and then to its return. *Anna Karenina* moves from the high hopes of relatedness to its failure. *Resurrection* moves toward the recovery of relatedness from the past. The overall thematic action of these fictions is repeated paradigmatically in the parts. *Resurrection* is the clearest example. Many of the scenes open with the hero awakening from sleep and then going out on a journey into the world to uncover some truth about that world and how he has resided in it. Often the narration shows the mental processes of the hero while he is on his journey through that world. This action of awakening, uncovering, and forward movement into the world is the action of resurrection, the redemption which is the eternal process of growth in life through the restoration of love. What *Resurrection* does obviously and obviously emblematically, the other novels do more subtly. Natasha and Kitty at the ball, the Rostovs and Levin on a hunt, Prince Andrew and Pierre on the raft, the steeplechase in *Anna Karenina*—these and many other delineated segments repeat paradigmatically the thematic action of the works. These paradigmatic actions are emblematic in the sense that they are particular things which embody and reveal the whole. The parts of the fictions, therefore, are not just the components or building blocks of the whole structure. The delineated segments participate in the theme of the whole work. The relationship of part to whole in Tolstoy's fiction resembles the relationship of part to whole in his metaphysics.

Some paradigmatic actions participate in the whole work through a system of similes and metaphors. Similes, of course, are a major feature of Tolstoy's fictional style, extended and epic in *War and Peace*, shorter and more suggestive in the other works. In the two major fictions, however, the similes and metaphors are woven together into a network which is generated by a particular emblematic element. The hunt scene in *War and Peace* is not only a paradigmatic action of the novel and an emblem of the world of war, but from the hunt and only after it in the narrative there is produced a series of similes which relate the experience of war to the experience of being hunted. In *Anna Karenina* this relationship between emblematic elements and the system of similes and metaphors is a major stylistic feature of the work. The violent mishap not only gives birth to the guilt-ridden dreams that haunt Anna and Vronsky but in its violence to life is related to a whole series of similes of violence and pain used throughout the story of Anna's romance: the comparison of Karenin to an ox with head lowered, waiting for a blow from the raised axe, and of Vronsky's passion to murder are but two examples of this. The banquet scene of the theory of love establishes food as the primary image of love, and then in a series of similes and of scenes depicting meals this theme is woven into the texture of the whole work. Almost all the similes used in the entire novel relate either to violence or food, to love which destroys others or is taken for its own pleasure. It is in this context that Seryozha's stolen peach or the dirty ice cream Anna sees in her final journey of discovery take their full meaning. The similes in Tolstoy's longer fiction are shaped by paradigmatic and emblematic moments in his realistic narratives.

The main characters enter the fiction on a mission. As in allegory, they are on a quest. The action begins *in medias res* and we do not learn much of the characters' story before the opening of the tale. Nekhlyudov in *Resurrection* is the exception because it is a story of redemption through recovery. In their missions there is a sense that the characters are driven toward something not clear to them. Often they seem obsessed with this something. The mission almost always involves a departure from the world in which they have resided. They leave home. On their journeys, they often encounter, as in allegory, secondary figures who seem to be images of their best or worst selves; from these figures they learn. In the end they may meet up with an emblematic resident who, as in the schematic *Notes of a Madman*, reveals to them a significant truth which reorders their way of seeing and being. This mission away from home is the action necessary for the uncovering of their spiritual being and hence their way to love. This is the meaning Tolstoy finds in the teaching of Christ, the one without a home. "A person who lives by the spirit has no home. Animals have homes, but a person lives by the spirit and therefore can have no home. Christ says that he has no place appointed to him. To fulfill the will of the Father he does not need an appointed place. It is everywhere and always possible" (24,419-20;1884). The mission away from home leads to a new sense of the world in which the characters reside. At the end, therefore, the mission is accomplished, but never in the way the characters originally intended. Olenin does love Maryanka, but in an unexpected way, and then he leaves. Prince Andrew finds love through forgiveness. Pierre learns that the "science of the whole" leads to God, and he marries Natasha. Levin finds faith. Ivan Ilych experiences pity. Brekhunov uncovers his divine self. Nekhlyudov resurrects love in himself. For Anna, as always, the experience is twisted: her love turns to hate. The culminating moment for all releases the character from the mission to go onto another, perhaps even after death. The emblematic missions end with the beginning of a new life even in death.

At the center of each work, which is the middle of the character's life in the narrative, the mission is redirected or redefined. What was understood in a concrete or physical sense may take on new spiritual dimensions. Masha gets married. Olenin redefines his concept of self and love. Natasha sins, suffers, and forgives. Pierre encounters the sky as the emblem of the whole he must grasp. Levin admits his own lack of faith. Anna accomplishes her mission of reconciliation, but not really. Nekhlyudov and Maslova forgive each other, but not completely. Ivan Ilych learns that he is dying. Brekhunov learns that he is alone. The center of the work is like the conversion in Tolstoy's own life: it reveals more clearly the way to love. The perfect type of this structural element in Tolstoy's fiction is the late (1904) story *The Counterfeit Coupon*, a work which tells all the evil that accumulates from one evil deed in the first half and then all the good that accumulates from one good deed in the second half. In Tolstoy, just as the later clarifies the earlier, so the form elucidates the content.

The journeys of discovery occur in two different modes. One is the story of a quest for a love never had but which is discovered in the end to be the solution to one's life. This discovery is a reversal, the experience of Olenin, Pierre, Levin, and Brekhunov. The other is the story of a love which is lost, abandoned, or betrayed and then recovered in a new key. The recovery is a return: the experience of Nikolenka, Masha, Prince Andrew, the madman, Ivan Ilych, Nekhlyudov, and negatively of Anna. The stories of reversal are narratives of the quest for God; the stories of return are narratives of sin and forgiveness. *War and Peace* and *Anna Karenina* weave the two stories together. These fictions, then, are emblems of God's life coming to be, told as tales of the eternally growing soul in the stages of that career of redemption which is the salvation called deification through that cleansing process of clarifying guilt and fostering forgiveness which is called reconciliation.

CHARACTER in emblematic realism is conceived in relation to the moral and spiritual values assumed inherent in reality. While the major figures are placed within the social, economic, and historical milieu of Russian life, they are also imagined as specific moral and spiritual types. Each is essentially a "relationship to the world," a quantum of love, for better or for worse. The two extremes of these types are what I have called the man of the flesh and the man of the spirit or of faith. The man of the flesh lives for himself, his own purposes, pleasure or profit. Often he is represented in pursuit of sex or food. Pierre and Nekhlyudov enter the novels as such men of the flesh. Stiva is the perfect example. Anna is the female version, and remains so throughout the novel. These characters define themselves by their body, their animal urges. They are types of personality. There is also another type of personality, however, which I have called the mind of the master. This type is not associated with the body or physical pleasure. These characters define themselves by their controlling mind. They may be intellectuals or rationalists or idealists. They tend to react with outrage or despair at what goes contrary to their conception of reality. Prince Andrew and Levin both suffer from the mind of the master. But both learn from their suffering and discover another level of self. This other level is the divine self. The man of the spirit or of faith is the one who defines himself by this divine self. He knows or learns (although not necessarily consciously) that he is a particle of the divine love called the All. All the major male figures in the novels in the end become men of faith. Since *Master and Man* is the perfect type of Tolstoy's art, it is not surprising that Brekhunov is represented as a man of the flesh who has the mind of the master, while Nikita is a man of the spirit. Tolstoy's conception of character is always theological. It is important to note here, although I shall return to this later, that Eastern Christian anthropology sees three categories of the person: body, mind or soul, and spirit. Tolstoy imagines his characters according to this Eastern Christian model of human experience.

The major characters, however, are not simple theological abstractions, as one would expect in allegory. They are represented in their milieu with an inner life and, importantly, they change. Major characters are fluid and full. But most figures in Tolstoy are not fluid and full; they are fixed and flat. The fixed, flat characters are more abstract versions of this theological conception of human beings. Helen

Kuragin is the body who loves for her own pleasure and profit; Varenka is the spirit who never loves for her own pleasure or profit. Helen is total self-indulgence; Varenka is total self-sacrifice. Levin's brothers are emblems of the body and the mind. Nicholas, however, is not represented as the body in pursuit of its pleasure; he is the body in decay. And Sergey Ivanovich is not represented as the controlling mind of the master; he is the ineffectual intellectual removed from life. They represent the inevitable outcome of a materialist or rationalist understanding of human existence, a dead body or empty words.

The major male characters are all in quest. Their female partners, Natasha, Kitty, Katyusha, are not. They are, however, fluid and full: each has her story of sin and forgiveness. But the female characters are not represented in pursuit of faith. They are the ones who love all and, as such, are emblems of the divine self. They are not unlike Nikolenka's "she" and Olenin's idealized Maryanka. Their function, as I have noted, is to reveal the way to love to the heroes. In this they resemble not only Nikita and Gerasim, but also Pierre's Bazdeev and Platon Karataev, Levin's old men, Nekhlyudov's man on the raft. These male emblems of the divine self tend to be less fluid and full than their female counterparts. Most are fixed and flat and the latest of them, Nekhlyudov's man, is baldly emblematic. But these fixed and flat emblems of the divine self do not fall outside the poetics of emblematic realism. They are simply less realistically embedded. In emblematic realism, we can say, therefore, that there are three types of represented characters. All fluid and full characters are embedded in the social, economic, and historical reality. Some fixed and flat characters are also realistically embedded. But some fixed and flat characters are not; they tend to be baldly emblematic.

Tolstoy's theological conception of character is the source of his method of representing figures by one significant feature. The physical leitmotif that accompanies a character through the work tells of his "relationship to the world": Prince Andrew's dry features; Pierre's corpulent body, spectacles, and open, kind smile; Princess Mary's luminous eyes and the red blotches on her neck and shoulders; Helen's classical shoulders and her half-bared bosom; the dimming light and sparkle in Anna's eyes; Vronsky's thighs, teeth, and thinning hair. In the major heroes these significant features are embedded in a complex of features; in the secondary characters they are less so. A totally emblematic character has a single baldly abstract feature: Bazdeev's wizendness of body, Platon Karataev's roundness of body, Gerasim's healthiness of body. Whether or not the character is represented in psychological fullness and fluidity, the leitmotif embodies and reveals his moral and spiritual meaning to the reader. In Tolstoy character is represented realistically and emblematically.

In realistic fiction the human being is represented within a world of man-made objects from a particular time and place. Clothing and habitats are rendered in some detail to locate the characters within the cultural and historical order, even to imply the derivation of their mode of being from that order. These details may also have a symbolic function. Tolstoy uses detail mainly for its symbolic purposes. Clothing becomes emblematic. The women in white are the most obvious instances of this: Maman and "she," Natasha at Prince Andrew's dying, Katyusha at Nekhlyudov's downfall. But other examples abound: Olenin's Cossack costumes of false identity, Pierre's various costumes of assumed identity or his white hat of innocence on the battlefield, Natasha's simple dresses or elaborate gowns, Stiva's formal wear, Levin's uncouth garb, Karenin's top hat, Brekhunov's fur coats, and Nikita's tattered jacket. These items of clothing speak not simply or even necessarily of the characters' social or economic status. The clothing reveals the characters' way of being in the world. Likewise human habitats. What is striking about Tolstoy's representation of dwelling places is not just that the exteriors of houses are not described, but that the interiors as well are usually left to the reader's imagination. The characters dwell in empty spaces, the perfect example of which is the madman's narrow, square, and white room. Tolstoy replaces descriptions of interiors with emblematic objects: the mirrors and lights at any ball; the sphinx on Natasha's bedpost; the bronze clock (Peter the First style) in Karenin's drawing room; the ladder and drapery that are Ivan Ilych's downfall, as well as the divan on which he lies and the blank wall to which he turns; the sumptuous appointments of Nekhlyudov's apartment; and the velvet seat in the train compartment. The details of interiors may be more or less realistically embedded; as always, of course, the later the work, the balder the emblem. It is in this context that the commonly repeated image of the doors must be seen. While Tolstoy does not describe interiors, he often represents character moving out through open doors. The open door is the image of a new and better life. Prince Andrew leaves home through the doors. Anna as always twists the meaning: she opens the door of her train compartment and steps out into the story of her passion which is a new but not better life.[7] The closed door creates the world of the closet, the emblem of the banishment from the life of human relatedness. In emblematic realism, we can say, therefore, details of clothing and habitat embody and reveal the moral and spiritual meaning of the characters' lives to the reader. Sometimes, as with the women in white or the madman's white room, these emblems speak also to the character.

Objects in Tolstoy's emblematic realism likewise reveal meaning. This is most obvious in Katyusha's bar of soap "large, fuzzy, and Russian." But Anna's crocheting or Sergey Ivanovich's fishing line function in the same way. Examples of such objects abound: the snuffboxes in *War and Peace*, the leaf in Anna's hand or her red handbag, the moth at the lawyer's office, Brekhunov's watch, and cigarettes in general. Items of food almost always are emblems of sharing: Platon's potato or Petya's raisins. Some of these details are used in just one delineated segment; others occur in several. What is significant in the use of these details is that they are singled out for attention. They reveal meaning to the character or reader or both because they are isolated from the context. Objects in Tolstoy's realism tend not to be verisimilitudinous but baldly emblematic.

While Tolstoy represents interiors as empty spaces in which the characters dwell and the objects in their possession as bald emblems of their being, he represents the world of nature in sumptuous, at times even poetic, detail. Nature is the privileged place in his fictional universe. Nature is the world in which the Resident resides. Significantly, Tolstoy depicts no nature which is by itself destructive or in any way suggestive of malevolent forces within God's world. Only the snowstorm is fatal to man, but even that is so because man chooses to go out into it for his own pleasure or profit. In the fiction nature gives life, sustains life, and renews life. Nature is the emblem of God's life in this world. Olenin encounters the mountains and sees the "whole of God's world." Characters who have no genuine expe-

[7] The symbolism of open and shut doors in Tolstoy has been discussed by Galagan, *op.cit.*, pp. 84, 96-99, 131-136. She rightly sees the connection between the fiction and Tolstoy's understanding of the image of open doors in the Gospels. One should add that the liturgical tradition of Eastern Christianity often refers to the redemption as Christ's opening of the doors to the new life of heaven.

rience of this life-giving nature in a profound sense do not live. Ivan Ilych is the obvious example; Anna, Karenin, and even Vronsky, the perfect types, and urban dwellers the typical class. These characters are isolated from the source of life, and they have no God. The privileged moment in Tolstoy's fiction is the characters' encounter with the expanse of nature. They discover the world in which they reside. Moments of movement outward and toward this expanse are emblematic of the characters' discovery of the Divine. The longer fictions all contain one emblem from the natural world which calls characters to it: the garden in the trilogy, the mountains in *The Cossacks*, the sky bathed in light in *War and Peace* and *Anna Karenina*, and the revived world of Spring and the revivifying summer rainstorm in *Resurrection*. At some significant point the characters experience an interaction with this expanse of nature: they move outward and toward it, while nature pours light or rain toward them. In these moments the characters, alone and removed from human interaction, discover the Divine within. They feel the sudden joy of life. In emblematic realism the experience of nature is a moment of grace. In the encounter with the expanse of nature the characters' inner spiritual life is born. To this world of inner experience we now turn in the second half of this book.

Part Two

STATES OF HUMAN AWARENESS

Self-perfection is life itself because it is
the expansion of consciousness.
(55,143;1905)

Chapter Five

THE WAYS TO KNOW

Man is but a center of consciousness which perceives impressions.
(58,10;1910)

Life is the expansion of consciousness.
(55,31;1904)

FOR TOLSTOY the fundamental questions—who am I? where am I going? what is good? what bad? what is life? what is death?—are the questions that the thinkers of his time could not and would not answer. The materialist assumptions of the positivists and their growing faith in science and technological progress were leading the human race, he thought, into an intellectual and moral impasse. The natural and social sciences, while capable of elucidating particulars in great detail, seemed to see the world only in fragmented bits and answered only unnecessary questions. What was even worse, Tolstoy felt, was that modern thinking people had no concern for what was good or bad. All criteria for moral behavior were evaporating with the pursuit of empirical truth. And the truth that the empirical sciences found was a form of determinism which robbed the human being of his freedom and responsibility. Man had lost his meaning. If I am but a speck of dust blown by the winds of time through the caverns of space, why should I go on living? If whatever I do is determined not by me and destined to be blown away by time through space, then why should I do anything at all? The post-Enlightenment world of positivism and scientism in which Tolstoy lived seemed to him to destroy the possibility of meaning in life and to pronounce the death of God even before Nietzsche coined the phrase.

Tolstoy himself, however, is a man of the mid-nineteenth century. He shares with his time an empiricist and positivist view of reality. He had a mechanico-corpuscular conception of a reality which is advancing progressively toward its fulfillment. This model of life, which has its origins in the eighteenth century, does not change throughout his life. Rather, it is transformed by his ever clearer and clearer belief in a spirituality embodied in this physical reality. This spiritual reality he uncovered in the phenomenon of consciousness. The positivists, he believed, tripped over one question. How could a product of matter and movement pose these very questions of faith? What is the meaning of the fact of human consciousness which itself is what allows man to ask about meaning? To Tolstoy the phenomenon of human consciousness is the stumbling block of all materialisms. Tolstoy first raised this question in *War and Peace*, where his religious world-view does battle with modernity. But the ideas which govern the world of *War and Peace* and come to a certain expression in the second half of the work are not, as Tolstoy himself said, "some chance paradox" (61,195;1868). His "thoughts on the boundaries of freedom and necessity" and his "view of history" are, rather, "an inseparable part of his view of the universe" (*mirosozertsanie*), which was the "fruit of all the intellectual labor of my life." He, of course, continued this labor throughout the rest of his life in ever-clearer articulations of that view. In *War and Peace* the science of history stands for all the natural and social sciences, and the battle with the historians is a battle about the ways to know human experience, about cause and effect, about subject and object, about the limitations of empirical knowledge and the possibility of knowledge of the Divine. The central philosophical issue in *War and Peace* is the problem of knowledge. In his battle over epistemology Tolstoy turns away from the empirical ways to know toward the phenomenon of human consciousness itself. In the experience of human consciousness Tolstoy found his answer to the materialists and the determinists. From his understanding of the epistemological moment he shaped his characters' inner lives and the modes of narration in his own fiction.

THE TYPES OF KNOWLEDGE

Beginning with his earliest attempts at philosophical writing in 1847 and continuing through his life, Tolstoy worked with a typically eighteenth-century model of human psychology based on an empiricist epistemology. The human being, in this view, is conceived as a hierarchy of four "parts": the "body," "feeling," "mind," and "will" (1,292,339;1851). The body is all that we generally consider "material" in ourselves, and as such it does not differ from the "external world" (1,234;1847). The most important and complex part is the realm of "feeling." For Tolstoy the word *chuvstvo* translated here as "feeling" has two different but related meanings. On the one hand, *chuvstvo* refers to the senses and the sensations experienced through them; on the other hand, *chuvstvo* refers to a mood, emotion, or feeling which is usually understood to be produced by the sensations through the experience of the senses. Using his empiricist model, Tolstoy imagined that the sensations and feelings were the effects or "influences" of matter, both the matter of the external world and of the body itself. Tolstoy imagines that this matter impresses itself on the so-called "faculty of receptivity" (*sposobnost' vospriimchivosti*) which relays the "impressions" (*vpechatlenija*) to the faculties of "memory" and "imagination," which store the impressions. When memory or imagination reproduce the impression, we experience a sensation. What causes this reproduction in what circumstances is a major question for this epistemological model.

From his earliest days Tolstoy yoked memory and imagination and saw both as a kind of storehouse of experience. He once whimsically imagined the mind filled with "boxes" of stored sense data divided into two groups, good and bad, and separated by an empty "corridor" (60,228-30;1859). In everyday experience the boxes of sense data shuffle from the good and bad groups along the corridor in varying proportions, giving us our ordinary sense of reality. What interests Tolstoy in this casual description of the workings of the mind are the extraordinary moments when "fine weather, flattery, good digestion, etc., press the catch" which controls the boxes of good sense data and releases them in a flood into the corridor or when "rain, bad stomach, or truth" does the opposite. Such moments abound in Tolstoy's fiction. Pierre gestures to the sky and thereby presses the catch on the good sense data stashed away in Prince Andrew's mental storehouse. In such situations the narrator often just lists the bits of experience that then flood the corridor. From such moments Tolstoy believes we deduce our philosophies of life:

My liver hurts; it's hard for me to live, and life therefore is represented to me as a course toward death, in comparison with eternity a paltry thing. But then the bile settles down, I am loved and

I love, and death is represented to me as an extreme (infinitely small) point serving as the boundary of life. I need not think about death; it would be stupid to think about it. There is only life, which I have to live through the best way possible, and on it I must expend all my energies. Both views of life and death are diametrically opposed, yet indubitably correct, because feeling transfers the mind from one point of view to another, but to the mind there is only representation. (48,121-22;1870)

The views of reality, be they of the Stranger or the Resident, follow from a "feeling," a mood which takes its source in physical experience and alters the point of view with which one interprets experience and hence knows the world. Therefore in Tolstoy's hierarchy of the four "parts," "feeling" is central. It is the body or matter as we experience it when we experience it, not necessarily as it is or when it is. We never know or experience the body or any matter in itself, only our sensations of the impressions.

Thus the world that we know, for Tolstoy—and this long before he read Hume, Kant, or Schopenhauer—is the mental representation of our sense experience. Our five senses determine the world as we know it. As he observed many years later, a flea might see it differently (55,155;1908). Certainly dogs do: "The whole world for me, a human being, is visual; I see everything. I touch, listen to, smell only what is unclear to my eyes. When a dog barks at a visual object which it has not smelled, it is the same as when I seek with my eyes what stinks so" (56,112;1908). In the end Tolstoy used this limitation to the truthfulness of empirical knowledge to condemn science.

All these sciences, with the exception of mathematics, do not satisfy our curiosity because while studying phenomena which take place in the inanimate world or in the animal and vegetable worlds, these sciences build all their studies on the false assumption that everything that is represented to human beings in a certain fashion actually exists just as it is represented to them. This assumption that the world is in reality as it is known (poznaetsja) by one of the innumerable beings of the world—man—through the external senses sight, smell, hearing, taste, touch with which this being (man) is endowed, this assumption is completely false and capricious. It is capricious and false because for any being endowed with different sense, as for example a crab or a microscopic insect or many, many beings known and unknown, the world is completely different (38,140;1909).

For Tolstoy the world as it is cannot be known through empirical observation of it, and hence science cannot lead to any ultimate truth. "The knowledge that is most unstable and subject to error is knowledge based on observation, on experience" (55,215;1906).

The third formative "part" of human knowledge is the "mind," which governs the faculty of "inference" (zakljuchenie). As enumerated in his philosophical fragments of 1847 and with little later modification, Tolstoy isolated five processes involved in the workings of the mind: "representation" (predstavlenie, Tolstoy often closely associates or equates this with "imagination"), "memory," "comparison," "deductions from the comparisons," and systemization of the deductions (46,271;1847). The first two of these processes, representation (or imagination) and memory are, as we have seen, closely associated with "feeling" since they involve directly the mental translations of the sensations. The results of these processes are what is kept in the mental storehouse called memory and imagination. The last three processes—comparison, deduction, and systemization— are the mental activity, most strictly speaking, since they involve the modes of relationships among the represented or remembered sensations stored in the mind. By the powers of "reason" (razum) the mind (um) attempts to understand them by comparison and deduction. Reason understands the feeling which is a sensation of the impression of the body. What reason knows is twice removed from matter and in this sense less than the thing itself. But in its independence from the influence of the impressions of matter, reason gains a certain power. In the comparisons and deductions from the comparisons, reason creates order and controls reality as known. Reason removed from the material object gains the illusion of power and control over it. This empiricist reason is the source of scientific thinking.

Tolstoy's model of human cognition is a simplified, if not simplistic, version of the empiricism so popular in eighteenth-century England and so influential among the philosophers of the French Enlightenment, including Tolstoy's beloved Rousseau, whose Vicar of Savoyard assumes a similar model of human knowledge. Tolstoy's version of empiricist cognition lacks the intricacy of Locke's "simple" and "complex ideas" or "primary and secondary qualities," just as it fails to distinguish clearly between Hume's "impressions of sensations" (immediate sense-experience) and "impressions of reflection" (feelings which result from the memory of sense-experience). What is significant in Tolstoy, however, is that he used this model to delimit the possibilities of science and to downgrade the role of reason in the epistemological event. As we have seen, to Tolstoy science is not based on facts. "There are no facts. There are only our perceptions of them. And therefore the only scientific approach is the one that speaks of perceptions, of impressions" (54,172;1903). We can know the "laws" of history or nature because these laws are the inductions from our perceptions of reality; they are our understanding of reality and our mental events. We cannot know scientifically, however, the cause of events in history or nature, because that cause is not available to our perception, if only because it goes too far back in time. Reason, which induces by the comparison of sense data, which are representations of sense experience, knows only abstract ideas, and the relationship of these abstract ideas to reality is by no means certain. Tolstoy's critique of empiricist epistemology is aimed, therefore, at the two enemies of religious faith, as he understood them: the positivist science of his day, whose advocates he called the "materialists" and the "determinists," and the Enlightenment's heritage of self-sufficient, individualistic, critical reason. He will reassert the free spiritual dimension of human existence by reshaping his epistemological model.

To reshape the empiricist epistemology Tolstoy turned to the fourth component in his model, the "will." This will, he noted as early as 1851, is even in the empiricist model the "essence of the soul." "I recalled that the basis of the new philosophy consisted of the fact that man consists of a body, feeling, reason, and will, but that the essence of the soul is will. Descartes (whom I had not read) said in vain *cogito, ergo sum*, for he thought because he wanted to think, therefore one should say *volo, ergo sum*" (1,339;1851). This "will" is then in the epilogue to *War and Peace* said to be known within by what Tolstoy calls "consciousness" (*soznanie*). This concept of consciousness becomes central to his whole epistemology. By this word, which can also be translated as "awareness," Tolstoy refers to many things: the fact of awareness, the act of awareness, awareness of self, awareness of others, and the content of consciousness. In the epilogue Tolstoy introduces this term as a counter to empiricist reason. With this consciousness the human being can find the self lost by the positivists. "Consciousness is a source of self-knowledge (*samopoznanie*), which is separate and independent of reason. Through reason man observes himself. He knows himself only through consciousness" (E,ii,viii). The self that man observes is what the later Tolstoy calls the personality. The personality knows through empiricist observation and reason. It sees in space and time, experiences itself as the impressions made upon contact with the limits it calls matter and the external world, and it feels that it is shaped by the external world. The personality is determined. The "reason" of the personality sees activity in a causal nexus and understands reality as the effect of an infinite series of causes. There is no freedom. There is also no responsibility. The reason of the personality also knows reality only as an "object of observation." All particular things, including human beings, are known precisely as objects, as entities whose inner reality is closed to the knowing subject. But still, and here is the paradox, with reason the personality orders and controls the impressions of the things observed and therefore, while determined by the external world, the knowing subject with its reason controls that world.

The self perceived through consciousness knows itself and the world differently. In *War and Peace* the major features of this self-knowledge in consciousness is, as already noted, the awareness of oneself as a being with free will. "In order to understand, observe, and draw inferences, a person must first of all be conscious of himself as living. To know himself as living, a person must know himself as willing; he must be conscious of his will. His will, which expresses the essence of his life, a person is conscious of and can only be conscious of as free" (E,ii,viii). What this self knows in its freedom is that it has no limitations. There are no temporal or spatial boundaries. And this self does not seem caused by anything else. What is discovered in the consciousness of self as a free being is a dimension of reality outside space, time, and causality. Tolstoy notes, however, that "a being that finds itself beyond time and independent of causes is no longer a person." Consciousness is the mode of knowing of what later is called the divine self. Tolstoy uses this idea of knowledge of the free self in consciousness to battle the assumptions about knowledge made by empirical science. History explains events by a causal principle which asserts that leaders make things happen. But this view, Tolstoy argues, results from the epistemological assumptions of the historians. "All knowledge [in empirical science] just subsumes the essence of life under the laws of reason." Through observation and what one induces from observations by the manipulations of reason one cannot get to any truth. This empiricist knowing always sees a world without freedom in which everything is held prisoner by the principle of causality. "Necessity is the form" of all existence as viewed through reason. The content of existence, Tolstoy argues, is freedom, the essence of life, the movement of reality, the flow not divided up by the mind which knows with an empiricist epistemology. Like the God of the ancients or the concept of a hero-ruler modeled on that totally transcendent God, this empiricist mind always stands outside the flow. It removes itself from events in order to know them. To Tolstoy this is a violation of reality because the knower is also in the event, just as a hero is part of the action and God dwells in the world. The separation of the subject and object is a fiction of the knowing mind. Everyone co-exists in the event, as the Russian word for event implies (*sobytie* etymologically means "co-existence"). In any genuine epistemology there can be no such opposition of knowing subject and known object. This mode of knowledge is what Tolstoy refers to as consciousness.

In his battle with historians in the epilogue, Tolstoy is not simply or perhaps not even writing a theory of history. He is working out a new theory of knowledge. The hidden agenda, however, is theological. The epilogue is an early version of his doctrine of God and creation. The self that knows itself as free in consciousness he calls in the drafts to the epilogue a "soul," and he defines these souls as "infinitely small moments of freedom in time" (15,239). But in the same drafts God is defined as the "infinitely large sum of the moments beyond time" (15,240). The reality Tolstoy speaks of is this freedom, the individual flow of God into time, God's life. The experience of this flow of God into time he had represented in his fictional images of Olenin and Pierre. The vagueness of the epilogue results from Tolstoy's failure at this time to articulate as an idea his doctrine of God. To this doctrine of God as the flow into time I shall turn in the last chapter of this book.

THE MODE of knowledge called consciousness is associated, not with the intellect, but with the will. With its consciousness the self knows itself as a living, willing being. To Tolstoy we should recall, however " 'to love,' 'to want' ('to desire,' the 'will'), and 'to live' all mean the same thing" (62,229;1875). The self that knows itself in consciousness is a particle of love; it is a striving soul which reaches out beyond itself outward and toward the other. The mode of knowledge called consciousness casts away the conception of self as a knowing subject imagined as some blank slate upon which are imprinted the sensations received from the external world. In consciousness the self moves out to become, to be for, and to belong.

> Consciousness. In man the only thing that is free is consciousness, i.e., the capacity to be conscious, to transfer one's whole self, one's attention, one's feeling, onto one thing or another. In its simplest form this consciousness is the consciousness of one or another member of one's own body. I can direct, transfer consciousness onto my hand, leg, the left one, the right one, a finger, an ear; I can transfer, direct consciousness onto other beings. This transferral of consciousness onto others is the cause and condition of the possibility of love. . . . No determinists will prove to me that I cannot right now become conscious (transfer consciousness) onto my left heel or my lower lip. This seems unimportant, but nevertheless in this consciousness is founded the freedom, divinity, non-temporality, and non-spatiality of life and therefore of every reasonable and kind view of the universe (*dobroe mirosozertanie*). (56,357;1908)

The passive knowledge of the empiricist epistemology is replaced by the active knowledge through attention. The sense data do not bombard the mind. Rather, the self goes forth to seize the other. Consciousness moves outward and toward the object of knowledge. It transcends itself. Self-transcendence is the defining feature of attending consciousness. Movement from self outward and toward other is what consciousness is. This capacity to transcend itself demonstrates the freedom of the self. The empiricist model of knowledge portrays a self that is shaped by the external world. The mode of consciousness portrays a self that can choose to abandon its home in order to grasp the other. In consciousness the self is free. What is most significant for Tolstoy, however, is that this phenomenon of attending consciousness is seen as "the cause and condition of the possibility of love." With the empiricist consciousness the self is passive, capable of being loved but not loving. In attending consciousness the self is active; it goes forth from itself to other. This going forth in knowledge is the "cause and condition of the possibility" of giving forth in love. The mode of knowledge called consciousness makes possible the mode of life called love.

In Tolstoy the empiricist model of knowledge co-exists with the mode of knowledge called consciousness.

> There are two methods of knowing the external world. One is the very crude and unavoidable method of knowing through the five senses. With this method, however, the world which we know would not be formed and there would remain chaos, giving us various sensations. The other method consists in first having known yourself by loving yourself and then knowing other beings by loving them, by transferring yourself by thought into another person, animal, plant, even a stone. By this method you know from within and form the whole world as we know it. This method is what is called poetic talent; it is also love. It is the re-establishment of the unity among beings which has been as it were destroyed. Go out of yourself and into another. You can go into everything. Everything (*vsë*); merge with God, with the All (*Vsë*). (52,101;1893)

Tolstoy does not retreat from the maya of the material world into some Eastern idealism. He is not interested in denying physical reality. Tolstoy wants to rescue the world from its enslavement to this physical reality. The mode of knowledge called consciousness allows him to call a stone a stone yet merge with it to find his God. Knowledge by attending consciousness merges. It is most important to note that the phenomenon of attending consciousness becomes the way to love for Tolstoy the artist. He sees attending consciousness as the cause and condition of the possibility of both love and artistic creation. Furthermore, Tolstoy sees in attending consciousness an antidote to the fragmentation in the empiricist opposition of subject and object. In attending consciousness the self merges with the other and therefore reestablishes the unity of being. Consciousness is the mode of knowledge appropriate for a redemption which is a restorative deification.

Attending consciousness can be called the "consciousness of life." (51,66;1890). The main characteristic of this consciousness of life is its "striving to seize as much as possible." This consciousness is primary in the sense that it exists before there is an object it would seize and regardless of any external object. It is an expression of an apparently spontaneous and unmotivated going forth from self. Attending consciousness is the primary experience of the question of faith, where am I going? The striving of this attending consciousness, therefore, is precisely what "love is, the striving to embrace more, everything—to be God, the striving toward God." Attending consciousness is a primary experience of self-transcendence which has as its final term the All called God. It is this attending consciousness of life that moves Olenin in the mountains to the experience of a love for all God's world which is his "greatest possible seizure of the Divine." Attending consciousness, therefore, is the "insight (*prozrenie*) of the spirit" (56,24;1907). It seeks to see the All in all.

The combination of the empiricist model of knowledge with this attending consciousness gives Tolstoy three kinds of knowledge:

> I know myself, my whole self before the veil of birth and after the veil of death. I know myself by the fact that I am I. This is the highest or rather the most profound knowledge. The next knowledge is knowledge gained by sensation (*chuvstvo*): I hear, see, touch. I do not know what it feels (*chuvstvuet*) about itself, what it is conscious of. The third knowledge is less profound; it is knowledge by understanding (*rassudok*): knowledge deduced from one's sensations or passed on by words from other people; reasoning (*rassuzhdenie*), prognostication, deduction, science.
>
> The first: I feel sad, pained, bored, happy. This is certain.
>
> The second: I smell violets, see light and shadows, etc. Here there can be error.
>
> The third: I know that the earth is round and revolves, that Japan and Madagascar can exist, etc. All this can be questioned.
>
> Life, I think, consists in transferring the third and second kinds of knowledge into the first, when one experiences everything in himself. (55,29;1904)

In this epistemological system the three kinds of knowledge reflect two basic types. One type is empiricist. This knowledge comes in two forms, the sense data experienced more or less directly and the abstraction from sense data known in the mind through reason's manipulations of stored data. Both these kinds of knowledge are expressed in sentences which oppose subject and object. The world is known in separation. This type of knowledge sets up a barrier between self and other. There is no "life." The other type of knowledge leads to "life." It unites what is separate from itself by grasping it and bringing it home. The action of transcending, attending consciousness reverses and returns. This knowledge not by reason but by life is expressed with no subject-object opposition. In Russian "I feel sad, pained, bored, happy" (*mne grustno, bol'no, skuchno, radostno*) is expressed here, and it is normal for the language, with an impersonal adverbial form, as well as a logical subject in the dative. The knowledge that is certain comes only when I am not I. The epistemology of life breaks down the barrier between self and other. Consciousness merges. "There is an 'I,' there is an 'it,' the relationship of 'I' to 'it' is 'thou,' 'thou' is life" (56,356;1908).

War and Peace tells the story of an epic battle for life between the strangers and the residents presided over by two emblematic leaders. Napoleon is the absolute Stranger. He embodies and reveals the separated, isolated individual with its way of knowing and loving. He is the emblem of the empiricist world-view and Western individualism. His error is twofold. By intellect he knows the external world separate from him only as the object of his observation which by reason he believes he can control, while failing to see the control this world has over him. He is the epitome of empiricist knowledge. By will he feels himself free from that external world, while remaining blind to any will that exists outside him. He is the personality. Kutuzov is the absolute Resident. He embodies and reveals the common divine self with its way of knowing and loving. He has a religious consciousness and experiences human relatedness. His power, therefore, is that by intellect he intuits the being of the external world and by will he attunes himself to that being. He has an attending consciousness.

Napoleon enters the novel as a topic of conversation: he is, according to Anna Sherer, a "murderer," a "villain," the Antichrist" (I,i,i). He first appears in the novel standing above the wounded Prince Andrew, who sees him as a figure who in the face of death loses his grandeur. We see him most in the process of arranging and planning the battle. In the end Napoleon stands in Moscow as a stranger to its life, awaiting the deputation from the city to recognize him. This is his last moment after which he disappears from the text. In the epilogue he is characterized as "a person without convictions, customs, traditions, or a name, not even a Frenchman" (E,i,iii). He is the individual separated from human relatedness. The descriptions of him in the novel focus on his physical being: his rotund stomach, his heavy thighs, his short hair, his white fleshy neck, his youngish full face, his extended chin. He is the body. We know him in weakness and ill-health, usually enveloped in an aura of eau de cologne, always aware of his appearance. He loves only himself. Because he is closed to the spirit, we do not see his eyes or his smile. Napoleon is a man of the flesh.

Napoleon is totally self-enclosed. "Only what was happening in his own soul had interest for him. Everything in the world (*mir*) seemed to him to depend on his will" (III,i,vi). From the point of view of the will, Napoleon stands in opposition to all that exists. He sees the battle for life as a "game of chess" in which he moves the figures (III,ii,xxix). From the point of view of the intellect also, Napoleon stands in opposition to all that exists. He is the subject; everything else is the object. He sees the battle for life through his telescope, and as a result "he does not know where what he saw is" (III,ii,xxxii). To him everything is abstract from life. He believes the "field of battle" (*pole srazhenija*) can be pictured on his maps and that the course of the battle can be directed by his "instruction" (*razporjazhenija*). From his "deductions" from what he sees he determines the "positions" (*pozitsii*) in battle and his "dispositions" (*dispozitsii*) for the battle (III,ii,xxvii). His way of knowing issues forth in empty words, marked in the narration by these puns. He is known for his "definitions" of profound vapidity: "The act of war is the art of being stronger than the enemy at a given moment in time" (III,ii,xxx). He lives in an "artificial world of the phantoms of his own grandeur." As a result his "mind and conscience" are so "darkened" that he has no awareness of "truth, beauty, and goodness," nor any sense of the "meaning of his actions" (III,ii,xxxviii). This individual, who sees life only at the end of his telescope in the reduced images he believes he can control, stands outside the battle for life in a self-imposed but profoundly false isolation. He has the mind of a master.

The icon of this isolated individual's way of knowing and loving is the portrait of the "king of Rome," Napoleon's own illegitimate son, painted to look like the Christ in the Sistine Madonna. It is presented as a gift to Napoleon just before the battle of Borodino begins. The Christ-Son of Napoleon, who for no understandable reason has become known as the "King of Rome," is depicted playing stick ball, but the ball is a "sphere" (*shar*) which "represents the earthly sphere" and the stick is the King of Rome's "sceptre" (III,ii,xxvi). The child is shown spiking the ball with his stick. "This allegory" is an image of Napoleon's physical issue seen in the game of conquering the earthly sphere by penetrating it from outside. The image stands in opposition to that other earthly sphere, Pierre's globe of life no one is outside of. This portrait of the King of Rome is the icon of the offspring of the individual personality, a picture of an isolated illegitimate person playing at life while outside its sphere. In the contemplation of his own physical issue, which he then presents for the admiration of all before the battle of life, Napoleon reveals the true meaning of his self-centered existence.

Unlike Napoleon, Kutuzov does not experience life isolated from others or wrapped up in the contemplation of himself. He enters the novel in a "review" (*smotr*) of the troops, a moment in which he "goes out to meet the regiment" with a "smile on his lips" (I,ii,ii). In the midst of the review he "suddenly" takes note of the red-nosed, inebriated Captain Timokhin, whose "position" he has understood, for whom he "wishes every good," and at whom he smiles. "We all have our weaknesses," after all. Blind in one eye, Kutuzov enters the complex reality of life and sees it with compassion. Even to the rowdy Dolokhov, reduced to the ranks for his misbehavior, he holds out hope. Kutuzov's review of the troops, because it is marked by his compassion, ends in a scene of song and dance, a moment of resonant harmony in which Kutuzov and his retinue "take pleasure in the bold, merry feeling" aroused by the song, and the experience of all is shaped by the rhythm of the dance. Kutuzov enters the novel like Natasha on a spontaneous and unmotivated mission to create the harmony of all together.

Once the battle for life is accomplished, Kutuzov knows his mission is over and dies. The culmination of his mission, however, is his "speech" (*slovo*) to the troops (IV,iv,vi), delivered but a few pages before his acceptance of the end of his mission in death. He thanks the troops for their loyal service. The troops shout "hurrah," and Kutuzov's "eye begins to shine with a meek, seemingly mocking glow."

But then this man for whom "thoughts and words used to express them are not what move people" (IV,iv,v) delivers himself of a speech. "Suddenly his voice and facial expression change."

> So that's it, my dear brothers. I know things are difficult for you, but what can we do? Be patient. It'll be over soon. Let's guide our guests out, and then we'll rest. For your service the Tsar will not forget you. Things are difficult for you, but still you are home, while they—just look at what they've come to, worse than the lowliest beggar. While they were strong, we did not take pity on ourselves, but now we can take pity on them, for they too are human beings. Isn't that so, my chums? (IV,iv,vi)

These words, which do not cause but give expression to the victory of the residents, are received by them with "sympathy," and this reception transfigures Kutuzov's image: "his face became brighter as the old man's meek smile wrinkled the corners of his lips and eyes into stars." The scene closes with the resounding accord of the soldier's "joyful shouts" and Kutuzov's unexpected sobs. Transfigured Kutuzov represents the best of all in each.

Just as Kutuzov's mode of being in the world is in loving accord with others, so is his mode of knowing the world. True, blind in one eye, he does not see as others do, and he listens to his generals' reports with a "piece of tow" in one ear (III,ii,xv). But this is because, as Prince Andrew understands, Kutuzov has a "contempt for knowledge and the mind." Kutuzov knows "something different, independent of knowledge and the mind." As Prince Andrew comes to understand Kutuzov, his "other father," he sees that in Kutuzov there is an "absence of everything personal" and "instead of the mind (which groups events [sobytija] and makes deductions) there is just the capacity for the calm contemplation of the course of events" (khod sobytij) (III,ii,xvi). Kutuzov knows through consciousness. This consciousness does not stop at the boundary of his personal interest. "He understands that there is something stronger and more significant than his will." This something is the "inevitable course of events," the sum total of all will with which he can live in accord only when by a negative action he "renounces his personal will." Kutuzov "will have nothing of his own." But when Kutuzov renounces his personal will, he thereby allows the expression of the will of all to come to be. He does not sacrifice himself, however, because he too is part of the

All, so that in this renunciation of the personal Kutuzov transcends himself and thereby expresses his own true will in accord with all. The ground and condition of this expression is the "contemplation" of the "inevitable course of events," that transcending awareness which goes forth from self in its seizure of everything, the consciousness of life. Kutuzov has "insight (*prozrenie*) into the supreme laws" (IV,iv,v). He knows the will of all. This will of the All he knows is represented as the patriotic feeling of the residents, who must rid themselves of the enemy of life and is expressed by him in his "directing all his energies away from killing and exterminating people and toward saving them and taking pity on them." Kutuzov, therefore, is not a hero in the European mold. He is not the leader of the people but their servant. Kutuzov is the Russian hero who has a saintly insight into the will of the residents, which is the divine will coming to be in all.

Just before the battle of Borodino, then, as with Napoleon but unlike him, Kutuzov too is presented with an image of his issue. The Smolensk icon of the Mother of God is brought out onto the field in procession. "When it got to the top of the hill, the icon stopped. The warm rays of the sun beat down directly from above; a faint, fresh breeze toyed with the hair on the bared heads and with the ribbons that decorated the icon; the soft chanting resounded beneath the open sky" (III,ii,xxi). Before the battle Napoleon was shown in his tent. Kutuzov moves into the expanse of nature, which is filled with light and song. This is the world in which he resides. Weighed down by his old, heavy, tired, and weak body, the one who has no erotic passions left, his head covered with the white hair of his years, with great effort Kutuzov approaches the icon, blesses himself, bends down, touches the earth, and sighs heavily. The icon of the one who has done the will of the Lord and hence gives issue to the Divine embodies and reveals Kutuzov's mode of being in the world. In his negative acts of rejection of his personal will and serving submission to the course of events he gives issue to the divine will coming to be. Before the battle of Borodino, in his loving adoration before the icon of the Mother of God, grounded in reverence for the earth and childlike adoration for the Divine, Kutuzov the "old man" with the exhausted body reveals his religious consciousness of life.

Napoleon and Kutuzov, the European hero and the Russian servant, embody and reveal the two opposed modes of knowing and loving which govern the universe of *War and Peace*. Many of the other characters in the work reflect in more detail one facet of these archetypal figures. Helen Kuragin as the body, her brother Anatole as the self-centered will, Berg as the self-interested relative, Rostopchin as the self-interested leader, and Speransky as the one who knows by reason alone—all reflect aspects of Napoleon. Natasha in both her knowing and loving, Princess Mary in her lack of anything personal, Bazdeev in his wizenedness, and Karataev in his attunement with the course of events—all reflect aspects of Kutuzov. In the end the one who comes most to resemble Kutuzov is Pierre, the one who never quite meets Kutuzov. In his captivity, when he is forced to confront the physical limitation of his being, Pierre discovers his inner freedom. In his "joyful consciousness of freedom" Pierre finds religious faith, "the God who is right here and everywhere." This God he knows "not by words, not by reasoning, but by direct feeling" (IV,iv,xii). In his moment of subjection to necessity and control of the external world, Pierre turns inward to consciousness. He "throws away the mental telescope" with which he had "looked over the head of people" and learns "to see the great, eternal, and infinite in all." Removed from the ordinary conditions of life, freed from his endless pursuit of plans and schemes for life, he learns "to contemplate the ever-changing, ever-great, incomprehensible, and infinite life around him." Pierre resembles Kutuzov and finds his God.

THE CHARACTER'S KNOWLEDGE

The kinds of knowledge by which Tolstoy believed we can know reality are tried out in the fictional images of his characters. Knowledge through empiricist reason's deduction from sense data, knowledge through sensory experience, and knowledge through consciousness are the ways by which Tolstoyan characters themselves know reality. To be sure, the way a character knows is itself known by the reader through the narrator's representation of the character's knowing. The question of the character's knowledge inevitably raises the question of the reader's knowledge. To the details of Tolstoy's narrative technique I shall soon turn, but first we must explore the kinds of knowledge tried out in the fictional representations of the character's knowledge.

The trilogy *Childhood, Boyhood, Youth* poses a unique and telling problem in the representation of a character's knowledge because it is a first-person narrative. The narration is complicated further, as we have already noted, by the double-layered telling, the story told by Nikolenka and the story recalled by Irtenev. Despite this complication, however, the trilogy, as a first-person narrative, represents the character's ways to know unmediated by any outside narrator. The character himself tells, and therefore his ways to know are embodied and revealed in his narration. In the trilogy what stands out are the two extremes of knowledge, through empiricist reason and through consciousness.

In *Childhood*, as one would expect, the central figures in the life of the young boy are his father and mother. But the character does not know his parents in the same way, and the way he tells about his parents reveals how and what they mean for him. Each parent is first presented in separate chapters told by Nikolenka, scenes which represent a significant moment to him. But then, later in the work, the narration returns to the parents to capture their meaning for Irtenev. In a chapter entitled significantly "What kind of a person was my father?" Irtenev tells what he knows.

> *He was* a person of the last century and *possessed* that exclusive character, common for that century's youth, which combined chivalry, initiative, self-confidence, amiability, and revelry. . . . *He knew* the extreme measure of pride and presumption that would raise him in the eyes of society without offending others. *He was* eccentric, but not always and *he used* his eccentricity as a means, as a substitute for breeding or wealth. . . . *He was* a connoisseur in all things conducive to comfort and enjoyment and *he knew* how to use them. . . . *He was* sentimental even to the point of tears. . . . His nature was such that to do a good deed he needed an audience. (x;*ital. mine*)

For Irtenev papa does not exist; he can only be summed up. He cannot be recalled, even though he can be remembered. Papa exists outside Irtenev's consciousness. The way Irtenev tells reveals the distance between him and his father. The obviously repetitive syntactical structures relying on the simple sentence—he was, he knew, he used—tell us only about papa, not about the narrator's experience of papa. Papa is the subject of the sentences but only an object for Irtenev. The narration does not represent papa through sense data; it sums up deductions from the prior experience of papa. Papa is known as an abstraction from what he did and felt. He is known by his "nature." The narrator who tells of papa is isolated within himself, separated from the alien observed world. He does not seem close to his father and bears no affection for him.

Irtenev's knowledge of Maman related in the chapter entitled "Childhood" (xv) reveals a totally different relationship between the subject and object, the child and the parent.

> Having had your fill of running about, you sit in your highchair at the tea table. It's already late, you have long since drunk your cup of sugared milk, sleep is weighing heavy on your eyes, and you do not budge from your place, you sit and listen. And why not? Maman is speaking with someone and the sound of her voice is so sweet, so inviting. The sound alone says so much to my heart. With eyes dimmed by drowsiness I gaze into her face and suddenly she becomes ever so little, so little, her face no larger than a button, but still as clearly visible as ever to me. I see her look at me and smile. I like seeing her tiny like that. I squint my eyes even more and she becomes no larger than the little spots I see with closed eyes. But I move and the spell is broken. I narrow my eyes, shift my position, and try any way I can to revive it, but to no avail.

For Irtenev this is a moment of memory, a memory which "refreshes and elevates his soul and serves for him as the source of his finest pleasure." The moment, however, is imagined as a repeated event, as something that happened many times. The verbs are controlled by the untranslatable modifying adverbial particle (*byvalo*), which marks repeated action in the past, even when used with present-tense forms as here. Furthermore, the passage divides in two, the first half told in the second-person singular form without the pronoun, equivalent to the French "on," and the second half told in the first person. The first half focuses on the narrator's recollection of the circumstances and surroundings of the experience, the place and objects in the place, culminating in the sounds of Maman's voice which came to him. The second half focuses on the narrator's going forth from himself in an act of knowledge of the other as he looks at Maman and "suddenly" sees her transformed by him into a being he bears within his knowing consciousness and for whom he has great affection, expressed in the reduplicated adjective, "so little, so little." The surrounding objects and the impression of the sound of Maman's voice and her beloved image transformed by him all now exist in the narrator's recollecting consciousness. But then when Irtenev looks at Maman's face transformed by him, she looks back at him with a smile. In this moment they coexist for each other in mutual love, and from this moment she exists within him, just as do the spots he sees with his eyes closed. Even as Maman is both subject and object for the narrator's sentences, so she is a subject and an object for his knowing consciousness. He sees her and he experiences her love for him within him. The narrator who tells of Maman is at one with her, and in his recollection she resides in him. Moreover, as the passage moves from the second to the first person, the effect of the particle of repeated action gets lost and the recollection of Maman becomes her presence. Remembered, Maman is recalled into being, only to be lost again by a chance change in perspective. The narrator's recollection of his perception brings Maman back to life for him. Thus the passage which relates the character's knowledge of Maman paradigmatically reiterates the theme of the work, the loss of love and its resurrection through memory.

Irtenev knows papa as an idea deduced from his experience; Maman lives with his memory as the "source of his finest pleasure." The epistemological mode of affective memory which represents knowledge not as abstract ideas about sense data, nor as impressions from sense data, but as the result of an act of going forth from self into other to seize the other for the self, this affective memory is Tolstoy's first representation of a character's knowledge through "consciousness." He uses it again, perhaps less successfully, in *Youth* (not in *Boyhood*) in the scene of return to the family residence, the garden encounter with "she," and also in *Family Happiness*. Affective memory occurs only in first-person narrations. In third-person narration this knowledge through consciousness is not represented as affective memory but as affective awareness. The narrator represents the character in a moment of meaningful internalization of the other. Olenin is on his way to the Caucasus. The more he distances himself from the circumstances that defined and confined him, the "more and more merry" he becomes (iii). The new people he meets now seem to be "simple beings with whom he can simply chat and joke without considering what class they belong to. They all belong to the human race, which is in its totality dear to Olenin, and they all relate to him in a friendly manner." Olenin experiences for the first time on his journey of discovery and in a vague way a sense of love for all and love from all. This moral experience is then followed by an experience of affective awareness which transforms the moral experience into a metaphysical one.

As he enters the Cossack territory proper, Olenin, delighting in the warm spring weather, feels "even more merry." He is anxious to get a view of the mountains about which he has heard so much. Indeed his coachman does once point them out as they stick out from behind the clouds, but the "something grey, white, and fleecy" that he sees does not correspond to his received ideas about them, and he dismisses the "completely unique view and particular beauty of the snowy mountains" as one of those fictions of civilization, "like the music of Bach or *love* for a woman." But then the next morning, in the clarity of day, he happens to glance outward and toward these mountains.

> Suddenly but twenty steps away or so it seemed in the first instant he caught sight of gigantic pure white masses with delicate contours and of the fantastic, distinct airy outline of the summits against the distant sky. When he had realized the whole (*vsju*) distance between him and the mountains and the sky, the whole immensity of the mountains, and when he felt (*pochuvstvovalas' emu*) the whole infinity of that beauty he began to fear that it was a phantasm or a dream.

In this glance, Olenin sees the mountains not simply as colors and shapes out there. The mountains themselves are part of a totality; the word "whole," which is the adjectival form of the pronoun "all" (*vsë*), is repeated three times. Indeed it is the outline of the mountains against the distant sky which makes this totality available to his experience. But this experience of this totality is not an experience of an object out there. The awareness of the totality brings Olenin to an awareness of himself in relation to the totality, his distance from it while he is in it. Furthermore, only in this awareness of the totality does the experience become affective and Olenin "feels" the beauty. This "feeling," however, is not something he does, as a subject of a verb does its action; the verb is in the reflexive form, the pronoun "subject" in the dative case, and the "feeling" is expressed grammatically, as is quite possible and even common in Russian, as something not that he does or has, but something that happens to him. But then, the "more and more he peered at that chain of snowy mountains which grow right out of the steppes and runs off into the distance, he little by little began to penetrate that beauty and *felt (po-chuvstvoval)* the mountains." The beauty that happens to him he now himself "penetrates," and the mountains themselves become what he feels. This "feeling" is now expressed with the transitive form of the verb, the object of which is a concrete thing, a less usual usage in Russian and marked by Tolstoy in italics. The "mountains" exist within Olenin's affective awareness, and as a result "from that moment everything he saw, everything he thought, everything he felt acquired for him the new and sternly majestic character of the mountains." His whole Moscow past is transformed by this "new character" and "a solemn voice seems to say to him 'Now it has begun.' " Olenin has come to a primary intuition of the All.

What has begun, then, is a whole new way of knowing the world. The awareness of himself within the All marked by the mountains that outline the sky penetrates and transforms everything he sees. The external world exists within his consciousness as his affective experience of that totality.

> The road, the outline of the Terek just becoming visible in the distance, the villages, and the people all now no longer seemed trifles. He'd look at the sky and remember the mountains. He'd look at himself or Vanyusha and again the mountains. Two Cossacks ride right by *(vot edut)*, their guns in their cases swaying rhythmically on their backs and their horses shuffling their white and bay legs—and the mountains. Beyond the Terek smoke from a Tartar village is visible—and the mountains. The sun rises and glistens on the Terek now visible from beyond the reeds—and the mountains. From the village comes a wagon, women pass by, beautiful, young women—and the mountains. Warriors roam the steppes and I am driving along and do not fear them, I have a gun and strength and youth—and the mountains.

In this remarkable passage, which closes the delineated segment of the discovery of the mountains, the narrator looks at Olenin's internal experience of the world. He begins with a statement about a change in awareness. Then he defines the area of Olenin's general and repeated vision: whenever he looks at the sky or himself he has in his consciousness the feel of the mountains. The mountains permeate the totality of the experience, of himself and of the sky within and abroad. At this point the narration shifts from the general to a specific moment and two Cossacks "ride right by" (the adverb *vot*, here translated "right," is a verbal gesture indicating immediate presence). Olenin experiences their movement and the shuffling colored images of the horses' legs, as if in a closeup. The reader is thrust into the process of the character's knowing as Olenin moves along through the scene and things move into the sphere of his awareness. Each new thing seen is followed by the refrain of affective awareness "and the mountains." But then at the close of the passage the narration again shifts and we move further into Olenin's psyche: he speaks in the first person, although not as a quotation marked with punctuation (the English translations are wrong here). The meaning of the mountains for him becomes a reality in his own mind: the consciousness of the mountains in him transforms his sense of self and he feels full of strength and youth. Olenin is alive with a new life within the sphere of the mountains which outline the sky. It is this sense that "the old life has been wiped away and that a new life has begun, a completely new life" which contains the real meaning of the experience of the mountains within (xi). For Olenin the internal awareness of the presence of the mountains in all that he knows and does creates the "youthful feeling of the joy of life without cause." His "new life had begun not as he expected when he left Moscow, but it was unexpectedly good. The mountains, the mountains, the mountains, were sensed in everything he thought or felt." This delineated segment of the discovery of the mountains is a journey of the mind toward its awareness of a new sense of "life," a life lived in the consciousness of the All. In the mountains Olenin experiences the sudden joy of life.

Olenin's new way of seeing leads to a new way of being. His discovery of the mountains begins the process by which he redefines love. This redefining of love, which is the purpose and process of his journey, however, is nothing other than the discovery of his true self, his love for all which is God's love in him. The mountains which outline the sky are an emblem of God. This is precisely how Tolstoy reinterpreted this very experience some thirty years later.

The devil almost got me in his clutches most terribly. When working on my Catechism he suggested to me that I could get along without the concept of God, the God who is at the foundation of everything, the God by whose will we live in this world, by whose will our divine essence is imprisoned in personality for some purposes of His and that I could retain just the God who is manifested in our life, and suddenly I was overcome with dejection and terror. I was horrified, I started to think and to check, and I found the God I had almost lost. As it were I discovered Him anew and came to love Him. No matter what sad or different things may happen or be thought, one has just to recall that God exists and it becomes joyful. Just like in the Caucasus there was the physical impression—and the mountains! so here a spiritual one—and God! (52,149;1894)

For Tolstoy knowledge by that attending consciousness which seeks to seize everything and become God is the way to life and love. In his fiction the representation of a character in the process of going forth outward and toward the other in an act of knowing through this consciousness which grasps the totality within embodies and reveals the path to God. The representation of the mind's journey of discovery is the emblem of the soul's search for God. Olenin's encounter with the mountains is autopsychological.

KNOWLEDGE through affective awareness is a way of knowing the reality in which one exists. It does not oppose a knowing subject and a known object out there. The subject exists in the reality and the reality exists in the subject's consciousness. Such knowledge is knowledge by participation: the subject goes forth into reality, takes part in it and takes that part of it back into itself. To be conscious of my finger, I must go forth from my center of awareness, where I reside, into my finger, become aware of the finger and then return that awareness to my center of consciousness, where now we both reside together. The process is a reversal and a return. Empiricist knowledge opposes the subject and the object. The knowing subject does not participate in the reality it knows; the objects out there impress themselves on the subject, but the subject does not take part in their reality nor actively take their reality into itself. In *War and Peace* this notion of participation is what relates the epistemological event to the moral event. How one knows the field of the battle for life is related to how one participates in the battle for life. Napoleon is the absolute minimal participant in the battle for life; he tells the strangers what to do. Kutuzov goes forth into the battle for life through his sympathetic awareness of those who participate in the event; he allows the residents to be. The two moments, the epistemological and the moral, are brought into focus when Pierre enters the field of battle. On his way, as he encounters "Cossacks, infantry and cavalry, wagons, boxes, and cannons" all around, Pierre is overcome with a "joyous new feeling, the feeling of the necessity to undertake something and sacrifice something, the pleasant feeling of the awareness that everything that comprises human happiness, the comforts of life, riches, even life itself, is rubbish which in comparison with something else would be pleasant to throw away" (III,ii,xviii). What this "something else" is Pierre does not know; at this point the "sacrifice itself comprises his joyous new feeling." This "something else" is what Pierre will find in the battle for life.

His mission, he believes is to go "to the army," to "take a look," "to participate in the battle," to find out where "the position itself" is. But Pierre is bothered by the "strange thought" that the men he encounters, "condemned to wounds and death," are mainly absorbed by his white hat even as they are filled with gladness and warmed by the sun (III,ii,xx). "Tomorrow they may die, how can they think of something other than death," he wonders. "And suddenly by some secret connection of thought he imagines the carts with the wounded, the ringing bells, the slanted rays of the sun, and the song of the cavalry soldiers." The "secret connection of thoughts" reveals a truth Pierre has yet to understand. Pierre goes to the field of battle in conflict between his mission to find the "position itself" and his "strange thoughts" about the soldiers in whose facial expression he sees, not concern for "personal success," not "personal questions," but the "general questions of life and death" (III,ii,xxii) and the "latent warmth of partiotism" (III,ii,xxv). The epistemological mission is accompanied by an existential moral concern for life.

Pierre gets out of his carriage and goes up onto a hill from where the "field of battle is visible" (III,ii,xxi). The sun is shining overhead, and in the "pure, fresh air" the "panorama" opens out before him as if it were an "amphitheater." Pierre looks upward, outward, and toward, but "nowhere is there the field of battle he is expecting to see."

He "cannot find the position." Later he returns to the hill again to look for the field of battle.

> Pierre looked directly in front of himself and was transfigured with rapture by the beauty of the spectacle. It was the same panorama he had admired from this hill the day before. But now the entire area was covered with troops and smoke clouds from the guns, and the slanting rays of the bright sun, which had risen to the left behind Pierre, were casting on it through the clear morning air a penetrating light in shades of gold and rose and long, long dark shadows. In the distance the forest which marked the end of the panorama seemed carved from the same precious, yellowish-green stone and was silhouetted against the horizon by the curved outline of the treetops. . . . Nearby glittered golden fields and copses. To the front, to the right, to the left, there were troops to be seen everywhere. Everything was vivid, majestic, and unexpected. (III,ii,xxx)

Just before his initiation into the battle for life, Pierre looks out onto a thing of beauty. From his lofty distance, the world before him is transformed into an aesthetic object. The "slanting rays of the bright sun" turn the forests into precious jewels glittering in their brilliant color. Pierre resembles Olenin, who entered the Caucasus and could not find the spectacular mountains he knew as an idea in books, but then turned to the mountains and saw their beauty. Pierre begins to discover his position in the universe when he sees the world he is in, transfigured by the rays of the sun which had also gladdened his vision of the wounded soldiers.

What distinguishes Pierre's view of the panoramic spectacle is the vantage point of the narration. In the spectacle, we are looking at Pierre as he looks directly in front of himself. The panorama is viewed in relation to the viewer and filtered through his aestheticising consciousness. In the passage that follows we lose sight of Pierre as observer, but look at his observation as it is happening. We do not see the aesthetic object known out there; we see the sense data as and when they are being experienced. We are thrust into the character's psyche.

> *Poof!* suddenly a round compact bit of smoke reflecting violet, grey and milky-white colors became visible and *boom!* there re-

sounded in a second the sound of that bit of smoke. *Poof! Poof!* two bits of smoke arose bumping into and blending with each other and *boom! boom!* the sounds confirmed what the eye saw.

The narration slows down the action; the experience of the gun-smoke "and strange to say its sounds" is represented in slow motion. This slowed narration focuses totally on empiricist knowledge by observation, the sense data impressing themselves through the senses onto a perceiving mind which is just a blank knowing subject. The "view of the field of battle" is known through bits of sound and sight. To emphasize this knowledge through sense data, Tolstoy translates the experience of the sense data of sight and sound for the reader into words (sounds) which are conventional signs designating each individual sense datum. "Poof!" translates for the reader the sight of the smoke; "boom" the sound heard after the "poof!" is seen (do not confuse the sound "poof" with the English "puff"). The narration thus reduces the experience of the field of battle to two bits of sensory experience; what is sight and sound for the character becomes two sounds for the reader. In the representation of the character's knowledge the reader experiences the character's impressions as he does. The empiricist epistemological event of "observation" is presented in slow motion and in the abstract. The narration thrusts the reader into the experience of knowledge through sense data, "sensation" in general. We are made to be present in this experience. As readers we participate in the act.

The narration then again turns to Pierre, now to look at him as he experiences the gunsmoke.

Pierre glanced round at the first bit of smoke which he had taken for a round, compact ball but immediately in its place there were spheres of smoke spreading to one side and poof . . . (with a pause) poof-poof there arose three more, four more and after each with the same intervals boom . . . boom-boom-boom responded the beautiful, firm, precise sounds. These bits of smoke now seemed to rush, now to stand still, while the woods, fields, and sparkling bayonets seemed to rush past them. From the left, along the fields and brush, these big bits of smoke with their triumphant echoes continually kept on rising, and nearer still, along the hollows and the woods, little bits of smoke which had not succeeded in rounding themselves out kept on bursting forth from muskets and likewise giving forth their own little echoes. Trakh-ta-ta-trakh crackled the muskets frequently and feebly in comparison with the cannon shots.

Pierre immediately mistakes the bit of smoke for a ball. From the sensation he makes the wrong deduction. But then as the sensations continue, he is drawn into the experience itself and we see Pierre in the process of perceiving the impressions. It is a closeup.[1] We again enter Pierre's psyche. True, we do not see him in the process of making deductions; we do not see how the external impressions are related to the inner self, to his emotions, attitudes, or beliefs; there is no apperception of the event. All we get is, as it were, an empiricist train of thoughts, the sense impressions from the external world: the sight of the bits of smoke and the sounds "poof . . . poof-poof," "boom . . . boom-boom-boom," and "trakh-ta-ta-trakh." We observe Pierre observing. The narrator knows somewhat more than Pierre, of course, and sees the muskets, but Pierre experiences only the bits of smoke and the sounds which have no meaning for him. His experience throughout, therefore, is totally limited to perception through the senses. What Napoleon knows with his empiricist reason and therefore thinks he can order and control, Pierre knows with his empiricist observation and therefore feels is beautiful. In either case, the knowledge is divorced from human reality, the moral world in which people are killing people. The narration observes Pierre observing because Tolstoy wants to show the flaw of knowledge which is divorced from moral value.[2]

But Pierre "wants to be where these bits of smoke, those glistening sabres and cannons, that movement, those sounds are." No sooner does he start to enter the field of battle, however, than his perception changes. "For the first time" he takes note of the wounded. As he approaches the center of the field of battle, furthermore, he has no sense

---

[1] In this book I have borrowed and expanded the comparison of Tolstoy's technique to the art of film, first discussed by Pavel Gromov in his very fine books on Tolstoy's style. See *O stile L'va Tolstogo: stanovlenie "dialektiki dushi"* (Leningrad, 1971) and *O stile L'va Tolstogo: 'dialektika dushi" v "Vojne i mire"* (Leningrad, 1977).

[2] The epistemological and moral significance of this sequence was first analyzed in detail by Leon Stilman in his important article "Nabljudenija nad nekotorym osobennostjam kompozitsii i stilja v romane Tolstogo *Vojna i mir*," in *American Contributions to the Fifth International Congress of Slavicists, Sofia 1963* (The Hague, 1965), pp. 332-335.

that he is, at the center, and "this place precisely because he is in it, seems one of the most insignificant places in the battle," and he feels "out of place and without a task" (III,ii,xxxi). At the center he is an outsider. The others, the soldiers "occupied with their task" here at the center, seemed to "experience a kind of family animation, the same in each and common to all." But slowly the soldiers' "hostile distrust" of the "man in the white hat" is transformed into an "affectionate, bemused sympathy" (*uchastie*) not unlike the feeling they have for their mascots, and they "accept Pierre into their family." The battle rages on, and Pierre sees that with each burst shell and "each loss" the "animation flames up more and more."

> As from an approaching stormcloud, lightning flashes of a latent flaring fire blazed up more and more intensely and rapidly on the faces of all, as if in resistance to what was taking place. Pierre did not look directly at the field of battle nor interest himself in what was happening there. He was entirely absorbed in the contemplation of that fire flaming up more and more, which he felt was flaring up in the same way in his soul.

This is Pierre's first moment of participation. The "latent warmth of feeling" he had noticed from the beginning on the soldiers' faces now flares up as the very spirit which animates the family of men. Pierre shares in their experience and knows as Kutuzov knows. In the face of death, they give forth what they have without forethought or intention and regardless of what is happening. Pierre's participation in the "family animation," his sense of residing and belonging, releases or increases his capacity to participate, and so when the cannon fire reaches the family circle and "suddenly something happens," Pierre without forethought or intention spontaneously responds to the call for ammunition. "I'll go." Confused and frightened he rushes, giving forth of himself he knows not quite how or why. In this moment Pierre finds that "something else" he was seeking and participates in the battle for life. The Stranger becomes the Resident.

After this moment Pierre sees the battle anew. Now he sees the enemy and stands directly "face to alien face" with him (III,ii,xxxii). But then he returns to his "family circle" only to find some of his family dead. At this moment the real meaning of the battle for life comes to Pierre's awareness. Pierre sees the field of battle no longer as an aesthetic object transformed by the gladdening rays of the sun.

Once he has shared with all others the inner sense of the event and, moved by this sharing, once he has given forth of himself to the event—that is, once he has participated in reality in knowledge and love—then he experiences the existential and moral value of life. "No, now they'll stop it, now they'll be horrified by what they've done," he thinks as he leaves the field of battle, assuming that what he has learned in his participation all will now know. As Pierre leaves the field, the sun still shines, but now it no longer transforms his vision of the world; instead, he hears the sounds of the battle which have "increased to desperation like a man who, over-straining himself, shrieks with all his remaining strength." Pierre now knows. The delineated segment of Pierre at Borodino begins with his hopeful intention to express his relatedness but paradigmatically turns into a moment of estrangement only to be transformed by his participation in the "family animation." In *War and Peace* paradigmatic actions are often representations of a character's knowledge.

THE FIRST representation of the experience of war in the novel, Nicholas Rostov's participation in the crossing of the Enns River, is just such a representation of a character's knowledge. It begins on a harmonic note. "Und die ganze Welt hoch" cries the German farmer in whose cottage Nicholas and Denisov are staying, as he takes off his cap and waves it above his head. "Und vivat die ganze Welt" shouts Nicholas in reply, likewise waving his cap. The two men, who have "no reason for such joy," then "look at each other with joyful ecstasy and brotherly love, shake their heads as a sign of their mutual love and part smiling" (I,ii,iv). This moment of human relatedness opens the first scene of war, but it is quickly dispelled. Rostov goes off into the cottage and is thrust into a state of discord, a conflict between his sense of honesty to himself and his sense of honor for the others in his regiment. In his cottage Rostov learns that Telyanin has apparently stolen Denisov's money. Rostov goes off to confront Telyanin and make the theft known. He is chastized by the senior officer Bogdanych for thus violating the honor of the regiment, but Rostov stands up to Bogdanych for calling him a liar. He now sees Bogdanych as his "enemy" (*vrag*), and it is this personal enmity which he brings into the battle at Enns with the public enemy (*neprijatel'*), the French. In the context of this state of enmity, therefore, Denisov's love-letter observations on life, which Denisov reads to

Rostov, seem but sentimental drivel: "Until we love, we are asleep. We are chidren of dust. But once you have loved, you are God, you are pure, as on the first day of creation." In the ensuing battle Rostov is to learn that this sentiment contains a truth, even as he recovers in a new form the joyful ecstasy of mutual love with which his experience of battle begins. The delineated segment of the crossing of the Enns is a paradigmatic action reiterating the basic rhythm of experience of the whole work.

There are two primary participants in the battle, the aristocratic Prince Nesvitsky and Rostov, and the crossing of the Enns is represented through the experience of each of them. For Nesvitsky, the battle begins with a picnic, as he treats his fellow officers to some piroshki and doppelkümmel. We see him chewing them in his "beautiful, moist mouth" (I,ii,vi). He has a "weighty body." As he chats with his fellow soldiers during the picnic, he masks his fear of the coming events with masculine bravado, joking with innuendo about the nuns in the convent on the hill. This preoccupation with food and sex embodies and reveals his experience of life. He is a man of the flesh.

As Nesvitsky approaches the bridge over the river, not surprisingly, then, this man of the flesh cannot grasp the meaning of the events: he experiences only the fragments of the world around him. He catches bits and snippets of conversations and takes note mainly of the crude remarks made to an attractive German girl fleeing for her life. Standing on the bridge, Nesvitsky sees only the "waves" of images that pass before his perceiving consciousness.

> Looking down over the rails, Prince Nesvitsky saw the rapid, noisy, little waves of the Enns chase each other along, merging, rippling, and eddying round the piles of the bridge. Looking on the bridge, he saw equally monotonous, living waves of soldiers, shoulder straps, covered shakoes, knapsacks, bayonets, long muskets, and under the shakoes faces with broad cheekbones, sunken cheeks, and listless, tired expressions, and feet moving through the sticky mud that covered the planks of the bridge. Sometimes through the monotonous waves of soldiers, an officer in a cloak and with a look on his face different from the soldiers' would squeeze through, like a spurt of white foam on the waves of the Enns; sometimes a hussar on foot, an orderly, or a

townsman would be carried across the bridge through the river; sometimes an officer's or a company's baggage wagon, hemmed in on all sides, piled high, and covered with leather, would float along the bridge, like a log floating down the river. (I,ii,vii)

To Nesvitsky these images are all the same. In all their variety these fragments of reality have for him the same monotonous meaning. What is in the river and on the bridge merge for him in his consciousness and for the reader in the similes. All that is seen are bits and pieces floating along in this closeup. Nesvitsky can make no sense of his experience.

When the first shot is fired, then, Nesvitsky "suddenly hears a sound still new to him, a sound of something rapidly approaching, something big, something that splashes into the water." He does not know what his experience is, and we are shown him in the process of experiencing in one sentence this new sound from the moment of the sound to the sense of its movement toward him, to the sense of its size, to its final sound when it splashes in the water. It is another closeup. Only from the reaction of others does Nesvitsky later realize that what he experienced was the sound of a cannon ball. Nesvitsky's knowledge is knowledge by sense data. In the representation of this man of the flesh, the narrator observes him observing: "Nesvitsky looked around and saw some fifteen paces away, separated from him by a living mass of moving infantry, something red, black, shaggy, with a cap set on the back of his head and a cloak jauntily draped over his shoulders: Vaska Denisov." This sentence captures Nesvitsky's way of knowing. The standard word order, subject, verb, object, is maintained, and the sentence ends with the object "Vaska Denisov." Everything that modifies the object precedes it in an order determined by the process of seeing itself: first the measure of distance from the object is given, then the object is represented as if seen when moving toward the subject, first the bright color, then the dark color, then the texture, then the details of clothing, and only then the person recognized, "Vaska Denisov." The strange, even strained syntax of this sentence is designed to imitate the action, the very process of seeing an object that is moving toward you. The narrator observes the character observing. Prince Nesvitsky, a man of the flesh who knows only by sense data, observes but does not understand the meaning of war or death or life.

Rostov enters the battle obsessed with his private war. To him the battle makes sense. It is, he believes, a personal test of his bravery. He assumes that his enemy, Bogdanych, is watching his every move and thus Rostov plays out his private rivalry on the public battlefield. If Nesvitsky cares for the flesh and sees only sense data, Rostov cares only for his reputation and sees the battle as his private affair. What reveals the true test of these men is their first encounter with the ravages of war when a soldier gets wounded before their eyes. To understand this event, however, we must now look to its larger context.

The delineated segment of the crossing of the Enns river opens with an abstract yet factual statement about the event which is happening: "Kutuzov fell back toward Vienna, destroying behind him the bridges over the river Enns (at Brunae) and Traum (near Linz). On October 23 the Russian troops were crossing the river Enns. At midday the Russian baggage train, the artillery, and column of troops were moving slowly through the town of Enns on both sides of the bridge" (I,ii,vi). The segment begins as a chronicle. The narrator knows what, where, and when events happened. The statement is removed from the human experience of the event and the natural world in which events take place. There is no attempt to understand why what happened, happened. The narration tells what the mind knows through empiricist reason, as one knows that Madagascar exists.

In the very next paragraph the narration changes its focus. Now the narrator moves into the scene in which the event is to take place. The narrator is a character there. This narrator locates the event in the expanse of nature.

> The day was warm, rainy, autumnal. The expansive perspective that opened out from the elevated spot where the Russian batteries were guarding the bridge was at times suddenly veiled by a muslin curtain of slanting rain and was at times suddenly expanded so that in the light of the sun objects became *visible* clearly in the distance, as if covered in lacquer. There could be *seen* down below a little town, with its white houses and red roofs, its cathedral and bridge troops. There could be *seen* at the bend of the Danube, vessels, an island, and a castle with a park surrounded by the waters of the confluence of the Enns and the Danube. There could be *seen* the rocky left bank of the Danube

covered with a pine forest with bluish gorges and a mysterious distance of green peaks. There could be *seen* the turrets of a convent which stood out from behind a wild, seemingly untouched pine forest, and way ahead in the distance on a mountain on the other side of the Enns there could be *seen* the horse patrols of the enemy. (italics added)

The narrator now seems to stand with the Russian batteries on their elevated spot as they guard the bridge. He is one of them, any one of them. The panorama is not filtered through any particular consciousness. The panorama is not aestheticized. This is simply and solely what is seen by all, and this seeing is marked verbally. This panorama of the world beyond, the narrator's glance outward and toward, provides the background for the battle; it is the world in which the crossing takes place. Nesvitsky, who indulges his fantasies about the nuns in the convent, thinks it is a "fabulous place." As Nesvitsky and Rostov move into battle, however, the struggle on the bridge consumes their attention, and the world in which they reside is lost from their vision.

But then a shot is fired which hits one of the men. It is the first war casuality in the novel. Nesvitsky grabs the arm of a fellow officer standing next to him and shouts, "Oh, oh, look, one of them has fallen, has fallen, has fallen." He then "turns away" (*otverachivajas'*) from the scene, pronouncing to all "If I were the Tsar, I should never go to war." The smoke of battle flows over the bridge and Nesvitsky sees no more. He disappears from the text and the focus shifts to Rostov. Absorbed in his private battle, Rostov is shocked to a new awareness only when he sees a hussar fall. "Together with the others Rostov runs up to him." He hears the shout for stretchers and the wounded man's pained cries.

Nicholas Rostov turned away (*otvertilsja*) and, as if in search of something, he began to gaze into the distance, at the waters of the Danube, at the sky, at the sun. How beautiful the sky seemed! How blue, how calm, how deep! How bright and august the setting sun! How tenderly and lustrously shone the water in the distant Danube! And still more beautiful were the distant mountains bluish beyond the Danube, the convent, the mysterious gorges, the pine forests bathed to the tree-tops in mist. It is peaceful and happy there. "I'd want nothing, nothing at all would I want if only I were there," thought Rostov. "There is so much happiness in me alone and in that sun but here, groans, suffering, terror, and this uncertainty, this hurry. Now again (*vot opjat'*) they are shouting something and again everyone has begun running back somewhere and I'm running with them and here it is, here it is, death, above me, around me. An instant and I shall no longer see that sun, that water, that gorge." (I,ii,viii)

Unlike Nesvitsky, Rostov spontaneously rushes forth to the wounded man, and when he does "turn away" he does not deliver himself of some empty pronouncement, but "as if in search of something," he looks outward and toward the expanse of nature. The sky, the emblem of the All in which everything resides, appears for the first time in the novel. Now, however, the narration itself zooms in on the inner experience of the character. The reader is impelled into the psyche. What is represented is Rostov's affective awareness of the totality in which his experience is taking place. The syntax of exclamation embodies and reveals this affective awareness. The repeated exclamatory remarks create the effect of an increasing fervor and involvement which culminates in the statement, "It is peaceful and calm there." The images which evoke Rostov's affection are, of course, the very images that appeared in the narrator's panorama of the scene. The landscape has become internalized, and the world beyond lives in the world within. Rostov has grasped the world in which he resides and now knows by consciousness.

This inner experience of the peace and calm "there" is then followed by Rostov's thoughts, set off in quotation marks. We are thrust into another level of the character's knowledge where his judgment and assessment of his situation are made within the context of his affective awareness. Reality is divided into "there" and "here." But the immediacy of the experience of this dichotomous reality is expressed in the consistant consonance (in "s") of the verbal signs which comprise the content of "there" and "here": on the one hand "sun" (*solntse*) and "happiness" (*schastie*); on the other hand "groans" (*stony*), "suffering" (*stradanija*), "terror (*strakh*), "uncertainty" (*nejastnost'*), "hurry" (*pospeshnost'*), "death" (*smert'*). Rostov recollects his reality. But then the world outside intrudes upon his recollecting consciousness ("now again") and Rostov focuses on himself as he is running into and toward death. The meaning of his experience comes to him through his affective awareness, and he realizes that in an instant "I shall no longer see that sun, that water, that gorge." In his affective awareness of the sun in the sky, his internal consciousness of the luminous totality in which he exists, Rostov comes to an awareness of death and hence of the meaning of life. Without his affective awareness he is dead; with it he lives.

The delineated segment of crossing the Enns is narrated in three fundamentally different ways. There is the chronicle of events which opens the scene and tells but little. This is knowledge by reason and understanding, knowledge "passed on by words from other people," the third kind of knowledge. The greater part of this segment is told by a narrator who is on the scene and reports what he observes or observes the characters observing. This narrator knows by "external knowledge," as do the characters whose knowledge he represents. But with Rostov's encounter with the sun in the sky we have another kind of knowledge, the "highest or rather the most profound knowledge," knowledge through attending, affective consciousness. The delineated segment of crossing the Enns embodies and reveals these three kinds of knowledge. In its representation of the characters' knowledge it is an emblem of life, that life which "consists of transferring the third and second kinds of knowledge into the first, when one experiences everything in himself." When Rostov measures himself against the totality in which he resides, he goes forth in attending consciousness to seize all within. Through consciousness he regains the moment of harmony with which he began his forray into battle. What began as a giving forth of self in an enthused moment of "mutual love" ends as a going forth from self in a moment of affective awareness. Rostov's knowledge resembles Olenin's. His mind's journey of discovery in the sky, and hence of the meaning of life as he rushes toward death, is an emblem of the soul's search for God.[3]

THE READER'S KNOWLEDGE

Tolstoy's theory of knowledge is tried out in the images of his characters' moments of knowing. This epistemological system, as we

[3] Gromov's three modes of narration, the "dialectic of behavior" (character presented from the vantage point of another character), the "dialectic of authorial attitude" (narrator as character present), and the "dialectic of the soul" (the psyche, not the scene) captures some of this method. Gromov does not explore the relationship of the narrative technique to epistemological assumptions. See, *Stanovlenie*, passim.

have seen, however, also shapes the modes of narration in his fiction. Tolstoy assumes that his characters and readers know in the same way. His techniques of narration, therefore, reflect his attitudes to the two types of knowledge. The privileged mode of narration in Tolstoy thrusts the reader into the character's psyche. The reader is forced to go out of himself to merge in knowledge with the character. Anna has returned from her Italian fantasy romance to her own world of Petersburg to see her son. She rushes into his bedroom, sees him smiling his "blissful, sleepy smile," and whispers his name, "Seryozha."

> During the period of separation from him and in that flood of love she had been experiencing of late, she imagined him to be the four-year-old boy she loved most of all. But now he was not even as she had left him. He was even farther from that four-year-old, more grown up, slenderer. What has happened? How thin his face is, how short his hair! How long his fingers are! How he has changed since I left him! But it was him, the same shape of his head, his lips, his dear, soft neck (*shejka*), his broad little shoulders (*plechiki*). (V,xxxix)

The narrator tells the reader about Anna's anticipation and the imaginary quality of her love for her son. The boy she loves is a remnant in her imagination and her moment of encounter a discovery of his changed reality. But as the narrator moves to the moment of encounter, he shifts the mode of narration, moving inside Anna's mental world. The reader sees Seryozha when Anna sees him and as Anna sees him in her affective awareness. This affective awareness is here marked in the exclamatory sentences which express Anna's shock of non-recognition and then in the diminutive forms which reveal her affection in her recognition. The reader is impelled into the character's psyche and the character's affective awareness is the reader's knowledge. In such a moment the reader is in harmony with the character. He shares in the character's affective awareness; he has no other knowledge. To this mode of narration which thrusts the reader into the character's psyche we shall return in the next chapter.

The most common narrative technique in Tolstoy thrusts the reader into the scene, not the psyche. The character may still be present at the scene, but the narration does not focus on the character's experience. The narrator looks with the character at the event.

Prince Andrew attends the epic council of war. He is present at the generals' deliberations when the "dispositions" about the "position" are read. He observes:

Count Langeron was sitting closer than the others to Weyrother and, with a subtle smile that never left his typically southern French face during the whole reading, he gazed at his delicate fingers, which were rapidly twirling by the corners a gold snuffbox on which there was a portrait. In the middle of one of the longest sentences, he stopped the rotary motion of the snuffbox, raised his head, and, with an unpleasant politeness on the corners of his thin lips, he interrupted Weyrother and tried to say something. The Austrian general, continuing to read, frowned angrily and jerked his elbows, as if to say, "Later, you can tell me your views later, but now be so good as to look at the map and listen." Langeron raised his eyes in an expression of perplexity, turned around to Miloradovich as if seeking an explanation, but, encountering his impressive but meaningless gaze, Langeron lowered his eyes sadly and again took to twirling his snuffbox. (I,iii,xii)

The narration does not thrust the reader into Prince Andrew's psyche. He is, of course, standing off in a corner, but we do not observe him observing. Rather, the narration looks at the scene Prince Andrew is seeing. The moment is told as it were in slow motion. But only certain actions and objects are seen. Langeron's mouth and eyes tell of his whole being. His inner life is relayed by the changes that take place in these two parts of his face. His smile is "subtle" and the "corners of his lips" reveal "an unpleasant politeness"; he raises his eyes in "perplexity" and lowers them "sadly." Langeron's attitude to the dispositions read at the council of war is embodied and revealed in the snuffbox he twirls in his hand. We see the snuffbox close-up. It has a portrait on it, and Langeron is holding it by the corners. The snuffbox, which is the emblem of Langeron's profound disagreement and annoyance, opens and closes the moment. The whole scene is narrated by a very attending consciousness. The narrator takes the time to see precisely what is before him, and he tells what he sees in a step-by-step narration. Furthermore, what he sees in the moment is isolated from the context. He does not take note of Langeron's hair or cheeks; he does not look at his physique or clothing. This isolation of objects and actions invests them with meaning. It is, as I have noted, the way Tolstoy makes things emblematic. Still, what the narrator tells is what Prince Andrew sees. The moment is brought into focus because it is a part of Prince Andrew's knowledge. He is learning that the generals in war do not agree with each other, nor listen to each other. The dispositions do not reflect a harmony of mind, any more than they are adequate to the reality of the position. Kutuzov sleeps through the reading. At the council of war, therefore, Prince Andrew begins the process of learning what war is by learning what it is not. He sheds some covers and asks the big question: "Could it really be possible that court and personal considerations lead to risking the lives of tens of thousands, and my life, my life?" Langeron and his snuffbox reveal to Prince Andrew a flaw in his theory of war and therefore in his way of being in the battle for life.

The techniques of slow motion and closeup need not be related to the character's knowledge. The narrator's attending consciousness may be turned toward the reader. Brekhunov is approaching his moment of terror. He is about to discover that he is alone in the storm. He grasps for his matches and cigarettes. He would quell his fear with his stupefying drug.

> Vasily Andreich had meanwhile unfastened his coat and, while holding its skirts up for protection, he struck one sulphur match after another on the steel box. But his hands were shaking and one match after another was blown out by the wind, either just before it burst into flame or at the very moment he raised it to the cigarette. At last a match did catch and its flame lit up for a moment the fur of his coat, his hand with the gold ring on his bent forefinger, and the snow-covered oat straw that stuck out from under the drugget. He lit the cigarette. He took two puffs, inhaled the smoke, then let it out through his moustache, and would have taken another drag, but the burning tobacco was torn off and whirled off toward the straw. (vi)

This is Tolstoy at his best. It is a most characteristic moment of narration. The tempo is slowed down and action is presented step-by-step. We see the match at the moment it bursts into flame and the cigarette as it is lit; we see the precise number of puffs taken and the smoke as it is exhaled, not from the nose but through the moustache. We need not know that to Tolstoy a cigarette is a stupefying drug because the attending consciousness which focuses on the smoking as it is in process makes this clear to the reader. By isolating the image, Tolstoy reveals its meaning. But here Tolstoy reveals more than why a man stupefies himself. When the match finally bursts into flame, it lights up Brekhunov. The narration zooms in on the emblems of his being: his fur coat, which is the sign of his self-enclosure; his "hand with the gold ring on his bent forefinger," which is the sign of his economic status and his separation from the world of genuine labor; and the horse's drugget he had used for himself, which is the sign of his self-centered way of being. In one luminous moment Brekhunov is revealed for what he is by these emblems which embody the moral meaning of his life. But they reveal not to Brekhunov. The slow motion closeup reveals Brekhunov to the reader.

The mode of narration which thrusts the reader into the scene, not the psyche, creates for the reader an effect of presence.[4] The reader participates, not in the character's inner knowledge, but in the character's experience of the event as the character is experiencing the event. In the opening chapter of *Boyhood*, Nikolenka describes the village where they will stop to rest on their way to Moscow and his boyhood.

But here's (*vot i*) the village where we are going to have dinner and rest. Already (*vot uzh*) the village smells are in the air—smoke, tar, bagels—and we hear the sound of talking, footsteps, and wheels; the sleigh bells no longer sound the way they did in the open fields, and on both sides we glimpse huts with thatched roofs, carved wooden porches, and little windows with red and green shutters from which there protrudes here and there the face of an inquisitive old woman. Here are (*vot*) peasant boys and girls in nothing but their smocks, with eyes wide open and arms outstretched they stand stock-still in one place or with their bare feet prancing through the dust; despite Fillip's threatening gestures they run after the carriage and try to climb onto the trunks strapped on the back. And here (*vot i*) come some red-haired innkeepers running up to the carriage, trying with inviting words and gestures to outdo each other in luring the travellers. Whoa!

[4] The phrase "effect of presence" has been borrowed from Gromov. He sees its importance in Tolstoy's style, but not its relationship to Tolstoy's epistemological concerns. See *Stanovlenie*, pp. 129 ff.

the gates are creaking, the cross-bars are scraping the gate posts, and we are driving into the courtyard. Four hours of rest and freedom! (i)

The first-person narrator does not tell of a place or relate in any way his affective awareness of the place. He is riding into the village and tells what he sees as he sees it. There are many details. But he points out the bits of sensory experience to the reader, as though the reader were travelling along with him. The paragraph is composed of five sentences and a summary phrase. Each of the first four sentences begins with the indicator particle *vot* which is a verbal gesture pointing out location and presence; in the first and last instance the particle occurs in the phrase *vot i*, implying a desired expectation, thus adding a tone of fulfillment to the utterance. But the reader is drawn into the character's carriage, not his psyche. The reader is forced through the scene with the character, first the smells, the sounds, the sights, then the people. The reader is present at the scene and when toward the end the narrator shouts "whoa!" the reader slows down with him, as he hears through onomatopoeia the sounds of the creaking (*skripjat*) and scraping (*tsepljaut*). The end of the passage and the attainment of the goal of the journey are expressed by the word "rest," repeated from the opening in order to close the paragraph. In this passage the reader shares the character's knowledge, not because the narrator observes an observer observing, nor because the narrator impells the reader into the character's psyche, but because the narrator assumes the reader is present with him.

In this first-person narration the reader is drawn into the scene by the narrator's verbal gestures. The character speaks to the reader directly. In third-person narration the character and narrator are not the same, and so obviously the effect of presence cannot be achieved through any communication between character and reader. The reader cannot be drawn into the scene by verbal gestures. Anna and Betsy are chatting, waiting for Liza Merkalova and the rest of the croquet party to arrive. Betsy accuses Anna of looking at things "too tragically," but Anna continues to wonder whether she "is worse or better than others" (III,xvii). Removed from Vronsky's and Karenin's presence, she is inclined to declare herself "worse." Her mood for the moment is self-critical. Betsy thinks Anna is a "terrible child" but the guests come.

Footsteps and a man's voice, then a woman's voice and laughter were heard and then the expected guests entered: Sappho Stoltz and a young man glowing with a superabundance of health, the so-called Vaska. It was evident (*vidno*) that he flourished on underdone beef, truffles, and burgundy. Vaska bowed to the ladies and glanced at them but only for a second. He came into the drawing room behind Sappho, following her across the room as if he were tied to her, and not taking his sparkling eyes off her, as if he wanted to eat her up. Sappho Stoltz was a black-eyed blond. She entered with short, brisk little steps in high-heeled shoes and shook hands with the ladies firmly, like a man. (III,xviii)

The narrator represents Sappho and Vaska from the vantage point of "the ladies." The order of the images is the order of their perceptions, first the sounds, then the sight of the entering couple. Even though Vaska enters second, "the ladies" take note of him first, seeing his healthy but fleshy body and noticing his failure to pay attention to them, obsessed as he is with Sappho. The reader sees what the ladies see, as they do and when they do. Bemused for a moment with this man of the flesh, the ladies dismiss him from their purview and turn their attention to the object of his attention, Sappho Stoltz with her bleached blond hair and her modish shoes. The paragraph ends when Sappho greets the ladies with her amazon grip. The reader knows this scene from the point of view of the ladies, but he does not enter their inner world. He is made to be present at their experience of the event. The reader may surmise from the tone of the narration that the ladies are a bit miffed that the "so-called Vaska" has only a glance for them. The reader may surmise that the ladies look down with propriety upon Sappho and her "completely new manner" (xvii). But the reader knows this, not because the narrator tells him directly, but because the reader shares the experience with the ladies. The reader is present with them. But still the reader has no access to their minds. He is impelled into the scene, not the psyche.

In the very next paragraph the narrator shifts the focus from the ladies to Anna.

Anna had never met this new celebrity before, and she was struck by her beauty, the extreme to which the fashion of her costume was carried, and the boldness of her manners. On her head there was such a pile of soft, goldenish hair, her own and artificial, that her head equaled in size her shapely, well-developed, and much exposed bust. The abruptness of her forward movements was such that with each step the shape of her knees and thighs were distinctly discernable (*oboznalis'*) through her dress, and involuntarily the question arose as to where on that undulating piled-up mountain behind, the real, slender, and graceful body came to an end, so naked was the body above and so hidden was the body behind and below.

Anna is obsessed with Sappho's external appearance, her sense of fashion and manners. Most of all, however, Anna sees the flesh: her eyes equate the size of the pile of hair on Sappho's head with the size of her bust. But Tolstoy does not show the inner workings of Anna's mind. He shows us rather what Anna sees. When Anna sees the shape of Sappho's knees and thighs through her dress, her mind begins to wonder about the whole body, but Tolsoy does not represent Anna's musing over this "question." Anna just stares. The syntax of the last sentence is calculated to stress Anna's fixated focus on the physical, visible "body" in relation to its coverings: in the original the sentence, and hence the whole paragraph, ends with the word "body," preceded by a host of modifying adjectives and adverbs, participles and prepositional phrases, all of which point out what Anna sees. The reader shares the experience with Anna and thus is thrust into the presence of this bleach-blond image of Anna's worst fear about herself. The reader may surmise that Anna sees this woman of the flesh as the incarnation of herself. The reader may surmise that Anna feels degraded in the presence of these bodies who are now to be her society companions and to whose world she is now expected to belong. But the reader knows this, not because the narrator tells him, nor because he is privy to Anna's secret thoughts, but because through the narration the reader is impelled into the scene, present there with Anna, seeing from her angle of vision.

Sappho Stoltz, an incidental figure who appears only once in the novel, is represented in two stages. The narrator shifts the point of view from the ladies to Anna. Through this shifting of the point of view, the narrator reveals to the reader the significance of the character. As the object of Anna's attention, Sappho becomes the emblem of the "new manner," the cheap body who even in her clothing has separated herself from the norms of the society. Had the focus not shifted, the reader would still have been present at the scene, but not with Anna, and the meaning for her would have remained obscure. Through such variations in point of view, the narrator determines the ways of the reader's presence in the scene and therefore shapes the degrees of conviction in the reader's knowledge. When the narrator turns to Liza Merkalova a few paragraphs later, for example, he does not show her being seen; he tells of her being seen.

> To Anna's taste Liza was much more attractive. To Anna Betsy had said of her that she took on the manner of an ingenuous child, but when Anna saw her she felt that this was wrong. She really was an ingenuous and depraved, but meek and nice, woman. True, her manner was the same as Sappho's; as with Sappho, there walked behind her as if sewn to her two admirers devouring her with their eyes, one young, the other old, but in her there was something better than her surroundings; in her there was the radiance of real diamond amidst pieces of glass. This radiance shone from her alluring, truly inexplicable eyes. The weary yet passionate look of these eyes surrounded with dark circles was striking in its complete sincerity. To anyone who looked in these eyes it seemed that he knew her completely and having known her could not but love her. Upon seeing Anna her whole face suddenly lit up with a joyful smile.

The reader does not see Liza in the way he sees Sappho, even though they are compared. The reader is told Anna's idea of Liza, her deduction about her; he is not shown Anna's experience of her. For Anna Liza is the image of her highest hope for herself, just as Sappho is the image of her worst fear for herself. Liza is not the body, but the radiance in the eyes which reveal the inner, better self. The reader, however, does not see the radiance any more than Betsy does, because he does not see it with Anna. He knows only that Anna sees it. The reader is impelled, not into the scene, but the psyche. True, the narrator does not show the psyche in action, as he did with Rostov at Enns. But still the reader is thrust into the world of what Anna "felt." That what Anna feels about Liza might be a rationalization or some form of self-justification the reader may well suspect, especially given the argumentative tone of the narration: the use of "true" to open the third sentence; the generalized statement about what "anyone" must seem to know. But what the reader knows for certain is his direct experience of Sappho the body and Anna's conviction about Liza's radiant eyes. In the representation of these two incidental characters, who are variations on the artist Mikhaylov's "personifications of physical and spiritual life," Pilate and Christ, the reader knows for himself, because he is present in the scene, only the personification of physical life. For the spiritual life he must trust Anna, if he does.

In the representation of Sappho Stoltz there is a kind of detail which might seem excessive to the incident. This seemingly excessive detail, Tolstoy's so-called "saturated realism," is calculated, not to create an effect of verisimilitude, but the effect of presence. As with the closeup, the reader is drawn into the character's world by observing that world with him. But detail thus observed from a character's point of view reveals its meaning for the character to the reader. In this way, as we have seen, the realia of the human world take on moral and spiritual meaning. Levin and Stiva are returning from a short hunting trip, during which Stiva lets Levin know that Kitty was jilted by Vronsky. The hunting trip, which had begun somewhat unfavorably for Levin, culminates, after this gladsome news about Kitty, in the downing of a snipe by the simultaneous shots of the two hunters, and the men ride home buoyed in spirits by the catch they made "in common" (II,xv). But then, as they approach the estate, the conversation turns to Stiva's announced intention to sell some wooded land to the merchant Ryabinin,who is awaiting them. Although Ryabinin appears only once in the novel Tolstoy devotes a whole paragraph to describing him.

> At the porch stood a little cart tightly (*tugo*) held together with leather and iron and tightly hitched with wide straps to a well-fed horse. In the cart there sat a completely (*tugo*) bloodshot and tightly belted clerk who served as Ryabinin's coachman. Ryabinin himself was already in the house and met the friends in the hall. Ryabinin was a tall, skinny middle-aged man with a moustache, a protruding, clean-shaven chin and prominent dull eyes. He was dressed in a long-skirted blue coat with buttons very low down at the back and in high boots, crinkled at the ankles and smooth over the calves, over which were pulled large galoshes. He wiped his face all around with his handkerchief and, after adjusting his coat, which already hung very well, he greeted the

new arrivals with a smile, extending his hand to Oblonsky as if he were trying to catch something. (II,xvi)

Such detail seems at once excessive and insufficient. As a description for the reader, it is certainly lacking: Ryabinin has no ears, nose, mouth, or hair. Although we know that Ryabinin's blue coat has buttons on the back, we do not know if there are any on the front nor if Ryabinin has anything at all underneath the coat. The first two sentences in the paragraph do not even speak of Ryabinin, whose cart and clerk stand in his stead. Clearly the purpose of this description is not a verbal picture. Ryabinin is the object of a perceiving consciousness. His portrait is composed of a list of attributes, physical features, and objects which are his sum. The syntax recalls the description of papa: "Ryabinin was . . . , he was dressed in, . . . he wiped . . . , he greeted. . . ." The subject of the sentence is the object of a consciousness about which we know nothing. Although we know Ryabinin as he exists in the world beyond the perceiving consciousness, not within it, we know him while he is being known, but not by whom he is being known. The structure of the paragraph imitates the action of perception: we accompany Levin and Oblonsky as they approach the estate, encounter the cart and the clerk, enter the hallway, and are met by Ryabinin. We see what they see, but we do not enter their psyche. In knowing the details, however, the reader is present in the scene, just as they are.

We enter the scene, not the psyche. The method, we could say, is cinemagraphic. The reader sees what a camera moving with Stiva and Levin would see. When the narrator observes an observer observing, the camera is focused on the character; when the narrator impels the reader into the scene, the camera moves with the character. We know as and when and what Stiva and Levin know, but not filtered through their consciousness—not as Anna sees Sappho, nor as Anna knows Liza, but as the ladies see Sappho. With Ryabinin, however, the narrator captures the hidden fears of the men in what they see. The reader knows this through a characteristic word repetition which is itself a pun. The cart and clerk, we have noted, stand in Ryabinin's stead in the opening two sentences of the paragraph. Each of these sentences in turn is divided into two, and each of the two resulting parts is marked by the repeated adverb *tugo*. What Stiva and Levin see, however dimly, is Ryabinin's "tightness": the word *tugoj* means not only strongly, fully, or completely bound or stretched or blown up, but also "slow" in making decisions, "covetous" of money, "difficult," and "hard" to bear. The cart and the clerk suggest the worst: Ryabinin the merchant, tight-fisted to the end, drives a slow and hard bargain. The scene ends, then, with the merchant, his cart and clerk, as they depart seen by no one but the camera and the reader: "An hour later, after carefully adjusting his overcoat and fastening up his coat with the agreement in his pocket, the merchant got into his tightly fitted cart and drove home." The reader is left, then, with this emblematic image. The whole description of Ryabinin, his cart and his clerk, is calculated to convey the feeling of being caught by an alien being. Images of binding, buttoning, enclosing, and grasping predominate. The handshake with which Stiva is greeted becomes the gesture of conquest by the merchants, who have the gentry in their tight grasp. Impelled into this scene, we are confronted by this compelling image of our conqueror in the process of putting us in chains. The scene in which the reader confronts this emblematic image, furthermore, itself reiterates the paradigmatic action of the novel, from the moment of hopeful accord to the experience of hopeless disharmony, and in this sense, then, the deal with Ryabinin is an action emblematic of the whole work. All this is the reader's knowledge.

In Tolstoy's fiction the reader knows in many different ways. There is a narrator-chronicler who conveys information about events and characters. There is no reason to be suspicious of this knowledge; this narrator is very reliable. But this information appeals only to the reader's "reason." Much of Tolsoy's narration is narration from a limited point of view. This limited point of view may be that of a narrator imagined present at the scene or of a particular character in the scene. In either case, what is epecially common for Tolstoy is the attempt to use this point of view to thrust the reader into the scene, to draw the reader close to the event or the experience of the character. Tolstoy does not limit his narrator to one consistent point of view; he is not interested in creating a world which is simply the function and revelation of character. Tolstoy wants to create in his reader the sense of presence in a world in all its variety, in a life which is experienced by many characters. The effect of presence is designed to involve the reader, to force him to share the moment with the character and the life of many characters. The extreme of this tendency is the representation of affective awareness, when the reader knows only what the character knows solely as and when the character knows: the reader is thrust directly into the character's psyche. The highest aim of Tolstoy's narrative technique—his prophetic intent—is to create in the reader a sense of at-onement with the represented character or event. In Tolstoy's fiction the reader's knowledge tends toward an internalization of the represented experience. The represented world enters the reader's consciousness, not as knowledge about something alien, but as something the reader himself is experiencing. In this sense the reader knows the other as himself. This is knowledge by consciousness. How Tolstoy knows is how Tolstoy tells.

THE THEOLOGY OF CONSCIOUSNESS

Tolstoy understood Christianity as a religion with a firm metaphysics and ethics. The ethics were derived from or logically followed from the metaphysics. What was clearest in the Gospels, however, was the ethical vision because this is what the life and teaching of Jesus Christ embodied. Jesus Christ is understood as the "personification of the one who does the will of the Father." His actions and words, then, reveal the moral imperative. In this understanding of Christ there is no need to talk of his divinity. Christ is the type of divine love. This Christ is the person known as Jesus Christ who lived in time and did the will of God.

But there is, for Tolstoy, another Christ. This is not the human being who lived two thousand years ago. This is "Christ, the logos, the understanding," and "He is in everything" (50,54; 1889). This is the Christ-logos of the prologue to the Gospel of St. John, which Tolstoy used as the preface to his own version of the Gospels. This Christ Tolstoy identified with the phenomenon of consciousness (55,251;1906). In his analysis of this phenomenon, Tolstoy explored the implications of the awareness of self and of other, all that the "contemplation of the contemplator" revealed (55,262;1902). To Tolstoy in consciousness one discovered one's freedom to act and do, coupled with the capacity to reflect on this action. In consciousness one becomes aware of others and of the relationship one should have with others. In consciousness one finds both judgment and love, conscience. But in consciousness one also becomes aware of oneself.

Tolstoy answers his questions of faith by turning inward to the phenomenon of consciousness.[5]

The consciousness of self as willing, living, loving, striving toward the other whose term is God is a primary mode of self-knowledge which precedes all objectification and hence is not reducible to any words about it. This original self-consciousness focuses its attention on the self as it goes forth to other. It transcends itself. Paradoxically, it is a self that loses itself. Along with this transcending, attending consciousness however, there is another kind of self-consciousness, equally as primary and equally as unavailable to words about it. This self-consciousness is the same transcending, attending consciousness but diametrically opposed in its direction of movement. This consciousness turns inward, away from the other. This is the "consciousness" that is aware that "all these organs are mine, that all this is me and all the rest is not me" (56,140; 1908). Attending, transcending consciousness turned outward is the primary experience of the question of faith: where am I going? Attending, transcending consciousness turned inward is the primary experience of the question of faith: who am I?

To Tolstoy this consciousness which pays attention to itself is an "amazing phenomenon" (56,113;1908). He wants to know "what it means that certain combinations of matter are conscious of themselves as separate from all others." Just as the consciousness of self in its transcendence was to be the ground and proof of its freedom and hence Tolstoy's answer to the "determinists," so this consciousness of self in its presence to itself will be the ground and proof of its non-material nature and hence Tolstoy's answer to the "materialists." In

---

[5] The turn to the phenomenon of consciousness in natural theology was made by Friedrich Schleiermacher and expounded in his monumental work *The Christian Faith* (1822). This turn was prepared for, of course, by the whole tradition of theology. Tolstoy knew Hegel only vaguely. He rejected him. To my knowledge he did not read Schleiermacher's theological works. In my presentation of Tolstoy's theology of consciousness I have borrowed some terms and observations from Karl Rahner, who follows in the German tradition and, now under the influence of Heidegger, grounds his theology in the phenomenon of consciousness in a manner similar to Tolstoy, although Rahner is, of course, much more sophisticated in this than Tolstoy. See Karl Rahner, S.J., *Foundations of Christian Faith, An Introduction to The Idea of Christianity* (New York, 1978), pp. 1-89. In the Russian context, it is important to note that Tolstoy's theology of consciousness anticipates the work of the great Russian philosopher and religious thinker S. L. Frank, especially his *Predmet znanija* (Petrograd, 1915), *Dusha cheloveka* (Petrograd, 1916), and *Nepostizhimoe* (Paris, 1939).

the phenomenological experience of attending consciousness in its presence to itself and in its transcendence Tolstoy will find for materialists and idealists alike the ground and proof of the existence of God.

This consciousness attending to itself, the awareness of self as an entity, is a defining feature of human existence and contains for Tolstoy a great secret. In his earliest writings he identified this phenomenon with the soul. "The essence of the soul is self-consciousness. The soul can change with death but self consciousness, i.e., the soul will not die" (46,146;1852). Throughout his years he asks where and what this sense of self was before death and where and what consciousness will be after death, where or what it is in sleep or in a fainting spell, in moments of insanity or passion. That it can disappear and then reappear, as when we go to sleep and awake from sleep or fall into passionate outbursts and then return to our senses, suggests to Tolstoy that this consciousness of self is independent of the conditions of space and time (54,182;1903). This independence of self-consciousness is even more evident in the subsequent moment, when the awareness of self as an entity turns in on itself. This is the moment of self-reflection. The self that knows that it is itself is the self that asks itself who it is.

> The soul is consciousness. . . . What is consciousness? The fact that I ask myself, "Who, what am I?" and answer "I am I." But then I ask myself "Now who is this second I?" and there is only one answer, "again I" and no matter how much I ask it's always "I am I." It is clear that the "I" is something beyond space and time, the only thing that really is. Everything physical could result from the conditions of space and time, but not consciousness. And consciousness is everything. (58,43;1910)

When the primary consciousness which pays attention to itself turns in upon itself in an act of reflexive consciousness, the self is both subject and object, even though in this secondary act the self that is the object is not yet objectified into a concept about the self. This reflexive consciousness which breaks the barrier between subject and object is for Tolstoy the ground and proof of the mode of existence beyond space, time, and causality and, of course, secondarily of the participation of the self in this mode.

The world beyond space and time is not this life; it is true life, God's life, the All in which everything participates. In the act of self-consciousness both in the primary presence of self and in the secondary self-reflection, the self that is always present is the self that participates in true life. "True life is consciousness of self. . . . I am conscious of myself. Who is that I who is conscious of self? It is the divine, eternal principle which I can participate in" (55,170;1905). The subject, the self that is always present and conscious of itself as object but never as subject, is "the spiritual, divine essence" in me (56,47;1907). The subject of the act of self-reflection is God. "I am conscious of my body, I am conscious of my soul, but I am not conscious of that which is conscious of the one and the other. That is He, God, Love" (56,37;1907). The ground and proof of the existence of God is the subject that goes forth to itself in an act of self-awareness. "What I am conscious of in myself in a limited state, I call in its totality God" (56,383;1908). This God is the only thing that really is. "There is only God, God the spirit as I am conscious of it in myself, (I), the subject, and God whom I am not conscious of but whom I am in touch with, the universe of beings, the object" (54,81;1901). God is the All which all beings participate in as subjects, but I know God as subject only in myself; in other beings God is for me a subject separated from me by objective existence, the bounds of space and time.

In this analysis of consciousness as a proof of God's existence Tolstoy reflects the Eastern Christian understanding of man. In Eastern Christian anthropology there is little of the tendency toward a simple dualism of body and soul or mind that is characteristic of Western modes of thinking even before Descartes. Rather, in the East, as I have already mentioned, man is made of body, soul or mind, and spirit. The soul or mind is unique to each individual, but the spirit is common to all. The Eastern Christian tradition always imagines being all together at one in this common spirit. Tolstoy and his heroes, as we have seen, seek to experience this common spirit in all in a variety of realms of life. In his theology of consciousness Tolstoy answers the riddle posed by the "contemplation of the contemplator" by turning to the common spirit within. The implications of this common spirit we shall explore in the last chapter of this book.[6]

[6] To my knowledge there is no comparative study of Eastern and Western Christian anthropologies, nor even a comprehensive study of this aspect of Eastern Christian anthropology. The distinction is my own observation. The most direct way to the subject of Eastern Christian anthropology I know of is through Father George Florovsky's excellent studies of the Greek Fathers, *Vostochnye ottsy iv-ogo veka* (Paris, 1931) and *Vizantiiskie ottsy v-viii vv.* (Paris, 1933).

For Tolstoy this world of space and time, as we have seen, is not illusory as with some idealist philosophers. It is the condition of this life. Yet, he argues, this world of movement and matter itself depends, in some sense, on subjective consciousness. The relationship between consciousness and the world of space and time is dialectical. "Only the consciousness of my unchanging, non-material 'I' gives me the possibility of perceiving the body, movement, time and space and only the movement of matter in time and space gives me the possibility of being conscious of myself. One determines the other" (58,96;1910). In this life, then, the consciousness of self as present to itself needs all that is not always present, the world of space and time, in order to be conscious of itself as always present, and all that is not always present needs something always present in order to know that it is not always present. This is the dialectic of this life. In Tolstoy A and non-A always coexist. From this it follows, however, that in true life there can be no consciousness of self as present to itself; in true life there is only the consciousness of self in its transcendence; in true life there is only the eternal going forth from self to other. This is God's life seen from the vantage point of intellect rather than will.

In the dialectical act of consciousness the self comes to the fundamental experience of reality in separation and belonging. In this life the self is both Stranger and Resident.

Life is consciousness. There are two consciousnesses, one, the lower consciousness, the consciousness of one's separation from the All, and the other, the higher consciousness, the consciousness of one's participation in the All, the consciousness of one's being beyond temporality and spatiality, of one's universality (vsemirnost'). The first consciousness, that of one's separateness, I call lower because the higher, spiritual consciousness is conscious of it (I can understand or be conscious of myself as separated). The second consciousness, the spiritual one, I cannot be conscious of. I am conscious that I am conscious and so on to infinity. The first consciousness (the lower) gives as a result of its separateness the concept of physicality, of matter (and of movement and therefore of space and time); the second consciousness does not know physicality, nor movement, nor space, nor time;

it is not limited by anything and is equal to itself. (54,179-80;1903)

On the one hand, this dual consciousness of "separateness and unity with the All" is itself a dialectical experience (55,234;1906). One feels oneself "at one and the same time as the *all* and as a separate part of the *All*. If a person did not feel himself as the *all* he would not be able to understand what a separated part of the *All* is, the very thing he feels himself to be. If he did not feel himself a separate part, he would not be able to understand what the All is. This double feeling gives a person knowledge about the existence of the All and about the existence of his separate being" (89,157;1909). On the other hand, separateness may seem primary. "The basis of everything is my separateness. The consciousness of separateness is the consciousness of oneself as separated and that from which one is separated" (57,48;1909). It is from this vantage point that Tolstoy makes his oft-repeated statement that "to be conscious of oneself as a separated being means to be cognizant (*poznat'*) of the existence of that from which one is separated, to be cognizant of the All, of God" (55,230;1906). To be cognizant of the God from whom you are separated is not quite a consciousness of God within. However, this primary experience of separated consciousness, and this is what we first come to upon the awakening of self-awareness in this life, for it is what primary self-awareness consists in, is in a most real sense grounded in our unity with the All in true life. "That we are conscious of ourselves as separated is only an illusory or 'temporal' consciousness, but in reality we do not stop being one with the All. In religious language this means that God lives in us" (57,21;1909). The consciousness of self as a separated being is our consciousness of our life in our space and our time; the consciousness of self as a participant in being beyond space and time is our consciousness of God within us.

THE DIVINE SELF, the subject, the center of consciousness, is not a static *tabula tasa* which in empiricist fashion is imprinted with impressions from the external world. The irreducible "I" which is always present to itself and the subject of the act of self-reflection is not an abstract knowing subject. Rather, this subject always actively knows an object; it always directs its attention onto something.

There is no entity called subject which is separate from its action. A subject exists in relationship. The subject is a point of going forth from self to other. Therefore, "everything depends on what consciousness is directed at" (53,213;1898). In self-knowledge there are two basic possibilities and hence two consciousnesses of self. The subject can direct its consciousness at the self as a total entity separated in time and space from other entities. This is the personality's consciousness, "an animal, temporal consciousness" (55,170;1905). Or the subject can direct its consciousness at itself beyond limitation of space and time in the moment of self-presence or self-reflection. This is the divine self's consciousness, a "spiritual, non-temporal consciousness." My understanding and experience of life depend on my mode of self-consciousness. The personality's consciousness sees itself in its isolation, pitted against other such isolated beings in a struggle for this life. The divine self's consciousness sees itself in its relatedness with all other such consciousness in the unity of true life. As a result "consciousness directed at the animal 'I' paralyzes and kills life; consciousness directed at the spiritual 'I' surpasses and liberates life. Consciousness directed at the animal 'I' increases and enkindles passion, produces fright, struggle, and the terror of death; consciousness directed at the spiritual 'I' liberates love" (53,213;1898).

The personality's consciousness is always understood as a screen which obscures the consciousness of the fundamental, divine self. It is the crust of animality which must be removed. In this sense the task of life is the "clarification of consciousness, a liberation from the covers which obscure the soul, the divine spark of truth" within (54,194;1903). This process of clarification is a "cleansing of the glass through which a person looks at the world." With such a clarification and cleansing, "a spiritual being knows no passion or desires and therefore is conscious of its unity with everything. Such consciousness of unity with the beings of the universe is love" (55,243;1906). The saint, purged of passion in a state of seeming *apatheia*, is the one who can really find the truth which is love, the relatedness of self and other.

> To the extent that they are not saints, people for the most part think not in order to find truth but only in order to justify and exalt themselves. Only a saint can think completely correctly

and only the thought of a saint is fruitful. Sinful people are full of desires, repulsions, expectations, and predilections, and their thought is in the service of them. So in order to understand an object one needs not to scrutinize it, think about it, analyze it; one needs to cleanse one's heart of desires, predilections, and worldly hopes, of sin, and hence to increase love, as when in order to see through glass covered with frost one needs not to strain one's vision nor draw closer to the glass, but to defrost it and clean it. (51,112-13;1890)

Empiricist knowledge which knows the object out there through the analysis of sense data assumes an abstract knowing subject divorced from will. For Tolstoy there is no such abstract knowing subject. Every subject has a relationship to the object; every self is related to other. The epistemological event cannot be divorced from this moral reality. All affective attitudes to other which are expressions of needs or frustrations turn the other into an object for the self. The self cannot be for or belong to the other; the other is expected to be for or belong to the self. It is a relationship of utility or possession. The saint does not know in this way. The saint purges himself of his passions and fears and lets himself be for and belong to the object.

The saint's knowledge in one sense, then, seems to contradict the fundamental notion of consciousness, the act of going forth from self into other. The cleansing and clarification are not actions directed outward and toward other: they do not transcend. But knowledge through consciousness in its presence to itself does not stand in opposition to knowledge through consciousness in its transcendence. Rather, Tolstoy imagines the knowing self as a dynamic point of attention going forth from self but separated from the other. What divides this dynamic self from other has two names, depending on the vantage point. When the barrier that divides the self from other is seen out there in the other, it is the bound (*predel*), the limit the other sets to the self; when the barrier is seen from within in the self, it is the cover (*pokrov*) under which the self hides from the other. To know the other as the self requires as it were a seemingly dual action, a positive striving of the self beyond the bound into the other and a negative removing of the cover which allows the other to enter the self. This assumes that every being—whether understood as subject or object, and that is just a relative understanding—is a point of attention going forth from self to other. And every self is separated from all other beings by its cover which is their bound. To be conscious of the other within the self, then, requires the negative cleansing and clarification of self which is a purging of passion and fear and a positive striving of self to the other which is an overcoming of the other's passion and fear, a forgiveness of its resistance to be for and to belong. In the act of consciousness, this negative and positive movement combines and the self goes forth to the other self which goes forth to it. In the present moment, when nothing is separated by time or space or passion or fear, the act of consciousness is a mutual act, right now. The self knows the other as the other knows the self. This act of consciousness is the cause and condition of the possibility of love, the negative purging of passion which releases the positive giving forth of self to other self which right now gives forth to it. As we know, so we love.

Knowledge by consciousness entails knowledge by intellect and will. Consciousness is an act of mind not divorced from heart. Consciousness, that is to say, includes conscience.

> What is conscience? Conscience is that supreme law of everything living which each is conscious of in himself not only as the recognition of the rights of everything living but as love for it. The demands of conscience are what in Christian language is called the will of God and therefore the meaning of life and the answer to the two questions, what is one to live for and what is one to do to have the right to live, consist in fulfilling the will of God which we are conscious of in our conscience. . . . That will demands two things, constant self-perfection and constant collaboration in the establishment of the Kingdom of God on earth, . . . the increase of love in yourself . . . and the increase of love in people. (67,51;1894)

Every living thing, and for Tolstoy everything is in some sense living, has within it the supreme law of love for everything. Conscience, then, is really nothing other than the consciousness of the divine self within. "This inner law is we ourselves. This inner law is what we call reason, conscience, love, the good, God" (53,68;1895). Since this inner law is we ourselves, furthermore, "it does not coerce us but rather liberates us when we follow it, because in following it we become ourselves." In our consciousness of our conscience, we find our identity and vocation, who we are and how we are to relate to others, the meaning and purpose of our life. It is this conscience which speaks "suddenly" to Tolstoy's characters, as it did so often to him.

Most particularly and most usually, Tolstoy describes conscience as the unity of "reason" and "love" (52,103;1893). But this reason is not the empiricist reason maligned in *War and Peace*. This "reason is the divine force of the soul which reveals to it its relationship to the universe and to God; . . . by destroying temptations this reason liberates the essence of the human soul which is love and gives it the possibility of manifesting itself" (68,161;1895). This "reason" which Tolstoy sometimes equates with "consciousness" and in *On Life* combines with "consciousness" in the concept of "reasonable consciousness" (*razumnoe soznanie*) is understood as the logos of the universe, the divine reason in all, and as the capacity in man for critical analysis of reality, critical reason. From the point of view of logos reason, "conscience is the manifestation of the supreme divine reason" (54,21;1900); from the point of view of critical reason, "conscience is the coincidence of one's reason with the supreme reason," with "God's reason" (54,28;1900). Man's critical reason can err; it often is used to justify his own actions. But when this critical reason coincides with the divine reason, then man becomes conscious of the supreme law and releases his love for all. This is what in Christian language is called doing the will of the Lord.[7]

For Tolstoy man has an inherent knowledge of good and evil, of what ought to be and what he must do, because man is that divine self within, the consciousness of all which is his conscience before all, his love for all revealed to him by the divine reason in him. The young Tolstoy rejected along with the empiricists any notion of "inherent ideas" (1,236;1851), but at the same time he insisted, unlike the empiricists, that human beings were born with "inherent tendencies" (1,221;1851) to the good. Fifty years later, after much phenomenological analysis of human consciousness and love, he could say, as he did many times, that "every person comes into the world with a consciousness of his dependence on a mysterious, all-powerful principle which has given him life, with the consciousness of his

[7] In these discriminations of Tolstoy's use of reason I have appropriated the terms used by Tillich in his excellent analysis of this confusing concept. See Paul Tillich, *Perspectives on 19th and 20th Century Protestant Theology* (New York, 1967), pp. 29-34.

equality with all people, and of the equality of all people among themselves, with the desire to be loved and to love others and with the need for self-perfection" (34,305;1902). Such an assessment of the human situation is, for Tolstoy, a secondary, derived position grounded in the phenomenon of the consciousness and conscience which is love, the task given to the eternally growing soul to assist in the creation of the Kingdom of God.

TOLSTOY'S description of metaphysical reality always wavered back and forth between two sets of terminology, one related to consciousness, the other to love, the language of intellect and the language of will. In Tolstoy Life and Love can be described with either language or a mixture of both, even though in the final analysis such a division is artificial. Intellect and will can never be separated. Still, for Tolstoy the metaphysics of Life and Love is grounded in the phenomenon of consciousness. The phenomenological experience of self in its relation to the self and to other embodies and reveals the reality and truth of life. The capacity of consciousness to cast its attention on to other, to go forth from self to other, is always understood as the cause and condition of the possibility of love.

From his analysis of self-consciousness Tolstoy derived a description of reality in terms of consciousness. "All beings are conscious of themselves or are included in someone's consciousness. The universal being, God, is conscious of everything that exists" (51,68;1890). Or, to be perhaps more precise, "the consciousness of the All is the life of God" (54,155;1903). In this view of reality from the point of view of consciousness, God, the All, remains the ever-indefinable and incomprehensible single being who is in any logical analysis a contradiction in terms. To Tolstoy it is clear that the phenomenon of consciousness, either of self or other, implies a separation or division which could not be in the one living God (54,159;1903). In God and in eternal life there is no movement or time, and no going forth from self to other. From the human point of view, however, God can be understood as a center of consciousness which goes forth from self in knowledge to embrace in its attention everything that exists. This going forth in attention, however, is not what God is in his essence; the center remains ever unknowable. The act of consciousness is God's life, his pure act, eternally and forever accomplished. In this pure act of eternal and true life God encompasses all others in his consciousness, and this consciousness of all is God's self-consciousness. God is a center of consciousness that knows all other as itself. This is what is revealed to Pierre in his dream of the globe of life. At the center of this sphere of life is God. Yet "life is all, life is God. Everything shifts and moves and that movement is God. While there is life, there is pleasure in the self-consciousness of the Godhead" (*samosoznanie bozhestva*). God's life is the subject's embrace of the total object, the one Divine Self's eternal embracing of all other divine selves in a unity and plenitude of all being. In this sense and in this context God can be called "universal consciousness" (53,198;1898). God is the consciousness that attends to all.

If "God is the consciousness of all life," the universal consciousness, then "my consciousness of life is God" (51,66;1890). But such a consciousness of life which is God is not simply the consciousness of self as living, willing, loving. That is the primary, transcending consciousness whose term is the All called God. In order to attain the consciousness of life which is God, the self must transfer its consciousness from itself as entity or personality to itself as spiritual "I." "Physical egotism" must be replaced by "spiritual egotism"; the self must transform its consciousness "into the spiritual, universal 'I' " (57,64;1909). This is accomplished by shedding the crust of animality, the rejection of personality. "Rid of personality . . . my consciousness will be the consciousness of everything" (51,67;1890). The "death of the personality" which releases the self into universal consciousness is the way "to be conscious of all other as self" (51;68). This consciousness of everything as self, however, is precisely what God's consciousness is. My consciousness of self as spiritual "I," then, is my consciousness of God which is God's consciousness of all in me. Or, to say it from a more logical point of view: "You can be conscious of God in yourself; when you are conscious of God in yourself, then you are conscious of Him in other beings (and especially vividly in people); when you are conscious of Him in yourself and in other beings, then you are conscious of Him in Himself" (58,120;1910). Strictly speaking, of course, this consciousness of God in Himself is not full knowledge of God in His essence. In this consciousness we are aware of God's life and the "soul of the world" (57,83;1909). The aim and fulfillment of all life is the transferal of self-consciousness into the universal consciousness, the uncovering of the consciousness of all as self within.

Life, then, is the "growth of consciousness" (56,122;1908). Such life and growth, are not to be understood as limited to this life, the mode of existence in time and space. "Life, and consequently consciousness, can and do grow infinitely, always drawing nearer to God . . . and in that approximation it can pass through worlds, i.e., states in which the limitations and therefore the growth take place in conditions other than space and time." The perfection of the eternally growing soul is what eternal life is, the endless "expansion of consciousness" (55,143;1905). From this point of view God is the "universe, the All which is immobile and non-temporal and which gradually reveals itself to me, a separated being. The covers which hide Him from me are removed, my consciousness expands and is liberated and in that is my life." (55,150;1905). In the remainder of this book we shall explore the varieties of moments in which consciousness expands or contracts as the eternally growing soul journeys toward its God.

Chapter Six

RECOLLECTIVE CONSCIOUSNESS

I am the recollection of my life.
(55,137;1905)

THE REPRESENTATION of the character's knowledge is one of the central features of Tolstoy's fiction. Moments when the characters confront themselves or something outside themselves are singled out and scrutinized with a microscopic focus on the process of knowing. Often such moments are telling in the lives of the characters, so that the psychological eavesdropping is a part of the general psychological analysis of character. But even so at times, from the point of view of the development of the story, the detail may seem excessive for this purpose. The narration stops, and the author indulges in an exploration of a particular state of awareness almost for its own sake. Pierre's experience of the battle of Borodino is a case in point. But this excess of detail, like the excess of detail in the description of Ryabinin, has its function. For Tolstoy these moments of knowing are in a most fundamental sense moments of faith, assessments of identity and vocation, momentary answers to the questions "who am I?" and "what must I do?" The detail brings this central Tolstoyan moment of recollection and decision into focus. The representation of a character's knowledge shows us how and when a character decides to become who he will be before he even knows he is deciding. These representations of moments of assessment illustrate the basic principle that the mode of seeing determines the mode of being. This is so even and especially at the moment of death. Because these moments of assessment are moments of faith, they provide Tolstoy with the model for his own life of prayer.

How Tolstoy knows is how Tolstoy tells. He assumes that the character and reader know in the same way. The process of reading, therefore, must resemble the process of knowing. The organization of material in a work of fiction must be adequate to the epistemological experience as Tolstoy understands it. But this means that the character's text is not the same as the reader's text. The character's text is based on the assumption of an eternally growing soul moving from crisis to crisis through time and space. But the reader's text is based on the assumption of an extended moment in the process of knowing. To Tolstoy such extended moments are imagined as inward journeys which recollect one's past in order to assess identity and vocation. In Tolstoy, therefore, the reader's text requires an act of reading which is a kind of assessing recollection.

THE READER'S TEXT

From the very beginning of his writing career Tolstoy adopted a manner of organization of material which he considered especially suited to him. He divided the material up into "little chapters," and "each chapter is supposed to express only one idea or one feeling" (46,217;1853). This "method of writing" which he used in *Childhood* makes "plot a secondary matter," subject to the concern for exhaustive treatment of an idea or a feeling (47,203;1857). The primary feature of Tolstoy's method is the atomization of reality, the exhaustive focus on a bit of information at the expense of the details of the temporal progress of a story. In *Childhood* this is most evident. The story covers two days in time, but the events of those two days are not presented in sequential order, nor is what is presented limited to those two days. Toward the end of his career, in an attempt to articulate the method of writing he needed in *Hadji Murat*, Tolstoy drew an analogy with a peepshow, "There is an English toy called a 'peepshow' which shows under a glass now one thing, now another. That's how the person of Hadji Murat must be shown: a husband, a fanatic, etc." (53,188;1898). This method would create a "work of art in which the fluidity of a human being could be clearly expressed; the fact that he is now one thing, now another, now a villain, now an angel, now a savant, now an idiot, now a powerhouse, now a weakling" (53,187). This conception of "fluidity" of human experience and the peepshow organization of literary material considered adequate to that experience is fundamentally no different from the assumption underlying Tolstoy's earliest work. The image of "fluidity" assumes a oneness or wholeness of being, but it focuses on discrete elements in that being snatched from the flow. Except in special moments of assessment, a Tolstoyan character is not represented as many different facets simultaneously in conflict; he is only serially so. Now Anna feels her vengeance toward Karenin, now she feels her love toward Seryozha, now she feels her resentment of Vronsky. Character is atomized and so is the literary work which represents it. In Tolstoy's work each delineated segment is delineated in order to explore one meaning, and the reader's first task is to ascertain the meaning of the delineated segment.

The reduction of plot and the atomization of reality lead to inevitable problems of organization. If the organization of material is not grounded mainly in the temporal movement inherent in a story and inherent in the reader's perception as he goes from word to word in time, what is the ordering principle and the purpose of that order? Some writers, of course, fragment the plot line simply in order to weave in other plots, subordinate and perhaps auxilliary to the main one. They still organize by plot. Other writers reorder the temporal progression to manipulate the reader's knowledge: to imitate the chaotic way one gets information in real life, to create suspense, to mystify or confuse. But not Tolstoy. He tells several full plots simultaneously, with one focal character in each plot, but he does not organize his material by these plots and he does not desire to create suspense or confusion. At its simplest, the ordering principle can be found in the method of some early works which are made of several short delineated segments. In *Two Hussars* Tolstoy juxtaposes two character sketches; in *Three Deaths* he juxtaposes three different experiences of death. Such juxtaposition, by its nature, the parallelism of different things, invites comparison and contrast. The juxtaposed character's texts provoke the reader to a relative measurement. They demand assessment. Such a juxtaposition of delineated segments, therefore, calls the reader to crisis; the reader must make a judgment, a decision, an evaluation of meaning for himself. The dice may be loaded and only one decision may be assumed possible, but still reality is but several dice, one of which the reader is called to cast for himself. The parallel delineated segments of these early tales are as it were spatial forms of the temporal journeys of crisis and conversion. In these early tales the reader is called to the crisis; in the later tales of conversion, the character is called to crisis. *Master and Man* combines the juxtaposition of delineated segments devoted separately to Brekhunov and Nikita and the story of Brekhunov's conversion to Nikita's service; it is in this sense too the perfect type of Tolstoy's art. The reader's relative measurement of the juxtaposed delineated segments makes the character's crisis and conversion meaningful and believable.

The three major fictions are built on this same atomization of reality and juxtaposition of non-temporally sequential delineated segments. In them, several journeys of discovery are related together, but the stories are broken into many bits and interspersed among each other. Of course, the general outline of story and plot time are intact, but it is still a secondary matter. What really matters is the atomization and juxtaposition. No story is related in its temporal unfolding from moment to moment. Nothing is seen as a whole. Rather, a delineated segment focuses on a minute moment within the total journey, and the whole work is made of such juxtaposed moments. In any one journey of discovery the time lapse between the represented moments can vary; it may be a day or years. What happens between moments is blank. The time between moments on any particular journey of discovery is taken up by another represented moment from another journey of discovery. When the narration returns to a journey of discovery after a lapse, the narrator does not fill in the blank, even in summary, although he may sum up the series of prior moments to recall them for the reader. This is how Tolstoy creates the effect of growth and change. Your sister you see from day to day does not seem to change, but let her go away to college for a year, and my how she has changed! Natasha with dirty diapers in hand illustrates this effect most adequately. The act of memory required in order to make one story out of the disassociated bits of information brings the process of change and growth into focus. Tolstoy's characters seem to grow because we do not see them grow. Atomization and juxtaposition serve Tolstoy's prophetic intent, which is to create in the reader a sense of change and growth and hence of time moving swiftly forward toward the moment of inevitable crisis before the scarecrow of death.

For Tolstoy the conscious purpose of atomization and juxtaposition is self-expression.

In almost everything I have written, in order to express myself I was guided by the need to gather together ideas linked among themselves. But every idea expressed separately by words loses its meaning; it becomes terribly debased when it is taken alone out of the linkage in which it was found. This linkage itself is based not on an idea, I think, but on something else and to express the basis of that linkage in any way directly is impossible; it is only possible indirectly, with words describing images, actions, situations. . . . For the criticism of art we need people who would show the absurdity of seeking out ideas in an artistic work and who would constantly guide the readers in that infinite labyrinth of linkages in which the essence of art consists and toward the laws which serve as the foundation of those linkages. (62,269;1876)

In this statement, made apropos of *Anna Karenina*, Tolstoy sees atomization and juxtaposition as his organizational method, but he focuses on the broader problem of the interrelationship of the delineated segments. The whole work of art is imagined as a chain, a "gathering together" of bits of information, "images, actions, situations," which are "linked" among themselves by a certain "law" of linkage. Or, in another articulation apropos of *Anna Karenina* and in regard to the two main plot lines, the whole work of art is imagined as a building, a structure in which the "vaults are joined in such a way that you cannot notice where the keystone is; . . . what holds this structure together is not the plot, not the relationship (acquaintances) of the characters but an inner connection" (*svjaz'*) (62,377;1878). In order to express himself Tolstoy needs "ideas" which are "linked among themselves," by some hidden, "inner connection." In the hidden connection which links the pieces of the chain lies the whole meaning. In Tolstoy's longer fictions this hidden connection is the paradigmatic action. Each work is made of delineated segments which reiterate paradigmatically one rhythm of experience; the paradigmatic actions are guided by one law. Structurally the paradigmatic actions are what the parts have in common with each other. The actions, therefore, express the spirit of the work. Tolstoy organizes his work by a principle of inner spirit which unites not by logical connection but by a unity inherent within the variety. This structure is like life itself.

Discrete segments in the reader's text are also connected by the repetition of words and images. The phrase "new life" is used to refer to Anna and Vronsky and to Kitty and Levin as they begin the second half of their journeys in the novel. Anna's "triumph" over Vronsky in the scene that leads psychologically to her suicide stands next to Kitty's "triumph" of giving forth life in the scene that leads Levin psychologically to his reassessment of faith. In each case—and there are many in both major novels—the characters do not know of the others' experience, and from the point of view of plot there is no relationship between the juxtaposed scenes. Yet this connection epitomizes the whole theme of the reader's text: the love that leads to hatred and death shocks one to the awareness of a love that leads to faith and life. To grasp this, the reader must remember the linked and connected "images, actions, and situations." Reading is, in this sense, recollection.

The most dramatic example of this method of unification of the parts is the repeated image of the sky in *War and Peace*. All three male heroes confront the sky and find a meaning in it. The sky they see is unique to each, and none knows the experience of the other. To the reader this sky encompasses all their meanings: Rostov's shining sun of warmth and security back home; Prince Andrew's abstract, empty, yet kind expanse; Pierre's All filled with light yet centered in a luminous point. The image embodies and reveals the high value and idea of the whole work. Not surprisingly, then, the sky reappears in the final war scene of the novel in which none of the heroes is present. Kutuzov has given his speech to the troops. The Russian soldiers are huddled around a fire. About to lie down to sleep, one of them glances up at the Milky Way and exclaims, "Look at the stars. It's wonderful how they shine! You'd think the women had spread out their linen" (IV,iv,viii). Sounds are heard and two Frenchmen appear, Rambaille and Morel. They are hungry, tired, and beaten. The Russians receive their enemy into their open arms and take them into their hut. The Frenchmen sing a song and the Russians join in (in a Cyrillic version of the French text). The Russians then share their porridge with their enemy, saying in Kutuzov's words, "They too are human beings" (IV,iv,ix). "O Lord, O Lord, how starry it is! It's tremendous," they exclaim, and "everything becomes still." The narrator then turns to the sky. "The stars, as if knowing that now no one would see them, got carried away, sporting in the black sky. Now flaring up, now dying out, now quivering, they busily whispered to one another something joyful and mysterious." The war closes with a scene of the Christian love of enemy which is imaged in the sharing of food, set to the tune of a harmonious song of all together, and placed in an expanse of nature emblematic of that life which is eternal growth in love toward the all in all. For the reader the "images, actions, and situations" of the whole novel converge in this epiphanic moment when the epic value of human life is revealed to the reader's recollecting imagination.

IN ORDER to see how Tolstoy links "images, actions, and situations" and how the reader finds the meaning in the linkages, let us turn to one extended text, albeit still a part of a whole work. The large segment is part three of the third book of *War and Peace* (Book Eleven in the Maude translation). This segment depicts the time after Borodino, when Napoleon enters Moscow and the Muscovites leave Moscow. It tells the story of the triumph of the residents, and so we can call it by that name. The section is made of thirty-four chapters which for simplification can be grouped into sixteen discrete segments.

1. Discourse on movement (i)
2. Kutuzov's decision not to give battle (ii-iv)
3. Count Rostopchin's plans (v)
4. Helen returns from Europe (vi-vii)
5. Pierre returns from Borodino (viii-xi)
6. The Rostovs leave Moscow (xii-xvii)
7. Pierre plans to stay in Moscow (xviii)
8. Napoleon in Moscow (xix)
9. Moscow is like a beehive (xx)
10. Chaos in Moscow (xxi)
11. Mavra Kuzminishna's act of charity (xxii)
12. Chaos in Moscow (xxiii)
13. Count Rostopchin's ordeal (xxiv-xxvi)
14. Pierre and Captain Rambaille (xxvii-xxix)
15. Prince Andrew's delirium (xxx-xxxii)
16. Pierre saves lives (xxxiii-xxxiv)

The physical center of this section is the image of Moscow as a beehive without its queen. "There is no life." The hive has become a foul place filled with theft and murder, a hovel in the process of self-destruction, a home in which there is no relatedness. What immediately precedes this epic simile, the longest in the novel, is the scene depicting Napoleon in Moscow. He will save Moscow's life by taking over the institutions of charity and making them his own, sentimentally dedicating them all to "ma chère, ma tendre, ma pauvre mère." Napoleon mentally rules Moscow with his announced charity given forth to all but for himself and not even from himself. What immediately follows the central epic simile are two scenes of chaos in Moscow, the pilfering and murdering of everything, which is the realization of the metaphor of the queenless beehive. These two scenes of chaos are themselves separated by the image of Mavra Kuzminishna, the remaining resident at the Rostovs. Regardless of the consequence of this time of utter uncertainty, she, the servant, spontaneously and unmotivatedly gives forth of her master's bounty to one of his relatives unknown to her, not for herself but because he is a relative of the master and because that is what the master would want. But, unlike Napoleon, who waits in vain for the "deputation from the city" to receive him, Mavra Kuzminishna gives away what is left, regardless of the consequences, but then is overwhelmed with an "unexpected flood of maternal tenderness and compassion for the officer who was unknown to her." For her act of love she is rewarded with the feeling of love. At the center of the "triumph of the residents" amidst the chaos of destruction and death, Mavra Kuzminishna stands as the principle of life and the only hope of the salvation of life. The victory over the enemy comes with a giving forth, right here, right now. At the center is the meaning of the segment, but the reader, of course, can come to this realization only after he knows both the beginning and the end in an act of recollection.

The "triumph of the residents" opens with a metaphysical discourse on movement. This digression is itself one of a series of articulations of the metaphysical and epistemological views that obtain in the work. This particular articulation stresses the error in understanding reality when it is divided into discreet units seen in a causal relationship. In reality there is only uninterrupted movement, the flow of the Kingdom of God coming to be. In the historical realm, this movement is manifested through the sum total of "human wills" which together bring about history in this life and—to the extent that these wills are expressions of the divine will—the Kingdom of God or true life, which is the salvation of this life. The discourse on movement is the philosophical introduction to the theme of the "triumph of the residents."

The image of Kutuzov which follows the introduction illustrates this. Kutuzov is the one who believes he "has been predestined to save Russia." He knows that "events and time do not wait" for an abstract analysis of them, even if that were feasible or desirable, and he acts with trust and assurance in giving his order "right now, right this minute." Kutuzov's order is not to give battle. He accepts the inevitable but mysterious fact that Russia's life can be saved only if it is lost. He wonders "who is guilty," but he has no answer. All he knows is that there is only one action to save Russia, a negative one, a non-action against the enemy, non-resistance to evil. Count Rostopchin, who is introduced after Kutuzov, is cast as his opposite. Rostopchin believes, not in negative action, but in resistance to the enemy; he would not abandon Moscow. The two leaders, the head of the army and the leader of the Muscovites, represent opposed ways to salvation.

Like Rostopchin, Pierre too would resist the enemy. Like Kutuzov, he too believes he is to save Russia. "L'russe Besuhof" has been called to kill the apocalyptic beast, 666, the Antichrist himself, Napoleon. Toward the end of the "triumph of the residents," after a night of drunkenness, Pierre awakens to this mission and, disguised as a peasant, rushes off to kill the enemy and save Russia, carrying his "intention" to kill Napoleon "within himself as something terrible and alien to him." But on the way he gets sidetracked by the cry of a woman whose child has been abandoned in a burning building. In immediate response to this woman's need, Pierre changes his direction and rushes off to "save the child." No sooner does Pierre rush off when, "as if suddenly after a long fainting spell he awoke to life. He raised his head higher and his eyes shone with the sparkle of life." Furthermore, the saving of the child only makes him want "to go again to save someone else," which he does when he protects the beautiful Armenian woman from the advances of the enemy and himself ends up thereby a prisoner of the enemy. In these salvific acts Pierre sacrifices not himself but his intentions and his assumed identity and loses this life to discover his true self. But this true self is his act of unmotivated giving forth to his neighbor, the one he is with right now. This is the salvific act which follows from the clearing from within himself of his assumed identity and of his intention to kill the enemy. The negative action becomes a positive one: release from hatred of the enemy releases the life and love within. The "triumph of the residents" closes with Pierre's salvific acts. They are the fulfillment of Kutuzov's negative action which opens the delineated segment and a reenactment of Mavra Kuzminishna's act of charity which stands at the center. At the three defining points life is saved from the enemy within, be that enemy Napoleon, the brutal selfishness of the robbers and murderers, or Pierre's self-centered intention.

In the "triumph of the residents" the two figures associated with Pierre stand in opposition to him, his wife Helen and Captain Rambaille. Rambaille arrives on the scene by forcing his way into Pierre's quarters; he almost gets killed in the process, but Pierre protects him. Pierre encounters the enemy in Moscow and saves his life. The two, Frenchman and Russian, then become friends and in the drunken evening that ensues Rambaille treats Pierre to the lurid stories of his peculiar sexual perversions which are for him the salt that flavors "l'amour." He concludes his tales of "l'amour" with an incident in Poland where "he saved the life" of a Polish man who then in reward gave Rambaille his wife, "Parisienne de coeur," and went off to join the French army. "Moved by magnanimity," Rambaille returns the man's wife untouched with these touching words: "Je vous ai sauvé la vie et je sauvre votre honneur." This is Rambaille's highest image of salvation; it brings a tear to his eye in the telling.

Helen returns from Europe to Petersburg with "another new task in her career" of love. Two men are now pursuing her, and she, though still married to Pierre, wants to find a way to marry them both. To accomplish this task of "being able to do what she wants," Helen resorts to her basic principle: "she puts herself in a position of justness, in which she sincerely believes, and all others in a position of guilt." She accomplishes this by converting to Roman Catholicism, a religion which in her Jesuitical view allows her "to observe the familiar proprieties while satisfying her human desires." For Helen this new task is an act of loving sacrifice: "Mais c'est que j'aime l'un et l'autre, je ne voudrais pas leur faire de chagrin. Je donnerais ma vie pour leur bonheur à tous deux." Helen's new task seems to her the salvation of others' lives.

Helen and Rambaille resemble Napoleon. They all have come from Europe to Russia. They all speak in French. Like Napoleon,

Helen acts for her own self-interest, her career, but masks it as sacrifice for others. Like Napoleon, Captain Rambaille considers the salvation of a woman's honor the highest salvific act. Whatever they do, all three do for their own gratification. Salvation and religious conversion are transformed into actions accomplished with a conscious eye to some personal purpose. Pierre's wife and friend resemble his enemy.

Helen and Rambaille are also like Rostopchin, even as they are placed next to him in the reader's text. Count Rostopchin lives, he supposes, for the good of other people, "le bien publique," but he plays the "beautiful role of the leader of the people's feelings, the role of the leader of the heart of Russia." Thus although, like Kutuzov, Rostopchin knows that Moscow has to be abandoned, he does not accept it, because he believes his role is to "arouse in the residents the very feeling he himself feels, patriotic hatred for the enemy and confidence in himself." The one who lives for the general good is in fact totally centered in himself. So when people leave, "showing by their negative action all the power of their feelings," Rostopchin's chosen "role suddenly turns out to be meaningless. He suddenly feels alone, weak, ridiculous, and angry." He needs to find an enemy who, he can believe, caused the people to act against his will. He finds this scapegoat in Vereshchagin. The violence and cruelty Rostopchin unleashes allegedly for "le bien publique," but in fact to attempt to reestablish his role, occur in the most gruesome and repellent scenes in the whole novel. Vereshchagin is murdered and Count Rostopchin rides off to see Kutuzov. But on the way a madman appears on his path, shouting, "Thrice have they killed me, thrice did I rise from the dead. They beat me with stones, they crucified me, but I shall rise from the dead." Frightened but undaunted Rostopchin rides up to Kutuzov only to blame him for the abandonment of Moscow. Kutuzov responds in enigmatic words. "Yes, I shall not give up Moscow without giving battle." That is all. "And a strange thing happened. The commander of Moscow, the proud Count Rostopchin, picked up his whip, went to the bridge, and started yelling to get unstuck the carts that had gotten jammed up." In his encounter with Kutuzov, Count Rostopchin goes through a miraculous conversion. The administrator has died, but in hearing the voice of conscience, the insane resident speaking the truth, Rostopchin is reborn to life and participates in the abandoning of Moscow. Instead of hating the enemy, Rostopchin now takes part in the salvation of life.

In the "triumph of the residents" the salvation of life entails conversion. Before the scene of Rostopchin's conversion and after the scene of Helen's, the Rostovs depart from Moscow. Petya and Natasha are alone, oblivious to the events, "joyful and happy." In their relatedness, they live. But Natasha cannot participate in the preparations for departure. She sits on the floor of her room in all its disarray, "immobily staring at the floor while holding in her hand her old ball gown (already out of fashion, the very gown she wore at her first ball in Petersburg)." Staring at the emblem of her worldly self, she cannot help with the packing. But, then, she hears the servants running around in excitement; she hastens to the window to see what is happening; and she discovers "a whole huge caravan of wounded men" right outside on the street. She rushes out to them and her gown is abandoned forever; it disappears from the text. In the courtyard she hears Mavra Kuzminishna telling one of the officers that they might stay there when the masters leave, but the officer doubts that his commanding officer would allow it. Natasha turns to the commanding officer. "May the wounded stay in our house?" she asks, so seriously that he eventually says they may. Natasha then throws herself into the packing. She is converted to life only when the departure will give forth their world to the wounded.

But the wounded also want to depart from Moscow. When the Count comes out and is asked by a wounded officer for a space on a cart, he readily replies "yes, yes, yes," which angers his wife, who sees this as a threat to the financial and material security of their children. Berg arrives. As he walks past the many carts, he takes out his white handkerchief and ties a knot in it. No sooner in the house, he begins his high-flown babble about the "Russia not in Moscow but in the hearts of her sons." In the midst of all the cant, Berg takes out his handkerchief, recalls his mission regardless of the wounded, and with that "tone of joy in his own comfortable situation" he tells the Count of the "chiffonier" he saw on the way. If the count would let him have a cart, he could surprise Verochka with it. The Count blows up and walks out. Natasha runs off, blurting out: "It's vile, it's loathsome." To her Berg's chiffonier surprise for her sister recalls her mother's own desire to keep the carts for themselves. Natasha's righteous anger at this love for a chiffonier regardless of others shocks her mother into the recognition of her own selfishness and, after she begs forgiveness for her anger, they all agree to give their carts to the wounded. Berg simply disappears from the text. The rest are converted to the task of life. Natasha throws herself into unpacking in order to give away the carts, while Sonya catalogues what is left behind, "trying to take with them as much as possible." They depart, the wounded Prince Andrew, unbeknownst to Natasha, "in front of all." And on the way out amidst the throngs of residents abandoning what is theirs, Natasha sees Pierre disguised as a peasant and absorbed in his mission. The scene closes with her "affectionate, somewhat bemused, joyful smile beaming at him," as she rides off with an eye to the cart in front of all. Like Helen, Natasha now has before her, and for the only time, the two men who love her and whom she loves, but not like Helen.

The scene with the Rostovs reiterates the theme of the whole segment. There is only one appropriate action, the negative action of giving up or abandoning what is yours, which is also a giving forth of yourself to others. In this rests the salvation of life. This is what Natasha knows and does. She packs or unpacks only when it is a giving forth. Count Rostov in his desire to "leave, leave, leave" lets this happen, Countess Rostova in her fear for the future would not, and Sonya in her unfailing failure of spiritual understanding helps it to happen for precisely the wrong reason. What Natasha knows is what Berg does not. He would add to what is his and take from others to do it. The scene with the Rostovs not only reiterates the basic negative action; it also rehearses the positive action of the conversion of the residents. Countess Rostova is brought to see what must be done, and they all decide to do it together. What Natasha reveals to her family, what she embodies for Prince Andrew and beams forth to Pierre, is what Kutuzov reveals to Count Rostopchin. This theme of conversion to the salvific act of life and love, of which Helen is the negative image, links these scenes with all those that follow the central images of chaos: Count Rostopchin's ordeal, Prince Andrew's delirium vision of love, and Pierre's final salvific act. Thus Natasha, as always, is the guiding figure. She embodies and reveals the principle of life, represented in the servant Mavra Kuzminisha and the commander Kutuzov.

The "triumph of the residents" is a characteristic reader's text. The major fictions, in their parts and on the whole, are made like it.

As with *Three Deaths*, the text is composed of delineated segments placed next to each other. The contiguity of parts simultaneously similar and different evokes comparison and contrast. The similarity becomes evident through the intensive reiteration which the reader experiences in a continuing act of recollection. In reading forward he looks backward. The reader's text in Tolstoy is not like the reader's text in fiction based on plot; such fiction requires that the reader not forget as he reads forward. Nor is the reader's text in Tolstoy like modernist fiction which the reader cannot read but only reread. In Tolstoy the reader's text needs to be continually and consciously recalled in order to be read. In Tolstoy reading is an act of glancing backward while moving forward, a continual assessment. In Tolstoy the reader's text is a gathering together of "images, actions, and situations" "linked among themselves" into a chain along which, to find the meaning, the reader must trace the pattern of connections in a continuing act of recollection. The structure is essentially lyrical.

THE INWARD JOURNEY OF DISCOVERY

The psychology of the reader's perception in which the reader's text is grounded is the psychology of empiricism. This empiricist epistemology was modeled after the Newtonian universe of atoms, held together and moved about by the law of attraction. The external world, it was believed, was experienced mentally as molecules of sensations. These mental images or impressions, "ideas," as Locke called them, were seen to cohere and move about in the mind according to definite and logical laws of association. This psychology of the association of ideas, born of the British empiricists, was fundamental to the French Enlightenment and commonplace to the nineteenth century. It pervaded that century's assumptions about the process of knowing. The sentimentalists built their literary structures around the laws of association; in *Tristram Shandy* Laurence Sterne put them to comic use. In their colloquies with self and God the romanticists assumed them even as they transformed them. For Tolstoy, as for the romanticists, the empiricist model obtains even when it is transcended.

This empiricist epistemology imagined that as the outer eye moved over a scene or anything seen, an "inner eye" was bombarded with millions of atoms of sensation which appeared in a series according to the order and manner of the movement of the outer eye. This series of mental images was called a "chain" or "train of ideas." Tolstoy illustrated such a moment of an empiricist experience of a train of ideas in his representations of Pierre's knowledge at Borodino. This notion of a train of ideas reduced the problem of knowledge to that of finding the laws of the association of ideas in the "train": how the atoms of sensation come together to make what we experience as simple and complex ideas, as feelings, images, and concepts, as the whole content of our mental world, how "poof" and "boom" became an exploding cannonball which can kill me. The central metaphor which dominates this epistemological theory is the "bond" or "link." Philosophers spoke of linking the atoms into a chain or binding them together, as it were, into larger molecules. By conjunction, fusion, or union the separate atoms are connected and thus become whole ideas or images. These new images, now what we ordinarily think of as mental images, also move along on a "train" and associate with the fellow passengers they meet there. The mind, then, is conceived as a container of discrete mental images which move along an ordered path, not unlike Tolstoy's boxes and corridors. Each new experience of the external world is then dumped into this container and finds its place in the chain by the laws of association.

These laws of linkage can be reduced to three central principles: (1) contiguity, (2) similarity, (3) intensity. "Contiguity" includes the experience before or after each other. "Similarity" includes the association of one mental image with another mental image which resembles it. "Intensity" can affect either of the two preceding principles, for the strength and length of the sensation as well as the frequency and recency of the experience of resemblance or contiguity play a role in the association of mental images. In Tolstoy the reader's text is constructed according to these very laws of association. Discrete "images, actions, and situations" are connected by contiguity, related to each other by similarity, and bound together by the intensity resulting from frequent repetition of similar or contiguous discrete units. The reader's text is based on an epistemology which assumes that knowledge is made of stored units which need to be unified to have meaning. Meaning resides not in the individual unit of experience but in the units linked together into a whole. Linkage makes the world coherent. It is because he assumes such an epistemology that Tolstoy could say that art is a labyrinth of linkages connecting ideas linked among themselves according to the laws of linkage.

How Tolstoy knows is how Tolstoy tells. The representation of a character's inner knowledge is based on the same laws that govern the reader's text. Such representation was recognized by Tolstoy's contemporaries as a defining feature of his literary interest, and one description of this peculiar representation of knowledge has itself become the *locus classicus* for all later criticism. In 1857, basing his observations on *Childhood, Boyhood*, and several of the early war stories, N. G. Chernyshevsky saw in these works something completely new which he called the "internal monologue," thereby introducing this phrase into the vocabulary of Russian literary discourse.[1] Of course, Chernyshevsky observed, many writers had been interested in the dynamics of their character's inner psychological life, but they tended to be analytical: a feeling was broken down into its component parts or the shift from one feeling to another was portrayed by giving, as Chernyshevsky said, the two extreme "links in the chain" (*zvena tsepi*), the simple juxtaposition of the two terminal points in the process of change. Tolstoy is different, and Chernyshevsky describes this new internal monologue he perceived.

> Count Tolstoy's attention is primarily turned to examining how certain feelings and thoughts develop out of others. He is interested in observing how a feeling (*chuvstvo*) that arises immediately out of a given situation or impression (*vpechatlenie*) turns into another feeling when it is subjected to the influence of memories and the power of combinations represented by the imagination (*sochetanija predstavljaemye voobrazheniem*), then turns into other feelings and then returns to its point of departure and then again and again wanders, while changing, along the whole chain (*tsep'*) of memories. [He is interested in observing] how a thought, begotten by the first sensation (*oshchushchenie*) leads to other thoughts, is carried further and further, blends reverie with real sensations, and dreams of the future with reflections on the present. . . . Count Tolstoy is primarily in-

[1] N. G. Chernyshevskij, *Polnoe sobranie sochinenij* (Moscow, 1947) III, 421-431.

terested in the psychic process itself, its forms, its laws, or to express it in a defining term, the dialectic of the soul.

This dialectic of the soul, however, is nothing other than a vulgari-
zation of the empiricist notion of the association of ideas. The psychological process which Chernyshevsky observed so astutely is a
process which, as he himself said, has laws and forms which are "responsible" for the "association of ideas" (*assotsiatsija predstavlenij*).
Chernyshevsky was able to perceive and describe the inner monologue because he shared with Tolstoy the general assumptions and
even the language of associationist psychology.

To illustrate his thesis about this new kind of internal monologue,
Chernyshevsky quoted a passage from the second Sebastopol sketch,
Sebastopol in May. This passage, which describes the death of Praskukhin, can serve us too as an introduction to Tolstoy's method of
representation of a character's inner knowledge. Praskukhin is a mi-
nor figure in the tale, and we know only little of him. The following
facts of biography do single him out, however, from the other officers
he seems to resemble. Praskukhin has a reputation for not being particularly honorable and is shunned by the other officers. He repeatedly jokes with sexual innuendo about a certain sailor's daughter.
The night before the fatal battle while with a group of officers who
had not invited him along, Praskukhin had sung a gypsy song along
with one of the other officers, but sang it so well that they asked him
to repeat it. As he approaches the battle, Praskukhin is afraid of every
sound but even more afraid that others will think he is a coward.
Throughout the story he is coupled with Captain Mikhaylov, whom
he considers his inferior, even though he drinks Mikhaylov's wine
and vodka and owes him twelve and a half rubles lost in a card game.
We know virtually nothing of Praskukhin's personal life or his inner
experience until this passage, which thrusts us into his psyche.

> No sooner did Praskukhin begin to come to life a bit, while walk-
> ing along with Mikhaylov . . . and approaching a less dangerous
> spot, than he saw a streak of light flash brightly behind him and
> heard the sentinel shouting, "A shell" and one of the soldiers
> walking behind him saying, "It's coming right here into the bat-
> talion." . . . Someone shouted out in a frightened voice, "Get
> down!" Mikhaylov fell onto his stomach. Praskukhin automat-
> ically bent down to the ground and began to squint. All he heard

was a shell somewhere very near, smacking into the hard earth. A second passed, but it seemed more like an hour. The shell didn't explode. Praskukhin was afraid that he may have felt cowardice in vain; perhaps the shell had fallen far away and it just seemed to him that the fuse was hissing right here. He opened his eyes and with self-assured satisfaction saw that Mikhaylov, to whom he owed (*dolzhen*) twelve and a half rubles, was much lower down and lying on his belly immobile, pressing up against him right near his feet. But just then, scarcely a yard from him, his eyes met (*vstretilis'*) for a moment with the sparkling fuse of a whirling shell. Terror, that icy terror which excludes all other thoughts and feelings, possessed his whole being. He covered his face with his hands and fell on his knees. (xii)

This passage, which comprises the first third of the sequence of Praskukhin's death, is made of four moments marked by Praskukhin's changing physical positions and ways of seeing: (1) walking with Mikhaylov, (2) bending down and squinting, (3) opening his eyes and seeing Mikhaylov, (4) seeing a shell coming toward him and falling on his knees. In order to focus on the psychic process, Tolstoy slows down the movement of time and divides action into discrete units. In the first section Praskukhin is represented experiencing not the chaos of battle, but only isolated bits of it, and these bits, as it were, are presented in a temporal sequence: a flash of light, caught phrases, the soldier next to him falling down. In the second section Praskukhin is totally absorbed with one sensory event, the shell bursting near him, but this moment, a second that seems like an hour, is represented as a moment of reflection on his own fear. This reflection takes the form of a concern about cowardice, indeed a cowardice felt "in vain" because there was no explosion and hence no real reason for cowardice or bravery. It is this convoluted reflection which is the cause of the felt length of the second, even as it is the content of that second. In the third section Praskukhin opens his eyes and sees Mikhaylov lying down on the ground. This man whom Praskukhin considers beneath him, even as he drinks his liquor and borrows money from him, is groveling at his feet. The debt he owes Mikhaylov—and this is the only concern about Mikhaylov he has— reminds Praskukhin of his own failure to be accepted by those he looks up to, and the image of Mikhaylov at his feet gives Praskukhin vengeful satisfaction. Praskukhin is concerned only with himself. He even takes "self-assuring satisfaction" in seeing Mikhaylov at his feet: better him than me. At the moment Praskukhin has this self-consoling thought, his eyes meet the sparkling fuse of another shell; the fourth section contains the reaction of fright.

The whole passage moves through discrete moments and positions, with each moment represented as a different level of awareness of self and the external world. The passage moves in sudden shifts of awareness. It opens with Praskukhin "coming to life a bit" as he walks along with Mikhaylov. Each succeeding change in position and way of seeing is accompanied by a sudden change in awareness of himself: his cowardice, his debt, his fear of dying. The external world is reduced to isolated bits of sensation, and Praskukhin's knowledge is represented as attention to very particular sensory data which then become associated with a stored feeling, image, or idea he has about himself. The scene is a closeup in slow motion. In each case, though, the psyche is still represented at a distance; the narrator tells what is happening, but does not show it happening. In this the first part of the monologue differs from the second.

> Another second passed, a second in which a whole world of feelings, thoughts, hopes, and memories flashed in his imagination.
>
> "Who'll it kill, me or Mikhaylov? or both together? If me, then how? If in the head, then it's all over, but if in the leg, then they'll cut it off and I'll certainly ask for chloroform, and I can still remain alive. Maybe only Mikhaylov will get killed; then I will tell how we were walking together, how it killed him and splattered me with blood. No, it's nearer me, it's me."
>
> Then he recalled (*vspomnil*) the twelve rubles he owed (*dolzhen*) Mikhaylov; he recalled another debt (*dolg*) in Petersburg which should have been paid back (*zaplatit'*) long ago; the gypsy song he sang the night before came back to his mind; the woman he loved appeared in his imagination in her bonnet with lilac ribbons; he remembered (*vspomnilsja*) a man who insulted him five years ago and whom he had not repaid (*otplatil*) for the insult—although inseparably together with these and thousands of other recollections, the sensation of the present, the expectation of death and terror, did not leave him for a moment. "However, perhaps it won't burst," he thought, and with desperate decisive-

ness he tried to open his eyes. But at that moment, still through his closed eyelids, a red flash struck his eyes; with a terrifying noise something hit him in the middle of the chest; he started to run somewhere, tripped on a sabre which happened to be under his feet, and fell on his side.

This passage moves into the "imagination" itself. It does not focus on the relationship between sensations from the external world and associated mental images. In the first part of this passage Praskukhin's thoughts about "him or me" are represented as a mental conversation with himself, in quotation marks. Praskukhin considers the possibilities and alternatives awaiting him. But, then, as he realizes that the shell is coming toward him (even though this is not represented), the level of awareness shifts. Again the debt to Mikhaylov returns and spawns a train of recollected images revolving around the notion of indebtedness and revenge. The narrator limns a sequence of images linked among themselves: the debt to Mikhaylov recalls a similar unpaid debt; these images of failure recall his moment of successful acceptance the night before while singing the gypsy song; this recalls another such acceptance, the woman he loves; this distant acceptance recalls a distant rejection still not revenged. We are totally in Praskukhin's "imagination," watching his association of images. All the laws of association are at work: the "intensity" of the experience of indebtedness, the "similarity" of the images, even in the language the narrator uses to speak of them (*dolzhen, dolg; zaplatil, otplatil*), the "contiguity" of this moment with the night before. This state of awareness is broken when the external world impinges on his psyche right through his closed eyes. The shell bursts, but we do not see this. Only the flash that penetrates through the eyelids and the sensation in the chest are shown. We are inside Praskukhin's psyche, virtually cut off from the world around him, just as he is. The sequence ends only when Praskukhin falls down on the ground.

This second part of Praskukhin's internal monologue moves through two distinct stages: the quoted thoughts about death and the sequence of associating images in the imagination. In comparison with the first part, the section represents a more inward layer of the psyche. But, even in the first part, the process was represented as a movement inward, from the external world to some sense of self. In its parts and in the whole, then, the psychic process is represented as a continuing process of increasing interiority, an examination of consciousness and conscience. In the last part, as Praskukhin lies on the ground, the focus turns even more inward, but not toward more consciousness of self. It moves toward the extinction of consciousness. Praskukhin thinks he is just wounded. The soldiers running above him "flit by in his eyes" and he "unconsciously counts" them: "one, two, three, there's one with his coat tucked up." Then a streak of light again "flashes in his eyes."

> He thought what are they shooting from, a mortar or a cannon? Must be a cannon. Here's some more shooting, here's some more soldiers, five, six, seven, they're still going by.

The psychic process near unconsciousness is again represented as thoughts and interaction with the external world; only now the thoughts and words are direct quotations without quotation marks. This experience of things flitting and flashing in the eyes which are closed to the world, and this expression of words that are unconscious and quoted but not quoted, are meant to convey the peculiar state of semi-awareness near the moment of death.

Finally, the words yield to words Praskukhin would speak but cannot. The verbal level ends with Praskukhin trying to shout out "take me along"—which turns out to be a moan that frightens even him. The moment of dying is represented only as the experience of the weight of falling shrapnel: "it seemed that the soldiers were putting stones on him; the streaks of light jumped less and less, the stones they were putting on him weighed more and more, he made an effort to get the stones off, he stretched out, and no longer saw, nor heard, nor thought, nor felt." As Praskukhin approaches total loss of consciousness, the verbal level becomes less and less distinct, the "imagination" no longer bodies forth images from its storehouse, and finally there is only the sensation of the body. The three parts—mind, sensation, body—shut down in descending order. For Praskukhin the whole process yields no real new insight. He goes through the mental review of himself, but fails to get a final view of himself. He dies as he lived, not being accepted by the soldiers, who just run over him and pelt him with stones. Praskukhin does not see through his own self-image. The psychic process reveals what he has been, his past identity and vocation in all his failure. In his final assessment he makes no discovery of his true self.

AT THE CENTER of Praskukhin's knowledge is an act of assessing recollection. The sensory data from the external world enter the psyche, bump up against other data stored there, and issue forth as images recollected in a series of associations. Four times the text repeats words referring to recollection. To Tolstoy, as he later articulated it, this act of recollection is the foundation of the act of faith, the ascertaining of identity and the actions that follow therefrom.

> I receive an impression. It does not exist in the present. It exists only in recollection, when by recalling I begin to consider it, to unite (*soedinjat'*) it with other impressions and thoughts (55,136;1905). . . . This recollection is a certain (obviously not material) act by means of which I ascribe two or more different events or impressions to myself. I feel and say that both states are my state (54, 175;1903). . . . What is this "I"? It is certainly not the body or the consciousness of the body in the present, but the consciousness of everything that is united (*soedino*) into one by my recollection. These recollections are given through the sensations of the body, but the being I call myself in no way is the body (55,136). . . . This consciousness of the unity of various states is the beginning of spiritual life. Once he has reached this consciousness, a person understands that he is a spiritual being separated from everything else. . . . The consciousness . . . of one's separateness from the All begins with recollection. (54,175-76)

Just as the act of consciousness which goes forth from self to other is the cause and condition of the possibility of love, so the act of recollection which unites into one the isolated atoms of experience is the ground, proof, and condition of the existence of the true self. Through recollection we begin to discover our identity and find our vocation.

Nicholas Rostov has great devotion for the tsar, and, he believes, a need to prove his loyalty and bravery in battle. For him the battle for life has brought on a personal crisis, and he has to learn where best he will realize himself, in the skirmishes of the public arena or in some realm of calm more in the private domain, rushing along "here" toward death or "there" in that happiness which resides in the sun and in himself alone. At Austerlitz, right after the delineated segment of Prince Andrew's affirmation of his Toulon, of his need for "glory," the "love of the people for him," Rostov is shown in a moment of self-discovery that reveals to him the meaning of his conflict between that here and there. Rostov is on guard duty, making the rounds with his fellow hussars. But he is sleepy. So, since he must keep himself and his horse moving with the fellow guards, he tries "to surmount the sleep which is insurmountably overcoming him" (I,iii,xiii). The whole sequence is presented in alternating states of drowsy awareness and aware drowsiness. He is surrounded by a hazy and dark distance into which he peers but sees nothing.

> His eyes were closing and in his imagination there were represented now the tsar, now Denisov, and now his Moscow recollections and he again hastily tried to open his eyes, and he saw right in front of him the head and ears of the horse on which he was sitting, at times when he came within six paces of them, the black figures of the hussars, and in the distance that same hazy darkness.

In his drowsiness Rostov shifts between an awareness of the external world and attention to the contents of his imagination. His knowledge of the external world is represented as it appears to him in his slouched and sleepy condition. His internal world, at this point independent of this external world, contains three sets of recollections: his duty in the war and his attitude to the tsar, his relationship with his friend and fellow hussar Denisov, and his whole life before the war. His conscious concern is his need to prove himself in war and gain recognition by the tsar. In a passage not quoted here he fantasies an imagined encounter where he demonstrates his bravery and loyalty by beating an enemy soldier right "before the tsar's eyes." "Suddenly a distant shout arouses" him from his fantasy; he opens his eyes, and asks the question of faith, "Where am I?" He comes out of his drowsy state enough to realize he is on guard duty, but his thoughts return to the tsar. He then shifts his position in the saddle, takes off on another round, and slips off into another level of awareness.

> It seemed to him that it was getting lighter. To the left was visible an inclined slope bathed in light and opposite a black knoll which seemed as steep as a wall. On that knoll there was a white spot (*pjatno*) which Rostov could not understand (*ponjat'*) at all:

was it a glade in the wood lit up by the moon or some snow which had remained or white houses? It even seemed to him that something began to move over that white spot. "It must be snow, that spot, *une tache*," thought Rostov, "but that's not tash (*ne tash*)."

As Rostov moves again through the hazy darkness, his attention focuses on light. His fantasies fade away as his consciousness singles out one bit of white lit up by the light, but this bit of white has no meaning for him. It is a pure sensory impression with no apperception, like Pierre's pure sounds. This state of awareness is marked by the narrator's pun: *pjatno-ponjat'*. But as Rostov tries to grasp what this bit of white is, the "spot" becomes a pure mental event dissassociated from the sensory perception. The "spot" gets translated into French *une tache*—Rostov like all Russians of his class and time spoke French and Russian—and then this *tache* is mentally transliterated into the Cyrillic *tash*. We are in the imagination watching the association of ideas through conjunction and similarity. But this moment of empiricist knowing releases another inner layer in Rostov's imagination. There is a sudden shift of awareness.

"Natasha, my sister, black eyes. Na—tasha—(won't she be surprised when I tell her I saw the tsar!) Natashka, the sabretache (*tashka*), grab it." "A bit more to your right, sir, there are bushes here," said a voice of a hussar whom Rostov was riding past as he was falling asleep. Rostov suddenly raised his head, which had already sunk down to the horse's mane, and pulled up next to the hussar. Youthful, childlike sleep was insurmountably overcoming him. "Yes, now what was I thinking? I mustn't forget. How I'll speak to the tsar? No, not that, that's tomorrow. Yes, yes. On the sabretache (*na tashku*), to stomp on it (*nastupit'*), to dull us (*tupid' nas*). Who? The hussars. The hussar and moustaches (*usy*). That hussar with the moustache, I thought of him again, was walking along Tverskaya street right opposite Guryev's house, good old Guryev. Oh, Denisov's a great guy! But that's all nonsense. The main thing now is that the tsar is here. How he looked at me and how he wanted to say something he did not dare. But that's nonsense, and the main thing is not to forget that I was thinking something necessary, yes. Na—tashka, to dull us (*nas—tupit'*), yes, yes, yes. That's good." And he again let his head fall to the horse's neck.

In this passage, one of the most daring Tolstoy ever wrote, we enter the mind muddled by drowsiness and follow the train of associations along its three-fold track. The spot that is "not tash" becomes Natasha, and this linguistic association releases the Moscow recollections. But then the memory of his sister collides with the recollection of the war. Rostov seems to begin a sentence about his sister (her name appears in diminutive form in the accusative case, *Natashku*), but he then changes the direction of his thought as he drops the first syllable from her name and gets "sabretache" (*tashku*). Just as he starts to think about grabbing the sabretache, his thought is interrupted by the words of a passing hussar. He then starts to think again of the tsar but recalls his train of thought, which he "must not forget." The sabretache again appears, but now as the object of the preposition "on" (*Na tashku*), which makes it the phonetic equivalent of his sister's name in diminutive form, accusative case. This phrase, furthermore, is apparently the object of the verb "to stomp" (*nastupit'*), but the verb appears as an afterthought and could well be meant in isolation from the phrase, thus having its primary military meaning "to charge, to advance." Then this verb is itself broken up, the first three phonemes being separated from it and put after it, producing the phrase "to dull us (*tupit' nas*). As the sounds move about in the mind, they evoke Rostov's dilemma, for the world of war here, with its stomping and charging and dulling, is not like there back home with Natasha, the pure white spot of the world to which he belongs. But, still, right now for Rostov the world to which he belongs is the hussar world, and his mind now turns to them who are "us." By phonetic association (and visual image) hussars recall moustaches (*gusary, usy*), and Rostov recollects seeing a certain hussar with a moustache back home. This reminds him of his friend Denisov. But all this is not the "main thing," for in this moment of recollection Rostov has uncovered what it is "necessary" not to forget: he sums up the whole experience by repeating the key words which have a phonetic resemblance, only now his sister's name is grasped in its fullness, which includes the sabretache (written *Na—tashka*) and the act of war is seen as inherently harmful to "us" (written *nas—tupit'*). Rostov is torn between war and peace, between here near

death and there back home with his image of the world of relatedness
where he feels he belongs. In his recollection he glimpses for a moment his dilemma and his heart's desire. The mental assessment reveals his quandary of identity and vocation.

DURING his moment of recollection on guard duty, something happens to Rostov. His discovery of his dilemma is not really new. That
he uncovered at Enns. But on guard duty this dilemma is seen at a
new level, with fuller understanding, with an eye to the broader implications. At Enns the dilemma was metaphysical; on guard duty
the dilemma is social and psychological. The "happiness" within
and in the sun becomes the whole world of home, friendship, and loving relatedness. These two represented moments of consciousness
are the central and determining experiences in Rostov's life. In these
moments, quite unbeknowst to him, he is deciding his fate. The representation of a character's knowledge in Tolstoy is the representation of the character's moment of decision, his act of choosing his
destiny. For Tolstoy all such moments of decision long precede any
active decision to act or any enactment of the decision.

> The chief work actuating the whole of human life does not take
> place in the movements of human hands, feet, or backs, but in
> consciousness. Before a person can accomplish anything with
> his feet or hands, a certain alteration has first to take place in his
> consciousness. This alteration determines all his subsequent
> movements. But these alterations are always minute, almost
> imperceptible. . . . True life begins where there take place infi-
> nitely small alterations which seem to us tiny, tiny. True life
> does not take place where large, external alterations are accom-
> plished, where people move about, clash, fight, and kill each
> other; it takes place only where tiny, tiny, infinitesimally small
> alterations are accomplished. . . . Many material alterations may
> result from what happens when a person has taken a decision
> and begun to act; houses, riches, and peoples' bodies may perish,
> but nothing more can result than what has already settled in a
> person's consciousness. The limits of what can take place are
> given by consciousness. (27,279-81;1890)

Tolstoy breaks up the process of moral decision into minute and
discrete shifts in awareness. Just as the epistemological event is re-

duced to the impression of atoms of sensation, so the moral event is reduced to atoms of alteration in the psyche. In everything he does Tolstoy extracts from the flow the significant bits which embody and reveal even as they determine the direction of the flow. This atomization of everything can be seen even in the style of his expository writing, in his diary entries, letters, and in his essays, as in the above quotation, which is from his essay on the relationship of consciousness to mind-altering substances, *Why Do Men Stupefy Themselves?* The sentences follow each other with what seems a stupefying repetition of the same words and the same ideas over and over. But in reality each sentence adds one discrete new observation or idea, nothing more, nothing less. This manner of writing makes for less than exciting reading, but it is not designed to arouse; its purpose is to guide the reader in slow motion through the tiny, tiny shifts in his awareness which will lead him to decision. It is the style of step-by-step articulation.

In the fiction, moments of moral decision are represented not as moments of active decision to act but as moments of tiny, tiny alterations of consciousness. Because to Tolstoy these moments are the significant ones, he brings them into focus and shows them in process and slow motion. The moments of alteration of consciousness are represented as journeys of self-discovery, the uncovering of layers of motivation and desire which will then release the active decision to act at some subsequent time. Because these moments of tiny, tiny alterations are not active decisions, Tolstoy represents them as moments of an unusual psychic order, near death or near sleep. Anna is returning to Petersburg after her visit to Moscow and her encounter with Vronsky. Throughout her sojourn in Moscow she has been tormented by her attraction to Vronsky and his pursuit of her. Her affair began, one could say, with the first glance she gave Vronsky at the railroad station, but the tiny, tiny alteration in her consciousness which releases the eventual active decision to act takes place on her journey home, on the train back to Petersburg and Karenin's big ears. The active decision itself is never represented. Instead, Tolstoy gives Anna's daydream on the train. Thankful that "it's all over," Anna settles into her seat on the train next to her servant Annushka, covers her legs with a blanket to keep warm, places on her knees a pillow she has taken from her red handbag, and takes note of a stout old woman who is wrapping up her legs to keep warm and discussing the heating on the train with the other passengers (I,xxix). Anna refrains from conversation, turning her attention to the contents of her hand-bag, the English novel she is about to read and the paper-knife she will use to cut its pages. The sequence is represented in five clearly delineated sections of increasing interiority. Each section represents a sudden shift in awareness.

> In the beginning she did not feel like reading. At first the hustle and bustle disturbed her; then when the train started up it was impossible not to listen to the noises; then the snow beating against the window to her left and sticking onto the glass, the sight of the conductor as he walked past, bundled up and covered with snow on one side, and the conversations about the terrible snowstorm outside distracted her attention. Further on it was all the same, the same: the same jolting and knocking, the same snow in the window, the same rapid transitions from steam heat to cold and back to heat, the same flashing of the same faces in the semi-darkness and the same voices, and Anna began to understand what she was reading.

This representation of the character's knowledge begins as do the others with the focus on the character's experience of sensations from the external world. These sensations impinge on Anna's psyche and disturb her ability to concentrate: she is not able to read. The passage itself is divided by the two long sentences into two parts, before and after the train begins to move, but the movement only results in an intensification of the sensory experiences to the point of boredom. They all become "the same," a phrase repeated eight times in the second long sentence. The repeated sensations dull the mind, and Anna turns inward. The first level of awareness ends as it began with a reference to Anna's reading. The second level of awareness turns to the reading itself.

> Anna Arkadyevna read and understood, but it was unpleasant for her to read, that is, to follow the reflection of other peoples' lives. She too much wanted to live (*khotelos' zhit'*). When she read about the heroine in the novel taking care of a sick man, she wanted (*khotelos'*) to move about noiselessly in the sick man's room; when she read about a member of parliament giving a speech, she wanted (*khotelos'*) to give the speech; when she read

about Lady Mary riding after the hounds, teasing her sister-in-law and astonishing everyone with her boldness, she wanted (*khotelos'*) to do that herself. But there was nothing to do, so twisting the smooth little knife (*nozhichek*) in her tiny hands, she forced herself to read.

Anna reads and understands what she is reading, but her attention is focused on herself. What is uncovered in her reading is her desire to live. What this desire to live entails Anna does not know. She experiences it as capricious identification with others. She could play nurse or lady or member of parliament. She wants to be someone, but there is no *one* she wants to be. Anna's desire to live is her way of experiencing dissatisfaction with herself. Her desire is not an active affirmation of a goal, but a vague feeling expressed grammatically by the impersonal reflexive form of the verb with the subject in the dative (not *ona khotela*, but *ej khotelos'*), a form repeated four times in this passage. She just feels like wanting to live, just as at the beginning she did not feel like reading (*chitalos'*). Because Anna just feels like wanting to live and because this desire to live means only to be like someone, anyone else, it seems to her that there is nothing to do. Because any option seems better than what she has and not one preferable to another, she is stymied by the possibility of choice, even in her fantasy. This second level of awareness, the moment of self-dissatisfaction measured by the fantasy of unlimited possibility, ends as Anna toys with the paper-knife and once again turns to her reading.

The hero of the novel had already begun to attain his English happiness, a baronetcy and an estate, and Anna desired (*zhelala*) to go together with him to that estate when suddenly she felt that he ought to be ashamed and that she was ashamed of the same thing. "What have I to be ashamed of?" she asked herself with outraged astonishment. She put down the book, leaned against the back of the seat, and gripped the little paper-knife (*razreznoj nozhik*) tightly in both hands. There was nothing to be ashamed of. She went over all her Moscow recollections. They were all good, fine. She recalled the ball, she recalled Vronsky and his enamoured, submissive face, she recalled all her relations with him: there was nothing shameful. But still just at that point in her recollections, the feeling of shame increased, as if some inner voice were saying to her right when she was remembering Vronsky, "Warm, very warm, hot." "Well, what is it?" she said to herself decisively as she shifted her position in her seat. "What does it mean? Could I be afraid to look straight at it? Well, what is it? Can it be that between me and this officer-child there exists or could exist some sort of other relations besides those that occur with every acquaintance?" She laughed contemptuously and again took up the book, but now she definitely could not understand what she read.

Anna does not simply read; she now forces herself to read, as if in reading she can hide from her dissatisfaction. Now her attention shifts from the heroine to the hero, but it still remains centered on herself. She would go off with him to his English happiness. But this fantasy is not something Anna just feels she wants; this she actively desires (*zhelala*). At the moment this active desire emerges in her consciousness, the pronominal reference to the hero shifts to Vronsky, and Anna "suddenly" feels that he ought to be ashamed, even as she herself feels shame. Her voice of conscience speaks. But then she immediately tries to extricate herself from this momentary flash of responsibility that outrages her. She puts down the book and grasps the knife that can cut (*razreznoj*). Now, with her attention totally on her self, she shifts, like Rostov, from fantasy to recollection. But Anna's recollection is designed to justify herself to herself; she recalls not her interested glances or her conflicted feelings, only Vronsky's enamoured, submissive face at the ball. He ought to be ashamed, not me, yet still I feel shame. At this point her recollection is interrupted by the voice of the stoker who is checking the temperature in the compartment, "Warm, very warm, hot." But only these words break through into Anna's recollecting consciousness. To her they must seem like some inner voice of conscience, speaking in the well-known words of the children's guessing game and telling her that she is close to the truth. She shifts her position. No sooner does she begin to "look straight at it" than she deposes Vronsky from his heroic status, reducing him to the "officer-child" of whom his mother knows and tells. With a contemptuous laugh at such a possibility, she again tries to hide in her reading, which now she no longer understands at all. In this central episode in Anna's inward journey of discovery there is uncovered the kernel of her whole being: her active desire, her failure to admit her responsibility in her desire, and her penchant for shifting responsibility for her desire onto others. Her tragedy follows from this moment. Now that she has realized her desire, she will, in what follows, make her desire real.

> She traced the paper-knife (*nozh*) over the windowpane, then placed its cold, smooth surface on her cheek, and almost began to laugh aloud from the joy which suddenly without cause took possession of her. She felt her nerves being stretched tighter and tighter like strings on some sort of pegs that were being screwed in. She felt her eyes opening wider and wider, her fingers and toes twitching nervously, something inside constricting her breathing, and all the images and sounds in that swaying semi-darkness impressing her with unusual clarity. Moments of uncertainty kept on coming over her: was the train going forward or backward or standing completely still; was that Annushka next to her or a stranger? "What's that on the hook; is it a fur coat or a beast? And what am I myself now? Am I myself or another?" It was terrifying for her to yield to this oblivion (*zabyt'ë*). But something was drawing her into it, and by her own will (*proizvol*) she could yield to it or resist. She got up to clear her head (*opomnit'sja*), removed the blanket, and took off the cape from her warm outfit. Her head cleared (*ona opomnilas'*) for a moment, and she understood (*ponjala*) that the thin peasant who had come in wearing a coat without buttons was the stoker, that he had looked at the thermometer, that the wind and snow had rushed behind him in through the door, but then everything got confused (*vsë smeshalos'*) again.

Anna abandons the book for the knife. Again she experiences a sudden shift in awareness, from the recollected past and shame to the sensuous present and joy. She is still centered on herself; only now that self is her body, which she feels in all its tenseness, and her impressions of the external world, which she feels in all their vividness. This state of loss of former self is both attractive and threatening. This new level of awareness of self and other confuses Anna, however, and she begins to lose sight of who she is or where she is going. Turned into the joy of her body, she comes to a crisis of faith, a necessary decision about identity and vocation. The knife has finally touched her, but as it has moved from hand to cheek it has grown in menacing proportions, each time dropping a diminutive suffix (*nozhichek, nozhik*) until now the bare root of knife (*nozh*) cuts right through her. At this point Anna gets up to clear her head of her crisis. For a moment she does, and Tolstoy marks the moment of clear vision with a characteristic pun (*opomnilas'*, literally, "recalled herself," and *ponjala*). But the clear vision of the peasant stoker in his coat is also a reminder of the conductor bundled up against the cold, who is also a reminder of the peasant-watchman bundled up against the cold, the ill omen of Anna's romance regardless of others. Again everything gets confused.

> The peasant with the long waist started to gnaw at something in the wall; the old woman began to stretch her legs through the entire compartment, and filled it with a black cloud; then something terrifying began to squeak and knock as if someone were being torn apart; then a red flame blinded her eyes; and then everything was closed off by a wall. Anna felt that she had collapsed. Yet all this was not terrifying but joyful. The voice of a man all wrapped up and covered with snow shouted something in her ear. She got up, cleared her head, and understood that they had arrived at the station and that this was the conductor.

Anna's attention switches from her body to the external world. But her experience of that world is transformed by her tense confusion. The peasant-stoker starts gnawing at the wall. The old woman becomes all body, filling and fouling all space. Sights and sound become more and more violent until they reach a climax, as Anna collapses. Anna has reached her body's desire. The knife and Vronsky too have disappeared from her consciousness. The journey comes to a halt, the train arrives at a station, and the conductor all wrapped up and covered with snow is there shouting in her ear. Her clear vision returns, once again marked by repeated puns: she got up (*podnjalas'*), cleared her head (*opomnilas'*), and understood (*ponjala*). Anna goes out through the door for some fresh air, and, "as if it had been waiting for her, the wind began to whistle joyfully and almost picked her up and carried her away." The "terrifying storm" raging around her now gives her pleasure, and she strolls off into it only to encounter Vronsky. From this moment of recollective consciousness there is no turning back. It is not all over. It has just begun.

Anna's inward journey of discovery is Tolstoy at his best and most characteristic. Everything is realistic, everything is emblematic. The ride on a train is the journey within. The red handbag is the container of her desires: her pillow, the novel with its fantasy scenarios, and the knife that cuts in two (Vronsky). The old woman concerned with the temperature and her spread legs filling and fouling the whole place embodies and reveals Anna's animal self; the stoker-conductor bundled up against the storm, gnawing at the wall, and shouting in her ear, is the voice of her gnawing conscience, her divine self whose call to clear vision she will not hear. The arrival of the train at a station is Anna's coming and climax, the aim and end of her journey, the fulfillment of her erotic need. And the storm, of course, is the passion to which she now yields for the first time, but not yet as an active desire and decision. Furthermore, the entire sequence, which recalls Anna's arrival on her mission and prefigures her departure from life, is itself a paradigmatic action: at the center of the journey within, just as at the center of the novel, is the question of guilt, but it begins with the high hopes that it is all over and ends with a certain awareness that these hopes were false. In this sequence the character's knowledge is represented both realistically and emblematically, but this method is not new, just a clearer articulation of the method used to represent Olenin's encounter with the mountains or Rostov's vision of the pure white spot. In all, the character comes to some new understanding of self in an act of assessing recollection.

ANXIETIES OF ASSESSMENT

Anna's inward journey of self-discovery is a daydream that culminates in a psychic state that borders on an hallucination. It combines material from Anna's present (her reading and her environment) with material from Anna's recent past (her Moscow experience and especially the violent mishap at the beginning). This violent mishap itself, however, also generates a series of dreams: both Anna and Vronsky dream of a peasant with a dishevelled beard, bent over while doing something and speaking unintelligible words in French. This recurrent dream is an image of the violent mishap which is an ill omen: the mangled, crushed body which foretells something. It is the only recurrent dream in Tolstoy's fiction.

Vronsky sees this dream only once. It occurs after Anna has admitted her pregnancy and Vronsky has seen his feared image of himself in the foreign prince, the "stupid hunk of beef" (IV,i). It is a time when Anna blindly believes that "her position will be unravelled" (*razvjazhet*) while Vronsky fears that his "feeling" for Anna is "tying (*privjazyvaet*) him to her more and more" (IV,ii). The delineated segment is characterized by words made from the root meaning "to tie" or "bind" (*vjaz-*). This is the point in the novel when Vronsky becomes aware that his relationship to Anna is deciding his whole life. To Vronsky, then, the dishevelled figure is associated with Anna and appears as a peasant whose job is to go along on a bear hunt to help surround and catch the animal to be killed (*muzhik obkladchik*). The dream does not show Vronsky coming to this awareness; it does not represent his consciousness in process. The dream assesses for a moment the meaning of Vronsky's actions for him and expresses the fears he cannot verbalize to himself. In his relationship with Anna he is being surrounded and caught.

Anna sees his dream twice, first in the scene which directly follows Vronsky's dream. Because she feels neglected, Anna sends Vronsky a note telling him she is not feeling well and asking him to come to see her, even though such direct meetings at home have been forbidden by Karenin and she is not really ill. Vronsky finds Anna in hysterics: "No! No! If it is going to continue like this, then it will happen much, much sooner" (IV.iii). He has no idea what Anna means by this not-so-veiled threat. But they seem to come to an understanding and agree that "it's now over" (*konchilos'*). But it is not all over. "Scowling," Anna picks up her crocheting (*vjazan'e*) from the table and "without looking at Vronsky takes out the crochet hook" and says, "That's the way life always is for all of you young men, isn't it?" This is the first represented moment of Anna's jealousy, and the scene is built on the dynamic of guilt and resentment. In what follows, the drama is played out. Anna resents Karenin for not letting her see Vronsky and feels guilty before Karenin for now seeing Vronsky; she resents Vronsky for not seeing her and feels guilty before Vronsky because she resents this. The entire meeting called by Anna is designed to unravel these feelings by projecting them onto others. It is in this context that Anna tells Vronsky of her dream. She ties the knot tighter as she sits there crocheting, the emblem of her raveling what she could unravel.

In his first dream Anna sees herself running into the bedroom "to get something, to find out something." In the corner she sees the peasant who is "bent over a bag and ruffling something" in it, while saying, "Il faut le battre, le fer, le broyer, le pétrir." Terrified, she wakes up within the dream and is told by her servant that this means she will die in childbirth. Anna does not transform the image of the peasant nor associate it with Vronsky. Rather, she sees the peasant in relationship to two objects, a bag and something iron (suggests a railroad, in Russian literally "iron road," *zheleznaja doroga*). For Anna the dream is grounded in the violent mishap, but it proceeds from her hallucinatory journey: the bag from which she takes her desires and the knife (something iron) that cuts in two reappear. As with Vronsky, Anna's dream is an image of her conscience reacting in panic to her pregnancy: the fantasies she took out of her bag are getting ruffled. But for Anna her conscience now tells her two things: the knife that cuts in two must be crushed, and she will die. Her conscience, which speaks in two voices from two different people, tells her what she must do and how she will be punished. As with Vronsky, the dream assesses for the moment the meaning of Anna's actions for her and expresses the fears she cannot verbalize to herself. In the scene in which the dream is told, Anna acts on these fears by directing them at Vronsky: her death will be his punishment.

The second time Anna sees the dream occurs toward the end of the novel, after a whole day, the first ever, spent in estrangment from Vronsky, "not an argument but an obvious recognition of a complete cooling off" (VII,xxvi). Anna passes the time imagining all the cruel things Vronsky wanted to say to her and then will not "forgive him for what in reality he did not say." She tells the servants to inform Vronsky upon his return that she has a headache, but when he returns and does not come to see her, she takes this as a sign of the end, "it's all over" (*vsë koncheno*). She entertains conscious desires to punish him with her death and realizes that "before she could speak to him of her love, she would have to prove to him that he was guilty before her." Anna is desperate and in her despair, as always, she tries to make Vronsky guilty in order not to feel guilty herself. Only now Anna fears that this will no longer work. The dream marks the end of her control over Vronsky. The peasant appears as an "old man" who is "bent down over some iron"; he "pays no attention to her" and is doing "something terrible in the iron over her." The peasant is now an image of Vronsky grown cold to her, paying no attention to her but doing something to her. The bag of her pleasures has disappeared. While in the first dream the images referred to Anna and what she must do, in the second the images refer to Vronsky and what he is doing to her. The victimizer now becomes the victim. As with the other recurrent dreams, then, this dream assesses the meaning of Anna's actions for her and expresses the fears she dare not verbalize. The actions in her waking life are meant to stay this course of the affair, but they in fact enact and ensure this course of the affair. The fears turn out to be desires.

The recurrent dreams in *Anna Karenina* reflect the inevitable results of the romance commenced at the violent mishap and conducted regardless of others. Although they are dreams about the relationship, they never show care or concern for the other. Rather, each instance of the recurrent dream captures a moment of inner assessment of some failing or flaw in the relationship which is threatening or destructive to the character. They are anxious measures of their misgivings. These dreams, then, are not representations of the stages in the growth of consciousness, as with Olenin's moments of heightened self-awareness, nor are they representations of the process of knowing, as with Rostov at Enns or Pierre at Borodino, nor are they representations of the process of recollective consciousness, as with Rostov on guard duty or Praskukhin at death. These dreams are recollections of the past transformed by the present. Dreams in Tolstoy are the measures of the "level of one's growth" at this time, the "essence of one's life" at this moment (55,18;1904). The dream is the revealing moment of assessment.

Pierre's dream at Mozhaysk is just such a revealing assessment. He leaves Borodino for Mozhaysk, where he hopes to find some semblance of "normal conditions," a "state" in which he can "understand himself and everything he has seen and experienced" (III,iii,viii). He has yet to grasp the meaning of his fear of death or the "family animation" he felt in the heat of the battle. Still in a state of great agitation and anxiety, he lies down on the ground near his carriage. As he covers his head to go to sleep, Pierre thinks of *them*, the soldiers he encountered in battle. "To be a soldier, simply a soldier," he thinks. "To enter into that common life with my whole being, to be penetrated by what makes them that way. But how can I cast from myself all that is superfluous and of the devil, the whole burden of the external man?" With these thoughts of moral reform and this image of the soldier as the perfect participant in life, Pierre falls asleep.

And the dinner at the club at which he challenged Dolokhov and his benefactor at Torzhok flashed in Pierre's imagination. He saw a solemn dining lodge. This lodge was taking place at the English Club. Someone, a close, dear acquaintance, was sitting at the end of the table. Yes, that's him! That's my benefactor. "But didn't he die?" Pierre thought. "Yes, he died, but I did not know that he is alive. How sorry I am he died and how happy I am that he is alive again!" At one side of the table sat Anatole, Dolokhov, Nesvitsky, Denisov, and others like them (the category of these people in the dream was just as distinctly defined in Pierre's mind as the category of those people he called *they*), and these people were shouting and singing loudly; but from behind their shouting was heard the voice of his benefactor speaking incessantly and the sound of his words was just as weighty and uninterrupted as the din of the battlefield, but it was pleasant and comforting. Pierre did not understand what his benefactor was saying, but he knew (the category of thoughts was also quite distinct in his dream) that the benefactor was speaking about the good (*dobro*), about the possibility of being what *they* were. And *they* with their simple, kind (*dobrye*) firm faces surrounded his benefactor on all sides. Yet, although they were kind, they did not look at Pierre; they did not know him. Pierre wanted to turn their attention to him so he could speak. He got up, but at that moment his legs grew cold and bare. He felt ashamed and with one arm covered his legs, from which in fact his cloak had slipped.

Pierre's dream coalesces two distinct events in his life: (1) his first crisis at Torzhok when, just after his duel with Dolokhov, he met Bazdeev and subsequently joined the masons and (2) his recent experience at Borodino. The link between the two events is death. Bazdeev had counselled the "love of death," and "they" are the ones who in their moment of latent warmth of patriotism seem to embody a love of death or at least an enthused acceptance of its inevitability. These two events, both of which are in some sense moments of Pierre's failure to face death, then themselves expand in the dream into two separate worlds represented by two sets of men seated on opposite sides of a table, those who shout and sing loudly and the simple, kind soldiers who surround in iconic fashion the central figure of Bazdeev, who speaks of the good, which means becoming one of the soldiers. Pierre is present in the dream but not at either side of the table. The dream image of this "dining lodge" with its two sets of beings facing each other, one raucous, the other speaking incessantly of the good and audible above the raucous din, represents Pierre's two opposed images of himself: Pierre the rake, the one he is, and Pierre the reformed, the one he would be, the one who lives for himself, the man of the flesh, and the one who would belong, the man of the spirit. The "dining lodge" that is taking place at the English Club reflects this same opposition. This is the banquet of the animal selves and the divine selves, of those who sit separately, have distinct names, and bear the burden of what is superfluous and external, and of those who sit surrounding a central figure, experience "common life," and share one simple interiority. This banquet shows Pierre's estrangement from both groups: he pays little attention to the distinct figures, but the common group pays no attention to him. The dream reveals Pierre's hidden wish in all its depth, his failure and his desire for conversion, even as it follows in the reader's text the delineated segment of Helen's conversion (the life of the flesh) and precedes the departure of the Rostovs (the life of the spirit). The emotion on which this dream is based, therefore, is shame: the recognition of failing before others, coupled with the realization that he can be otherwise. The central figure in the dream, not surprisingly, then, and as in the recurrent dream in *Anna Karenina*, is a figure who speaks incessantly, an image of the voice of conscience always present, alive even when thought dead. What distinguishes Pierre from Anna, and this is significant, is that Pierre, after covering his bared legs, makes an effort to fall back into his dream in order "to hear and understand the words of his benefactor," words which later Pierre became convinced "someone outside him was saying to him." To Pierre the dream is a revelation.

"War is the most difficult subordination of human freedom to the laws of God," said the voice. "Simplicity is submission to God; from Him you cannot escape. And *they* are simple. *They* do not speak; they act. The spoken word is silver; the unspoken is golden. A person can control nothing so long as he fears death. To him who fears it not, everything belongs. If there were no suffering, a person would not know his boundaries; he would not know himself. The most difficult thing (Pierre continued to think or hear in his dream) consists in being able to unite the meaning of everything in one's heart (*dusha*). "To unite everything (*vsë*)?" Pierre said to himself. "No, not to unite. It's impossible to unite thoughts, rather to yoke (*soprjagat'*) all these thoughts together—that's what is necessary. *You've got to yoke; you've got to yoke,*" Pierre repeated to himself ecstatically, feeling that by precisely these words and only these words what he wanted to express was being expressed and that the whole question that was tormenting him was being resolved.

What "is revealed to Pierre during his dream" is nothing other than the moral meaning of what he will later see as his metaphysical vision of the globe of life. Those who participate in life are those who do not think of themselves as individuals. They are the "simple" ones who in their acceptance of suffering and death in some sense know that suffering is the inevitable result of the experience of limitation by boundaries, which is the mysterious but inevitable law of this life. The laws of this life always limit the individual's freedom. To fear suffering or death is a denial of this reality and of these laws; to accept them is to belong to this reality. One accepts this life, not by some verbal affirmation of it, but by living it without hesitation, going forth and giving forth without thought or word about it. Pierre's dream tells of his moral failure in the face of death and of his desire to overcome his fear of death and hence to face his ability to go and give forth and hence to belong. But for Pierre this is not yet clear. The dream represents his anxious assessment of the level of his growth just before he goes on his mission of salvation which ends in his spontaneous giving forth of self. The dream of the globe of life which follows that salvific act reveals Pierre's next level of growth and his final image of the whole universe.

The dream at Mozhaysk ends with Pierre's desire to figure it all out, to yoke together his "thoughts." "Yes, you've got to yoke; it's time to yoke," he hears or says. "You've got to harness up; it's time to harness up" repeats "some voice," and Pierre awakens to his groom's shouting in his ear. Just as the first half of the dream seems to emerge from its final moment of shame at his bared and cold legs, the moment which contains the dream's major emotion, so this second half of the dream emerges from the groom's statement about the need to "harness" (*zaprjagat'*), which word is but one phoneme re-moved from the word "to yoke" (*soprjagat'*). The dream emerges from Pierre's basic need for an image of the whole universe. The content of each half of the dream is related to its final moment, which is the moment of slipping from sleep to awakeness. The material from the distant and recent past is recollected, reorganized, and pushed to dream consciousness by some stimulus from the external world which is actually arousing the sleeper from his sleep. The dream takes place at the moment of awakening. In this Tolstoy saw great meaning.

> Everyone knows and everyone has taken note of these strange dreams that end with an awakening from some external influence on the sleeper: a knock, noise, touch or fall . . . which happens in reality takes on in the dream the character of a concluding impression after many others which seem to prepare for it. . . . We all know such dreams and are surprised that this event which has just happened now and has awakened me could have been prepared in the dream by everything I dreamt before it, by everything that led up to the momentary event which has just happened. The deception of time, in my opinion, has a very important significance. (57,139-40;1909)

What Tolstoy sees is that the dream does not take place in time, but only at the instant of awakening when "we see united into one what was broken up through time" (55,19;1904). The dream world is a world that exists outside the categories of the mind. In dreams "there is no personality, no time, no space, no causality" (55,20). One figure may appear in various guises: the peasant-stoker and the conductor in Anna's hallucination or the peasant speaking in French and Korney predicting death in Anna's recurrent dream. Things separated by space coalesce: the lodge meeting takes place in the English Club and discrete spatial objects like the knife and something iron replace each other. Simple causality and logic fade: Anna goes to the bedroom to get something or to find out something, and not being seen means not seeing. Pierre's dream of the globe of life is constructed according to these same principles. He is aroused from the dream by someone shouting out, "Vous avez compris, sacre nom?" which in the dream appears as the voice of his old geography teacher, "long for-gotten and as if alive," asking him if he understood the lesson of the globe of life, "vous avez compris, mon enfant?" This dream, like the one at Mozhaysk, has two parts, a sequence of thoughts and a dream image; only here the thoughts precede the image. The dream does not follow the laws of space, time, or causality: Bazdeev's liquid imagery merges with the past images of the sky; the teacher from Switzerland knows about Karataev and seems to be Bazdeev; the sphere has no dimensions and yet a center. Dreams represent a mode of existence beyond space, time, causality, and personality. Because this dream world exists, it is the proof, if not the ground and revelation, of that mode of existence.

In all the represented dreams the dream image is dominated by a central figure who speaks forth some words. These words may be enigmatic or highly abstract, but, as with Pierre, these words seem to come forth from someone other than the dreamer. In the dream world the dreamer hears another voice. In this dream world, which does not abide by the categories of our waking mind, we learn some truth about reality and especially about ourselves. In dreams we see "the weaknesses we consider ourselves free of when awake, the weaknesses we fear when awake but no longer have, and what we are striving toward" (55,18). In dreams we find our failings, our anxieties and our wishes, our conscience and our conductor. For Tolstoy dreams occur in an instant of awakening from sleep to life and reorder events from the past into a recollected image to reveal where we have been and to speak of where we would or should go. Dreams assess our identity and vocation now.

THE DREAM that is the moment of assessing recollection of the past and of an awakening to life provided Tolstoy with a model for grasping the psychic experience at the moment of death. In the death of Praskukhin he explored the first half of this process: the instantaneous reordering of images from the past which reveals to Praskukhin who he has been. In *Childhood*, telling of the death of Maman, Tolstoy looks at the other half of this process, the awakening to a new life. The scene is represented not directly, but in Maman's words addressed to her husband and scribbled down at a moment shortly before she dies, when her "thoughts," she insists, are "extremely clear," not "unreal, confused presentiments" (xxv). For Maman the issue is not the past but the future because she has always looked at "death as a passage to a better life."

Will my love for you and the children end with my life? I have understood that this is impossible. I feel too strongly at this moment to think that that feeling without which I cannot understand existence might sometime be destroyed. My soul cannot exist without love for you, I know that it will exist eternally by the fact that such a feeling as my love could not have come to be if it had to come to an end sometime. I will not be with you, but I am firmly convinced my love will never leave you, and this thought is so joyful to my heart that I calmly and without fear await my approaching death.

For Maman death is a passage from this life, her personal existence, to another life when "I will not be," but her eternally growing soul, her *love for*, will live forever. What distinguishes Maman from Praskukhin, then, is the moral character of their lives reflected in their psychological state at death. Maman knows that she is dying; indeed, she believes "God has been pleased to reveal this to her." She does not want to die and regrets having to leave this life, but she accepts the fact that this life includes by definition a terminal point which is also a transition to another state where the *love for* she has accomplished in this life will be preserved, even if her personality "will not be." She has no regrets about what she has done and hence no fears for what will be done. But Praskukhin, shot down by a shell, bleeding, and only half-conscious, remains convinced that he is not about to die. His moment of death is all regrets, a past made of rejection by others and unpaid debts. He fears for this life which is what the fear of death is. All Tolstoy's depictions of the at-death experience follow from these two early representations: the fear of the end of this life that had no *love for* and the passage from this life of *love for* to another and greater life of *love for* when, however, "I will not be."

Like Maman, Natalya Savishna dies without regret for her life or fear of the next. She too knows that she will die: she prepares a white dress for the occasion and chooses the site of her burial. What distinguishes her death from Maman's, however, are her rituals of giving forth and forgiveness. "From all the household servants she begged forgiveness for the offenses she might have caused them, and she asked her confessor, Father Vassily, to tell all of us that she did not know how to thank us for our kindnesses and that she begged us to forgive her if by any stupidity of hers she had upset anyone" (xxviii).

To the very end Natalya Savishna is concerned with the distribution of her meager savings, and when at last she manages to find ten rubles to give to the poor, she then "blesses herself, lies down, and sighs for the last time, pronouncing God's name with a joyful smile." Maman dies sentimentally with a touch of the metaphysics of love on her lips; Natalya Savishna dies with her sense of love, as she had done all her life. Maman looks to the future life, but Natalya Savishna recollects her past, as she gathers it all together to forgive and give away.

Like Maman and Natalya Savishna, the peasant Fyodor in *Three Deaths* knows that he is dying. Like Natalya Savishna, his last act is to give away what he has: a young boy asks for Fyodor's new boots, which now that he is dying he will no longer need, and Fyodor without hesitation or thought of himself tells the boy to take them. But Fyodor, the peasant, unlike Maman, has no consoling metaphysics to draw upon, and so he requests of the boy a favor: he wants a gravestone put on his grave in return for his act of charity. Fyodor accepts his death but wants to be remembered in the future. In this he differs from the tree at the end of the story. The tree of course cannot know it is dying or be conscious of itself as having lived or being remembered; it just dies. But, unbeknownst to it, the tree in falling to the "damp earth" releases a calm, joyous majesty in the world around it even as it provides the boy with the wood for a cross which he will put on Fyodor's grave instead of the stone he cannot afford. At death both the peasant and the tree yield of themselves and thus create a new life for those around them. According to Tolstoy's own interpretation, they live and die in "harmony with the whole world" (60,266;1858).[2]

Unlike the peasant and the tree, Marya Dmitrevna lives and dies in "discord." *Three Deaths* opens with a scene showing this "lady" with a "dry, deadly whiteness to her skin," riding along in her carriage on a journey to save her life. But, like Praskukhin, Marya Dmitrevna, who is sick unto death, does not know that she is about to die. She believes that if she gets to Italy her health will return, and the very mention of death frightens her. Near death she blames her hus-

---

[2] Maman, Natalya Savishna, and Fyodor all die a variation of what Philippe Ariès calls "the tame death." He claims this tame death is the oldest ritual death in Christian society. It is always characterized by a knowledge of the imminent death, a regret for loss of life, and the rituals of confession, forgiveness, and giving away of possessions. See Philippe Ariès, *The Hour of Our Death* (New York, 1981), pp. 5-28.

band for her illness and, "suddenly remembering something," calls him in to chastize him for not getting her the best doctors. When her cousin comes to pay her last respects and leans over to kiss her hand, Marya Dmitrevna exclaims, "No, don't kiss me there; only the dead are kissed on the hand." Marya Dmitrevna does not understand mortal life. As a result at her death she gives nothing away and forgives no one, although she believes God will forgive her because she has "suffered so." Throughout her dying, as throughout her life, Marya Dmitrevna has concern only for herself. Death frightens her because her life has been totally self-enclosed. She has never experienced that giving forth or forgiveness which creates new life, and so she cannot imagine any loss of self that is not completely self-annihilating. In her dying Marya Dmitrevna is the opposite of both Maman and Natalya Savishna.

Ivan Ilych resembles Marya Dmitrevna. He too has led a self-enclosed life, and he too has not understood mortal life. But in his illness and suffering Ivan Ilych discovers mortal life and thus comes to know that he will die. Once he knows that he is dying, he recollects his life only to regret it. This regret for a life lived wrongly increases his desire to live. Ivan Ilych's moment at death is characterized by this glance backward and forward, by the new vision of his past and a new hope for his future. It thus combines the two moments of recollection and passage. The representation of this death, furthermore, combines the two methods used in the earlier representations of death: in Ivan Ilych's death the reader is thrust into the scene, as he is with Maman, Natalya Savishna, Marya Dmitrevna, the peasant and the tree, and into the psyche, as with Praskukhin. In the scene Ivan Ilych meets death with the ritual of giving forth and forgiveness. In his agony but an hour before his death, Ivan Ilych accidentally touches his son's head. His son grabs the hand and kisses it. At this moment Ivan Ilych for the first time feels "pity" for his son and would ask forgiveness. "At the very same time" (xii) that Ivan Ilych goes through these rituals of *love for*, in his psyche he slips from that "deep, narrow black bag" (ix) which he has been struggling to get through in his suffering, to the "light" at the end (xii). "In one moment" the fear of death disappears, death disappears, and there is only "joy" and "light." The psychic experience at death is represented, not as Praskukhin's recollection of the past ending in nothingness, but as Maman's passage to another life. With Ivan Ilych,

however, we see the psychic experience: the dark tunnel and the beam of light that mark for Ivan Ilych, as apparently for many, the passage out of this life.

Prince Andrew dies as does Ivan Ilych: we see both the scene of his dying and his psychic experience of it. Prince Andrew's experience of dying is represented in two parts: a delirium vision and a near-death dream. The delirium is an abnormal state of consciousness in which "all the forces of his psyche (*dusha*) were more active and clearer than ever, but beyond the control of his will. . . . At times his thinking process would suddenly begin to work with a strength, clarity, and depth it never had in a normal state, but then suddenly in the midst of its work it would break off, be replaced by some unexpected image, and he had not the strength to return to it" (III,iii,xxxii). This delirium, then, is represented, as are Pierre's dreams, by an image and a sequence of ideas. The ideas are of the divine love which is the essence of the soul, and they recall to his mind Natasha. The image is the mental, visual representation of the sounds of a fly buzzing around his face as he lies in his delirium state:

> Suddenly the course of his thoughts was broken, and Prince Andrew heard (not knowing whether he heard it in his delirium or in reality) a soft whispering voice repeating incessantly to a beat: "I piti-piti-piti" and then "i ti-ti" and again "i piti-piti-piti" and again "i ti-ti." Along with this, to the sound of this whispering music, Prince Andrew felt that a strange airy structure was being erected out of needles or splinters right above the middle of his face. He felt (and this was difficult for him) that he had to try to keep the balance so that this structure that was being erected would not collapse (*zavalivalos'*), but nevertheless it kept on collapsing and again being slowly erected to the sounds of the steady whispering music.

This delirium image of a structure which is all air yet made of many particular "needles or splinters" that keep coming together and falling apart to the tune of "whispering music" recalls, of course, Petya's death dream of his fugue music and Pierre's dream of the liquid globe of life. It is Prince Andrew's imagination of the whole universe (*mirozdanie*); this structure (*zdanie*), which is his final emblematic expanse of nature, he has difficulty keeping in balance. This difficulty is reflected in the representation of Prince Andrew's delirium consciousness: he keeps on moving back and forth between his inner world of mental events and his feverish apprehension of objects in the external world around him. It is during this delirium state of sudden shifts of awareness, through the emblematic image of the expanse, that Natasha appears to Prince Andrew. Natasha has the answer to the riddle of the universe that he cannot quite hold together. Prince Andrew awakens from his delirium, extends his hand to her and tells her that he loves her. She begs his forgiveness.

The final near-death moment epitomizes Prince Andrew's most characteristic, if paradoxical, way of being in the world: he does not hide from death, as did Marya Dmitrevna or Ivan Ilych, but rather he sees it everywhere, and still he would live. Death is for him the end of all life, and he would hold on. He dreams a characteristic dream of ideas and images. The ideas are about the all-uniting love that is life and a God that is the "eternal source" to which the soul returns at death, a conception of the universe so held together that it remains whole and cannot collapse into nothing. The dream image represents the anxious struggle to accept this death that leads to new life. In the dream he sees himself lying in the same room as in reality, only he is not wounded. There are a lot of people there, and he is involved in a discussion with them, impressing them with his witty words. Slowly and imperceptively the people begin to disappear, and Prince Andrew's attention is focused on a closed door.

> He got up and went to the door to bolt it and lock it. Everything depended on whether he could lock it or not. He walked, he tried to hurry, his legs wouldn't move, and he knew that he could not lock the door, but still he painfully strained all his powers. A tormenting fear took hold of him. This fear was the fear of death: beyond the door there stood *it*. But while he was crawling toward the door, weak and clumsy, that terrible something was pushing the door from the other side and forcing it open. Something non-human, death, was forcing the door, and it had to be kept in place. He took hold of the door, made a final effort just to keep it in its place; to lock it was no longer possible; but his efforts were weak and clumsy and the door, pushed by something terrible, opened and closed again. Again it pushed from the other side. His last, superhuman efforts were for nought, and the door opened without a noise. *It* entered and it was death. Prince An-

drew died. But at the same moment that he died Prince Andrew remembered that he was sleeping, and at the same moment that he died he made an effort and awoke. "Yes, that was death. I died, I awoke. Yes, death is awakening!" It suddenly grew light (*prosvetlelos'*) in his soul, and the veil that had till then hidden the unknown was lifted from his spiritual vision.

In the dream Prince Andrew is not sick unto death. He is alive and healthy as he had been through life. And this is what he sees, his life spent impressing others with his clever words about what was not important. From this image of his life recollected he then turns to the closed door. In his anxiety vision at the moment near death he sees reality divided between here and there; the door is an image of the boundary between this life and true life. But to Prince Andrew, who has lived enclosed in himself and has only just now experienced that love which accepts the other without fear, this other appears in his dream as the abstraction of his lifelong awareness of a "threatening, eternal unknown and distant presence," the sky not as the great All but the great Nothing. The other is *it* (*ono*), the neuter pronoun referring to this unknown presence (and not to the feminine noun "death"). The other is the "it" that stands in opposition to the personal "I." Prince Andrew's fear of death is overcome only when, despite his efforts to shut out the other, it rushes in and engulfs him. The experience, however, is not obliterating; death is not the terminal point. Within the dream when he is dead he recalls that he is sleeping and simultaneously wakes up. This dream experience reveals to him, then, the meaning of his idea of love: to die is to slip into another mode of awareness, an awakening from this life to another where, as Maman firmly believed, his love exists eternally even though "I will not be." Only after he has experienced that love which forgets the self in an act of forgiveness can Prince Andrew understand the death that awakens to life.

Prince Andrew's experience of levels of loss of self and return to awareness provide him with a model for understanding the experience of death, as they did for Tolstoy himself, whose own experience some ten years earlier served as a model for Prince Andrew's.

I dreamt that in my dark room the door suddenly opened terrifyingly, and then closed again. I was terrified, but I tried to believe it was the wind. Someone said to me, "Go, shut it," and I

went and at first tried to open it; someone was persistently holding it from behind. I wanted to run, but my legs would not go and
an indescribable terror seized me. I awoke, I was happy in the
awakening. Why was I happy? I got consciousness back and lost
what was in the dream. Might a person not be happy that way
when dying? He loses consciousness of the "I," it is said. But
didn't I lose it when sleeping, and still I am alive. But isn't personality, what is individual, lost? Nothing dies, nothing is non-
individual. Therefore both the skull and the skeleton are alive
and individual. This individuality speaks for little, it will be
said. But what is a lot and what a little in comparison with the
eternity in time and the infinity in space which this life participates in . . . Nothing dies, and I will never die, and I shall be eternally happier and happier. Consciousness kills happiness and
strength (*sila*). (48,75;1858)

Tolstoy associates his own dream of the opening door with the idea
of loss of consciousness of self as personality and the conviction that
in dying this loss will be a gain. Death is the passage to eternal life
which is imagined as eternal growth. But Tolstoy's dream of the door
leads him also to perceive the very process of awakening from dream
to consciousness as an analogue of the at-death experience. Prince
Andrew's dream of the door is the autopsychological image of Tolstoy's own experience. After the image comes the articulation. The
process of awakening from dream to consciousness becomes, therefore, for Tolstoy the model of the experience of both death and life:
"A dream with its periods of complete unconsciousness and semi-
awakenings of consciousness, which provide the material for the recalled dreams, and finally complete awakening is the perfect analogy
of life with its unconscious periods, its manifestations of consciousness which are recollected and become clearer and clearer, and finally with death, complete awakening. . . . Death not only does not
destroy [true life]; it just discloses more of it" (57,162;1909). Furthermore, the process of awakening from dreams helps explain what happens at birth: "Birth is the awakening from sleep. Dreams from that
sleep are almost all forgotten; all that life is composed into one and
remains united in the form of a real character in this life, just as at
awakening from a dream everything seen in the dream is gathered
into one. The same thing, one must suppose, will happen at death:

everything experienced will be composed into one, and with that you will enter into that life. Our everyday falling to sleep and awakening are models of the transition from one [form of] life to others. . . . Awakening leads out of the self, and leading out of the self it leads into the life of all" (57,140-41;1909). The experience of consciousness, its loss and gain in sleep and awakening, finally, becomes the model for understanding our experience of the eternal life which is the life divine.

> As in this life dreams are the states during which we live by the impressions, feelings, and thoughts from the life that has preceded them and gather forces for the life that follows, so precisely our whole life now is a state during which we live by the "karma" of a more actual life that has preceded it and during which we gather forces, work out the karma for the following life, that more actual life whence we came. As we experience thousands of dreams in this life of ours, so this life of ours is one of a thousand such lives into which we enter from that more actual, genuine, real life from which we came upon entering this life and to which we return upon dying. But that more real life is only one of the dreams of another, still more real life, and so forth to infinity, to the one last real life, the life of God. (66,155-56;1892)

Thus in its final articulation the experience of awakening from dream to life with its double focus backward and forward serves not only as the model of the at-death experience, with its recollection of the past and its passage to the future, but also as the image which embodies and reveals that eternal life, the eternal growth and resurrection which is the life of God. It is this image which Prince Andrew sees as the airy structure which keeps collapsing and coming together again. The metaphysics of life and love is grounded in the experience of consciousness in its moments of resurrection from its death called sleep.

Tolstoy never doubted the notion of eternal life. He was obsessed with trying to understand it. He did not believe in any form of "personal" survival after death, let alone in any resurrection of the flesh, no matter how conceived. In death, thus, he would confront the unknown ever-present to him. Life after death is not imagined as total annihilation of consciousness, for then there would be no confrontation with the unknown; rather, death is the loss of consciousness of self as entity, a merging with the other in some new mode of existence. The fear of death for Tolstoy, therefore, takes two forms: the moment of recollection and the moment of awakening. Death recalls the past: the thought of death leads to a measurement of one's life, an examination of conscience and an appraisal of one's mission and task. The fear of death is the assessment of failure. Death also calls to the future: the idea of death reminds one of the inevitable loss of self-awareness that awaits us, the awakening from the sleep of life to another mode of being when "I will not be." The fear of death is an anxiety of annihilation. In either case the fear is overcome only through love: love is the only mission and task in which one gives forth of self in a moment of loss which is simultaneously a moment of gain, a loss of self which finds itself in the other. The representation of death in Tolstoy, therefore, is grounded in the concept of love. Those who remain enclosed in themselves recollect their past with a sense of failing and fear of death; they experience no passage and have no sense of eternal life or even eternal memory. For them death is an anxiety of assessment. Those who love, even if only at the last moment, overcome their fear and their failing and pass on.

THE THEOLOGY OF PRAYER

All moments of recollective consciousness, whether they take place at sleep, in dreams, in delirium, or at death, include a glance backward and forward, a clarification of identity and vocation. But this state of assessment is not consciously induced, and the psychic event often seems to come upon the character because of extraordinary psychological and physical circumstances. The moments occur "suddenly." In content and moment these states of recollective consciousness resemble what Tolstoy understood as a state of prayer. In his *Christian Doctrine* Tolstoy distinguished two modes of prayer: perpetual prayer, which is the constant awareness of the presence of God, and "true temporary prayer," which is a "clarification of a person's awareness of the truth about his life, about his relationship to God, and about his destined purpose in the world" (*mir*) (39,185-88). Unlike perpetual prayer, which is a state of consciousness induced by repeated verbal utterance and designed to enable a person to avoid

the occasions of sin, true prayer takes place "at moments of lofty spiritual awareness" which come upon a person "through suffering, at death, or sometimes without any external cause at all." In these special moments of lofty spiritual clarity, as in the moments of recollective consciousness, a person confronts himself. The moments of recollective consciousness represented in the fiction are the literary image of what becomes Tolstoy's articulated idea of prayer.

Tolstoy prayed throughout his life. His early diaries record his youthful dissatisfaction with rote prayer and his enthusiastic moments of prayerful solitude in nature. In his fiction he represents Natasha in prayer at church, Princess Mary in prayer before an icon, Levin in spontaneous cries for divine help at moments of crisis, and Nekhlyudov in conscious evocation of divine guidance. In his later diaries Tolstoy analyzed his own moments of prayer and composed his own prayers. "He who prays to an idol," Tolstoy came to believe, "is ignorant and unenlightened, but he who does not pray at all is both unenlightened and stupid" (56,29,1907).

Prayer for Tolstoy is the encounter of self and God, a moment and an experience of truth: "Prayer is the only situation in which a person, because he is standing face to face with God, must be honest with himself" (54,30;1900). Prayer, therefore, can take place only in private and must be removed from the distractions of life. By definition prayer is not what happens in church.

> They say that prayer is necessary, that we need the tender feeling evoked by the liturgy—the singing, reading, entoned prayer, and the icons. But what is prayer? Prayer is contact (*obshchenie*) with God, the highest state of the soul. Can it really be that this state of the soul can be reached by effects on the external senses, effects used to evoke the lowest feelings, to stupefy? Is it not more likely that the prayerful state can be reached only in rare, exclusive moments and definitely in solitude? Even Christ said that, and Elijah saw God, not in a storm, but in the gentle fluttering of the wind. (53,101;1896)

The moment of truth can be reached only "when you have severed all relations with people . . . even when among them" (55,245;1906). The moments of communion with God require the exclusion of the world. Prayer seems to be a form of estrangement from others.

For Tolstoy the state of prayer has two stages. The first stage is verbal prayer, the repetition of "words of wisdom" (57,97;1907). This repetition of words enlightens and instructs. The words of the prayer are not entoned to induce another state of consciousness; the prayer itself is to be reflected upon. Furthermore, these words of wisdom are polysemantic so that, despite the repetition, prayers are "capable of having various meanings and therefore can affect and exalt the soul in various ways." Prayer leads to growth in knowledge of the Divine. Prayer, thus conceived, however, does not appear to be communion with God. Such prayer seems to be a form of "auto-suggestion, a kind of talking to yourself" (54,13;1900). But the self to which one talks in prayer, Tolstoy argues, is "not the lower self, nor the whole self, but that divine, eternal, loving self which is in me, and it hears me and answers me." In verbal prayer through reflection on words of wisdom one communicates with the divine self within. This verbal form, however, does not imply that one is communicating with a personal God. "Prayer is addressed to a personal God, not because God is personal, but because I am a personal being" (53,102;1896). Verbal prayer is the form of "address to God which is characteristically human" (56,51;1907).

Verbal prayer assesses. It glances backward and forward. "Prayer is prayer only when all the words pertain to past and future life" (51,70;1890). "True prayer consists in the assessment of our soul, our acts and desires, according to the demands not of the external conditions of the world, but of the divine principle which we are conscious of in our soul" (45,282;1910). Prayer, which "assesses past acts and indicates the direction of future acts," is a kind of "confession" that gives "succor, strength, and elevation to the soul." Tolstoy's own prayers, however, are not cast in the form of a confession. The prayer of assessment may be a reaffirmation of faith:

I know that if I love, You are in me and I am in You. And therefore I want to love always and everyone in thought, word, and deed.

I desire nothing in the future because I know that everything that will be, will be good. . . . I know that I am dying, and in the sight of death I cannot desire anything external in that life from which I am departing. . . . But I cannot help desiring and do desire one thing: to love everyone always and in the same way in thought, word, and deed, every minute and to the last minute. (57,23-25;1909)

Or, the prayer of assessment may take the form of an address to God requesting his aid and presence:

Help me, Father, to cleanse myself spiritually so that You might be able to live in me in order that I might live through You.

Help me, Lord, to destroy myself so that You might be able to live in me, to pass through me in order that I might be Your manifestation. (56,122;1908)

Whether the prayer of assessment takes the form of reaffirmation or supplication, however, it has the function of recollection of identity and clarification of vocation. In such a prayer "a person is transferred from the realm of the petty details of life to the awareness of the true meaning of life and death and of his duty on earth before the heavenly Father who has brought me into the world" (64,68;1887). The verbal prayer "reminds me of who I am and what I must do" (57,24;1909).

Supplicatory prayer that is not transposed into a prayer of assessment, however, thrusts a person back into the petty details of life. Prayers which ask for health or wealth or less pain or more rain, Tolstoy believes, are as far removed from true prayer as is liturgical prayer. True prayer is neither petition nor plaint. "One cannot ask God for anything. It is not that God does not want to, but He cannot change anything because He has established a law according to which all are equal. Any change would be an injustice. But we are like children who are envious that others have better toys or who cry at the pain when our fleas are being combed out" (55,240;1906). All such supplicatory prayer—whether they be positive requests for help or negative requests which border on complaints—may well be signs of "weakness, a failure of faith" (53,225;1899). "What is most similar to faith, supplicatory prayer, is really a failure of faith, a failure to believe that there is no evil, that there is nothing to ask for. If things are bad for you, then this just shows you that you have to correct them, that what is happening is the very thing that must be and the very circumstance in which you must do what must be." Prayers of petition and plaint are prayers of false assessment, which reveal a misunderstanding of both identity and vocation.

The perfect type of the prayer of assessment is the Lord's Prayer. Tolstoy believed this prayer was "as it were a repetition of all the Gospels" (64,68;1887). Indeed, after completing his own translation and harmonization of the Gospels, he discovered to his "amazement and joy" that the "so-called Lord's Prayer is nothing other than the entire teaching of Christ expressed in a most compressed form" (24,803;1883). Furthermore, he saw that the twelve separate statements which he perceived in the prayer corresponded in both meaning and sequential order to the twelve chapters in his arrangement of the Gospels. In this reading the Lord's Prayer contains a complete assessment of faith. The prayer and the Gospel chapters alternate statements of identity with statements of vocation.

1. Our Father	Man is the son of the infinite principle, the son of the Father, not in the flesh but in the spirit,
2. Who art in heaven	and therefore man must serve that principle in the spirit.
3. Hallowed be Thy name	The life of all people has a divine principle; it alone is holy,
4. Thy kingdom come	and therefore a person must serve that principle in the life of all people. That is the will of the Father.
5. Thy will be done	Only service to the will of the Father of life gives true, i.e., reasonable life,
6. On earth, as it is in heaven	and therefore the satisfaction of one's own will is not necessary for true life.
7. Give us our daily bread	The temporal life of the flesh is the food of eternal life, the material for reasonable life,
8. This day	and therefore true life is beyond time; it is only in the present.
9. Forgive us our trespasses as we forgive those who trespass against us	The deception of life in time, of life in the past or future, hides the true life of the present from the people

10. And lead us not into temptation	and therefore a person must strive to destroy the illusion of past and future life.
11. But deliver us from evil	True life is not only life beyond time, life in the present, but also life beyond personality, life common to all people and expressed by love,
12. For Thine is the kingdom, the power, and the glory.	and therefore one who lives the life common to all in the present is united with the Father, the principle and foundation of life. (24,802)

The prayer addressed to the Father is transformed into a statement which is at once metaphysical and moral. Each assessment of human reality in the context of the Divine is followed by an ethical imperative. The Lord's Prayer thus becomes a series of backward and forward glances, moving from clearer and clearer assessments of the source and sense of life to clearer and clearer indications of the direction and goal of life. It ends where it begins, with the Father, the "principle and foundation of life." This articulation of the Lord's Prayer (and it is only one of many) not only summarizes Tolstoy's understanding of the Christian message; it imitates in its structure the fundamental action of faith, the ever clearer, step-by-step articulation of identity and vocation. Thus read, the Lord's Prayer "can renew in you the spirit of the Gospels," at least as Tolstoy himself lived them (64,68;1887). Thus read, the Lord's Prayer embodies and reveals the pattern of the experience of life of both Tolstoy and his literary heroes. Thus read, the Lord's Prayer articulates the assessing action of recollective consciousness.

THE PRAYER of assessment may be the prelude to a moment of communion.

Today, being alone after my work, I asked myself what to do. Since I had no personal desire (except the physical needs which arise when you feel like eating or sleeping), I felt the joy of the consciousness of the will of God so clearly that I did not need or want anything except to do what He wanted. This feeling arose as a result of the question which I have asked myself when alone in silence: who am I? why do I exist? And it was answered of itself so clearly: whoever I may be, I am sent by someone to do something. So let's do it! And I really felt so joyously my own merging with the will of God. (53,158-59;1897)

Tolstoy experiences what Natasha prayed for in church: "I want nothing; I desire nothing. Teach me what to do, how to use my will. Just take me, take me," she prayed, "expecting that right now some invisible force would take her and release her from herself" (III,i,xviii). But for Tolstoy this moment of awareness follows upon the uttering of the fundamental questions of assessment. The "merging with the will of God" is the resolution of identity and vocation, as indeed Natasha too expects it to be. Tolstoy says of his own moment of merging, however, that it is "second vivid (*zhivoe*) feeling of God." In the first one, he tells us, he "felt God, . . . that only He exists and that I am in Him, Him both as something limited in the unlimited and as surrounded by beings in which He is" (53,154;1897). The first vivid feeling of God is not a moment of assessment or dependence. It is the experience of an awareness of divinity. The prayer of awareness is the articulated form of the epiphanic experiences of the All in the fiction: Nikolenka in the garden, Olenin in the mountains, and Pierre's sky in him and around him.

This prayer of awareness is another kind of prayer. "Prayer is the consciousness (however it be manifested) of one's divinity. The one who prays to himself, through himself, is conscious of himself as a part of God" (55,259;1906). The prayer of awareness of divinity is grounded in the logic of the All. The verbal type of this prayer of awareness is not the Lord's Prayer, but the Orthodox morning prayer so often alluded to by Tolstoy.

Heavenly King, Comforter, Spirit of Truth, Who art everywhere and fillest all things (*vsja*), the Treasure of blessings (*blagikh*) and the Giver of Life, come and dwell in us, cleanse us of every impurity and save our souls, O Thou Blessed One (*blazhe*).

This prayer is addressed to the Holy Spirit, the good (*blago*) and source of all good. This Spirit is everywhere and in everything. It is

the All. This Spirit is truth and gives life. This prayer, thus, contains
the model for Tolstoy's metaphysical understanding of the relationship between God and man. The Divine manifests itself within man
as "truth" and "life." This "truth" is the consciousness that goes
forth from self to other in conscience. It is a truth that fills "all
things," a knowledge that cannot therefore be attained from outside
it, because everything is in it. This "life" is the love that gives forth
of self to other in freedom, a life given to be given away. The Spirit
that is within and abroad is the Spirit of Truth which is the ground of
the Giver of Life, whose result is the Treasure of Blessings.

This prayer addressed to the Spirit-Life-Truth, however, is a supplication which asks for what is indeed already given. The supplication thus functions as a call to awareness of the Life and Truth that
is within and abroad. "Come and dwell in me," Tolstoy comments
on this prayer. "But You already do dwell. You are already me. My
task is just to become conscious of You" (53,178;1898). The accomplishment of this task is the experience of "love for love, not only
love for all people, but love for everything, love for God"
(56,12;1907). Such experiences of love for God, when recorded in the
diaries, are likely to be followed by some reference to this Orthodox
morning prayer. Tolstoy would recall and retain the moment of
awareness of divinity: "God help me to live in that love," he added
after recording the above experience, "come and dwell in me." (See
also 55,130;1905.) These moments of awareness of divinity are Tolstoy's finest articulations of his identity and vocation.

The moment of awareness of divinity is an experience of ecstasy.
"Since morning I have been experiencing an inexpressible, tender joy
of the consciousness of the life of love, of love for all and for the All.
What joy! What happiness! How can I not thank That, The One (*To,
Togo*) Who has given me this!" (56,76;1907.) These ecstatic moments
of communion with the God of love invariably call forth expressions
of joy and thanksgiving. "Yes, I thank That, The One Who has given
and does give me life and all its blessing (*blago*). . . . Everything is
good and joyful" (58,63;1910; see also 55,275;1906). Communion
with the Giver of Life bestows a Treasure of Blessings. To Tolstoy,
furthermore, these moments of the "consciousness of God" are
themselves life-giving: "Do not think that this destroys the energy of
life, that it leads to an ascetic, mental prayer and to staring at the end
of your nose; on the contrary, it gives an energy not comparable to

ordinary life, fearlessness, freedom, and kindness" (55,49;1904). This awareness of divinity releases one from all restrictions of the personal self. "The separated being bursts forth from its bounds, like compressed gas; its life consists in first becoming conscious of its spiritualness, of its unity with the All, and then striving to unite with it. In this striving, in this intensification (*usilenie*) of consciousness there is the fluttering of divine life" (55,91;1904). The self released from its restrictions feels itself at one with God, participating in the divine life. The prayer of awareness, therefore, is a form of mystical prayer: "While taking my walk yesterday, I was praying, and I experienced an amazing feeling—probably like what mystics arouse in themselves through spiritual acts. I felt that I was just something spiritual and free, tied to the illusion of a body" (53,141;1897). Such moments of mystical freedom from earthly bounds, not accompanied or induced by any verbal words of wisdom and characterized by a sense of merging with God and a feeling of love for God and thanksgiving for His blessings, are the final articulations of Tolstoy's first recorded moment of prayer. They are the perfection of the twenty-three-year-old man's "desire to merge with God" and "feeling of love for God . . . which unites everything in itself" (46,62;1851). In his prayer life Tolstoy realized his need to merge with all.

Tolstoy experiences the mystical union with God in a moment felt to be beyond time and space. "In order to live with God and through God and in God one must not be guided by anything external (*izvne*), not by what was, nor what may be; one must live only by the present, only in it does one merge with God" (53,186;1898). This experience of the awareness of divinity occurs "only at one point," the present moment. The mystical union contains no glance backward or forward. In this experience there is no assessment and no restriction by the assessing mind. "When you live by true consciousness, then you live beyond time, i.e., always in the present, in that moment when you are free" (55,47-48;1904). The mystical moment is, in Tolstoy's understanding, the moment of freedom from all restrictions and hence a moment of release from the personality. "Personality is just recollection of the past and desires for the future. As soon as neither the one nor the other exist, there is no time, just life in the atemporal moment of the present, and there is no personality. There is only the foundation of life, love, God" (56,166;1908). The moment of aware-

ness of divinity is a moment of the resolution to the question of identity and vocation. Who am I? What must I do? are no longer problematic. Furthermore, the moment of awareness of divinity entails death to the personality even though it is grounded in life. In the mystical moment, one experiences life unhindered by death and unrestricted by anything outside oneself. In the moment of awareness of divinity, therefore, one partakes of "eternal life (here, now)" (53,182;1898). In the prayer of awareness which transcends assessment Tolstoy finds the secret in Christ's teaching: he lives in the present and discovers himself and his God.

The moment of awareness of divinity consists in a sense of love for God and all people. But the "loving contact (obshchenie) with the source of all, with God" is the "basic feeling" (56,41;1907). It includes within it "loving contact with all people." Love for people is "derivative" of love for God. Just as consciousness which goes forth from self to other is the cause and condition of the possibility of love, so the "consciousness of one's spiritualness is the cause of love." (54,186;1903). This "consciousness demands love; it produces love." As a result Tolstoy seeks to develop the state of awareness of divinity in order to increase his experience of love for humanity. "You should pray upon entering into contact with any person, Tsar or beggar" (56,80;1907). In any such encounter you should "recall that there is before you a manifestation of God, and you should evoke in yourself the highest spiritual state you can" (57,69;1909). But since the person encountered is a manifestation of God, the contact with the person is a contact with God. "Prayer is the evocation in oneself of the highest spiritual state, the recollection of one's spiritualness. Contact with a person is the sacrament of contact with God, Communing (prichashchenie)" (57,59;1909).[3] The moment of removal from others in awareness of divinity leads to and creates the experience of loving belonging.

---

[3] To my knowledge this is the only reference to a sacrament of communion in all of Tolstoy's own theological writings. In the system of his thought, however, the concept of communing plays a large role. The Russian word for the act of making one's communion (prichashchenie) is related to the idea of participation (prichastnost') upon which so much of Tolstoy's theological thinking depends. The relationship between man and God imaged as "part" (chast') and All is based on this idea of participation. What I have called the experience of residence is the experience of "being concerned with, being involved with, being connected with" which in Russian is byt' prichastnym.

Prayer in which one experiences "eternal life (here, now)" and which creates the experience of loving belonging is not a static state of awareness. In such prayer one feels a sense of growth. "For me prayer is on the one hand the consciousness of my relationship to God and on the other hand an increase in my spiritual power" (*sila*) (65,20;1890). Prayer is a moment of "intensification" (*usilenie*) (55,91;1904). Participation in the divine life through prayer entails a sharing in the eternal growth and progress of becoming that divine life is. This means, however, that each particular moment of prayer seems different from the last one, something *new*, something experienced *for the first time*. One year before he died, therefore, Tolstoy could record the following moments.

> God is love. To love God is to love love. I have experienced for the first time a feeling which I can call similar to the love for God. (57,33;1909)

> Yesterday or the day before I became conscious of my relationship to God for the first time in a new and better way than before. . . . For the first time I understood that I am one of the infinitely small manifestations of life in relation to the infinitely great life, and therefore that I have just one relationship: I am almost nothing, but I am in relation to the All. (57,98-99;1909)

> Yesterday for the first time I experienced a very joyous feeling of full devotion to His will, a full indifference to what will happen to me, of an absence of any desire except one—to do what He wants (I am experiencing this right now). . . . I thank Thee. How good I feel . . . so joyful that tears are coming to my eyes. (57,81;1909)

The prayerful moments are themselves articulations of tiny-tiny alterations in consciousness, just as the inward journeys of discovery are for his characters. Moments which seem to repeat central ideas of Tolstoy's metaphysical vision of the universe seem to him "new" and experienced "for the first time" because they are known at another level of awareness, deeper within his own experience, with more certitude and conviction. What may have seemed abstract and intellectual now brings tears to his eyes. The young man who felt "love for God" now seems to feel "love for God" "for the first time" because this love is greater. As knowledge not by reason but by life

grows in ever clearer articulation, so does prayer. Prayer partakes of the very principle of life, "greater and greater awakening, greater and greater enlightenment" (53,191;1898).

The "new spiritual state" which Tolstoy experiences "for the first time with a new and unusual clarity" is understood as a "step forward toward the liberation of the only thing that is, LOVE" (56,89;1907). But this means that the new state arises from a state of lack of love. There is a "change in the state of the soul, a transition from confusion and suffering to clarity and peace" (53,183;1898). And "this is precisely what prayer is: you have to be hiding something or fearing something, something is tormenting you or something is lacking, and suddenly there is nothing to hide, nothing to fear, nothing to be tormented about, nothing to desire." Prayer is a sudden shift in awareness "from human judgment to divine judgment." In prayer Tolstoy finds the answers to the sudden questions of faith, and he experiences the sudden joy of life. The sudden shift, however, does not last, and the moment of prayer is inevitably lost.

In the beginning I experienced as never before a vivid (*zhivoe*) consciousness of God in myself and of the divine life of love and therefore of freedom and joy. This lasted powerfully for a week; then it began to weaken and the newness, the joy of the awareness of that feeling, disappeared, but there remained, there certainly remained, the ascent to the next, not very large step of the unconscious state which is higher in comparison with the former unconscious state. (56,44-45;1907)

Tolstoy's prayer life moves forward step by step, but each step up into "consciousness" is followed by a fall backward into a state of "unconsciousness." This state of "unconsciousness" into which he slips back, however, is itself a rung higher on the ladder of ascent toward God. The life of prayer is a continuing series of reversals and returns. The pattern that shapes the life of Tolstoy's heroes as they move up to their peak moments of enlightenment and fall back into the routine of their lives is autopsychological. It traces the path of Tolstoy's own life of prayer. This pattern is the structure that follows from life understood as eternal resurrection.

Chapter Seven

INTOXICATED CONSCIOUSNESS

Drunkenness is necessary in life. If not the drunkenness of
pleasure, then the drunkenness of labor.

(47,210;1857)

A sober person is ashamed.

(27,272;1890)

TOLSTOY'S psychology of human consciousness is grounded in
the acts of remembering and forgetting. Recollective consciousness
discloses and reveals who we are and where we are going. To the extent that this recollection turns one toward the divine self within, it
is an act of faith or a moment of prayer. However, there is another
kind of remembering, diametrically opposed to this state of awareness. For Tolstoy the recollection of self as personality blocks the
awareness of the divine. This is the consciousness of self that to the
young Tolstoy was the "greatest evil" (46,66;1851). This self must be
forgotten.

> I am convinced that there is in man an infinite, not only moral
> but even physical force (sila), but that along with this there is
> placed a terrible brake on that force—love of self or rather the
> memory of self which produces impotence. Yet as soon as a per-
> son tears himself away from this brake he gains omnipotence.
> . . . Omnipotence is unconsciousness; impotence is memory of
> self. One can save oneself from this memory of self by means of
> love for others, by means of sleep, drunkenness, work, etc., but
> all human life passes in quest of this forgetting. . . . Where do
> clairvoyants, sleepwalkers, people in delirium or under the in-
> fluence of passion get their power (sila) from? Why is the most
> horrible punishment invented an eternal solitary confinement
> in which a person is deprived of everything that can make him
> forget himself and left with an eternal memory of himself? And

how does the person save himself from this torment? He forgets himself if only for a moment in a spider or a hole in the wall. True, the best salvation from memory of self, the most in conformity with life in common with all mankind, is salvation through love for others, but it is not easy to acquire this happiness. (5,196;1857 italics added)

Tolstoy is highly ambivalent about this search for oblivion: while it can be a positive quest for happiness, it can just as well be a negative escape from unhappiness. Concentration on one's work can be a source of creativity or a stay against boredom. Service to others may be a genuine outpouring of yourself or an attempt to assuage your conscience or obtain a reward. The loss of self can lead to life or death. The perfect type of this ambiguous oblivion is love. "According to my theory," Tolstoy wrote, "love consists in the desire to forget oneself," to which he added that "therefore like sleep it comes more often when a person is dissatisfied with himself or unhappy" (60,221;1857). But the love that Tolstoy is speaking of here is not the love for others which is most in conformity with life in common with all. Here he means passion-love. In such passion, Tolstoy believes, the oblivion is caused by the attraction to the object. The self is not given away to the other but is captivated by it. The loss of self is brought about by something external to it. In this sense, passion is like an intoxicant which alters your awareness or an infection which raises your temperature. Something is done to you. Passionate loss of self is the opposite of self-oblivious love for all. "If you are infected with some passion, then remember that this passion is not your soul, but something completely alien to it which hides your real soul from you and from which you can free yourself" (40,371;1909). Only liberation from external influence will release true love.

In his fiction and in his theology Tolstoy explored this ambiguous quest for forgetting. In his novels and stories he portrays characters in various states of oblivion and ecstasy. He came to understand the aesthetic experience itself as a most powerful form of this loss of self and hence both very important and very dangerous. Indeed, finally he saw all cultural forms of human experience as formative and therefore potentially deforming. In the end human society seemed to him grounded in coercion and human institutions designed to force one into oblivion. From this vision he forged his theology of anarchism.

STATES OF INTOXICATION

Pierre Bezukhov arrives in the novel from abroad with no sense of what he is to do; he spends his time in drunken dissipation. Then suddenly this bastard son of Count Bezukhov is about to become an orphan. His father is dying, and Pierre, it seems, "will not be Pierre but Count Bezukhov" (I,i,xviii). The naive Pierre is not aware of the intrigues surrounding his father's death: he does not know that Prince Vassily is conspiring with Pierre's cousins to keep Count Bezukhov's title and inheritance from his son; he does not know that Anna Mikhaylovna wants to extract from the dying Count a promise of funds for her son; he does not even know that he is about to become Count Bezukhov, nor what this new status would entail. Circumstances thrust Pierre into a crisis of identity and vocation, but he does not know what is happening.

The carriage carrying Pierre and Anna Mikhaylovna draws up to the home of the dying Count with the sounds of the "carriage wheels softly scraping against the straw spread under the windows" (I,i,xix). Thus Pierre is thrust into his fateful moment. When he was told of his father's imminent death or how he reacted to the news or what he is now feeling, we do not know. We last saw him dancing with Natasha and now "he is sleeping in the corner of the carriage." Anna Mikhaylovna awakens him, and as he steps out of the carriage he "begins to think about the encounter with his dying father, which awaits him."

> He noticed that they have driven up to the rear entrance rather than the main one. As he was getting down from the carriage steps, two men dressed as tradespeople ran hurriedly away from the entrance into the shadow cast by the wall. Pierre paused and discerned some other men like that in the shadow on both sides of the house. But neither Anna Mikhaylovna, nor the footman, nor the coachman, who could not have helped seeing these people, paid any attention to them. Therefore that's how it has to be (*nuzhno*), Pierre decided, and he followed Anna Mikhaylovna. She rapidly ascended the dimly lit, narrow, stone staircase, beckoning Pierre, who was lagging behind, to follow. Although he did not understand why he had to go to see the Count at all or even less why he had to go by the rear staircase, yet judging by Anna

Mikhaylovna's assurance and haste, Pierre decided that it necessarily had to be (*neobkhodimo nuzhno*) that way. Halfway up the stairs they were almost knocked over by some men who came running down toward them, carrying pails and clattering with their boots. These men pressed closely to the wall to let Pierre and Anna Mikhaylovna through and did not show the least surprise at seeing them.

What is strange is that Tolstoy does not show here (or anywhere) Pierre's thoughts about his dying father or his father's dying. In their stead we are given Pierre in the process of walking from the carriage to the inner quarters. We observe Pierre observing. Strange men lurk in shadows and rush along the stairway, but Pierre has no sense of who they are or what they are doing. Nor does he ever find out. The mysterious men never reappear after this moment and serve no function in the story other than to be seen by Pierre. To Pierre the world he enters appears as aimless, disruptive, and threatening commotion. He sees what is happening, but does not understand what is happening. Nothing makes any sense. Pierre has awakened into a state of disorientation. This moment of disorientation, however, is represented, as it were, in slow motion, and we see the walking and the observing broken down into bits. Each change of place is accompanied by an observation of confusion. Each new level of disorientation is followed by a new level of resolve simply to follow Anna Mikhaylovna. These decisions, which stem from the disorientation, however, provide no real resolution to it. They are decisions to acquiesce. As Anna Mikhaylovna opens the door at the landing on the staircase, Pierre follows "submissively." He "understands nothing. Again it seemed to him even more firmly that everything must (*dolzhno*) be that way." Pierre yields more and more, even as the modals increase in intensity from necessity to obligation (*nuzhno, neobkhodimo nuzhno, dolzhno*). The movement up the stairs traces the stages of decision to let himself be led on. Pierre chooses not to understand.

Anna Mikhaylovna leads Pierre into his father's reception room and directs him to a sofa while she goes off to her intrigues.

He noticed that the eyes of all in the room were trained on him with something more than curiosity and sympathy. He noticed that they were all whispering to each other and casting glances at him with a kind of awe and even servility. They showed him a kind of respect they had never shown before: a lady he did not know, who was speaking with the priests, got up from her seat and offered it to him; an aide-de-camp picked up a glove Pierre had dropped and handed it to him; the doctors became respectfully silent when he passed them and stood aside to make room for him. At first Pierre wanted to take another seat so as not to trouble the lady; he wanted to pick up the glove himself and to walk around the doctors, who were not even at all in his way. But suddenly he felt that on this night he was a person obliged to perform some aweful rite expected by all, and therefore he had to (*dolzhen*) accept all their services. He silently accepted the glove from the aide-de-camp, he sat on the lady's seat . . . and decided that all this just had (*immeno dolzhno*) to be and that on this evening in order not to become flustered and do foolish things, he had to act, not according to his own ideas, but that he must (*nadobno*) yield himself completely to the will of those who were guiding him.

Once Pierre has "decided to obey his guide in everything," the focus of attention shifts. We observe Pierre observing himself being observed. Pierre is now confused by the commotion he himself seems to cause. In the eyes of others he has become someone else. The moment of disorientation passes into a moment of crisis of identity and vocation. But this moment of crisis is itself broken up into bits: the observation ("he noticed . . ."), the self-assertion ("at first . . ."), the decision and acquiescence ("But suddenly"). On the staircase the observation of confusion was itself a form of self-assertion, a statement of who I am right now. In this moment of approach to the sofa, the observation and self-assertion become separate acts. The crisis of identity is thus brought into focus. This crisis, however, leads nowhere, for Pierre has already decided not to understand and has chosen to yield. In this moment at the sofa Pierre's paradox becomes clear. He is at once totally estranged from the world in which he exists and totally in acquiescence with it. He belongs not enough and too much. He exists for these people whom he does not know and who never appear again in his story. He does what the strangers want, but at the same time it is not he but some "person" who is doing this. In choosing what others want, Pierre loses his sense of self. He de-

cides to have no will of his own. Pierre forgets himself in order to please others. In his disorientation he is not lured on; he chooses to be led on. Pierre fails to be responsible to himself.

Estranged involvement is Pierre's characteristic way of being in the world. He next appears in the text some one hundred and fifty pages later, but his mode of being has not changed. Now Prince Vasily has taken charge of him: the new Count Bezukhov has been made a Gentleman of the Bedchamber; he has been moved to Prince Vasily's Petersburg; and he has been thrust into the social world of the class to which he now belongs. Now a rich man and a count, Pierre "feels himself so surrounded and busy after his recent solitude and carefree existence that only in bed could he be by himself" (I,iii,i). Everyone is solicitous, and even those "who used to be hostile had become kind and loving."

> He constantly felt himself in a state of mild and cheerful intoxication. He felt that he was the center of some important and general movement. He felt that something was constantly being expected of him, that if he did not do such-and-such he would annoy many people and deprive them of what they expected, and that if he did such-and-such and such-and-such everything would be fine. So he did what they demanded but that something fine always remained in the future.

In Petersburg Pierre is not disoriented, but overwhelmed. Once having decided to yield to those who guide him, he gets caught up in their world. Pierre's forgetting reaches a new stage. His drunken orgies are replaced by a social whirl, but he is still intoxicated. In this state of intoxication Pierre is the object of everyone's affection, which he feels he must keep on earning. He is compelled to please others. He does nothing for himself, can scarcely be by himself, and ends up feeling dissatisfied and yet ever hopeful. The paradox of Pierre's intoxication with the social whirl is that he lives totally for the expectation of others yet keeps on expecting "something fine" for himself.

Prince Vasily has designs on Pierre. He wants to marry him off to his daughter Helen and thereby ensure his family's financial position. So Pierre is invited to one of Anna Sherer's evenings, where he is pushed into Helen's presence and maneuvered into a conversation about a snuff-box. Pierre reaches for the box to get a better look. At just that moment the snuff-box is passed toward him right over Helen, who has to lean forward to get out of the way. She smiles. Pierre's reaction is given in this closeup.

Her bust, which always seemed like marble to Pierre, was so close to his eyes that his near-sighted eyes could not but perceive the living charm of her shoulders and neck and was so close to his lips that he need only have bent his head a little to have touched her. He was aware of the warmth of her body, the fragrance of her perfume, and the creaking of her corset as she breathed. He saw, not her marble-like beauty forming a complete whole with her dress; he saw and felt all the charm of her body covered only with her clothing. And once he saw this, he could not see it otherwise, as we cannot recapture an illusion we have already seen through. She turned, looked directly at him and, with dark eyes glistening she smiled. . . . At that moment Pierre felt that Helen not only could but must be his wife, that it could not be otherwise. . . . Pierre lowered his eyes, raised them again, and tried to see her once more as that distant alien beauty he had seen every day before, but he could no longer do this. . . . She was terribly close to him. She already had power over him. And between him and her there were no barriers except the barriers of his own will.

In this moment of reaching for the snuff-box, Pierre discovers "something fine" for himself. He is totally carried away by Helen's physical presence and becomes fully absorbed in what is immediately before him. His consciousness is seized by the minute details of Helen's being. Pierre's experience of the world is reduced to the aroma of her perfume and the crackling of her corset. He is possessed. In this moment of possession Pierre's perception of reality is completely transformed. Helen is forever stripped of her revealing clothing and her marble hardness. Her body now controls him. He decides that she must be his wife, but this decision is again a form of acquiescence. In the acquiescence, however, there is still a moment of self-assertion. Pierre is possessed, but he does not abandon himself to his possession. He still has his will.

In his total absorption in the moment of erotic attraction, Pierre resembles the passionate Masha from *Family Happiness*. Her mo-

ment of possession by the Italian Marquis is also presented in a closeup.

> His moist, burning eyes right next to my face looked with passion at me, at my neck, at my bosom; both his hands were stroking my arm; his opened lips were saying something, saying that he loved me, that I was everything to him, and those lips came close to me and his hands pressed my arm more firmly and warmed me. . . . Suddenly I felt a kiss on my cheeks, and all trembling and cold I stopped and looked at him . . . that narrow, slanted brow visible under his straw hat, like my husband's, that beautiful, straight nose with dilated nostrils, that long slickly pomaded moustache and the beard, those smooth cheeks and the tanned neck. I hated and feared him, so alien was he to me, but at that moment the agitation and passion of that hateful, alien person so strongly aroused me! So irresistibly did I want to yield to the kisses of that crude and beautiful mouth, to the embrace of those white hands with the delicate veins and rings on the fingers. (viii)

Like Pierre, Masha is totally absorbed by the physical presence. Her consciousness is filled only with the blown-up details of the Marquis' face and hands: his opened lips, his dilated nostrils, his greasy moustache, the veins and rings on his fingers. In her erotic moment she almost forgets herself. But for Masha the details of the sensuous being are simultaneously attractive and repulsive. She would "throw herself headlong into the abyss of pleasures that has suddenly been opened up and is attracting her," but instead she rushes off, back to her husband. Masha is afraid because she knows she can be seduced. She could easily yield to the abyss of pleasures and fears the consequences.

Unlike Masha, Pierre is not repelled in his moment of attraction. But also unlike Masha, Pierre cannot be seduced. He cannot yield himself to any abyss of pleasure because his will divides him from it. Pierre does not run away from his attraction, he does battle with it. He argues with himself that marriage to Helen would be disastrous: she is stupid, and he does not love her. The "image of her feminine beauty," however, has already decided. Pierre is invited to a dinner party where, it is expected, he will at last ask for Helen's hand. Everyone present expects this of him.

> Pierre felt that he was the center of everything, and this position both pleased and inhibited him. He was like a person completely absorbed in some occupation. He did not see, understand, or hear anything clearly. (I,iii,ii)

Again Pierre is estranged from a world which demands something from him. Again he finds himself in a moment of confusion of identity.

> And here he was sitting next to her as her betrothed, hearing, seeing, feeling her nearness, her breathing, her movements, her beauty. Then suddenly it seemed to him that it was not she but he himself who was so unusually handsome, that that was why they were looking at him so, and, flattered by this general admiration, he expanded his chest, raised his head, and rejoiced in his happiness.

For the moment Pierre has found "something fine." Bewitched by the admiration, he is transformed. In his state of possession, he now possesses. But still Pierre remains indecisive and estranged. "It seemed to him that here next to Helen he was occupying someone else's, a stranger's place." Prince Vasily decides for him. Pierre is congratulated, and the betrothal becomes a fait accompli. "It all had (*dolzhno*) to be that way and could not have been otherwise," Pierre decides. He at last yields his will, takes off the glasses from his near-sighted eyes, and, as he leans over to kiss Helen, he is struck by the "changed, unpleasantly dismayed expression on her face." "Now it's too late, it's all over, and besides I love her," he thinks, as he says what must be said, "Je vous aime." In his possession Pierre finally capitulates.

Pierre is simultaneously removed and involved. For him the analyzing mind does battle with erotic attraction. He cannot be seduced. He can only decide to let others decide. Although he cannot be seduced, he is the type who would let someone rape him. He lives to fulfill the expectation of others, even when this does violence to himself. In his possession Pierre does not lose his sense of freedom. He gives up his freedom only when others choose to take it away. Pierre, then, is not like Eugene Irtenev, the hero of the story *The Devil* (1889). True, like Pierre, Irtenev is an "open person loved by all" (i). True, like Pierre, Irtenev enjoys his moments of debauchery which, Irtenev believes, ensure his health and freedom. True, like

Pierre, Irtenev's story opens with the death of his father and the need to pursue his career. True, like Pierre, Irtenev is near-sighted. But Irtenev, in an attempt to regulate his erotic life, arranges an encounter with a peasant woman Stepanida. His story tells of the loss of his freedom to think and act, as he becomes more and more obsessed with his passionate desire for the peasant woman. Irtenev gets married, but the illicit passion does not go away. He but sees Stepanida with his near-sighted eyes, and "passionate desire consumes him" (xii). He seems to live "by the will of someone alien to him." Unlike Pierre, Irtenev is totally possessed, believing that "against my will she has taken possession of me." Irtenev is "not free." To him, therefore, the object of his desires is the total cause of them: Stepanida is the "devil" who has lured him away from himself. Irtenev removes himself from his involvement by projection and rationalization. He is not free because he fails to take responsibility for his actions, but, unlike Pierre, he does not acquiesce to please others; he is seduced by his own passion and pleasure. He is compelled to please only himself. Pierre lets others make his decisions, Irtenev blames others for his decisions. Both fail to be responsible and in this sense live in a state of forgetting.

"TO TURN a person into a beast," the young Tolstoy observed while serving in the army, "all you need is a uniform, separation from the family, and beating on a drum" (47,204;1857). Disorientation accompanied by external stimuli can transform the human psyche. Dressed in the new uniform of his court position, removed to Petersburg and into Prince Vasily's family circle, and aroused by the stimulating social whirl, Pierre in his state of mild and cheerful intoxication in some sense resembles the beastly soldiers of Tolstoy's diary entry. In the military extreme, this disorientation accompanied by arousing stimuli is what makes possible the regimental forces, the marching column of men who have yielded their freedom and will to the group. Prince Bagration is about to review the troops. He hears "the heavy, weighty tread of a whole mass of men marching in step" toward him before he espies the company commander, who thinks he is in charge even as he thinks of himself (I,ii,xviii).

All the powers of his soul seemed to be directed toward the passing by the commander in the best way possible and, feeling that he was doing it well, he was happy. "Left . . . left . . . left," he seemed to repeat in response to every second step, and with stern but various faces the wall of soldiers burdened with knapsacks and muskets marched in time to this, each of the hundreds of soldiers seeming to repeat in response to every other step, "left . . . left . . . left." A fat major stepped out of the way of a bush on the path, panting and falling out of step; a soldier who had lagged behind, his face alarmed at his carelessness, ran at a trot to catch up with the company; a cannonball pushing through the air flew over the heads of Prince Bagration and his suite and hit the column to the beat of "left . . . left . . . left." The soldiers marched in a semicircle around the place where the cannonball hit, and an old trooper, a non-commissioned officer on the flank who had stopped beside the dead men rushed to catch up with his line, jumped in pace, switched legs, fell into step, and looked around angrily. "Left . . . left . . . left" seemed to be heard through the ominous silence and the monotonous sound of the earth being regularly beaten by feet.

Like Pierre, the company commander exists to please others; in this is his happiness. To do this, however, he has to focus all his attention not on himself but on being at one with the marching mass. The rhythmic beat of the marching regiment is the music of absolute and coerced belonging. The company commander exists only to belong to this beat. And so does everyone else. Nothing must intrude upon this moment of regimentation. Neither a physical object in the path, nor a moment of inattention, nor even the death of their fellow soldiers, suffices to break for long or good the rhythm that totally absorbs the psyche of these marching men. In a sense in this state of regimentation no one exists; rather, the state of regimentation exists through the participation of each in it. They all lose themselves in the beat that pervades their whole being, even as it pervades the whole paragraph. The sound of the march seizes the consciousness of all, and each in order to be has to leave the unity of them all. If one person disoriented and subjected to the beat of a drum becomes a beast, in aggregate these people become a deadly, threatening machine without heart or mind. They are compelled by the count of their own stomping feet.

Marching to the rhythmic beat and thus subjecting their bodies to

movements which influence their psyches, these soldiers are com-
mitting what the older Tolstoy called the sin of intoxication. In his
Christian Doctrine Tolstoy distinguished six cardinal sins, all of
which "hinder the manifestation of love": self-indulgence, sloth, ac-
quisitiveness, love of power, lechery, and intoxication. (39,132). Last
in the list, intoxication is the fundamental sin, the first to be conquered if the others are to be controlled. As with all Tolstoy's sins,
intoxication is a perversion of a natural proclivity, in this case the
proclivity of the human being "in an animal state" to take pleasure
in a state of arousal caused by external influences. In its perverted
form this arousal is brought about by the ingestion of mind-altering
substances, by frenzied movements of the body, or by the effects of
public rituals and spectacles. Cigarettes, alcohol, drugs, dancing,
gymnastics, bicycle riding, paintings, music, ceremonies, and artistic performances can all put one in a state of "arousal which strength-
ens the false consciousness of separate life and weakens the consciousness of the true 'I' " (39,171). Intoxication of any form hinders
the "activity of reason" and thus opens the path to false understanding and flawed living. Intoxication befogs conscience. Furthermore,
in intoxicated consciousness a person is attracted and affected, lured
and led on by something foreign to it. Intoxication, thus, is a false fac-
simile of going forth or giving forth. In the state of arousal one is
drawn into participation. In the moment of intoxication the sense of
who I am and where I must go gets blurred. Stupefied, one forgets
one's identity and vocation.

Natasha is in despair. Prince Andrew has told her that their engagement must be postponed for a year. And this afternoon was a
great fiasco. She has gone to meet Prince Andrew's father and sister
not without some misgivings. "It's not possible that they won't love
me," she had thought on the way. (II,v,vii). "Everyone has always
loved me." But Princess Mary disliked her "from the first glance,"
and Prince Bolkonsky was simply rude. Thus twice rejected, betrayed, insulted, unwanted, and unloved, Natasha goes off to the opera. She is disoriented. On the way, lost in thought and staring at the
lights that flash through the carriage window, she "forgets whom she
is with and where she is going" (II,v,viii). In the opera house everyone
stares at her in her over-revealing costume, and she is both pleased
and displeased at the "swarm of memories, desires, and trepidations"
that are aroused. The center of attention but "indifferent to every-

thing that surrounds her," she resembles Pierre in Petersburg. She sits "unconsciously crumpling her program to the beat of the overture." Insult is added to injury when she sees Julie Karagina and Boris Drubetsky publicly together, now that they have announced their engagement. The Natasha whom everyone loves is now the Natasha whom no one has anything to do with.

Turned in on herself, estranged from the world she finds herself in, unloved and wanting love, Natasha does not experience the opera. She does not follow it, nor listen to the music; she just looks at the stage. Natasha's knowledge is reduced to the visual, and the narrator tells us what she sees, not what the opera represents but what is on the stage. Natasha's knowledge of the opera is estranged because she is in no mood to participate in it. She is at the opera but not in the theater. To her, then, all there is on stage are cardboard images of trees, a girl in white, a man in tights, and singing in solos and duets. She knows what "all this is supposed to represent," but in her moment of estrangement it seems to her "unnatural" (II,v,ix). She looks at the audience which is involved in the opera. "It must (*dolzhno*) be that's the way it has (*nadobno*) to be," she thinks, like Pierre. And then while watching others involved in the opera

> Natasha little by little begins to enter a state of intoxication. . . . She did not remember who she was or where she was or what was happening in front of her. She looked, and the most strange thoughts unexpectedly, without connection, flashed through her mind. Now it occurred to her to jump onto the stage and sing the aria the actress was singing; now she wanted to tap the old man sitting near her with her fan; now she wanted to lean over toward Helen and tickle her.

In her intoxication Natasha wants to move out of her isolation at the opera, to enter the world of the theater around her, even to participate in the opera. Most of all she wants to shock others into recognizing her. So, when during this first act of the opera Anatole Kuragin enters the theater, taking note of Natasha and pronouncing to Helen "Mais charmante!" Natasha cannot help but pay attention "just because he said that she was charmante." The first act ends with this reorientation: Natasha has been noticed. In the intermission Boris comes in to invite Natasha to the wedding. Natasha chats "with the man whom she had formerly loved" about his impending marriage with a "cheerful and coquettish smile" on her lips just like Helen's. "In her state of intoxication this all seemed simple and natural." Her sense of rejection is hidden by her smile. In this first intermission, as at the ball, the men in Natasha's life pass by. Only now, when Natasha talks to Pierre, she hears Anatole's voice in the next box and turns her eyes toward him. In this moment of looking and being looked at begins Natasha's moment of belonging to Anatole.

In the second act the opera seems to represent a girl's loss of innocence, but Natasha pays no heed. Instead, she keeps looking over to Anatole because "it was pleasant to see that he was so captivated by her." In the pleasure of her power she sees "no evil," in herself or on the stage. The second act ends, and Natasha goes over to Helen's loge. In the middle of the opera she changes her position and angle of vision. So when the third act begins and the girl in white, now dressed in just a smock and somewhat disheveled, stands before the throne of the king and queen, apparently begging for her life in vain, Natasha like the rest can turn attention, not to the drama of lost innocence, but to Duport's brilliant dancing and finds herself in agreement with Helen and everyone else. It "no longer seemed strange." In the third intermission Anatole enters Helen's loge. "His nearness, self-assurance, and the kindly affection of his smile," conquer Natasha, and she smiles (II,v,x). When he smiles back, however, "she feels terror that there is no barrier between him and her." As the curtain rises for the fourth act, Natasha feels "completely subordinated to the world in which she finds herself." Gone are her thoughts of Andrew's betrayal, of Princess Mary's rejection, even of life back in the country. "All that seemed a long time ago." All Natasha sees is a devil in the opera and Kuragin in the theater.

Natasha at the opera resembles Pierre at Borodino. Both are estranged from the world they enter and as a result disoriented in the new environment. Both are represented observing the world they are in, but not involved in. Both see this world in some sense freed from the conventional interpretation of it. In the course of the event both move from estrangement to involvement, and as a result of their involvement both change their view of the world they are in. But Pierre, who has never before experienced war, moves from an isolated, aestheticized vision to existential engagement. Natasha goes to the opera disoriented, not because she has never been there before, but because she has lost her orientation in the world: she is not loved, and there is no one for her to love. The delineated segment of Natasha at the opera, thus, tells the story of the results from the fall from grace. Once love is lost, Natasha is easy prey for the alluring charm of the atmosphere in the theater: she is quickly intoxicated by the sights and sounds and soon loses all sense of who or where she is. The loss of love is the cause and condition of the possibility of intoxication. Once she is intoxicated, the new and false sense of self allows for the seduction to a false love. In the enslavement to this false love, the world grounded in it, both in the opera and in the theater, becomes intelligible and acceptable. The world of convention and culture is diametrically opposed to the world of love. The first step toward acceptance of and the enslavement to the conventions of culture is the intoxication of consciousness. "A ˏsober person is ashamed." Natasha at the opera resembles most, not Pierre, but the soldier of Tolstoy's diary note: like him she is removed from her family, dressed in a uniform, and subjugated to the beat of a drum, and thus becomes a beast.[1]

NATASHA at the opera is a moment of self-forgetting. We observe the character observing, and we see her in the process of becoming intoxicated and seduced. Pozdnyshev, in *The Kreutzer Sonata* (1889), lives in a state of chronic intoxication. He understands well the function of this stupefaction. "Man's salvation as well as his punishment," he believes, "lies in the fact that when he lives incorrectly he can befog himself so as not to see the poverty of his position" (xvii). We meet Pozdnyshev some time after the "critical episode" in his life, when he killed his wife in a rage of jealousy (ii). He believes that only when he saw the body that he had deformed and destroyed did he "for the first time see in her a human being" (xxviii). But he also believes that his whole married life was passed in a state of stupefaction. His wife, he says, "tried to forget herself in her intense, hurried preoccupation with housekeeping, decoration, her wardrobe and the

---

[1] This passage, and many others, is often interpreted as an example of Shklovsky's "defamiliarization." This concept is not, in my opinion, particularly useful for interpreting Tolstoy, although it is true that he often does "defamiliarize" conventional perception. The fact that Shklovsky and others could generalize this idea into an aesthetic theory suggests to me that it does not capture the uniqueness of Tolstoy. My idea of estrangement (the experience of reality as *chuzhoj*) is not the same as "defamiliarization" (*ostranenie*), nor was it suggested to me by Shklovsky's work.

children's, with the children's lessons and health," while he "had his own drunkenness, the drunkenness of work, hunting, and cards" (xvii). *The Kreutzer Sonata* is the story of a man who has spent his life hiding, in a state of intoxication, from the poverty of his position.

The form of the story, however, is unique. It is presented as a conversation with a traveller on a train ride, reported to the reader by a faceless narrator who is a fellow passenger on the journey. In a sense, then, this is a first-person narrative told by a person about whom we know nothing and of whom we learn nothing, nor do we care to. The narrator serves as an observing eye, the camera that captures Pozdnyshev's noises and words. Through this narrator the reader is thrust into the train and the conversation with the traveller; the reader sees Pozdnyshev's peculiar twitches and hears his "strange noises that resemble muffled sobs" (xvii). The bulk of the story consists of Pozdnyshev's tirades reported by the narrator verbatim, so that it seems as though this is Pozdnyshev's first-person narrative. The faceless narrator thus creates an effect of presence for the reader, who encounters Pozdnyshev in all his threatening peculiarity.

Pozdnyshev casts his story in the form of a journey of discovery. In the end, he believes, he learned the truth about life and himself. He now "knows," and on the train he tells what he knows (xv). His life, he believes, has been ruined by a chronic obsession with sex. This obsession took hold with his first sexual encounter with a woman because, he thinks, in this encounter he was divorced of any responsibility toward the woman. Like Nekhlyudov in *Resurrection*, he used her and left her. Once he experienced sexual pleasure without responsibility, he became addicted. "I became what is called a lecher. To be a lecher is a physical condition similar to the condition of a morphine addict, a drunkard, or a smoker" (iv). Sex became the motivation for everything he did. Furthermore, Pozdnyshev believes that he is not alone in this. Everyone in society is obsessed with sex. Wherever he looks he sees a lurking id: in his wife and, when he appears at the center of the story, in his rival. Indeed, for Pozdnyshev social customs, cultural values, and industrial productions all serve this ever-present, ever-needful urge to copulate.

But because he sees the world around him so obsessed with sex, even if this is his projection, Pozdnyshev also believes that he is not responsible for this addiction. This is what they taught me, he argues. They told me it was good for my health and that everyone else did it. Thus Pozdnyshev sees himself as an addict whose addiction is caused by others. He is simultaneously obsessed with his own actions and paranoiac of what others do to him. He feels guilt and resentment. At one moment he exclaims in exacerbated resentment of his wife, "why didn't she leave me!" (v) and in the very next moment, overcome by his sense of guilt, he admits, "it served me right" (vi). Pozdnyshev is both victim and victimizer. This dualistic sense of self colors his vision of the world. Everyone seems to be simultaneously the oppressor and the oppressed. Women are traps or bait on a hook, and they are also slaves at an auction (viii). Women resemble Jews, who "pay back by their financial power for their own oppression" (ix). When the alleged rival appears on the scene, he is imagined as both seducer and seduced, just as is Pozdnyshev's wife. Pozdnyshev switches back and forth between these two images of himself and others with maddening speed, and the logic of his tirades is subordinated to this splintered vision of a world in which everything is evil and everything is justified.

Pozdnyshev does not see the poverty of his position because he is totally self-centered. He cannot escape from his projections and has no sensitivity to others. Even at the beginning, when he hears complete strangers on a train mention the words "critical episode," he assumes they are speaking of his. He "knows," he says, but in his self-centered isolation he cannot see clearly. His life is in fact a drama of self-defeat told as a story of oppression. But since he cannot take responsibility for what he does, even though he "knows" that he killed his wife, he must hide from his conscience in an intoxicated stupor. As he tells his story he smokes incessantly and gulps down tea so strong that it is "really like beer" (ii). Pozdnyshev is like the people described in *Why Do Men Stupefy Themselves?* who "do not so much want their consciousness to work right as they want what they do to seem right, and so they consciously use substances which destroy the right work of consciousness" (27,281-82). The more Pozdnyshev reveals what he knows, the tipsier he gets. To this intoxication is added the jolting and arousing movements of the train which agitate and aggravate him. The rhythm of his story, therefore, builds a crescendo toward a moment of acute intoxication, arousal, and annoyance. This peak moment on the train coincides in time with Pozdnyshev's story about his ride on the train to the scene of the murder.

That eight-hour ride on the train was for me something so terrible that I'll never forget it all my life. Either because once I got on the train I vividly imagined myself already arrived or because the railroad arouses people that way, but as soon as I settled in the train I no longer could control my imagination. Without stop and with unusual clarity I began to draw pictures which enflamed my jealousy. . . . I burned with indignation, spite, and a particular sense of thrill in my own humiliation. (xxv)

The moment on the ride to the murder corresponds to the moment of the telling of it. He forgets where he is. As then, now Pozdnyshev burns with indignation over what his wife has done and thrills in his own humiliation. As he rides alone intoxicated and aroused, he works himself into a state in which he reexperiences the murder. On his drunken journey Pozdnyshev has returned to his crime, and indeed in his self-centeredness he seems compelled to do this. He "knows," but he has not resolved his guilt or his resentment. At the end his wife would not forgive him, and even now he cannot forgive himself. The story ends with his final request to be forgiven, now by the narrator, but it is not certain for what, for the murder or the telling of the murder. The narrator gets off the train with just a farewell, and Pozdnyshev rides on, perhaps once again to tell what he knows in the hope of finding forgiveness. Otherwise he will keep on smoking and gulping down tea so as not to see the poverty of his position.

STATES OF ECSTASY

Pierre, Natasha, and Pozdnyshev all suffer from a sense of dislocation. Their former routine of life is shattered, and they are thrust into an alien world. The drama of their disorientation is played out variously, but each for some time and in some sense loses himself in the intoxicating atmosphere which surrounds him. But dislocation does not necessarily lead to intoxication. Kitty is about to give birth, and Levin is in a state of panic. Everyone else seems indifferent, while Levin is consumed by his "attention to all that is to be done" and feels compelled to "break through the wall of indifference" if he is to "attain his goal" (VII,xiv). He loses his sense of measure and patience. In his panic Levin sees only the frightening event in which he is totally involved but which he does not understand, and others do not seem to notice. Even though he is among people, he is isolated in his anxious terror. Thus totally involved in the moment and yet totally removed from his surroundings, Levin has no perspective on himself or others. "All the ordinary conditions of life without which one cannot imagine anything no longer existed for Levin. He lost his consciousness of time. . . . Where he was at that time he knew just as little as when something was." In his panic Levin is dazed.

He saw the Princess, red, overwrought, her grey hair out of curl, and in tears which she swallowed intensely while biting her lips; he saw Dolly and the doctor, smoking thick cigarettes; and the midwife with a firm, resolute, and calming look on her face; and the elderly Prince pacing the hall and frowning. But when they came and went, where they were he did not know. The Princess was now with the doctor in the bedroom, now in the study, where there had appeared a table set for a meal, now it was not the Princess but Dolly. Later, Levin remembered being sent somewhere. First they sent him to move a table and sofa. He did it with zeal, thinking that it was needed for her and then only later learning that he had prepared a place for himself to sleep. Then they sent him to the study to ask the doctor something. The doctor answered and then began speaking about disorders in the duma. Then they sent him to the Princess' bedroom to get an icon in the silver-gilt frame, and he and the Princess' elderly maid climbed onto a cupboard to get it, and broke the vigil light, and the Princess' maid tried to reassure him about his wife and the vigil light, and he took the icon and placed it at the head of Kitty's bed, carefully slipping it under the pillows. But where, when, and why all this was done he did not know.

Levin at the moment of Kitty's giving birth seems to resemble Pierre at the moment of his father's dying. Like Pierre, Levin sees what is happening in great detail, but he does not understand it. Like Pierre, Levin does not know what to do and so does what he is told to do. But disoriented Levin does not yield his responsibility nor acquiesce to the will of others. Only after the moment does he remember that he did what others told him to do. Dazed, Levin does not decide to do anything. In his dislocation Levin loses the capacity to order reality according to temporal and spatial categories. As a result, his sense of the world is transformed. While "outside the ordinary conditions of life" Levin experiences "as it were in this ordinary life an opening through which something higher" is revealed. Through his disorientation Levin is released from the mind of the master and reduced to the state of prayer. "Lord, forgive me and help me." At the moment of Kitty's giving birth Levin experiences the whole world in two diametrically opposed ways. In his state of "forgetting" Levin sees, but his mind does not understand what his mind sees. The world is reduced to people coming and going, talking and doing, but none of it makes any sense. And Levin himself is lost in this meaninglessness. What shocks Levin out of his disorientation is the reality of Kitty's giving birth. "In her presence" he is all compassion and prayer.

Levin at the moment of Kitty's giving birth is not at all like Pierre at the moment of his father's dying. Pierre is disoriented because he does not know the proper rituals and does not care enough to realize he is being led on. His father's dying has no meaning for him, and in the experience Pierre learns nothing. He does not awaken to the terror of death or to life lived in the face of death. Levin's dislocation releases a sudden revelation of the meaning of ordinary life when confronted with the extraordinary event of life. In his disorientation Levin is thrust to the brink, where the words and deeds of daily living seem senseless in the face of the mystery of our ultimate coming and going. Levin's forgetting when he loses his awareness of time and place turns out, on the one hand, to be an intensified moment of life lived in the mindless routines of this world. Only later, does he remember that he just did what he was told. Dazed, Levin has no faith. But, on the other hand, when his soul soars to the heights of life understood not by reason but by life itself, Levin suddenly sees who he is and what he must do. Beyond the categories of space and time, he loses his sense of self as personality and finds himself in a state of ecstasy.

Captain Tushin on the battlefield cannot forget the limitations of personality. "If it were possible to know what comes after death, then none of us would fear death" (I,ii,xvi). But fear of the unknown overtakes us, the philospher Tushin argues, because "no matter how much they say the soul goes off to heaven, we know that there is no heaven, only the atmosphere." The agnostic's voice is then suddenly interrupted: "A whistling sound was heard. Nearer, nearer, faster and louder, louder and faster, and a cannonball which seemed not to have finished everything it had to say splattered the dirt with inhuman force, as it crashed into the earth not far from the shed." Tushin rushes out into the battle, his face "pale." Once in the fray Captain Tushin becomes so totally involved in his task that he seems beside himself. "Despite the fact that he remembered everything, put everything together mentally, and did what the very best officer in his position could do, he was in a state similar to a feverish delirium or in the state of a person who was drunk." In battle, Tushin the philosopher disappears. In his stead there is "a little man with weak, awkward movements who over and over again demands from his orderly 'another pipeful for that one,' as he puts it, who charges forward scattering sparks from 'his pipe,' and who looks at the French by shading his eyes with his little hand." As he runs from one gun to another, puffing on his pipe, Tushin shouts in his "weak, shrill, and irresolute voice," but his "face grows more and more animated." He is all "concentration and activity." Unlike the philosopher Tushin, Captain Tushin "does not experience the slightest unpleasant feeling or fear, and the thought that he could be killed or seriously wounded does not enter his head." He just "grows more and more cheerful" until it seems to him that "the patch of the field on which he is standing is a long familiar native place" (*davno znakomoe, rodstvenoe mesto*). His men, "like children," so look to him that his facial expression becomes "reflected" on them. In battle, the battery becomes a family to which they all belong. Captain Tushin finds his home right here, right now.

In battle, Captain Tushin steps right out of the world in which he resides. In a state of ecstasy, he discovers and creates a new world of his own.

> From (*iz-za*) the deafening sounds of his own guns all round him, from the whistling and thud of the enemy's shells, from the sight of the flushed and perspiring crew bustling around the guns, from the sight of the blood of humans and horses, from the sight of puffs of smoke from the enemy's side (always followed by a flying shell which struck the earth, a person, a gun, or a horse), from the sight of all these objects there had taken shape in his head a fantastic world of his own. In his imagination the enemy's guns were not guns but pipes from which occasional puffs

of smoke were blown by an invisible smoker. "There, he puffed again," Tushin muttered to himself as a puff of smoke rose from the hill and was burned off in a streak to the left. "Now look out for the ball, we'll throw it back. . . . Come on, Matvevna," he said to himself. In his imagination the farthest gun, which was large and old-fashioned, became the daughter of Matthew (*Matvevna*). The French swarming around their guns seemed to him to be ants. In his world the handsome drunkard Number One of the second gun's crew was "uncle"; Tushin looked at him more than at anyone else and took joy in his every movement. The sound of the muskets cross-firing at the foot of the hill, now diminishing, now again increasing, seemed to him like someone's breathing. He listened intently to the flaring up and flickering out of these sounds. "See, she's begun to breathe again, to breathe again," he said to himself. And he himself seemed to be an enormous, powerful man who was throwing cannonballs at the French with both hands.

Like Pierre at Borodino, Tushin sees the puffs of smoke and hears the sounds of the shots. But he does not turn the battlefield into an aesthetic object outside him, nor do we observe him observing. Captain Tushin is in the fray, and we see him taking part. In his participation, however, Tushin transforms the whole world. The little man smoking his pipe sees everything in his own image. The puffs of smoke come from pipes being smoked by an invisible smoker, and the noise of the shells sound like breathing. Inanimate objects become animate and an unknown soldier a relative. The cross-fire of battle is turned into a game. Tushin is no longer a member of an isolated battery, but somewhere back home with relatives and friends playing catch. Having forgotten the philosopher, Captain Tushin now gives his all, participates in the moment, belongs to his family, and resides in his native place. In ecstasy he finds his true self.

IN HIS ECSTASY Captain Tushin stands outside the "little man with weak, awkward movements" to become an enormous, powerful giant. Nicholas Rostov undergoes a similar transformation, but not in battle. He has long waited to get a look at the tsar, and finally the time has come. Alexander is to review the troops at Olmütz.

A group was seen approaching directly ahead from Olmütz. And at that very moment, although the day was still, a light gust of wind fluttered over the army and slightly ruffled the streamers on the lances and the unfolded standards, which began to flap against their staffs. It seemed that with this slight movement the whole army expressed its joy at the Emperor's approach. One voice was heard. "Attention!" Then, like the crowing of cocks at sunrise, voices from various directions echoed it. Then everything became quiet. In the dead stillness only the trotting of horses was heard. This was the Emperor's suite. The Emperor rode up to the flank, and the sounds of the trumpeters from the first cavalry regiment burst forth as they began to play the general march. It seemed that it was not the trumpeters playing, but that the army itself, rejoicing at the approach of the Emperor, naturally issued forth these sounds. Midst these sounds there was distinctly heard only the youthful, affectionate voice of Emperor Alexander. He pronounced a greeting, and the first regiment roared "Hurrah!" so deafeningly, continuously, and joyfully that the people themselves were frightened at the multitude and power (*sila*) of that vast mass which they constituted. (I,iii,viii)

This first half of the representation of Rostov at the Emperor's review of the troops focuses on the general experience of all present. It is a moment of anticipation and attention. The moment is presented in stages: first the slight movement of the wind permeating the masses and expressing the joy of anticipation, then the resounding call to attention which echoes through the whole, then the stillness which is roused to life by the trumpets, which again express the joy of anticipation that seems to emanate from the whole, then the exchange of greeting between Emperor and troops which culminates in a joyful "hurrah!" astounding in its cumulative power. Each stage is composed of a stimulating movement of air or sound which then engulfs the whole. This is a movement, then, of ever-increasing intoxication. No individual member of the troops is singled out, but all together are aroused more and more. The second half of the representation of the Emperor's review of the troops then moves the camera onto Rostov, and the focus becomes more inward.

Rostov . . . experienced the same feeling that every person in that army experienced, a feeling of self-forgetfulness, and a proud awareness of might and passionate attraction to him who was the cause of this celebration. He felt that at a single word from this man that entire vast mass (and he who was connected with it, an insignificant grain of sand) would go through fire and water, commit crime, die, or perform deeds of highest heroism, and therefore he could not help but tremble and his heart stood still at the sight of that approaching word. "Hurrah! Hurrah! Hurrah!" thundered from all sides, and one regiment after another received the Emperor with the strains of the general march, then "Hurrah!" the general march and again "Hurrah!" and "Hurrah!" growing ever stronger and fuller and merging into a deafening roar.

This focus on the individual experience, however, paradoxically represents the experience of all. Rostov loses his sense of self, but in this he is like everyone else. Furthermore, this "self-forgetfulness" in Rostov and apparently in everyone else releases a feeling of strength in himself and an attraction to the Emperor. He would give forth of himself. Rostov does not now recall the world of *love from* where he belongs; he himself experiences *love for*. And, later, when the Emperor gets within twenty feet of him, Rostov "experiences a feeling of tenderness and rapture like he had never experienced before." The Emperor smiles, and "Rostov himself automatically begins to smile and feel an even stronger flood of love for his Emperor." The Emperor speaks, and Rostov feels "he could die for his tsar." The soldiers shout "Hurrah!" and Rostov joins in, "hoping to harm himself by that shout, just to express fully his rapture for the Emperor." His flood of love is so great that when he spies Prince Andrew with whom he had quarreled the day before, his anger is dispelled. "In such a moment of love, rapture, and self-renunciation, what do our quarrels and resentments mean? Now I love and forgive everyone." The delineated segment of Rostov at the Emperor's review of the troops is a paradigmatic action in which harmony is restored once again.

Rostov's experience of self-forgetfulness has a particular structure. He feels himself an "insignificant grain of sand" within the "whole vast mass" and yet filled with a "proud awareness of might." In this too Rostov shares the state of awareness common to all at that moment. "Every general and soldier felt his insignificance, being conscious of himself as a grain of sand in that sea of people, and at the same time felt his might, being conscious of himself as a part of that gigantic whole" (*tseloe*). A force that is outside them all yet comes from within them all engulfs them all, but each has a sense of a simultaneous diminution and aggrandisement of self. In the totality each feels himself less and more. Each is in a state where "I will be no more" but where his love will exist forever. In the intoxicating rapture of the military parade all experience the fundamental double consciousness of insignificance and strength, of separateness and participation, of loss and gain, of estrangement and belonging. Unlike the soldiers in the regimental march, they do not have to leave the rest to be. Rather, they are at their best because they are all together. At the Emperor's review of the troops everyone experiences what Prince Andrew sensed when he heard Natasha sing and what Nikolenka discovered in his anticipation of "she" when the garden at night lit by the moon took on another meaning and he felt a love for God. Three days later Rostov sees the Emperor Alexander again, and this very nearness once again dispels in Rostov "any thought of himself" (I,iii,x). "He is as happy as a lover when the long-awaited rendezvous has arrived." To Rostov Emperor Alexander seems like the sun that "spreads rays of tender and majestic light around itself," and Rostov "feels himself seized by these rays." In his ecstasy Rostov "loves and forgives everyone." In his self-forgetting Rostov stands outside himself, and God's love for men wells up in him. In his moment without "any thought of himself," Rostov is seized by the rays which emanate from the sun and penetrate everything, even himself. Rostov's enraptured love for the Emperor in concert with everyone else is an emblem of the experience of that "seizure of the Divine" which is God's love for all in all.

Rostov at the Emperor's review of the troops resembles Natasha at the ball when in her happiness she feels "completely kind and beautiful and does not believe in the possibility of evil, unhappiness, or grief." For both, the moment of intoxicated enchantment releases a swell of love for all. They are like the narrator of *After the Ball* (1903) who, when his lady fair bestows on him a feather from her fan, tells of his moment of enchanted rapture: "I was not only cheerful and satisfied; I was happy and blessed (*blazhen*); I was kind (*dobr*): I was not me, but some being not of this earth who knew no evil and was capable only of good." All three are transformed by the experience of what seems to be reciprocated preferential love and attraction to another. In this moment of love they are set free from this world and transported to another level of existence.

Levin and Kitty experience the magical, non-verbal declaration of love. Then Kitty departs. "Alone," Levin is all anticipation of the next day, when he will make the formal declaration (IV,xiv). He feels the need to "talk with someone so as not to remain alone." He catches up with Stiva, who is on his way to another party and tells him that "he is happy and that he loves him." He returns to his brother Sergey Ivanovich, declares his "happiness," tells him that he loves him "very much," and offers to go off to a meeting with him. At the meeting he sees the secretary reading the minutes with "embarrassment" and takes this as a sign that "he is a nice, kind, fine person." The meeting turns into an argument about some statistic-laden reports and the laying of some pipes.

> Levin listened to them and saw clearly that none of that existed, not the enumerated sums, not the pipes; he saw that they were not angry, that they were all such kind, fine people, that everything among them was going nicely and well. For Levin it was remarkable that they were all now visible through and through. By small, formerly unnoticed signs he now recognized the soul of each and saw clearly that they were all kind. Now they all loved him very much, especially him, Levin. This was evident from the way they spoke with him, from the affectionate and loving way even strangers looked at him.

Levin, who detests meetings and rarely gets along with his brother or his brother's friends, is beside himself with love. The barrier he sets between himself and others falls down. He then leaves the meeting and returns to the hotel. Now the servant Yegor, whom he "had not noticed before," seems "very intelligent, good, and, what matters, a kind person." Levin feels compelled to share his new discovery of love with him. "With love you are always happy because happiness exists only in yourself," he says. Yegor does not quite grasp Levin's point; the words are scarcely adequate to the idea. But Yegor does understand because Levin's love is catching: the servant is "infected" with the master's "enraptured state," just as "people are infected by a yawn." Yegor himself is transformed and immediately begins sharing his private, inner life with his new friend. The master's love given forth releases the servant's love given forth in a right-now mutual moment of happiness. Levin belongs because he loves.

But then Yegor leaves and Levin is alone again. He goes to the window, opens it, and sits down on the table to gaze outward and toward.

> Beyond the snow-covered roof there was visible a fretwork cross covered with chains and above it the rising triangular constellation Charioteer with the bright yellow star Capella. He looked now at the cross, now at the star, breathed in the fresh frosty air which was flowing in a steady stream into the room, and as in a dream he followed the images and memories that arose in his imagination.

Looking outward and toward the sky Levin is filled with the frosty air streaming into the room. He breathes in the air, and "images and memories arise in his imagination." Alone, Levin now communes with "the whole world," but what he finds is his own love. He hears the gambler Myasnik coming home from the club. "The poor, unfortunate man" thinks Levin, and "tears of love and pity for this man come to his eyes." He wants to "comfort him." And again he looks outward and toward the sky "to bathe in the cool air and gaze at that wonderfully shaped cross, silent but full of meaning for him, and at the bright yellow ascending star." Levin at the window experiences love anew. Before, his loving glance not blocked by words saw all others as loving him. Now that loving glance simply gives forth in compassion with no expectation of return or reward. Still, in the moment at the window Levin is filled with the cool air of the world beyond, and he does see its marvellous beauty. In the love that expects no reward he discovers a new and transformed world.

Levin in love enters a state of ecstasy in which he forgets himself and is rewarded with a new sense of himself and the whole world.

> All that night and morning Levin lived completely unconsciously and felt himself completely removed from the conditions of material life. He did not eat all day, he did not sleep for two nights, he spent several hours half-dressed in the cold air outside and felt not only freshened and healthier than ever before but completely independent of the body: he moved without the effort of his muscles and felt that he could do anything. He was certain that he could fly upward or knock down the corner

of a house if that were necessary. He spent the remaining time pacing the streets, constantly looking at his watch and gazing all around. What he saw at that time he never saw again. He was particularly touched by the children going to school, the grey doves that had flown from the roof to the sidewalk, and the loaves of bread sprinkled with flour and placed outside the baker's window by an unseen hand. These loaves, the doves, and the two boys were beings not of this earth. Everything happened at once: the boy ran up to the doves and glanced at Levin with a smile; the dove fluttered its wing and flew off glittering in the sunlight midst the snow just quivering in the air; from the window came the smell of fresh-baked bread and the loaves were placed out. All this together was so unusually beautiful that Levin began to laugh and cry with joy. (IV,xv)

In love Levin enters a world beyond space, time, and causality. He is all-powerful and yet not conscious of himself. In this independence from material existence, he gains power and freedom. Like Natasha, he even believes he can fly up into the sky. There are no limitations. In love Levin can do anything. In love, however, Levin does not do anything. Rather, he experiences a not so tiny shift of awareness. He sees the world itself, himself included, "at once" and "all together." Everything is related to everything else in the moment that transfigures the boy, the dove, and the bread. In his ecstasy of love Levin sees the world harmoniously fit all together, and it is beautiful. In love Levin discovers the harmony of the spheres not in the sky but right here, right now incarnated in the boy, the dove, and the bread, the "beings not of this earth" that he sees on this earth. He knows the joy of life.

In love Levin is the opposite of Anna at her moment of hate. In her journey to her suicide she too exists in a state in some sense beyond the ordinary conditions of time, space, and causality. Disoriented, she rides through the streets, not knowing where she is going or even who she is. She too sees the world beyond transformed. On her journey to death she is obsessed with her unfulfilled need to be loved, and she sees hatred everywhere. In her ecstatic hatred everything falls apart. Images impinge upon her consciousness in maddening disarray and arouse the chaos in her soul. She has no sense of freedom and power; she is compelled and driven. The terrible break of memory of self has reduced her to impotence. In everything she sees she is conscious of herself. No matter how hard she tries, Anna cannot forget herself. Everything she sees, and even how she sees, is very much of this world.

R O S T O V at the Emperor's review and Levin in love were both led out of themselves by their attraction to another. Neither the Emperor or Kitty, however, consciously or actively did anything to affect a change in Rostov's or Levin's psyche. To be sure, Rostov, is aroused by the intoxicating atmosphere of the review, and Levin is enchanted by Kitty's presence, but neither is lured or led on. There is for Tolstoy, however, another kind of ecstatic moment. We might recall that in his enraptured state Levin encounters the servant Yegor, who is "infected" with Levin's enraptured state, just as "people are infected by a yawn." In this encounter the servant automatically becomes like the master. Levin may not quite do this intentionally, but still in effect he transforms the other into the self. One person becomes like another in a moment of automatic imitation.

Times are hard for Rostov. He loves Sonya, and Sonya loves him, but his best friend Dolokhov also has an eye for his girl, and, besides, for financial reasons his parents have forbidden him to marry his poor relative. Indeed, his father has just given him his last bit of allowance until spring, and, hoping to escape his fiscal realities, Rostov has decided to gamble at cards, with the hopes of winning at least enough to buy his mother a name-day present. So they play not "for fun" but "for keeps," and Rostov starts to lose (II,i,xiii). "At that moment his home life—joking with Petya, chatting with Sonya, singing duets with Natasha, playing piquet with his father—appeared before him with such force, clarity, and charm as though it were a happiness long past, lost, and priceless." This paradise must be regained. Rostov loses and returns home. At home the usual "loving, poetical atmosphere" still reigns, but Nicholas finds himself alienated from the innocent games and songs that mark the Rostov residence (II,i,xv). "I'm dishonorable, a goner. A bullet in the head is all that's left, but songs, no." Natasha senses Nicholas' estrangement, but dismisses her brother's mood because "at that moment she herself felt so cheerful, she was so far from grief, sadness, and reproaches that (as often happens with young people) she deceived herself. 'No, I feel too cheerful now to spoil my own gladness with sympathy for another's (*chuzhoe*)

grief. . . . No, surely I'm wrong, he must feel cheerful, just as I do!' "
Thinking of "nothing or no one" she moves to the middle of the room
and begins to sing.

"What's happened to her? See how she's singing today!" thought
Rostov. And suddenly the whole world (*mir*) became centered for
him in the anticipation of the next note, the next phrase, and
everything in the world became divided into three beats: "O mio
crudele affetto—one, two, three, one, two, three, one—O mio
crudele affetto—one, two, three, one. O this senseless life of
ours," thought Nicholas. "All that, the unhappiness, the money,
Dolokhov, anger, and honor, all that is nonsense. But this, this is
real. Now then, Natasha, now then, my dear, now then, my dar-
ling. How will she take that, si? She took it. Thank God!" And
without himself noticing that he was singing, to strengthen her
si, he joined in a third below the high note. "My God, How fine!
Did I really take it? How wonderful," he thought.

O, how that third vibrated, and how touched was something
that was finest in Rostov's soul. And that something was independent of everything in the world and above everything in the
world. What are losses and Dolokhov and one's word of honor!
That's all nonsense. One can kill and rob and yet be happy.

Natasha's song infects Rostov. The despairing gambler, broken and
broke, "suddenly" finds himself in a new but not alien frame of
mind. In harmony with Natasha, the goner is glad. In accord he recovers his best self and feels free from the world of money and power.
But Rostov's psychological state is precisely the one Natasha consciously attempts to instill by her song. His mood is her gladness experienced and expressed as she stands like a ballerina and sings out
with her "untrained" but "velvety" voice. In her gladness Natasha
knows her brother's broken state, yet refuses to let another's grief
dispel her gaiety. When she sings she thinks of "nothing or no one,"
but her song is coercive. In his harmony Rostov may be "independent
of everything in the world," but he is not free from Natasha. Yet Rostov does not feel that he has been coerced, any more than Yegor does
when infected with Levin's rapture. While coercive, Natasha's infectious song does not violate Rostov's being, even though it changes
his mood. Natasha evokes what is already hidden in Rostov. His experience of infection, therefore, is for him a moment of liberation

from the power of Dolokhov's hairy hands. In harmony with Natasha, he feels free, liberated from his oppressor, truly himself. He then confesses his sin to his father, and all is forgotten. Rivalry and anger are transformed by love and forgiveness. The moment of ecstatic infection is a paradigmatic action in which discord is dispelled by harmony restored.

The moment of Rostov's infection is told, as it were, in three parts. In the beginning the camera zooms in on Rostov's psyche. Rostov experiences reality as does Natasha: her singing goes forth from herself to him and transforms his understanding of the world. Rostov shares Natasha's idea of "everything in the world" and now knows what is "real." But then Rostov joins in. Now he goes forth from himself to her, and the two singers merge together in the moment of harmony. Once this harmony is attained, the narration changes direction. In a new paragraph, the narrator speaks as it were in Rostov's voice but not in the first person and without quotation marks. The language becomes affective. Now the narrator seeks to draw the reader into Rostov's experience. We are not just thrust into the psyche, and we certainly are not observing him observing. In the final section of this moment of infection the reader himself knows and sees the world as and when Rostov does. The narrator's voice merges with Rostov's, and the reader is not only present at the scene but at one with Rostov. The reader, thus, is not infected with Natasha's song, but united with her and her brother in their shared vision of harmonious gladness. With this effect of presence we are all in accord.

Moments of intoxication resemble moments of ecstasy. In each there is a sense of loss of self. Pierre reaching for the snuff box and Rostov at the Emperor's review both undergo an alteration in their everyday way of being in the world. Natasha at the opera and Levin in love both undergo an alteration in their everyday way of seeing the world. The company commander marching to the tune of the regiment and Captain Tushin playing ball with the relatives both enter a world unlike the world around them. Intoxication, however, is not ecstasy. In intoxication the external world impinges on a person's psychological and physical being: one is aroused and loses a clarity of consciousness. Things, events, and people take over one's body and mind. As a consequence, in the intoxicated state one feels impelled or compelled, driven or drawn. Intoxicated, a person is not free to be himself. In ecstasy, on the contrary, a person steps outside his everyday routine and finds himself. Released from his usual way of being and seeing, the person discovers a new world to which he feels he belongs. In intoxication one is drawn to or driven by others. In ecstasy one is set free to be with and for others. Both are states of relatedness, but intoxication is the foundation of sin, while ecstasy resembles prayer.

THE ART OF INFECTION

Infection resembles both intoxication and ecstasy. Rostov at the moment of Natasha's song is both coerced by the music and liberated from his oppression. He is compelled to be glad, but in the gladness discovers his true way of being and seeing. The infectious quality of Natasha's song, therefore, is very powerful. Music can change one's way of being and seeing. This power to transform is precisely what makes music so threatening to Pozdnyshev in *The Kreutzer Sonata.*

> In general, it's a terrifying thing, music. What is it? I do not understand. What is music? What does it do? And why does it do what it does? They say music has an exalting effect on the soul. Nonsense! Not true! It has an effect, a terrible effect—I speak for myself—but not at all of an exalting kind. It has neither an exalting nor a debasing effect on the soul, but an agitating one. How can I put it? Music forces me to forget myself, my true position; it transports me into some other position not my own: under the influence of music it seems to me I feel what I really do not feel, that I understand what I do not understand, that I can do what I cannot do. I explain this by the fact that music has an effect like yawning, like laughter. I don't feel like sleeping, but I yawn if I look at someone yawning; there's nothing to laugh about, but I laugh if I hear someone laughing. It, music, immediately, directly transports me into the psychological state of the person who composed the music. My soul merges with his, and together with him I am transported from one state to another, but why I do this I do not know. (xxiii)

For Pozdnyshev music is not infectious but intoxicating: he loses clarity of consciousness and is aroused to activity not of his own initiation. Identity and vocation get blurred. He is not set free but coerced to be what he feels he is not. The effect is automatic, like a yawn or a smile. This power of music, indeed of any art, frightens Tolstoy himself as well. It violates one of his fundamental principles. "One of the most important rules in life is not to yawn when others yawn" (55,34;1904). Yet Tolstoy constructed his whole theory of art around its capacity to have an effect upon the human "propensity toward imitation (the yawn)" (50,125;1889). The paradox of Tolstoy's art of infection arises from the conflict between the independent self opposed to all others and the common self that belongs to and with all others.

Tolstoy worked out his essay *What Is Art?* during the time he composed *The Kreutzer Sonata*. The two works are closely related. In each Tolstoy singles out a subject of long interest to him. In *The Kreutzer Sonata* he explores in fictional form the nature of sexual attraction and the power of lust and jealousy to transform the psyche. In *What Is Art?* he explores in essay form the nature of the aesthetic experience and the power of art to change one's mood. In the story Tolstoy unmasks the concept of "love"; in the essay he unmasks the concept of "beauty." Furthermore, each work sees its subject in terms of the other: in *The Kreutzer Sonata* lust is occasioned by feminine beauty and evoked by music; in *What Is Art?* most art is seen decked out as a prostitute and devoted to lustful occasions. Both works bump up against the problems of pleasure and power. Both works raise the issues of freedom and identity in moments of human relatedness. But Pozdnyshev, despite his admission of guilt, sees the world as the victim. He views art, therefore, from the vantage point of the audience. In *What Is Art?* Tolstoy speaks from the point of view of both audience and artist.

Tolstoy dismisses the concept of beauty from his discussion of art. He turns his attention from the notion of "pleasure" (*naslazhdenie*) received by the audience to the "destined purpose" (*naznachenie*) of the asthetic experience (v). His primary interest is the function of art in society. For Tolstoy humanity in its present state is "incomplete and disparate" (*razroznennyj*), and human beings are "hostile" to each other (v). The purpose of art is to overcome this state of estrangement. By its nature art unites people. "The real work of art works in such a way that in the consciousness of the perceiver the division between himself and the artist . . . as well as between himself and all people who perceive the same work is destroyed. In this liberation of the personality from its separation (*otdelenie*) from other people, from its aloneness (*odinochestvo*), in this merging of the personality with others, consists the chief attractive force and characteristic of art" (xv). Art connects and creates harmony. In the moment of connection, furthermore, the "perceiver merges with the artist to such an extent that it seems to him that the object he is perceiving was made, not by the artist, but by himself and that everything expressed by that object is the very thing he had so long wanted to express." The artist expresses himself, but the audience experiences his self-expression as its own. There is one common feeling, yet "each experiences it in his own way" (*kazhdyj po-svoemu*) (xii). In the aesthetic moment there is no contradiction between unity and multiplicity. This liberation from personality, attainment of harmony, and discovery of the self is precisely what Rostov experienced when he heard and joined in Natasha's song.

Art connects, but it is not coercive. Art does not force you into a position not your own, as Pozdnyshev claimed. Rather, art leads you into your own position. In the aesthetic moment you discover your identity. "All the arts, but especially music, are good in that they unite people, i.e., they lead them temporarily into that state which is characteristic of their nature" (56,347;1908). Art returns men to their natural state of harmony. "The main significance of art is the significance of unification (*ob"edinenie*). The 'I' of the artist merges with the 'I' of all the perceivers who merge into one" (57,132;1909). In the aesthetic moment artist and audience become one whole, and there is nothing else. Tolstoy understands the aesthetic experience in the same way he understands the religious experience of belonging to the All. Indeed the aesthetic experience, as Tolstoy describes it in *What Is Art?* is a moment of mutual love for all.

> It happens that people who find themselves together are if not hostile then alien to each other in moods and feelings, and suddenly a story, performance, picture, even a building, but most often music, unites these people as if with an electric spark and instead of their former disparateness, often even hostility, all these people feel union and love for each other. Each rejoices in the fact that the other experiences what he experiences; each rejoices in that communication (*obshchenie*) which has been established not only between him and all those present, but also

between all living people who will receive that impression; what is more, each feels a mysterious joy of communication beyond the grave with all people of the past who had experienced that same feeling and with all people of the future who will experience it. (xvi)

This is truly an experience of total unity. In the aesthetic moment one jumps right out of time and space in an act of rejoicing embrace of the whole human race as it was, is now, and ever shall be. The aesthetic experience resembles ecstatic prayer. But the ecstatic moment of love for all is a solitary event. The infectious experience of art is communal. In the aesthetic moment one is united with all, not just in feeling but in an act of participation. Aesthetic experience is not perception of an alien object out there but participation in the event of art. The aesthetic experience is not what one feels about something or in response to something. In the aesthetic moment each in his own way feels the same thing all together at one. Art has a religious function, then, not primarily because of its potential for moral teaching. Rather, the nature of the aesthetic experience is paradigmatic of all experience of true life. The aesthetic experience is a form of religious experience. In the aesthetic moment we all become aware that we belong to each other right here, right now.

Pozdnyshev did not experience Beethoven's "Kreutzer Sonata" this way, perhaps because to Tolstoy Beethoven's music, especially of the later period, is not real art. Real art by definition effects belonging. False art does not. False art is simply intoxicating. False art bombards the senses with sounds, shapes, or colors which are selected (1) because they have been used before in earlier works of art, (2) because they resemble sounds, shapes, or colors from the world of nature or culture, (3) because they are striking in effects achieved by contrast, spectacle, extreme realism, or sheer inventiveness, or (4) because they draw exclusive attention to the content or to the form. False art seeks to "borrow" or "imitate," to be "striking" or "diverting" (xi). The mannerisms of false art have no relationship to the artist's experience, so there can be no moment of belonging. The audience may all experience one feeling, each in his own way all together at one, but in the false aesthetic moment the audience is everyone else except the artist. False art in fact "affects the audience by hypnotizing it, in the way a person would be hypnotized by listening for several hours to the babbling of a madman pronounced with great oratorical artistry" (xiii). False art can make you feel anything whatsoever. It can coerce you into being what you are not. "One can achieve that more quickly by drinking wine or smoking opium." False art intoxicates; true art infects.

Infection is a function of the "discreteness" of the emotion expressed, the "clarity" of the expression, and the "sincerity" of the artist in his expression (xv). It has nothing to do with the moral quality of the emotion. In order for art to infect, the work of art must simply express a discrete, particular emotion clearly. There must be one pronounced feeling of a kind that all can share each in his own way. This all, however, includes the artist himself. The requirement of sincerity, therefore, is grounded in the communal nature of the aesthetic experience. When the audience senses that "the artist himself is infected with his own work and writes, sings, or plays for himself and not just to affect others, then the audience is infected by the psychological state of the artist." When Natasha sings, we should recall, she thinks of "nothing or no one." Such sincerity guarantees that there is no conscious coercion. But, and here is the paradox of infection, although there must be no attempt by the artist to induce a psychological state in the audience, real art "infects people against their will" (v). So, of course, does false art. But false art intends to induce a psychological state: its purpose is to change the psyche of the audience, not to unite artist and audience in a communal moment all together at one. Still, true art is dangerous because it is infectious. All moral limitations on art stem from its inherent capacity to infect.

Art's capacity to infect, in the final analysis, depends on the artist's sincerity: the clear and distinct feeling follows from this "inner need to express the feeling to be transmitted" (xv). But this sincerity of the artist is not understood simply as a lack of deceit or duplicity. Sincerity entails an immediate, unmotivated, and spontaneous expression. From the point of view of the artist, "the activity of art consists in evoking in oneself a feeling already felt before and, having evoked it in oneself, by means of movement, lines, colors, sounds, images expressed in words, to transmit that feeling in such a way that others feel the same feeling" (v). The true aesthetic act has four moments: (1) an original (or vicarious) experience, (2) the reexperience of that experience at creation, (3) the expression of that experience in external signs, (4) the resultant experience of the perceiver. What is significant is that the artist must reexperience the experience while creating. Tolstoy imagines the aesthetic act as a performance. The reexperience of the experience while expressing it ensures communication, just as an actor's inner becoming of the character guarantees the creation and projection of a believable character or a singer's feeling of the emotion while letting the sounds flow forth ensures the listener's shared feeling. It is because the feeling expressed in art is reexperienced at the moment of expression that Tolstoy assumes that "expression" (*vyrazhenie*) entails "infection" (*zarazhenie*). Technique is taken for granted, but technique does not guarantee infection. The external signs seem to preexist or flow forth automatically with the feeling. There is no effort or act of mind in the moment of creation. What matters is sincerity, understood as the immediate, unmotivated, and spontaneous experience of a feeling while expressing that feeling in external signs. The paradigm of the aesthetic act seems to be the performance of a folk song: the words and tunes are given and themselves embody the feeling which the performer himself must feel while performing if he is to reveal the feeling to the audience and compel the audience to feel. When Tolstoy the writer writes of art, he always thinks of a musical event. Tolstoy's art of infection is the art of a good performance.

BUT A YEAR before he died Tolstoy recorded a moment when he was overcome with an urge to break through the barriers to expression inherent in written words. The old forms now seem impossible, but still he feels duty-bound to write. "A megaphone has been placed in my hands, and I am obliged to take control of it and use it. Something is being suggested to me, but I don't know if it will succeed. I feel that I should write without any form at all, not as in articles, or dissertations, or literary works, but by speaking out, by pouring out (*vylivat'*) however you can what you strongly feel" (57,9;1909). The urge is not new. Almost sixty years earlier, at the very beginning of his writing career while in the Caucasus, Tolstoy was struck with a similar sense of frustration with the expressive limitations of written words.

A wondrous night! The moon had just moved out from behind the knoll and lit up two low, thin, little clouds; behind me a cricket was chirping its plaintive, uninterrupted song; in the distance a frog could be heard, and near the village now Tartars shouting, now a dog barking; and again everything quieted down and again just the transparent cloud rolled past the near and distant stars.

I thought I would go and describe what I saw. But how can you write that down? You have to go and sit at a table buried in inks, pick up a piece of grey paper and take some ink, dirty your fingers, and trace letters on the paper. The letters make words, the words, sentences, but can you really transmit a feeling? Is it not possible upon seeing nature to pour (*perelit'*) one's view into someone else? Description is insufficient. (46,65;1851)

Tolstoy is not interested in recording details for the purpose of verisimilitude. He does not want to create a verbal picture. His frustration with written words, therefore, is not that the words cannot capture a picture, either, as with Lessing, because they are experienced in time while the picture exists statically, or because they are but signs of sounds and thus appeal fundamentally to the sense of hearing, even though primarily to the eye. What concerns Tolstoy is the expression of his affective awareness of the "wondrous night." He needs to communicate verbally his inner experience to the reader. His purpose is to "pour out his feeling" and "pour his view" into another. By this he wants to attain that "merging of souls" (*slivat'sja* means literally "to be poured together, to flow together") which, as he said in *What Is Art?* is the "essence of art" (xiv). This is his prophetic intent. Tolstoy's first concern as a writer, therefore, is the recreation of his or a character's emotion in the reader. His main concern is not the creation and analysis of character, nor the dissection of moral and social behavior, nor the depiction of the natural and social milieu. All this he does and does masterfully. But for Tolstoy the audience must be made present at his words, and the task of these words is the creation of the narrator's or character's feeling in the present audience. If in his narration Tolstoy strives characteristically to draw the reader into the scene, to create the effect of presence, then in his verbal style he strives characteristically to get the reader to share a feeling or response with the narrator or character, to express in order to infect. To infect, the narrator performs his narration for the audience.

Presence and infection are not mutually exclusive, and commonly in the description of a character at a particular moment, the two effects merge. This is how Helen Kuragin first appears in *War and Peace*.

> Rustling slightly in her long white dress trimmed with moss and ivy and gleaming with the whiteness of her shoulders and the sparkle of her hair and her diamonds, she went through (*proshla*) the men who made way for her, and not looking at anyone but smiling to all as if graciously granting each the right to admire the beauty of her figure, her shapely shoulders, her bosom and back very much exposed, as was the fashion, and as if bringing the glamour of the ball with her, she went toward (*podoshla*) Anna Pavlovna. (I,i,iii)

This one sentence—and it is a characteristically Tolstoyan sentence—represents Helen as she walks up to her hostess, but Helen exists grammatically only as the bald pronominal subject "she" at the center and end of the sentence, and her main action of walking is expressed in the two verbs of motion with prefixes of direction (*proshla, podoshla*) which follow the pronominal subjects. Upon this simple structure Tolstoy piles the rest of the sentence, which presents the reader with details of sight and sound, of the manner of walking and smiling. Helen walking across the salon to her hostess is replaced by the heap of detail. The subject and predicate of the sentence are buried by the physical and psychological attributes of the character who is thus represented as a physical presence whose meaning the reader is given to experience. Helen becomes for the reader the gown, the body, the self-centered inviting smile, and the self-assured bearer of everyone's pleasure. But this sentence is a performance in which the narrator recreates verbally not the subject and its simple action, but the feel of the character's presence. The whole burden of the sentence falls on the adverbial participles (rustling, gleaming, looking, smiling, granting, bringing), which are arranged to create the effect of Helen's approaching the perceiver from across the room: first the sounds, then her general appearance, then her facial expression, then the manner of her approaching, and finally what she is bringing. The reader is made to feel Helen approaching, even as he is told that she is approaching. This peculiar syntactical ordering of the words is accompanied by an organization of the sounds which enhances the verbal meanings: the rustling is reproduced in onomat-

opoetic alliteration (*slegka* sнumja svoeju), the sumptuousness of
the gown is suggested in the rich consonance (веloju вal'noju roвoj
uвrannoju), complemented by a full variety of stressed vowels
(e,a,o,u), and the movement of the men making their way for Helen
is heard in the words telling of it (мezнdu rasstupivsнimisja мuzн-
cнinaмi). Sound repetition especially marks the key phrases: the
beauty of her figure (*krasoта svoego sтana*), shapely shoulders (роl-
nykh рlech), the glamor of the ball (вlesk вala). The special effects
Helen uses to make herself present to her audience are translated
into auditory signs which make her present to the reader.

Presence and infection may be achieved in direct contrast to this
sentence by focusing on the action itself. Count Rostov and Marya
Dmitrievna are dancing the Daniel Cooper. Natasha is all excited
and shouts, "look at papa," as she fills "the whole room with the flow
of her resonant laughter" (I,i,xvii). Count Rostov takes in a deep
breath and shouts to the musicians to "play faster."

> Faster, faster, and faster, more, more, and more boldly twirled
> the Count around Marya Dmitrievna, now on tiptoe, now on
> heel till finally returning her to her place he completed the last
> step, raising his light foot backward, bowing his sweating head
> with its smiling face, and swirling his right arm around midst
> thundering applause and laughter, especially from Natasha.

This sentence does not just describe the action; it recreates it. The
sentence divides into two parts, the first half depicting the dance, the
second the ritual of ending the dance. The sentence begins by picking
up the word of Count Rostov's command, "faster," transposing it
from a characterization of the music to the dancing. The two pairs of
thrice-repeated comparative adverbs which open the sentence imitate the rhythm of the crescendoing twirling movements (*skoree,
skoree i skoree, lishe, lishe, i lishe*), just as the changing positions
from toe to heel are kept in balanced rhythm by the repetition of the
particle of serial action "now . . . now" (*to . . . to*). The syntax recreates the dance. The ritual ending is then captured after the final main
verb in the series of adverbial participles "racing," "bowing," "swirling," which open clauses of increasing length, creating thereby the
rhythm of the dramatically grandiloquent gesture which closes the
dance amidst the onomatopoetically recreated applause and laughter
(groкнoта ruкopleskanij i кнокнoта). The syntax of this sentence

is designed to imitate the action of which the sentence tells. If you read the passage carefully, your foot taps to the beat of the dance and you feel the triumph of that last grand gesture. This imitative syntax, and it is used commonly by Tolstoy, serves to draw the reader into the event so that the reader and characters "merge in soul."

Imitative syntax often surfaces in descriptive passages. The world is viewed in motion, and the narration attempts to create the effect of its presence. Pierre at Borodino is in search of the "position." He first looks out and finds an aesthetic object. He looks again and sees the "field of battle itself" (III,ii,xxx).

> Beyond the Kolocha, in Borodino and along both sides of it, especially to the left, where the Voyna flows between its marshy banks into the Kolocha, there had settled a mist which seemed to melt, dissolve, and become translucent with the rise of the bright sun, as it magically colored and outlined everything that was visible through it. The smoke from the guns mingled with the mist, and through the mist and smoke there sparkled everywhere the flashing rays of the morning sun on the water, on the dew, on the bayonets of the troops crowded together on the banks and in Borodino. Through this mist a white church could be seen and here and there roofs on huts in Borodino, dense masses of soldiers, green ammunition chests, cannons. And all this was moving or seemed to be moving because the mist and smoke extended over the entire expanse. Just as around Borodino in the area of hollows covered with mist, so outside it, higher and especially to the left along the whole line, along the woods, and along the fields, in the hollows and on the summits of the high ground, the swirls of cannon smoke continually kept on arising out of nothing, alone, in mass, a few, a lot, and swelling, breaking, swirling, merging they could be seen along the whole expanse.

This most remarkable passage represents Pierre's knowledge of the place where the battle for life will occur. He has found the position, but the position turns out to be no fixed place. It is alive. The language of the whole passage is designed to embody and reveal movement. The mist is not a fixed entity; it changes. It seems "to melt, dissolve, and become transparent." This changing process is embodied in these three verbs. The first is simple and short: "melt" appears in a bare unprefixed form (*taet*). The verb expresses the negative action necessary for life: the removal of the limits to let flow. The next verb is complex. "Dissolve" (*rasplyvaetsja*) is prefixed by the morpheme of dispersion (*ras*) and has as its root the morpheme of floating or swimming which is part of a whole group of verbs (including "to melt") related to the liquid imagery especially associated with Pierre (and his namesake Petya). Another form of this verb surfaces in Pierre's dream of the globe of life. This third verb is also complex. "Become translucent" in the original is made of a root meaning "light" and a prefix meaning "through"; the verb means literally "let light get through" (*prosvechivaetsja*), as does "translucent" etymologically. This verb is part of a whole group of words related to the light imagery associated with the sky. The changing mist that Pierre sees becomes emblematic to him of the world of liquid and light that he will discover as his true residence, even before he can be aware of this.

The movement of life that Pierre sees in the position at Borodino is expressed directly by the syntax. Repetitions of syntactical forms create a sense of expansion: "the flashing rays of the morning sun *on* the water, *on* the dew, *on* the bayonets of the troops crowded together *on* the banks and *at* Borodino." The first three repeated prepositional phrases beginning with "on" (*po* may also be translated "along") are marked by the particle of serial action (*to . . . to*, "now . . . now"), which further adds to the sense of expansion. The second set of prepositional phrases is also marked, but now by sounds. "Crowded together on the banks and at Borodino" repeats the sounds from the first set of phrases (то по in то*lpivshikhsja* по). "Banks" and "Borodino" are also related phonetically (*bere-*, *Boro-*). This pattern of a set of three prepositional phrases beginning with *po* followed by a second marked set of two prepositional phrases is repeated later to locate the expansion of the swirls of cannon smoke "along (*po*) the whole line, along the woods, and along the fields, in the hollows and on the summits." The mist thus merges syntactically with the smoke. The effect of all these repetitions is to enhance the sense of the moving and spreading action that is what Pierre sees.

This vision of the movement of life is then fully captured in the remarkable closing of this passage. The swirls of cannon smoke which arise "alone, in mass, a few, a lot" are referred to in the original by four adjectives all in the same form. (This rhetorical device called homoeoteleuton is one of Tolstoy's favorites.) Each adjective is preceded by the particle of serial action (*to*), which enhances the sense of the expansion and movement. These adjectives, futhermore, are arranged in two sets, in which the first looks at one small bit (alone, a few), the second at the whole bit (in mass, a lot). The effect of this series of four adjectives, which precede the noun "swirls" in the original, is to create the sense of continuing growth by the merging of a small entity into a larger entity, like the drops in the puddle of the aphorism. This sense of growth then surfaces in the four adverbial participles, which follow the noun in the original "swelling, breaking, swirling, merging." The first two of these participles are prefixed by the morpheme of dispersion (*raz*); the second of these has as its root the morpheme of growth, which resembles the morpheme of dispersion phonetically (*rast*). This second participle, therefore, not only repeats the morpheme of dispersion from the first participle; it also reduplicates it within the root. The verb imitates phonetically the action of dispersion (*razrastajas'*). But this action of dispersion is what melting is, and the ending of this participle contains the adverbial participle of the verb "to melt" (*taja*). The one word embodies and reveals the action of eternal life, eternal growth, eternal resurrection. The last of the four participles is made of a prefix which is the morpheme of togetherness (*s*) and a root which is the morpheme of pouring or flowing. This last is related to the liquid imagery, and the word appears in Pierre's dream of the globe of life. The word is "merging." The whole sequence thus ends with the key term which expresses the action of going forth and giving forth of self to other called love. The verbal and syntactical levels combine to embody and reveal that movement which is life.

Tolstoy also uses syntax to draw the reader into the emotional experience of a character. The simplest example is the description of Ivan Ilych's pain. "Suddenly he felt the old, familiar, hollow, gnawing pain, persistent, silent, serious." The piling up of adjectives, four before and three after the noun, creates the very effect of the relentlessness of the pain. Even after the noun it goes on and on. And this persistence is accompanied by the sameness of the feeling marked by the incessant homoeoteleuton, the repeated accusative case ending on all seven adjectives (*uju*). The syntax does not in any way imitate an action; it expresses a feeling. The homoeoteleuton creates the effect of a wailing sound. By this expressive syntax the reader is infected with Ivan Ilych's relentless suffering.

Expressive syntax is Tolstoy's most effective device for infecting the reader. With it he makes the signified feeling palpable. Prince Bolkonsky has received a letter from Kutuzov, informing him that from the lack of evidence to the contrary it is safe to assume that Prince Andrew is dead. Prince Bolkonsky does not tell Princess Mary of the letter or its contents, but she reads the message from the look on his face. What Princess Mary reads is what the reader feels.

> On her father's face, not a sad, not a beaten, but an angry face controlling itself unnaturally, she saw that right now there hung over her, about to crush her, a terrible misfortune she had not yet experienced, the one irreparable, incomprehensible misfortune, the death of one you love. (II,i,vii)

The sentence is divided in two by the simple subject and verb "she saw," which in the original surrounds the statements about what she saw on her father's face. What she saw is conveyed by four adjectival forms, all modifying the word "face" and having the same endings, "sad, beaten, angry, controlling itself." The first two of these adjectives are qualified by the negative particle. The second half of the sentence, all that follows the connective "that," renders Princess Mary's interpretation of what she reads on her father's face. It is what it means to her. This half of the sentence is introduced by the reduplicated particle of immediate imminence translated "right now" (*vot, vot*). What is immediately imminent is "misfortune," which in the original is the negated form of the important Tolstoyan word "happiness" (*neschast'e*). This word is repeated three times and itself is modified by three adjectival forms, all of which are themselves negated (*ne ispytannoe, ne popravimoe, nepostizhimoe*). These words are arranged in a crescendoing effect, so that the negatives resound as it were louder and louder until they burst forth in the end in the appositional phrase which defines their real meaning, "the death of one you love." The syntax thus moves toward the revelation of the meaning accompanied by the resounding negative to create the feeling of that "terrible, worst" misfortune. The sentence is performed by the narrator to pour Princess Mary's feeling into the reader.

The narrator's performance may take the form of a reenactment of the character's experience, so that the emotion of which the narrator tells seems to come directly from the character. Petya has gone off to war; the Rostovs are about to leave Moscow; and Countess Rostova is now concerned for the life of her youngest.

> While Nicholas alone was in danger, it seemed to the Countess (and she was even repentent of this), that she loved her eldest more than all her other children, but when the youngest, that naughty boy Petya, who studied badly, broke everything in the house, and pestered everyone, that pug-nosed Petya with his merry black eyes, his fresh rosy complexion, and that fuzz just coming out on his cheeks, when Petya ended up there with those big, terrible, cruel men who fight *something* there and find something joyful in it, then it seemed to his mother that it was him she loved more, much more, than all her children. (III,iii,xii)

This delightful sentence is made of an uneven contrast. In the first part the narrator tells of Countess Rostova's former favoritism. It is stated as a fact, something she regretted but something she did feel. In the second half of the sentence, the narrator turns to the present moment, but he does not just tell of the mother's present special love for her youngest. This part of the sentence is made of the characteristic three-fold repetitions, but it is not really the syntax as such which conveys the emotion. Rather, here the narrator begins to speak as if he were Countess Rostova. The mother's recollections of her youngest son are told as if by her, and they bring to the fore her feelings as she imagines her son "there with those big, terrible, cruel men." To her the enemy is not the French, but those grown men who have taken away her child. The war is seen through the eyes and in the words of a loving mother back home, ignorant of the cause and purpose of war, but not of its dangers. She knows they fight "something" (Tolstoy emphasizes her exasperated ignorance with italics) and that they find some mysterious pleasure in this, but this has nothing to do with her world and her love for Petya, which is right now "more, much more" than any other love she has had. In the entire second half of the sentence, the narrator no longer tells: he performs, he becomes Countess Rostova, he reexperiences what she feels and expresses this feeling as it were in her words. For a moment the reader is drawn into the Countess' sphere of experience; he shares with her her way of being in the world.

Tolstoy's narration by performance can be contrasted with Dostoevsky's narrative technique. In Dostoevsky the narrator stumbles over his words as he tries to get out what he has to say. He seems to be speaking spontaneously. His words gush forth with all the quirks and inconsistencies and irrelevancies that make for the delight of Dostoevsky's manner of writing. It seems that reality is so vast and varied that the narrator cannot put it all into words and certainly not at this moment. But in Dostoevsky this moment is all-important. All is narrated at a fever-pitch. This sense of urgency is fundamental to Dostoevsky's narrative technique. Tolstoy is not interested in a sense of urgency. His narratives are highly controlled. Tolstoy rewrote *War and Peace* many times over a period of nearly ten years. For Tolstoy the words are already at hand, and he wants to communicate the full feeling of which the words speak. The words do not gush forth. They are highly organized, as though they must be in precisely this order. It is this precise order of sound and rhythm that Tolstoy needs in order to express feeling. He performs his sentences by means of complex phonetic, verbal, and syntactical organization.

This complexity of organization which results in a narrative performance is what lies behind the peculiar stylistic feature of *War and Peace*, the extended and obviously contrived sentence. Rostov's moment at the Emperor's review of the troops is preceded by two such sentences, one right after the other. The narrator sets the stage for Rostov's intoxicated ecstasy of self-forgetting by presenting the reader with this image of the troops moving into their review formations. The two sentences reiterate the movement from general to particular experiences that characterized the representation of Rostov at the review. The first sentence depicts the mass formation.

Now moved thousands of feet and bayonets with their banners unfurled, and at the officers' commands they halted, did an about-face and lined up in ranks, while going past other (*drugie*) such masses of infantry in different (*drugikh*) uniforms; now the rhythmic hoofbeats and clanking of the showy cavalry in blue, red, and green braided uniforms sounded forth with the smartly dressed band mounted on black, roan, and grey horses in front; now spreading out with its bronzy clatter of the polished, glistening cannons shaking on their carriages and its smell of linstock, the artillery crawled between the infantry and cavalry and took up its appointed places. (I,iii,viii)

This sentence is made of three parts. Each section focuses on a different military group: infantry, cavalry, artillery. Each section is introduced by the particle of serial action, "now" (*to*). In each section what immediately follows this particle characterizes the whole part: (1) the general sense of movement which is stated by the verb "moved" and then expressed in the three following verbs, which stand side by side and are themselves followed by an adverbial participle made from a prefixed verb of motion; (2) the physical sensation of sound, "the rhythmic hoofbeats and clanking" which then bursts forth from the "band in front" (3) the "spreading out" of the physical sensations from sound to smell. Each section ends with a repetition which marks some secondary aspect of the perception of the military divisions: the variety of types in the infantry signaled by the twice-repeated word "different" (*drugie, drugikh*); the variegated colors of the cavalry, expressed in the two series of color adjectives; the interspersal of the artillery among the other divisions, marked by the repetition of their names next to each other (*mezhdu pekhotej i kavaleriej artillerija*). This last repetition sums up the sentence in abstract terms even as it closes it with a sense of finality and totality. This sense of totality is the aim as well as the end of this sentence, which is contrived to convey the feel of the whole mass coming into being. The one sentence contains all its variety in the one unit.

This combined sense of variety and unity also characterizes the second sentence, which turns from the depiction of the army to the experience of the men in the army.

Not only the generals in full parade uniform with their thick and thin waists drawn into the utmost, their red necks propped up by their decorations, not only the pomaded officers dressed to the hilt, but every soldier with his washed and shaven face and his weapons polished to the fullest possible shine, and every horse groomed till its coat glowed like satin and its wetted mane lay smooth hair upon hair—all felt that what was taking place was serious, significant, and solemn.

This sentence divides in two, the first half being the complex and variegated subject which is then summed up by the word "all" and followed by the simple predicate which unites everyone in the one feeling. The subject comprises four groups of beings which are presented in hierarchical order and are themselves divided into two parts. The sentence opens with the phrase "not only" which precedes the "generals" and is repeated again in reference to the "officers." This introductory phrase serves to isolate the commanders from the masses and yet to imply that they all belong together. The second half of the subject also repeats an introductory word, but the distributive "each" shifts the focus from the group to the individual members of the group. The commanders are characterized by their costumery and cosmetics: their bodies are covered and contorted by their clothing and medallions. The narrator brings their physical appearance into focus by the sound repetition: "p" in the "full parade" uniforms (*polnoj paradnoj*), "t" in "their thick and thin waists drawn in" (*peretjanutymi . . . tolstymi i tonkimi talijami*) and "sh," "f," "kh" in "necks . . . wearing scarves and all their decorations" (*shejami, v sharfakh i vsekh ordenakh*). The similarity in the group is marked by homoeoteleuton: the piled-up instrumental plural endings associated with the generals (*peretjanutymi, tolstymi i tonkimi talijami i krasnevshimi, podpërtymi vorotnikami, shejami*) and the twice-repeated past passive participles which modify the "officers" (*pripomazhennye, rasfranchënnye*). The masses, which include both men and animals, are characterized by their well-groomed preparedness, marked by the thrice-repeated past passive participles made with the same prefix (*vymytym, vychishchennoj, vykholennaja*). The focus turns from the costumes to the body. This hierarchy, as always in the novel, moves from the pretentious to the natural. This movement from the superficial above to the real below is what distinguishes the second sentence from the first. If the first sentence represents the formation of the troops in all their variety, but still all together at one in one sentence, the second sentence looks to the authentic experience of this moment: what it feels like to be all together in one formation. The mark of the authenticity of the "serious, significant, and solemn" sense of the moment is not just its all-encompassing embrace, but its capacity to touch even the honest goodness of a horse. This second sentence, then, pronounces a judgment. The narrator values such an experience of total unity, even as he clearly does not approve of the decked-out and decorated commanders. The syntax and sound organization of this sentence are calculated to pronounce sentence on the experience of these men. In the performance of the words, the narrator speaks forth his opinion about what he describes. He also prepares the reader for Rostov's experience of being "a part of that enormous whole" by these two sentences which are performed as a prefiguration and paradigm of Rostov's self-forgetting moment of belonging.

Judgmental tone is common in Tolstoy's narrative voice. It is often combined with the contrived sentence to create an ironic performance. In contrast to the lady who just gathered up "her Negroes and her jestors" and left Moscow, thereby "simply and truthfully doing that great deed (*delo*) which saved Russia," Count Rostopchin is described as helpless despite all his efforts to help (III,iii,v). The following sentence closes the section which characterizes this man.

Count Rostopchin, who now shamed those who were leaving, now had government offices removed, now distributed useless weapons to the drunken rabble, now had processions displaying the icons, now forbade Father Augustine to remove any icons or relics of the saints, now seized all the private carts in Moscow, now had the balloon being constructed by Leppich removed on one hundred and thirty six carts, now hinted that he would burn Moscow, now related how he had burned his own house and had written a proclamation to the French in which he solemnly reproached them for destroying his orphanage, now claimed the glory for burning Moscow, now repudiated it, now ordered the people to catch all the spies and bring them to him, now reproached them for all this, now let Madame Aubert-Chalmé, who was the center of the whole Moscow French population, remain in the city, but ordered the venerable old postmaster Klyucharev to be arrested and exiled for no particular offense, now assembled the people at Three Hills to fight the French, now to get rid of the people gave them a man to be killed while he himself drove away through a rear gate, now said that he would not survive Moscow's misfortune, now wrote in albums French verses about his participation in it, this person did not understand the significance of the event that was being accomplished, but wanted just to do something himself, to shock someone, to accomplish something patriotically heroic and like a little boy he gamboled over the momentous and unavoidable event, the abandoning and burning of Moscow, and with his little hand tried now to stimulate, now to stay, the enormous popular tide that bore him along with it.

The sentence falls into two parts. In the first half the narrator lists the many and contradictory efforts that Count Rostopchin made in his attempt to be the administer of the Russian heart. The whole list is a relative clause with the many verbs having the one subject "who." Each verb is preceded by the particle of serial action, "now . . . now" (to . . . to). This consistent coupling of contradictory actions in a series of seemingly endless repetitions creates the effect of massive confusion. The whole phrase which lists Rostopchin's efforts is itself an effort without any apparent end or purpose. The syntax conveys this endless and purposeless effort. In its obvious cumulative effect, however, the phrase conveys an attitude to the effort, a growing impatience, disrespect, even annoyance, for the one who does such consistently contradictory things. The narrator's judgment speaks through the syntax even before it is stated. This statement of assessment comprises the second half of the sentence. What is striking is the narrator's image of the little boy gamboling through the flow of history, trying to direct it with his little hands. The disproportion between the labored efforts told in a labored manner and the frivolous reality conveyed by the image becomes clear. The whole first half of this sentence is designed to appear overwhelming, so that when this appearance is revealed for what it is, the contradictory "stimulating" and "staying" of the flow, which is the sum meaning of the relative clause and in its syntax and expression a repetition of it, the reader himself will feel the sense of the futility of the effort in face of the flow of the tide. The sentence is top-heavy with effort and in the end topples over in an inevitable collapse that bears the relative clause away with it. Such syntax is expressive of the narrator's own feeling. It conveys its judgment as it tells it.[2]

---

[2] The peculiar features of these extended sentences in *War and Peace* have been imaginatively described by S. Solov'ëv in "O nekotorikh osobennostjakh stilisticheskogo masterstva Tolstogo," printed in the useful collection of essays edited by S. Mashinskij, *O mire Tolstogo* (Moscow, 1978), pp. 454-475. Tolstoy's verbal style is also discussed by A. V. Chicherin, *O jazyke i stile romana-epopei "Vojna i mir"* (Lvov, 1956) and *Idei i stil'* (Moscow, 1965), pp. 216-261. See also A. N. Kozhin, *Jazyk L. N. Tolstogo* (Moscow, 1979). All analyses and interpretations of Tolstoy's style are my own.

This tendency to convey judgment through the manner of the telling results in the satirical tone that is so common in Tolstoy. But expressive syntax is not the only source of this tone. Often Tolstoy conveys his judgment through a kind of word play that borders on the pun. Ivan Ilych is ill, and his wife has had to put up with his "difficult character" (iv). She learns that it is best to suffer in silence and then puts "her humility to good use."

> Having decided that her husband had a terrible character and that he made life unhappy, she started to pity (*zhalet'*) herself. And the more she pitied herself, the more she hated her husband. She started to wish (*zhelat'*) he were dead, but she could not wish that because then there would be no salary (*zhalovan'e*). And that just made her more annoyed (*razdrazhalo*) at him. She considered herself unhappy just because even his death could not save her, and she got annoyed, tried to hide this, and this hidden annoyance of hers increased his annoyance.

This passage displays Tolstoy's power of psychological analysis at its height. His devastating dissection of the relationship between self-pity and resentment is clear even as it breaks through the proprieties of behavior and feeling to reveal a terrible self-interest in the face of death. It would be tragic if it were not satiric. The narrator stays the tragic with his punning words. He has a contemptuous smile on his lips. Only at the end, when he turns his focus from the wife to the victim, does the real import of her drama of self-pity and resentment come to the fore. She makes her husband suffer all the more. The puns do more than show contempt, however. The repetition of the morpheme of pity-love (*zhal-*) and its transformation into its etymologically related word "salary" and then into "desire" (*zhel-*) and finally "annoyance" (*razdra*ZHAL) creates an effect of inevitability, as though Ivan Ilych's wife were an actor in a drama which was being played out through her. The paratactical syntax adds to this sense of inevitability. That the punning words reiterate the central theme of work—the life lived by the "inertia of salary" leads to the sickness of self-pity until death is seen and one takes pity on others—only adds to this sense of inevitability. In this passage the narrator expresses through his language both contempt for the wife and horror at this inevitability, although none of this is stated as such. In the verbal

performance the narrator conveys his feelings about what the words signify.

Puns, obviously contrived syntax, whether expressive or imitative, and focus on the sounds and rhythms of the words—all combine in Tolstoy to create an infectious language. Such infectious language does not turn the reader away from the signified world, as in ornamental or lyrical prose, where the language itself becomes the object of the reader's attention. Infectious language resembles more the language of oratory or homily. That Tolstoy's best articles on religion resemble sermons may be a telling point. Infectious language makes use of rhetorical devices in order to be convincing. It wants to convey a truth, be it called a feeling, image, or idea, which the reader will automatically internalize as his truth. Infectious language does not allow for analysis or dissection even when it itself analyzes and dissects. Infectious language does not argue or persuade; it coerces The reader is left no choice; for the moment he feels what the narrator or character feels. As Tolstoy said, "The aim of the artist is not to resolve irrefutably some question, but to make (*zastavit'*) people love life in all its infinite, inexhaustible manifestations" (61,100;1865). Infectious language is what gives Tolstoy's fiction this compelling quality which *makes* people feel what the author wants them to feel.

The following sentence from *War and Peace* combines the many devices at Tolstoy's disposal to create through such infectious language one compelling image which contains and expresses the fundamental crisis around which the novel is built and to which the characters are called to respond. It is in a sense the novel in miniature, a characteristic example of its style, a reiteration of its theme, and an expression of its existential feeling.

> On the narrow dam at Augesd on which for so many years the old miller in his tassled cap used to sit peacefully with his fishing line while his grandson with his short sleeves rolled up would fiddle with the floundering silver fish in the pail, on that dam along which for so many years Moravians in shaggy caps and blue jackets used to drive along peacefully on two-horse carts loaded with wheat, and covered with flour drive away on that same dam on white carts, on that narrow dam now midst wagons and cannons, underneath horses and between wheels men thronged disfigured with the fear of death, crushing each other,

dying, stepping over the dying, and killing each other just so that having gone a few steps they themselves could likewise be killed. (I,iii,xviii)

This sentence is divided into three parts, the first two of which are past images "on the narrow dam" and "on this dam," which stand in contrast to the final and present image, "on this narrow dam." These introductory prepositional phrases point out the place, even as the last one combines the first two and delineates the place anew. The temporal contrast divides the images, not just into past and present, but into a past both frequentative (*sizhival*) and of long duration, "for so many years," and a present that is in progress "now." The past images are pictures of peace marked specifically by the adverb "peacefully" (*mirno*), repeated after the first main verb of each of the first two parts of the sentence. The first past image is static; peace is imagined as the restful labor of fishing and the playful idling of fiddling with the fish. In this static image of peace there is a picture of essential life, the gathering of food and the relatedness of the generations. Each of these participants in the task of life is marked by his own sound leitmotif: the old man by *s,l,k* (*sizhivaʟ v koʟpake starichoк meʟ'niк s udochкami*) and his grandson by *r,v,b,p* (*ʀukava ʀuʙashki peʀeʙiʀal . . . seʀeʙʀjanuju tʀepeshchushchuju ʀyʙu*). This sound focus enhances the idyllic quality of the picture and places the grandfather and grandson in the reader's presence. The second past image is dynamic: the two main verbs are verbs of motion, affixed with prefixes of direction which isolate the coming and going of essential life, the transforming of crops into food. In contrast to these past images the present image is chaotic. After the temporal indicator "now" in the place of the repeated adverb "peacefully" there are three adverbial prepositional phrases modifying the main verb: people throng everywhere, "midst," "underneath," "between." In the present image, however, the focus is not on the main verb, but on a series of adverbial participles which depend on it, "crushing," "dying," "stepping over," "killing," "having gone" and the past passive participle "be killed," which ends the whole sentence, even as it is the aim and end of the action. This is what is happening. This focus on the crushing, killing, and dying is enhanced by sound organization: alliteration (*ɒavja ɒrug ɒruga*), homoeoteleuton (*umirajа, shagajа . . . ubivajа*), and consonance (*ʙyt' tochno tak zhe uʙitymi*). The aim and end of the action is marked by the pun, "could . . . be killed" (*ʙyt'* . . .

uʙɪᴛ*ymi*), which in the original embodies and reveals the existential dilemma between life (*byt'*, "to be") and death (*ubitymi*, "be killed"). In the chaos of the present crush of humanity, human relatedness, stressed by the twice-repeated "each other," has gone awry: life has been replaced by death. In the war there is no peace, just dying. However, the word dying (uᴍɪʀ*aja*, uᴍɪʀ*ajushchikh*) itself contains the very root for peace (*mir*) which supplied the adverb "peacefully" in the past images and thus in punning fashion sees the scene anew. This whole sentence, with its considered syntax, sound organization, and poignant puns builds to a compelling image of killing and being killed. With its infectious language it pours into the reader the horror of war in contrast to life-giving and life-sustaining peace. The narrator's verbal performance is calculated to evoke the reader's knowledge of this existential feeling.

What unites all the unique elements in Tolstoy's style is a kind of repetition in which there is an element of sameness and an element of difference. The parallelism of delineated segments is designed to create this paradoxical effect of variety and unity: death is death, but in the story there are three deaths. The paradigmatic actions also achieve this same effect, for each action is different, yet they all share the paradigm. Units in Tolstoy's fiction are yoked by repeated phrases which also unite what is disparate, in a sentence, a paragraph, one delineated segment, or several. The most common kind of sentence is made of several repeated syntactical units, and adjectives and adverbs come piled up usually in threes: the forms are the same, the content is different. And Tolstoy loves both puns and homoeoteleuton, which are the purest verbal form of this unity in variety available to prose (poetry has rhyme and meter). At every level of his fiction Tolstoy strives to create a sense of oneness within variety. His prophetic intent is to pour out his sense of life in all its fullness in order to infect his readers with his feel for the oneness of all being. "Unity in variety" is Tolstoy's definition of life. It can also serve as a definition of his verbal style of life.

THE THEOLOGY OF ANARCHISM

In intoxication and infection, consciousness is seized by some foreign agent and whisked off to some alien land. The going forth from self to other in transcendence is perverted by an act of coercion which invades the privacy of the self and distorts the vision of one-self. To the extent that the self is led out of its isolation and back to its native residence with all its relatives all together at one, but each in its own way, the coercive act is a covert form of the free going forth which is the foundation of every self. Mostly, however, this coercion seems to be an unfortunate and not necessary condition of life in common with others.

Tolstoy's first image of this common life, itself the source for Pierre's globe of life, stresses this potential for coercion. In this image, which appears in a variant text of the essay *Who Learns To Write from Whom?* (1862), Tolstoy imagines the self as a "perfect, mathematically correct, living sphere developing by its own power" (*sila*) (8,433). This sphere is the "first image of righteousness, of correctness" (*pervoobraz pravednosti, pravil'nosti*) and itself a metaphor for the child who is, as Tolstoy said in the essay, the "first image of harmony, truth, beauty, and goodness" (8,322). Rousseau's "great words," that "man is born perfect," are taken to mean literally that each child is thus conceived, and then these words are translated into the language of Eastern Christian thought, with its "first image," its classic universals of truth, beauty, and goodness, and its ideal of "eternal harmony" (8,434). This child is to be father to the man. But, once born into this world, this harmonious sphere must coexist with the "aggregate" of like, living, developing spheres. Each sphere in the aggregate grows according to an "immutable law": its "task" is to grow while retaining its perfect "form." Like the liquid drops in Pierre's globe of life, the spheres bump into each other, causing "compression" (*szhatie*) and "expansion" (*rasshirenie*), but the ideal form of each, Tolstoy insists, can be maintained. No matter how distorted by life's hard knocks, "the original features of eternal harmony always remain," and one can always "hope to attain at least some rapprochement with the correctness of harmony." If the spheres are allowed to take the knocks as they come, this freedom will let the "inner power" retain the original harmonious shape. What destroys this harmonious growth is "coercion" (*nasilie*). One sphere tries to guide or shape another. This is what happens in most forms of rearing and education which Tolstoy characterized in his essay *Education and Culture* (1862) as the "compulsory, coercive effect of one person on another with the aim of forming the kind of person we think is good" (8,215). Society shapes and distorts the individual.

This conception of coercion, the exercise of power by some over others, is what unites Tolstoy's theories of education and government. In his essays on education he writes of ways of rearing children and imparting knowledge which are free of this coercive element. The child should be guided by his "inner power." In his later essays on government Tolstoy sees coercion as the cohesive force that keeps people together. All power is traced to the threat or reality of violence (*nasilie* means both "coercion" and "violence"), and freedom can be achieved only by the elimination of this violence. Non-resistance to evil in this context means the refusal to fight violence with violence and the rejection of coercion as the glue of the commonwealth. Freedom means tearing off the chains of the social bond to release the "inner power" which is assumed will find its accord with all others in some sort of providential harmony. Tolstoy measures all social and political organization of life against this theological ideal of harmonious community.

In this life "every arrangement" of human life "is founded on coercion and supported by coercion" (56,9;1907). "The state is just the product of coercion by conquests. All theories of social contract, etc., are justifications après coup" (55,110; 1904). For Tolstoy this is true, regardless of the form of state government, none of which escapes his penetrating and indiscriminating sarcasm: "When out of 100 one person rules over 99, that's unjust; it's despotism. When 10 rule over 90, that's just as unjust; it's oligarchy. When 51 rule over 49 (and then only in one's imagination, in effect it's once again 10 or 11 of those 51); then it's perfectly just, it's freedom" (76,55;1905). While Tolstoy has especial contempt for democratic forms of government because in his opinion they are the most deceptive, he also argues against Marx's assumption that in communism "capital will be transferred from the hands of the private individuals to the hands of the government, which represents the people, to the hands of the workers" by asserting his one major political axiom upon which his criticism of all forms of state government rests: the notion that the "government represents the people is a fiction, a deception" (53,206;1898). "If there were an arrangement in which government actually expressed the will of the people," Tolstoy argues against Marx's theory but in essence against all theories of representative government, "then in that government there would be no need for coercion, there would be no need for government in the sense of rule" (*vlast'*). For Tolstoy there is no way in which government can represent people. "The government is a den of thieves" (55,10;1904).

How this den of thieves maintains the fiction that it represents the people and therefore can retain the power to rule over them is accomplished by what Tolstoy calls, in *The Kingdom of God Is Within You*, the "circle of coercion" (28,152;1893). The circle begins with a "deterrent": the government of whatever form is made to seem "sacred and immutable"; attempts to change it are punished by expelling the perpetrators from the community and confining them in solitude, where they perish and are forgotten (28,152-53). Most forms of modern technology, such as "railroads, telephone, telegraphs, and photographs," serve the police and other government administrators in their work of deterring those who would threaten the rule of the government. The second form of coercion combines slavery and bribery. The government administration levies taxes on the working people which force the people into financial servitude to the administrators whose own livelihood is derived from these very taxes. The working people are forced to follow the will of the administrators, and the administrators are bribed to do what the government wants. The third form of coercion is the most pervasive and effective. The government uses a method of "hypnotization organized in a most complex way" to control the minds of all its subjects. Through education, through state forms of religion, through patriotic sentiment, through control of printed matter, the state shapes the minds and views of its subjects. One of the most effective forms of this hypnotization is the media event: "As soon as an event, the result of accidental circumstances, becomes significant and therefore stands out slightly, then the organs of the press single out the significance of the event, and then the public pays even more attention to it. The public's attention causes the press to consider the event with more attention and detail. Public interest increases even more, and the organs of the press competing with each other respond to the demands of the public" (35,260;1904). Such media events result in mass hysteria, where people will believe anything at all, even that the government that oppresses them represents them. Their function is to keep people from thinking clearly about anything at all.

Most hypnotization is accomplished through intoxication: people are kept in a "state of stupefaction" through religious ceremonies, political spectacles, popular entertainment, prostitution, and legalized mood-altering substances themselves taxed by the government (28,154). Such intoxication usually follows the Tolstoyan law that as a "general rule, not a paradox, the more stupid, often the more immoral something is, the more it is surrounded by the festive: the popes, archbishops, parliaments, liturgies, coronations, theaters, operas, bordellos" (55,19;1904). Through intoxication the splendiferous masks stupidity and sin. This particular process of intoxicating hypnotization is then applied in a special way to one group which guarantees the coercion of all others.

> They take people at a young age when no clear conceptions of morality have managed to take shape in them. Once these people have been separated from all natural, human conditions of life such as home, family, native land, and sensible labor, they are locked up together in barracks, dressed in special garb, and under the influence of shouts, drums, music, and shining objects they are forced daily to perform special movements designed for this and by these means are brought into such a state of hypnosis that they stop being people and become insensate machines subjected to the hypnotist. (28,154-155)

With this return of the intoxicated Tolstoyan soldier from the diary entry of 1857, the "circle of coercion is closed." The army is the strongest glue in the commonwealth.

The most effective form of coercion, however, is self-coercion. The fiction and power of government is maintained in the final analysis because the people need to believe in it. What happens in society is that the attempts to intoxicate the people become so effective that everyone eventually lives in a state of total stupefaction, blind to the fact that the emperor has no clothes.

> The intoxication experienced by people during such events as parades, crusades, ecclesiastical ceremonies, and coronations is a temporary, acute state, but there are other chronic, constant states of intoxication which are experienced by people who have some sort of power, ranging from the power of the tsar to the policeman on the beat, and by people subjected to power and thus in a state of intoxication through servility, justifying their state as all slaves have done and do by ascribing the greatest significance and dignity to those whom they obey. (28,253)

Thus everyone in the state is brought into accord through some sort of participation in power. The overt power over someone provides a sense of strength and worth. The "inner power" (sila) to become oneself is replaced by one's "power" (vlast') over others. What is more, society is a hierarchy of power, and most people are subject to people above them. This servility itself, however, helps perpetrate the myth of power: "We respect and idolize people—courtiers, the tsar, clergy, the hierarchy, etc.—only because the higher the one we submit to (for our own benefit), the more we are justified not only in other people's eyes, but also in our own" (54,6;1900). We are all oppressed, and we all pay homage to our oppressors, not out of fear, however, but because of self-interest. The lofty master raises the lowly servant's self-esteem. Power is sustained because we adulate the powerful in order to feel powerful ourselves. The fiction of government rests on a failure of self.

Tolstoy's view of the governed society betrays a revealing paradox. On the one hand, he sees the whole social and political arrangement in any society stemming from a few alien individuals who usurp the power to rule from each member of that society who seems to possess that power naturally. The "den of thieves" are foreign conquerors who have established all the "external laws" that "now hinder people from living according to reason" (55,229;1906). A few coerce the many. On the other hand, Tolstoy believes that in a governed society all are responsible for the coercive social and political arrangement, but no one wants to see this clearly. Instead, "all people bound by the state order transfer responsibility for what they do onto others" (28,252). They "lose the moral awareness of their responsibility" because they are convinced that what they do is commanded by someone above whom they revere, or needed by someone below whom they wish to help. Those who blindly accept that political order and those who rebel against it, as well as those who would make it better, all end up affirming the fundamental dualism that splits any society into the oppressors and the oppressed. Conservatives reaffirm the old coercion. Radicals and revolutionaries establish a new form of it. Democratic liberal reformers, worst of all, play a "child's game" of upholding the old and then taking pot shots at it "with its own weapons" (55,10;1904). While a few coerce the many, all participate in the power of coercion. The only escape from this circle of coercion is a negative action. The harmonious community begins,

not with reaffirmation, revolution, or reform, but with the rejection of any idea or act of coercion.

The rejection of coercion means primarily the absolute refusal to participate in it. This rejection does not guarantee freedom from being coerced by others, only freedom from coercing others. This negative freedom from coercing others, however, is always assumed to release the fundamental freedom to be yourself. "A person who endures acts of violence can be free, but not a person who commits them" (56,85;1907). The paradox of power is that "people who submit to any power (*vlast'*) whatsoever are beyond any comparison freer than people who participate in power" (55,288;1906). In fact, participation in power harms the participant. "The power of one person over another ruins first of all the one who exercises the power" (55,223;1906). The victimizer is the victim. Power corrupts because it makes a person seem independent and self-sufficient. He becomes self-interested and self-enclosed. "The usual corrupting effects of power are self-importance, pride, vanity, and mainly disrespect for the person" (55,206;1906). Participation in power cuts off the flow of *love for.*

The exercise of power, coercion, or violence is a violation of the true self. It is the source of the "immorality" and "indifference" of both Europeans and Americans, Tolstoy argues, because they are corrupted by living in "constitutional states," which implies their "participation in the government" (55,131;1905). The Russian people, however, Tolstoy agrees with the slavophiles, "avoid power" and are "ready to leave it to bad people rather than dirty themselves with it." In this they are right, Tolstoy believes, because "the position of a person under the rule of a tyrant promotes moral life much more than the position of a voter, a participant in power." Furthermore, Tolstoy affirms that not just Slavic people, but "all people inherently," have this "awareness" of the necessity to avoid power. This is, after all, implied by the very notion of the true self. The paradox of this inherent need to refuse to participate in power, however, is that "the possibility for despotism is based on it." The negative action on which the harmonious community is grounded is itself the foundation for the possibility of the divided community of governed society.

"My anarchism," Tolstoy said, "is only an application of Christianity to human relationships" (55,239;1906). The first principle of this anarchism, as we have seen, is the "ignoring of any external political forms of life" which always divide people, coupled with life lived "by each for his spiritual rather than physical 'I' " (56,27;1907). Community is achieved, regardless of the social and political order, through the unhampered expression of each individual will. In this community all are free and equal. It must be remembered, of course, that the "Christian concept of equality understood with pride rather than humility leads not to the unity but the disunity (raz"edinenie) of people" (56,33;1907). This unhampered expression of each individual will which guarantees freedom and equality, therefore, means nothing other than the expression of pure *love for*. This *love for*, however, not only is the ground for the possibility of despotism; it is that spontaneous, unmotivated giving forth that is all content unlimited by form. There is no form, structure, or arrangement of life that can contain it. "Every form of life is not only spiritual stagnation but an encumbrance to true life" (63,411;1886).

No social order, it would seem, could be adequate to this metaphysical ideal of *love for*.

> The life of each of us rests not in this or that arrangement but in the common rather than the personal good. The common good is obtained not by an arrangement with arguments, anger, and coercion, but only by love. The main thing is that this is possible. It is in my power and characteristic of my nature. An arrangement is not in my power and against my nature. (56,120;1908)

To Tolstoy there is no political arrangement of the community that does not divide and coerce; yet what must be sought, if there is to be a common good, is unity. In the human community, however, there not only can be no division or coercion; there can be no conscious attempt to achieve unity or freedom. Community cannot be arranged.

> The attainment of cooperation, communism, community (obshchestvennost') ... will come not from organization—we can never predict future organization—but only from each person following the undarkened urge of his heart, conscience, reason, faith, the law of life, or call it what you will. Bees and ants live socially (obshchestvenno), not because they know the arrangement which is most advantageous for them and follow it—they have no idea of the expediency, harmony, or rationality of the

beehive or anthill as they appear to us. Rather, they yield to the instinct (we say) placed in them; they submit to their law of life, being wise not slyly but simply. I imagine that if the bees could think up a better arrangement of their social life through something above their instinct (as we call it), above their consciousness of their law, then they would think up a life in which they would perish. In this consciousness of the law there is something less and more than reasoning. It is given just to lead to that single, narrow path of truth along which man and humanity must go. (52,9-10;1891)

The human community does not come from some external structure which is first thought out or reasoned about and then applied to the lives of people as some external law to which they must submit. The community comes from each individual's following the "undarkened urge of his heart." Each human being must free himself from the intoxicants and passions that stupefy his "consciousness of the law" so that, like the animals and the insects, he can be "wise not slyly but simply." Community can be achieved only when man abandons his rationalizations and organizations and becomes attuned to his inner reason. Community comes to the pure of heart.

As in much Eastern Christian thought, the animal for Tolstoy is the image, not of some non-rational and therefore dumb beast, but of a being whose knowledge is not divided by the darkened urges of a reasoning mind. The ants and the bees yield to their inner law of life and attain "cooperation, communism, community." With "organizations" they have individual freedom in the sense that each follows his inner law, and this freedom results automatically in unity. There is no clash between the individual urges of the ants and bees. The "undarkened urge" called instinct in animals and conscience, reason, faith, the law of life in man is darkened by man's own self-interest, and so it seems that "each has his own reason" (50,82;1889). While the ants and bees seem to be and act all in agreement even as they follow their own inner law, human beings listen to their darkened reason and find themselves in discord. They have no common truth and cannot find the single, narrow path along which they must go. Unlike the ants and bees, human beings are divided by their reasoning and cannot agree about the truth, "not because there is no such truth, but because they do not all agree." The truth along whose path mankind must go is a truth whose certitude is assured by common agreement. The community of freedom and unity must be a community of all together, at one in truth. When all agree on the truth, all will be united and free.

> The world is a huge temple in which light falls in the center. All people who love light strive toward it, and from the various directions of the world they gather there in the center and unite. Unity is achieved only when you seek, not unity, but truth. Usually people gather at the dark side-altars, and, with unity as an aim, they round up and attract people to them. But at another side-altar other people are doing the same thing. Seek truth and you will find unity. Seek unity and you will retreat from truth. (50,92;1889)

The image that provides Tolstoy with his clearest vision of the human community, of all together at one in truth, is the living organism. The individual and society are related as cell to body.

> The closer the state of a society is to an organism, the more tightly its parts are bound together in such a way that each part is concerned about the good of the whole (*tseloe*), the more the form depends on the content and vice versa. In that union of people when all members united together participate in the decisions common for all and freely submit to them, as it happens in small communes, the form which flows from the nature of the union, from the content, will always be the same: the equality of all members and the free fulfillment of positions established by common agreement. In the union of people where not all people participate in common decisions and are compelled by force, as in ancient Greece, Rome, Turkey, France, England, and Russia, the forms, since they flow from chance or the will of one or several people, will be infinitely variable and not dependent on the content. (76,39-40;1905)

Underlying Tolstoy's vision of anarchistic community is the assumption that the individual is not a self-enclosed and self-interested monad seeking its own good with assurance that the firm hand of providence will guarantee the harmony of all. This is not Adam Smith's world. To be sure, Tolstoy believed that in order "not to fear non-rule (*bezvlastie*), anarchism" one has to believe that "God gov-

erns the universe" (*mir*) (55,243;1906). But Tolstoy's God is everything that exists all together at one in the harmony of truth and every
individual to the extent that he is open to all and in accord with all is
a manifestation of that God. Anarchistic community is possible because human beings are not individuals, at war each with each. They
are, by their nature and for their own good, concerned with the
whole. They are monads of *love for*, the content from which the form
of their community must flow. Each individual, like each cell, lives
for itself, but this self can live only to the extent that it is related to
and in harmony with all other cells that comprise the one body, the
form which flows from the cellular content. Only such a society
could be adequate to the metaphysical ideal of *love for*. The Tolstoyan anarchist society is a vision of a transfigured universe of all
together.

> Man has to do consciously what animals do unconsciously. Even
> before attaining bee or ant communes, man has to get to the
> level of the beast from whom he is still so far off: he must not
> fight (wage war) over nonsense, nor overeat nor indulge in prom-
> iscuity, and then he will have to get to the level of the bees and
> ants, as is now beginning to be done in communes. First the fam-
> ily, then the commune, then the state, then humanity, then
> everything living, then the whole universe, like God
> (51,88;1890)

Life in this world, in culture and governed society, has lost the
original paradisical community of *love for*. The purpose of life is to
return to this state of unity. The loss of this loving unity is the cause
and condition of the possibility of intoxication. The self that goes
and gives forth loses its freedom to *love for*, and, instead of striving
toward the other, the self is lured and attracted. This capacity to be
led on and ruled by others in a state of loss of self, which resembles
so closely the free going and giving but is its opposite, makes social
life and political organization possible. The kingdom of unity and
freedom that man is called to reestablish on earth begins with the
sobering of consciousness that follows the withdrawal from the state
of intoxication.

The link between Tolstoy's aesthetic and political theory rests in
his vision of the human community of all together, each in his own
way. The anarchist community of human relationships that Tolstoy

envisions as the political ideal is attained in the moment of aesthetic experience when the isolation and enmity of this life is suddenly transformed into the loving unity of the shared common feeling. In this ideal moment, as in that ideal society, the self is most fulfilled and true when it freely participates with all others in this moment or in that society. The images in Tolstoy's fiction which are the exemplary types of these two ideals, aesthetic and political, are Petya's dream of his fugue music (IV,iii,x) and the guerrilla warfare that assured the Russian victory. In both images each particular entity, be it sound or person, expresses itself and thereby something in common with all others: in Petya's fugue all the sounds and tunes express Petya's music; in the war all the soldiers express the spirit of the army. All are together, but each in his own way. The perfect type of this Tolstoyan community, an image which combines as it were the aesthetic and political moment, is the final moment of the hunt in *War and Peace*: Each hunter hunts for himself, yet the victory is common to all and expressed in Natasha's resounding squeal of delight. Tolstoy's aesthetic and political theories are the articulations of these images, which express his fundamental sense and highest ideal of the way to belong in this world or any other.

Chapter Eight

SELF-CONSCIOUSNESS AND THE KNOWLEDGE OF GOD

I am of two parts; I am but one thing spiritual.
(1,226;1847)

A human being is the divine spirit in a body.
(45,433;1910)

To know God, one has to merge with Him. To merge with Him, one has to fulfill His Law.
(55,187;1906)

THE VAST majority of people in Tolstoy's fictional universe have no moment of recollection, intoxication, infection, or ecstasy. We see them only for brief moments in their lives, and they are represented in one unaltered state of awareness. They do not grow or change. These people do not seek to know themselves or find God. In contrast to these people, the central figures change. They do not have a fixed identity, and they are in quest of their vocation. Unlike the static souls, these people have an awareness of themselves. This consciousness of themselves varies, and itself can go through stages, but self-consciousness in some form and in some sense is the first requirement of life. "Until a person is conscious of himself, he does not know if he is alive or not, and therefore he does not live" (53,58;1895). To be unconscious is to be dead.

The task of life is to become self-conscious. But in Tolstoy's understanding of man there are always two selves and two ways of being self-conscious. The task of life in this context is to learn which self to be conscious of and what the relationship of this self to the other must be. This task is accomplished through practice and is learned in the perfection of the way to love.

In the end all life is understood as the movement from the "physical" to the "spiritual," so the proper growth of self-consciousness leads to an awareness of the Divine. In the perfect disclosure of yourself you find and know God. The paradox of this disclosure, however, is that it cannot be attained simply through practice. No human effort will guarantee contact with the Divine, but there is no knowledge of God without effort. Furthermore, no human knowledge of God can be adequate to God, but in the effort and despite it there is a sense in which we do know God. This knowledge of God is the goal of life and the salvation of life. This knowledge of God is the true consciousness of self and the perfection of our participation in the divine life. This knowledge of God is what is given us to be accomplished.

CONVENTIONAL CONSCIOUSNESS

War and Peace opens with a soirée. The conversation and the human encounters which take place at this soirée are subject to the conventions of the salon. All who come must pay their respects to *"ma tante"* and conduct themselves according to the unspoken rules of behavior appropriate for this form of being together. The harmony of the moment is orchestrated by Anna Pavlovna Sherer, the hostess of the salon. Her task is to control the moment and keep the guests together. She performs her duties with mechanical precision. "As the foreman of a spinning mill, once he has settled the workers in their places, walks around the plant, and, whenever he notices a stopped spindle or one that is making an unusual, excessively loud squeaking noise, rushes up to it and stops it or fixes it, so Anna Pavlovna would walk around her salon, up to a group that had grown silent or one that was talking too much and with one word or rearrangement would again start the steady, proper, conversational machine" (I,i,ii). The salon is a world, like so many, in which people are expected to act according to someone else's rules. In such a world Pierre appears as a potential disruptive force because he does not know the conventions and acts on his own. His presence threatens the established order and causes Anna Pavlovna "anxiety and fear." The machine works only when all the spindles whir together under the foreman's rule.

Anna Pavlovna's role as hostess is to rule the salon. She achieves her control by emanating an electric involvement in everything. She is an enthusiast. But "to be an enthusiast had become her social position and sometimes, even when she did not feel like it, she became an enthusiast in order not to disappoint the expectations of the people who knew her" (I,i,i). Anna Sherer is trapped in her role: she is herself ruled by the convention of her position. She performs her life for others even when she does not feel like it. The people who know her, then, do not really know her; they know only her conventional position—and likewise the reader. Who Anna Pavlovna is or where she is going no one knows, not even she. Her consciousness is conventional.

Prince Vasily speaks his words "by habit, like a wound-up clock," not even caring if he is believed. He is like an "actor" playing a "role in an old play." He resembles Anna Pavlovna in his lack of concern for authenticity to himself, but the role he plays is different from hers. He does not project an image of enthusiasm. He performs his life as a proper man of society, stable, self-assured, respectful of others. With the narrator, the reader can see Prince Vasily in a different light. We see his flattery of those in high position, his machinations for his children, his obsession with his family's future. But Prince Vasily sees none of this because he lives only in his conventional awareness.

> Prince Vasily did not deliberate over his plans, still less did he think of doing ill for his own advantage. He was just a man of society who had succeeded in the world and who had made a habit of that success. His whole life-interest consisted of various plans and schemes which constantly arose from the circumstances and people he encountered but which he was not well aware of. Of these plans and schemes he had not one or two in his head but dozens, some just beginning to take shape, others nearing fulfillment, others already disintegrating. He did not say to himself, for example: "Now this person here has power; I must gain his confidence and friendship and through him arrange the payment of an allowance," nor did he say to himself "Now Pierre is rich; I must lure him into marrying my daughter and lending me the forty thousand I need." But when he came across a person with power, at that very moment instinct told him that this person could be useful, and Prince Vasily approached him at the first op-

portunity, without preparation, by instinct; he flattered him, became friendly with him, and spoke about what he needed."

(I,iii,i)

Prince Vasily has so mastered his performance of himself that he is no longer aware of what he is doing. His role has become habitual, as if an instinct. How he became who he is, no one seems to know, he least of all. He just acts out his role of conniving, not even knowing that he is conniving. All his feelings and actions flow from the role he plays in life. Since Prince Vasily has no self-awareness, he has no sense of the moral implications of his behavior and therefore no need to justify himself to himself or others. He does not live threatened by guilt or thwarted by resentment. He seems whole and undivided.

In his blind self-assurance Prince Vasily resembles Princess Betsy Tverskaya. In *Anna Karenina* Betsy is the norm for all society women. She follows the conventions of social life without question. Like many other society women in the novel she is married, and she has a lover. This causes her no conflict or division of interests. The effect of her adultery on her husband is not mentioned, nor would it occur to her as a topic of discussion, any more than she would speak of the plight of Liza Merkalova's similarly afflicted husband. To her such discussion is unseemly, like talking about the details of one's toilet. In Betsy's world of convention not talking about something makes it go away. This silent observation of society's conventions provides a public role which justifies her to others and to herself. So long as life is performed according to the conventions of marriage, family, and salon, regardless of her actual behavior, there will be no possibility for inner conflict.

A conventional consciousness has no conscience. Betsy does not ask questions about life or wonder about her own fate. When Anna begins to examine her own behavior, Betsy dismisses Anna's self-examination as a "tragic" view of life which ends up causing one's own suffering (III,xxii). Betsy believes life should be viewed "simply and cheerfully"—which really means that it should not be viewed at all. Betsy raises no moral questions and has no religious views. When at one point she quotes ironically from the Sermon on the Mount, she believes she remembers having "heard someone say something like that" (II,v). With no religious sensibility and no moral awareness, Betsy has no compassion. She cannot see suffering. When Vronsky

relates the telling tale of the Titular Councillor whose wife was "pursued" by Vronsky's army pal Petritsky and Kedrov, a tale which ironically repeats the story of Karenin, whose wife is "pursued" by Vronsky, Betsy has no sense of "tragedy" in the story, either the pain of the husband and wife or the potential harm to the regiment. Betsy's initial impulse is to retell the story to the first lady who appears on the scene. For Betsy all events in other peoples' lives are reduced to anecdotal material to be used in the salon.

Betsy plays by the rules, and therefore she is always at ease and always sincere. As a hostess she can sit behind a samovar and pour tea, while letting others talk, she can with equal aplomb control the flow of conversation. But in neither case does she show a preference or reveal a personality of her own. She just follows the rules and plays the role. Still, Betsy is sincere. Even though she herself cannot distinguish the soprano Nilson's voice from the commonest chorus girl's, Betsy is truly shocked that Vronsky would walk out on a performance by the soprano. All Betsy's feelings flow from the conventions. Therefore, when Vronsky makes even the slightest verbal allusion to the possibility of an affair with Anna, Betsy is genuinely offended for her friend, whose honor is being sullied by words that ought not to be spoken. To cope with this indiscretion Betsy then pretends not to understand the allusion, thereby making what ought not to have been disappear. The issue is not truth or moral behavior, but loyalty to her friend. Consequently, Betsy experiences no deception. When she herself speaks about Vronsky in polite society, she uses her "natural, simple tone" of voice, and, although Anna knows that Betsy knows what is really going on, even Anna cannot hear in Betsy's words the slightest touch of insincerity. For Betsy there is no deception because honesty to herself comes in following the rules. Betsy knows no doubt, and her voice conveys the assurance of her conviction. Betsy Tverskaya's paradox, however, is that while she lives by the rules made by others, she does what she wants. With her conventional consciousness there is no felt conflict between self and other, and what she desires guides her every action even as she obeys the rules. Princess Betsy Tverskaya, therefore, embodies the principle of the personal self: that way of being in the world which sees all purpose for living located in the satisfaction of one's own desire. She is a grown-up child. The good is what pleases her. All means used to attain this pleasure are justified by this end. Even though Betsy is unaware of it, the role of the conventional social lady is the mask she wears to hide this self-centeredness from others and from herself.

Anna's cousin by marriage and Vronsky's by blood, Princess Betsy Tverskaya becomes the center of Anna's new life and seems the source to which she turns for stability and sanity. Prior to meeting Vronsky, however, Anna devoted herself to Countess Lydia Ivanovna, the "conscience of Petersburg Society" (II,iv). In *Anna Karenina* Countess Lydia Ivanovna, with her "almshouse" world, is the foil of the conventional society women in the novel. She was married young and was loyal to her husband. But he mysteriously rejected his young wife after their first month together, and for the rest of their life together he treated her with mockery and hostility. Yet Lydia Ivanovna never takes a lover. With no seemingly happy marriage and no lover, Lydia Ivanovna is the opposite of Betsy Tverskaya. Lydia Ivanovna is not alone, however, because she is always "in love with someone." "She was in love with several people at once, both men and women; she was in love with all the new princesses and princes who married into the Tsar's family; she was in love with a metropolitan, a vicar, a priest; she was in love with a journalist, three Slavs, and Komissarov; a minister, a doctor, an English missionary, and Karenin" (V,xxiii). Lydia Ivanovna's mode of being is "being in love." She must live for others. She has no other self.

Unlike Betsy, then, Lydia Ivanovna has compassion and sees the suffering of others. Her whole relationship with Karenin revolves around his suffering and her concern for his suffering. She does not want Anna to visit Seryozha because this would cause Karenin pain. In Karenin's willingness to allow a visit, Lydia Ivanovna sees a martyrdom from which he must be saved. In her attempts to alleviate Karenin's suffering, Lydia Ivanovna becomes the cause of Anna's woe, thereby gaining for Karenin the revenge he could not allow himself to seek. This desire to hurt Anna, of course, conflicts with Lydia Ivanovna's sense of love, but she does not see this conflict. She is, she believes, only protecting those for whom she cares. Everything she does she does quite sincerely for others. Her whole life is a performance of self-sacrifice. Not surprisingly, then, Lydia Ivanovna is religious. She is a pietist who finds "peace, comfort, salvation, and love" in the Christ Who "dwells in your heart" (V,xxii). This is a religion with which Lydia Ivanovna can give to others, all the while insisting that it is not she but the indwelling Christ Who gives support and sol-

ace. Lydia Ivanovna moves into Karenin's life, takes it over, directs his activities, tells him what to think and do, yet she asks not to be thanked because "I am not doing it myself." This pietist faith in the indwelling Christ thus justifies her existence: whatever she does, she has no sins, since she, after all, does not do it. With this faith Lydia Ivanovna need not question her life or confront any conflicts. To her her religious belief is sincere, and her prayers seem genuine even to the doubting narrator. She does not feign or pretend. Lydia Ivanovna lives for others, but makes all the rules herself. Her religion serves her, as society's conventions do Betsy. Because Lydia Ivanovna believes in the Christ Who dwells in her heart, she can play the role of the pious matron sacrificing for others, all the while conniving, not knowing she is conniving.

Anna Pavlovna Sherer, Prince Vasily, Princess Betsy Tverskaya, and Countess Lydia Ivanovna all resemble each other in their lack of self-awareness. Each character plays out his life according to an adopted social role. They all measure their activity as well as the actions of those around them from the vantage point of their conventional consciousness. The role becomes a mask which screens their inner reality from others and from themselves. What these characters do in the salon and private drawing room, however, is at bottom no different from what all people do in governed society. They become what Tolstoy calls, in *The Kingdom of God Is Within You*, "conventional people": "The conventional positions established centuries ago, accepted for ages, recognized now by all around, designated by special titles and special dress, and enhanced by every sort of ceremonious affect on the external senses, are so suggestive to people that, forgetting the customary conditions of life common to all, they begin to look at themselves and all people only from this conventional point of view, and by this conventional point of view alone are they guided in their evaluation of their own and others' actions" (28,155). Such conventional people are intoxicated by the historical and social conditions in which they live. The forms of life dictated by economics, class conditions, religious beliefs, popular customs, and political institutions shape their very being to the point where such "people represent themselves to themselves and others no longer as who they are in reality, people, but as particular, conventional beings, that is, noblemen, merchants, governors, judges, officers, tsars, ministers, and soldiers who are no longer subject to ordinary human obligations, but above all else and before all things human" are subject to the obligations which arise from their conventional positions (28,254). What is done in the salon is done throughout society. Conventional people can coerce, connive, and condone their own self-interest, not knowing they are coercing, conniving, and condoning. Conventional people make possible the inhumanities of governed society, its wars, its penal colonies, its mass poverty, its abject slavery. Conventional consciousness leads to the circle of violence.

The circle of violence made by conventional people would truly be vicious if there were no way out. But in Tolstoy's universe no one is necessarily trapped in himself forever. Princess Anna Mikhaylovna Drubetskaya is a conventional society lady. But, widowed and impoverished, she is suddenly confronted with the material realities of life. Dismayed that her beloved son Boris will no longer have the privileges and opportunities that he and she assumed were his rightful heritage and real domain in life, Anna Mikhaylovna is forced to fight for her son's future. She gets what she wants for him and cares not what others think of her. The society lady adopts the role of a conniving mother. But this confrontation with economic and social reality teaches Anna Mikhaylovna something about herself. Unlike Prince Vasily, she has violated the conventions of her customary role, and this break with convention makes her see herself differently. There is an Anna Mikhaylovna who exists beyond the role she plays. This Anna Mikhaylovna peeps forth in one poignant moment when in desperate need of cash to buy Boris a uniform she is forced to accept a gift from her old friend Countess Rostova. The society lady and conniving mother fade away, and we see a bit of the human being hidden behind the roles: "Anna Mikhaylovna was already embracing her and weeping. The countess was also weeping. They were weeping because they were friends and because they were kind and because, friends from youth, they were concerned with such a base thing as money and because their youth had passed. . . . But their tears were pleasant to them both." (I,i,xiv). The repeated word "weeping" and the cumulative syntactical construction of "because" clauses yoke together complex and varied feelings and mark the high emotion of this moment of authenticity. In her pleasant tears Anna Mikhaylovna senses her life beyond her role. We get a glimpse of the real Anna Mikhaylovna and so does she.

A break with convention leads toward truth. Tolstoy understood this early on. "When a person plays a role, and especially a grand role," he wrote in 1853, "the slightest infringement on his grandeur, if it does not anger him, will force him, even while he continues in his role, to speak his heart" (46,279). Such infringement upon the role is characteristic of Tolstoy's representation of conventional people. Even Prince Vasily is forced by the facts of life to confront for a moment his own reality. At the height of his conniving for his family at the death bed of Count Bezukhov, just before he learns of the Count's death, Prince Vasily is shocked into an awareness of the sordid death-bed drama. "How much we sin, how much we deceive, and all for what? I am near sixty, dear friend," he says to Pierre, who is struck by a "sincerity and weakness he had never observed before." "But I too, everything will end in death, everything. Death is awful" (I,i,xxi). In the face of death even a conventional consciousness is awakened. Even Napoleon's grandeur is infringed by death. At Borodino he is suddenly overcome by the realization that by some "unfortunate accident" he might be defeated by the Russians (III,ii,xxxiv). Later at the "terrible sight of the battlefield covered with corpses and wounded men" this possibility of failure turns into the thought of death.

> He sat on his campstool, his face sallow, swollen, and heavy, his eyes dim, his nose red, and his voice hoarse, listening involuntarily with downcast eyes to the sounds of the firing. With pained anguish he awaited the end of the action of which he considered himself the cause but which he could not stop. For a brief moment a personal, human feeling took over that artificial phantasm of life he had served so long. He internalized the sufferings and death he saw on the battlefield. His heaviness of head and heart reminded him of the possibility of suffering and death even for himself. At that moment he did not want for himself either Moscow, or victory, or glory (what need did he have for more glory?). The only thing he wanted now was rest, calm, freedom. (III,ii,xxxviii)

What is striking in Tolstoy's representation of Napoleon is that he allows him this "human feeling." In the face of death Napoleon may not quite sympathize or empathize with others, but in his glance backward and forward he is allowed to see the vanity of his past life and to hope for a new and better one in the future. Pushed to the limits, Napoleon reveals a capacity for assessment that contradicts his entire self-centered experience.

For Tolstoy no one can be completely reduced to a role or trapped by a convention. Everyone has the potential for self-awareness inherent in the fact of human consciousness. In Tolstoy's fiction conventional people of whatever class or role may be brought to a moment of awareness by the sight, thought, or threat of death: Prince Bolkonsky sheds his eighteenth-century armor as he dies, begging forgiveness from Princess Mary; Karenin is shocked out of his bureaucratic self into a moment of Christian forgiveness at the sight of his dying wife; Brekhunov breaks out of his merchant mentality from fear for his life. From this point of view *The Death of Ivan Ilych* is the paradigmatic story of all conventional people. For conventional people death is the last hope for the moment of self-awareness.

THE PRACTICE OF SELF-CONSCIOUSNESS

In their lack of self-awareness conventional people do not grow. They live by "tradition, inertia, and imitation" (57,23;1909). They do either "what everyone else does" or "what they did yesterday" (50,152;1889). Their life in their role is just a habit. For Tolstoy, however, "a person's entire life is an unceasing process of giving birth to a new life, a constant, endless growth" which results from the struggle with the "habits" of his former state of life (26,646-47;1888). He believes that "people who have not been resurrected to life are always busy, but only with the preparations for life, of life there is none. They are busy eating, sleeping, studying, resting, continuing and bringing up the species" (50,87,1889). For such people, however, "one thing is missing—life, the growth of one's own life." Our task, Tolstoy therefore advises, is "like the task of a nurse, to make grow what is entrusted to us, our life." For Tolstoy this notion of growing one's own life "is no metaphor" (50,88;1889). People who do not grow their own life "have no life exactly as a tree has none, if it decomposes food but does not assimilate it." As always for Tolstoy, however, life is not understood simply as the biological process of life. Human life consists in acts of self-creation and self-overcoming. Such acts of self-formation, however, should not be understood as "egoism. To make your own life grow is to serve God" (50,87;1889). If the young Tolstoy felt that the "aim of philosophy is to show how a person should form himself," the later Tolstoy saw clearly that life is a process of self-transformation in which egotism is constantly being overcome in moments of struggle which give birth to new life (1,229;1847).

Nikolenka in *Childhood* is not a conventional person, but death brings him to a new level of self-awareness. The child's mother has just died, and the narrator recalls himself as a young boy looking at the body of his dead mother. Tolstoy records what Nikolenka sees in a closeup.

> I stopped by the door and began to look, but my eyes were so swollen from weeping and my nerves so distraught that I could not make out anything. Everything somehow strangely merged together: the light, the brocade, the velvet, the tall candlesticks, the pink lace-trimmed pillow, the frontlet, the cap with ribbons, and something else of a transparent, waxen color. I got up on a chair to examine her face, but in the place where it was located there again appeared that same pale-yellow, transparent object. I could not believe that this was her face. I began to peer at it more closely and gradually to recognize in it the dear familiar features. I shuddered with horror when I realized that this was she. But why were the closed eyes so sunken? Why that terrible pallor and on one cheek the blackish spot under the transparent skin? Why was the expression of the whole face so stern and cold? Why were the lips so pale and why did their shape, so beautiful and so majestic, express such an unearthly calm that a cold shiver ran down my back and through my hair as I peered at them? (xxvii)

The moment is represented as a series of stages of recognition. Nikolenka does not just receive impressions from the external world; he tries to grasp their inner meaning for himself. Each sentence in the paragraph presents a different stage in the process, which ranges from the blur of an object, to the identification of the object, and finally to the meaning and emotional impact of this recognition. Furthermore, the dual mode of narration characteristic of *Childhood* also affects the representation of this awareness: the narrator is recalling albeit very vividly a past experience, and thus throughout this moment of awareness it seems as though the boy already knows what he is in the process of learning. In this chapter, "Grief," Nikolenka does not learn that his mother is dead; he is shown in the process of becoming aware of the meaning of her death for him.

In this first paragraph the camera focuses on what Nikolenka sees. The narrator "looks" (*smotret'*) and "examines" (*rassmotret'*). The verb "to peer" (*vgljadyvat'sja*) surrounds the second half of the paragraph. In the next paragraph depicting Nikolenka's awareness of his mother's death, the camera moves inward from the realm of sight to Nikolenka's "imagination."

> I looked and felt that some incomprehensible irresistible force was drawing my eyes toward that lifeless face. I did not take my eyes off it, but my imagination had for me pictures blossoming with life and happiness. I forgot that the dead body which lay before me and at which I was looking blankly as at an object having nothing in common with my memories was *her*. I imagined her now in one, now another, situation: lovely, gay, smiling. Then suddenly I was struck by some feature on her pale face on which my eyes rested, and I remembered the terrible reality, and then again the consciousness of reality destroyed my fantasy. Finally my imagination grew tired and stopped deceiving me; the consciousness of reality also vanished and I became oblivious to everything. I do not know how long I stayed in that state; I do not know what it consisted of; I know only that for a time I lost consciousness of my own existence and experienced some sort of exalted, ineffably fine, and sad delight.

As Nikolenka turns from the object out there to the image stored in his imagination, he enters a new state of consciousness, "blossoming with life and happiness." He recovers his love. Maman has entered Nikolenka's awareness, and now she is alive again, "lovely, gay, smiling." As always in *Childhood* memory restores the lost paradisical past. But then the present reality of death once again seizes Nikolenka's consciousness, and with this sense of loss the child shuts off both the external world and the images stored in memory. What happens, however, is that by this action Nikolenka does not enter a state of blank unconsciousness. Rather, he enters another state of consciousness which he experiences as a loss of self which is "ineffable delight." Turned in upon himself but oblivious to himself, the child discovers a new sense of self. This state in which he is not conscious of his own separate existence, but still feels exalted, is then destroyed by another intrusion from the external world. Nikolenka slips back into an awareness of himself. The ecstasy of loss of self is replaced by an agony of egotism, and Nikolenka doubts his grief and his love. At the moment of his awareness of his mother's death, Nikolenka thus experiences a loss of self which is the highest moment, the final revelation of his love untainted by any self-awareness. The representation of this moment records what became for Tolstoy the defining process of life, "the process of transition from a lower sphere of consciousness to a higher one," an endless process of growth in self-awareness which culminates in the sense of the Divine (55,37;1904). Nikolenka's moment of grief is an emblem of the "expansion of consciousness" which is the growth of new life (55,143;1905).

Father Sergius (1891) tells the story of a man whose life is indeed an unceasing process of giving birth to new life. In this story Father Sergius moves through a series of roles, all of which are conventions of the world of Russian Orthodox piety. He continually changes his image of himself and what he must do by trying to act out these roles. But Father Sergius is a perfectionist in the sense that wherever he is and whatever he does he must see himself as "the first," or "perfection" (i). He needs to feel superior. Yet at the same time Father Sergius needs some ideal and perfect being whose image guides him in his own quest for perfection. His way of being in the world is to look simultaneously "down from above" (sverkhu vniz) and "up from below" (snizu verkh) (ii). Whenever the ideal image to which he aspires fails him or he fails it, he is thrust out of his role in search of a new one. His sense of failure spurs him on.

With such a failure his religious life began. A characteristic Tolstoyan orphan, his father having died when he was twelve, Prince Stephan Kasatsky moved from his home to Petersburg but never felt a part of life there. In the world of aristocratic society in which the tsar was his ideal image and his fiancée a favorite, this prince "was a stranger" (chuzhoj). He knew that there were those who felt "at home" (svoj) there, but in that world "he was not at home" (ne svoj). Yet "Kasatsky wanted to be at home there." Before entering the monastery, then, Prince Kasatsky's problem was "that he was accustomed to being first but in this society he was far from it." Recognition by the tsar and social entrée attained in marriage to a court favorite were the means by which he would attain his goal of belonging. When he learns that his fiancée has indeed been the mistress of the tsar, his plan for himself falls apart even as his ideals of perfection and purity fall before his eyes. With wounded pride, he abandons the world for the monastery.

In the monastery Kasatsky, now Father Sergius, finds a new ideal to guide him. The abbot becomes his spiritual director. This abbot is a starets in the hesychast tradition of Paisius Velichkovsky and himself the pupil of Father Ambrose, the renowned starets of the Optina-Pustyn monastery. He teaches, therefore, a life of inner prayer based on the recitation of the Jesus prayer accompanied by controlled breathing, a yoga-like regime designed to turn consciousness inward on the peace (*mir*) in the heart within. In this peace one has contact with the Divine. The first stages of this quest for the Divine consist in the training of the body, and Father Sergius devotes his early years in the monastery mainly to the development of control over himself. He concentrates especially on obedience to his starets. Obedience becomes the new perfection he must attain. In this "ever greater and greater submission of his will" to the starets, however, Father Sergius receives his own rewards (iii). He feels no responsibility for what happens and quells his critical view. "It's not my business to judge." Whatever happens Father Sergius feels only "joy." This joyful state is interrupted, to be sure, by moments of doubt when he feels that in the submission of his will to the starets he is "not in his own power, nor in God's but in the power of someone alien" (*chuzhoj*) to him. Still, Father Sergius continues to learn from his starets until "everything that had to be learned (*uchit'sja*), everything that had to be attained, he attained and there was nothing more to do." Father Sergius is content until his life becomes a "habit," and then he gets bored. "No sooner does he get one thing than he takes on another" (i). His sense of success, as well as failure, spurs him on. The perfectionist never stops growing his life.

The abbot of the new monastery that Father Sergius is sent to, is no disciple of that hesychast movement which created the golden age of Russian mysticism in the nineteenth century. The new abbot is a "worldly, clever man who is making a spiritual career," and Father Sergius does not like him at all (iii). To this abbot he submits, but "in the depth of his heart he does not cease to judge him." The new monastery, headed by this worldly abbot, is filled with "visitors, gentlemen, and especially ladies"; Father Sergius turns his attention away from the abbot by concentrating on controlling his reactions to this disruptive world the abbot fosters.

> He tried not to see them, not to notice what was happening, not to see the soldier accompanying them while pushing the people away, not to see the ladies point out the monks to each other, often even him and a certain handsome monk. By putting blinders as it were on his attention, he tried not to see anything except the glitter of the candles at the iconostasis, the icons, and the monks, not to hear anything except the song and spoken words of the prayers and not to experience any feeling except a forgetting of self (*samozabvenie*) in the consciousness of the fulfillment of duty which he always experienced when he listened to or repeated the prayers he had heard so many times.

Father Sergius cuts off the impression from the external world, but what he discovers in this state of inwardness is not peace. Rather, by focusing his attention precisely on what he is doing at the moment, he enters into a state of loss of self in which he is aware of himself fulfilling his duty. Despite the disruptive world about him, he at least is doing what he ought. Father Sergius has learned to control his attention only for his own purposes. In his self-forgetting he is concerned only with himself. At the moment of this controlled attention, the abbot breaks through his focus and beckons to him. A general from Sergius' former regiment has come for a visit and the worldly abbot plays the host and reintroduces them. Sergius is outraged at this intrusion upon his attention, which Tolstoy marks with a closeup.

> The abbot's face, all red midst the grey hair, and smiling as if approving what the general had said, the general's well-groomed face with its self-satisfied smile, the smell of wine from the general's mouth, of cigars from his sideburns, all this infuriated Father Sergius.

In an "outburst of anger" Father Sergius reprimands his superior. The next day, repentant, he "begs forgiveness" for his "pride" and writes to his starets of the incident. From him he learns that the anger means he in fact believes he "needs no one," that he accepts himself as he is and "humbles himself not for the sake of God but for his own pride." Sergius looks down from above even when he looks up from below. The starets sends him off to the life of a hermit in Illarion's cell so that he can "humble his pride." At the new monastery, therefore, Father Sergius discovers his fatal flaw: in his outburst of anger he reveals the mind of the master who would have the world arranged only for himself. This perception of failure again spurs him on.

Six years pass in Illarion's cell. Father Sergius' reputation as a holy man begins to grow. Then one day a "lost" woman ("not in the metaphorical, but in the literal sense," she says with a smile) arrives at his hut in need, she claims, of a place to stay (v). Father Sergius believes she is the devil and not without justification, for this woman has come on a bet that she can seduce this most holy man. He allows the woman in, but all the while retreats into himself, reciting the Jesus prayer both inwardly and with his lips: "Lord Jesus Christ, Son of God, have mercy on me a sinner, have mercy on me a sinner." The woman does all she can to tempt him; he keeps on reciting the prayer. She goes behind the screen to lie down, takes off her clothing, and then cries out for help, "O come to me, I am dying." "Yes I'll go," Sergius thinks, "but I'll do what that holy father did when he put one hand on a prostitute and the other into a brazier." But he has no brazier, so Father Sergius picks up an axe and chops off a finger. Flooding his consciousness with pain, he approaches his temptress in complete control of his passion. At the center of the story, this incident is the high point in Father Sergius' career to control his attention. His moment of freedom from his desires releases the charity within. The woman is so impressed that she begs forgiveness, leaves, and a year later becomes a nun. This success thrusts Father Sergius into a new awareness of himself and a new crisis in his quest for perfection.

Seven years pass. Father Sergius becomes a famous man. He heals the sick and comforts those of little faith. Everyone comes to see him. In his hermitage he has become the first, the perfection, the ideal to which all others look up from below. But Father Sergius is dissatisfied because the more "he gave himself to his life, the more he felt that the internal had been transformed into the external, that the source of living water had dried up in him, that he was doing what he was doing more and more for people, not for God" (vii). In his success he feels failure. Yet he persists. He assists at the liturgy, despite the crowds of women who came just to see him. "That's how the saints do it," he thinks. What he had realized one moment long ago he now discovers is true. He "wants to be saint" (v). Furthermore, in his success and fame he is amazed that "he, Stephan Kasatsky, has gotten to be such an unusual holy man and indeed a worker of miracles, but he has no doubt that he is such: he cannot help believe the miracles he himself sees" (vii). In his simultaneous sense of failure and success, Father Sergius sees himself both as a holy man and playing out the role of a holy man in order to get attention. He looks simultaneously up from below and down from above at himself. Thus doubly self-conscious in his fame (*slava*), he discovers his vanity (*tshcheslavie*). "The love from them was pleasing and necessary, but he felt no love for them. Now he had no love, nor humility nor purity." If he is conscious of himself as a saint, then he is not one. He has only been playing a role.

But if Father Sergius is not a saint, then he has not attained perfection. He has failed. In his failure he begins to doubt God. There may be no ideal to which he can aspire. But he prays himself into a state of peaceful assurance, reciting in full the Orthodox morning prayer so loved by Tolstoy. He decides to receive a merchant's daughter who has come to be healed. But she seduces him, and he yields. With this proof that he is no saint, he is thrust into disbelief near suicide. At this point he has his revelatory dream in which he recalls from his youth the much maligned and disabused Pashenka. When he visits her, he discovers a person who "lives for God, imagining that she lives for people" (viii). Pashenka does not exalt herself nor see herself a saint. She sees her failure but never her success. She looks up from below at others but down from above at herself. She plays no role to gain approval, and in her acts of charity she has "no thought of reward." Pashenka becomes Father Sergius' new ideal. But Father Sergius has also again turned his own failure into his success. Whether he can become a "servant of God" and be unconscious of being a "servant of God," however, is unclear. His story may well end in a failure to become like his ideal. But Father Sergius succeeds because his life is an unceasing process of self-transformation in which egotism is constantly being overcome in moments of struggle which give birth to new life.

FATHER SERGIUS may have to go through a series of identities to find himself, but he knows that his life's vocation is the increasing of love in himself. Furthermore, although he is a monk devoted to the contemplative life, Father Sergius lives within a religious tradition which sees that the body is the instrument used to reach out to the Divine. Tolstoy himself understood this well. "Nothing spiritual is acquired spiritually, neither a religious sense, nor love, nor anything. The spiritual is created through material life, in space and time. The spiritual is created by doing" (*delom*) (54,121;1902). Like Father Sergius, Tolstoy sees the "doing" which creates spiritual life as a process of repeated doing, an asceticism understood in the Eastern Christian sense of training (Gr. *askesis*, "exercise," "training" as of an athlete), not mortification of the flesh. Spiritual life is acquired through practice. "To love is to transfer yourself into another's soul, to live by their desires. I cannot do this. So learn (*uchis'*)," Tolstoy instructed himself in his diary and then continued characteristically addressing this instruction to the world. "One has to learn to practice (*uprjazhn-jat'sja*) loving, that is feeling another's feeling. We not only do not learn this; we often learn the opposite . . . to extinguish this sensitivity in ourselves, in business, games, hunting, war" (51,82;1890). Of course, Father Sergius failed in his practice, for he looked down from above at another's feeling and therefore could not feel it himself. But, moved by his perfectionism, he does keep on trying. In this he resembles Levin in his mowing.

The mowing scene (III,iv-v) divides into three parts which represent the three stages of Levin's learning his task. In the first section Levin mows with his mowing tutor, Tit. But as Levin takes the scythe Tit has honed for him, an "old man" (*starik*) says to the astonished peasants: "Take a look at the barin, he's got himself in for it now. He'd better not fall behind." This breaks the ice of disbelief. Levin begins, several peasants offer advice on how to place the body, and the "old man" continues his jocularly gentle, supportive remarks. Thus helped and encouraged, Levin keeps mowing. But as it were miraculously, just when Levin is at the point of exhaustion, Tit stops to hone the scythes. This rhythm of rest and work continues to the end of the first row. The peasants' sensitivity to Levin's pace keeps him going: they seem to know what he feels. Still, it is very hard. And Levin's strokes are irregular, his grass falls unevenly, but he does not fall behind. He pays total attention, which Tolstoy marks with a closeup.

He thought of nothing, desired nothing, except not to fall behind the peasants and to work as well as possible. He heard only the swish of the scythes, and he saw right before him Tit's receding, erect figure, the convex half circle of the grass he just mowed, the strands of grass and tops of flowers tumbling slowly in the waves round the blade of his scythe, and ahead of him the end of the row where he would find rest.

Levin is right there, doing his job, unaware of others looking at him. When he "remembers" what he is doing and tries to do it, he loses the ability to do. But, emptied of thought and emotion, devoted to his task, he "forgets" what he is doing in the doing, loses all "consciousness of time," and does. Rain falls and he experiences it solely as pleasure, joyously shaking his shoulders in its refreshment, until the "old man" reminds him that it is time for breakfast and, wrenched out of his attention, Levin, now his old self, realizes that it is raining and his hay may be spoiled. This old self is the mind of the master whose view of nature is pragmatic. The world is his estate, to be run by his calculation and decision. When, earlier, Levin had asked a peasant if it were the right time to mow, he was perplexed when the peasant answered that the right time depends on the church calender and God, not on his judgment: "God provides and the grass is good." In his moment of attention, Levin forgets his controlling mind. He also learns the first lesson of all genuine labor, concentration. Work cannot be done with any immediate purpose other than itself. The only aim is the work itself, the very doing, the only reward the cessation of that work, the stopping of doing called rest. The paradox of this concentration is that Levin is totally present in his attention, yet totally absent of thought or feeling. Angered at Sergey Ivanovich's grandiloquent words about the "common labor" of the peasants, Levin had begun mowing as a "personal task" to rid himself of his anger, but how can it be "personal" when the person seems to get lost?

When Levin returns from breakfast he starts work anew, not at "his former place" behind Tit, but between the "old man" and a "young peasant" mowing for the first time. Levin is neither master nor novice, just in between, entering the intermediate stage of his learning. The young peasant is all "effort": he works very hard at working and, aware of others looking at him, he keeps on smiling. He has no ease or concentration. In contrast the "old man" gets so lost in his work that he seems to be "playing," as though "not he but the scythe itself whizzed through the juicy grass." And now Levin too attains such "blessed moments," "moments of forgetting," that "unconscious state" when "his hands no longer waved the scythe but the scythe itself moved (*dvigala*) his body, which was full of life and conscious of itself." The paradox of concentration is raised to a new level. The body does not "move" the instrument but becomes the instrument, and the "unconscious state" turns into a state of heightened awareness of "life," a life which fills the instrument while the task is being accomplished. The "personal" thinking, feeling self has been transformed into a being which acts unconsciously and in some sense not of its own accord, but which remains aware of the action taking place through it.

Levin has not yet attained the level of his master, however. Tit, we will recall, had a special feel for Levin's moments of exhaustion: he was attuned to Levin's rhythm. The "old man" not only moves with Levin but reaches out to him: "Here, have some of my kvas. 'S good, ain't it," he says, winking as he offered Levin a drink of water. This openness and generosity of spirit characterizes the "old man's" style of mowing. Whereas Levin loses his concentration the moment the terrain becomes uncertain and the rhythm has to change, the "old man" responds with ease to all change and is open to all events. Furthermore, while mowing

> he looked everything over and observed what was revealed before him: now he plucked a stalk of sorrel and ate it or offered it to Levin; now he tossed aside a branch with the point of his scythe; now he examined a quail's nest from which the hen bird had flown out right from under the scythe itself; now he caught a snake that had gotten in his way and, raising it on his scythe as though on a pitchfork, he showed it to Levin and tossed it away.

Levin's concentration forces him to limit his vision and action. He moves and sees, but the world around him determines his movement and limits his vision: he could not "change his movement and at the same time observe what was before him." The "old man," having totally mastered the movement of his body, can now proceed outward into the world to respond to it. He harvests it, remakes it, takes it, and enjoys it. But, most importantly he shares it: "whenever he

found a mushroom, he would bend over, pick it, put it in his pocket, and say 'Another treat for the old lady.' " To him nature exists to be shared. Sergey Ivanovich views nature for his pleasure; Levin uses it for his own profit. But the "old man" is the one who is in touch with nature, because he reaps it to give it away. This generosity of spirit guides all the "old man's" actions, so that when dinner time arrives he offers Levin some of his simple fare of bread moistened with salted water. Levin is delighted with his meal and gets involved in an absorbing conversation with the "old man." "He felt closer to him than to his own brother and involuntarily smiled for the tenderness he felt for this person." In a novel filled with meals marred by failures of sharing—Levin's and Stiva's luxurious repast at the Moscow restaurant, Vronsky's beefsteak snack intruded upon by the leering homosexual officers, Dolly's dinner with Anna at Vronsky's estate, Levin's supper devoured by Veslovsky during the hunt, and Anna's dirty ice cream—this is a scene of communion, simple, direct, honest. Enjoyed because of the labor done but not as its reward, this meal crowns Levin's lesson in caring and sharing. The "old man" does not view mowing as a "personal task."

As with so many Tolstoyan characters, Levin wakes up to a new awareness: "he looked around and did not recognize the place." The mowed meadow had been transformed into parallel rows of grass glowing in the evening light. "It was all completely new." This vision of the world transfigured inspires Levin to work more. He immediately begins to figure out how much has been done and what more might be done. He consults the "old man," and it is decided they will finish this spot and move on to Mashkin Heights. The pace quickens, and the work becomes a race. When they reach the Heights, the style of mowing once again changes.

> The grass cut with a juicy sound and smelling like spices fell in high ridges. The mowers, crowded together in short rows, their tin boxes clinking, resounded all round now with their scythes striking against each other, now with their merry shouts urging each other on.

While all the preceding images of mowing were represented as pedagogical experiences, this one depicts a communal event. The peasants work harmoniously together at their "common labor" attuned to each other and their task. The auditory imagery suggests a kind of music made from the sounds of their common action. The paragraph opens with the "juicy sound" of the grass being mowed and closes with the "merry shouts" of the workers. The plural presentation— the peasants are seen as a group—does not preclude individual action but allows for the sound of one whetstone honing, even though it does draw attention to the one group in its harmonious interaction: the paragraph ends with "each other." No thoughts or feelings are ascribed to the individual mowers, nor do they observe the world around them. Rather, one mood of merriment infects them all, and they express this mood in their music. The "old man" too is infected with this merriment, and the mowing scene closes as he "freely" and "merrily" moves through the field unimpeded by any change in terrain, while Levin following behind, trying to keep up, thinking that maybe he cannot, in the end "did what he had to do. He felt that some external force was moving (*sila dvigala*) him." This last experience crowns Levin's learning. No longer solo but in chorus, Levin finally discovers that his work is not a personal affair. Not he, but a "force"—be it of the merriment around him—does the work through him. Mowing is not a personal but a common task. He has experienced the "force of life" (*sila zhizni*) he feels his brother lacks.

The lesson Levin learns in the mowing scene is the lesson of love. Through mowing he dispels the anger and enmity which has caused the "disagreement" (*raznoglasie*) between brothers, and he remembers his nanny. The action of the mowing scene is the fundamental action of the task of life, that replacing of enmity with harmony which Levin thought his book was to accomplish. But in the mowing scene Levin learns this love by practicing how to relate to the world around him. He has to master the placement of his body so that it lets the scythe mow. To do this Levin must learn how to "feel another's feeling," to do which—and it is what is most difficult for him—Levin must be ever open to the variety of the world about him, the furrows and hillocks he must maneuver. He has to learn that feel for the scythe, the terrain, and the other mowers that he sees so developed in Tit and the "old man." Levin does not fully master this feeling in the mowing scene, but he does practice it, and in this sense the mowing scene is an emblem of the practice of love.

In the mowing scene Tolstoy focuses on Levin's inner awareness of what is happening to him: he explores Levin's consciousness. As he mows, Levin moves through three stages of awareness of self and

other. These three stages follow an abstract paradigm, articulated somewhat later by Tolstoy: "First of all in man there awakens the consciousness of his separateness from everything else, i.e., the consciousness of his body; then the consciousness of what is separated, i.e., the consciousness of his soul, the spiritual foundation of life; and then the consciousness of what that spiritual foundation of life is separated from, i.e., the consciousness of God" (54,149;1902). In the first stage of consciousness, Tolstoy believes, a person sees his "separate, material existence," his body which he seems to be able to "control with his thoughts," in opposition to the "whole surrounding universe from an insect to Sirium which he cannot control" (88,317;1904). The first stage includes the consciousness of self as personality and the mind of the master challenged by the reality around it. At this first stage of separateness, furthermore, the person has not yet taken into account that before he awoke to consciousness "he did not exist," and he just assumes that what is, is "his body and the whole universe beyond his body." In this first stage, awareness is limited to time and space, movement and matter, and the person in separation does not confront the fact that there was a time when he did not exist and there will be another time when he will not exist: the facts of birth and death. Levin, afraid of encountering his dying brother and far from experiencing the birth of his child, is living only as such a "separate, material being" concerned only with his "personal task." In all his appearances in the novel up to the mowing scene he has been the outsider, alienated from other people's lives and isolated in his own world of domestic personal interest and intellectual endeavor, buoyed up by his fantasy of family happiness. In the first stage of self-consciousness Levin is his "body."

In the learning of concentration, however, Levin stumbles up against the contradiction inherent in his personal consciousness: if there is awareness of material existence, then there must be something non-material that is being aware. A entails non-A. There is an "internal contradiction" between the concepts of a material being and a "consciousness" of that being that "cannot be derived from it" (88,318). In the heightened impression he receives in the closeup vision, coupled with his experience of his body "conscious of itself full of life," Levin discovers himself as a separate but spiritual being, an acting, ordering, knowing principle that perceives and rules the body. In this awareness, the self is not the body but that which is conscious of the body. It is not material or spatial. This self, furthermore, seems to exist only in the moment of the closeup, or any other moment of full concentration. It does not seem to endure in movement or through time. In concentration and closeup Levin experiences the contradiction which Tolstoy later articulated in this question: "What constitutes his real being, his body or that which controls his body and can change it (even to the point of destroying consciousness of it)?" In closeup and concentration Levin learns the inevitable Tolstoyan answer to this question: "the essence of his life is a spiritual being which receives impressions not only of the external world but of its own body." This second stage of awareness of self as a consciousness which receives impressions is the empiricist sense of self as a separate knowing subject, and Tolstoy believes this second stage is "Berkeley's idealism." In the second stage of self-consciousness Levin is his "soul."

The second stage of self-awareness, like the first, contains a contradiction: this soul, which by definition is something non-spatial and non-temporal, is considered to be "bounded by space and time" and to "comprise a part of something." The union of soul and body, as ordinarily understood, makes no sense. Levin experiences this contradiction in his mowing: he becomes aware of himself as a spiritual being not bounded by space and time, yet he receives all his impressions from this separate world of space and time and is limited in movement by that world of space and time. This sense of separation and limitation of something by definition not subject to separation and limitation leads to the final state of awareness in which a person is "conscious of himself as a separate, material being (the first stage) who is not a separated being" but one of "an infinite number of forms (beings)," "contiguous" (*sopredel'nyj*, literally "co-bounded") with each other and mutually "limited," yet all "manifestations of the one, infinite, eternally alive being." In this third stage, even though I am still a flesh and blood human being, "I do not exist." What exists is "the eternal, infinite divine force (*sila*) acting in the world through me, through my consciousness." This "force" is what is common to all: it is the spirit in which there is no separation or limitation. Mowing all together at one to the music of their "merry" shouts, Levin experiences that sense of self as spirit when not he but "some external force moves him." He comes to a state of self-awareness in which, like Maman at death, "I do not exist" but in

which he is conscious of a "force" that acts "through" him. In learning how to mow, Levin is practicing how to know himself. In the perfection of his self-awareness, he knows God. The mowing scene, then, is an emblem of the articulation of identity through the doing of life's task which is the practice of love and hence the participation in the life of God.

What Levin experiences when he mows is what Father Sergius goes through in his career of perfection. His quest to be first and Levin's practice of self-consciousness both end with the discovery that "I do not exist." Stephan Kasatsky is not Father Sergius; he is a "servant of God." What Levin experiences when he mows is also what Olenin learns on his journey of discovery. Olenin, we might recall, leaves Moscow with a desire to love. He considers himself an "egotist." In his encounter with the mountains that mark the sky he has a primary intuition of his physical being separated from everything else and enters the Cossack world looking for romance. In the lair hidden from the mountains he reassesses himself. Either he is an "animal and nothing more" or a "frame in which is placed a part of the one divine being." From this he concludes the equality of all such distinct animals and frames and derives a morality of self-sacrifice for others. The "egotist" now lives not for himself but for others and for their approval. Then in the letter, again before the mountains that mark the sky, he senses himself not a distinct, framed being but an "integral part of the whole of God's joyful world" and believes some "elemental force loves . . . through" him. He knows himself as spirit. Olenin moves through the three stages of life because he goes through three different stages of self-consciousness. These three stages of self-consciousness are the cause and condition of the possibility of the three stages of life which comprise the career of life (55,40;1904). In each stage the mode of seeing determines the mode of being. What Olenin discovers is what Levin practices and Father Sergius seeks to perfect.

THE THEOLOGY OF PERFECTION

"To love God," Tolstoy said, "means to love perfection" (56,90;1908). This "perfection," as always in Tolstoy, has a metaphysical and moral meaning. On the one hand, there is the perfection of the God of Life and Love, which is the state of total accomplishment and successful completion: the word "perfection" (*sovershenstvo*) is an abstract noun denoting the quality which results from the process of accomplishing or completing (*sovershenie*). Both nouns are derived from the very common Tolstoyan verb "to accomplish" (*sovershat'*). This metaphysical conception of perfection is what philosophers mean by the absolute, the complete fulness of being, unlimited, unconditioned, and self-determined, total freedom to be and final realization of being, the ultimate ground of everything that is. Perfection is complete *love for* and the All that has come to be. On the other hand, perfection is the "ideal" which gives "direction for all that exists, the model of a life ruled by reason which is love" (58,6;1910). This is the perfection found in "Christ," "the light, the ideal" (56,55;1890). This moral ideal, like the metaphysical principle in which it is grounded, cannot be fully realized in human experience. While the "task of life is perfection" (52,140;1890), "the ideal is always ahead, and I am never calm unless I not so much attain it as move toward it" (65,166;1890). Life is the "struggle" to attain what is unattainable.

This struggle is what Tolstoy calls the "process of perfecting" (*sovershenstvovanie*) an abstract noun formed from the verb "to make better, more perfect" (*sovershenstovovat'*). From his earliest days Tolstoy believed the purpose of life was the continual quest for perfection. What changed with the years was the object of the process and the content of the perfection. In the beginning both the world and the self were to be developed to their perfection; in the end the world was to be brought to perfection through the perfecting of the self. Toward the end of his life it became fully clear to Tolstoy, as it does less fully to his heroes at the end of the fictions, that life is the "process of self-perfection in love before God," which is what "the peasants call the salvation of the soul" (54,66;1900). The process of perfection becomes Tolstoy's way of understanding the notion of salvation as deification, "the greater and greater deification (*obozhestvlenie*) of the soul, the increase in oneself of the major divine attribute, love" (77,15;1907). How there can be or why there need be a "process of perfection of the soul" when the soul is "divine and therefore perfect" is the central problem raised in Tolstoy's conception of salvation through perfection (56,91;1908).

Salvation through self-perfection in its apparent self-centeredness seems to contradict Tolstoy's belief that "we must be saved all together" (71,307;1898). Self-perfection, however, always goes hand in hand with the "perfection of the world" (*mir*) (56,103;1908). "Life is the participation in the perfection of self and life. Be better and make life better" (53,3;1895). "True life," then, is seen in "movement forward, in the betterment of self and the life of the world through the betterment of other people" (53,4;1895). Anything else is "*not life.*" But the perfection of others, as Pierre and Nekhlyudov learn, cannot be attained through anyone's attempt to perfect others. "To realize the Kingdom of God," all you can do is "to make yourself better" (55,199;1906). If you see someone drowning, Tolstoy argues, then you will not save him by running along the beach and shouting, nor by jumping in with your clothes and shoes on, but by "undressing and carefully working your limbs to swim over to the person drowning" (50,165;1889). "Everything a person can do for another is always done by him himself, by his activity, his energy directed at his own activity." Self-perfection is not "egotism" nor a self-centered interest in one's own salvation. Rather, self-perfection assumes that "God will do through me what He needs and as He needs it" (55,199;1906). Providential harmony reigns. "The master of life gave each of us separately some work, the accomplishing (*sovershenie*) of which is a most fruitful thing. And he himself uses and directs this work; He gives it a place and meaning. . . . My task is to do, but He knows what it is necessary for and uses it" (53,121-22;1896). This, Tolstoy believes, is what the peasants mean when they say, "Man walks, but God leads." Self-perfection is a process which is guided by perfection itself.

Salvation through self-perfection also seems to contradict Tolstoy's notion of eternal life and the eternally growing soul. The moral conception of life lived more and more according to the "demands of God, one's conscience, one's highest nature (all one and the same)" seems to mean that in this life one "prepares his soul for the transition to a better world" (53,180-81;1898). But this only seems so because the process is looked at and expressed "in time." "To perfect oneself does not mean to prepare oneself for a future life, although we say it that way for convenience and simplicity of speech." More precisely, one should speak of "merging one's life with its timeless principle, with the Good, with love, with God." In this sense "to perfect oneself means to draw close to the foundation of life for which there is no time and therefore no death." Since one can never become this foundation of life, however, to believe in self-perfection implies a "process of self-perfection" which cannot "be broken" (54,28;1900). To Tolstoy the "process of self-perfection and the eternity of life" go hand in hand and "flow from one source," his very conception of God as the All that has come to be in which we participate in our coming to be (54,21;1900). A "paradise where people are perfect and therefore do not grow" seems but a "childish idea not thought through" (56,90;1908). In such a paradise people "do not live." Self-perfection is the eternal process of eternal growth.

Salvation through self-perfection does not mean the "preparation of the soul for another, better life beyond the grave" because "nothing *will be*, everything (*vsë*) is" (56,156-57;1908). Eternal growth, eternal life, is all that has come to be in which we participate in our coming to be now. "Self-perfection, the increase of spiritual power (*sila*), liberation from the body, approximation (*priblizhenie*) to God . . . is accomplished (*sovershaetsja*) only in the present moment." The past is but the "material for self-perfection," the future only the result of what I do now. "There is only the present in which I can accomplish my own task of life." In the present moment, however, one cannot know the aim, purpose, or result of one's actions. "What will come" of my task of self-perfection "is not given to me to know." I cannot know the purpose or result for "the world" or "my soul." In the present moment, therefore, I experience the "true joy of the good," good done for its own sake with no ulterior motive, even the motive of perfection. In the process of perfection there can be no personal interest. "It has been so arranged that we do not see the success of our activity (Moses did not enter the promised land) in order that we might act, not in view of success, but for the salvation of our soul, i.e., not being guided by external, deceptive motives, but by internal, certain ones" (54,4;1900). The theology of perfection is understood outside the categories of time, space, causality, and personality.

Salvation through self-perfection also does not mean the quest for sinlessness. "It is a great and harmful effort to think that it is possible to live without fault or sin" (58,66;1910). The "full realization" of perfect love "is impossible; if it were accomplished, there would be no life" (57,65;1909). Life and self-perfection entail the assumption that "a person can never be good" (56,96;1908). "Humility is a necessary condition of life." Self-perfection is, therefore, understood within the context of the fluidity of human experience. "Like an accordion, all life goes on by being squeezed together and stretched out, then squeezed together again, from the bad to the good and back to the bad. To be good means only to desire to be good more often" (55,174;1905). To be bad creates "the possibility for self-perfection" (54,28;1900). Sinfulness is the "condition" necessary "for self-perfection" (53,226;1899). As with Father Sergius, success and failure spur one on toward the good.

Salvation through self-perfection means only one thing: "the approximation to perfection in everything" (58,14;1910). The "task of life consists in this approximation to perfection" (57,65;1909). What matters, therefore, is not the perfection but the task itself. "What is valuable is not the level of moral perfection you achieve, but the very process of perfecting" (*protsess sovershenstvovanija*) (54,133;1902). "What counts is not what you do but your movement toward the good" (53,210;1898). This "movement toward perfection" is "happiness (*blago*) itself" (28,42;1893). Therefore "Christ, having in mind that full perfection would never be obtained," taught both that "striving for full, infinite perfection would continually increase people's happiness" and that "this happiness therefore could be increased to infinity" (28,77). Self-perfection means infinite and eternal approximation toward perfection.

What follows from this conception of salvation as the process of unceasing perfection is not just that the fulfillment of Christ's teaching is reached through "incessant movement, through grasping ever higher and higher truth, through even greater and greater realization of that truth in oneself by ever greater and greater love and outside oneself by ever greater and greater realization of the Kingdom of God" (28,42). What follows from this conception of salvation is a complete transformation of our understanding of man and his moral life. The Christian teaching of infinite perfection assumes a human being for whom "it is characteristic to strive at will" toward the perfection of the Heavenly Father, regardless of the "level of imperfection at which he finds himself" (28,76). Everyone can be saved, right here, right now. Furthermore, since what matters is not the level of moral perfection but the process of improving, "a person standing on a lower stage but moving (*podvigajas'*) toward perfection is living better, more morally . . . than a person standing on a much higher level of morality but not moving toward perfection" (28,79). This is the very meaning of the parables of the lost sheep come back, the lost coin found, and the prodigal son returned. "The fulfillment of the teaching is in the process of movement from self to God."

This conception of salvation, not through the attainment of deification, which is after all impossible, but through the participation in the process of deification, distinguishes Christianity from both the Judaic and the Graeco-Roman understanding of the good. First of all, the Christian teaching, which assumes an inherent striving toward perfection, guarantees salvation from within. Christ is the "model of inner perfection, of truth and love" and the Kingdom of God is the "result of that inner perfection attained by people," a world in which all will be "united by love and the lion will lie down with the lamb" (28,41). The Christian teaching of the eternally growing soul eliminates the need for external "rules" of religious behavior characteristic of the Jewish religion and for the external "laws" of a governed society characteristic of the Roman world and its legacy. No one needs to be forced, coerced, or lured on to the good because the good, the "truth" which Christianity teaches, is the "truth" within known through the realization of that truth in life. One need only love to know the truth of love. The theory is known in the praxis, and the motivation to practice this theory, to strive at will toward the perfection of the Heavenly Father, is characteristic of our nature. We all want to be all together and at one.

The doctrine of salvation through participation in the process of deification not only changed the conception of the nature of man and hence the means to human relatedness; it altered the concept of human virtue. The pagans conceived of finite perfection only. "Plato, for example, used justice as the model of perfection" (29,59; 1892). Christ, on the other hand, "used as his model the infinite perfection of love." This change from perfection understood as the attainment of finite virtues to a perfection which is infinite, unattainable, yet always to be attained, transformed the way we measure human value.

> According to the pagan teaching, the attainment of the highest virtue is possible and every step of attainment has its relative significance: the higher the step, the more value, so that from the pagan point of view people are divided into the virtuous and the non-virtuous. According to the Christian teaching which established the ideal of infinite perfection, this division is impos-

sible. There cannot be higher and lower steps . . . ; all the steps
are equal among themselves in relationship to the infinite ideal.
The pagan understanding of value consists in that step reached
by man: Christian value consists only in the process of attaining,
in the greater or lesser speed of the movement. From the pagan
point of view a person who possesses the virtue of prudence
stands higher in moral significance than a person who does not
possess that virtue; a person who possesses prudence and bravery as well stands even higher; a person who possesses prudence,
bravery, and justice as well stands even higher. A Christian cannot consider one person lower or higher than another in moral
significance; a Christian is just more a Christian the more rapidly he is moving toward infinite perfection, independent of the
step on which he is to be found at a given moment. The immobile (*nepodvizhnaja*) righteousness of the Pharisee is lower than
the movement of the repentant thief on the cross. (29,59-
60;1892)

The doctrine of salvation through self-perfection implies and guarantees the possibility of the moral equality of all people. No one can
accumulate virtues in the way that a rich man accumulates money.
Virtue is not a whole made of the sum of its parts, any more than the
All is simply composed of particular things. Virtue is an ideal, an abstraction, the good, love, which nevertheless is a real being, the
source of all good and love, the giver of life to all who participate in
it. The measure of value is not the accumulated wealth of virtues,
but the rapidity with which you are moving from yourself to the
source of your self. Everyone is equal in his capacity to participate in
this process, but some choose to participate more fully and hence are
"more a Christian" than others. This distinction between the more
or less virtuous, however, can be made only in the present. One is
more or less a Christian "in a given moment." The Christian measure of human value, therefore, is the rate of a person's approximation
toward the perfection of love for all right here, right now. In the moment of change from non-love to love, which is to say in the moment
of repentance and forgiveness, you are saved because you do love. As
so often in the Eastern Christian liturgy, for Tolstoy the image of the
redeemed Christian is the repentant thief. Since not even the repentant thief can love perfectly, however, for Tolstoy it is more precise

to say that you are saved in the moment when you try to love. Therefore Tolstoy's theology of perfection, which guarantees the possibility of equality for all by the promise of salvation to all who attempt
to love, is a theology of the practice of the virtue of love.

TOLSTOY'S theology of perfection is a theology of work. He speaks
of life in terms of a "task" to be done, and "to accomplish" is one of
his common verbs and major values. The "entire life of all people is
work" (50,67;1889). The Count Leo Tolstoy, who never had to work
for gainful employment, considers work the only employment of life
gainful of salvation. He believes that Christianity, in its call to perfection, called for a transformation of "Hebrew civilization" in
which "idleness was the condition of paradise" (56,38;1907). In the
"new, more rational order of social life people will be amazed that the
necessity to work had been considered evil and idleness good"
(55,172;1905). Tolstoy believes that when Christianity finally gets
rid of the Hebraic ideals, it will so reevaluate work that "punishment" would consist in the "deprivation of work." Labor is the common task in which all are called to participate.

The theology of perfection is the answer to the question "What
must I do?" The necessity of work is related to the concern for vocation. On the one hand, Tolstoy believed that each person had a particular vocation. The work he had to do is derived from some given
talent. Everyone pursues perfection but each in his own way. Tolstoy
saw his own vocation as a writer and teacher in this sense. On the
other hand, everyone is given the same talent, the common *love for*
he is called to reveal in its perfection. Tolstoy saw his own inner life
in this sense. The two understandings of the vocation of perfection
in work coalesce in the fictional heroes he creates, whose stories tell
of a quest for love, and in the non-fictional essays and preachments,
which teach of the way to love.

The way and the quest which are the "movement" and "approximation toward perfection" consist ultimately in "work on one's
soul" (55,206;1906). This work, as always, Tolstoy understands
as the "gradual approximation toward an established goal" (55,
269;1906). This gradual approximation is accomplished by repeated doing which Tolstoy thinks of as practice and training for the
attainment of an established goal. For example, Tolstoy practices the
elimination of that concern for the opinion of others that he consid-

ers a major source of limitation to all *love for*. This practice consists in testing himself by courting approval and disapproval. "When with someone it is useful to practice not doing acts you will not do in front of people [but might alone], such as killing flies or getting angry at your horse, etc., and doing in front of people acts that you know they will judge you for but which you do not consider bad" (58,92;1910). Tolstoy thus consciously tries not just to do good but to eliminate the other person from his awareness as he performs his exercises in doing good. Thus he tests himself as he practices.

But Tolstoy also often feels that he is being tested by others. He reads a newspaper article critical of him, and the mind of the master responds with rage at the one who does not agree with him. Then he recalls that this is "my test," the "material for my work" (57,60;1909). This moment of test upon reflection in the diary then recalls an incident from the day before. Tolstoy was riding his horse in the woods, and the horse was acting too timidly for his taste, so he "got angry and started to take revenge" on her by pulling at the bit. Then the angry master "recollected" that the "spirit of life" in all is "in the horse" as well and that "he must treat her religiously, with love." He calmed down and calmed down the horse. From this Tolstoy now concludes that "the relationship to animals is very important" because "better and easier than anything else, it prepares for a loving relationship to people: people are vain, tell lies, hurt others on purpose, and mostly feign wisdom, and it is even harder to hold oneself back with them. If you get accustomed to animals, it will be easier with people." By practicing not getting angry with his horse, he will not only accomplish this but prepare himself for the more difficult task of not venting his rage at people who are not in accord with him. Tolstoy not only practices the elimination of his awareness of others who approve or disapprove, but he also works toward the control of himself, the mind of the master who responds to others with rage. At any moment he can test himself or turn the test given him into a preparation for the attainment of his goal. Each bit of experience is a moment of crisis and a call to work and "rework" (58,109;1910).

Tolstoy's angry moment with his horse is most characteristic of his piety of self-perfection. He encounters opposition, disagreement, or disapproval to which he responds with the mind of the master: he rages or sulks, blames others or feels sorry for himself, wallows in re-

sentment or guilt. But then he recollects himself, sees his own relations as his limitations, and restores peace within himself and harmony with others. He practices over and over again that grand "task
of life," which is to replace discord with concord everywhere. What
is most significant in this incident with his horse, however, is not
this obsessive practicing but that Tolstoy sees his "material for
work" right here, right now. His theology of perfection moves the
time and place of the pursuit of salvation not only out of the monas-
teries into the family circle and place of labor, as had Luther, but into
the given unfavorable circumstances of his immediate present. An
unruly horse or an annoying beggar are the "material for the work of
loving those who do not love you or are not pleasing to you"
(57,58;1909). The "Gospel definition of the activity of life" is expressed for Tolstoy, then, in the images of "the cross, or even better
the yoke" which means "the place in your work" (51,71;1890). For
Tolstoy this "yoke" is most often the complex of difficulties with his
wife and family which resulted from his conversion. Thus when Tolstoy speaks in his diaries about "loving the enemy," the enemy may
be a disapproving critic, but usually it is, as with Karenin, his own
disapproving wife. Tolstoy, however, turns his marriage into the
"place in his work," and his failings in his marriage into the "material for work." He does this not to improve his marriage, although he
hoped it would help in this, but to work at the cultivation of his own
soul right here.

Tolstoy's "work on his own soul" is based on a conception of activity as habit and self-perfection as the acquisition of "good habits"
(53,220;1899). His theory of behavior modification assumes that acts
are habits, but divides all acts into three groups depending on their
relationship to consciousness and will: (1) acts we do unconsciously,
not aware of their moral significance, (2) acts we do against our judgment or judge we want to do but do not, (3) acts done in accordance
with our own judgment (65,167-68;1890). The first group will move
into the second "in accord with the movement of our life"; the third
group has moved from the second and become the "property of our
moral nature." The first group, therefore, is the "material for reworking life"; the third group, products "lying in the storehouse." The second group, where I do what I would not and would what I do not, "as
St. Paul says," is the "realm of life" (51,89-90;1890). This is the
"place in your own work." In his theory of behavior modification

Tolstoy pays no attention to motivation for acts. And for the moralist, surprisingly, even the consequences of acts "are not important. What is important is the act which makes for an evil or good habit" (55,258;1906). All acts are the result of former acts which become habits. Change is possible only when one becomes conscious of the habitual act and therefore able to judge it. All behavior moves progressively toward perfection, inevitably toward the scrutiny of conscience and through conscious scrutiny toward perfection by practice.

Tolstoy's theory of behavior modification revolves around two seemingly contradictory concepts, consciousness and habit. Consciousness, which is the "glance at yourself" where you "see yourself as an outsider," is directed at your "activity" (55,75;1905). This scrutiny stops the action, but "only for a time." To change a habit one has "to stop by means of consciousness and then continue activity passed through consciousness." What happens in this process is that one learns to do unconsciously what is "passed through consciousness." The newly acquired habits are as unconscious as the former ones. They are done freely and easily. Tolstoy takes pleasure in such "free, unconscious, almost perfect acts which formerly were done with effort" because they are the measure of his "growth of life, like a mark on the wall" (54,144;1902).

The best example of such a consciously learned unconscious habit is physical labor, like sewing or mowing. Levin at his best mows, unconscious of what he has learned to do consciously. He is all attention to the task, but unconscious of the task. He forgets himself. It is this state of self-forgetting which is total attention that Tolstoy most prizes. "You can forget yourself in plowing, mowing, or sewing. And in this way you must forget yourself in all of life, in the divine task. Don't ask yourself what will come of my labor, what will become of me after death, but give yourself to the task with the same—be it love or desire to do good—with which you plow or sew" (51,76;1890). He believes a person should learn "to do the task of life" with the same "attention" with which he plays chess or reads music (53,151;1897). For Tolstoy, then, the spontaneous and unmotivated *love for* is what is to be learned. And "the task of life is to work out in oneself a conscious love which of itself is transformed into an unconscious love" (54,128;1902).

Tolstoy's theory of behavior modification, with its seeming contradiction of habits that are conscious and unconscious, recalls the scholastic distinction between a spontaneous, unreflected act which is some primal or instinctual drive (*potentia*), a conscious act reflected upon (*actus*), and a spontaneous, unreflected act which is learned through some transformation of self (*habitus*). Tolstoy values highly not the naive, unreflected act which is unconscious, but the act of consciousness and the unconscious habit. The spontaneous and unmotivated giving forth of self can be a learned habit, as for Marya Pavlovna in *Resurrection* (III,iii). All the contradictions in Tolstoy's usage of the words "conscious" and "unconscious" fade away when seen in the light of his theory of behavior modification. Natalya Savishna in *Childhood* does what is right unconsciously, not quite because of some primitive instinct for good, but because she has learned through a hard life lived well how to do what is right unconsciously. The scholastic distinction, however, does not quite fit because it assumes that what is there in the primal potential drive (*potentia*) has need of transformation either to correct it or to make it valuable in human terms. For Tolstoy, however, what is there in Natalya Savishna or any of us is not a primal drive that needs to be transformed. What is there is the *love for* that needs to be revealed. When a person attains perfection "he will do without effort what his nature attracts him to" (51,20;1890). The habit of love does not reshape the self nor add something to it; the habit of love uncovers the true self through the very effort of loving.

Tolstoy's theory of perfection hinges on the will. It assumes that all behavior can be traced back to our "thoughts" and that we can "control" our body, feelings, and acts "by our thoughts" because "thought is the source (*nachalo*) of everything" (53,222;1899). To control our thoughts, and hence our body, feelings, and acts, requires, however, an act of will, what Tolstoy calls "effort" (*usilie*). The "infinite struggle with oneself" which always assures the "joy of work" is waged by acts of effort. The joy of the struggle comes, however, not with the victory but with the exertion of the effort. "Just as the animal being in a person needs happiness from outside himself, so the rational, spiritual being needs only effort (the effort of consciousness) from within" (55,139;1905). "Human life is true life," for Tolstoy, then, "only when it is conscious and consists of efforts of thought, as well as of word and deed" (56,269;1907). This effort is "what is demanded of you right now" (52,49;1891). Regardless of your past, no "repentance" over it will change it (41,224;1910). What must be done is to exert a "real and patient effort" to change right now. This effort to change your thoughts, as well as words and deeds, is what "repentance" (Gr. *metanoia*) really means. On this effort at repentance, all true life depends. "A person's entire life, no matter how awful or virtuous it was in the past . . . is for him the x of the remaining bit of life on which everything depends and which will . . . make the evil good or the good evil. Whether you are Judas or the thief depends on that x" (51,50;1890). While good habits can be stacked away in the storehouse, neither virtue nor vice can be accumulated. Thus good habits may give you some security, but your life depends on the effort of will right here, right now. The movement and approximation toward perfection is endless and relentless.

The effort in the infinite struggle with ourself is to get rid of sin. "I have not undertaken to be sinless," Tolstoy reassured himself in a moment of failure, "because there is no existence without sin; rather, I have undertaken and must undertake to rid myself of sin" (55,208;1906). The "effort" that is required, therefore, is "not to do anything against His will" (57,14;1909). "Effort is always negative" (58,45;1910). It makes possible the process of the "liberation" of life which "is being accomplished." "Effort" is "not doing what hinders this liberation." The theology of perfection, which seeks "greater and greater deification of the soul" even as it assumes that the soul is "divine and therefore perfect," resolves this dilemma in part by a negative conception of deification (77,15;1907). "A person cannot increase love in himself because love is the very essence of life. A person can just destroy the encumberments to the manifestation of love and . . . on that he ought to direct all his efforts" (56,87;1907). These efforts include "first liberation from feeling, then from suggestion [by others], then from one's own reason," and culminate in "submission to the one, eternal reason, God" (54,203;1903). The effort of perfection requires a continuous negative act of will which begins with "abstinence" and moves up the "ladder of virtue" toward "self-control" by an increasing rejection of the personal feelings and desires which block *love for* within (29,73;1891).

"Effort" is Tolstoy's answer to "fatalism" (54,74;1900). The theology of salvation through the process of approximation to perfection stands in argument with both materialistic "determinism without God" and "ecclesiastical or rather dogmatic, supernaturalistic Christianity." These "two most terrible plagues" with which "people have been innoculated in childhood" and which have been "sustained hypnotically till death" teach the same thing: "all effort to be good or do good are idle and empty." Materialism, with its "mechanical, physical, chemical, biological, and even psychological laws," maintains that any "effort exerted on yourself is useless because everything is done by the organization or the milieu" (53,153;1897). The dogmatic church, likewise, teaches that "effort is a sin because it is pride, reliance on your own powers" (sily). To do this the church has had to subvert the teaching of Christ by reverting to an Hebraic world-view. In the ancient days, according to Tolstoy, when people "felt the path they were following was not the real one," they did not put all their "attention and energy" into "finding the right one" (50;94-95;1889). Instead, "fearful for their mistake," they felt "that they had perished, that they would be punished" and so they "turned to the unseen powers (sily) of Elohim," attempting to "propitiate Him" by "begging forgiveness" and "offering Him sacrifices (in the original sense)." The prophets attempted to change this by "denouncing the sacrifices" and "affirming that if there are unseen forces, then they demand only that one go along the right path." Christ taught the same thing, saying that "he was on the path." But then because people were so accustomed to the old ways, the teaching of the prophets and of Christ was turned into a doctrine of sacrifice (zhertva) in which Christ himself is the victim (zhertva) who offered Himself, and "the people are left in their former state of quest for forgiveness." As a result of this new doctrine of sacrifice, "some recognize forgiving, cleansing grace in the sacraments" which are "something like sacrifices" offered and a "redemption by Christ's sacrifice. Others recognize only Christ's sacrifice." The effect has been that "both have remained in the first world-view" where "departure from the path" is a "sin for which one must gain forgiveness." Those who look to "grace" received from "sacraments" which are "like sacrifices offered" end up relying on something "external" to themselves in order to find the right path. They do not use their own powers. Those who believe in redemption through Christ's sacrifice consider themselves "a cleansed, new Adam," and "all new" they "stop struggling." "Redemption [through Christ's sacrifice] is the liberation of oneself from effort" (50,166;1889). Thus the modern doctrines of sanctifying grace and salvation by faith alone, as Tolstoy

understood them, have thrust humanity back into the hands of the "unseen forces of Elohim."

Tolstoy's theology of perfection through effort rests on a belief in freedom. It assumes that regardless of external conditioning and despite the enslaving charity of sanctifying grace a human being in whatever state or condition can always make an effort to be better. What matters is the "effort" (usilie) to love, the "increase and strengthening" (usilenie) of our love (26,419;1887). This is always possible, whatever the external or internal circumstances. Tolstoy's stress on effort with its assumption of freedom, however, bumps up against his firm belief that the life of any person and of the whole world "willy-nilly goes forward toward the better," since "life is that movement" (53,170;1897). All life moves toward perfection. What the church calls "salvation and redemption through Christ" is for Tolstoy the "natural course of life" (56,22;1907). What kind of freedom is there or need there be, if the "natural course of life" is the eternal progress toward the source from which all life comes? In what sense are we free, and why should we make the effort? Who is this God of perfection, and what is the relationship between Him and the world?

GOD AND THE FORCE OF LIFE

"We feel that we are free," Tolstoy concluded toward the end of his life, "but we are not free" (55,36-38;1904). "The illusion of the possession of freedom comes" with the movement through the three stages of consciousness. On the lowest level, aware of self only as physical body separated from all other bodies, a person does not feel free. He is limited by everything else. "As he moves higher in his awareness, he feels himself freer and freer." When a person becomes conscious of himself as a "manifestation of God, he feels completely free." But the procession through the three stages of consciousness, what Olenin traverses in his travels and Levin moves through in mowing, takes place "according to the law of life." It is "what life consists in." Nothing can stop it, and no effort is needed to make it happen. This "incessant movement of life . . . from a lower region of consciousness to a higher one, from less freedom to more freedom, from less happiness (blago) to more happiness" is simply a "process which is constantly being accomplished" (*sovershaetsja*) in each individual and in the whole universe. Life is the movement from the physical to the spiritual, the inevitable progress of the "spiritualization" (*odukhotvorenie*) of everything.

Still, there is a sense in which it can be said that man has free will. Certainly not, however, in the sense of "doing what he wants" because "he who does what he wants is the slave of everything" (55,268;1906). Nor can free will be understood as "volition" in the manner of materialist psychology, where this "will" is really "something derived from impressions, emotions, etc., according to immutable laws" (55,183;1906). This materialist "volition" assumes that "man is an automatic (*samodejstvujushchaja*) machine" which reacts to "stimuli" but forgets about "what makes the machine act" in the first place. "What force (*sila*) is that?" For Tolstoy the answer is certain but not at once clear. "Free will is the action of the divine force (*sila*) in man" (52,50;1891) and therefore "what is called freedom of the will is life itself" (57,30;1909). By this Tolstoy means at the least that although in the materialist realm man is not free, "in everything spiritual he is free" in the sense that "he can love or not love, love more or less" (53,230;1899). A person can always "direct or not direct his power (*sila*) to the service of God." Even though the movement toward God is inevitable, at any moment a person can choose or not to "participate in the general spiritualization" of everything (58,33;1910). "Effort" (*usilie*) is the choice to participate and belong. To the extent that a person chooses to participate in this inevitable progress toward the spiritualization, he is "doing that task which has been predestined" for him. To the extent that a person "manifests his spirituality," he also feels the "happiness which spiritualization, perfection, the increase of love bring: he himself loves (which is the best happiness) and he is loved" (56,268;1906). If a person does not choose to participate in the process of spiritualization, this process will go on despite him. Man is free to love or not to love, but love will inevitably progress to fulfillment because that is the life and law of the All. "Free will is the possibility of acting not by some external, alien will, but by one's own will in accord or not in accord with the law of the All" (56,101;1908).

This "law according to which everything big and small is accomplished is the only real and certain thing, the will of God" (52,8;1891). The content of God's will is in one sense simple. God wills that "it be good not for me alone but for everyone" and everything (55,289-90;1906). Man is the one sent by God to do His will and thus "create true, spiritual life" (51,109;1890). In this is man's creative freedom. But how can man do God's will? In any specific moment, he cannot know what is good for everyone and everything. Man cannot "grasp the entire will of God" (50,142-43;1889). So man must look to his inner feelings to find some "signs" that he is "fulfilling God's will." These signs are three: (1) the absence of suffering, (2) the absence of hostility in oneself or toward oneself, (3) the sense of movement or growth. Tolstoy compares man's life to a horse that draws his master's cart. At first he "lives for himself, for his own will" (54,89;1901). He pulls at the bit, rebels at the bridle, and goes nowhere. But then later he calms down, forgets his own will, and draws the cart. When the horse draws the cart, he feels free from the suffering and free to move. He is fulfilling the will of the master. At this point Tolstoy's analogy breaks down because his God gets where He wants to go even if the horse does not draw the cart. All happens according to His will, so that in life all we can do is "to draw or be drawn" (53,230;1899).

Man's vocation in life is to do the will of God. Historically, for Tolstoy this represents a major change in the relationship to God. He believes the understanding of worship and service has been completely altered. What has happened, Tolstoy argues, is that as time has passed the conception of God has become "more and more unlimited and less and less anthropomorphic" (55,184-86;1906). In the beginning, when gods were more "like human beings," the relationship between man and God was close: there were sacrifices, covenants, thanksgiving, and praise. But as man has become aware of the "total immeasurability of what we call God" and the "total insignificance, the infinite smallness of man in comparison to God," the relationship based on such contact with him has become untenable. The new conception of God, represented by the "Hebraic Jehovah, the Christian Father, the Bhrama, and the Chinese heaven" did not at first change the relationship of men to God because people did not grasp the full "grandeur" of the conception. Worship and service still meant singing praises, making sacrifices, and building buildings. But the real meaning of this grand conception of God is that worship and service consist in the "fulfillment of the task which has been entrusted to us." This relationship of doing God's will "puts man in his real place (*mesto*) and gives him his true happiness which consists only in fulfilling his destined purpose" (*naznachenie*). Man need not affirm, nor praise, nor know, nor pray to God; he need only fulfill God's will. Only when life is understood as the "fulfillment of the will of the one who has sent [us] do death and life after death acquire meaning" (52,87;1893).

This conception of man's vocation does not mean, however, that God is a "despot, a tyrant" (54,43-44;1900). True, in the past the stoics and the Buddhists conceived of a God Who required the doing of His will at man's expense. They understood the "merging of one's will with God's will" to mean a kind of self-denial in which a person ended up "having no will or desires." "Why do I have desires," Tolstoy asks, "if I am to renounce them?" A "God who sent us into the world" to deny ourselves everything "is such a despot, a tyrant." But the Christian God is different. He too "demands self-denial and merging with the will of God," but this merging is "what gives life meaning," and the self-denial is a "redirection of our desires to what God wills, to the establishment of the Kingdom of God on earth, i.e., the replacement of struggle and violence with love and accord." Since Tolstoy assumes that accord is man's true innate desire, he believes that in fulfilling God's will man has "more and more joy." Such a God is not a despot but "a kind master for us, his workers."

Tolstoy's conception of human freedom in relation to God's will reflects the Eastern Christian understanding of the relationship of man to God. In the West St. Augustine cast this relationship into the two-tiered mold of nature and grace. In response to the Manichaean heresy of the two determining forces of good and evil, which he believed eliminated human responsibility, St. Augustine insisted that nature as nature is good. But in response to the Pelagian heresy of voluntarism, which he believed denied the human propensity to evil despite the will to good, St. Augustine insisted that nature of itself is insufficient for salvation and has need of a grace added onto it. Nature is thus something separate from grace. Furthermore, this grace does something to nature, so that human freedom is in some sense limited, if not eliminated. St. Augustine bequeathed his conceptions of nature, grace, and human freedom to the Western tradition, which has been shaped by his two-tiered mold. Eastern Christianity did not know St. Augustine, who after all wrote in a language foreign to it. In the East there is only God and creation. The relationship between God and creation, and most especially man, is said to be "synergistic." God wills and gives, and man "collaborates" or fails to collaborate with God's willing and God's giving. This conception of the collaboration of man with God preserves human freedom and ensures God's autonomy. Tolstoy himself calls the exercise of free will in accord with the divine will "collaboration."[1]

Tolstoy's conception of man's freedom to collaborate with God's will culminates in this vision of the creation of God's life.

> Through me and an infinite number of beings God lives and gives joy, the happiness (*blago*) of life to me and all those beings. What we call free will and what freedom is is the allowance or non-allowance of God into my self so that He might through me create life, live. The non-allowance of Him into myself deprives me of the happiness of life, but His life cannot be hindered since He lives in an *infinite* number of beings, which is *incomprehensible* for me. Beside that, He lives even in those beings who consciously do not allow God into themselves, and living in them He attains the same aims. What is significant is that man, each of us, while having the unconscious happiness of life can also have the greatest conscious happiness of being an instrument of God, uniting directly with Him, creating at the same time His life and our own. (57,74;1909)

God creates the universe and brings it to the perfection of spiritualization through His creatures, the "beings" who are the atoms of the All. These "beings" may not "allow God into themselves," but, regardless, He is there and His life is growing. Man is free, but only to recognize or not the presence of God and then do what follows therefrom. Yet, recognized or not, God's life will come to fruition. Tolstoy illustrates this articulated understanding of the creation of God's life with this telling comparison.

> The rain waters the fields, woods, steppes, and the grasses that grow on them. The trees and the grass have as a result of the acceptance of the moisture the joy of growth, flowering, and frui-

---

[1] Tolstoy uses mainly the verbal form *sodejstvovat'*, "to collaborate" or "to assist." The reader should recall that the fundamental action of replacing discord with harmony is the task by which man collaborates in "God's establishment of His Kingdom." The noun *"sodejstvie,"* which Tolstoy rarely uses, is the technical, theological word for "collaboration." The Russian word is a calque of the Greek *sunergeia*, "synergy." The clearest discussion of this concept of synergy is in V. Lossky, *Mystical Theology*, pp. 197-199.

tion, but the moisture, the rain acts also on the bare earth, softening it and preparing it for the possibility of accepting seeds and growing them. So it is with people. They consciously participate in the divine life, and they are not conscious of God but nevertheless participate in His life, not even knowing it themselves.

What is telling about this comparision is that the image from the world of nature does not just clarify man's position in the universe. The trees and the grass are themselves "beings" who "consciously" or "unconsciously" allow God's will into themselves. To Tolstoy the world of nature is not fundamentally different from the human world nor separate from the Divine. Nature is not just an emblem of God's love for man or a revelation of God's love for man; nature itself is a manifestation of God's love coming to be. It is significant, then, that this simile, as well as the image of rain in *Resurrection* which it resembles and the other numerous fictional images of rain and light which it recalls, presents the world of nature in terms of giving and receiving, rather than taking and destroying. The Darwinian vision of a Hobbesian war of each against each does not enter into Tolstoy's conception of nature because Tolstoy looks beyond to God's providence reigning over nature. Tolstoy chooses to see in nature moments of the recognition and reception of God's gift of life—liquid and light—because in these moments he sees the creation of the Kingdom of God. Man and nature willy-nilly live because they are given God's life, but men truly live when in recognition of the reception they choose God's will for their life. Tolstoy sums up this understanding of the relationship of creation to creator with the "beautiful idea," very characteristic of Eastern Christian thought, that "God is the light of the sun and man the object which absorbs the rays of light, of God" (56,55;1907). In this view "man's body is those rays of God which man has not absorbed." And the purpose of "life for man is more and more absorption of the divinity." Salvation through deification means the total absorption of the will of God, resulting in a complete transfiguration of the self.

The person who chooses the will of this God Who is not a despot but a kind "master" (*khozjain*) is a "worker" (*rabotnik*) of the Lord. To be a "worker of the One by whom I live," however, means that "I do not exist" (57,183;1909). In place of the personality there is "just the worker, and all his interests" lie in his master's "task." "Perfection" means "being a good worker" for the master. This metaphor of man as worker, which informs *Master and Man* (*Khozjain i rabotnik*) clarifies the synecdochic image of man as part of the whole. In both views the "self as an individual being is an illusion," and "there is no 'I' " (57,56;1909). But the image of man as a "cell" or "organ" of the All, the whole body, stresses the relationship of the part to the whole. It turns on the issue of belonging. The image of the worker casts the focus from the issue of belonging to the functional relationship. "Individual life, personal life is an illusion. There is no such life. There is only a function, an instrument of something" (53,220;1899).

In this functional conception of man's relationship to God, organic metaphors are replaced by instrumental ones. "Human beings are instruments of the Supreme Force" (57,127;1909). This "force which does everything uses me to do its work" (55,195;1906). Man's identity, therefore, is to be "just an instrument." This sense of man as an instrument of some force is precisely what Levin discovers in mowing, for at his best moments the scythe moves the body, not the body the scythe, and in the end he feels that "some external force is moving him." Mowing, Levin does not exist; he becomes the instrument of something else. The mowing scene, therefore, because it is an emblem of life's task, the practice of love, and the establishment of identity, is an emblem of becoming an instrument of the Lord.

If man's identity is to be "just an instrument," then his vocation is "to keep himself in repair, like a scythe or an axe that could hone itself." "I am a self-moving saw or a living spade whose life consists in keeping the blade clean and sharp. It will do the work, and the work is necessary," Tolstoy observes of himself and then characteristically goes on to exhort himself. "Get it sharp and keep on sharpening and sharpening. Keep on making yourself better and better" (54,122;1896). Man's vocation is the articulation of the self. But the self that is to be honed and sharpened is not the divine self. It is the personality. "The personality is the instrument for the perfection of the soul. Only through the personality and its work can the soul be perfected and become proximate to God" (52,154;1894). In a sense, then, I do not articulate myself. Rather, through the negative actions which train the personality I allow it to be used by "the one who is not the instrument, who is not material, who is beyond bounds, God in me" (53,119;1902). Thus it can be said that "all the efforts which I can make and which are characteristic of me consist only in opening an access for God into my soul, in giving Him space for his activity by suppressing myself" (57,100;1909). And it must be remembered that "He Himself will help me to the extent that I open for Him an access into my soul" (54,168;1903). When I open an access to God in myself, I know Him. "There is only one good deed, the one good deed, the one which has as its aim the discovery (*otkrytie*) of God for one-self, the opening (*otkrytie*) of a window through which God is visible. Only through that window, if it is gotten open, will you see God and through it will God act in you" (51,44;1890). The knowledge of God comes with the efforts of perfection which clear the coverings of self-love and make way for "God in me." Thus the instrument of the Lord seems to be called to become His container. "One must construct in oneself an abode (*obitalishche*) worthy of God that He might come and dwell" (51,48;1890). Man is called to be the place where God resides.

This container of the Lord, however, must give Him forth. The "highest happiness" is "to absorb into myself and contain in me as much as possible of the divine will in the form of love" and "to be as much as I can a conductor of that will" (54,72;1900). The clearest metaphors of identity are instruments of transmission. "The soul is a glass, and God is the light passing through the glass" (45,41;1910). Man is a "channel through which the immobile, non-material, non-temporal, non-spatial principle passes in this life" (57,172;1909). Man is an "opening through which life passes (a turbine)" (89, 45;1906). "Man is a vessel with two openings" of uneven size; into the larger one "love enters (from God) and through" the smaller one "love leaves (like a teapot)" (56,79;1907). Man is "just an instrument of transmission through which the divine force acts" (55,146;1905). In the synecdochic understanding of the relationship of man to God, the key word was "part" (*chast'*); in the instrumental understanding the key word is "through" (*cherez*). "God lives in me or rather through me or rather it seems that I exist but what I call me is only an opening through which God lives (55,6;1904). The purpose of all these glasses, conductors, channels, transmitters, turbines, and teapots is to keep the openings and byways clear so that God's life, love, and will might pass through. That is the goal of salvation. "They speak of saving the soul. One can save only what can perish. The soul cannot perish because it alone exists. One need not save the soul but cleanse it of all that has darkened and defiled it, enlighten it so that God might more and more pass through it" (45,42;1910).

Salvation through deification thus means salvation not through the acquisition but through the transmission of the divine life. "In life we are frozen, stopped-up vessels whose task is to open up and overflow, to establish communication with the past and the future, to become a channel of and a participant in the common life" (50,13;1888). Man's vocation is to let the divine content flow through him. "The entire wisdom of the world" teaches that one must "transfer his life from the form to the content and not direct his energies (*sily*) toward preserving the forms, but toward flowing" (53,19;1895). "All that I can do if I understand my position in the universe is to submit to the law of the disclosure of myself, of my spiritual essence. I can swim with the flow, not take a stand against the flow or hold on to anything in opposition to the flow. . . . All a person can do is just for himself to submit to the will of God, the LAW" (55,214;1906).

In discussing the synecdochic metaphysics of the part and the whole, I defined Tolstoy's "beings" as "an act or an action, a movement which goes out of itself toward something other, uniting this other to itself." This definition must now be clarified, for Tolstoy's "beings" are not just those atoms of energy, going outward and toward. They are the vessels of the waves of energy going outward and toward. God, man, and nature are all energetic movement, but man and nature transmit the energy of God. "The life of the universe appears to me as follows: through innumerable pipes of all different kinds there flows liquid or gas or light. This light is the whole force of life (*sila zhizni*)—God. We are the pipes, all beings. Some pipes are completely stationary (*nepodvizhny*), others almost so, others less so, and finally we are completely mobile (*podvizhnye*) pipes. We can allow the light through completely or we can block it for a while" (50,190;1889). Tolstoy's "universe of living beings," which he imagines as "one organism," is the receiver and transmitter of the "force of life, God" (55,26;1904).

The doctrine of God implied by this "universe of living beings" turns on a paradox. It is important to remember, first of all, that for Tolstoy the "divine force in and of itself without any form is only my representation and obviously inexact, false, incomplete" (50,192;1889). On the one hand, however, "this divine force moving and directing the forms of life, i.e., what lives in forms, is not an idea but reality (*dejstvitel'nost'*) itself." On the other hand, "this common life, the force of that organism, is not God; it is only one of his manifestations; just as our planet is a part of the solar system which in its turn is part of another, higher system, etc., so also the force of the spirit is only one of the manifestations of God" (55,26;1904). In this way Tolstoy tries to save his doctrine of God as the Force of Life from a form of vitalistic pantheism. He insists that "God is always inaccessible." But Tolstoy must also keep his God of becoming from the realm of change. The "force of life" is not the same as the "source" of the force, any more than the light of the sun is the sun. The inaccessible God, for whom "even the pronoun HE somehow diminishes HIM" does not change and therefore cannot be energetic movement (44,264;1910). "What we call God is the infinite spiritual, non-spatial, non-temporal being which we know as that which exists," (54,187;1903). Thus, just as the doctrine of the God of Life and Love rests on the paradox of the All which unifies itself by a process of separation from everything else, so the doctrine of God as the Force of Life hinges on a vision of God Who is at once all energy and the one essential source of all energy.

Tolstoy's doctrine of God as the Force of Life has deep roots in the Eastern Christian tradition. In Western theology, the doctrine of God usually rests on the notion of abstract being, and God can be defined as the Being whose essence equals existence. This God may be pure act, but the conception is static. God seems separate from all reality, its ground and cause, but not its fabric and life. The model is Aristotle's Unmoved Mover. In the East God is all energy and movement. He is the God of Life, physical and spiritual. God is not abstract but all act, and there is no actor separate from the action. This Eastern doctrine of God does distinguish between God's "essence" and His "energies" and God remains unknowable in His "essence." But in His "energies," both "uncreated" and "created," God exists in the world, *ad extra*, available to all because He is the energy of all. The dominant image of this divine energy, one of God's "manifestations," is light, and created light is understood as a physical form or expression of the uncreated light. In the piety of Eastern Christianity, sanctity is marked, not by stigmata (no Eastern saint has ever had them), but by a transfiguring light which permeates and emanates from the body (as with St. Seraphim of Sarov who lived in the time of

Pushkin). Dostoevsky's slanting rays of light from the sun and Tolstoy's sky permeated with light emanating from a central source are literary images of this Eastern Christian doctrine of God.[2]

For Tolstoy the energy that flows through the universe is not the unknowable God, the source of the force ever inaccessible, but the manifestation of God whom we experience as the "force of life" and can call the "force of the spirit." From a young age Tolstoy believed that the "Holy Spirit in the Gospels is an unconscious force living in all people, acting in each against his striving, but in accord with the common good and truth" (48,74;1858). This unconscious force that the Gospels call the Holy Spirit and Tolstoy calls the "force of life" is not a simple element. The "foundation of the divine essence," Tolstoy came to believe, is comprised, as it were of three elements, "life," "reason," and "love." (53,32;1895). In this doctrine of God "life is the power (sila) of movement, original (creative) power. Unenlightened by reason it is just a force (sila). Enlightened by reason it is love." Of course, "life," "reason," and "love" are just three names for Tolstoy's "basic concept" of God, but, still, in establishing the relationship between these three elements in the divine essence Tolstoy has let the Christian triune God in by the back door. He too has a creator (the "creative power"), a logos ("reason"), and a spirit of life ("love"). But in his understanding of God, as with all his "basic concepts," Tolstoy imagines the discriminate elements all together at once. The "elemental force" for him is a force which draws all things together into harmony (55,118;1905). The "force of the spirit" acts to unite everything.

This "elemental force," which unites everything, orders nature. The universal organism is made of beings which transmit this elemental force of unification through the so-called inorganic world by "gravity" and "attraction," through the vegetable world by "reproduction," and through the animal world by "reproduction" and "social interaction" (56,148-49;1908). All of nature, inorganic and organic, receives and gives forth this elemental force. But not all of nature transmits without resistance. Resistance to the elemental

---

[2] The clearest discussion of this Eastern doctrine of God and the attendant conception of creation is in V. Lossky, *Mystical Theology*, pp. 67-113. This doctrine runs throughout Eastern Christian thought, but it finds its best expression in the work of St. Gregory Palamas. For a discussion of the Palamite synthesis of this doctrine, see John Meyendorff, *A Study of Gregory Palamas* (Bedfordshire, 1947), pp. 202-227.

force is what makes natural evil, the movement at odds with the force of life which results in particular things at odds with each other. To the extent that "beings" are non-resistant to the force of life, they are "immobile." The force just flows through them, or, to say it another way, they flow with the force. These totally transmitting beings are immobile, however paradoxical this may seem at first, because, as Tolstoy astutely observed in his comment on Newtonian physics, "movement *is not* in opposition to rest; it is the opposition of directions of movement. The movement of everything in the same direction is rest" (48,135;1872). All of nature moves toward this rest, which is the movement of all together at one. But this immobile yet moving and harmonious universe of at-onement which receives and transmits the "force of life" itself does not truly exist in time and therefore does not truly move or change. "The universe (*mir*) seems to move. Upon strict consideration, however, I see that it is not the universe that moves but that I do not know it all at once (*ne vdrug*). Nevertheless, the universe does not move, nor does it originate as in Darwinism; it is. It just seems to me to be originating, and what I think of as geological and cosmological upheavals only seem so because of the structure of my mind; they have no reality at all" (55,221-22;1906). To the personality the universe comes to be in this life. But the divine self senses the universe as it exists beyond the categories of space, time, and causality bounded only by the logic of the All.

Within this universe, as manifested in this life, man is the completely mobile being. "What we call our life, our personal life, is the capacity to stand in the way of the light, not to let it through" (50,190;1889). In this sense man's life is always prone to moral evil, because "sin is just the deviation from the life of the spirit which is inevitably being accomplished" (56,89;1908). Still, despite his mobility, man is made in the image of the triune God, whose divine energy is not only beyond but within. Of this energy within man Tolstoy says that "the divine force which moves life is love. Not enlightened by reason, this force is love for self, enlightened by reason; it is love for beings, for people, for truth, for good, for God" (53,66;1895). In man, however, the three elements do not exist all together at one. Although God "placed in him His reason, which liberates love," man uses that reason only to love himself (53,92;1896). This self-love results in that separation from beings which ultimately leads to coercion and violence. Man's vocation is to be enlightened by God's reason and in this life thus attain true life. To become enlightened man must make the effort not to block the "force of life" which is God's gift of life, reason and love. Thus Tolstoy's conception of the relationship of God, man, and the universe and hence his whole understanding of religion and moral life turns on his doctrine of God as the Force of Life. There is God in His essence, the "Supreme Force" (*Vyshaja Sila*) and God in His energies, the "force of life" (*sila zhizni*). All action against this divine force is the violation of it that is called coercion or violence (*nasilie*). All action in collaboration with the force is called effort (*usilie*). All human existence consists in actions which attempt to go along with the divine action or to go against it. Sin comes in deviation from the force; salvation comes in collaboration with it.

Man's collaboration with the "force of life" leads to true life, but this true life is man's most paradoxical state. "True life is the capacity to stand so that we can let the light through, not hold it back. But when a person takes such a stance . . . the movement (*dvizhenie*) of life ends. He feels that he has done everything he ought to have only when he has removed himself, *as if he did not exist*. When a person is cognizant of this negation of his personal existence, then he transfers his life into what is passing through (*cherez*) him, into God" (50,190;1889; ital. added). Man's vocation is to reach the stage where the " 'I' approaches the non-'I' " (52,36;1891). This is Levin's third stage of consciousness, when I do not exist, but all there is is "the infinite divine force acting in the world through (*cherez*) me, through my consciousness" (88,318;1904). Man finds harmony with the force of life not just when "I do not exist" but when "His force which is love passes through (*cherez*) me" (50,44;1889). This, then, is the real meaning of Olenin's moment in the mountains, when he sensed a loss of "control of my will" and felt that "some elemental force loves [Maryanka] through (*chrez*) me." At that moment it seemed to him that "the whole of God's world, all of nature, was pressing that love into my soul," and he believed that "formerly I was dead; now I am alive." In the mountains Olenin experiences Tolstoy's God.

What distinguishes man from nature is precisely the paradoxical capacity consciously to experience the loss of self. Like Nekhlyudov in *Lucerne*, Tolstoy believes that "the force of life is one and the same in everything, in the grass and the buds on the trees, in the flowers, insects, and birds" (57,61;1909). Only man, however, has the "characteristic of being able to be conscious of this force in himself, when he . . . submits to it." Man is aware of this force only when he is not aware of himself. But man need not submit to the "force of life called God" which "he knows in everything and especially clearly in beings most like himself" (56,121;1908). He can live a life which is oblivious to or aware of the force. "The difference between these two lives is that in the first I live one limited life surrounded by hostile beings, while in the second, beside the limited life, I also live the life of all similar beings near me, becoming more and more conscious of [the force] also by means of their love." This is the difference between Anna and Levin.

In man this paradoxical conscious loss of self leads to the knowledge of God. "What seems to me the movement of my personal life is the movement of my form of life when I stand at an angle to the direction of divine life. . . . The movement of my life is the wavering of that form which was standing at an angle to the direction of the force and little by little is adjusting to that direction. When the identity of direction is established, the movement stops, the fleshly, personal life ends and *I pass into the force which is passing through me.* . . . When I stand in the direction of the divine will and it passes through me, ceasing to move me, then illusion fades and I am conscious that I, my life, is nothing other than the divine force. . . . The consciousness of life is transformed from the moving form to the source (*istochnik*) of the force, to the divine will itself, eternal and endless. From the consciousness of the form I move to the consciousness of life itself. . . . I am conscious of myself as the very force of life which passes through me" (50,191-92;1889; ital. added). To be conscious of the force of life in oneself, then, is to go forth from self to other in a spontaneous swell of love which surges back upon the self. The knowledge of God as the force of life comes in a moment of reciprocity which is a mutual passing through of self to other. In the loss of self, there is a return to the self. In this reversal and return rests the knowledge of God.

This knowledge of God is grounded, then, in the fact of consciousness. The mode of awareness which transfers attention from self to other to let the other pass into one's awareness is the model for the way to know God. This knowledge of God, furthermore, is realized concretely in the experience of mutual *love for.* In that love for others

wherein we give forth of self to other in a right-now reciprocal feed-
back event, we experience that creative force of life enlightened by
reason releasing love. This knowledge of God bestows ultimate belonging, for when "I pass into the force which is passing through me"
and "what goes through me is not me but the force endless and
whole," then "I have stopped being a part of the whole" (50,191-
92;1889). The "isolation which consisted of the form through
which" the force "was passing is over and I have united with the All."
In this knowledge of God I find my true residence. "I have merged
with the All." And, finally, with this knowledge of God, "I know that
death is not terrifying to me" because I see that "when I die I shall in
no way die, but I shall be alive in everything else . . . and everything
that will be, will be I . . . so that perishing, destruction, death do not
exist."

What Tolstoy learns in the knowledge of God which comes with
the loss of self is what Maman knows intuitively, Prince Andrew discovers in dying, and Levin learns in mowing. It is what Nikolenka
finds in the garden, when the "force of life" in nature takes on another meaning and he senses the "source of all beauty and bliss" and
feels "as though nature and the moon and I were one and the same."
It is what Olenin discovers in the mountains. And it is what Pierre
learns in captivity when, embued with the "force of life," he looks to
the sky and sees that "all that is mine, all that is in me, all that is
me." With this knowledge of God in the moment of loss of self Tolstoy, like his heroes, resolves his fundamental questions of identity
and vocation. Personality and death are eliminated. The part rejoins
the whole and, dispersed throughout, the "I" finally reaches the
"non-I" and lives in everything, in a loving seizure of the All. In the
loss of self man achieves salvation through deification.

Conclusion

THE ESTRANGED RESIDENT

LEO TOLSTOY is a Russian Christian artist and theologian of the second half of the nineteenth century. His task was to create an image and idea of life as understood in the Eastern Christian tradition but freed from what he believed were ecclesiastical misreadings of dogmas and from what he felt was the pompous and meaningless jargon of most philosophical and theological discourse. His two guiding ideas are freedom and unity, and over these he saw himself at odds with both the religious and secular sectors of the world in which he lived. The Russian Orthodox Church and the traditional piety it fostered to him were at best a "crude form of the abstract, purely spiritual relationship to the Principle of life" and at worst with the doctrines of grace and redemption in violation of freedom and with the insistence on a unique orthodoxy in violation of unity (55,243;1906). The secular sector was his greater enemy, the "determinists" being in basic opposition to freedom, the "materialists" assuming the existence of multiple, particular things devoid of any inherent unity. Doing battle with the major forces of intellectual and spiritual life in nineteenth-century Russia, Tolstoy thus stands alone, a stranger in his native land.

But, while estranged, Tolstoy is still a resident in the world in which he dwells. Although in opposition to ecclesiastical life and to official interpretations of dogma, Tolstoy shares many of the assumptions of his fellow Eastern Christian thinkers, both his predecessors in the Greek and Byzantine tradition and his contemporaries in modern Russia. He views the world in the Greek and Platonic tradition (middle and neo-) which divided Eastern Christian thought from the more Aristotelian and Roman West. With this Eastern tradition Tolstoy shares the fundamental assumption of a higher unity to which all particular things are subordinated: the general takes precedence over the particular. With these thinkers he makes the correlative assumptions that the intuitive, "mystical" apprehension of reality is primary to empirical knowledge and that only dialectical thinking can acccommodate the unity which overrides all particularity. In his doctrine of God he walks the same tightrope of transcendence and immanence as those thinkers who insist that God is unknowable in his "essence" yet known in his "energies." His model of salvation is the Eastern Christian idea of deification, and he shares the belief in human collaboration in the task of salvation. To him salvation is a restoration of and a return to the primary unity of all creation. For him, as for the Eastern Christian tradition as a whole, sin is separation from this unity and redemption entails the realization of the inevitable reality of God all in all. Tolstoy may not be an Orthodox thinker, but certainly he is an Eastern Christian artist and theologian within the culture of Russian Orthodoxy.

Tolstoy's world-view, not surprisingly, then, resembles in many ways the teachings of his contemporaries and successors in modern Russian religious thought. The dominant idea of that tradition is the total unity of all that is. Tolstoy's metaphysics of the All stands beside the highly influential metaphysics of total unity created by his younger contemporary, Vladimir Solovyov (1853-1900). In the famous *Lectures on Godmanhood* (1878) Solovyov, a mystic and encyclopedic philosopher, detailed a metaphysical world of particular "beings" which he thought of as a synthesis of the concepts of idea, atom, and monad. These beings he imagined as "mutually penetrating," particular beings, yet all in all, sharing in a "wholeness" and "total unity," an "All" which is and is not the Divine Being. Even the more technical philosopher Nicholas Lossky (1870-1965), who does not quite subscribe to the metaphysics of total unity, has elaborated a metaphysical system of ideal being composed of "substantival agents" which resemble Leibnitz's monads, except that their windows and doors are all open: each agent is free and particular, yet consubstantially united with all others. For Solovyov, Lossky, and many others the model of this metaphysical reality is the Trinitarian God which is simultaneously many and one, composed of distinct beings which are "neither separate nor merged," to use the commonly quoted apophatic phrase from the doctrine of Christ's person as defined at the Council of Chalcedon (A.D. 451). Modern Russian metaphysics takes its source in the doctrine of the Trinity. Tolstoy, who considered this doctrine so much hogwash, still managed to create a similar metaphysics which differs from the more orthodox thinkers only in the description of the redemption of particularity as "merging"; it should be remembered, however, that this merging is understood by Tolstoy as growth, not simple loss of particularity. Tolstoy thus stands within the Russian tradition of metaphysical total unity.

The metaphysics of total unity inevitably stumbles over the hard fact of the material world. Solovyov tried to ensure the unity of Creator and Creation by resurrecting the ancient, mystical idea of Sophia, the Divine Wisdom, which he understood variously but most often as a sort of Platonic idea of passive existence. This idea of passive existence he imagined united in metaphysical wedlock with an idea of active, energizing, and unifying life, which he called the Logos and the Christ. Metaphysically, Sophia is uncreated, but physically it is the created world. This created world, however, has marital problems, and life is the process of the restoration of the ideal relationship between Sophia and the Logos. Solovyov's doctrine of Sophia in its various forms proved fruitful to Russian theologians because it portrayed a world intimately united with the Divine, at odds, to be sure, but not estranged. While the systematic theology of Sergey Bulgakov (1871-1944), which is based on this sophiological conception of God and creation, seems to some Orthodox thinkers a touch heretical (because Sophia appears to be a fourth element in the divine trinitarian life), the sophiological view of reality is important to the modern Russian tradition because it preserves the world from any inherent evil tendency: sophiology creates a picture of the world appropriate for the doctrine of man as image and likeness and makes possible a theology of culture. At first glance Tolstoy seems far removed from the recondite views of the sophiologists, but with them he shares a view of the world which is by nature good even when dominated by evil and at bottom always united with the Divine: for Tolstoy the umbilical cord is not broken. His images of nature are without exception sophiological. His understanding of the Force of Life, created and uncreated, we might say, resembles the sophiologists' Logos, which gives life to an assumed existing reality. Tolstoy shares with sophiology a panentheistic doctrine of God.

In the moral rather than the metaphysical realm, the vision of total unity emerges in the philosophy of Tolstoy's nearly exact contemporary, Nicholas Fyodorov (1828-1903). Fyodorov's moral vision is based on one principle: "one must live not for oneself (egoism) and not for others (altruism), but with all and for all." His sense of moral total unity is expressed in his "common task." For him to live with and for all means "the unification of the living (the sons) for the resurrection of the dead (the fathers)." Unlike Tolstoy, Fyodorov, a kind, meek polymath, did not do battle with the positivists of his day; he joined their ranks. He would harness all scientific knowledge to "regulate" nature in order to accomplish the one common task of realizing salvation on earth, which he understood to be the harmonious living of literally all together. He shares with Tolstoy the rejection of a simplistic altruism, the notion of human collaboration in God's salvation of man, and the high ideal of the salvation of all together on earth. Tolstoy's moment of aesthetic perception when the living, the dead, and those to come are united in the aesthetic experience partakes of the maximalism of Fyodorov's vision of moral total unity. Tolstoy believed Fyodorov was a saint and claimed to be proud to live in the same century with such a man.

The moral and metaphysical visions of total unity always assume a radical freedom for all. The trinitarian model which ascribes an independent active power to all three persons of the one God but allows for no conflict shapes the world-views of most Russian thinkers. They postulate an ideal world in which there is no discord among the free members of the community. To Alexey Khomyakov (1804-1860), a seminal thinker in the modern tradition, the free concordance of all is the only measure of truth. He saw this principle at work in the early church councils and called this principle of truth 'councilarity" (sobornost'). On this principal of free communion he built his ecclesiology. With anarchist thinkers freedom only seems to take precedence over community. Nicholas Berdyaev (1874-1948), of the modern Russian thinkers the most known in the West, imagines a primordial, creative free unity out of which is born God, Whose love is that creative freedom. From this same freedom God creates the world, but all existence in this world entails a loss of freedom and unity. The "objectified world" must recognize the necessity of law and the division of subject and object. But man as person retains an element of the creative freedom (Berdyaev thus reworks the doctrine of man as image and likeness), and in his creative love he can attain unity with others, fusing with them yet remaining his unique self. When he so loves, he is saved. In such an "existential moment" of free creative union man attains the Kingdom of God now. All other experience is in the objectified world of space, time, and causality. Berdyaev's world-view reflects many aspects of Tolstoy's. The concept of the objectified world resembles Tolstoy's beings separated from the All, existing in the world of space and time, following the law of causality. Berdyaev's notion of "existential time," with its "moments of eternity" now, is Tolstoy's "living in the present" with its "right-now" idea of time. Berdyaev's creative freedom is Tolstoy's Divine Love and the Force of Life. Both significantly alter the doctrine of creation *ex nihilo*. Both share a theology of redemptive love. Both stress freedom but press it into the service of unity.

Russian epistemology is grounded in moral and metaphysical total unity. It often assumes that the subject in the subject-object relationship is what Solovyov called the "divine principle" within, and it wants to establish a relationship of equality and mutuality between the subject and object. Father Pavel Florensky (1882-1952?) in his seminal work *The Pillar and Foundation of Truth* (1914) cast the epistemological event into the mold of love. "Cognition," he says, "is the knower's real going forth from self and what is the same thing the known's real going into the knower, a real union of known and knower." Florensky, a trained mathematician and physicist, believes Western epistemology, which assumes the identity of a thing with itself, turns all beings into dead objects. With his "antinomian" logic in which A in order to be A must be a correlative of non-A, he would resuscitate all beings by giving them the power to transcend themselves in each act of knowing the other. In this way each "impersonal 'non-I' becomes personal, another 'I', i.e., THOU," The "other" (*drugoe*) is the "friend" (*drug*). Lossky's intuitivism, a philosophically more sophisticated epistemology, grounds the act of knowing in the fact of attention which is understood as a "coordination" between subject and object with no causal connection or subordination of one to the other. Tolstoy's epistemology combines empirical knowledge, which Florensky would see as a Western epistemology of "lifeless immobility," with knowledge by consciousness, which strongly resembles Florensky's love-knowledge and as with Lossky is grounded in the fact of attention. What I have called Tolstoy's logic of the All, which assumes that for a thing to be it must coexist with what it is not, is a precise example of Florensky's "antinomian" thinking.

Russian epistemology assumes a center of knowing, what philosophy calls a subject, which is an active principle inherently connected to or capable of direct connection with all other. This assumption can be traced to the doctrine of man as image and likeness of the Divine, but filtered through Solovyov's idea of Godmanhood which in effect uses the doctrine of Christ's person as the model for the doctrine of man: in each person the center of being and center of knowing is the "divine principle" neither separate from nor merged with the human principle. The human principle, the personality, is understood as a hypostasis or substance which has this divine principle as its center of being and knowing. As the philosopher and religious thinker of great distinction, Simon Frank (1877-1950), would say, the personality is the "created bearer of the image," and the whole tradition assumes that the purpose of life is to let this "image of God" (*lik Bozhij*) shine through the "personality" (*lichnost'*). In epistemology the center of knowing is seen as a special cognitive faculty called "integral reason" or "free willing reason" by Khomyakov, "mystical knowledge" or "direct perception" by Solovyov, "spiritual experience" by Berdyaev. This special cognitive faculty works, however, only when the center of knowing is in harmony with the center of being and both are in accord with all being; right knowledge requires moral goodness. Tolstoy shares with this tradition the assumption of a special cognitive faculty that he calls "reasonable consciousness" or simply "reason" (but not of the empiricist kind), and he too grounds this faculty in a "divine principle" (he even uses that phrase) which he understands to be neither separate from nor merged with the personality. With his fellow Russians, therefore, Tolstoy firmly believes that right knowledge requires moral goodness. In his epistemology, as in his moral and metaphysical vision of total unity, Tolstoy reveals himself a product and creator of the culture of Russian Orthodoxy.[1]

The icon of this Orthodox view of life is Dostoevsky's Father Zo-

---

[1] The generalizations about particular thinkers and the interpretations given to them are all based on my own readings in Russian religious philosophy. Since there are no interpretive studies of this rich but short-lived tradition, the running commentary in the three volumes *Russian Philosophy*, edited by James M. Edie, James P. Scanlon, and Mary-Barbara Zeldin (Chicago, 1965) may be useful, even though this anthology emphasizes the more strictly philosophical concerns of the writers and thus does not bring into focus the religious concerns which in most cases were the primary ones. Gustave Wetter, S.J. in *op.cit.*, has given a helpful general schema for understanding Russian religious thought, although with perhaps too much emphasis on the Hegelian parallel. The best statement on the nature of Russian religious thought is the short seminal piece by the now deceased but much beloved and much missed Mary-Barbara Zeldin, "Chaadayev as Russia's First Philosopher," *Slavic Review* III (1978), 473-480.

sima. In contrast to the Western Grand Inquisitor, who sees a world of rebellious, separated individuals in need of unification by something external to them, and thus sets himself up as a controlling power, ruling by miracle, mystery, and authority over a "unanimous and harmonious anthill," the Russian Father Zosima sees present human reality only as a necessary "period of human isolation" (*uedinenie*) during which each individual, because he "wishes to secure the greatest possible fullness of life for himself" ends up "aloof" from others, "hiding himself and what he has," "repelled by others and repelling them." This sense of individual freedom leads to slavery. For Zosima each person, acting as a "unit" (*edinitsa*) has "cut himself off from the whole" (*tseloe*) and can find redemption only in that "common human integrity" (*ljudskaja, obshchaja tselostnost'*) which is a "feat of loving fraternal communion" (*obshchenie*). Zosima believes this "isolation" has resulted from the "distortion" of "God's image and His truth" which is "in" all and that the redemption of all entails the restoration of the "beautiful" (*blagolepyj*) image. The moral unity of men comes with the expression by all of God's love which is in all. For Zosima this divine image within is the pledge of a total unity with all of reality, physical and metaphysical. On earth we may be "as it were astray," but we have been given a "precious mystic sense of our living bond with the other world, with the higher, heavenly world, and the roots of our thoughts and feelings are not here but in other worlds." We all have a God-given special cognitive faculty which enables us to grasp reality in its total unity. While Zosima believes we are but "seeds from different worlds" sown on earth, which is "God's garden," for him what grows stays alive only through the "feeling of its contact with other mysterious worlds." Without the contact the "heavenly growth will die away in you" and "you will be indifferent to life and even grow to hate it." Right knowledge entails moral goodness, and therefore contact is maintained through "active love" which in its complete "self-forgetfulness" is a "semblance of divine love and the highest love on earth." This active love is expressed particularly in the love for a sinner, but should include "love of all God's creation, both the whole (*tseloe*) and each grain." If you love "each leaf and each divine ray of light, if you love everything, you will perceive the divine mystery of things." In his epistemology, as well as his vision of moral and metaphysical total unity, Father Zosima is an image of the religious idea of life in the culture of Russian Orthodoxy. This culture saw the great meaning of the Christian religion, not in the Passion and Crucifixion, but in the Resurrection: the joy and gladness of eternal life in the face of the death of everything is the Good News. Father Zosima regrets the loss of "joy" during the period of isolation and calls all to "pray to God for gladness." The tone of his piety, as well as the tenor of his moral and metaphysical views, epitomize the Russian version of the Christian religious experience. Estranged from Father Zosima's church and monastery, Tolstoy dwells in his universe.

"Active love" is Father Zosima's name for the redemptive act required of all. *The Brothers Karamazov* tells the story of three brothers in pursuit of their redemption through love. Alyosha, who loves the father and never doubts the father's love for him, is the normal human being, weak but by nature inclined toward active love. Dmitry and Ivan are the types of distortion, the sinner and the man of little faith. These distorted brothers can regain their normal humanity only when they restore within themselves the image of love: Dmitry has to experience the dream of the babe and the gift of the pillow; Ivan has to experience genuine concern for the drunken peasant. The salvation of life comes with the spontaneous and unmotivated act of love for other. The theological vision of life in *The Brothers Karamazov* thus resembles the idea of the salvation of life in *War and Peace*, even as *Anna Karenina* explores the two distorted types of human experience, the sinner and the man of little faith. Father Zosima's active love, which is understood as God's love in us given to be expressed and when expressed redemptive of life, a theological vision of great hope and promise, stands in total agreement with Tolstoy's theology of redemptive love. The verbal icons of the two major Russian novelists of the nineteenth century thus assume St. Gregory of Nyssa's beautiful idea that "Christianity is the imitation of the divine nature" and the Eastern Christian liturgical notion that the Divine by nature is the "Lover of Man." In this tradition of the God of Love Tolstoy resides unestranged.

Bibliography

The following bibliography represents only the works important for my study. It is not meant to be a complete bibliography on Tolstoy criticism or on Eastern Christian theology.

I. TOLSTOY

Aksel'rod-Ortodoks, L. I., *L. N. Tolstoj, sbornik statej*. Moscow, 1922.

Aldanov, Mark, *Zagadka Tolstogo*. Berlin, 1923.

Ardens, N. N., *Dostoevskij i Tolstoj*. Moscow, 1970.

Babaev, E. G., *Ocherki estetiki i tvorchestva L. N. Tolstogo*. Moscow, 1981.

———, *Roman L'va Tolstogo "Anna Karenina."* Tula, 1968.

Bayley, John, *Tolstoy and the Novel*. London, 1966.

Benson, Ruth Crego, *Women in Tolstoy*. Chicago, 1973.

Berlin, Isaiah, *The Hedgehog and the Fox*. New York, 1957.

Bilinkis, Ja., *O tvorchestve L. N. Tolstogo*. Leningrad, 1959.

Bocharov, S., *"Mir v 'Vojne i mire,' "* *Voprosy literatury* VIII (1970), 76-90.

———, *Roman L. Tolstogo "Vojna i mir."* Moscow, 1963.

Bulgakov, V. F., *Khristjanskaja etika, sistematicheskie ocherki mirovozrenija L. N. Tolstogo*. Moscow, 1917.

———, *Tolstoj—moralist*. Prague, 1923.

Bursov, B., *Lev Tolstoj, Idejnye iskanija i tvorcheskij metod (1847-1862)*. Moscow, 1960.

———, *Lev Tolstoj i russkij roman*. Moscow-Leningrad, 1963.

Chicherin, A. V., *Idei i stil'*. Moscow, 1965.

———, *O jazyke i stile romana-epopei "Vojna i mir."* L'vov, 1956.

Christian, R. F., *Tolstoy, A Critical Introduction*. Cambridge, 1969.

———, *Tolstoy's "War and Peace."* London, 1962.

Ejkhenbaum, B., *Lev Tolstoj, Kniga pervaja, 50-ye gody*. Leningrad, 1928.

Ejkhenbaum, B., *Lev Tolstoj, Kniga vtoraja, 60-ye gody*. Moscow, 1931.
———, *Molodoj Tolstoj*. Petersburg-Berlin, 1922.
———, *O proze*. Leningrad, 1969.
———, *Lev Tolstoj, Semidesjatye gody*. Leningrad, 1960.
Ermilov, V., *Tolstoj—romanist*. Moscow, 1965.
Fejn, G. N., *Roman L. N. Tolstogo "Vojna i mir."* Moscow, 1966.
Galagan, G. Ja., *L. N. Tolstoj, Khudozhestvenno-eticheskie iskanija*. Leningrad, 1981.
Gifford, Henry, ed., *Leo Tolstoy, A Critical Anthology*. Middlesex, England, 1971.
Ginzburg, Lidija, *O literaturnom geroe*. Leningrad, 1979.
———, *O psikhologicheskoj proze*. Leningrad, 1971.
———, "O romane Tolstogo *Vojna i mir*," *Zvezda* I (1944), 125-138.
Gromov, Pavel, *O stile L'va Tolstogo, "Dialektika dushi v 'Vojne i mire."* Leningrad, 1977.
———, *O stile L'va Tolstogo, Stanovlenie "dialektiki dushi."* Leningrad, 1971.
Gudzij, N., *Lev Tolstoj*. Moscow, 1960.
Ishchuk, G. N., *Problema chitatelja v tvorcheskom soznanii L. N. Tolstogo*. Kalinin, 1975.
Jackson, Robert L., "The Archetypal Journey: Aesthetic and Ethical Imperatives in the Art of Tolstoj; *The Cossacks*," *Russian Literature* XI (1982), 389-410.
———, "Chance and Design in *Anna Karenina*," in *Discipline of Criticism*, ed. by Peter Demetz. New Haven, 1968, pp. 325-329.
Kamjanov, V., *Poeticheskij mir eposa, O romane L. Tolstogo "Vojna i mir."* Moscow, 1978.
Kandiev, B. I., *Roman-epopeja L. N. Tolstogo "Vojna i mir."* Moscow, 1967.
Khrapchenko, M. B., *Lev Tolstoj kak khudozhnik*. Moscow, 1965.
Kozhin, A. N., *Jazyk L. N. Tolstogo*. Moscow, 1979.
Kuprejanova, E. N., *Estetika L. N. Tolstogo*. Moscow-Leningrad, 1966.
Kvitko, D. Ju., *Filosofija Tolstogo*. Moscow, 1930.
Leont'ev, K., *Analiz, stil' i vejanie*. In *Sobranie sochinenij K. Leont'eva*. Vol. VIII. 1912.
Mashinskij, S., ed. *V mire Tolstogo*. Moscow, 1978.
Matlaw, Ralph E. ed., *Tolstoy, A Collection of Critical Essays*. Englewood Cliffs, N.J., 1967.

Mooney, Harry J. Jr., *Tolstoy's Epic Vision*. Tulsa, Oklahoma, 1968.

Odinokov, V. G., *Problemy poetiki i tipologii russkogo romana XIX v.* Novosibirsk, 1971.

O religii L'va Tolstogo. Moscow, 1912.

Plakhotishina, V. T., *Masterstvo L. N. Tolstogo-romanista*. Dnepropetrovsk, 1960.

Posse, V. A., *Ljubov' v tvorchestve L. N. Tolstogo*. Borovichi, 1918.

Potapov, I. A., *Roman L. N. Tolstogo "Vojna i mir."* Moscow, 1979.

Saburov, A. A., *"Vojna i mir" L. N. Tolstogo, Problematika i poetika*. Moscow, 1959.

Sakulin, P. N., ed., *Estetika L'va Tolstogo*. Moscow, 1929.

Shklovskij, Viktor, *Materjal i stil' v romane L'va Tolstogo "Vojna i mir."* Moscow, 1928.

Simmons, Ernest J., *Introduction to Tolstoy's Writings*. Chicago, 1968.

Skaftimov, A., *Nravstvennye iskanija russkikh pisatelej*. Moscow, 1972.

Sorokin, Pitirim, A., *L. N. Tolstoj kak filosof*. Moscow, 1914.

Steiner, George, *Tolstoy or Dostoevsky*. New York, 1959.

Tolstoj—khudozhnik, Sbornik statej. Moscow, 1961.

Vinogradov, V., "O jazyke Tolstogo (50-60 gody)," *Literaturnoe nasledstvo* 35 (1939), 117-220.

Wasiolek, Edward, *Tolstoy's Major Fiction*. Chicago, 1978.

Weisbein, Nicolas, *L'Evolution réligieuse de Tolstoi*. Paris, 1960.

Zajdenshnur, E. E., *"Vojna i mir" L. N. Tolstogo*. Moscow, 1966.

II. EASTERN CHRISTIAN THOUGHT

Averintsev, S. S., *Poetika rannevizantijskoj literatury*. Moscow, 1977.

Benz, Ernst. *The Eastern Orthodox Church, Its Thought and Life*. New York, 1963.

Berdyaev, Nicholas, *The Beginning and The End*. New York, 1952.

———, *The Destiny of Man*. New York, 1960.

———, *Ekzistentsial'naja dialektika bozhestvennogo i chelovecheskogo*. Paris, 1952.

———, *Opyt eskhatologicheskoj metafiziki (Tvorchestvo i ob"ektivatsija)*. Paris, 1947.

Berdyaev, Nicholas, *The Russian Idea*. London, 1947.

——, *Samopoznanie (Opyt filosofskoj avtobiografii)* Paris, 1949.

——, *Slavery and Freedom*. New York, 1944.

——, *Tsarstvo dukha i tsarstvo kesarja*. Paris, 1951.

Bolshakov, Sergius, *Russian Mystics*. Kalamazoo, Mich., 1977.

——, and Pennington, M. Basil, o.c.s.o., *In Search of True Wisdom, Visits to Eastern Spiritual Fathers*. New York, 1979.

Bulgakov, Sergej, *Svet Nevechernij*. Moscow, 1917.

——, *Kupina Neopalimaja*. Paris, 1927.

——, *Filosofia khozjastva*. Moscow, 1912.

Bychkov, V. V., *Vizantijskaja estetika*. Moscow, 1977.

Cavarnos, Constantine, *Byzantine Thought and Art*. Belmont, Mass., 1968.

Chaadayev, Peter Yakovlevich, *Philosophical Letters*, and *Apology of a Madman*. Knoxville, 1969.

Christoff, Peter K., *An Introduction to Nineteenth-Century Russian Slavophilism: Khomjakov*. The Hague, 1961.

Daniélou, Jean, S.J., *Gospel Messages and Hellenistic Culture*. London-Philadelphia, 1973.

——, *Origène*. Paris, 1948.

——, and Musurillo, Herbert, S.J., eds., *From Glory to Glory, Texts from Gregory of Nyssa's Mystical Writings*. Crestwood, N.Y., 1979.

De Grunwald, Constantin, *Saints of Russia*. London, 1960.

Edie, James M., Scanlon, James O., and Zeldin, Mary-Barbara, eds., *Russian Philosophy*. 3 vols. Chicago, 1965.

Evdokimov, Paul, *L'Art de l'icone, théologie de la beauté*. Paris, 1972.

Fedorov, N. F., *Filosofija obshchego dela*. 2 vols. Verny, 1909/Moscow, 1913.

Fedotov, G. P., *The Russian Religious Mind, Kievan Christianity*. New York, 1960.

——, *The Russian Religious Mind, The Middle Ages*. Belmont, Mass., 1975.

——, *Stikhi dukhovnye*. Paris, 1935.

——, *Svjatye drevnej Rusi*. New York, 1960.

——, ed., *A Treasury of Russian Spirituality*. New York, 1948.

Florenskij, Pavel. *Stolp i utverzhdenie istiny*. Moscow, 1914.

Florovskij, G. V., *Vizantiiskie Ottsy V-VIII vv*. Paris, 1934.

———, *Vostochnie ottsy iv-ogo veka*. Paris, 1931.

Frank, S. L., *Dusha cheloveka*. Paris, 1964.

———, ed., *Iz istorii russkoj filosofskoj mysli kontsa 19-ogo i nachalo 20-ogo veka*. Washington, D.C., 1965.

———, *Nepostizhimoe*. Paris, 1939.

———, *Predmet znanija*. Petrograd, 1915.

———, *Real'nost' i chelovek, Metafizika chelovecheskogo bytija*. Paris, 1956.

———, *S nami Bog*. Paris, 1964.

Gregory of Nyssa, *The Life of Moses*. New York, 1978.

Jaeger, Werner, *Early Christianity and Greek Paideia*. London, 1969.

Kadloubovsky, E. and Palmer, G.E.H., trans., *Early Fathers from the Philokalia*. London, 1954.

———, *Writings from the Philokalia on Prayer of the Heart*. London, 1951.

Kormiris, John, *Synopsis of the Dogmatic Theology of the Orthodox Catholic Church*. Scranton, Pa., 1973.

Koyré, Alexandre, *Études sur l'histoire de la pensée philsophique en Russie*. Paris, 1950.

Ladner, Gerhart B., *The Idea of Reform*. New York, 1967.

Le Guillou, M. J., O. P., *The Spirit of Eastern Orthodoxy*. New York, 1962.

Lossky, N. O., *History of Russian Philosophy*. New York, 1951.

———, *Svoboda mysli*. Paris, n.d.

———, *Uslovija absoljutnogo dobra*. Paris, 1949.

Lossky, Vladimir, *In the Image and Likeness of God*. Crestwood, N.Y., 1974.

———, *The Mystical Theology of the Eastern Church*. Cambridge, 1957.

———, *Orthodox Theology, An Introduction*. Crestwood, N.Y., 1978.

———, *The Vision of God*. Bedfordshire, England, 1963.

Lot-Borodine, Myrrha, *La Déification de l'homme*. Paris, 1970.

Maloney, George A., S.J., *Man the Divine Icon*. Pecos, N.M., 1973.

Meyendorff, John, *Byzantine Theology*. New York, 1974.

———, *Christ in Eastern Christian Thought*. Crestwood, N.Y., 1975.

———, *St. Gregory Palamas and Orthodox Spirituality*. Crestwood, N.Y., 1974.

———, *A Study of Gregory Palamas*. Bedfordshire, England, 1974.

Mochulskij, K., *Vladimir Solov'ëv, zhizn' i uchenie*. Paris, 1951.

Origen, *An Exhortation to Martyrdom, Prayer, and Selected Works*. New York, 1979.

Ouspensky, Leonid. *Theology of the Icon*. Crestwood, N.Y., 1978.

Papademetriou, George C., *Introduction to Saint Gregory Palamas*. New York, 1973.

Pascal, Pierre, *The Religion of the Russian People*. Crestwood, N.Y., 1976.

Pelikan, Jaroslav, *The Spirit of Eastern Christendom (600-1700)*, vol. II of *The Christian Tradition*. Chicago, 1974.

Poltoratskij, N. P., ed., *Russkaja religiozno-filosofskaja mysl' XX veka*. Pittsburg, 1975.

Prestige, G. L., *God in Patristic Thought*. London, 1952.

Schmemann, Alexander, ed., *Ultimate Questions, An Anthology of Modern Russian Religious Thought*. New York, 1965.

Solov'ëv, Vladimir Sergeevich, *Sobranie sochinenij*. 12 vols. Reprint: Brussels, 1966-69.

Stephanou, Eusebius A., *Charisma and Gnosis in Orthodox Thought*. Fort Wayne, Ind., 1975.

Stremooukhoff, D., *Vladimir Soloviev and his Messianic Work*. Belmont, Mass., 1980.

Trubetskoj, Evgenij, *Smysl zhizni*. Berlin, 1922.

———, *Umozrenie v kraskakh*. Paris, 1965.

Tsirpanlis, Constantine N., *Greek Patristic Theology*. New York, 1979.

Walicki, Andrzej, *A History of Russian Thought from the Enlightenment to Marxism*. Stanford, 1979.

Ware, Timothy, *The Orthodox Church*. Middlesex, England, 1964.

Young, George M. Jr., *Nikolai F. Fedorov: An Introduction*. Belmont, Mass., 1979.

Zander, L. A., *Bog i mir*. 2 vols. Paris, 1948.

Zander, Valentine, *St. Seraphim of Sarov*. Crestwood, N.Y., 1975.

Zeldin, Mary-Barbara, "Chaadayev as Russia's First Philosopher," *Slavic Review* III (1978), 473-480.

Zenkovsky, V. V., *A History of Russian Philosophy*. 2 vols. London, 1953.

Index

This book forms part of the STUDIES OF THE HARRIMAN INSTITUTE, successor to:

STUDIES OF THE RUSSIAN INSTITUTE

ABRAM BERGSON, *Soviet National Income in 1937* (1953).

ERNEST J. SIMMONS, JR., ed., *Through the Glass of Soviet Literature: Views of Russian Society* (1953).

THAD PAUL ALTON, *Polish Postwar Economy* (1954).

DAVID GRANICK, *Management of the Industrial Firm in the USSR: A Study in Soviet Economic Planning* (1954).

ALLEN S. WHITING, *Soviet Policies in China, 1917-1924* (1954).

GEORGE S.N. LUCKYJ, *Literary Politics in the Soviet Ukraine, 1917-1934* (1956).

MICHAEL BORO PETROVICH, *The Emergence of Russian Panslavism, 1856-1870* (1956).

THOMAS TAYLOR HAMMOND, *Lenin on Trade Unions and Revolution, 1893-1917* (1956).

DAVID MARSHALL LANG, *The Last Years of the Georgian Monarchy, 1658-1832* (1957).

JAMES WILLIAM MORLEY, *The Japanese Thrust into Siberia, 1918* (1957).

ALEXANDER G. PARK, *Bolshevism in Turkestan, 1917-1927* (1957).

HERBERT MARCUSE, *Soviet Marxism: A Critical Analysis* (1958).

CHARLES B. MCLANE, *Soviet Policy and the Chinese Communists, 1931-1946* (1958).

OLIVER H. RADKEY, *The Agrarian Foes of Bolshevism: Promise and Defeat of the Russian Socialist Revolutionaries, February to October, 1917* (1958).

RALPH TALCOTT FISHER, JR., *Pattern for Soviet Youth: A Study of the Congresses of the Komsomol, 1918-1954* (1959).

ALFRED ERICH SENN, *The Emergence of Modern Lithuania* (1959).

ELLIOT R. GOODMAN, *The Soviet Design for a World State* (1960).

JOHN N. HAZARD, *Settling Disputes in Soviet Society: The Formative Years of Legal Institutions* (1960).

DAVID JORAVSKY, *Soviet Marxism and Natural Science, 1917-1932* (1961).

MAURICE FRIEDBERG, *Russian Classics in Soviet Jackets* (1962).

ALFRED J. RIEBER, *Stalin and the French Communist Party, 1941-1947* (1962).

THEODORE K. VON LAUE, *Sergei Witte and the Industrialization of Russia* (1962).

JOHN A. ARMSTRONG, *Ukrainian Nationalism* (1963).

OLIVER H. RADKEY, *The Sickle under the Hammer: The Russian Socialist Revolutionaries in the Early Months of Soviet Rule* (1963).

KERMIT E. MCKENZIE, *Comintern and World Revolution, 1928-1943: The Shaping of Doctrine* (1964).

HARVEY L. DYCK, *Weimar Germany and Soviet Russia, 1926-1933: A Study in Diplomatic Instability* (1966).

(Above titles published by Columbia University Press.)

HAROLD J. NOAH, *Financing Soviet Schools* (Teachers College, 1966).

JOHN M. THOMPSON, *Russia, Bolshevism, and the Versailles Peace* (Princeton, 1966).

PAUL AVRICH, *The Russian Anarchists* (Princeton, 1967).

LOREN R. GRAHAM, *The Soviet Academy of Sciences and the Communist Party, 1927-1932* (Princeton, 1967).

ROBERT A. MAGUIRE, *Red Virgin Soil: Soviet Literature in the 1920's* (Princeton, 1968).

T.H. RIGBY, *Communist Party Membership in the U.S.S.R., 1917-1967* (Princeton, 1968).

RICHARD T. DE GEORGE, *Soviet Ethics and Morality* (University of Michigan, 1969).

JONATHAN FRANKEL, *Vladimir Akimov on the Dilemmas of Russian Marxism, 1895-1903* (Cambridge, 1969).

WILLIAM ZIMMERMAN, *Soviet Perspectives on International Relations, 1956-1967* (Princeton, 1969).

PAUL AVRICH, *Kronstadt, 1921* (Princeton, 1970).

EZRA MENDELSOHN, *Class Struggle in the Pale: The formative Years of the Jewish Workers' Movement in Tsarist Russia* (Cambridge, 1970).

EDWARD J. BROWN, *The Proletarian Episode in Russian Literature* (Columbia, 1971).

REGINALD E. ZELNIK, *Labor and Society in Tsarist Russia: The Factory Workers of St. Petersburg, 1855-1870* (Stanford, 1971).

PATRICIA K. GRIMSTED, *Archives and Manuscript Repositories in the USSR: Moscow and Leningrad* (Princeton, 1972).

RONALD G. SUNY, *The Baku Commune, 1917-1918* (Princeton, 1972).

EDWARD J. BROWN, *Mayakovsky: A Poet in the Revolution* (Princeton, 1973).

MILTON EHRE, *Oblomov and his Creator: The Life and Art of Ivan Goncharov* (Princeton, 1973).

HENRY KRISCH, *German Politics Under Soviet Occupation* (Columbia, 1974).

HENRY W. MORTON and RUDOLPH L. TÖKÉS, eds., *Soviet Politics and Society in the 1970's* (Free Press, 1974).

WILLIAM G. ROSENBERG, *Liberals in the Russian Revolution* (Princeton, 1974).

RICHARD G. ROBBINS, JR., *Famine in Russia, 1891-1892* (Columbia, 1975).

VERA DUNHAM, *In Stalin's Time: Middleclass Values in Soviet Fiction* (Cambridge, 1976).

WALTER SABLINSKY, *The Road to Bloody Sunday* (Princeton, 1976).

WILLIAM MILLS TODD III, *The Familiar Letter as a Literary Genre in the Age of Pushkin* (Princeton, 1976).

ELIZABETH VALKENIER, *Russian Realist Art. The State and Society: The Peredvizhniki and Their Tradition* (Ardis, 1977).

SUSAN SOLOMON, *The Soviet Agrarian Debate* (Westview, 1978).

SHEILA FITZPATRICK, ed., *Cultural Revolution in Russia, 1928-1931* (Indiana, 1978).

PETER SOLOMON, *Soviet Criminologists and Criminal Policy: Specialists in Policy-Making* (Columbia, 1978).

KENDALL E. BAILES, *Technology and Society under Lenin and Stalin: Origins of the Soviet Technical Intelligentsia, 1917-1941* (Princeton, 1978).

LEOPOLD H. HAIMSON, ed., *The Politics of Rural Russia, 1905-1914* (Indiana, 1979).

THEODORE H. FRIEDGUT, *Political Participation in the USSR* (Princeton, 1979).

SHEILA FITZPATRICK, *Education and Social Mobility in the Soviet Union, 1921-1934* (Cambridge, 1979).

WESLEY ANDREW FISHER, *The Soviet Marriage Market: Mate-Selection in Russia and the USSR* (Praeger, 1980).

JONATHAN FRANKEL, *Prophecy and Politics: Socialism, Nationalism, and the Russian Jews, 1862-1917* (Cambridge, 1981).

ROBIN FEUER MILLER, *Dostoevsky and the Idiot: Author, Narrator, and Reader* (Harvard, 1981).

DIANE KOENKER, *Moscow Workers and the 1917 Revolution* (Princeton, 1981).

PATRICIA K. GRIMSTED, *Archives and Manuscript Repositories in the USSR: Estonia, Latvia, Lithuania, and Belorussia* (Princeton, 1981).

EZRA MENDELSOHN, *Zionism in Poland: The Formative Years, 1915-1926* (Yale, 1982).

HANNES ADOMEIT, *Soviet Risk-Taking and Crisis Behavior* (George Allen & Unwin, 1982).

SEWERYN BIALER and THANE GUSTAFSON, eds., *Russia at the Crossroads: The 26th Congress of the CPSU* (George Allen & Unwin, 1982).

ROBERTA THOMPSON MANNING, *The Crisis of the Old Order in Russia: Gentry and Government* (Princeton, 1983).

ANDREW A. DURKIN, *Sergei Aksakov and Russian Pastoral* (Rutgers, 1983).

BRUCE PARROTT, *Politics and Technology in the Soviet Union* (MIT Press, 1983).

SARAH PRATT, *Russian Metaphysical Romanticism: The Poetry of Tiutchev and Boratynskii* (Stanford, 1984).

STUDIES OF THE HARRIMAN INSTITUTE

ELIZABETH KRIDL VALKENIER, *The Soviet Union and the Third World: An Economic Bind* (Praeger, 1983).

JOHN LEDONNE, *Ruling Russia: Politics and Administration in the Age of Absolutism 1762-1796* (Princeton, 1984).